Science and Technology Advice to the President, Congress, and Judiciary

D0162419

Science and Technology Advice to the President, Congress, and Judiciary

Edited by William T. Golden

Transaction Publishers
New Brunswick (U.S.A.) and London (U.K.)

SALVE REGINA UNIVERSITY
LIBRARY
NEWPORT, RI 02840-4192

Second printing 1995
Copyright © 1993 by William T. Golden.

All rights reserved under International and Pan-American Copyright Conventions. No part of this book may be reproduced or transmitted in any form or by any means, electronic or mechanical, including photocopy, recording, or any information storage and retrieval system, without prior permission in writing from the publisher. All inquiries should be addressed to Transaction Publishers, Rutgers—The State University, New Brunswick, New Jersey 08903.

This book is printed on acid-free paper that meets the American National Standard for Permanence of Paper for Printed Library Materials.

ISBN: 1-56000-829-6
Printed in the United States of America

To the future of our beloved country

Contents

PART 2: CONGRESS

PART 3: JUDICIARY

PART 4: APPENDICES AND INDEX

Acknowledgments to the Second Edition

William T. Golden

I seize this opportunity to reiterate my gratitude to those who helped and inspired me in the preparation of the first edition of this book.

And with equal warmth I thank those friends who have been helpful in the preparation of this second edition. I start with David Hamburg who contributed an important new preface and whose vision and participation led to the creation and achievements of the Carnegie Commission on Science, Technology, and Government.

And I am grateful to other friends and colleagues who have helped in varied ways: David Z. Beckler, Joshua Lederberg, Helene L. Kaplan, David and Nan Robinson, Maxine Rockoff, Mark Schaefer, Steven G. Gallagher, J. Thomas Ratchford, Richard S. Nicholson, William G. Wells, Jr., my resourceful and devoted assistant Christie Van Kehrberg, and Ellen Rosenblatt and Eugene Gorman of my staff.

William T. Golden

New York, NY
July 1, 1993

William T. Golden designed the first Presidential Science Advisory organization for President Truman in 1950. He is Chairman of the American Museum of Natural History and Past Chairman of the New York Academy of Sciences, and is Cochairman (with Joshua Lederberg) of the Carnegie Commission on Science, Technology, and Government. He has served in the US Navy (World War II), the Atomic Energy Commission, the Department of State, and the Executive Office of the President. He received the Distinguished Public Service Award of the National Science Foundation (1982) and a Special Tribute of Appreciation (1991). Mr. Golden is an officer and trustee of the American Association for the Advancement of Science, the Mount Sinai Hospital and Medical School, and the Carnegie Institution of Washington; and is a member of the National Academy of Public Administration, the American Philosophical Society, and the American Academy of Arts and Sciences.

Acknowledgments to the First Edition

My gratitude goes first to the authors of these essays, patriots all.

George Bugliarello, President and George Schillinger, Professor, of Polytechnic University, and Editors of the journal, *Technology In Society,* encouraged the project, and its predecessor, from the moment of conception; and Martha Miller Willett, Managing Editor of *Technology In Society,* has been editorial ancillary *par excellence*.

Then I thank the friends who have been encouragers and helpers. Notable among them are David A. Hamburg, M.D.; Helene L. Kaplan; D. Allan Bromley; H. Guyford Stever; William D. Carey; Michael L. Telson; David Z. Beckler; and J. Thomas Ratchford.

Members of my office staff—loyal, resourceful, and tireless—were essential. Without them this book would have been leaner and later: Georgia Phelps, Christie Van Kehrberg, Cynthia Brink, and Eugene Gorman.

This collection of essays is dedicated "To the future of our beloved country." Surely, every one of its authors would endorse that expression of devotion. On a more deeply personal basis, I think of my grandparents, steerage immigrants a century ago, who found freedom and opportunity in the United States of America, as did countless others, and I think of my late parents, S. Herbert Golden and Rebecca Harris Golden; my late brother, Barry; and my late wife of forty-five years, Sibyl, ever-loving and supportive; my cherished daughters, Sibyl Rebecca and Pam; and certain friends. They are my inspiration and my reward.

William T. Golden

Olive Bridge, New York 12461
October 1, 1987

PREFACE

David A. Hamburg

In the second half of the twentieth century, the pace of advance in basic scientific knowledge—of the structure of matter and life, of the nature of the universe, of the environment, and even of the human species—has accelerated dramatically. These scientific advances have provided an unprecedented basis for technological innovation, especially in the context of political and economic freedom. Such innovations have pervasive, world-wide effects that extend far beyond the bounds of prior experience.

Science and technology bear upon war and peace, health and disease, the economy and society, resources and the environment—indeed, our the entire human future. The international economy, for example, is increasingly driven by scientific and technological developments: witness telecommunications, biotechnology, computers, and the technical upgrading of established industries. No reminder is needed of the immense impact that weapons development and distribution have on society. The issues involve not only the existence of new hardware but the *uses* of that hardware.

These trends are intrinsically worldwide in scope. Many problems historically considered to be internal might better be viewed as domestic instances of international problems. Moreover, the opportunities and problems arising out of modern science and technology cut across traditional disciplines and sectors of society. Thus, institutional innovations

David A. Hamburg, M.D., has been President of the Carnegie Corporation of New York since 1983. He served as President (1984–85) and Chairman of the Board (1985–86) of the American Association for the Advancement of Science. He was Professor and Chairman of the Department of Psychiatry at Stanford University from 1961–72; President of the Institute of Medicine, National Academy of Science, 1975–80; and Director of the Division of Health Policy Research and Education and John D. MacArthur Professor of Health Policy at Harvard University, 1980–82. Dr. Hamburg is a Trustee and Vice Chairman of the board of Stanford University, a Trustee of the Rockefeller University, of the American Museum of Natural History, and of the Mount Sinai Medical Center, New York. He has served on many policy advisory boards, including the Chief of Naval Operations Executive Panel and the Advisory Committee on Medical Research of the World Health Organization.

are needed that can transcend traditional barriers—disciplinary, sectoral, and geopolitical.

Clearly, wise policy and administrative decision-making in each sphere of life depend on access to the best available knowledge and advice in the various fields of science and technology. Sound advice requires analysis, and analysis requires a broad base of research and development on which informed decisions can be made. Governmental decision-makers, moreover, need to understand the major facets of the scientific enterprise itself.

The rapid and pervasive transformations induced by science and technology call for strengthening the governmental capability to objectively analyze critical issues and make informed decisions based on a broad foundation of knowledge and experience. That requires the establishment of dependable mechanisms for analyzing policy questions in ways that take adequate account of their scientific and technological aspects. In the current process of world transformation, studies are needed to tackle vital and complex issues analytically rather than polemically. This means that leaders should have access to a wide range of high-quality information, analyses, and options. Jumping to conclusions, or using a heavy ideological filter, can easily lead to major mistakes, missed opportunities, and even disasters.

In the early 1980s, I became increasingly aware of the profound difficulty facing governments who sought to meet the challenge of accelerating scientific and technological developments. These concerns led me to convene a group of distinguished scientists at Carnegie Corporation of New York. They shared my concerns and strengthened my inclination to organize a Carnegie Commission on Science, Technology, and Government. A crucial step in the development of the Commission occurred when I was able to enlist the distinguished leadership of Joshua Lederberg and William T. Golden as co-chairs. These appointments ensured that the Commission's work would be of very high quality and that it would be germane to the emerging problems of both American society and the international community. In the years since its establishment, the Commission has deepened our understanding of the important role science and technology can play in meeting the challenges of the human future.

Bill Golden has been a leader worldwide in strengthening mechanisms of analysis and advice for the highest levels of government—striving always to illuminate, to open eyes and minds, to speak truth to power. He has enlisted superb people from all parts of the world in this effort. The result is a publication of enduring value. Like the work of the Carnegie Commission, these insights and suggestions can help people everywhere in the vital quest for wise and humane uses of science and technology.

For a description of the work of the Carnegie Commission,
see W.T. Golden's article beginning on page 505.

Introduction to the Second Edition

William T. Golden

In preparing this second edition of the 1988 volume, there was a need to review, an opportunity to recant, and encouragement to revise. The original 85 articles especially written for the volume by outstandingly experienced and well qualified authors were timely, remain apposite, and are reprinted unchanged. There is nothing of consequence I feel disposed to alter in my Introduction or in my article, "Then and Now: Personal Reflections."

The establishment of science and technology advisory organizations to the top levels of governments, formed along the general lines of the American model, with variations, has spread to many countries of the world.[1,2,3,4] Several multi-national meetings of top-level science and technology advisers and ministers have been held in recent years. Originally brought together by the Carnegie Commission on Science Technology and Government, the science advisers and ministers of G-7 countries (United States of America, Canada, United Kingdom, France, Germany, Italy, and Japan), Russia, and the European Community have now established themselves as the "Carnegie Group." They have met five times, semi-annually, in different countries, and they plan to continue in this mode. Meetings of top-level and high-level advisers of many Western Hemisphere countries have been held on two occasions, a little over a year apart, in Mexico under the auspices of President Salinas. And a large group of advisers from African countries held their initial meeting early in 1993 in Nairobi, Kenya, under the leadership of Thomas Odhiambo, President of the African Academy of Sciences.

The world has been changing, largely along trajectories that were evident in 1988. The cold war is over, which has created both new opportunities and diverse problems. The nuclear threat has diminished but is still with us, as is the latent, problem-ridden opportunity for peaceful nuclear energy. Population perils persist. Global awareness of the environment increases. Communications and competition accelerate. Education is becoming increasingly important for survival and progress. Wars, small but bestial, including civil wars, arise from old tensions. Weak bonds rupture. Human nature does not change.

The Introduction to the first edition of this book began:

"This book has a purpose. It aims to attract attention to the necessity for quality advice on science and technology issues to the President of the United States, to the Congress, and to the Judiciary. And it aims to provoke thought, to stimulate discussion, and to encourage action. Emphasis is on reconsideration and improvement of existing organizations and mechanisms, mindful of the need to adapt to changing circumstances.

"A related purpose is to provide a compendium of facts and opinions useful to government officials and staffs in all three branches; to journalists; to scholars and students of political science, of science policy, and of the history of science; to the industrial and financial communities; and to the concerned citizenry."

Though progress has been made, those are still the main purposes of this second edition. The task is unending. The social and political climate changes, and there will always be need for adaptation and improvement.

An important development in the United States since the 1988 publication of the first edition of this book, was the creation of the Carnegie Commission on Science, Technology, and Government by the Carnegie Corporation of New York, inspired by its president, David A. Hamburg, M.D., who was influenced by this book in its developmental, *in utero* phase. With Hamburg's leadership, an extraordinarily able, distinguished, dedicated, and hardworking bipartisan group of Commissioners and Advisory Council members was quickly recruited for a 5-year undertaking. Joshua Lederberg and I served as harmonious, mutually stimulating cochairmen. A small and outstandingly capable staff was recruited by David Z. Robinson, Executive Director, and Maxine Rockoff, Senior Administrator. The staff have been thoughtful, resourceful, dedicated, and tireless. They are generally young, with a leavening of experienced, youthful-spirited elders.

The Commission has been concerned with the organization and decision-making mechanisms of the three branches of our federal government and with the availability and utilization of science and technology knowledge and advice in the formulation and execution of government policies in all their aspects. With offices in New York City and Washington, DC, the Commission has organized and staffed task forces of Commission and Advisory Council members and other well-qualified individuals to study major topics. It has published some 30 papers, including 18 task force reports, and has distributed more than 200,000 copies of these reports. Of great practical importance, it should be noted that during the preparation of these studies, it has consulted, assisted, and on occasion cajoled government officials at working levels and at exalted levels. In this process, it has both learned and taught.

The Commission has aimed for action, not just for publication of papers. It has been influential (for example, in the elevation of the position of the Science Adviser to the President to Cabinet rank and in the reestablishment of the President's Science Advisory Committee), and it believes its efforts will continue to be beneficial. Though formally dissolved on June 30, 1993, after five years of existence, as planned at its genesis, it will persist informally in its efforts for progress. It will continue to distribute its papers, and it may reconvene occasionally in subgroups or in plenary form if warranted. Though inherently bipartisan or non partisan (including former Presidents Ford and Carter on its team), several of its members and staff have been enlisted by President Clinton for important positions in his administration.

The Carnegie Commission on Science, Technology, and Government has been an important influence in the evolution of science policy, and the utilization of science and technology information by the federal and state governments in the US as well as worldwide. Its influence will continue. The article beginning on page 505 provides more information about the Commission and its activities and objectives with the executive, legislative, and judicial branches of the federal government and with the states.

1. D.W. Bronk, "Science Advice in the White House: The Genesis of the President's Science Adviser and the National Science Foundation," *Science*, Vol. 186, pp. 116–21, 11 October 1974. Reprinted in W.T. Golden, ed., *Science Advice to the President* (New York: Pergamon Press, 1980; Washington, DC: AAAS Press, 1993); also published as a special issue (Vol. 2, Nos. 1 and 2) of *Technology in Society*.
2. W.T. Golden, "Government Military-Scientific Research: Review for the President of the United States, 1950–51," basic documents, including precept, report, and memoranda, as well as interviews with about 150 appropriate individuals. Unpublished, 432 pages. Copies available at the Harry S. Truman Library, Independence, MO; the library of the American Institute of Physics, New York, NY; the Herbert Hoover Library, West Branch, IA; the Dwight D. Eisenhower Library, Abilene, KS; and the Library of Congress, Washington, DC.
3. W.T. Golden, ed., *Science Advice to the President* (New York: Pergamon Press, 1980; Washington, DC: AAAS Press, 1993).
4. W.T. Golden, ed., *Worldwide Science and Technology Advice to the Highest Levels of Governments* (New York: Pergamon Press, 1991; Washington, DC: AAAS Press, 1993), xiii + 430 pages.

Introduction to the First Edition

William T. Golden

> "Fools need Advice most, but only
> Wise men are the better for it."
>
> > Benjamin Franklin,
> > *Poor Richard's Almanac*

> "The way of a fool is right in his own eyes:
> but he that hearkeneth unto counsel is wise."
>
> > Proverbs 12:15

> "*E pur si muove*"
>
> > Galileo

PURPOSE

This book has a purpose. It aims to attract attention to the necessity for quality advice on science and technology issues to the President of the United States, to the Congress, and to the Judiciary. And it aims to provoke thought, to stimulate discussion, and to encourage action. Emphasis is on reconsideration and improvement of existing organizations and mechanisms, mindful of the need to adapt to changing circumstances.

A related purpose is to provide a compendium of facts and opinions useful to government officials and staffs in all three branches; to journalists; to scholars and students of political science, of science policy, and of the history of science; to the industrial and financial communities; and to the concerned citizenry. An earlier volume, *Science Advice to the President,*[1] with original essays by Presidential Science Advisors, members of the President's Science Advisory Committee (PSAC), and other especially qualified individuals, provides a valuable background for the present volume. This book concentrates on the future, mindful that the approaching 1988 elections create an important and timely first target of opportunity.

1

COMMENTS ON THE COLLECTION

Among some eighty-five essays comprising this volume, several are included as salutary anomalies, condiments as it were, to spice the collection. A few of them are essentially examples of issues for consideration by a science and technology advisory organization, rather than designs for such an organization.

An exception is made for a cogent paper by Hans Bethe and John Bardeen that appeared in *The New York Times* in 1986. It is reprinted, as an Appendix, because the authors' response to invitations to write papers for this volume was that the article still represents their views, concisely stated, and that "We would not write it differently today."

An extended interview, during his terminal illness, with George Kistiakowsky, Science Advisor (1959–60) to President Eisenhower, completed too late in 1980 for publication in *Science Advice to the President*, is also included as an Appendix. Its pungency, piquancy and wisdom are germane today; and it fills the lacuna in the collection of essays by Presidential Science Advisors in that book.

Noteworthy papers by George A. Keyworth II, President Reagan's first Science Advisor, and William R. Graham, his current Advisor, bring the series up to date. Except for Oliver Buckley, who was the first Presidential Science Advisor (President Truman's, located in the Office of Defense Mobilization), who died in 1959, every President's Science Advisor has written an article for one or both of these volumes.

The Appendices include an index to the 1980 volume which will be useful to readers of this one.

The articles are categorized broadly by areas of emphasis: President, Congress, Judiciary. Within each category the order is alphabetical by author.

Since 1951, a number of foreign countries have followed the lead of Presidents Truman and Eisenhower and have created science and technology advisory channels to the top levels of government. Initially, it was intended to include in this book a few relevant articles by appropriate individuals. In the course of preparing this American collection, however, it became evident that there is considerable interest here in the foreign practice and experience. For this reason and because so many foreign countries now have science and technology advisory organizations in various forms, it has been decided to assemble a separate international volume, to be published later.

THE AUTHORS AND THEIR RECOMMENDATIONS

The individuals invited to write papers were selected for wisdom, experience, and love of country, without regard to political affiliations. Many are independents in politics, as is the editor, who has served under both Presidents Truman and Eisenhower. Diversity of views was sought, and novel ideas were encouraged. Each author wrote independently, during mid-1987, without access to the essays of the other contributors.

President

It is noteworthy, therefore, that a strong consensus, but not unanimity, has emerged, favoring a strengthened Presidential science and technology advisory organization as an essential ingredient in policy formulation and decision-making on a broad range of issues woven into the fabric of modern life. Most of the articles focus on the President and his staff, reflecting perceived need, opportunity and tradition. As McGeorge Bundy expresses felicitously, "The next President will have a great opportunity to create for his country and for himself a wholly renewed process of effective connection between the scientific and technological communities and the Presidency."

With certain notable exceptions and numerous variations of detail, the preponderant recommendations are for the re-establishment of a Presidential science and technology organization in the Truman/Eisenhower pattern:[2] a full-time Science and Technology Advisor to the President (STAP) and a President's Science and Technology Advisory Committee (or Council) (PSTAC).

Among the thoughtful variations and alternatives on this basic theme are several suggestions (including one by Frank Press, President of the National Academy of Sciences, and former Science Advisor to President Carter) to elevate the President's Science and Technology Advisor to Cabinet rank, possibly as Secretary of Science without portfolio; that is, without the constraints and competitiveness of operating Departmental responsibilities (although a few writers, including Jay Keyworth, advocate an actual operating Department of Science).[3] A truly novel alternative (with which this editor disagrees) is Edward David's suggestions for creation of a not-for-profit corporation, a Federal Contract Research Center (FCRC), to provide science and technology advice to the President and his staff. Dr. David was the very able Science Advisor to President Nixon when the latter, contrary to Dr. David's advice, abolished the office in 1973. "The cook was a good cook, as cooks go; and, as cooks go, he went."[4] And PSAC went, too. And our country has been the poorer.

Congress

Less attention is devoted to the Congress, although its multiple resources are recognized—especially its dedicated committee staffs, which have grown in ability and size in recent decades, the Office of Technology Assessment, and the specialized staff of the Library of Congress. Specific attention is given to the effective, little-known Congressional Science Fellows Program.

Further development of Congressional science and technology sources is encouraged.

Judiciary

The essays on the different and growing needs of the Judiciary, of the federal and state Administrative agencies, and of the legal profession, all confronted increasingly with science and technology issues, may stimulate further discussion and creative approaches in dealing with the constraints inherent in the adversarial nature of our legal system. The growing awareness of these needs by the legal profession is salutary.

THE QUESTIONS

What organizational structures should be utilized by the President, the Congress, and the Judiciary—the three branches of our government—to utilize available knowledge most effectively and to evaluate and respond to the diversity of opinions, and self-interests, in our world of change? As Frank Westheimer has pointed out,[5] "Lack of knowledge will not prevent them from having opinions; it will only prevent them from having informed opinions."

What to do now? How adapt? How evolve? The essays in this volume address these issues thoughtfully, based on varied backgrounds, experience, and viewpoints.

REFERENCES

1. Golden, William T., ed., *Science Advice to the President* (New York: Pergamon Press, 1980); also published as a special issue of *Technology In Society,* Vol. 2, nos. 1&2 (1980).
2. Bronk, Detlev W., "Science Advice in the White House: The Genesis of the President's Science Advisers and the National Science Foundation," *Science,* October 11, 1974, Vol. 186, pp. 116–121; reprinted in Golden, *op. cit.,* pp. 245–256.
3. Re: a Department of Science, see a compendium of articles, Frederick Seitz, Guest Editor, in *Technology In Society,* Vol. 8, nos. 1&2 (1986).
4. Saki (H. H. Munro), "Reginold on Besetting Sins," *Reginold* (1904). Quoted in annual report of Paul Gross, president, Marine Biological Laboratory (Woods Hole, Massachusetts), August 1987.
5. Westheimer, F. H., "Are Our Universities Rotten at the 'Core'?," *Science,* Vol. 236, June 5, 1987, pp. 1165–66.

Then and Now: Personal Reflections

William T. Golden

The world was, or seemed to be, a simpler place in mid-1950, when, after the outbreak of the Korean War, President Truman, with strong encouragement from Congressional leaders, asked me to serve as a special consultant to advise him on the organization and utilization of the government's scientific research activities. Emphasis was to be on the military aspects. The study involved discussions with some 150 scientists, government officials, academic leaders, and industrialists. My recommendation, dated December 18, 1950, "for the appointment of an outstanding scientific leader as Scientific Advisor to the President,"[1,2] was promptly approved by President Truman.

The pace of change has quickened in the intervening years, and the prospect appears to be for continued acceleration. Among the well-recognized factors distinguishing the world from what it was at the end of World War II are faster communication, faster transportation, computerization, the opening of the new world of space, progress in biomedical science, the further internationalization of industry, commerce, and finance, the unequal growth of populations, the rise and decline of nations* and the ferment of the developing world, the overhanging danger of a nuclear holocaust, the expansion of armaments and the contagion of terrorism, the increasing indus-

---

*"Many shall rise that now are fallen; and many shall fall that now are held in honor." Horace, *Ars Poetica*

William T. Golden designed the Presidential Science Advisory apparatus for President Truman in 1950. He is President of the New York Academy of Sciences. He has served in the US Navy (World War II), the Atomic Energy Commission, the Department of State, and the Executive Office of the President. He received the Distinguished Public Service Award of the National Science Foundation (1982). Mr. Golden is an officer and trustee of the American Association for the Advancement of Science, the American Museum of Natural History, the Mount Sinai Hospital and Medical School, and the Carnegie Institution of Washington; and a member of the National Academy of Public Administration and of the American Philosophical Society.

5

trialization of agriculture, growing concern for the environment, greater sense of societal responsibilities, and the increasing participation of women and minorities.

Yet human nature changes slowly and certain principles remain unchanged, even as scientific and technical factors increasingly influence virtually every aspect of life on Planet Earth. Thus, more and more, every level of our government (including states and municipalities) must take science and technology factors into account in policy formulation and in long-range and day-to-day decision-making.

Science and technology advising has experienced ur^ulations of popularity and, like life itself, has responded in an evolutionary way to changing circumstances, adapting with more or less successful mutations to a varying environment.

Modifications will continue to occur, stimulated by changes in the personalities of the Presidents and in the competitive strengths of the several Departments of the Executive Branch and of their Secretaries. The Congress and the Judiciary will, of course, be affected by comparable factors. Also influential will be the progress of science and technology and their increasing involvement in virtually every aspect of human life, throughout the world; and the changing national and international political, military, societal, and economic environments.

Science and technology advising has a long history,[3] going back to Adam and Eve.[4] Adam and Eve were the first executives (and co-investigators). The serpent was, of course, the first Science Advisor. Were it not for that primordial research project, these essays would not have been written. Original sin or initiation of scientific research, the outcome should not discourage the quest for knowledge. Indeed, the episode supports the need for a President's Science and Technology Advisory Committee (or Council [PSTAC]), of diverse experience and wisdom, to supplement and buffer a single full-time Science and Technology Advisor to the President.[5] For, however talented the Advisor may be, and however close the Advisor's rapport with the President, he or she cannot be omniscient and will also need a PSTAC, as PSAC served in the past, to provide scope, collegial discussion, and loyal opposition.*

All PSTAC members should be men and women of stature, ability, scope, independence, and patriotism. They would command the respect of the members of the Cabinet, notably the Secretaries of State, Defense, and Commerce; and the President's National Security Adviser, the Directors of the Office of Management and Budget and of the National Science Foundation. All would be Presidential appointees and would be inspired by that

---

*"Where no counsel is, the people fall: but in the multitude of counselors there is safety." Proverbs 11:14

distinction and responsibility. All would understand that they are chosen to represent the best interests of the United States as a whole, not any special interests of the scientific and engineering communities, or any political party, or geographic area, or ethnic group. They would be there to serve the President, and the President to serve the people.

All would realize that they are members of the President's staff, responsible to him; and that their effectiveness and survival depend on the President's confidence in them, both for wisdom and for discretion. Their advice will be sought and should also be volunteered. It will not always be taken. Presidential attitude and action will be the resultant of many forces, political and economic as well as scientific and technological. Realists will understand that. Much of the advice will be influential rather than decisive. Much of it will be of long-term value, long-term influence on policy issues that may involve no immediate decisions. Fire prevention may be more effective than fire-fighting.

There is a lesson for us in the Roman observation: *"Tempora mutantur, nos et mutamur in illis."* ("The times are changing and we are changing in them.") Or, to paraphrase Charles Darwin, "Adapt or perish." Let us change course thoughtfully.

REFERENCES

1. Golden, William T. *"Government Military-Scientific Research: Review for the President of the United States, 1950–51,"* 432 pages, unpublished. Available at the Harry S. Truman Library, Independence, Missouri 64050; the Herbert Hoover Presidential Library, West Branch, Iowa 52358; the Dwight D. Eisenhower Library, Abilene, Kansas 67410; and the American Institute of Physics, New York, New York 10017.
2. Bronk, Detlev W., "Science Advice in the White House: The Genesis of the President's Science Advisers and the National Science Foundation," *Science*, 11 October 1974, Vol. 186, pp. 116–121; reprinted in Golden, William T., ed., *Science Advice to the President* (New York: Pergamon Press, 1980), pp. 245–256.
3. G. Allen Greb, *Science Advice to Presidents: From Test Bans to the Strategic Defense Initiative* (San Diego: University of California Institute on Global Conflict and Cooperation, 1987).
4. *Genesis* 3:1–24.
5. Golden, William T., "Science Advice to the President: Past, Present, Future," *Proceedings of the American Philosophical Society*, Vol. 130, no. 3, 1986, pp. 325–329.

PART   1

PRESIDENT AND EXECUTIVE BRANCH

Science Advice at the Cabinet Level

Richard C. Atkinson

On December 18, 1950, William T. Golden, then serving as a special consultant to the White House, drafted a memorandum to President Truman recommending ". . . the prompt and immediate appointment of an outstanding scientific leader as Scientific Advisor to the President."[1] He reasoned that the proliferation of uncoordinated scientific programs of the individual federal agencies dictated the need ". . . for centralization of knowledge of all scientific programs in one independent and technically competent individual to whom the President can turn for advice."

If Golden's argument about the need for independent, technically competent science advice at the Presidential level was worth serious consideration thirty-seven years ago, it is obviously even more compelling today. The scale and complexity of both the government and non-government stake in science have increased to a level undreamed of in 1950—or in 1957 when President Eisenhower accepted the essence of Golden's recommendation by creating a President's Science Advisory Committee (PSAC) and designating its Chairman as his special assistant for science and technology. More important, whereas throughout the 1950s and up to the mid-1960s science advice at the Presidential level was considered important primarily because of its military significance, today the impact of science on all sectors of national concern and its importance to the nation's global obligations and opportunities is widely acknowledged. Science intersects with virtually all policy areas that regularly concern the President and his top advisors. These areas include, for example, regulatory policy, economic policy, industrial policy, relations with state and local governments, and foreign affairs.

Unfortunately, while the importance of scientific considerations in helping to clarify and resolve national policy issues may be widely acknowledged, there is still no consistent mechanism for bringing scientific insights to bear on decision-making at the Presidential level. The Director of the Office of

Richard C. Atkinson has been Chancellor of the University of California, San Diego, since 1980. Previously, he was Director of the National Science Foundation (1975–80), and was a Professor of Psychology at Stanford University (1956–1975). He is a member of the American Philosophical Society and of the National Academy of Sciences.

Science and Technology Policy (OSTP) holds the statutory position as Presidential Science Advisor. The Congress has assigned detailed oversight, coordination, planning and evaluation functions to OSTP to ensure that its Director's advice can be well informed.[2] The President, however, need not and very often does not seek the OSTP Director's advice except in those instances when he and his top policy advisors recognize that a particular issue does have scientific implications.[3] Moreover, while it is obviously important for the President to have competent, independent science advice, the number of significant issues with scientific components has now become too great to command close Presidential attention in all but the most exceptional cases. For that reason, science-related policy issues need to receive consistent attention across the government and in the context of consistent Presidential policies. Thus, there is clearly a need to update Golden's 37-year old recommendation by asking how the concept of "independent and comprehensive science advice" on a range of important issues can be institutionalized in the light of contemporary complexities.

In an illuminating 1976 memoir, David Beckler, who served as Executive Secretary to PSAC from its inception until it was abolished in 1973, assessed PSAC's accomplishments and speculated on the causes of its demise.[4] The principal reason given by Beckler has to do with the increasing divergences between PSAC and Presidential-level policies. Public notice of these divergences became acute in the case of the anti-ballistic missile and even more so in the case of the supersonic transport. A second, often overlooked problem cited by Beckler has to do with the increased scope of PSAC's interests. For approximately ten years, PSAC was concerned primarily with military and space-related issues. But by the mid-1960s, the desirability of exploring a much broader range of problems had become compelling. These included, for example, the status and long-range needs of US research universities, and the impact of science and technology on health, safety, and the environment. Beckler suggests, by implication, that the effectiveness of PSAC (and the Office of Science and Technology that provided its primary support staff) was diluted by attempts to gain Presidential attention for such a wide range of issues. On the other hand, it is certainly true that PSAC would not have been fulfilling its independent advisory function adequately if it had simply ignored those issues.

Congress attempted to solve some of the problems identified by Beckler and others when it established the present science advisory system in 1976.[5] It tried to improve the Science Advisor's access to the President by designating that individual as head of an Executive Office agency (*i.e.,* OSTP) in parallel with, for example, the Director of the Office of Management and Budget (OMB) or the Chairman of the Council of Economic Advisers (CEA). Congress sought to protect the science advisory system against the political hazards experienced by PSAC by mandating specific functions for OSTP that would be subject to Congressional oversight. It attempted to provide OSTP with sufficient staff (and access to additional staff from the federal line agencies) so that it could deal with a broad spectrum of issues without diluting its effectiveness. Finally, in recognition of the pervasive character of science, the 1976 Act that created OSTP sketched out the elements of a national science and technology policy identifying ten areas of national importance that, by implication, defined the substantive context of the Science Advisor's mandate.

Despite the evident craftsmanship of the OSTP Act, Congress has been unable to guarantee that the scientific implications of national policy issues will receive sustained attention not only by the President and his political advisors, but also by senior policy level officials throughout the federal government. One recurring proposal for solving the related problems of improved coordination and oversight of federal science activities and enhanced visibility for science-related policy problems has been to create a Department of Science.[6] Although the most recent versions of that proposal differ somewhat in detail, most would combine, in a Cabinet-level department, the National Science Foundation (NSF), the National Bureau of Standards (NBS), the National Oceanic and Atmospheric Administration (NOAA), and units within several other agencies, including the National Aeronautics and Space Administration (NASA) and the Department of Energy (DoE).[7]

The wisdom of such proposals is questionable. First, combining diverse agencies into a Department of Science would further erode the unique pluralistic federal support system that has been an important factor in the spectacular success of US science since World War II. Second, it is not obvious that more coherence would result by combining under one roof, for example, NSF, whose sole mission is to support basic research and science education, with other entities that both conduct and support research (*e.g.*, NBS and units within NASA and DoE), and still others involved primarily in operational matters (*e.g.*, other units within DoE and NASA). Indeed, the current federal system for supporting research in universities could be seriously weakened by combining research-support and operational functions in a single department. Finally, none of the recent proposals for a Department of Science would incorporate either the National Institutes of Health (NIH) or the science and technology units of the Department of Defense (DoD). And by failing to do so, they fall far short of their objective of improving coordination and oversight of the federal science and technology effort.

The most appealing aspect of proposals for a Department of Science is that its Secretary, as a Cabinet member, would have regular access to the President as well as to the heads of all other federal departments and agencies. The problem of institutionalizing access for the President's Science Advisor to various units within the White House circle such as the National Security Council or the Domestic Policy Council received some attention during Congressional hearings that preceded passage of the OSTP Act. Suggestions by several witnesses that the OSTP legislation should designate the Science Advisor as a member of one or more of those bodies were rejected primarily because of assurances given by the Ford Administration that the Science Advisor would frequently be asked to sit in on their meetings.

The merits of those suggestions are worth reconsidering. The stakes have now increased sufficiently, however, to question whether anything short of Cabinet membership for the Science Advisor is adequate. Cabinet membership is not restricted to the Secretaries of the principal departments of government; in addition, several other Presidential advisors, including the Ambassador to the United Nations and the Director of OMB are members. The stature and visibility of the OSTP director, as well as his sustained access to senior policy level officials, would be enhanced considerably if that individual were a member of the Cabinet without portfolio. One decided advantage in granting the President's principal Science Advisor Cabinet-level status without creating a Department of Science would be to spare him the administrative headaches that would inevitably result from having to manage a large and probably cumbersome bureaucracy, thus allowing him and his staff to focus their attention on policy problems.

Despite considerable changes in the scale and complexity of both science and government since 1950, one aspect of Golden's original proposal needs to be reemphasized: the need for independent and technically competent science advice at the highest policy levels of government. Whatever institutional arrangements may be made to improve the Presidential science advisory system, no system can be effective unless the Science Advisor is a respected individual who can command attention not only within government and the scientific community, but also within the many other sectors of the nation that rely increasingly on science and its wise and effective development.

NOTES

1. William T. Golden, *Government Military-Scientific Research: Review for the President of the United States, 1950–51* (unpublished memorandum), pp. 392–404.
2. *US Code Congressional and Administrative News, 94th Congress, Second Session, 1976*, Vol. I, 90 Stat., pp. 459–473.
3. See, *e.g.*, Ted Greenwood, "Science and Technology Advice for the President," in Kenneth W. Thompson, ed., *The Presidency and Science Advising* (Lanham, MD: University Press of America, 1996).
4. David Beckler, "The Precarious Life of Science in the White House," in William A. Blanpied and Gerald Holton, eds., *Science and Its Public: The Changing Relationship* (Amsterdam: Reidel, 1976).
5. *Op. cit.*, ref. 2.
6. The first proposal for a Department of Science was made by the Allison Commission in 1884 at a time when federal involvement in applied science and en-

gineering was rapidly increasing. A. Hunter Dupree, *Science in the Federal Government* (Cambridge: The Belknap Press of Harvard University, 1957), pp. 215–231.

7. A short summary of recent Department of Science proposals appears in General Accounting Office, *U.S. Science and Engineering Base: A Synthesis of Concerns About Budget and Policy Development* (GAO/RCED-87-65), Appendix III (March 1987); see also William T. Golden, "A Department of Science: An Illusion— PSAC: A Prescription," *Technology In Society,* Vol. 8 (1986), pp. 107–110.

Notes on Science Advising in the White House

W. O. Baker

Science and technology became part of our American expectations for social and economic and political progress only about a third of a century ago. Our leaders then remembered their role in winning wars, particularly World War II, and in introducing also new factors in the power of nations and the energy and material resources of the world (as shown through nuclear fission and fusion, substitution of synthetic material, such as nylon and rubber, for the world's natural fibers, metals, and minerals, and also for science and technology's important role in public health). So science and technology began to be recognized as essences of Vannevar Bush's "The Endless Frontier." In this broad sweep of global affairs, dominated as usual by national security and affected by nearly four decades of freedom from major-nation wars, the tendency to expect White House science and engineering to continue in earlier forms is widespread.

Nevertheless, the displacement of the White House Office of Science and Technology in the early 1970s was a signal for more pervasive change than has been assimilated. This was, however, recognized when Dr. Simon Ramo and the writer were assigned by President Ford the task of reviewing and reforming appropriate science and technology activities at 1600 and 1700 Pennsylvania Avenue. Accordingly, we did work out in collaboration with certain members of the House of Representatives and through the active participation of Vice-President Nelson Rockefeller, a statutory base. This embodied a feeling that the whole domain of science and engineering had grown to where expressed participation of the Congress should be assured. On the other hand, we had organized preliminary committees, one on An-

William O. Baker is Chairman of the Rockefeller University and Chairman of the Andrew W. Mellon Foundation, and has been Research Director, President and Chairman of Bell Laboratories. He is a Trustee of Princeton and Carnegie-Mellon Universities. Dr. Baker has been a member of the President's Science Advisory Committee and the National Science Board, is a member of the President's Foreign Intelligence Board, and has received numerous awards, including the President's National Security Medal and the National Technology Medal.

ticipated Advances in Science and Technology, chaired by the writer, and one chaired by Dr. Ramo, (these were combined as a Presidential Committee on Science and Technology—Dr. Simon Ramo, Chairman, W. O. Baker, Vice Chairman—when the new OSTP was in place) which sought to identify the scope and magnitude of issues facing oncoming Administrations. In this statutory structure, total involvement of national science, technology and engineering—academic, industrial and governmental—would be warranted, and was prescribed.

These studies, of course, emphasized economic and sociopolitical matters much more than national security, which had already achieved such expert attention and interest. But the other areas, ranging from energy supplies and its distribution, health affecting large and growing segments of our population, education, and a variety of other issues relating to vitality and competitive challenges in our industrial system, were transferred to the next stages of OSTP, in 1977. Since actions proposed on these have not yet been adequately reflected in terms of science, technology and engineering policies in our federal administration, there is a recurrent question of whether this can be expected.

This particular phase of White House Science activity has fortunately been so well documented by Mr. Golden's earlier collections,[1] by a special section of the journal about science policy, *Science, Technology, and Human Values*,[2] and by Thaddeus Trenn's book, *America's Golden Bough*[3] that almost every option for the next phases of the federal science office has been offered and discussed. Dr. Trenn has especially carefully reflected the views of a wide sample of the national scientific and technical community, so the context in which further remarks are offered should be known from these sources. A forthcoming study by Dr. Gregg Herken, "Cardinal Choices,"[4] also deals insightfully with the record and future of Presidential science advising.

Accordingly, in terms of the changed environ of public, academic, and industrial science and technology noted before, arising from world competition and social concerns, the values of pluralism in federal and other public science and engineering stand out. R. W. Nichols's wide-ranging essay on decentralization of R&D organization is an excellent survey[5]; see also W. O. Baker.[6] Namely, science and technology have so widely permeated our culture by the approach of the 1990s (ironically perhaps the more so as general literacy has declined) that a single agency such as a Department of Science or a single spokesman such as the Science Advisor to the President, could not adequately deal with what is required. These requirements range from providing a proper position for the President in teaching of kindergarten-to-twelfth-grade science and math to appropriate positions in international trade in super computers and the national values of planetary exploration to decoding of the human genome or pursuit of causes for ozone variation in the stratosphere.

POLITICAL PRIORITIES

Clearly, no coherent position of the national scientific or technical population can be expected from the White House on such complex and diverse matters. More importantly, the federal priorities assigned to them come through political rather than technical (or rational) considerations. Of course, this in no way implies that there should not be strong scientific and technical participation in both the political formulation and resolution of such matters, but such participation can hardly be centralized. Further, and most importantly, the validity of scientific and engineering positions taken in behalf of the public interest will gain from working experts being directly involved and having qualities recognized by professional peers, such as the national academies.

Indeed, such representation was intrinsic in our formation of the Council of Scientific Society Presidents and the cognate group affiliated with the Engineer's Joint Council, during the early 1970's. See also current suggestions for a "New Science Advisory Apparatus," NSAA, by J. Thomas Ratchford and William G. Wells.

Also, a special function of the eventual federal sponsorship and policy is to assure systems synthesis and analysis, to advocate the role of some form of systems engineering, in dealing with the broad issues which involve large segments of national science and technology resources. This, too, demands first-hand, on-site information.

New pathways to assure scope and vitality of this pluralism in science advising seem to be forming. We have emphasized the growing role of scholarly and professional societies (in the striking expansion and quality of the Materials Research Society, for instance) as well as the increasing public responsibilities recognized by industrial firms and such groups as the Industrial Research Institute, the Scientific Research Administrators Society, the Conference Board, and others. But in addition, local governments and particularly state-based agencies are bringing issues of science and education, and economy and technology of public ventures, including public engineering and health, ever more deeply into their basic operations and politics. Now, of course, it is unrealistic to expect that highly informed and coordinated findings about Super Colliders or vaccine programs or environmental improvement around cities, etc., will emerge from fifty localized and variable centers. Nevertheless, stimulated especially by the compelling urgency of educational reform and the restoration of literacy ("A Nation At Risk. . .", "To Secure the Blessings of Liberty", "Education Commission of the States Report on Undergraduate Education")[8] and by dislocations of industry and impact of foreign competition, the National Governor's Association has become a growing strength. It is building bases for mobilizing and expressing the widespread views of our expert populations, without having them molded into a conventional government format. (The National Science Foundation's Office of Legislative and Public Affairs, with the special attention of Joyce Hamaty, is conducting an analysis and listing of these state entities.)

THE ENDLESS QUEST

So as we have said before, the endless quest of how to make the culture of science (which C. P. Snow and Robert Oppenheimer and many others felt was hopelessly disparate from other human affairs), nevertheless part of a broader citizen participation may get significant aid from such new state-based activity. Our experience in New Jersey is encouraging. There our statutory State Commission on Science and Technology (in succession to a preliminary Governor's Commission on Science and Technology) is providing new linkages. These include specific operational politics (several of its members are members of the legislature and the Governor's Cabinet) while at the same time involving significant numbers of younger, directly active scientists and engineers from industry and universities. These serve in the formation and conduct of consortia and institutes for R&D in materials, biomedicine, food and agriculture, waste disposal and recycling, and other important capabilities.

Further evidence of major shifts in science and technology initiatives comes from our experience with the Health Effects Institute. This novel enterprise was organized independently in 1979 and 1980, with precisely balanced sponsorship by the federal government's Environmental Protection Agency and the automotive and engine manufacturing industry (worldwide). Its administration (sternly independent) benefits from *joint* government and private missions—a blend which can minimize the shortcomings of separate sectors. We believe that the future of American science policy and application for public benefits would gain notably by other locally engendered combinations of public and private initiative and management.

These ongoing endeavors are all related to our fundamental theme that modern science and engineering flourish from pluralistic policy guidance, intrinsically derived from often first-hand knowledge of diverse leaders who have earned professional respect of their peers. They must be sufficiently involved in the rational and ethical principles of scientific and engineering practice so that the often subjective and emotional dominance of technical matters through big politics is suitably modulated or contained. Indeed, this tactic will probably become increasingly desirable as the role of video in shaping popular human attitudes, from infancy through maturity, becomes ever more prominent. New generations of citizens could be led to expect bizarre roles of science and technology from political campaigning that "shows" medical marvels, automobile perfection, faultless plumbing. . .for public purposes. Our government should go ever more in direction of authentic dispersion of seeking counsel among a national community.

The role of the White House Science Office should move even further toward these positions we have discussed before, so as not to centralize the assessments and needs of all science and technology of public import. Rather, it should transfigure into appropriate scientific and engineering terms and meanings the major interests of the President at a given time. These would be expected constitutionally to have a large national security component (unlike earlier Science Advisor and OST, the OSTP has had little or no involvement in national security systems or budgets.)

LOOKING TO THE FUTURE

Hence, in the theme of looking to the future that William Golden has emphasized for these reports, we shall see new proposals for further decentralization, pluralism and diversity, in seeking ways for research and development to serve even more strongly the needs and interests of our people. Certain functions do, however, endure. The first official report of the President's Science Advisory Committee received by President Eisenhower was on the creation and distribution of suitable and widespread access of the record of understanding and discovery on which all science and engineering depend.[9] This matter of accumulated record, avoiding among other things a costly and futile repetition of the work of generations of engineers and scientists up to now, remains an ever-challenging need, but one which has been significantly unmet in recent years.

The challenge of knowing what is being done in both federal and independent sponsorship is already vast. But this is an area where machine aids and thought, augmented by enduring ties to evaluative resources such as the National Academies, the Engineering Society Councils, and the Council of Scientific Society Presidents, would yield new visions of what is going on and what is needed. One more reminder of the dimensions of these issues, looked at from this need for Executive branch perspective, accents the point. This year's national research and development spending will exceed $125 billion which is in current dollars more than 300% that of the spending of a decade ago, when we were pursuing the reconstruction of the OSTP. Although inflation reduces the steady value (the constant 1982 figure for this year would be about $105 billion), the actual management and spending of the funds have clearly surged. About $60 billion or 48% of this comes from the federal government and, of that fraction, about two-thirds is from the Department of Defense. About $65 billion or the remaining 52% comes from industry, academic, and other non-profit institutions. But of the total $125 billion, about 75% will actually be spent in industry.[10] Now everyone knows that in this combination of basic research (about $15 billion), applied research (about $27 billion), and development and engineering ($83 billion), the mechanisms of resource management and administration have reached such complexity and idiosyncratic diversity that the conventional notion of knowing the scientific and technical results related to the dollars administered for them is fantasy.

As we have said, we do not even have the comfort that we are avoiding extensive and corrosive repetition, to say nothing of whether quality and authenticity are surviving. The dimensions are such that naturally the agencies, particularly the federal bureaus and the Congress, are uneasy and have pursued vast hearings, such as those during 1986 from the Fuqua Committee of the House, on trying to see what has happened and what might be expected. (These followed the report of the Task Force on Science Policy, Don Fuqua, Chairman; H. P. Hanson, Staff Director; December 1984. This "Agenda for a Study of Government Science Policy" resulted in notable testimony from many segments of the national community.)

The White House needs far more incisive views of what is truly critical for national strength that any of the present processes offer. Indeed, those of us who moved some years ago into the billion dollar per year laboratory budgets of individual industries (these have now been notably exceeded and include in 1987 about $4 billion each for General Motors and IBM, $2.3 each for Ford and AT&T, and more than a billion dollars each for GE, DuPont and Eastman Kodak) know that even on that comparatively modest scale, special new tactics involving particularly substantive information or guidance of science and technology programs have become compelling. So it's not surprising that recurring unease about the national total is building. The General Accounting Office accented this in its current staff study.[11] This careful study, disputed, of course, by other agencies, such as the OSTP, brings together the old familiar criticisms of all kinds. These emphasize a stronger role in central planning, an aggregation of expertise, correlations with OMB, enhanced functions of the National Academies, and continuum of multi-year funding for research, etc. But there are other implications in the report connected with our themes of seeking a new grasp of what is actually being done. This, too, appears in the growing functions of the Office of Technology Assessment, in moving toward coalition and quality-weighting in the large range of initiatives coming from Congressional committees.

GROWING PROVINCIALISM

Similarly, on August 20, 1987, the National Academy of Engineering released a report undertaken at the request of the National Science Foundation, asserting growing provincialism in the US scientific and engineering community. It properly deplores language deficiencies and other skills which would permit our scientists and engineers suitably to participate in world advances. It notes that among the 30,000 Americans attending foreign universities, only about 3% are even studying technical subjects. In comparison, of the more than 317,000 foreign students enrolled in our academic centers in the US, about 180,000 are studying engineering and science. The various recommendations of the NAE panel wisely urge expanded overseas participation by American professionals and students, including the establishment by the government of "international technology assessment centers" at various US universities. This is another way of saying that the scientific and technical knowledge base of the world ought to be mastered in the US.

So, once more, we feel that a new shaping of the White House science advice should focus on information handling, on setting a pattern of assuring recognition for what is both new and true. These basic elements of science and engineering are easily (and presently) lost in the skittish frenzy of titillating the American people's instinctive and worthy interest in engineering, invention, science, and discovery through sensational headliners of super–everything. Indeed, the current experiences of The Scientists Institute for Public Information, which provides for the media a credible and expert-based information resource on current technology and science, further support the view that a highest level conscience is needed in this domain, both to support public understanding and the responsibility of the R&D community.

INFORMATION AND COMMUNICATION

The evolving situation—that the alleged findings of science and technology can not be taken at face value to the degree which has become accepted during much of the century—is ideologically regrettable. But it is an inevitable consequence of the range and size of the effort and the difficulty that human frailty has in dealing with it. Hence effective high-level science advising, in shifting from prescriptive to critical descriptive phases, warrants new attention to information resources and communication of knowledge. In fact, since many aspects of the Information Age derive from technical facilities themselves, it is fitting that science strategy and advising have a more sweeping connection with the knowledge base than has been attained or even been fashionable in recent years. Overall, we have not quite adopted knowledge as the basis for action sufficiently.[12] Indeed, the currently proposed Technology Competitiveness Act, (H.R.2916/S.907, 1987), (which includes among other related elements of national science structure making the National Bureau of Standards into the National Institutes of Technology and even one more attempt to make federal agents adopt the metric system by 1992) has emphasis on improved information resources. The HR2958/1223, "Economic Competitiveness. . .Act" carries forward the old theme of a new federal Department of Industry and Technology, including Advanced Civilian Technology Agency. While this idea of a new Department of Industry and Technology has not survived eventual Bill drafting, the hearings and statements also recognize strongly the role of information resources.

A significant common element of all this legislative movement is a feeling of information deficiencies, and an abiding unease that modern technology is inadequately applied to organizing knowledge for action in the public realm. This has taken specific form in HR1615 entitled "The Government Information Act" of 1987 on which hearings were held by the House Subcommittee on Science Research and Technology on July 14 and 15. This proposal would establish a Government Information Agency, absorbing the present National Technical Information Service of the Department of Commerce, and making the NTIS officially government owned. Such an activity would thus follow the departure from the White House Science Office of a once active Committee on Science and Technology Information in the original Federal Council of Science for Technology, which, in turn, has declined from its once lively responsibilities for information exchange among federal science and engineering bodies. It has become a quite different and diffuse "coordinating" and conversation symbol. But we should say again that just extension or restoration of effective information circulation, such as the functions of the former Science Information Exchange and Science Information Council, is not the essence of the present proposal. Rather a major shift in science advising is intended. In this, the content and ethics of new knowledge, and its potential for use are steadily assessed by expert leadership and support. This should be done in terms of the issues that a particular President and his Administration are pursuing. Certain potential elements of this have appeared since the 1976 reestablishment of the OSTP, when the National Academy of Sciences, for example, has presented overviews of COSEPUP and other studies of significant frontiers of science and engineering to the White House group. The assessment of existing knowledge bases, however, primarily the literature, and the relationships to Administration issues, have rarely been covered.

THE NSF SURVEY

The needs being considered are strikingly represented in a recent survey, sponsored by the National Science Foundation, of principal engineering advances of recent years. In this work, "National Science Foundation Support for Significant Advances in Fundamental Engineering Research as Shown in Publication Acknowledgements 1965–1985," apparently a group of well-qualified academic leaders judged, by publication quality and frequency (but seemingly not with the breadth of statistics provided by such effective bibliographic analyses as from the Institute for Scientific Information) what were thought to be important new findings. However, the judgments of such communities as the National Academy of Engineering, with appropriate industrial insights and particularly with a worldwide perspective, do not seem to have been involved.

In recent times, these trends have become much stronger and are attended by other tendencies in the national government which prompt further insight and adjustment of how science advising in the Executive branch should be shaped. For instance, in this Bicentennial period, the classical Constitutional bonds between the activities of the President and the Congress become especially relevant.

Direct connection of science and technology to the President has come from their role in national security and public health. Since the mid-century, however, the surging position of research and development for economic progress,[13] their predominant role in industrial gains and especially in modern world competition for both social and economic position, and the prominent part of science and engineering in education, especially post-secondary, have raised new issues. Although the principal post-World War II discoveries and industrial advances, such as materials science and engineering, the transistor and solid-state electronics, the laser and photonics, have occurred without initial government support or participation, the dramatic advances in the life sciences, pharmaceuticals, and medical therapy, have represented intermediate cases. There, the federal NIH in particular has provided, largely through its academic and federal laboratory programs, an interesting large and hybrid role also enhanced by vigorous innovation from the pharmaceutical and health care industry. Likewise, although much molecular biology beginning with molecular genetics and the discovery of RNA/DNA systems originated in private academic research, this area in recent years has represented a special move of entrepreneurship by academic leaders. Often their work was initially linked to the NIH, but they recently have formed many independent small companies.

So altogether, the mission of science and technology advice to the President and his staff has shifted drastically from earlier times. Then, huge defense programs; major issues of public health requiring concerted industrial action on new vaccines, therapeutic agents, etc.; and overall social programs, such as social security, access to education, environmental protection were the primary sociotechnical concerns.

DIVERSITY AND DECENTRALIZATION

Nowadays, diversity and decentralization become vital issues, so valid but vast realms represented by information, publication and bibliography provide examples that highest-level governmental science and technology advising should deal with usefully. For ways of assuring that the now vast national (and international) community can be informed about what is known and what needs to be known are needed, while similarly providing an authentic overview of whether groups know each other, and what sort of total resources are working in given areas of research and development.

This is especially significant for advances in engineering, where modern engineering systems can benefit very quickly and steadily from quite new and even incomplete scientific discoveries. In turn, if the OSTP and its Director maintain a keen awareness of the large movements in the literature around the world, they will be able to recognize important trends and to find the experts we have referred to with a confidence that they are not reflecting only the necessarily special interests of this or that federal agency. We have seen trends of the large sponsoring agencies toward claiming priority for both their programs and results. But significant new values can come from having science advice in the White House and Executive Office of the President that does not derive from or espouse particular programs, as merited as they may be. For instance, the tight coupling of the science of directed energy beams to the development of SDI is not necessarily a fruitful high-level tactic, nor is the emphasis of commercialization of superconducting solids the pathway to understanding the basis for electron movement in complex crystals. But there is a kind of over-wisdom that should be cultivated at the highest levels, about how discovery and knowledge are moving world-wide in science and engineering, and thus about what it is reasonable to *expect* in our total national effort.

Now these expectations often turn out to be the strongest catalyst for new findings, if they are expressed with credibility and care in the highest forms of national leadership. In fact, many of the successful elements of OST and PSAC, as established by President Eisenhower and pursued by a couple of Administrations thereafter, was in the published reports that established *expectations,* rather than Presidential commitment to a particular technical or political technical goal. The space program and the national materials program, both begun the latter part of President Eisenhower's tenure, are pertinent examples. PSAC reports were prepared by experts who were either working directly in the field and or had carefully evolved the best counsel. Then, statements of expectations, such as those of the Apollo mission forwarded by President Kennedy (without specific scientific or technical consultation, but based on wide-ranging political considerations), have appropriate significance in terms of what is known, or merely imaginable. This difference is the advice Presidents and other political figures truly need.

The present dimensions of science and technology require Presidential science advising combining disciplines and ranging over wider fields of knowledge and discovery than have been adequately covered. The strong tradition of science to specialize in disciplines is particularly limiting in the habits and experience of premiere Advisors. Likewise, integration of new and complex science with technology and engineering is allowed to languish over times which are often important in recognizing new movements in international security, economics, industry and social affairs. Hence, a challenge for the future is to make Presidential science advising a focus of information handling, supported naturally by the potentially powerful and unprecedented abilities of both the public and independent publication, and learned and professional society, knowledge basis. This will demand multidisciplinary interests and skills. So far, little has developed out of it, except for some special industrial resources. The increasing use of systems engineering in applications of science and technology is, however, a constructive factor in such development.

Nevertheless, much new effort and training will be needed in universities and other institutions to develop both the hierarchical coverage of new knowledge and trends and simultaneously to access the validity of what is alleged. Quality assurance, in recent years a byword in industrial competition, particularly with Japan, and for decades before that a necessary component of high technology operations in the industry where it was evolved, is pursued in the validation of discovery primarily by peer-review systems in publication. These vary so profoundly that the quality control of reviewing would itself be a major gain (but still astonishing). Overall, however, with a "publish or perish" doctrine still firmly dominant and with a proliferation of journals, circulars and bulletins anticipated, quality assurance on a knowledge base for national Presidential science and technology judgments remains for the future.

Indeed, the size of the task is not to reform research and development in 20th Century science, as appealing as that may be, but merely to provide for the head of government in the US some credible estimates of scientific and technical aspects of particular political positions. But the task is illustrated by the intensity of effort used by the Swedish Academy of Sciences in sorting out validity of exceedingly narrow and specialized fields for Nobel Prize designation, and of similar work in other groups such as the Wolf Prizes, the Welch Prizes in chemistry, and, on a broader scale, awards of the National Science Board, the National Academy of Sciences, the National Academy of Engineering, and others. And these judgments are usually made long after performance, whereas we now need such quality identification during the course of discovery and its earliest application.

The influence of scientific and engineering advice, critically conditioned as we have suggested, would, of course, challenge many of the fondest habits of the respective communities. That, too, could have values, however.

NOTES

1. William T. Golden, ed., *Science Advice to the President* (Oxford: Pergamon Press, 1980).
2. William T. Golden *et al.*, *Science, Technology and Human Values*, Vol. II, no. 2 (1986).
3. Thaddeus F. Trenn, *America's Golden Bough* (Cambridge, MA: Oelgeschlager, Gunn and Hain, 1983).
4. Gregg Herken, *Cardinal Choices* (pending publication, 1987).
5. Rodney W. Nichols, "Pluralism in Science and Technology: Arguments for Organizing Federal Support or R&D Around Independent Missions," in Frederick Seitz, ed., "Special Issue: A Department of Science and Technology: In the National Interest?," *Technology In Society*, Vo. VIII, nos. 1 & 2 (1986), pp. 33–63.

6. W. O. Baker in *Science, Technology and Human Values, op. cit.*
7. J. Thomas Ratchford and William G. Wells, *Science, Technology and Human Values,* Vol. 12, no. 1 (1987), pp. 73–79.
8. David P. Gardner, Chairman: W. O. Baker, *et al.,* National Commission on Excellence in Education, "A Nation at Risk. . ." (1983); Terrel H. Bell, Chairman; W. O. Baker *et al.,* National Commission on the Role and Future of State Colleges and Universities, "To Secure the Blessings of Liberty," American Association of State Colleges and Universities, 1986.
9. Panel of PSAC, W. O. Baker, Chairman, "Improving the Publication and Dissemination of Scientific and Technical Information in the United States," July 1958.
10. Data from the National Science Foundation (NSF87-303, 1987).
11. General Accounting Office, "U.S. Science and Engineering Base: A Synthesis of Concerns About Budget and Policy Development," RCED-87-65.
12. W. O. Baker, S. Lazerow Memorial Lecture, University of Pittsburgh, 1984; HR Committee on Science and Technology, Subcommittee on Oversight, Record of Hearings, September 29, 1981—"Information Centers As Basic Emergency Management Systems"; and The World Future Society Conference, New York, July 1986.
13. See R. Landau and N. Rosenberg, eds., *The Positive Sum Strategy* (Washington, DC: The National Academy Press, 1986).
14. M. MacCarty, *The Transforming Principle* (New York: The Rockefeller University Press, 1985).
15. W. O. Baker, "The Bridge," *National Academy of Engineering,* Vol. 16 (1987), p. 15.

Science, Technology and Democracy

Harry G. Barnes, Jr.

Science and technology questions have had an important place in the relationships between our country and the countries in which I have served as Ambassador: Romania, India, and Chile. My Foreign Service career, in fact, has been spent almost entirely in what are called developing countries, and my most recent Washington assignment, as Director General of the Foreign Service and Director of Personnel of the Department of State, involved me in the recruitment and assignment of Foreign Service employees around the world. It is against this background that I offer some thoughts for the future.

I start with some assumptions:

- The United States has an abiding and, therefore, vital interest in a world where democratic societies can flourish and where international disputes can be resolved by negotiation and not by force.
- The impact of disturbances in almost any area of the globe can be substantial for the United States and, therefore, what happens in developing countries can be of great consequence to us. How we, in turn, relate to these developing countries depends, in large part, on our ability to communicate effectively with them.
- The universality of science and the abundant applicability of technology makes scientists one of the most important channels of communication among countries, especially if they also have ready access as a community to those who make policy.
- A good part of the success of our own society, as seen from abroad, lies in our ability to share in the search for solutions to problems, which is, in turn, an inherent part of democracy. The equivalent in international

Harry G. Barnes, Jr., a career Foreign Service officer, served mostly in posts in South Asia and Eastern Europe until his most recent assignment as US Ambassador to Chile. When Ambassador to India (1981–85), he was actively involved in the development of the US-India STI (Science and Technology Initiative), launched by President Reagan and Prime Minister Indira Gandhi in 1982.

The views expressed in this article are the author's own, and do not necessarily reflect those of the US Department of State.

affairs is cooperating and sharing in areas which are mutually important, areas which science and technology are constantly addressing.

If these assumptions make sense, then the United States Government needs to be sure that there is a serious science component built into our relations with other countries. Obviously, with many developed countries, it is already there, often through private channels. With regard to developing countries, though, it is harder, because their science resources are usually scarcer and their governments often play a much larger role than does ours. This means that, perforce, we have to design different ways to relate to science policy-makers, scientists, and science-related issues in those countries. In the first place, we should consciously look at the relationship in terms of science interests (and potential for meeting the principal problems a country faces), as well as in terms of our more traditional commercial, political and military interests. It is a search, in other words, under a broader definition, for the interests we would have in common.

In Washington, this means careful selection of the individual who fills the role of Science Advisor to the President and a deliberate decision to involve that person in policy-making. It means, too, an equally deliberate focusing on those developing countries which are of particular importance to the United States and a determination of the relative priorities that should be assigned in the use of government science resources internationally. Thus, there should be a US science policy for each such country which all the various US Government agencies with programs in science and technology (coordinated by the State Department's Assistant Secretary for Oceans, Environment and Science) should help develop and then be expected to carry out.

Overseas, the counterpart would be a strengthening of the system of science attaches, and the incorporation into the Ambassador's goals and objectives of a significant science and technology component. In fact, were I back in my previous incarnation as Director General, I would also seek further ways whereby Foreign Service Officers would, regardless of their specialty, be kept regularly informed about scientific developments with potential foreign affairs impact. Throughout, the focus will have to be kept on problems of major concern and major potential benefit to both the US and the other country that can come from collaborative efforts. The work on the monsoon in India as part of the world weather system or on earthquakes in Chile with lessons for our own West Coast are cases in point.

With regard to the Congress, help can come in the form of more emphasis on developing countries in the excellent work done by the Office of Technology Assessment and what those countries can help us learn. Help can come, too, in greater recognition of the international dimension of problems like toxic wastes or the depletion of the ozone layer and the development of marine resources, by encouraging agencies like the EPA to increase their collaborative efforts with other countries. Similarly, the Fulbright program, which has a long tradition of Congressional support, could be provided funding to enable it to expand into the areas of the natural sciences, recognizing thereby the contribution that science and technology make to the improved communication and comprehension among peoples that the Fulbright exchanges have so long sought.

Particularly in the developing countries where the drive for change is so strong, those engaged in science and technology activities have a substantial role, and it is in our interest to enable them to be in continuing touch with their counterparts in the US. In countries where the political system is far from democratic, one of the healthiest elements for change is the scientific community where there is constant need for a freer atmosphere in order to be able to function effectively. We, as a country, benefit whenever the "space," as Latin Americans call it, for greater freedom and communication can expand.

The other great advantage to a stress on scientific collaboration, especially when coordinated with our assistance programs, is that we thereby can associate ourselves with the problems that are primary in the minds of the people in other countries. Too frequently we are apt to be seen as focused only on a narrow definition of our own interests, regarded as strategic and economic. Our interests have to encompass those aspects obviously, but we do ourselves a serious disservice if we forget the psychological importance of associating ourselves with people's basic aspirations. Those, especially in the developing world, are often in the area of improved standards of living and some greater sharing in the political process. Science and technology, because of their emphasis on problem-solving and on more open communication, greatly serve those ends, ends which ought always to be ours as well.

In short, an emphasis on science as a vehicle for broadening our relationship with developing countries to help promote their own progress helps us by bringing fresh experience and ideas for the solutions of some of our own problems. More broadly, it helps us, too, by making our relationships more mature and solid. And this, to take a concept from another era, one that is still vital for our own future, helps make the world safer for democracy.

Science and Technology in Presidential Policy-Making: A New Dimension and Structure

David Z. Beckler

The current fever of introspection concerning the nation's industrial/technological competitiveness is reminiscent of an earlier time. In 1957, the Soviets surprised the world by launching Sputnik, the first artificial satellite, and American complacency in its scientific and technological superiority was shattered. President Eisenhower responded with the appointment of the first full-time Presidential Science Advisor and the re-constitution of the President's Science Advisory Committee.

The Science Advisor served as Director of the Office of Science and Technology created by Reorganization Plan early in the Kennedy Administration. He also chaired the President's Science Advisory Committee which met monthly to consider a wide range of science and technology related issues, drawing on the expertise of some 200 scientists and engineers outside of government.

The White House science and technology advisory structure was terminated by President Nixon in 1973, shortly after his re-election, and its responsibilities were transferred to the Director of the National Science Foundation. The stated reason was the desire to steamline the White House staff.

David Z. Beckler was Executive Officer of the President's Science Advisory Committee and assistant to six Science Advisors to the President from 1957–1972. He served as Special Assistant to the President of the National Academy of Sciences from 1973–1976, and was Executive Assistant to the Academy's ad hoc *Committee on Science and Technology in its study of science and technology in Presidential policy-making. From 1976–1983, Mr. Beckler was Director for Science, Technology and Industry at the Organization for Economic Cooperation and Development in Paris, France.*

The underlying rationale had more to do with political considerations—the loyalty and faithfulness of an outside group of scientific advisors and their support of the President's positions.

The Congress reinstated the S&T advisory function in the Executive Office of the President by legislating the Office of Science and Technology Policy in 1976. The Science Advisor to the President heads that office. Although authorized by the same legislation, the President's Science Advisory Committee was not reestablished.

Developments since that time serve to underscore the need for a strong, independent source of S&T advice to the President. There is a serious challenge to the international competitiveness of American high technology industries. There has been a major setback of US outer space capabilities due to a failure of management oversight of the space program. There are deep differences of view on the technical feasibility of the Strategic Defense Initiative, between advocates within the military establishment and outstanding scientists and engineers outside of government.

Such developments reveal how much American security, economic performance, and world leadership depend on the quality of scientific and technical judgments at the highest level of government. Yet, the elimination of the President's Science Advisory Committee and the progressive narrowing of the scope and responsibility of the Science Advisor have significantly reduced the ability of the President to take soundly based S&T policy decisions. Policy objectives based on flawed S&T assumptions cannot be attained. Moreover, the pursuit of such policies can be dangerously counterproductive when they involve international commitments.

One could ask, as in the case of Sputnik, whether these developments and new challenges to American technological performance warrant a change in the White House science and technology advisory structure and whether it is adequately shaped to satisfy the needs of the President. Unlike the pre-Sputnik circumstances, there is a White House S&T mechanism in place. The burden is on those who assert that a change in structure is necessary. The burden is supportable.

This essay concludes that the requirements for S&T advice in Presidential policy-making call for a deepening and broadening of the S&T advisory function. It makes a case for the reorganization of the White House S&T advisory structure based on two propositions:

(1) Experience before and after the dismantling of the White House S&T mechanism in 1973 demonstrates that the requirements for authoritative and credible S&T advice in Presidential policy-making can better be met by the reestablishment of the President's Science Advisory Committee;

(2) The heightened importance of technology policy, including policy for improving the international competitiveness of American industry, calls for a reconstituted White House S&T advisory struc-

ture designed to integrate S&T considerations into a broad range of Presidential policies.

DEEPENING S&T ADVICE TO THE PRESIDENT: A CASE FOR REESTABLISHING THE PRESIDENT'S SCIENCE ADVISORY COMMITTEE

Since the demise of the President's Science Advisory Committee, the function of the President's Science Advisor has gradually become more akin to that of an individual member of the White House staff, rather than that of the head of a major policy office in the Executive Office of the President which Congress intended for the Office of Science and Technology Policy. The reasons for the decline in the S&T advisory function are not clear. It appears to have been downgraded in Presidential reporting channels. Whether the attenuated relationship to the President is the cause or effect of a weakened S&T advisory capability, the central question is how to restore its usefulness to the President. In the absence of a personal relationship between the President and the Science Advisor, backup and reinforcement by a Presidentially appointed Science Advisory Committee could help to make the Science Advisor more relevant and less remote in the White House decision-making process.

A President's Science and Technology Advisory Committee would be an important component of a reconstituted White House S&T advisory mechanism. The inclusion of technology in its title would emphasize its technology policy function. The committee could bring to bear in a common forum a blend of expertise ranging from science, engineering, economics, sociology and medicine. It would lend stature and authority to the Science Advisor and scientific and technical credibility to decisions of the President. The committee could also serve to promote public understanding of S&T policy issues facing the country.

Furthermore, there are dangers in relying on a Presidential Science Advisor for advice in the absence of a strong base of scientific and technical expertise to which he is also accountable for scientific and technical judgments. The President needs the best S&T judgments available. S&T advice that is not founded on thorough analysis, however, can be misleading and counterproductive, all the more worrisome when rendered at the pinnacle of government. Its specialized nature makes it less amenable to critical review by generalists on the White House/Executive Office staff. This is one of the reasons why the Presidential staff over the years has viewed with mixed feelings the presence of S&T specialists in the ranks of Presidential advisors.

Important as the establishment of the President's Science and Technology Advisory Committee would be, experience cautions as to the likelihood of its acceptability. In the past, there has been an aversion on the part of White

House staff to the institutionalization of outside S&T advisors within the White House. There has been concern about the possible requirements for public openness in its deliberations. There has been apprehension that the conclusions of outside consultants may not coincide with those of the President who may need to take a wider range of factors into consideration, and risk being undercut by his advisors.

A discerning President might weigh the advantages of a President's Science and Technology Advisory Committee differently. In this age of science and technology, it is inescapable that certain scientific and technical judgments affecting Presidential policy decisions must be weighed at the top of government, and cannot be relegated to lower levels. The President must have access to the expertise of the nation's most qualified scientists and engineers. This, in turn, requires that he have an authoritative body to judge their findings, and an able staff to bring those judgments to bear in the policymaking process. The White House/Executive Office organizational structure must recognize this reality. Second-best arrangements for S&T advice to the President are unlikely to be good enough.

BROADENING SCIENTIFIC AND TECHNICAL ADVICE TO THE PRESIDENT: A CASE FOR A COUNCIL FOR SCIENCE AND TECHNOLOGY POLICY

In judging the capability of the White House S&T mechanism to advise the President, it is necessary to distinguish between two distinct but related functions: policies *for* science and technology, and science and technology *in* public policies.

Policies for science and technology deal largely with matters internal to the S&T system, such as support of basic and applied research and programs for the development of military, space, and nuclear energy technologies.

Science and technology in public policies concern those policies having objectives outside of the S&T system, such as:

- the promotion of technological innovation,
- balancing the costs and benefits of East-West flows of technology,
- judging the technical assumptions underlying national security and arms control policies,
- weighing environmental controls over technology, and
- assessing the policy impacts of major technological advances, as in biotechnology and superconductors.

During the earlier years of the White House S&T advisory mechanism, there was substantial emphasis on science and technology in policy, for example, the organization of the civilian space program, arms control policies and negotiations, assessment of technology-related national security policies, and technology for developing countries. Such emphasis on broad policy issues has not been as evident in the activities of the White House/Executive Office S&T policy mechanism, particularly in recent years. Although there have been some technology policy initiatives, the "S&T in policy" function has not been systematic and sustained.

Since the formulation of White House policies that draw on S&T advice is primarily in the hands of policy-makers outside of the S&T structure, there is need for a strong S&T advisory mechanism that can inject an S&T perspective during the shaping of those policies, whether they be national security, domestic or budgetary policies.

Most of the issues on the President's desk are not perceived or framed in S&T terms. They relate to the ends served by S&T—national security, economic policy, environmental policy, trade policy, etc. Thus, person-to-person contacts with the President by the Science Advisor may be less frequent than other White House advisors. This does not necessarily lessen the value of the relationship of the Science Advisor to the President. Active involvement of the S&T mechanism in the policymaking activities of other offices in the White House/Executive Office provides a vehicle for making the Science Advisor's views known to the President in the context of broader policy discussions.

The need to integrate S&T policies with other national policies has been underscored by the Ministers of Science of the twenty-four industrialized Western countries who are members of the Organization for Economic Cooperation and Development ("Science and Technology Policies for the 1980's," Ministerial Declaration on Future Policies for Science and Technology, O.E.C.D., 1981). Such policy integration must be accomplished at a level of government where it is possible to deal in a horizontal manner with an array of policy concerns, *i.e.*, in the White House and the Executive Office of the President.

Thus, scientific and technical advice must flow into the overall White House/Executive Office policy-making process and be integrated in policy proposals and conclusions presented to the President. This requires close interaction between the White House S&T advisory mechanism and the other policy offices, presently the:

- Office of Management and Budget,
- Council of Economic Advisers,
- National Security Council,
- Office of Policy Development (Domestic Policy Council, Economic Policy Council),
- Office of the Special Representative for Trade Negotiations,
- Council on Environmental Policy,
- Office of Drug Abuse Policy, and
- Intelligence Oversight Board.

Methods of policy research and analysis and the techniques for conducting integrated policy analysis have greatly improved in recent years. It cannot be expected, however, that each of the offices in the Executive Office of the President will have specialists to analyze S&T/policy interactions. In some cases, the S&T advisory staff will need to bring to bear the requisite S&T economic, social, legal and other expertise necessary to take account of the full range of policy considerations.

The White House S&T mechanism can draw on excellent policy studies undertaken within and outside of government in integrating and analysing White House policies. Within the government, the Congressional Office of Technology Assessment has established the feasibility and utility of integrating science and technology with other aspects of public policy. The OTA has produced a highly useful body of policy analysis for Congressional committees and staffs. It is paradoxical that Congress has at its disposal an analytical mechanism for dealing with S&T policy issues that is not matched by a corresponding capability in the Executive branch. Both branches of government have need for policy oriented S&T analysis that is not distorted or constrained by the missions and parochial views of the various departments and agencies.

The National Research Council, operating under the umbrella of the National Academies of Science and Engineering and the Institute of Medicine, also produces significant S&T policy-oriented studies that raise issues and suggest policy approaches that should be considered at Presidential level, although they may be addressed to particular agencies of the government. The White House S&T mechanism can be a channel for initiating and facilitating such consideration.

Some policy studies that would have been undertaken by the White House S&T mechanism in earlier years are now being conducted by the Office of Technology Assessment and the National Research Council, *e.g.*, the OTA assessment of the policy implications of breakthroughs in biotechnology and the NRC review of NASA's plans to redesign the space shuttle.

These new S&T policy research capabilities have significant implications for the functioning of the White House S&T mechanism. First, they constitute important resources for S&T-related policy analysis that can be drawn on by the White House. Second, the S&T advisory mechanism must have a strong capability to assess outside studies and to utilize their findings in the White House policy-making process. Such outside studies do not reduce or replace the role of the White House S&T mechanism. It is in a position to be fully informed and to situate S&T policy conclusions in the broader setting of White House policy objectives, constraints and interactions.

The issue of the international competitiveness of American industry, particularly high-technology industries, gives a sense of immediacy to the question of the adequacy of the White House/Executive Office S&T advisory structure to deal with technology policy.

It is well recognized that technological innovation is strongly influenced by government policies outside of the S&T system, *i.e.,* economic and fiscal policies, trade, industrial, regulatory, social, and manpower policies. Structural impediments can blunt the effectiveness of macroeconomic policies in stimulating technological innovation, such as resistance to structural change in obsolescent industries, labor market rigidity, restrictive trade and regulatory policies, and reduced incentive to invest due to high interest rates. The design of integrated policies for fostering technological innovation must take the foregoing factors and policy interactions into account. Since many of the separate policies involved are developed and intersect in the White House/Executive Office, their effects on technological innovation need to be addressed by the White House S&T mechanism in cooperation with the other offices concerned.

Providing integrated S&T policy advice can best be accomplished by a White House S&T mechanism that has a council structure similar to that of the Council of Economic Advisers. The analogy is more than superficial. Like economics, the breadth and diversity of science and technology call for a blending of different expertise and viewpoints in coming to policy conclusions. The consultative nature of a council arrangement lends itself to an integrated approach to policy development. With all council members appointed by the President with Senate confirmation, its consensus on policy conclusions would have political as well as technical standing.

The top-down organization of the Office of Science and Technology Policy, with a Director and Associate Directors appointed by the President, is not well suited to arriving at policy consensus. Nor have the Associate Director positions been filled, with the lesser status that this implies for the OSTP.

A Council for Science and Technology Policy would embody in its membership the different kinds of expertise and experience required. The three or four members of the Council could be drawn from the fields of science, industrial technology, and biomedicine. An economist versed in the economic relationships of science and technology would be an important addition. The chairman of the council would serve as Science Advisor to provide a single point of contact with the President.

The Council for Science and Technology Policy could be a particularly effective instrument for intensifying contacts and communications with nongovernmental communities. This is an important consideration, since a shift in emphasis towards technology policy will entail a more outward looking approach. Technology policies depend heavily on the private sector for their identification and implementation, and there is a commensurate need for close communication between government and industry.

The council arrangement for scientific and technical advice to the President was proposed by a blue-ribbon Committee on Science and Technology convened by the National Academy of Sciences in 1974 "to assess arrange-

ments whereby scientific and technological judgments may best contribute
to the formulation of policy at the highest levels of the Executive Branch
of Government" ("Science and Technology in Presidential Policymaking: A
Proposal," National Academy of Sciences, 1974).

The establishment of a Council for Science and Technology Policy and a
President's Science and Technology Advisory Committee would be consistent with Presidential authority under the National Science and Technology
Policy, Organization and Priorities Act of 1976. The Act authorizes the President to appoint a Director of the Office of Science and Technology Policy
and up to four Associate Directors, by and with the advice and consent of
the Senate.

It is inevitable that increased attention will need to be given at Presidential
level to the arena of national technology policies. The present machinery
for S&T advice has moved slowly in this direction. Domestic needs and
international competition may dictate a faster pace. Unless it can broaden
its capabilities for technology policy, the existing S&T advisory mechanism
may find itself increasingly on the sidelines as other policy offices take
up the function without the requisite scientific and technical footing and
perspective.

Reorganization of the White House S&T mechanism would mark a break
with the past. It would signal the intention of the President to meet the
challenges to American technological performance, just as President Eisenhower moved to implant the earlier White House science advisory structure
in response to the Soviet Sputnik. With the establishment of a Council on
Science and Technology Policy and a President's Committee on Science and
Technology, the decline in credibility and influence of the White House
S&T mechanism could be reversed. Presidential leadership in guiding S&T
policy could be measurably strengthened.

The Limitations of White House Science Advice

William A. Blanpied

It seems paradoxical at first glance that the official science advisory system within the Executive Office of the President is currently held in such low esteem, even though a January 1987 Presidential message to Congress explicitly recognized the importance of US science and technology capabilities to the achievement of major national goals, including enhanced economic competitiveness.[2]

But the paradox evaporates when this rhetorical support is viewed in the context of several administration decisions (or non-decisions) in which strong, independent science advice should have played a role but apparently did not. Certainly it is wise policy (and probably good politics) to link strong science and technology capabilities to the achievement of national goals. On the other hand, it is questionable policy to consider early deployment of the Strategic Defense Initiative (SDI) in the face of reasonable scientific evidence that considerably more research is required even to make an adequate assessment of the feasibility of satellite-borne directed energy weapons[3], or to persist in trying to enforce several unworkable aspects of export control regulations despite strong evidence of their negative impact on US high-technology trade[4], or to make it needlessly difficult for US oceanographers to cooperate with their Soviet colleagues in non-sensitive research on the grounds that those colleagues might learn something about US computer technology.[5]

The point is not to question the sincerity or competence of the current Science Advisor, but rather to suggest that the provision of real annual in-

William A. Blanpied[1] is currently on leave from the National Science Foundation at the University of California's Graduate School of International Relations and Pacific Studies at La Jolla. At the NSF, he is a Senior Analyst in the Information and Analysis Section of the Division of International Programs. He received his Ph.D. in Physics from Princeton in 1959. Prior to joining NSF in 1976, he held academic appointments at Yale, Case Western Reserve, and Harvard Universities, and was Head of the Public Sector Programs Division of the American Association for the Advancement of Science.

creases in the aggregated federal budget for research and development does not constitute *prima facia* evidence that a President recognizes the importance of science and technology in national affairs. The low esteem in which the science advisory system is currently held is linked to the apparent failure of two successive Directors of the Office of Science and Technology Policy (OSTP) to convey that message to the President and his political advisers.

Before seeking options to improve the situation, it is useful to recall the intention of the Congress in creating the existing science advisory system. The National Science and Technology Policy, Organization, and Priorities Act of 1976 tried to do considerably more than simply establish OSTP and designate its director as the President's Science Advisor.[6] It also assigned to OSTP a number of specific coordination, evaluation, analysis and planning functions designed to provide its director with the in-depth knowledge about the entire federal science and technology system and the impact of its activities on the nation as a whole that would be required of an effective Science Advisor. More important, the Act attempted to articulate the elements of a broad science and technology policy in terms of specific national goals and needs, with the clear implication that the Science Advisor had the responsibility to provide advice in the context of a coherent science and technology policy. According to the legislative history of the Act:[7]

> The government has gone through decades of *ad hoc* situations, arrangements regarding science and technology which have not been based on any firm policy but have responded merely to the current crisis. The results have been a marked inconsistency in utility and effect. In some cases things have worked well; at other times they have worked poorly.

INSUFFICIENT RESOURCES

Against this background, the widespread perception concerning the ineffectiveness of the Presidential science advisory system derives in part from the fact that OSTP has never been given sufficient resources to carry out the broad coordination, evaluation, analysis and planning functions envisioned by Congress. But more is traceable to the failure of two successive Administrations to implement a consistent science and technology policy that would provide a framework for long-range planning in the development and use of the nation's science and technology resources, as well as a set of guidelines for coordinating the science and technology activities of the separate federal agencies and rationalizing their annual research and development budgets. The Science Advisor seems to be regarded by the President and his political advisers more as an in-house technician called upon when they recognize that a specific policy issue has scientific implications, rather than as an independent spokesman who is expected to articulate the relationships between science and technology and other significant national policy issues.

Of course, this situation could be reversed by a President who understood the broad significance of science and technology, attracted a person of stature and independence to the Science Advisor's post, insisted that that official's counsel be taken seriously by all White House and cabinet-level officials, and provided OSTP with sufficient resources to carry out all its Congressionally mandated functions. But that is just the point. The effectiveness of any OSTP Director as Science Advisor depends not only on his access to the President. More important, it depends on the President's willingness to understand that science and technology have complex interactions with virtually all important national and international issues, and to be willing to act upon that understanding.

Of course, the Science Advisor is not the only White House-level official whose effectiveness depends on the President's willingness and ability to grasp and heed complexity. The Chairman of the Council of Economic Advisers, for example, must gauge his effectiveness largely through the President's understanding of the complexities of economic policy. Short of reconstituting OSTP as an independent agency on the model of the Federal Reserve Board, there appears to be no simple way to resolve the dilemma of forcing a President to heed the downstream implications of complexity unless he wants to listen.

Part of the solution to the problem of effective Presidential science advice at the Presidential level is to recognize that even in the best of all possible worlds, the Director of OSTP, no matter how well qualified, is likely to spend most of his time on problems that the President and his political advisers regard as immediately important. That role is, of course, vitally important, and can be carried out effectively only to the extent that the Science Advisor can bring sufficient intellectual resources to bear against what will often be the discordant, often persuasive, special pleading of the government's line agencies. Some of those resources will be volunteered from outside OSTP, provided the Science Advisor and his senior staff have the requisite stature to command them.

But that is only a partial solution. What can be done about the more difficult problem of bringing Presidential—and Congressional—attention to bear on the long-term implications of a host of science and technology-policy issues? In particular, how can sustained, high-level attention be focused on the need to maintain the strength and effectiveness of the US science and technology base as the key to solving all other science- and technology-related issues?

Although informed opinion now acknowledges the importance of science and technology to the achievment of national goals, a full understanding of the structural and substantive problems that need to be addressed in order to maintain the long-term strength of US capabilities in those areas is generally lacking. These problems include, for examples: the decay of the university research infrastructure; chronic inadequacies in scientific and technical education, particularly at the pre-college and two-year college levels; an uncoordinated budget process for federal research and development that has led, for example, to commitments for several large projects, such as the Strategic Defense Initiative, the Space Station, and the Superconducting Super Collider, with little apparent consideration for the downstream effects of these capital expenditures on the future availability of broadly based research support; the virtual evisceration of the research programs of several agencies, including the Environmental Protection Agency, the National Bureau of Standards, and the National Oceanic and Atmospheric Administration; and the failure of the US Government to understand—or take effective actions relative to—the changing international context of US science and engineering.

A PUBLIC CONSENSUS

If, as seems reasonable, the strength of US science and engineering capabilities will retain its status as a viable policy issue, the development of a public consensus that would recognize and begin to deal with the complexities and interrelatedness of the above-noted problems would constitute a significant contribution to the national interest. The historical record suggests that when the National Science Foundation was created in 1950, the National Science Board (NSB) was expected to play a substantial role in helping the President and the Congress identify and deal with important problems associated with the overall strength of US capabilities in scientific research and education. For several reasons, the first boards declined to accept such a role, restricting their attention to issues directly related to the National Science Foundation's programs.

Since the demise of the President's Science Advisory Committee (PSAC) in 1973 and the failure of the Carter and Reagan Administrations to reestablish a similar advisory body as authorized by the OSTP Act of 1976, the National Science Board remains the sole Presidentially appointed advisory body specifically authorized and directed by Congress to oversee the state of the collective national effort in science and engineering research and education. Assertive but appropriately measured action by the NSB to focus public attention on critical, systemic problems associated with the long-term health of US science and technology capabilities would be welcomed by both the US scientific community and the Congress as a positive contribution to the national interest. If carefully negotiated with the Director of OSTP, the assumption of such leadership by the NSB could buttress his position as Science Advisor by enhancing the intellectual resources he requires to provide the best possible advice to the President on critical national problems.

NOTES

1. The opinions of the author are his own and do not necessarily reflect the policies of the National Science Foundation.
2. "The President's Competitiveness Initiative," White House press release, January 27, 1987; Mark Crawford, "Competitiveness Bill Goes to Congress," *Science*, Vol. 235 (February 27, 1987), p. 967.
3. Colin Norman, "Doubt Cast on Laser Weapons," *Science*, Vol. 236 (May 1, 1987), pp. 509-510.
4. Committee on Science, Engineering, and Public Policy, *Balancing the National Interest: U.S. National Security Export Controls and Global Economic Competitiveness* (Washington, DC: National Academy Press, 1987).
5. Colin Norman, "Soviets Disinvited to Join Drilling Program," *Science*, Vol. 236 (May 8, 1987), pp. 659-660.
6. U. S. Code Congressional and Administrative News, 94th Congress, 2nd Session, 1976, Vol. 1, 90 Stat. 459-473.
7. *Ibid.*, Vol. 2, p. 896.

Supporting the President's Need for Technical Advice

Lewis M. Branscomb

Traditionally, fathers were expected (by their wives) to advise their young sons on the "facts of life"—information many lads either didn't need, didn't want, or wouldn't believe. And sons submitted to the advice because they understood that fathers regarded giving it as part of their professional responsibility.

A grossly unfair parable on the issues involved in providing scientific advice to the highest levels of the political community? Perhaps. But it may serve to remind us that among those who most frequently worry and write about the state of science advising, scientists figure more prominently than Presidents.

The scientific community, or at least that portion of it deeply concerned with public policy relating to scientific matters, feels—with considerable justification—that the management of public affairs could be improved if political leaders dealt with the technical content of their decisions with greater knowledge, comfort and insight. In private, many politicians freely admit that they feel ill-equipped to take public positions on complex technical matters. Only a few have the time and interest to become expert on issues such as the technical feasibility of SDI deployment, public health strategies for dealing with AIDS, or determining what a multi-billion dollar space station or superconducting Super Collider facility might contribute to the nation's technological vitality and competitiveness. Presidents are expected to make decisions, or at least take responsibility for them on all such issues.

Lewis M. Branscomb is Professor at the John F. Kennedy School of Government at Harvard University, and is Director of the Science, Technology and Public Policy Program. Until his academic appointment, he was an Overseer of Harvard University. He has been Vice President and Chief Scientist of International Business Machines Corporation, Director of the National Bureau of Standards, Chairman of the National Science Board, and a member of the President's Science Advisory Committee and of the Board of the American Association for the Advancement of Science. Dr. Branscomb is a member of the National Academies of Sciences, Engineering and Public Administration, and of the American Philosophical Society.

Thus the first and most fundamental question: Why are the political traditions and institutional arrangements for providing expert technical advice to the President not more robust?

The President's Science Advisory Committee was disbanded by President Nixon, along with the location in the Executive Office of the President of the Office of Science and Technology, and its director, the President's Science Advisor. When President Ford brought OST (now OSTP) back into the Executive Office, the Congress provided for an advisory committee for one year, but it was not continued. President Reagan authorized establishment of the White House Science Council, which has a distinguished but smaller membership than that of the old PSAC. But this Council only advises the Director of OSTP, who himself reports via the White House Chief of Staff.

In 1981[1] the National Science Board studied its role in broader issues of science policy, and concluded that such a role was appropriate, but would not likely be effective without Presidential encouragement and sponsorship. The Board is again discussing this question in the summer of 1987. The question will be answered the moment the Board receives a specific request from the President for its advice.

Both President Reagan and President Carter were slow to the point of apparent reluctance to appoint a Science Advisor (and Director of the Office of Science and Technology Policy) when they staffed the senior positions in their Administrations. It is hard to conclude that Presidents, of either party, come into office with a conviction that they need strong scientific and technological staff support, together with access to formal processes for soliciting technical advice from persons outside government.

Does the President, or his chief of staff, Howard Baker, have any real difficulty getting advice if and when they want it? Surely the answer is "no." The entire structure of the Academies and the NRC, the National Science Board, other Presidentially appointed boards of technical experts, dozens of scientific professional societies, hundreds of universities, and thousands of technically competent individuals are ready and willing to respond to any White House request.

THE PROBLEM

What, then, is the problem?

Recent Presidents were apparently not wholly persuaded that the institutional provisions for such advice established in the past (a Science Advisor who is also Director of OSTP, plus a President's Science Advisory Committee—PSAC) are to their advantage, at least when first coming into office.

Presidents are always free to seek opinions from their personal friends, in and out of government, in whom they have confidence. They probably realize that this method of getting advice can trap them into idiosyncratic and erroneous views.[2] They are perhaps more concerned that they may be manipulated or constrained by the advisory system that is supposed to help them.

This concern about being constrained is likely to be accentuated in the presence of a broad public clamor from scientists who insist their advice should be heard.

The political official's problem must be, then, some combination of:

• Top officials do not know when they need to ask (*i.e.*, would benefit from asking) for early warning advice about potentially important issues not yet high on the political agenda.
• They would prefer the Presidency not to be presented with highly visible evidence of major national problems prior to the time a politically acceptable plan for dealing with the issue can be developed.
• They may not have confidence that the advice they might get is more competent and objective than that contained in the positions of the departments, agencies and other stake-holders; and
• They may not be comfortable with the context of political values in which the advice would be embedded, and regard the Advisors as yet another constituency with its own agenda.

Scientists are quick to agree that the first of these is a problem. "Early warning" is probably the least-often challenged justification for a Presidential science advisory apparatus. One has only to look back to history, at the AIDS epidemic, at the energy crisis, at the technical management problems leading to the Challenger accident, to wish that some competent group of scientists and engineers had directed the President's attention to the matter much earlier.

The problem of associating the President with major problems that have no straightforward solution is a kind of "Catch-22," in the sense that unless the issue (acid rain or ozone depletion, for example) achieves some political visibility, it is doubtful that meaningful actions can be taken. Thus the President brings pressure on himself without the prospect of early relief.

Scientists are only reasonably comfortable about assuring the President that a science advisory body can be formed with unimpeachable credibility. Scientists have their own differences about the quality of technical judgment exhibited by different committees, institutions, and even individuals. Wisely reluctant to accept credentials in place of evidence, the scientific community will prefer to rely on a process for advising that contains checks and safeguards. These, as we shall see below, force the process into public visibility.

CONSEQUENCES

Perhaps the most troublesome aspect of the relationship between political officials and scientists concerns the consequences of an advisory process that is not totally private and confidential. Many scientists regard the politician's concern for the ideological context of science advice as a suggestion that political consequences—as well as scientific evidence—are legitimate criteria for acceptability of advice. Resolving this conflict is easy, in principle: The scientist gives his advice as free of ideological baggage as he can, and makes explicit the values in which the analysis is imbedded. Then the politician is left to accommodate "truth" and "reality" as best he can. But quite apart from the naivete of this distinction, the public visibility of the institutionalized advisory process makes that division of responsibility impossible. That would be true even if there were no Freedom of Information Act, no Federal Advisory Committee statute, no sunshine laws, all of which make visible the difference between the scientists' position and the President's "balanced" decision.

Why not solve the problem by arranging a completely private advisory group for the President, not supported by statute or (as private advisors to the President personally) not subject to the Advisory Committee Act? The President is of course, quite free to do so. But both President and scientists need a structured institutional process for this advice, one that includes both a full-time technical executive (Science Advisor) supported by a competent staff, but also a formal mechanism for tapping the expertise in the nation at large (a PSAC).

The President needs such an institutional capability for addressing complex technical issues and for evaluating the technical content of policy positions advocated to him in which he can gain confidence. Only by institutionalizing the function can the President make the group accountable, both for political consequences and to their technical peers for the quality of technical judgments.

The President's key additional requirement is that the advisory group supports his needs as Chief Executive of the Executive branch, and does not view itself as having a constituency representation function. This is a difficult balancing act, since the effectiveness of the science advising process requires both institutional visibility and sensitivity to the President's problems as a manager.

For the President's scientific advisors to have political credibility, they must be credible within the scientific community. Thus they have a dual accountability—to the President and to their intellectual standards represented by their peers. The scientific community also requires development of an institutional capability for rendering advice, with processes for developing advice in which scientists have high confidence.

THE ROLE OF PSAC

The PSAC met this requirement at the time. Its members took their responsibilities very seriously. Their selection was remarkably free of political distortion. Its many panels reached out to a diverse collection of experts who were knowledgable about details of PSAC activity. Much of its work resulted in formal White House publications with fully detailed texts. To this extent, the committee was publicly accountable, even though its meetings were closed.

But those were simpler times. Fewer disciplines were needed on the committee to do its work. Most of the PSAC members were physicists, chemists or mathematicians. Today's technical issues reach further into areas of social and economic concern and are more intimately bound up with them. Engineering, economics, social impacts, foreign relations all must be dealt with by those evaluating technical issues. For a group of experts to be accepted as adequately broadly representative, people of many different professional backgrounds are required.

These trends not only make it harder to separate value judgments from technical evidence, but make the process of assuring technical credibility harder too. Interdisciplinary science advising suffers from the same difficulties as interdisciplinary research; it is hard to establish and protect standards of scientific rigor. At the same time, the number of alternative sources of science policy analysis has grown, and their capabilities matured. Thus the advisory process in the Executive Office will have competition unless it earns a privileged position by providing some unique value added to the President and the agencies.

Nevertheless, the need for competent, independent evaluation of the technical dimensions of national policy was never greater. Examples of functions served by a public advisory mechanism such as PSAC include the following, with a parenthetical example of each:

- early warning of emerging issues (ozone depletion);
- creating public agenda (world food problem in 1960s);
- assessing the health of the national technical enterprise (science education);
- weighing conflicting technical arguments (SDI);
- identifying and assessing new opportunities from science (superconductivity);
- analysis of policy alternatives (space exploration goals);
- enhancing economic values from federal R&D (innovation, productivity and competitiveness);
- evaluating the likelihood of scientific solutions to seemingly intractable problems (AIDS, cancer);
- addressing public concerns about hazards (nuclear waste disposal); and
- providing the technical component of policy in other areas (R&D incentives in industry, science for foreign policy).

THE SOLUTION

How might an institutional structure be developed that would have a higher probability of survival and effectiveness?

A part-time public advisory body of experts, such as PSAC, cannot be expected to succeed absent a strong technical executive within the White House to serve as its chairman and to provide its staff. Thus the first requirement is to modify the current Office of Science and Technology Policy (OSTP), both as to mission and function. This office should be seen as having not only a role in policy formulation, but also in effective management of the federal enterprise. That does not imply assigning to OSTP any operational responsibilities. It does require the Office of Management and Budget to share some of its management role with OSTP, and obligates OSTP to be a responsible partner in the Executive Office management team.

If the agencies carry out their technical missions incompetently, if cabinet officers are tempted—or forced by political pressure—to appoint unqualified people to the top technical jobs, if the President has difficulty in getting agency cooperation toward the implementation of an important policy decision involving technical issues, the Director of OSTP should be held accountable, together with the agency heads. He or she can only be accountable if given review and approval authority appropriate to the purpose.

In this management support role the Director of OSTP carries out, as a member of the President's management team, a function that is not publicly visible, but is, nevertheless, critically important. If given the needed authority and cooperation, the Director will earn the respect and support of the President and, importantly, his Chief of Staff.

The OSTP also needs much closer links with economic and national security policy. This requires the establishment of formal responsibilities for the Director of OSTP both within the OMB's budget process and within the National Security Council. One such proposal was presented [3] by E. E. David, who was Science Advisor to President Nixon during his first term. Dr. David presented his proposed strengthening of the OSTP office as a preferable alternative to a Department of Science.

The President's concern about technology is likely to focus on two large issues: how the United States can compete successfully with both the USSR (in the military sphere) and Japan (in international trade) simultaneously. The development of a strong national scientific and technological capability on which both economic and military security can be built will require OSTP and its expert advisors to be accepted into the strategic debates in the NRC and the Economic Policy Council. To facilitate that happening, the President's Science Advisor and Director of OSTP should be elevated to Cabinet rank.

Finally, the Congress should consider very seriously how the Advisory Committee Act might be modified to provide more confidentiality for advisory committees working directly for the President. It should be possible to compel disclosure after the fact of advice given (subject to national security considerations) without forcing the deliberative process to take place entirely in public. Unless progress can be made in that regard, it is very unlikely the President and the White House senior staff will share with such a committee the information it needs to give advice the President will want to receive.

NOTES

1. P. A. Smith, *The National Science Board and the Formulation of National Science Policy* (Washington, DC: National Science Foundation [NSB-81-440], 1981).
2. In 1952, Sinclair Weeks, newly appointed Secretary of Commerce in the Eisenhower Administration, was urged by Undersecretary Shaefer to remove Alan V. Astin as Director of the National Bureau of Standards. The Bureau's electrochemists were supporting a Post Office fraud case against the manufacturer of a battery additive, ADX2, whom Mr. Shaefer was seeking to help. Secretary Weeks turned to the source of technical advice with which he was most comfortable, the chief engineer of the United Carr Fastener Corporation, of which Weeks had been CEO. Quite by chance, the engineer had used the product ADX2 in batteries at the corporation, and had a favorable impression of its efficacy. On this advice, Weeks supported Shaefer. Later, he brought in the Academy of Sciences for a full-dress technical audit of the Bureau's technical work, and concluded that it had been faultless.
3. Edward E. David, Jr., "A Department of Science and Technology: Noah's Ark or Instrument of National Policy?," *Technology In Society,* Vol. VIII, nos. 1 & 2 (1986).

Issues in High-Level Science Advising

Harvey Brooks

The period from the appointment of James Killian as Presidential Science Advisor in 1958 to the assassination of President Kennedy in 1963 is generally regarded as the high-water mark for the prestige and influence of high-level scientific advisory committees. Reminiscences of participants of that period embody a sense of pride in having been a part of a great moment in history, and current writings on the subject look to that period as the model for what an effective science advisory system should be.

Yet there is a certain paradox in this, since the scope of scientific advice and the role of scientists was much more limited in the early 1960s than it has since become. Cynics would argue that the nation today is using science advice more, but enjoying it less than in the heady PSAC days of Killian, Kistiakowsky and Wiesner. Scientists are listened to and consulted much more at all levels of government, but, at the same time, granted much less deference than was the case in those early days. One of the questions addressed in this essay concerns the extent to which it is realistic to expect that the unique situation of those times can ever be expected again.

HISTORICAL BACKGROUND

High-level advice by scientists serving part-time from outside government has a long history in the United States, but it only became an important political phenomenon after World War II, when it grew hand in hand with rising federal support for extramural R&D. Prior to the war, virtually all federally supported research had been performed by full-time civil servants in government laboratories, but, during the post-war period, more than 80% of federally sponsored R&D came to be performed in non-governmental in-

Harvey Brooks is Professor of Technology and Public Policy, Emeritus, at Harvard University. Trained as a physicist, he was a member of the President's Advisory Committee and of the National Science Board in the 1960s, and served as Chairman of the National Academy's Committee on Science and Public Policy (COSEPUP) in the late 1960s and early 1970s.

stitutions through the instrument of the research contract or grant. It was the concomitant phenomena of extramural performers and non-governmental policy advisors that led Don K. Price to characterize the roles of science and scientists in government as a new "scientific estate" in a well-known book of that title.[1]

Robert Wood further characterized scientists in high policy advisory roles as a new "apolitical elite," which derived its influence in politics from the very fact of its perceived distance from politics—perceived, that is, by the general public and a majority of politicians.[2]

In the heyday of the President's Science Advisory Committee (PSAC), this perceived distance was symbolized by the unique continuity of the membership of PSAC in the transition from the Eisenhower to the Kennedy Administration in 1961 and, subsequently, to the transition from Johnson to Nixon in 1969. Appointments to the National Science Board, the General Advisory Committee (GAC) of the Atomic Energy Commission, and many other agencies were similarly insulated from partisan politics. Indeed, when the Congress moved to create its own scientific advisory apparatus with the establishment of the Office of Technology Assessment (OTA) in 1972,[3] the new institution's structure and procedures were carefully designed to emphasize both the appearance and reality of non-partisan, neutral competence.[4]

The general public acceptance of the "apolitical" model of scientific advising (and of neutral expertise more generally) in the US political system has a long history in the first half of the twentieth century. Philip Harter[5] has pointed out that, in the original philosophy of government regulation established in New Deal days, public servants were regarded as neutral interpreters of political directives established by the Legislature, and it was thought that general legislative guidelines could be translated into concrete administrative decisions in a value-free scientific way.

This image of the apolitical role of expertise in making legislative intent concrete was reinforced in the early 1960s by an apparently extraordinary degree of political consensus in the country over the overriding need to meet the challenge posed by the Soviet successes in space and the feared "missile gap." The atmosphere of a decade of Cold War had created a situation in which national debates were largely about appropriate means to achieve national ends, which were the subject of a degree of bipartisan consensus seldom achieved in the US except in actual wartime. Thus the scientific advisory apparatus was seen as a natural mechanism for sorting out the means to an agreed end "scientifically," and the President's Science Advisors were perceived as being above and outside the bureaucratic struggles between agencies inside government, particularly the rivalries among the un-unified military services.[6]

It is thus no accident that science advice first reached the highest levels of politics with respect to the military and space, where there was virtually no questioning of the desirability and necessity of the ends being sought. At the time, even the support of pure research and the education of technical manpower, from the lowest to the most advanced, was frequently justified politically in terms of its ultimate contribution to meeting the challenge of Soviet military-technical competition, and hence to the national security of the United States.[7]

The prestige acquired by the natural sciences, especially physics, as a result of their contribution to the war effort resulted in a generous interpretation of what was to be regarded as "means"—and hence in the domain of the experts—as compared to "ends" in the public discussion. Moreover, the space and defense activities which became the major focus of the advice provided by high-level scientific advisors did not *seem* to have large distributional consequences within the society, favoring some social groups relative to others; this fact undoubtedly contributed to the apolitical image of the Presidential Science Advisors. Thus, for example, the development of a defense strategy based on nuclear weapons and deterrence—which might have been seen as highly "political" under different circumstances—was treated as a means in which the public and the politicians could appropriately defer to the judgment of experts.

As the national consensus on foreign and security policy began to erode in the second half of the 1960s and virtually disappeared in the agony of the Vietnam War, the prestige of science began to decline. At the same time, the work of PSAC and the institutionalized Office of Science and Technology came to deal increasingly with issues that transcended defense and space, while space and defense themselves became more "political." For example, in space policy, the country was never again able to achieve the consensus on national goals that had driven the Apollo program through the vicissitudes of several disasters, such as the Apollo capsule fire which claimed the lives of three astronauts in 1965.

Moreover, the very success of PSAC and OST in their initial assignments led to greater and greater expectations, and to their taking on more and more a quasi-operational role in such areas as oceanography, atmospheric sciences, materials, and scientific information, wherever responsibility for technical activities seemed to cut across established departmental lines. Broadening of responsibility came to be inevitably accompanied by dilution, while more and more bureaucratic toes got stepped on. The endpoint of this process was the dissolution of OST and the abolition of PSAC at the beginning of 1973.[8]

CONTRASTING VIEWS OF THE SCIENCE ADVISORY ROLE

Commentary on the Science Advisor and PSAC has always been characterized by two quite different views of their roles in the governmental process. These contrasting views are perhaps best captured in the phrases "policy for science" and "science for policy." In the first view, the office of the Science Advisor should be primarily concerned with "policy for science," that is, with the allocation of the nation's scientific and technological resources and with the institutional vitality and social contribution of its R&D system. It should thus be looked upon as a sort of general staff for the nation's science and technology, aimed at producing a coherent and concisely stated "national science policy." In this sense, it should look outward from science and technology toward the government, seeking opportunities for science and technology to serve national goals, but also planning the grand strategy of the nation's scientific and technological institutions.

In this view, the Science Advisor and PSAC are, to some extent, substitutes for a Cabinet Department of Science and Technology which would manage most of the nation's technical resources. It was this view which was embodied in the 1976 legislation which re-established an Office of Science and Technology Policy (OSTP) as a statutory office within the Executive Office of the President, and required that it develop a Five-Year Outlook report, as well as an annual report to the Congress modeled after the annual reports of the Council of Economic Advisors and the Council on Environmental Quality, which would include a separate Presidential statement concerning the Administration's S&T strategy.

The alternative view is that of a staff resource to the President, whose priorities are set mainly by the policy interests of the President, and which works mainly on specific issues assigned by him, although it may also have an early warning function in alerting the President to S&T issues which may affect his policy agenda in the future. In this view, the Science Advisor's office is much less institutionalized, and is primarily accountable to the President personally. In setting its agenda, it starts from the policy interests of the President, and searches for ways of bringing to bear on these policy interests the scientific expertise available inside or outside the government. This is "science for policy." It downplays the institutional interests of science and technology, and simply treats S&T as a resource for the formulation of the President's general policies.

Of course, policy for science and science for policy cannot be separated in any neat and simple way. The focus of scientific or technological inputs on the resolution of a public policy issue may involve more than simply bringing together what is already known, and also require the allocation or re-allocation of existing R&D efforts to develop missing knowledge needed to bring a policy initiative to a satisfactory conclusion. Thus, for example, President Eisenhower's efforts to negotiate a comprehensive nuclear test ban with the Soviets in the 1950s ultimately required an extensive new research program to improve the technology of seismic detection, and PSAC helped design such a program, which was subsequently implemented in the Department of Defense under the auspices of the Advanced Research Projects Agency (ARPA). Concerns about depletion of stratospheric ozone—first due to the Supersonic Transport (SST) program and later due to the industrial production of fluorocarbons[9]—led to the mounting of an extensive new atmospheric research program on a government-wide basis, led by the Department of Commerce (the CIAP program). Thus initial considerations of science for policy led to new policies for science, *i.e.*, a new allocation of R&D resources.

Similarly, on-going research programs not undertaken for a particular extra-scientific purpose frequently turn up new results which have implications for policy, either as new opportunities to meet existing government goals, or as indications of environmental or safety hazards not previously known. In this case, what started as policy for science may end up as science for policy. The emergence of biotechnology as a new tool for the enhancement of agriculture, coming out of previous sustained federal support for molecular biology, is one example.

Which of these orientations is the appropriate one for the Science Advisor, and to what extent can both functions be reconciled in a single office? In the past, some of the difficulties encountered by the Science Advisor have been attributable to conflicts—or, at least, perceived conflicts—between the science for policy and the policy for science functions. For example, nonscientists on the White House staff often viewed PSAC as advocates for a "special interest" within the President's office, the special interest being the support of basic research, especially in the universities. No matter how hard PSAC members tried to remove their institutional hats when advising the government on the allocation of R&D resources, it proved impossible to convince hostile critics of their impartiality, and once this impartiality became suspect in areas where they had potential conflicts of interest, it became easier to challenge their impartiality in other areas where they had no obvious vested interests.

As the country became polarized on issues like the Vietnam War and arms control, the scientists became more and more identified with particular political positions. Before he abolished PSAC, Nixon came to regard PSAC and OST more and more as political enclaves of a hostile academic community within the White House political family—a feeling that was confirmed in his mind when several individual members spoke publicly against Administration policies on issues on which they were known to have provided expert advice within the Administration, as, for example, on the SST and the Safeguard ABM system.

One of the most important values of PSAC in its heyday lay in the fact that its members were respected scientists from the private sector with no natural allegiances to the various bureaucracies whose programs and policies would be most likely to be impacted by their advice. In the big defense and space technologies on which they were being expected to pass judgment, they had no economic and little professional stake in the outcome; their allegiance was entirely to the President. Yet this status of impartial outsider no longer obtained when they were asked to advise how much was enough to be spent on university research or graduate fellowships, or whether the government should invest in a new particle accelerator or radioastronomy array, or step up research in molecular biology or materials science. Not only did many members have potential conflicts of interest in such cases, but they were being placed in the position of having to take sides in controversies internal to the scientific community. Thus the very backgrounds and professional experiences which made the members of PSAC unusually credible in their dealings with "big ticket" technology issues tended to make their advice suspect when they dealt with broader issues of general national research strategy—suspect both with the public and among their own colleagues outside government.

Yet, what is the alternative? As I have indicated, there can be no sharp line between policy for science and science for policy, in practice. The alternative to combining both branches of science policy advice in a single mechanism would be to have separate bodies with separate reporting channels to the President and the Congress. Indeed, this was the situation which existed on paper when the Science Advisor and PSAC were revitalized in the White House after Sputnik before the Office of Science and Technology (OST) was institutionalized by Executive Order under the President's reorganization authority at the beginning of the Kennedy Administration.

Before Kennedy, the policy for science function was assigned by law to the National Science Foundation and, more particularly, to the National Science Board, while PSAC concentrated on science for policy tasks. In practice, however, the NSF was too weak a player among the government's science bureaucracies to be able to address national science and technology strategies for the whole government in a comprehensive manner. It controlled only a tiny percentage of the overall federal R&D budget, and that part was almost entirely basic research and academic science. Even in this domain, the NSF was dwarfed by several other agencies, especially the National Institutes of Health, the Atomic Energy Commission, and the Department of Defense. It was difficult for the NSF to act simultaneously as an arbitrator among competing claims for R&D investment and, as itself, a claimant for such funds when it was such an inconsequential player. It was this practical fact that led President Kennedy, in his reorganization, to assign the policy for science responsibility to be shared equally between OST and NSF.

But much water has gone under the bridge since the 1960s. The NSF's budget has grown by more than a factor of twenty, and it has gradually been taking on a more activist role in initiating policy for science and developing something resembling a national science strategy. The National Science Board (NSB) has become less exclusively academic in its orientation, its two most recent Chairmen having been highly respected industrial research directors with close contacts in both academia and industry. The present Director of

NSF is also an industrial scientist who is attempting to give the Foundation a much higher profile in a renewed national debate over federal R&D strategy. Together with the National Science Board and its recent Chairmen, the Director has taken steps to revamp the Foundation's role in engineering research and education, to stimulate university-industry collaboration in critical areas as a new feature of policy for science, and to support several new initiatives in interdisciplinary collaborative science. He has attempted to link all these initiatives to national economic and competitive strategies. Thus the elements of a more coherent general strategy for the federal R&D investment, as a whole, appear to be emerging from the NSF, and I think the stage has been set, not for a rigid division of responsibility between OSTP and NSF along science for policy and policy for science lines, but for a revitalized OSTP to concentrate on science for policy issues, supported by a rejuvenated PSAC and an activist NSF and NSB to develop a national strategy for science and technology. Such a dual structure does not seem implausible, provided the two agencies coordinate their efforts effectively.

At the beginning of the PSAC era in the late 1950s, there was created the Federal Council for Science and Technology (FCST), whose main purpose was to coordinate the R&D investments of the entire federal government. While this provided a useful forum for the discussion of federal policy, it was—like many other interagency groups—not very influential in the implementation of policy. Such a mechanism should obviously be continued, but, in my opinion, consideration should be given to having it chaired and staffed by NSF, rather than OSTP, thus further emphasizing the science for policy role of OSTP relative to the policy for science role of NSF.

Such a scheme would be consistent with the actual practice which was followed in response to the 1976 legislation setting up the present OSTP and its elaborate reporting system. Although the legislation called for OSTP to prepare both the Five-Year Outlook and the Annual Reports, both of these tasks were almost immediately delegated to NSF, which, in turn, subcontracted a portion of the staff back-up work to the National Academy of Sciences through its Committee on Science, Engineering and Public Policy (COSEPUP). This system has now fallen into disuse, but it should probably be revived with the NSF more clearly taking the lead role under the general aegis of FCST.

One possible objection to the general scheme outlined above, with the NSF, rather than OSTP and the Science Advisor, taking the lead in formulating national policy for science, is that the NSF Director would be both an overall coordinator and a competitive claimant in the division of federal R&D resources. This is the same problem that for so many years prevented the NSF from taking on the role envisioned for it in the original NSF enabling legislation of 1950.[10] I feel, however, that the situation is different today in view of the much enhanced size and stature of the NSF and the enhanced strength of its Congressional constituency.

EXECUTIVE PRIVILEGE AND CONFIDENTIALITY

An important reason why PSAC was not revived in its original form after the restoration of the Science Advisor's office and OSTP in the 1976 Act was the problems that were feared to be involved in operating such a sensitive formal advisory group in the new context created by the Freedom of Information Act and the Federal Advisory Committee Act. The original PSAC had operated very effectively behind the shield of Executive Privilege traditionally accorded to the President's personal staff. This enabled PSAC members to put forward tentative—and sometimes outrageous—ideas in committee discussions, and to hammer out a consensus, free of the risk of being held accountable at some future time for opinions that they had later modified in the light of new information or the arguments of colleagues.

It also protected PSAC members from being challenged by outside colleagues, especially those in their own disciplines, who felt that they should support the strongly held views of those colleagues in their advice to government. Confidentiality of PSAC discussions encouraged greater candor and collegiality, which would have been difficult in a more public forum. Thereby, it facilitated the reaching of consensus, and gave greater assurance to the President that whatever consensus was reached reflected his perspective, rather than that of some outside conventional wisdom. Particularly in the case of very large and expensive projects with big regional economic stakes riding on them, some PSAC scientists or consultants might have been reluctant to express candid opinions for fear of Congressional reprisals against the private organizations from which they came, which might be dependent on government funding in other areas.

The Federal Advisory Committee Act was perhaps even more problematical than the Freedom of Information Act, because it required that the agendas of advisory committee discussions be announced in advance and determined by a responsible full-time government employee. Thus it was thought that there would be a tendency to keep off the agendas issues that would embarrass the President (or other executives) politically if it came to be known that certain established policies were being challenged in the advisory committee. One of the most important functions of PSAC would be that of early warning, *e.g.*, warning the President in advance that certain of his policies were likely to run into future political trouble, because they were inconsistent with the developing technical situation. Although, in the case of PSAC, the President should usually be expected to set the broad agenda, it is important that it also be able to identify emerging issues for the President without the risk of premature publicity, thus enabling the President to take corrective action on his own initiative, rather than seeming to respond to outside criticism.

On the other hand, there is no question that the confidentiality of PSAC deliberations in the 1960s was frequently a source of frustration, not only to Congress and the press, but also to the Science Advisor himself. For example, PSAC members or the Advisor were often prevented from testifying to Congress or from defending publicly policies which had been hammered out through careful PSAC study and argument. Later on, after the shield of Executive Privilege had been partially removed by the creation of OST, the Science Advisor was able to testify using his alternate hat as statutory Director of OST.

This still left a good deal of ambiguity, however, in that Congress could never be confident of the degree to which the Science Advisor was expressing his own best judgment as compared with the White House "party line." The problem became even more complex in the Nixon Administration when certain members of PSAC testified against Administration programs (such as the SST and Safeguard ABM system), while attempting to completely separate their testimony from deliberations in PSAC or one of its panels.

It seems clear to me, in the light of the above discussion, that any reconsitution of PSAC will have to be accompanied by a much more careful and explicit delineation of the ground rules of confidentiality. The committee should certainly be accorded the possibility of having executive sessions whose deliberations are not subject to release through the Freedom of Information Act. At the same time, it should be careful to limit the use of such executive sessions, and should put on the record the final arguments and considerations which led to important policy recommendations or initiatives. At the same time, members of PSAC who participate in studies and discussions that are carried out behind the shield of confidentiality should not be able to claim the privilege of appealing to the public or to the Congress if their views are not finally accepted by the President, unless, of course, they are prepared to submit their resignations from PSAC.

SPECIALISTS VERSUS GENERALISTS

Specialized knowledge is one of the contributions that PSAC brings to high-level policy debate, but a more important role may be as an intermediary or "transducer" between the specialized knowledge of panels and study groups and generalist politicians and staff advisors. A very important function of PSAC as it operated in the 1960s was that of putting specialized panel reports into a broader context that could be understood and acted upon by generalist policy-makers. Fulfilling this role requires a more active role than simply receiving and interpreting panel reports. In addition, it requires a critical report review function, which frequently involves sending a panel back to the drawing boards to respond to questions and criticisms raised by the members of PSAC in a preliminary review of the findings and recommendations of the panel.

In this function, PSAC acted more like sophisticated laymen than experts. They had to understand the technical issues in greater depth than would be possible for any generalist political staff or policy advisor, but they also had to appreciate the policy issues and broader political context better than was possible for the report's authors. This intermediary function is likely to be even more important in the future than in the past. Members of a future PSAC should be able to ask probing questions of their panels, and to raise more general issues and implications than those likely to be thought of by the specialists.

This "generalist" role of PSAC has important implications for the criteria of selection of its members. While some distribution among disciplines is important to insure breadth of scientific perspective within the committee, this is probably a less important consideration than more general qualities of mind, healthy skepticism of conventional wisdom, and breadth of both technical and managerial experience. Given a wide acquaintance within its own disciplinary communities, the committee is always in a position to recruit specialized expertise for *ad hoc* studies on particular issues, as well as to make use of such outside groups as the NAS/NAE/IoM complex, but it needs other qualities for its own unique function. Therefore, apparent imbalances in representation on the committee, which were the subject of a good deal of criticism in the 1960s (especially with respect to the social sciences) should not be taken too seriously, especially if the alternative is an attenuation of the committee's capacity for collegial communication among its members.

Since one of the functions of a PSAC would be exploring the societal implications of new developments in science and technology, it is important to remember that consequences of new technologies are not always best foreseen by the experts in the particular technology, although such experts need to be on tap to fill in details which depend on the exact characteristics of the technology. This may even imply bringing into the committee's deliberations a few experienced laymen from non-scientific professions.

In the past, there has been criticism of PSAC for its domination by academic scientists, particularly physicists, and for inadequate representation of the engineering profession and of technical people from industry more generally. Again, my view is that these people should be selected primarily for their individual qualities of mind, and not to represent a particular constituency. In the future, as national science policy becomes more involved with questions of competitiveness and the enhancement of industrial technology, it is logical that PSAC should include more industrial scientists and engineers than it did in the 1960s, but evolution, rather than revolution, is in order.

THE PSAC ROLE IN NATIONAL SECURITY AFFAIRS

The involvement of PSAC and its panels in studies of military technology reached its peak during the mid-1960s, although the greatest impact was probably exerted during the early part of the Kennedy Administration. Since that time, the tendency has been to move OST or OSTP more and more out of national security policy. Since 1976, involvement of the Science Advisor in military technology issues has been minimal. The ostensible justification for this was that—as a result of the creation of the office of Director of Defense Research and Engineering (DDRE), ARPA, and the centralization of DoD's R&D management—the need for independent input to DoD technology planning has largely disappeared.

In fact, this is a dubious argument. The growing concentration of technical competence within DoD, especially since the post-1978 build-up of the military R&D budget, rather argues for the creation of competence outside the defense establishment that is capable of bringing to bear considerations outside the narrow military security context of DoD. The Arms Control and Disarmament Agency is the only other agency of government that is concerned with military technology, but has, in principle, little more than a narrow military security perspective on policy. There is thus a serious need for a technically competent group within the Executive branch capable of criticizing plans for military technology development and deployment from a broader perspective that includes not only military security, but impact on the civilian economy and industrial competitiveness, human resources development, and foreign policy.

PSAC did, to a considerable extent, fulfill such a role in the late-Eisenhower and Kennedy Administrations, but it has scarcely had the opportunity to do so since. It is surprising, for example, that the only independent studies of the Strategic Defense Initiative have been made by the Congressional Office of Technology Assessment or by non-governmental groups, such as the American Physical Society. The two official reports that were issued—those of the Fletcher and Hoffman panels[11]—were published as Department of Defense "white papers," and were carried out entirely by experts with close affiliations with DoD or its contractors and from a perspective of military security as interpreted in terms of the DoD mission.

In recent years, there has been increasing public discussion of the impact of defense spending—but particularly of defense R&D spending—on the civilian economy. Debate has grown as the defense share of R&D spending has grown from 50% of all federal R&D spending in the late 1970s to 70% in FY1986, with almost all the increase being in development rather than basic and applied research. This spending is frequently justified as a contribution not only to national security, but also to US competitiveness in the commercial sphere, but critics in increasing numbers also attack it as a prime cause of loss of competitiveness to other nations, particularly those—like Japan—with much smaller defense budgets than ours. At the present time, there appears to be no place in the government where this kind of issue—vital to future national science policy—can be sorted out in an objective manner, not suspect because of bureaucratic self-interest. It is not only (pos-

sibly, even, not chiefly) a question of the total *amount* of DoD R&D spending, but also the *manner* and decision criteria for spending and the institutional arrangements through which it is carried out.

The issue has become more important as some of the technologies which
are being utilized by the military are increasingly coming from civilian sources,
while other technologies being financed by the military in terms of military
criteria are claimed by some (including our foreign competitors) to have
major potential commercial applications. There are many who assert that we
can no longer afford two science policies, one for the military and one for
the civil sector, and yet, in the present set-up, there is no place in government where these two science policies are considered together. A PSAC by
itself would have the capacity to do this, but it could serve to initiate and
provide some of the ground rules for such a study, which is of critical importance for the future of the country.[12]

IS NATURAL SCIENCE DIFFERENT?

Much of the by now voluminous literature on science advising and the
utilization of natural science in public policy decisions seems to assign a
special role to natural science and engineering in comparison with other
fields of specialized knowledge which are equally important to public policy
and which often have a much longer history. Is there really a special quality
about natural science which makes it unique and different from other forms
of expertise in its interaction with the policy process? I am personally inclined to doubt it, although, to the best of my knowledge, there is almost
no literature which deals with the relationship between knowledge and policy
on a comparative basis among different fields of knowledge.

One might well seek parallels in other areas—for example, economics,
foreign policy (knowledge of the politics and culture of other countries),
foreign intelligence data and interpretation, and even legal interpretation
(witness the current surprising debate over the interpretation of the negotiating record in the 1973 ABM treaty).[13] If there is any difference between
these areas and the natural sciences, it must lie in the general perception—
whether justified or not—that the natural sciences are less accessible to quick
learning and understanding by policy generalists, primarily because they
usually rest on a deeper structure of abstract theory and inference than most
other areas that are studied by scholars and utilized by policy-makers. This
may be true in selected instances, but it is probably frequently exaggerated.

Another difference is that the natural sciences are often perceived by laymen as fields where questions have unique, precise and quantitative answers, not involving the subtle shades of judgment and nuances of personal
experience that influence conclusions in other academic fields. This perception is palpably false, but it is, nevertheless, pervasive. It is especially false
for those areas of natural science which are most involved in policy debate,

where incomplete and contradictory evidence, as well as competing theoretical models, are the rule, rather than the exception.

I think that much could be learned about science advising through careful scholarly studies of the utilization of expert knowledge in policy—particularly the utilization of different fields of knowledge in the same area of policy. An especially fruitful field might be the comparison of the use of intelligence data and scientific information in the formulation of policy for the acquisition of weapons systems. Such a comparison might help to bring about some demystification in both fields!

INSTITUTIONALIZATION OF SCIENCE POLICY

As we review the history of Presidential science advising, one recurrent theme is the progressive institutionalization of the process. Some saw the position of science at the highest levels of government as a precarious one, and actively promoted institutionalization as a way of insuring a permanent place for the scientific community in the highest councils of government, commensurate with the importance of science to the future of the country. Others, however, saw institutionalization as a threat to the free-wheeling, non-bureaucratic style of science advising which enabled so few to accomplish so much in the early days of PSAC, and which, indeed, was responsible for the success of scientists in both Britain and the United States in World War II. It is true that the debate over institutionalization partly reflected the dichotomy between policy for science and science for policy that I mentioned earlier. It was those who saw the science advisory apparatus as personal staff to the President who continued to favor the informal White House arrangements created by Eisenhower. In the words of E. R. Piore "the good intentions of the legislation are not sufficient when people must compete for the attention of the President."[14] Some scientists might "think they're losing some great privilege by getting rid of the law" and, therefore, favor institutionalization because it guarantees a hearing for science, but that is probably an illusion. Science will have to sell itself repeatedly to each new President in this view.

My own view is that the policy for science function should be institutionalized, as proposed earlier, but probably through NSF, rather than through an office in the White House. Policy for science does require a degree of permanence and continuity, but science for policy does not. Moreover, the continuity of policy for science should not be hostage to the political antagonisms that are likely to develop when science in the White House must become the messenger bearing the bad news to the President that the emperor has no clothes. The Science Advisor, in the long run, cannot be completely honest if he has to continually look over his shoulder to assess the impact of the reception of his political advice on the institutional fortunes of science in the federal government. If this means that the policy for science advisor sometimes comes into conflict with the science for policy advisor, I think this a risk worth taking for the sake of the greater intellectual integrity of the science for policy process, as well as for the continuity of rational science planning.

NOTES

1. Don K. Price, *The Scientific Estate* (Cambridge, MA: Harvard University Press, 1965).
2. Robert Wood, "The Apolitical Elite," in R. Gilpin and C. Wright, eds., *Scientists in National Policy Making* (New York: Columbia University Press, 1964).
3. Technology Assessment Act of 1972, Public Law 92–484.
4. Harvey Brooks, "Technology Assessment and Environmental Impact Assessment," in US-China Conference on Science Policy, *Conference Papers*, January 9–12, 1983, Committee on Scholarly Communication with the People's Republic of China (Washington, DC: National Academy Press, 1985).
5. Philip Harter, "Negotiating Regulations, A Cure for the Malaise?," *Environmental Impact Assessment Review*, no. 3 (1982), pp. 75–92.
6. D. Nelkin, "The Political Impact of Technical Expertise," *Social Studies of Science*, Vol. V, no. 1 (January 1975).
7. J. Merton England, *A Patron of Pure Science: The National Science Foundation's Formative Years, 1945–47*, NSF 82–24 (Washington, DC: National Science Foundation, 1982), Chapter 11, pp. 211–226.
8. Harvey Brooks and E. B. Skolnikoff, "Science Advice in the White House? Continuation of a Debate," *Science*, Vol. 187, January 10, 1975, pp. 35–41.
9. Harvey Brooks, "Stratospheric Ozone, the Scientific Community and Public Policy," Chapter 9 in F. A. Bower and R. B. Ward, eds., *Stratospheric Ozone and Man*, Vol. II (Boca Raton, FL: CRC Press, Inc., 1982).
10. England, *op. cit.*, Chapter 15, pp. 311–345.
11. D. L. Hafner, "Assessing the President's Vision: The Fletcher, Miller and Hoffman Panels," in "Weapons in Space," Vol. I, *Daedalus*, Spring 1985, pp. 91–126.
12. Harvey Brooks, "The Strategic Defense Initiative as Science Policy," *International Security*, Vol. II, no. 2 (Fall 1986).
13. Senator Sam Nunn, "Interpretation of the ABM Treaty," *Congressional Record*, Proceedings and Debates of the 100th Congress, First Session, nos. 38 (March 11, 1987) and 40 (March 13, 1987).
14. Emanuel R. Piore in William T. Golden, ed., "President's Science Advisory Committee Revisited," *Science, Technology & Human Values*, Vol. 11, no. 2 (Spring 1986).

A New Institution for Science and Technology Policy-Making

George E. Brown, Jr.

An analysis of how best to provide science and technology advice to the President is a matter of considerable importance in a world increasingly dominated by the technological fruits of an insatiable human curiosity about the universe. Broadening the analysis to encompass such advice to the other branches of government further increases its importance. Yet it would be unrealistic to believe that, from such an analysis, will emerge a consensus for some ideal, new institutional structure or process that will substantially enhance the quality of science and technology policy decisions. Forty years of effort have produced changes that are, on balance, modestly conducive to such improved decision-making, but they by no means assure that it will take place. Human beings, operating within diverse value frameworks, must still resolve policy issues, for better or for worse.

This is not to belittle the importance of structure and process. They are a necessary—but not sufficient—prerequisite for sound policy. The existence of a National Security Advisor and a National Security Council have not obviously solved the President's problems of developing balanced, coordinated and successful security policy. Nor have the existence of the Council of Economic Advisors and the Domestic Policy Council, with their frequent access to the President, elevated the level of policy decisions in these areas to new excellence.

One can probably assert with all due humility that, in the absence of such mechanisms, policy decisions might have been worse, longer delayed, or more difficult to achieve.

George E. Brown, Jr., has been a member of Congress from California since 1971 (and, previously, from 1962–70). He is the ranking Democratic member of the House Science, Space and Technology Committee, and also serves on several Subcommittees, including that on Science, Research and Technology. He is also a member of the House Permanent Select Committee on Intelligence and of the Congressional Technology Assessment Board. His degree from the University of California/Los Angeles is in Industrial Physics.

All policy-making, including policy in the areas of national security, the economy, and domestic programs, requires a balance of complex interests, represented institutionally by powerful government departments and agencies, and numerous quasi-governmental and private organizations. The Departments of Defense and State, the intelligence community, and others vie for the attention of the President and the Congress on security matters; and the Departments of Treasury and Commerce, the Federal Reserve Board, and a host of private organizations on economic policy. Most of the other Departments together with state and local governments and very large national constituency groups join in presenting alternative domestic policies.

The structure of the White House advisory apparatus, which includes the National Security Council, the Domestic Policy Council, and the numerous *ad hoc* advisory groups, was established primarily for the purpose of resolving institutional conflicts and differences, clarifying options, distilling arguments on various alternatives, so that the President can efficiently make informed decisions. Policy issues on which there is minimal institutional disagreement do not require the President's involvement. The most comparable process in the Congress is the public hearing process, followed by several levels of conflict resolution and consensus-building through subcommittee, committee, conference committee, and finally House and Senate debate and voting.

A HIGH PRIORITY

I would assert that science and technology policy today ranks in importance to the national welfare with security, economic, and domestic policy, and is closely intertwined with all of them. I shall elaborate briefly on some of the reasons for this importance below.

I would further assert that, as a consequence of this importance, science and technology policy requires both an institutional structure and a voice commensurate with those of other vital policy areas. I do not believe that this change would automatically guarantee the perfection of science and technology policy-making. But what it would guarantee is that—in the complex process of balancing competing ideologies and interests at the highest level, from which national policy emerges—science and technology considerations would compete on a more equal basis. From that better matched competition, there could emerge not only better science and technology policies, but better national security, economic and domestic program policies. This is, after all, the fundamental reason for analysing the process of science and technology advising.

I shall offer a suggested outline for a proposed structure and voice to illustrate my views.

The human condition is changing today at an exponential rate. This change is a direct correlation of the corresponding exponential increase in organized human knowledge (science), and the application of that knowledge to the satisfaction of human needs (technology). This reality is the foundation for the growing importance of science and technology policy.

Those who shape the direction of societal change, whether at the highest levels of government or as innovators and leaders in the many other sectors of society, cannot today fulfill their roles adequately without a more robust and dynamic system of science and technology advice. With that advice, they are better able to evaluate the impact of science and technology on their various areas of responsibility, and to direct that impact in constructive ways. Let me cite just two examples.

Researchers working in biological laboratories in the United States have recently created a new growth hormone which will revolutionize milk production in cows. The commercial introduction of that bovine growth hormone, now beginning, will drastically alter the structure and nature of the dairy industry throughout the world. Other breakthroughs in genetic engineering are expected to have similar or greater impact in other areas of agriculture. I know of no adequate policy response to these developments, despite a decade of high-level government awareness of the potential problems.

Within the past year teams of researchers in Switzerland, the United States and Japan have discovered new substances that were superconducting at high temperatures. Within the next year, scientists and engineers quite probably will produce new materials that may alter the nature of the electric utility and rail transportation systems of the world. These technological developments are more likely to occur in Europe and Japan than in the US.

These are but two examples of a world in change as a result of science and technology. Other examples can be identified in essentially every area of today's society. Indeed, there may be no more powerful and pervasive force in the world today than the advance of science and technology.

ENHANCING THE STATUS OF SCIENCE

Science expands the pool of human knowledge and invites all who desire to share in that knowledge. To engage in the scientific process, to solve old problems and find new ones, to answer old questions about the universe around us and find new ones, fulfills an important need in almost all human beings. For a select few, science not merely fulfills a need, but also becomes a higher vocation. Enhancing the status of science in our society is an intrinsically important challenge to high-level policy-makers.

Technology selects from the pool of knowledge created by science that which can be used to develop a new or better product, process or service for which there is or can be established a market. That market can be in national defense, health, consumer products, education or any other area. Given rational markets, this process enhances the quality of life for all people, and is thus likewise intrinsically important.

While science and technology profoundly affect all aspects of society, and must, therefore, be properly weighed by all who make or influence social policy, it is the national government (and its leaders at the highest level) that must be most concerned with science and technology. In the modern world, the state is by far the largest patron of science, and by its allocation of tax resources, determines the priority of major research areas, and the relative status of institutions and individuals engaged in that research, from human health to astrophysics. It is the state that also establishes and protects intellectual property rights. It is the state that provides the market for major technological developments, and regulates the conditions for use of almost all new technology. It is the state, through its economic and regulatory policies, that frequently determines the profitability of long-term investments in new technology.

The successes and the failures of our science and technology policy efforts during the post-war period have affected our national and world security, our quality of life, our balance of trade, and our economic prosperity and stability. Policy-makers in both Congress and the White House, dimly perceiving the growing importance of science and technology on our national lives, groped blindly for the new institutions and processes that would help them cope with intertwined policy issues. The history of this search has been treated elsewhere. The results, it is generally agreed, have been inadequate.

For all of these reasons, science and technology policy has become critical in today's world. The structure and process by which the leaders of government make that policy is now a matter of national and international importance.

If such is the case, what can be done? Let me suggest now in specific terms the outline of a structure and voice for science and technology policy which I believe could fundamentally improve the national policy process in all areas.

PROPOSALS

First, I propose that most of the scattered government organizations now engaged in the development and implementation of science and technology policy and programs be assembled into a Cabinet-level Department of Science and Technology. A tentative listing of such organizations would include:

- National Science Foundation;
- National Aeronautics and Space Administration;
- National Oceanic and Atmospheric Administration;
- National Bureau of Standards;
- National Research Laboratories of the Department of Energy, and related basic research programs;
- Environmental Protection Agency;
- National Technical Information Service; and
- Patent Office.

For many good reasons I would not suggest the inclusion of the science and technology functions of the Departments of Defense, Health and Human Services, Agriculture, Transportation, and Interior. These functions are basically mission-specific and are best carried out within these departments.

I would suggest the simultaneous creation of a Department of Trade and Commerce to focus policy attention on those important areas.

Second, I propose that the Secretary of Science and Technology establish an Office of Policy Planning, and that the present functions and staff of the Office of Science and Technology Policy in the Executive Office of the President be transferred to the Secretary of Science and Technology.

Third, I propose that the Secretary be designated Science Advisor to the President.

Fourth, I propose that the President be authorized to appoint a broadly representative President's Science Advisory Committee of approximately fifteen members, to advise him and the Secretary of Science and Technology on critical national science and technology issues. These members should be of a quality that distinguish them as among the best scientific minds in the country.

Fifth, I propose that the Secretary of Science and Technology or his designee serve as a member of the National Security Council and the Domestic Policy Council.

Sixth, I propose that the membership of the President's Council of Economic Advisers be expanded to include one person with a broad understanding of the effects of science and technology on the national economy.

Seventh, I propose that the Federal Reserve Board include one or more persons with a strong grasp of science and technology.

Eighth, I propose that the National Academy of Sciences (NAE, NRC) be strengthened by having an endowed base of funding. With that increased autonomy, it should be encouraged to analyze major science and technology policy issues on its own initiative, presenting its findings to the President, the Congress, the Judiciary and the public.

HIGHER VISIBILITY

The structure I envision would create a higher level of visibility for many science and technology programs within the government, but by no means all of them. The Secretary of Science and Technology, by necessity, would have to weigh priorities and evaluate the impact of programs on both the federal budget and the national welfare. The Secretary's responsibilities would require a familiarity with science and technology issues on both a national and global basis, involving government, private industry, and universities. The multiple roles of this official would provide him or her with numerous channels of communication with the President, other Cabinet members, and high-level administrators, and the Congress. The presence of qualified scientists on the Council of Economic Advisers and the Federal Reserve Board would enlighten economic policy areas which now give little or no consideration to science and technology issues, despite their economic significance. A strengthened National Academy of Sciences would provide further independent analysis of critical science and technology policy issues, with all its prestige available to policy-makers and public alike.

I have said above that a more robust and dynamic system of science and technology advice is a necessity for policy-makers. My proposal is only a beginning. Science and technology considerations will be more adequately presented at the highest levels of government, by institutionalizing scientific advice within the multiple sectors of the Executive branch. In addition, diversity of policy views will be protected, and more effectively reconciled.

I would even argue that my suggested structure would provide economies in administration, better coordination of programs, and greater protection against unreasonable fluctuations in support of vital long-range national science and technology objectives.

But a strong program must include components to improve the understanding and decision-making ability of individual policy-makers, in every branch of government. These components must be tailored to meet needs which are short-, medium- and long-range, and encompass every conceivable subject. One must consider ways, therefore, to encourage more interaction between the scientific and technical community and the policy-makers, through joint meetings, the appointment of science Fellows to key offices, and similar devices. The Congressional Office of Technology Assessment, which distills the policy differences of stakeholders in technical issues on a national basis, and suggests reasonable policy options, must be utilized more effectively. The expertise of the science policy staff of The Library of Congress, and the technical staff of the General Accounting Office can be used more effectively. Professional societies of scientists and engineers can encourage their members in every area of the country to interact with policy-makers to explore technical issues from both a local and national perspective. Ultimately, since elected policy-makers are influenced most by motivated constituencies, a technically literate public is essential to sound science and technology policy-making.

We will therefore be challenged by an unfinished agenda for a long time to come.

On Advising the Federal Government

S. J. Buchsbaum

I had my first bout with the vagaries of the Presidential advisory process when I served on the ill-fated President's Science Advisory Committee during President Nixon's first term. After that, I had the honor and pleasure to chair the Defense Science Board during President Ford's tenure and the Energy Research Advisory Board during President Carter's. I was also consultant to the Office of Science and Technology Policy (OSTP) during the Carter Administration and chaired several *ad hoc* advisory task forces for Frank Press, then the President's Science Advisor.

Since 1981, I have served as Chairman of the White House Science Council, first for Jay Keyworth and now for Bill Graham, both Science Advisors to President Reagan. All this makes me somewhat of a veteran in advising the Executive branch of the federal government.

I have learned some important lessons during all these years. One of these is that the apparent prestige of an advisory body does not assure its effectiveness.

During the Nixon days, for example, the PSAC was still held in high esteem by the scientific/technical community. Unfortunately, neither the power structure within the White House nor, indeed, the various departments and agencies of the government shared this attitude.

As a result, the Committee was largely ineffective. In those days, we had several standing and *ad hoc* panels, and issued many reports. For a while, I chaired the Ground Warfare Panel, which tried to keep track of the activities of the U.S. Army. I was also a member of the Air Traffic Control Panel. If memory serves correctly, not much of lasting value emerged from these efforts.

Looking back, the reason for failure was quite simple: Most—if not all—

Solomon J. Buchsbaum, Executive Vice President, Customer Systems, of AT&T Bell Laboratories, is a member of the National Academies of Science and Engineering; is Chairman of the White House Science Council; is a Trustee of the RAND Corporation; and, in 1986, was awarded the National Medal of Science.

of the work of the Nixon PSAC was self-initiated, so much so that we were meddling in the internal affairs of government departments; our work was not of burning interest to the policy- and decision-makers who then served in the government.

There is no question that many issues we tackled should have been of interest. The fact that they were not points to a potentially fatal flaw in any advisory mechanism: Unwanted advice is seldom heeded. Unless there is a rapport between the advisory body and its client, the system will not work. Rapport cannot be preordained. It has to be earned unless it already exists because of previous close association between the principals. The relationship between President Kennedy and Jerome Wiesner is a good example.

It was just such a lack of rapport, coupled with an absence of the discipline needed to handle two issues that were of burning interest to the Nixon White House—the ABM and the SST—that caused PSAC to botch them. This, in turn, led to PSAC's demise.

There is much moaning these days about the absence of a "truly Presidential" science advisory mechanism, that is, the absence of a PSAC. The White House Science Council is not being regarded as highly in some circles, presumably because it lacks the word "Presidential" in its title. I dare say that, even without a PSAC, Frank Press was at least as effective as a Science Advisor as some of his predecessors. Frank tackled fewer issues, but he selected those he could do something about.

A related issue has to do with the perceived status of the President's Science Advisor within the White House. That, of course, depends upon the personality and effectiveness of the incumbent. There is also moaning about the fact that, in the present Administration, the Science Advisor does not report "directly" to the President. I happen to know that Bill Graham has ready access to the President on issues Bill deems important enough to bring to him. The same was true of Jay Keyworth. Obviously, the vast majority of issues and problems with which the Science Advisor deals do not require the President's involvement, and are handled at lower levels of the hierarchy.

The critics expect miracles. These days, such miracles are harder to come by. After World War II and even after the shock caused by Sputnik, America's technological, military and economic power was of such magnitude that we could set our own—and even the world's—agenda and stick pretty much to it.

The world has caught up with us. We now have to react to agendas set by others. There is precious little opportunity to act on our own in relative isolation from the rest of the world. Issues are no longer as straightforward as placing a man on the moon or filling a missile "gap," real or imagined.

Fighting AIDS, shoring up our sagging industrial competitiveness, rebuilding the deteriorating educational infrastructure, or even deciding how best to proceed with SDI are all issues where the scientific/technological component pales in comparison with political, economic or social considerations.

Thoughtful scientific advice is still needed, of course, but it has to be provided just that way—thoughtfully. It also has to be mindful of the many other considerations which preoccupy today's decision-maker. Otherwise, there is little chance the advice will be considered, much less accepted and acted upon.

A Time for Renewal: The Next President Needs What Eisenhower and Kennedy Had

McGeorge Bundy

The next President will have a great opportunity to create for his country and for himself a wholly renewed process of effective connection between the scientific and technological communities and the Presidency. That connection has been strong and good only intermittently in the last fifty years, and as the Reagan Administration limps to its end, the connection is so thin and so badly skewed that there will be wide support for a fresh start. Only the few who have had personal and unofficial access to the outgoing President will be distressed by reform. The opportunity is clear.

So is the need. The President and those with whom he works in making major policy choices, both in matters of national security and in matters of domestic policy, have had no generally effective access to the best judgment of advisors not tied to any one department or service since the role of the Science Advisor was allowed to fade by Lyndon Johnson. The responsibility for this breakdown lies with successive Presidents—Johnson was in a curious way indifferent, and Nixon was mistrustful—but not with them alone. It is easy to give advice, even good advice, to political leaders in such a way that they will not ask for it again. That is what almost always happens if advisors take their case past the President to the public, and, in the Nixon Administration, there was a failure among the advisors in setting clear and recognized standards on public policy statements by active participants in the advisory process. The next President and his Science Advisor will need to find ground rules that will limit the damage from the built-in conflict between confidential advice and public candor. The first such ground rule should be that the Science Advisor himself has no public differences with the President, and the second should be that the President ought to be en-

McGeorge Bundy, Professor of History at New York University, was Special Assistant for National Security Affairs to Presidents Kennedy and Johnson (1961–66), President of the Ford Foundation (1966–79), and Dean of the Faculty of Arts and Sciences at Harvard (1953–61).

tirely relaxed about the public positions taken by others who serve on advisory committees but remain primarily private citizens—as long as they do not seek to make their own use of work done for the President.

It is an instructive irony that one of the most notorious cases of such public political use of a secret expert report—the leak of the Gaither Report of 1957—came just after President Eisenhower had wisely established a new and different advisory process led by James Killian as the first full-time Science Advisor. Those who leaked the Gaither Report—exaggerating its conclusions as they did so—were wrongly but passionately persuaded that there was a desperately dangerous "missile gap" just ahead. They thought Eisenhower insufficiently attentive to their conclusions, and they went public by anonymous leaks. With the help of Killian and his successor, George Kistiakowsky, Eisenhower successfully resisted the pressures created by the self-appointed leakers, while at the same time skilled attention was given to prudent measures of strategic modernization. Eisenhower's response on the level of public explanation was less effective, but that is quite another story. Substantively he sought, received, and acted on excellent advice, and he had taken the decisive step of appointing Killian before the Gaither Report was leaked.

Kennedy's Science Advisor was Jerome Wiesner, who had played an active part in the advisory process organized by Killian and Kistiakowsky. I think it is right to regard the six years between the appointment of Killian and the death of Kennedy as the period in which science advice to Presidents was at its best and most productive. All three of the Advisors of this period were good friends of mine, and I cannot claim to have a wholly dispassionate view of their achievements, but I do not think it is wrong to keep their ways of work in mind in considering what will be needed in the Science Advisor to the next President. The comments that follow are heavily dependent on what I know from both direct exposure and historical study about the work of these three men.

INDISPENSABLE QUALITIES

The qualities desirable in a first-class Science Advisor are many, but three are indispensable and interconnected. First, the Advisor must have and deserve the trust of the President. Without that trust, no advisor can help a President or any one else in the Administration in more than marginal ways. The White House is no place for any one who is not, in the President's view, on the President's side. All good Presidents are wary, and some have made that virtue a vice by overdoing it. Some have been intrinsically unable to trust men of truly independent mind. I do not think it an accident that the collapse of the Science Advisor's role came in the time of Richard Nixon. But the bright record of 1957–63 shows that two quite different Presidents, both wary politicians, were able to get invaluable help from three very different Advisors, Killian, Kistiakowsky, and Wiesner. None of the three was weak in will or lacking self-confidence, but each understood that his basic responsibility was to be helpful to the President, and the two Presidents knew that their Science Advisors had this view of their work.

I put first this requirement—call it loyalty—partly because it is frequently forgotten by people who assume that what is primarily at issue here is a voice for Science at the White House, as if the Science Advisor's primary function was to speak for Science to Power. Certainly one value of a good Science Advisor is that he can help others in the White House to understand some of the folkways of scientists, and it is not wrong that the world of science should have a knowledgeable friend close to the President, but that is not what is at the center of the job. What the President needs is an advisor to help him with questions of truly Presidential magnitude. I. I. Rabi, himself an experienced advisor to Presidents, and the man who persuaded Ike to get a full-time advisor in 1957, had it right when he remarked in a later essay that the advisor should be a spokesman *of* not *for* the scientific community. The Science Advisor can indeed help science and technology from his White House office, but only if he always puts first his task of helping the President.

The second requirement in a Science Advisor is a capacity to enlist serious working support from men and women who combine technical and professional talent with a capacity for analysis and judgment on operational choices. In its good years under Eisenhower and Kennedy the Science Advisor's office had the powerful reinforcement of the President's Science Advisory Committee (PSAC), a group of scientists chosen for their recognized combination of talent and good sense (two quite different qualities, both of which are necessary). PSAC was a powerful reinforcement to the process of analysis and advice, and the direct and serious interest of Eisenhower and Kennedy, made evident to the members of the Committee in relatively frequent and serious meetings, had a positive effect on the quality of the advisory effort. PSAC is not at all the only possible arrangement for widening and deepening the quality of scientific counsel to the President, but its successful operation under two very different Presidents, and the much less notable record of Presidents and advisors who have not had or have not used this reinforcement, makes me believe that both the President and his Science Advisor would be reinforced by the careful reestablishment and the serious use of such a Committee.

Third and not least important, the Science Advisor must be able to perform effectively in the President's world—the world of governmental choice and action. This is a political world, but, fortunately for Science Advisors, the politics of White House staffwork—and this is a White House staff job—are in no fundamental sense different from the politics of the academy. No two Presidents and no two Advisors will have identical ways of work, and the one who must adjust to the working methods of the other is the Advisor, but that is true also of relations within the academy (even the requirement of deference from Presidents to untouchable grandees exists in both places). The Science Advisor will need to learn to work effectively with other members of the President's staff, with the Office of Management and Budget, and with relevant officials of the great departments, especially their senior technical officers. He will also need ties of mutual confidence with the heads of such great centers of scientific capability as the National Academies, the National Science Foundation, and the National Institutes of Health. Obviously not all of these relations will be continuously free of friction, but once it is plain in Washington that the Science Advisor has the President's confidence, it is practicable, as it is certainly necessary, for him to have generally good relations with others.

THE NUCLEAR PROBLEM

Since the discovery of fission, the most important connection between science and government has been the threat to both national and human survival that is presented by the bomb. Since the President and Commander-in-Chief is inescapably the central figure on this enormous subject, it must also be the primary concern of his Science Advisor. The most notable contributions of Killian, Kistiakowsky, and Wiesner were in this field, both in the assessment of weapons systems and in the analysis of arms control issues. The questions of the present and future here are more complex than ever, ranging from the pros and cons of a complete ban on nuclear tests to the future of deployments of all sorts in space. The agreement on intermediate-range forces (INF) that seems in sight as I write has considerable political importance, but it does not address the largest questions that have opened up in the 1980s. The future of INF is a small and non-controversial matter compared to the future of strategic forces, both offensive and defensive.

The process of scientific and technical counseling in the White House will not be made easier for the next Administration by the powerful reality that there has been a sharp polarization of both technical and political opinion on these matters in the fifteen years since the first SALT agreements. It will not be possible to resolve this division simply by attention to the technical quality of the analysis done for the President. Ever since the Soviet Union, in the Nixon Administration, achieved a visible strategic parity that included missiles of unmatched size and carrying capacity, American Presidents have fallen short, in one way or another, in the task of explaining just what forces the United States needs—and why—and they have failed just as badly in explaining and defending their positions on arms control. In the Reagan years, the quality of public exposition by the President and his senior colleagues has been disgracefully low, and worst at the highest levels, those of the President and the Secretary of Defense. Science advice in 1989 will not be able to begin on a relatively level field like the one James Killian found in Washington after the sudden shock of Sputnik. Tendentious argument and sentiment unsupported by evidence have been rampant both in the Reagan Administration and among its polarized opponents.

The next President, no matter what he now thinks he thinks, will be well advised to undertake a fresh and deep examination of the central issues, and he will need the support not only of his own Science Advisor, but of such critically important officials as the people at the top of the Department of Defense, in and out of uniform. But there is reason to hope that such a good hard look will show ways of moving beyond our present impasse. I believe that within all the confusion that now bedevils both weapons programs and arms control negotiations there are sensible and hopeful choices that can command general and sustained support. But I do not think these choices can be defined and defended successfully until a new President has ensured a full renewal of the science advisory role at the White House.

The New Longevity: Case Illustration of Needed Science and Technology Advice to the Three Branches of Government

Robert N. Butler

All industrialized nations have gained approximately twenty-five years of average life expectancy in the twentieth century (the century is not over yet)—nearly equal to what had been attained in the preceding 5,000 years of human history! The implications are enormous. Nearly all societies, regardless of their political systems and socio-economic status, are concerned about the potential burdensome costs associated with dependent old age, possible stagnation of societal productivity, and the forecast of possible intergenerational conflicts over limited resources. Whether these concerns are ever realized or not, the chance of avoiding the adverse effects of "population aging" and experiencing the promise of this unprecedented increase in vital, robust life expectancy can best come about through appropriate investments in research and applications intended to moderate or eliminate various forms of debility and senility.

In addition, we must support the creation of effective pension and long-term care systems, introduce changes in education, work and retirement patterns, restructure cultural attitudes, and facilitate the new and pioneering roles of the elders of our society, etc. Demographers project the "aging of the aging" (the rapidly growing 85-plus age group). Gerontologists predict a spectrum of vigorous healthy older persons at one end and a hard core group of diseased and disabled (medicated survivors) on the other. Devel-

Robert N. Butler, M.D., is Brookdale Professor and Chairman of the Gerald and May Ellen Ritter Department of Geriatrics and Adult Development, Mount Sinai Medical Center, New York City, the nation's first medical school department of geriatrics. He was Founding Director of the National Institute on Aging (1975–82) of the National Institutes of Health. In 1976, Dr. Butler won the Pulitzer Prize for Why Survive? Being Old in America. *He is a member of the Institute of Medicine.*

opment of personal and social responsibility (often called "health promotion/disease prevention") and the use of private pension funds, already a powerful source of capital formation, are obvious opportunities to deal with the concerns of the longevity revolution—but planning of various kinds and at varied levels is required. This must especially and specifically include scientific aspects of aging and longevity.

The *New Longevity* then, illustrates a practical need for national planning that cuts across all private social institutions and governmental departments and agencies. The "baby boom" generation is growing older. There is no doubt that there will be unprecedented numbers and proportions of older persons that will begin to reach their maximum within the next thirty and forty years, which gives us very litte time, indeed, to plan (short of an extraordinarily adverse impact of AIDS). The rapidly rising numbers and proportion of older persons are world-wide phenomena. Thus, US scientific (and economic) planning should evaluate overseas opportunities.

In the context of planning, for instance, the health enterprise should be evaluated in the global economy. It is the number two industry with eight million employees. It might be driven by a variety of policies, not "cost containment" alone. We might decide to build up the health enterprise—products and services—for expanded export to other nations.

Often, we cannot plan because we cannot anticipate. We can also over-plan. But those two facts do not militate against a reasonable amount of planning, particularly when confronted by challenges, such as the new longevity, that do appear to be well-founded. Some are challenges in the form of scientific opportunities, such as super-conductors, mapping the human genome, Super Colliders. Others are undesired but compelling scientific needs such as Alzheimer's Disease and AIDS, and some even are actually a consequence of success, such as population aging.

A COORDINATING BODY

Beyond a strengthened science presence (considered elsewhere in this volume) in the White House, we should have a special unit in the White House reserved for those issues that have special national concern, and require the response of a variety of departments or agencies of government. This could mean a revitalized Domestic Policy Council. Medical scientific topics connected with aging, such as Alzheimer's and AIDS, for example, principally depend upon the Department of Health and Human Services, but population aging is much broader. Indeed, it requires the organized response of all private sector institutions and federal, state and local departments and agencies. At the federal level, both the Executive and Legislative branches need to be able to turn to well-developed data bases, and have analytic capability to assist in building policy. For a time there was a special Presidential Counselor on Aging, but this was abandoned by the present Administration.

The present Federal Council on aging should be strengthened by Congress. This body is appointed by the President with the advice and approval of Congress. Nearly all departments and agencies should establish research units focused on aspects of aging relevant to their departments and agencies, for example, environmental and prosthetic studies in the Departments of Housing and Urban Development and Transportation (DoT and HUD).

The National Advisory Council on Aging (NACA) of the National Institute on Aging is presently advisory to the Secretary of the Department of Health and Human Services. The role of NACA should be elevated to be advisory to the President and the Presidential Counselor on Aging. This would have a status somewhat similar to the Cancer Board, which is advisory to the President, but with added staff responsibilities to help consolidate research on both aging and longevity and aging-related problems. This would serve units relevant to aging in various departments and agencies, not just the National Institute on Aging. Of particular relevance to science and technology advice in the White House, however, would be NACA's help in coordinating research on aging and longevity. Morever, there are important data sources in government such as the Census Bureau, the National Center for Health Statistics, Social Security, etc., of critical importance to policy-making, including resource allocation, identification of emerging problems, and the like. NACA would, therefore, bring its scientific presence to the White House, and would have the opportunity to relate to the strengthened science presence (discussed elsewhere in his volume).

Political forces become important limiting factors. The roles of the US Senate and House Committees on Aging and the growing power of the 26-million-member American Association of Retired Persons (AARP) in the private sector have critical roles. Thus the dynamic interplay of legislative and executive forces is presently monitored and influenced by large organizations representing the elderly, such as AARP. Happily the aging organizations are now joining forces with the principal advocacy groups for children in sponsoring still another organization, Generations United, which should help pursue a more balanced course from the perspective of the generations.

Ultimately, of course, the influence of advice depends at least as much upon the openness of the recipient as it does upon the knowledge and wisdom of the provider. Here political ideology and personality come to the fore—and can weaken for all practical purposes, and, indeed, make impotent—all efforts such as those that have been described here to institutionalize science and technology advice, whether regarding aging or any other subject, and the relationship of aging to the science advising apparatus built in the White House and in the Legislative and Executive branches.

We always have to hope that reasonable people will see the prudent and national importance of such efforts—in this case illustration, we have suggested the needed national response to the unprecedented social change of the new longevity.

One reason that supports the idea of a separate Department of Science and Technology to help coordinate the billions of dollars of research funds devoted to science by government outside of the Department of Defense is that it provides a bureaucratic stronghold of science advocacy in an increasingly global economy. This is an approach that other nations have taken. It is an imperfect idea, as perhaps all efforts at institutionalization are. But Departments do build constituency interests. The obvious disadvantages of bureaucratization may be balanced by assured stability amidst changing forces.

We as a nation—and indeed the nations of the world—would be ill advised to wait until the swelling numbers of older persons overwhelm income maintenance, health, and social service systems. By 2045, there will be an estimated two hundred forty million Chinese over sixty and perhaps some seventy million in the US. We can not wait for a population crisis of this character to emerge before we undertake the necessary research to bring to an end at least some of the more awesome, devastating and expensive debilities of age and create cost-effective, high-quality options to reduce dependent care.

Science Policy: USA and USSR

William D. Carey

On a humid spring day in May 1987, bemused Washingtonians warily unfolded the morning newspaper to a headline reading "Administration Ozone Policy May Favor Sunglasses, Hats." The Interior Secretary, it transpired, had intervened to block White House action on a completed international agreement to restrict production of chlorofluorocarbons (CFCs). As reported by the *Post,* the Secretary was pained by the thought of Administration acceptance of regulatory restraint on manufacturers, and proposed instead that citizens be urged to ward off carcinogenic radiation with sunscreens.

I am not about to argue that, because a negotiated environmental initiative is grounded on scientific evidence and probability, it is entitled to safe passage through the heavily mined straits of policy evaluation. Wince though we must at the trivializing of a manmade threat to environmental health and safety, the Secretary was not out of line in asking whether alternatives had been weighed adequately. This is what one expects to complete staff work in other areas of national policy, with good reason, and it is only the aspect of farce in this instance that makes it hard to take.

In science policy, as elsewhere, homework counts. Plainly, the ozone agreement should not have foundered at the wrapup stage. The agreement did not, so to speak, come as a bolt from the blue. It had kept people in the State Department and the Environmental Protection Agency busy for years in tedious international negotiations with thirty-odd other governments. Where was the lateral coordination process within our own Administration that should have prevented the ultimate embarrassment of the United States at the hands of one unhappy Cabinet officer? How could matters have gone so far without engaging the notice of the President's own Science Ad-

William D. Carey, a former Assistant Director of the Bureau of the Budget, retired recently as Executive Officer of the American Association for the Advancement of Science. He is an ex-officio member of the Governing Board of the National Research Council, a member of the Institute of Medicine, and a Trustee of the MITRE Corporation, the Argonne National Laboratory, and the National Academy of Public Administration. Since 1973, he has been Chairman of the US Section of the US-USSR Science Policy Working Group. He is currently advisor to the Carnegie Corporation of New York.

visor, who appeared in the *Post*'s story as supporting the Secretary's position because of his own qualms over "uncertainties" in the scientific evidence? What did he know, and how, and when did he know it?

The peremptory sinking of an earlier international agreement on the Law of the Sea at the hands of the same Administration comes all too readily to mind, as does the prolonged stonewalling on measures to abate acid rain, another example of taking political refuge in misty allusions to scientific uncertainty. What runs through all of these environmental policy disasters involving international consensus is the telling evidence of the superior strength of commercial self-interest. In the ozone affair, producers of CFCs complained of inequitable ceilings on production. Sea-mining interests had little taste for a potentially unfriendly international system for managing rights to the ocean's economic resources. The economic costs of abating stack emissions figure in the stalling of a transborder agreement to control acid rain. Altruism in the realm of long-term environmental policy runs a poor second in a race with short-term economic self-interest and its powerful tools of representation.

EQUAL AND OPPOSITE ACTION

All this said, it is still the fact that the process of the open society hangs on the equal and opposite action of consensus and dissensus, and science policy takes its life in its hands when it steps into the oncoming two-way traffic. Congress may appropriate money to get on with the design of a superconducting Super Collider, but it is unlikely that the exquisite beauty of experimental particle physics moves them nearly as much as the joy of an economic shot in the arm for the region winning the siting contest. Billions thrown at a space station may or may not advance either general science or competitiveness, yet billions cannot be found for science and mathematics education, which surely would do more. It was Robert Lovett who once observed that, although we yearn for straight-line public policymaking, it has no chance in the American experience because the founders built "the foulup factor"—group and interest competition—into the national policy machinery at the start, and it is alive and well—and a very good thing, too.

Government's funding of scientific research and development is, at this point, on a path to its fourth doubling since the 1950s. Although the previous three doublings are stated in current dollars, the arc of the curve bears watching. What are we going to do with all this dough when we get it? No visible process is at hand with which to map investment choices, and it is not even clear that such a process would be universally welcomed. Even so, learned papers tell us that federally funded R&D is less beneficial to the general economy than its industrial equivalent, that the transfer of research results into new processes and products is waylaid by deficient manufacturing technique, and that advanced science and engineering education is not drawing its needed share of the brightest American graduates of four-year institutions. Would a fourth doubling of federal outlays for science be sensible, absent policies to reinforce the human and institutional base upon which the advancement of science depends?

As Lovett was telling us, our process for making up our minds is built close to the ground and it advances crabwise. Science has quite different dynamics, and it is hardly surprising that the more instrumental science becomes in the hands of government, the more its aims are confused and its destinations blurred. A few habitual worriers like myself fret lest yet another doubling of federal funding will end by completing the transformation of postwar science to a quasi-governmental enterprise at the mercy of the foul-up factor, no longer an endless frontier.

"LIMP MUSCLES"

This commentary began by criticizing the limp muscles of science policy arrangements at the Presidential level. It should be added that what passes for public science and technology policy plays junior fiddle to a robust array of senior policies, notably for defense, foreign affairs, and the political economy. That equation is unlikely to be rewritten, at least as far ahead as one can see. But if national security and a strong national economy presume a first-class technology base, and if the conduct of foreign policy presumes that the United States will be a reliable partner in cooperative undertakings, the management of the science component of the policy system takes on a centrality that oncoming Presidencies cannot ignore.

Does this foretell "more government" in science's affairs? It would be hard to cram much more government into the system than is already there, notwithstanding the landscaping that obscures it. The idea is not to invite still more governmental invasiveness, but to make it somewhat more possible for government and science to negotiate the confused terms of their mutual dependence. That bespeaks suitable checks and balances: restraint on government's side in politicizing science for nationalistic and military ends, and a rediscovery by science of the representational skills that served it so well in the immediate post-war years, only to subside as government outdid itself in successive doublings of financial nutrition. Putting more weight on the far end of the see-saw without compensating at the other would leave science kicking empty air.

One can be properly objective about the other superpower while still acknowledging its tenacity in pursuing science and in selectively exploiting its capacity for global advantage. The Soviets do this well, and they can be counted on to do it even better. In their political construct, science policy is *not* junior to a host of senior policies. Science is, first and last, the business of the state, and there is not much altruism in it. It is not a fluke of bureaucratic paperwork that the president of the Soviet Academy is paid more than the General Secretary of the Party. It is not accidental that science and mathematics are dominant throughout the school experience, nor is it surprising that students strive in the awareness that to excel is to earn amnesty from a lifetime of deprivation banality.

So it should not continue to come as a surprise to learn that science policy comes to the Central Committee as a matter of course and priority. The successive Five-Year Plans incorporate (and underwrite) more than 150 "main directions" for multi-year research and development, some of them for the dual military-civil economy. The Academy and the State Committee for Science and Technology carry both weight and accountability, while international scientific strategies are run by a ministerial Intercosmos Council. A European observer, taking his shocked eyes off the disarray and near-collapse of the American space science program, can see on the Soviet side an unambiguous space policy-in-place for the next decade and a half, ambitious and daring in the sweep of its planetary science intentions, and assured of massive financial support. True, not much of its rests on dreamy thoughts of the ennoblement of the human spirit. It is all eminently pragmatic and politically strategic, designed to nail down Soviet pre-eminence in global space leadership, to assure long-duration proficiency in the space environment, and to arrive first in the commercial economy of space services. Not the least collateral bonus of all this is the message sent around the world that space should be a theatre for international cooperation, in contrast with the adversary's focus on Star Wars. However unsuitable the Soviet science policy model may be for export, it tells us that we are in a game that we could lose.

American science and technology have had things largely their own way during four decades of primacy with the rest of the world as followers. That scene is changing rapidly as the Europeans, the Japanese, the Soviets, and eventually the Chinese make their moves. It is all very well to treat ourselves to visions of a Strategic Defense Initiative, an Orient Express fast airplane, and even the blessings of superconductivity. But we are seen as lax in science education, facing demographic cramps, protectionist toward our advanced technology, unreliable as international partners, and unbuttoned in our capacity for science policy. Today's text is borrowed from Thomas Wolfe: "A wind is rising, and the rivers flow."

A New Era in Science Advising

Ashton B. Carter

For many who care about the quality of technical advice guiding national policy, the model of effective advising seems to remain the President's Science Advisory Committee (PSAC) of the 1950s and 1960s. The PSAC era was indeed a golden age, or so it seems to those of us who did not witness it first-hand, but only read about it now in histories and in the reminiscences of the participants. Technical people of distinction had the attentive and trusting ear of Presidents. The advisors policed themselves for objectivity and for high analytic standards. Presidents, for their part, took their near national monopoly on organized technical policy advice as a solemn trust, not to be abused for tactical political advantage.

Yet however appealing the PSAC paradigm is, it belongs to a bygone era of American political history. The conditions under which PSAC flourished do not exist today, nor is there much prospect they will reemerge. Though many observers point to the tension between the loyalty of technical advisors to their President and loyalty to their scientific standards as the cause of PSAC's decline, it seems clear in retrospect that this was a proximate cause only. Deeper forces were at work.

One force was the rise of a public policy process less tolerant, rightly or wrongly, of what it perceived as "elitist" advisory groups. The public also grasped—correctly—that technical expertise is a necessary but far from sufficient type of expertise for handling most policy problems, particularly as technology becomes more deeply embedded in social life. The public is also less naive that questions of value can be separated from questions of fact, with the latter entrusted to technical advisors. In other words, less and less is it possible to identify a set of policy problems that would be the appropriate agenda for a 1950s-style PSAC.

Another force is the growth of other sources of technical analysis: in Con-

Ashton B. Carter is Associate Professor of Public Policy at Harvard's Kennedy School of Government and Associate Director of the Center for Science and International Affairs. His Ph.D. in theoretical physics is from Oxford, where he was a Rhodes Scholar. He has worked at the Rockefeller University, the Congressional Office of Technology Assessment and the Office of the Secretary of Defense.

gress (as in the Office of Technology Assessment), in public service organizations and lobbies, and in Executive branch agencies themselves. The Department of Defense, for example, has a small army of analysts of unquestionable competence in matters of technical detail (but not unquestionable independence) continuously under contract. These competitors mean that a PSAC today would be distinguished by the quality of its individual members and by its independence, but no longer by the kind of questions it posed or the way it went about analyzing them. Technical analysis is standard fare in the policy process.

For these and other reasons, PSAC cannot any longer serve as the paradigm of how to get good science advice into government. (Another reason, not discussed further here, is the fact that a growing fraction of the vital issues needing technically informed attention are not national but international in scope, for example, the ozone problem. In the absence of international mechanisms for making policy, though, there is little scope for good advice on these problems.) The problem today is not a weak signal—an absence of technical input to policymaking—but the small signal-to-noise ratio. Technical argumentation has become the preferred way to get a policy position across. Every policy position has analysts enlisted in the cause, ready to produce fat reports with at least the appearance of analytic soundness, and ready to produce refutations of opposing analyses with at least the appearance of cogency. The problem for a good piece of technical advice today is not getting a hearing, but distinguishing itself from the welter of other analyses. These other analyses can easily "look" just as solid, with the same density of graphs, equations, and technical terms. For the community of scientists committed to good science in government, therefore, the issue is not access, but authority: how does the scientific community at large arrive at and express a "consensus" technical judgment to stand against false claims? At times, these false claims are far from subtle, as with "scientific" creationism, "refutations" of tobacco's danger to health, and leakproof nuclear defenses. Though these are egregious cases, they point up the weak voice of technical consensus.

I do not know completely how to increase the signal-to-noise ratio in science advising. But I believe that the solution to the problem of authority will not be found in the PSAC model—a small and elite group of individuals with private and exclusive access to the President—but in its antithesis— advisory *institutions* that publish their analyses for *all* interested consumers. Institutions like the National Research Council and the Office of Technology Assessment do not achieve their authority by any one product, and pressure groups will always be able to produce self-serving analyses with as many graphs, equations, and technical terms as any analytic product of these institutions. These institutions gain their authority through a track record of good analysis on issue after issue. That authority is earned because, in time, the technical community develops a loyalty to them, helps them maintain high standards, and defends them against irresponsible attack. Their publication of reports offering their conclusions and the underlying reasoning for all to read is necessary because it is in the chaotic public debate of today, unlike the more private deliberations of the 1950s and 1960s, that society's "technical" decisions are made.

Though it is not as exciting as being a member of the elite PSAC, supporting technical solidity in today's open public fray is a needed role of today's Science Advisor, in addition to service in Executive branch councils. The old romance is perhaps gone forever. But it need not be true, as one physicist mentor of mine suggested to me, that "the country is getting so open that its brains will fall out."

Science Advice and Social Science Advice to Government

James S. Coleman

As one of only three social scientists who were members of PSAC during its existence (the others were Herbert Simon and Daniel Patrick Moynihan), I have had occasion to reflect on the question of what social scientists were doing there. Stated more broadly, is it useful for there to be advice to government from social scientists in the same context and setting as advice from natural scientists? Besides PSAC, there have been several such contexts in the US Government since World War II. There is the President's Science Advisor (as separate from PSAC, though he also served as Chairman of PSAC during its existence), the Office of Science and Technology, which has served as the staff to the Science Advisor, and the Office of Technology Assessment serving the Congress. In addition, there is the National Research Council, whose committee reports often serve policy advice functions similar to those addressed by these other institutions of government.

The question appears simple enough, but it is not so simple. It is really two separate questions, one about social scientists, and the other about social policies. First, if the scope of policies addressed by a body like PSAC remains confined to those with a high content of science and technology questions, is it useful to have (as PSAC did in the last few years of its existence) social scientists as members, or should any such body be confined to natural scientists and engineers?

Second, is it useful to have an expansion of the scope of the body to include questions of "social science policy"? This would include, alongside policies like funding for SST and NASA programs, the B1 bomber, and an

James S. Coleman has, since 1973, been a Professor of Sociology at the University of Chicago. Previously he was an Associate Professor in the Department of Social Relations at Johns Hopkins University. His Ph.D. is from Columbia University (1955). He is a member of the American Sociological Association, the National Academy of Sciences, and the Royal Swedish Academy of Sciences. He was a member of the President's Science Advisory Committee (PSAC), 1970–72.

ABM defense system, also policies like federal aid to education, income maintenance, housing allowances, health insurance.

Although these are two separate questions, it might seem at first glance that the answers would imply each other: A yes or a no to one would imply the corresponding answer to the other. Yet the two questions are quite different, and their answers may well be different. PSAC, in the latter half of the 1960s, began first by answering yes to the question of social scientists, as Herbert Simon was appointed to the Committee. But the Committee also began to examine problems related to social science policies. When I joined the committee in 1970, a panel of the Committee was studying problems of education—not specific to science education, but general problems of education.

Yet, despite the fact that these two expansions of the scope of PSAC occurred at about the same time, they illustrate well the independence of the two questions: Simon did not direct his attention principally to questions of social policy, and the panel on education was not chaired by Simon (who was not even a member of it), but by Frank Westheimer, a chemist.

In this short essay, I will not examine the question of the scope of the policies that are appropriately encompassed by a science advisory body. That is a subject for a separate essay. Here, I will limit myself to the question of social scientists as members of a science advisory body.

The social scientist question, undisturbed by the social policy question, may be put this way: Suppose we were to consider a science advisory body whose scope was limited to questions of policies with a high component of science and technology content. Should social scientists be among the members of such a body? If so, what kinds of social scientists, and for what kinds of purposes?

THE GM COMMITTEE

The answer I will give is based in part on PSAC experience, but in larger part on experience as a member (from 1973–1983) of another science advisory committee, the General Motors Science Advisory Committee, formed in the early 1970s, with Lee DuBridge, a former President's Science Advisor, as one member, and Charles Townes, a Nobel Laureate physicist, as its first chair. The GM Science Advisory Committee was established by GM's CEO in part to provide "early warning" on new scientific and technical developments which GM might profitably exploit, and in part to advise on technical problems with which the company was confronted. (For example, one early question was how to meet the prospective emissions standards: with a catalytic converter or by some other means? And if with a converter, a noble metal catalyst, [platinum and palladium] or a base metal catalyst?) The committee reported directly to the Executive Committee of the Board of Directors, both in writing and in meetings. It had the run of the corporation in investigating the problems it chose or was asked to examine. The Committee consisted of six members, and as in the case of PSAC, there was one "social science member."

This was a period before the Japanese automobile invasion, and the company was in fine fettle, except for some discomfort due to the increasing emissions and safety standards being imposed on the industry by government. By the time I left the committee, GM had been overwhelmed by the explosive Japanese invasion of the car market, and was belatedly attempting to change itself to meet the cost and quality benchmarks established by the Japanese.

Over this period, which encompassed a large number of major technological and scientific decisions by GM, what was the role of the Science Advisory Committee? One component of the answer is clear, not only to me as the social science member, but also to the others who were members of the committee when I was: Nearly all the problems which the committee investigated, though they initially appeared to be principally scientific and technical problems, became increasingly revealed as social and organizational problems the more deeply the committee went into the problem.

An aspect of this was the disparity between what was technically "known to be true" within the GM culture, and what was in fact technically correct. For example, it was "known" that there were no significant advantages to overhead cam engines, but for the engines GM was designing in the late 1970s, that was not a correct technical assessment. What prevented the correct assessment from being made was a pervasive technical culture which prevented certain questions from being raised anew as conditions changed. All organizations are subject to such cultural norms; it is characteristic of every collectivity engaged in a common endeavor. It arises from too great pressures toward agreement, a phenomenon found in organizations generally, but to differing degrees.

A related phenomenon is that of group decision-making which can lead to inferior decisions in certain types of problems. Irving Janis, in *Victims of Groupthink* (Boston: Houghton Mifflin, 1972) discusses this phenomenon, with examples, such as the Kennedy decision to invade Cuba at the Bay of Pigs which arguably was an incorrect policy decision given the information then available.

There are organizational devices, well known to social science, which can prevent such norms from obscuring technically superior solutions.

One of these, termed "structured dissent," is similar to what some US Presidents have introduced as an aid to policy decisions: Each of several possible policy alternatives for a given decision is assigned to a staff member, who then prepares a policy paper arguing the merits of this alternative. These papers are then presented and the positions argued, before the President and other relevant persons. Such devices were not present in the GM technical organization.

Another aspect of the social and organizational basis underlying scientific and technical decisions is exemplified by technological innovation at GM. Frequently, as a Japanese or European competitor would introduce a state-of-the-art technical innovation, the question would arise: Why did GM not introduce this? The first answer was ordinarily concerned with the quality of GM's technical engineering skills; but then it shortly became apparent that the problem lay elsewhere. For example, the use of MacPherson struts on smaller cars was an innovation by overseas competitors, although at the time of the innovation, GM was building small cars, and later began to use MacPherson struts on these GM cars. But the problem was not lack of technical expertise: MacPherson struts had been invented some years earlier by a Chevrolet engineer, but never used by GM—until forced to do so by competitors.

The committee found numerous similar examples of innovations which were known, or even developed, by GM engineers, but introduced only belatedly after competition forced the company to do so. Again, the apparently technical problem was instead a social and organizational problem. And again, it is a problem with which social science has extensive experience. The general class of such problems may be described as "incentive structure" problems: The incentives confronting an individual lead to organizationally non-optimal outcomes. In the case of MacPherson struts and similar cases, it is the incentives for the intermediate or lower-level managers who supervise technical staff (e.g., incentives for the supervisor of the Chevrolet engineer who invented the MacPherson strut). In cases of various other apparently technical problems, it is the incentives for persons in other positions.

We may pose another question, which appears at first to be primarily technical: Why not fewer product recalls of GM cars? Because of an incentive structure which is non-organizationally optimizing, an engineer is encouraged to use technical ingenuity to patch up a problem in production, for example, by reversing a bolt placement in the floor pan, a problem due to a design defect, rather than to correct the design defect, for short-term cost saving. The patch-up later returns as an organizationally expensive recall. Or why extensive cost overruns by suppliers? Again because of inappropriate incentives, this time for engineering units involved in outsourcing: They are not sanctioned for specification modifications, which increases costs to suppliers, and encourages inflated pricing at delivery. Why is the time expenditure by engineers on a new product development crowded into the later weeks of their time-window? Again because of incentives confronting them that make this the most reasonable course of action, despite their non-optimality for the Corporation. A simple question that is critical for the design and management of organizations, but is often not asked (and was too seldom asked at GM) is, for every employee in every position: "What are the incentives that this employee confronts in work-related actions?"

SOCIAL DECISIONS

This extended set of illustrations taken from experience on a Science Advisory Committee to the General Motors top management might appear to be irrelevant to questions concerning science advice to the federal government. Certainly the kinds of policy decisions involving science and technology in the government are different from those involving overhead cam engines, MacPherson struts, or floor pan bolts. Yet the difference in types of decisions makes the examples even more relevant: These are decisions which appear at first to be based *wholly* on technical issues; yet even they turn out out to be largely social and organizational in origin. Governmental policies involving science and technology ordinarily have, even on the surface, a component of social and organizational issues. They are less close to the technical extreme than the GM decisions and problems I have described. The question of whether the Defense Department should fund design of a joint aircraft for the Air Force and Navy or separate designs may hinge as much on knowing the competing forces within and between these two branches of DoD, and the impact of this on the force-specific technical modifications they will demand as on knowing the technical merits of the two alternatives. The benefits of a technologically advanced weaponry may depend as much or more on the skill levels and learning rates of the mix of servicemen who will use them as on the technical capabilities of the weaponry.

In short, policies involving science and technology are so replete with issues involving social science—that is, replete with issues concerning the persons and organizations who interface in some way with the science and technology—that they cannot be well addressed by a body lacking expertise in these areas. Such expertise is not, moreover, widely distributed among natural scientists, just as it is not in the general population. The questions of social science are not like those of religion, in which each can have his own private solution. There are, for example, organizational structures that, confronted with certain tasks, produce outcomes that come closer to an organizational optimum than do others. And the principles behind these structural differences, while not unknown to non-social scientists are not well-schooled in these matters, and may well find, as have scientists and engineers at GM in examples I have given, that technically inferior decisions are made for reasons that are not apparent, or that technically inferior outcomes arise from technically correct decisions, again for reasons that are not apparent.

The United States Has No Adequate Mechanism to Set Long-Range Research Policy

Dale R. Corson

This is a discussion of the nature of scientific and engineering research, about how we support it, and how we set our national priorities. The discussion is built around the following propositions:

- Science and technology are growing in an exponential manner and will continue to do so if we let them.
- Every exponential growth eventually encounters some limiting factor and research is no exception.
- The growth in research is already slowing through the unavailability of resources.
- The nation and the world have critical technical problems which can be solved only by better fundamental understanding.
- These problems are getting worse, some of them rapidly, as the world population also grows exponentially. There is potential for the explosive growth of some problem to overwhelm us.
- We have no adequate way to set national priorities and, in the meantime, we are "fiddling while Rome burns." Only strong science and engineering in all their branches can respond adequately to crises when they arrive.
- We need new mechanisms for setting national research policy.

Dale R. Corson, a physicist by training, is President Emeritus of Cornell University. He has been affiliated with Cornell since 1946, serving as a faculty member, Dean of the College of Engineering, and Provost. He has served on many Washington study and advisory committees, including service as founding Chairman of the Government-University-Industry Research Roundtable established by the National Academy of Sciences.

EXPONENTIAL GROWTH CHARACTERIZES OUR CIVILIZATION

Exponential growth characterizes this stage in the evolution of our civilization. The world population, for example, is doubling every thirty or forty years, representing an annual growth rate of 1.5 or 2%. Research achievement is also growing rapidly, and I want to make three points about it:

- The growth in research achievement has been enormous and it has been exponential.
- Research has become enormously expensive and cost has also risen exponentially.
- The exponential character of the growth in both scientific achievement and cost was inevitable, and the same explosive growth will continue in the future, if we let it.

An exponential quantity, incidentally, is one that increases ever more rapidly, always doubling in magnitude over a characteristic "doubling" time.

Space does not permit documentation of these assertions. Rate of growth in the number of technical journals or in the number of people engaged in research, however, supports the assertions.

The nature of research leads directly to the exponential characteristic. It is an example of the rate of change (in this case, of the amount of research) being proportional to the results already achieved—the classic exponential relationship.

The cost of doing research follows the same pattern. As scientific achievement progresses, the number of people requiring support grows, and the equipment becomes ever more complex and expensive. Today's research equipment is yesterday's research frontier. And the more rapid the progress, the more rapid the obsolescence of the equipment.

So where do we go from here? Will scientific productivity continue at the present rate, and will expense continue to grow in exponential fashion? Will society continue to support science at these levels?

SOME FACTOR WILL EVENTUALLY LIMIT THE EXPONENTIAL GROWTH

Any exponential growth must eventually encounter some limiting factor. Let us look at the population. Right now, we're doubling our numbers every thirty-five or forty years. It is easy to calculate how long until the amount of the earth's surface per individual is only one square yard, and that is about 500 years. That is the time since Christopher Columbus discovered America.

Obviously, the population will not continue to grow at the present rate for 500 years. Something will limit it. What will it be? Food supply? Climate changes? Inter-group conflict? New diseases?

What about the continued growth in scientific achievement? I assert that it, too, will encounter some limiting factor, and there is danger that we will not address serious problems adequately.

INADEQUATE HUMAN RESOURCES MAY BE A LIMITING FACTOR AT AN EARLY DATE

The obvious critical factor in our future progress is the availability of capital resources—human and financial. Right now, we are in danger of being limited by human resources. We are not attracting an adequate number of young people into scientific and engineering careers.

In physics, the annual number of new Ph.D.s is now about two-thirds what it was in 1972. It is stabilized at this level only because of the growing numbers of foreign nationals in our graduate schools.

There is gross underrepresentation of women and minorities, other than Asian minorities, in our scientific and technical disciplines. Only about 2% of the 30,000 American physics Ph.D.s are women. In 1985, only about 110 Ph.D.s in all the science and engineering fields went to black candidates; half of them were in biology, and thirty-three were in engineering and the physical sciences, which is fewer than one per state. The representation of black and Hispanic students in our science and engineering schools is low and it is falling, while the relative numbers of these groups in our population is growing. We are failing to tap a large segment of our talent pool.

Coupled with these concerns is the demographic factor: The number of 22-year-olds will fall by about 25% by the year 2000, further reducing the available pool.

SCIENTIFIC PROGRESS IS ALREADY LIMITED BY ALLOCATED RESOURCES

Gross National Product is a measure of our national resource base, and it grows a few percent per year—slower than the scientific achievement rate. At some stage, the cost curve must cross the resource line.

The investment in our research and graduate education enterprise, when measured in constant dollars, began to fall about 1968. We are no longer investing in people, for example, as we did in the 1960s. There are fewer graduate fellowships, one of the reasons, perhaps, why young people are turning away from science and engineering careers.

Since 1968, the research and graduate education infrastructure has deteriorated. Modern instruments of research are unavailable in adequate numbers. Slowly, but surely, our base for international competition is eroding.

What *is* the correct fraction of the GNP that can be profitably invested in research and graduate education? What level of investment will sustain our economic health and our place in the community of nations? What level of investment will assure our military security? What level of investment will produce a level of scientific achievement which will enrich our lives and contribute to an esprit that will make us a vital and admirable society?

THERE ARE GREAT OPPORTUNITIES FOR RESEARCH WHICH WILL ENRICH OUR NATIONAL LIFE

The opportunity for rapid scientific progress has never been greater. In biology, the understanding of biological processes, including ways to control some of these processes, has opened the door to greater food production and to elimination of disease. We are learning how to design materials which can lead to achievements never before possible. There are many other examples.

These scientific and technical developments can make our future safer, more rewarding, and less painful.

At this point, I will make three more assertions:
- As the world population grows ever faster, the stress in the lives of human beings everywhere increases, and there is ever more trouble in the world.
- Part of the stress is related to growing scientific and technical problems, exacerbated by the growing population, which must be solved if we are to survive in any kind of reasonable way. Some of these problems have the potential for overwhelming us through their explosive growth.
- The resources allocated to these problems are insufficient to deal adequately on a long-term basis, and the longer the underinvestment persists, the larger the problems become.

OUR FUTURE SURVIVAL DEMANDS THE SOLUTION OF DIFFICULT SCIENTIFIC AND TECHNICAL PROBLEMS

There are big scientific and technical problems which we must address if our civilization is to survive.

The problem which commands our highest national priority is our military defense. Defense is based on advanced technology, and it exploits the most recent scientific achievements. For our military defense to be assured, we must "run faster" in science and technology than our adversaries.

Air pollution is potentially devastating, because of the "greenhouse effect" and potential changes in the climate brought about by increasing concentrations of carbon dioxide in the atmosphere. Some predictions indicate a serious problem within the next fifty years.

Our energy supply presents another huge problem. Oil appears headed to exhaustion in another fifty years. We have a great deal of coal—enough to last for hundreds of years, but burning it puts carbon dioxide in the atmosphere. If the greenhouse problem proves serious, we will be unable to use the coal—at least, in a straightforward combustion mode. Nuclear power appears to be doomed for the time being by political forces—the public does not trust it. Conventional nuclear power could provide a solution for only fifty to 100 years, in any case, before the supply of uranium is exhausted. Breeder reactor technology, which could extend the useful life by a large factor, has hardly been considered in the United States. Fusion energy may well be our savior, but it will be decades before we can be sure.

For solar energy to meet more than perhaps a small fraction of our energy need, we would require ways to transport it long distances—from Arizona to New York, for example. Transmission losses and complexities are far too great to make that possible, however.

In the health area, we still have major diseases to conquer—the genetic diseases, for example, and new diseases, a prospect made real by the AIDS problem. Furthermore, the widespread use of antibiotics over the past forty or fifty years has led to the growth of mutant strains of bacteria that are resistant to our present array of drugs.

ADEQUATE TECHNOLOGY REQUIRES INVESTMENT IN ALL AREAS OF SCIENTIFIC ENDEAVOR

To sum up the situation: We have great opportunities, we have great societal needs, but we have limited resources. What can we do about it?

Perhaps we can decide which are the highest priority problems and direct our resources at them alone. But can research really be directed? Such an effort is, probably, at best, a short-term solution.

The real question is: "Can any field of science or engineering prosper long without opportunities to exploit the achievements in other—sometimes seemingly unrelated—fields?" I think not.

At this point, I will make another set of assertions:

- Major opportunities cannot be exploited and serious societal problems cannot be confronted successfully for long by directing resources to a limited set of priorities.
- The only way to assure a scientific and engineering base capable of addressing any technological problem likely to emerge is through investment in all promising scientific and engineering fields.

To know how to direct our resources most effectively, we must have informed political decision-making mechanisms. Let us look at the mechanisms we have.

SCIENCE POLICY DECISIONS WERE SIMPLY AND WISELY MADE IN EARLIER TIMES

Right up to World War II, research was investigator-driven. The scientist himself or herself decided where the pay-off areas were likely to be. The more competent the investigator, the better the judgment about the critical problems and about the best approaches to them. Fund providers had to rely on the judgment of the scientists.

The mechanisms for making research and development policy decisions in World War II were extraordinarily effective. A few wise people devised a national policy, and took it to the highest levels of government.

After the war, the public—and Congress—believed that science and technology could solve nearly every problem. When Vannevar Bush produced his *Science, the Endless Frontier,* his suggestions were implemented and a magnificent system of research support was established.

SCIENCE POLICY DECISION-MAKING NOW IS MORE COMPLEX

Today, the world is more complex. Decisions are more difficult, and the allocation of resources among competing claims is troublesome.

It was only with the advent of significant federal support in the post-war period that priorities began to be set by federal agencies and Congress. Other than the National Institutes of Health, only the Office of Naval Research supported research in a significant way in the years immediately following the war. With the creation of the National Science Foundation, the government took a large step toward supporting and guiding American research.

The reinvigoration of Truman's science advisory apparatus in the Eisenhower Administration, with a full-time President's Science Advisor and a President's Science Advisory Committee (PSAC) of distinguished individuals, provided us with an effective means for defining and recommending considered science and engineering initiatives. For two decades—until they were abolished in the Nixon Administration—the President's Science Advisor and PSAC played an important—and, in some matters, decisive—role.

Moves were made to restore the office to its former position in the Ford Administration, and we have had, throughout the Ford, Carter and Reagan Administrations, an Office of Science and Technology Policy and a President's Science Advisor, but no PSAC. From the end of 1985 until late 1986, however, there was no Advisor, and the influence of the Office appears to have deteriorated.

From the beginning, the role of the Science Advisor has appeared—to me, at least—somewhat ill-defined. There appears to have been confusion on whether the role of the Advisor was to bring carefully studied analyses and recommendations from the scientific community to the President and the Administration, or whether the role was to take positions already adopted to the scientists.

There are other means of bringing informed opinion to bear on important scientific and technological problems. The Office of Technology Assessment provides in-depth studies of problems directed to it by Congress. The

National Research Council (NRC) brings the best talent in the country to consider matters put before it by the government.

DECISIONS ARE NECESSARILY BASED ON POLITICAL EXPEDIENCY AND PERCEIVED NATIONAL NEED

Industrial competitiveness has become a symbol of perceived deteriorating American leadership, and there is overwhelming political priority for restoring that leadership. If research can play a part in the restoration, it can have a legitimate claim to its share of the federal dollar.

Questions of national prestige often enter into decisions about research and development priorities. Important elements in the priority debate these days are the "mega" projects: the space station; the superconducting, Super-Collider particle accelerator; the Strategic Defense Initiative; and the hypersonic airplane (the Orient Express). Prior to the Challenger accident, the Shuttle program appeared to be spectacularly successful, and the public, including Congress, viewed Shuttle activities as "science," although the amount of real science undertaken on Shuttle missions was small. Our space achievements represent American prestige and technical dominance, however. We are certain to continue support for at least some of these programs, whether or not they speak to our greatest needs.

Congress is one of the most important bodies, but it is particularly hard for it to make technically informed decisions. Few of the individual members are qualified to make independent judgments. Congressional committees and subcommittees, including policy-oriented committees, such as the House Science and Technology Committee, develop policies based on testimony in hearings. In spite of the committees and other mechanisms available to Congress, hundreds of millions of facility and research dollars have gone to various universities—some qualified, some not—over the past few years with no merit review at all.

SUMMARY AND CONCLUSIONS

And so I come to my conclusions and my final assertions:

- There are troubling problems on the horizon, and only a vigorous, long-term research program with assured resources can cope with them.
- We are not likely to see the light until we feel the heat. Our best defense, when the crisis comes, from whatever direction, will be strong science and engineering in all their branches. We are underinvesting in the research required to provide this insurance.
- Only the informed judgment of scientists and engineers working with political leaders can lead to reliable decisions about priorities and the required levels of funding. We need a more effective mechanism for achieving this decision-making partnership at the highest levels of government.

NEW INSTITUTIONS ARE REQUIRED

If we are to deal wisely with these problems, new institutions are required to supplement our present decision-making mechanisms. The goal is to bring objective consideration to the most serious problems we face, and to set priorities in ways and in directions likely to be effective.

We can ask first whether or not existing mechanisms could be made adequate. The most important body now in identifying long range, urgent problems and suggesting appropriate responses is the National Research Council. By and large, the various committees, commissions, study panels, symposia, and other means by which major problems are examined include the best people in the country, operating in the best national interest.

Properly organized, supported and operated, the Office of Science and Technology Policy could play a large and important role. It has long been too politicized, however, to do the objective and long-range job which must be done. If it can be restructured, its mission redefined, and if it can attract the best-informed people in the country, it can play a crucial role.

The funding agencies tend to be led by competent and wise people who have much to contribute to the long-range priority setting which is essential to our future health, if not our survival.

Congress, by itself, will always be consumed by the immediate problems. Political solutions tend to be crisis-driven. Nonetheless, the politicians are the ultimate decision-makers. The problem is how to provide the Congress with the help required if it is to make informed political judgments.

I believe that a mechanism is needed in which scientific and technical statesmen come together with funding agency leaders, other critical Executive branch officials, and Congressional leaders in a totally non-political, non-lobbying setting to examine issues, to explore likely approaches to particular problems, to identify gaps in our research programs, and to suggest priorities. The participants must be viewed as objective with no "axes to grind," and they must include the best scientific and technical wisdom the country possesses.

Obvious elements in such an effort include the leadership of the National Research Council, industrial research leadership, federal agency officials with budget authority, funding agency leadership, and Congressional leadership.

Such a mechanism should be institutionalized as soon as possible, but it would be a mistake to try to do it in the beginning. Nothing would ever happen. The way to begin is with a few dedicated people in Congress, in the Executive branch, and in the scientific and technical world discussing the problems in an informal manner. Experience would indicate the way to make the mechanism permanent, and to insulate it from the changing political winds which dominate the short-range decision-making process.

We must understand the explosive growth of the technical problems our exponentially expanding world bequeaths us. If we address these large problems in any way other than with the best objective, long-range thinking we can muster, the problems will consume us. We will be doomed to a slow, painful decline in our civilization.

White House Science Advising

Edward E. David, Jr.

Science advice for the highest levels of govenment—namely, the President and his immediate staff—has become topical again, as the Presidential election looms. The current mechanism is in question. Many people believe that scientific and engineering factors should play a larger role in Presidential decision-making, and that the current mechanism is not serving well. Is the idea of the White House science apparatus as an honest broker of rational problem-solving obsolete? To be less dramatic, are changes in order to improve the performance of that apparatus? To answer the question, let me examine several central issues: (1) science and politics, (2) modern demands on science advisors, (3) the position of the social and life sciences in advisory activities, and (4) the role of outside people in the advisory process. This examination will lead to a proposal for a revised White House mechanism.

SCIENCE, ENGINEERING, AND POLITICS

The White House is certainly "where science and politics meet." Indeed, this was the title of Jerome Wiesner's book, published after his stint as Science Advisor to the President. Science and politics may meet in the White House, but they don't mix well. When politics invades science or when science becomes politically active, personalities can be bent out of shape, and realistic policies can be replaced by wishful ones. This realization crystallizes a principal issue in the continuing controversy about science advice for the highest levels of government. That issue is whether it is productive

Edward E. David, Jr., was Science Advisor to President Nixon, is Acting President and a Trustee of the Carnegie Institution of Washington, and is President of EED, Inc., consultants to industry and government on technology and research management. He was Science Advisor to President Nixon (1971–73), and has been President of Exxon Research and Engineering Company, Executive Director of Bell Telephone Laboratories, and Executive Vice President of Gould, Inc. Dr. David is a member of the National Academies of Science and Engineering, the White House Science Council, and the New Jersey Commission on Science and Technology, and is US delegate to the NATO Science Committee.

for a science advisory person or group to advocate actions animated by politically loaded convictions.

While I was Science Advisor to President Nixon, I wrote a short piece entitled "Advocacy or Options, Science Advice for the President." The distinction is a critical one. Most engineers and scientists, I believe, think that it is their job to create technological options for government, business and society in general, but it is the job of politicians, managers and citizens to decide which options to pursue.

That simple idea is widely held outside the science policy cognoscenti, but it cannot be transferred bodily to the mechanism for advising the President about science. There are many reasons. An important one is that significant public policies or actions usually, perhaps always, involve technical issues for which science and engineering do not provide unequivocal answers. Thus Science Advisors find themselves constantly beyond the edge of the known and often in speculation and guesswork.

Furthermore, scientists and engineers are human. Their judgments are biased by their experiences and backgrounds and are hardly purely objective. It is easy for accomplished technical people to slip over into advocacy for deeply felt positions. The operation of the President's Science Advisory Committee (PSAC), 1957 to 1973, illustrates this well.

PSAC became part of the political fabric of the White House, and engaged in activities intended to sustain its recommendations by influencing Presidential decisions. Engineers and scientists outside the PSAC circle recognized this situation. There was wide disapproval, in part because the outside favored options, not advocacy. That was particularly so when PSAC positions went against the grain of those outside. The most prominent examples were in defense, arms control, space, environmental regulation, and pre-college education. The controversy has continued. The quality and quantity of science advice has been blamed for the SDI decision, the Challenger accident, and even the loss of US industrial competitiveness. The degree and intensity of PSAC politically involved activities probably accounts, at least in part, for the resistance by the scientific and engineering community itself to the revival of PSAC following its demise in 1973.

I saw this resistance at first hand during the deliberations of the pre-inauguration task force preceding President Reagan's first term. Many people on the task force regarded the PSAC mechanism as an anachronism. Yet scientists and engineers could hardly be against sound technical advice for the President. Why were they opposed? Probably because of their distaste for the previous experience and their lack of confidence that a new PSAC would or could give politically neutral, objective advice.

There may be other reasons arising from the unfortunate schisms among scientists and engineers themselves; unfortunate because, ultimately, they undermine the public's and politicians' confidence in science and scientific opinion as credible sources of advice. The earliest such schism of which I was acutely aware was the Oppenheimer-Teller division of the 1950s. That persists to this day—in print, on television, and in the SDI debate. Other schisms have arisen from the environmental regulatory scene, manned spaceflight, health effects of ethical drugs, and so on. These subjects have intense political polarities. There have even been organized groups of scientists and engineers who publicly favored certain Presidential candidates. So it has become the practice at the top levels of government to appoint advisory scientists and engineers according to the same criterion as for political appointments. That criterion involves both compatible political and economic philosophies and loyalty to the principal. The resulting mode of operation reduces scientific advice to merely another voice among many supplicants. This situation might be reversed, but that would take several political generations. Regardless, this involvement between science and partisan politics is not one to inspire support from the community at large.

Of course, science advice, no matter how objective, will often have political repercussions if it is followed. But, in my opinion, science advice should not be slanted to achieve political objectives. Nor should science advice be diluted for fear of its political fallout. Between these two alternatives is a narrow path for Science Advisors to tread.

Scientists are citizens, and are entitled to their political opinions. But those opinions should best be kept distinct from science-based advice. Ideally, engineers and scientists should not trade on their reputations to lend credibility to politically loaded positions. It is the seeming inability or unwillingness of scientists and engineers to keep the political and technical domains apart that has put science advice to the highest levels of government in the state that it is today.

SCIENCE ADVICE FOR TODAY

Even if science advice were kept out of the political rough-and-tumble, its function is much different today than it was fifteen years ago. The issues today are different, focused more on commercial competitiveness, primary and secondary education, and engineering, including manufacturing and design, and less on national security. Ethical and moral questions involving science have increased in intensity, bringing a broader dimension into science advising. There are genetic engineering, creation science, nuclear energy, and the AIDS epidemic to deal with in that context. There is also a burgeoning activity in regulatory science. Automobile and aircraft safety are major issues, for example.

The role of small business and new ventures has emerged. The SBIR program, initiated by Congress, is one of the broadest set asides ever enacted to favor an industry segment. The SBIR covers all agencies and departments of government that have substantial R&D programs.

The issue of small vs. big science has intensified with a vengeance. With the emergence of SDI, SSC, the space station, mapping the human genome, the DARPA advanced computer initiative, and specialized centers in universities, small science may well be overwhelmed by gargantuan programs. The real issue here is not small vs. big, but rather investigator-initiated vs. programmed research. The latter has become more and more dominant as federal administrators have followed the Mansfield Amendment philosophy. More and more, micromanagement of research by officials is evident. The balance between investigator-directed and sponsor-directed research is a rising issue.

At one time, the federal government dominated R&D funding. During the 1960s, federal funds were almost 70% of the total. Today they are less than half. Industry funding has increased more rapidly than federal in recent years. Commercial payoff has become the principal criterion for the largest share of R&D funding. Commercial activities are less new-technology-driven and basic research-dependent than federal programs are. This trend means that basic research is losing its identity. International commercial competitiveness has come to the fore, and so applied research is predominantly the industrial mode. Even Defense sees research as part and parcel of national policy, so fundamental research is de-emphasized. Industry-university couplings are increasingly sought, not only by the federal government but also by state and local governments in the service of economic development. So, the traditional activity of science, namely the search for knowledge, is becoming increasingly submerged by other objectives. The sustenance of fundamental research is increasingly difficult as these trends progress.

When the Science Advisory post was set up in the White House and PSAC established during the 1950s, it was a time when there was a paucity of technical talent and organization in the Executive branch, and little or none elsewhere in governments, federal, state, and local. The White House Science Advisor led by default. To the credit of those early advisors, that situation has changed dramatically. There are now responsible technical resources in NASA, in the Departments of Defense, Health and Human Services, Transportation, and Commerce, as well as in some state governments, and many other loci. The Congress has set up its own technical resource, the Office of Technology Assessment. Many states have science and technology commissions. City governments too, have science advisors. White House science is no longer the dominant operative.

Further, the relation between the scientific and engineering communities and the federal government has changed. Science advice in the 1950s and 1960s came from a cohort that had supported government policies unflinchingly. That was the legacy of World War II. Today the community has detached itself, and is looked upon as a critic, pursuing its own agenda. That was true in the Johnson, Nixon and Carter Administrations, as well as in the Reagan Administration.

Then there is the sheer size of the R&D activity in this country. It has grown many fold over the past twenty years. The federal laboratories alone are now budgeted at over $17 billion per year, while the total federal budget for R&D is pushing $65 billion. This scale is far beyond that handled by PSAC and the Science Advisor in the 1960s.

So the situation today bears little resemblance to times past. It is propitious to ask what the top levels of government think they now need in the way of science advice, because that is what is likely to emerge. I have not seen a clear statement of such needs, but discussions with White House officials, present and past, lead to the following. One need is for alerting. Decision-makers need to know what is going on technically, inside government and outside as well. In selected instances, the goings-on need to be influenced to support Administration policies. The Science Advisor and his office must provide analysis for such decisions and actions. The recent high-profile emergence of high-temperature superconductors is an example; what should the federal role be in furthering and exploiting the new possibilities they open? The President has attempted an answer in his recent speech on the subject. Thus significant technical events are matters to be highlighted for the President.

Large federal programs involving heavy use of science and technology are becoming ever more common, as mentioned earlier. The Science Advisor and his staff can and should monitor these to assure their goals are compatible with scientific and engineering realities, and that such programs are being managed and executed effectively. This function is particularly important when program elements are spread across several departments and agencies. Example are the current attempts by NASA, and the Departments of Defense, Transportation, and Commerce to re-establish access to space for the many military, commercial, and exploration payloads that hinge upon reliable launches.

Another example is the ongoing arms negotiations with the Soviet Union, where technical factors, particularly in treaty compliance verification, are crucial. Still another example is scientific cooperation with other nations as a part of US foreign policy. All these activities involve governmentwide interests and can benefit from a central focus in the White House.

The White House science apparatus needs to support decision-making in a variety of situations. Daily or weekly issues are handled by the White House staff on a time-urgent basis. Science staff work is required to support such decisions.

Finally, and certainly not least, there is the health of basic research and scientific and engineering education. These matters have been traditional concerns of the federal government. Appropriate policies and actions are a proper concern of the White House science office along with other agencies, particularly the NSF and the NIH.

If we take filling these five needs as the missions for science activity in the White House, there remains the question of how to best pursue those missions. A crucial issue, seldom addressed, is the desired qualifications for the President's Science Advisor. Clearly, he or she must have the confidence of the President and the technical community. Such confidence involves again both political and scientific factors. I believe, however, that there is one overriding requirement. The Science Advisor must be devoted to scientific and technological progress and that devotion should not be diluted by pseudo-sophisticated beliefs in political or economic doctrines.

SCIENCE BEYOND THE PHYSICAL

In its early incarnation, the White House science apparatus focused on the physical sciences and engineering. Defense and nuclear energy, followed by space, were principal concerns. Over the years, the scope of activity expanded, first into the life sciences, then into certain social sciences. Yet there was—and still is—a strain of opinion that particularly the social sciences are outside the competence of science and represent a hazard to its credibility.

This issue is a difficult call because the social sciences are exceedingly diverse, and can involve politically related controversy to a high degree. The levels of certitude are less than in physical sciences and engineering. It is more difficult to separate social science from opinion and speculation. Nevertheless, certain aspects of the social sciences, for example, economic modeling, experimental psychophysics in vision and hearing, educational methods, and demographics have agreed upon scientific claims. Furthermore, the importance of bringing objectivity to the social scene is increasingly important. Despite that, the pain caused the NSF over its 1970s foray into social science education recommends caution.

Of course, the life sciences have long since established themselves as principal components of science advisory activity. The AIDS epidemic and molecular biology are only the most recent examples. Health care, too, is a matter for scientific consideration as technology invades diagnosis and therapy. Nevertheless, such matters have strong political and social overtones.

So it seems that the scope of science advice should be broad, but also should be constrained to subjects where there is a potential scientific contribution.

OUTSIDE SCIENCE ADVISORS

One of the greatest strengths of the federal government has traditionally been active participation by citizens on a *pro bono* basis in activities from Presidential Commissions to informal consultation on matters where special insights are useful. Scientists and engineers in such roles have been particularly effective. There was PSAC and now WHSC, but, in addition, there were many panels and task forces to study pressing subjects and recommend actions. Involvement by individuals has a long history, punctuated by the famous letter from Einstein to the President on nuclear explosives. This tradition is especially worth maintaining and strengthening, a path made difficult by current practices concerning supposed conflicts of interest and the resulting disclosure requirements.

Closely related to these matters are the statutory requirements for public meetings under the Federal Advisory Committee Act. These requirements make it difficult for science advisory committees and panels to provide confidential viewpoints to the Executive unless the matters are officially classified. These requirements ought to be reviewed and modified to allow advisors and advisees to operate with reasonable privacy. Such steps seem unlikely, however, as distrust between Administrations and Congress grows.

A PROPOSAL

The Science Advisor and his office, OSTP, have no recognized function in the White House, despite the passage of the Science Advisory Act of 1974. The activity is only what the Science Advisor makes it, and what the White House staff will allow. If the science office had some budget authority (akin to Congressional authorization, for example), its effectiveness could be greatly enhanced. In particular, such authority could be used to pull together federal programs across all of government, as well as seeing that sound technical programs go forward and unsound technical programs do not.

Should such a function be established, the capability of the science office staff would become even more critical than it is today. Turnover of staff has been a problem for the science office in the past, and maintaining continuity has been difficult. This situation leads to the suggestion to establish a permanent and professional capability for the White House in the form of a Federal Contract Research Center (FCRC), replacing the OSTP. A FCRC is a private, non-profit corporation chartered to work exclusively for the federal government, in this case the White House. FCRC's have been around for many years. They have a good record in serving the government economically. They attract fine people and good leadership. Furthermore, many FCRCs have shown the level of good judgment required for sensitive positions of this kind. Yet they have maintained their integrity, a critical requirement. A White House FCRC might, under some conditions, contribute to activities in the NSC and other elements of the White House staff as well.

This arrangement could result in the flexibility for a President and his people to secure sound science advice in a variety of ways. The President would not have to appoint a Science Advisor. He could depend upon the President or Chairperson of the FCRC. Or, should he have confidence in a scientist or engineer known to him or recommended by a colleague, he could appoint such a person as his Science Advisor. Through the FCRC, the President or his Science Advisor could establish a Presidential Advisory Committee or special panels which could operate with the confidentiality appropriate to the subject. Perhaps the Board of Trustees of the FCRC could be called upon as a Presidential Advisory Committee. Conflicts of interest could be avoided and ethics sustained through mechanisms that have served the FCRC community well in the past. Of course, the FCRC could call on outside advisors extensively. It could also provide continuity and an institutional memory.

Such an arrangement would have some negatives as well. A science-based FCRC would be outside the President's official family, and might become isolated. FCRCs can become entrenched and require renewal. A mechanism for such renewal would have to be put in place. The mere existence of the FCRC might reduce the incentive for a President to appoint a Science Advisor to his personal staff. On the positive side, this arrangement would give some political insulation for the Science Advisor and his resource people. Regardless of these factors, a mixed arrangement of this kind should be studied, since it may be an important way of improving science advice to the highest levels of government.

Science Policy Advice to the US Government

John Diebold

Many factors that made for once-commanding American leads in international competition have eroded, from educational excellence to the commercialization of technologies to financial strengths. As a result, the US semiconductor industry has become the first in a series of industries (biotechnology is almost certainly the next) that could soon be lost to foreign competition—even though they were pioneered in the US.

The most crucial elements of a national high-technology strategy for the United States are 1) education, 2) basic research, and 3) mechanisms for bringing scientific discoveries from the laboratory to the marketplace. The development and application of scientific innovations has traditionally been a source of unique strength of this country. Today, it is an area that requires material improvement, if we are to retain our leading edge in international technological competition.

The kinds of changes we need to make are not industry-specific. Targeting the high-tech information industries through research or trade subsidies and other "quick fix" solutions would do more harm than good. And our obsession with Japanese competition is entirely misplaced, especially when Korea, Singapore and all the "little Japans" are forging new inroads into the US. We must look for long-range, systemic solutions to complex problems that cut across our entire industrial structure—in which high technology plays a pivotal part.

A few suggestions:

- Restore incentives to invest in the future. When capital gains are taxed at the same rate as other income—under the recent tax reform—there is less incentive to take risks by investing in entrepreneurial startups. Such investment is also discouraged by the high cost of capital, which is related

John Diebold is Chairman and founder of The Diebold Group, Inc., an international management consulting firm based in New York City. He is a specialist in information technology, and is the author of two books on automation and the future, and several collections of speeches and papers.

to the low level of our national savings rate. Congress should reconsider its tax revisions that discourage investing and saving, including the disastrous elimination of Individual Retirement Account (IRA) incentives.

• Support mechanisms to ease the transition from innovation to marketplace. Certainly, the time-lag between basic research and applied technology is becoming shorter. This underscores the need to understand the mechanisms that carry scientific discoveries from the laboratory to the marketplace. The Reagan Administration's policy of encouraging national laboratory scientists to market their ideas is the kind of innovation in transitional mechanisms that deserves support.

A related problem is the peer review process. For example, I am personally acquainted with a Nobel laureate who cannot get funding for research in neurobiology; he can only get peer approval for continuing research in the area for which he won his Nobel, even though he considers the neurobiological project far more important. The tendency of the peer review process to favor "safe" or proven topics of research—rather than radically new frontiers—only exacerbates the time lag problem.

• Rebuild the foundations of basic research. Laboratory equipment in our research institutions and universities is seriously outdated. The National Science Foundation has not budgeted funds for new laboratory equipment since the 1960s. NSF Director Erich Bloch has made a forceful case for doubling annual outlays for basic research to $4.3 billion, drawing the funds from the Defense Department's ample research budget to rebuild laboratories, replace old equipment, and support students. Moreover, experiments in the leasing of laboratory equipment and the encouragement of other private-sector financial innovations could provide a substitute for the heavy investment required to update university research facilities.

• Stop subsidizing our competitors by underwriting technical education for foreign students. More than half our graduate students in science and engineering are from foreign countries. While we may have an obligation to train scientists from around the world, we should charge fees to developed nations like Japan, Germany and France for the appreciable subsidies that are now borne by the US taxpayer.

• Encourage cooperation between business and universities, which has historically been an important element in US technological leadership. Not only should this relationship be studied as part of a national research strategy, but it undoubtedly is one in which further innovation would be fruitful. The computer science laboratories that IBM has funded at Carnegie-Mellon University, Brown University, and MIT emit an atmosphere of extraordinary excitement and fecundity. Although corporate funding of university research has often prompted concerns about academic freedom and integrity, these cooperative efforts show how productive the industry-university link can be.

• Encourage the application of the fruits of science in our educational structure. A national research strategy should not only seek to improve science education, but also the use of such technologies as personal computers and electronic networking throughout the entire education structure. The importance of electronic networking cannot be overstated when considering science education and the links between universities and industry. New intellectual communities are being formed around electronic information networks that link professors and researchers all over the country. The intellectual use of database services and electronic bulletin boards should be further explored and encouraged.

- Place a higher premium on science and engineering education. We could benefit from scholarships and prizes that attract attention and prestige to scientific research. Imaginative programs are especially needed to attract women and minorities to these fields, while at the same time reducing US dependence on foreign nationals in our graduate programs.

- Discard antiquated notions about job-related education and retraining. In an age when the volume of technical knowledge in industry is doubling every fifteen years, it is unwise to limit educational support to the young. Education should be continuing and lifelong, perhaps a part of the benefits package of employment. Ironically, the present tax system discourages meaningful career training: One can take a tax deduction for further training in one's present profession—even if it is a dead-end field—but one cannot take a deduction for training in a new growth field.

- Reduce the short-term bias in our financial markets. By focusing on quarterly profits, our financing structures reward short-term thinking. In the case of semiconductor manufacturers, the need to show a consistent profit forces US companies to lay off a substantial portion of the work force as each generation of chip dwindles in demand. Meanwhile, Japanese companies forego short-term profits in favor of long-term market share. Our business schools continue to teach short-term analytical techniques that often keep companies from strategic positioning necessary for long-term success.

- Review antitrust laws, particularly with regard to large companies' support of small innovative companies and the formation of research cooperatives. The Joint Research and Development Act of 1984 represents a step forward by breaking down anti-trust barriers to joint research, enabling US firms to pool their resources to battle overseas competition. Another avenue the Commerce Department might explore is facilitating aggressive export and overseas development of small and mid-sized US science-based companies. We need to foster trade policy that enables new and emerging "growth" companies to expand their enterprises to the same foreign markets, such as Japan and Korea, that have successfully penetrated the US.

I know that all these proposals are difficult and long-term. But a great deal can be achieved by a little of what I call "institutional inventing"—rebuilding the very machinery by which we, as a society, make decisions. If we can cultivate this strength—rather than resort to brute-force solutions—we can reverse the decline in our technological leadership and create a business climate conducive to innovation.

The best US example of institutional innovation and the greatest success story of American technology transfer is in the area of agriculture. The transfer of scientific knowledge, through technology, to practical application by the ultimate entrepreneur of the free-enterprise system—the farmer—was a process started by Abraham Lincoln with the Morrill Act of 1862. The Morrill Act created an organized network linking universities and farmers. The Hatch Act of 1887 established agricultural experiment stations, and the Smith-Lever Act of 1914 created cooperative extension programs in agriculture and home economics.

These political and institutional innovations resulted in such an increase in agricultural productivity and efficiency that the percentage of the US population engaged in farm labor fell from 40% in 1900 to only 3% in 1980. Today, agricultural exports sustain the United States in international trade competition, while providing the margin of survival for the Soviet Union and other food importing nations around the world. Few accounts of US technological leadership even mention this enormously powerful engine of agriculture.

While much past US success has been due to innovative government action of the kind exemplified by the encouragement of agriculture, some is the result of incentives and disincentives that have evolved over the years through the tax system, accounting rules, security market regulations, constraints on the banking system, bankruptcy laws, and other factors. Much has been due as well to unique social and cultural factors that have received relatively little attention.

One of the unheralded US cultural strengths is the fact that there is little social stigma attached to repeated failures in the launching of new ventures. By contrast, the social stigma attached to business failure in Europe, compounded by punitive bankruptcy laws, does much to discourage promising young people from starting new ventures.

In sum, I believe that any society should fund basic research to the fullest extent that it is blessed with first-class intellects. We clearly need better coordination of many different policymaking areas in drafting a national policy regarding science and technology. Moreover, any effective strategy must provide for continuous rather than one-time monitoring and coordination of programs.

The goal of the US science and technology policy should be to unleash the creative energies of our people: through incentive and disincentive systems, including regulations and tax policy, that ensure the maximum rewards for breaking new scientific ground. No small part of this effort should be focused on the institutional relationships and the transition mechanisms that bring new insights from laboratory to marketplace.

The US's ability to innovate has always been one of our great strengths. If we can cultivate this strength—rather than resort to brute-force solutions—we can reverse the decline in our technological leadership and create a business climate conducive to innovation.

Restoring General Science's Head: How the Science Advisor Could Lead

William Drayton

The public's deep concern with the country's ability to compete in the world may be creating a situation that will give the next President both the political leverage and the political incentive to lead the country toward important innovations in both the strategies and management of science.

If his Science Advisor can help him define a few generically important, practical opportunities, and then help build the necessary support, this political opportunity could bear very substantial fruit. For it to do so will, however, almost certainly require an Advisor with exceptional stature, vision, and political skill. Without very skilled leadership, inertia and the competing concerns of a thousand squeaking-wheel constituencies will probably once again leave little more than rhetorical room for science in the President's priorities.

How important and politically valuable are the opportunities for fundamental change in science? Is this an area where the next President's wisest *general* advisors will counsel him to press?

Science is so vast and complex a beast that anyone like the author who is familiar with only its tusks, ears and/or trunk should refuse to answer. What I have seen of its management in general and of its specific content in the public health, environment, and development fields, however, makes me very ambitious for the next President and his Science Advisor.

HEADLESS GENERAL

Environmental protection is a field that was called into being and that is constantly being redefined by science. Anyone who looks beyond today's

William Drayton was Assistant Administrator of the Environmental Protection Agency under President Carter, and has long been a management consultant with McKinsey & Company. He has taught at Stanford University Law School and the John F. Kennedy School of Government at Harvard. Dr. Drayton is a MacArthur Fellow, and is President of Askoka, which supports innovative individuals to effect social change in developing countries. He is also Chair of Environmental Safety, which monitors implementation of the public health and environment laws.

regulation or litigation recognizes that science is the general who commands this field.

Sadly, the general now seems virtually headless.

Let me cite several important, quite apparent strategy vacuums that are now costing the country dearly. In each case, I also give examples of what the country might do—not so much to advocate these ideas, but rather to show what strategy might accomplish.

Probably none of these specifics should directly engage the President. Restoring purposive consciousness to the important areas of science where it has been lost, however, probably should. The following examples illustrate the magnitude of opportunity:

• Several environmental statutes (notably including the Toxic Substance Control Act [TSCA] and the pesticides and drinking water laws) require that over one hundred thousand chemicals be tested for the full range of possible health risks—but this is impossible since no short, economical, reliable tests exist for any risk other than cancer. Animal substitutes for human epidemiological tests are slow, expense, uncertain and, in any case, generally don't cover many of the classes of possible effects at all well—e.g., behavioral or psychological effects. Almost nothing is now being done to clear this bottleneck and thereby to give these key statutes a chance. One promising way the government might break this bottleneck stranglehold is by: (1) identifying twenty to twenty-five first class teams of researchers; (2) giving each three or four of the major high-exposure, highly suspect chemicals in commerce and asking them to evaluate each for the full range of health risks as best they can; and (3) in the process, develop as many reliable short tests for different risks as possible. An investment of up to several million dollars per team over several years would at least give us the best possible reading on the risks of these major chemicals, thereby usefully focusing the regulators' agendas. Given the proper incentives, at least some of these teams should develop a first generation of new short tests for risks other than cancer.

• Given the enormous uncertainty affecting the hazardous waste field, the industry's firms have made it clear they cannot invest in basic research (since they cannot foresee demand sufficiently far into the future to assure a payback for such research). Imaginative use of research guarantees and partnerships might save billions in avoidably misdirected expenditures.

• Further billions in wasteful policy measures (e.g., banning all ocean or land disposal or deep well injection) could be avoided if researchers would only define for the major waste streams which treatment and disposal techniques are acceptable under what circumstances; which are too risky; and which can be used under certain conditions. Such characterizations should be reviewed and updated every five years.

- Environmental regulation has developed from the paradigm of painting the back of a rat with one substance and, if a bump develops, regulating that substance through that method of exposure. In fact, people are exposed to random complex mixtures of many substances through many avenues of exposure at once. Epidemiological work demonstrates that, at least in some cases, the synergistic effects of several pollutants is likely to be greater and different from the sum of the individual effects. Adequate development of the science of synergistic (and cumulative) health (and environmental) effects might ultimately well require a basic restructuring of the environment's legislative and regulatory approach. It would also very probably allow the effort to proceed in a better focused and, therefore, more cost-effective manner.

- Most people spend more time inside than out, and this is especially true for those who are sick or otherwise especially vulnerable. Concentrations of pollutants already regulated in the outside ambient environment are typically several times greater inside than outside. Moreover, typical indoor concentrations are as high in clean North Dakota as in heavily polluted New Jersey, suggesting that the problem is a function of what we have inside the modern home—pesticides, household chemicals, stoves, furniture, building materials, etc. Yet America regulates outdoor pollution and all but refuses to even look at indoor pollution. (The Administration has tried, year after year, often successfully, to eliminate entirely even the few million dollars supporting indoor pollution research.) The country needs a serious research investment in order to (1) define the exact extent and sources of the problem, and (2) begin defining possible preventative interventions.

If the President could help environmental science regain consciousness and boldly pursue its many very great opportunities, he would be doing far more for the field (and, therefore, economic efficiency and the public's health) than if he successfully championed four major new regulatory statutes.

How might the Science Advisor help the next President thus awaken and energize this and a host of other idling science engines? Ordering or funding a list of specific initiatives from the White House will only lose the President's opportunity in a chimera of sound and motion.

Startling science by experiments with new management tools designed to encourage innovation is one major area of opportunity.

Stimulating those in (and served by) the myriad fields of science to think and act more strategically about the ends, investments, and internal incentives of science is the ultimate prize. The President can use a powerful array of leadership tools to pursue this prize, including his bully pulpit, his line department science managers, his convening and ceremonial powers, his legislative leverage, and his international leadership. A very skilled Science Advisor is almost essential for the President to play such an orchestra.

GETTING THEIR ATTENTION

There are two reasons for shaking the established patterns of science management: (1) specific reforms will improve performance, and (2) doing so will capture the attention of a decentralized, even insular population who might otherwise barely notice the President's broader reforms.

Since almost every science reformer has a list of favorite management reforms, let me cite just a few examples to illustrate what an inspired (and management-literate) Science Advisor might help the President do:

- There is tremendous duplication of research across the government and beyond. If only it could be made effectively competitive, the most contributive and innovative researchers could be rewarded and overall effectiveness greatly enhanced. There are a host of mechanisms that could accomplish this result. For example, where research has identifiable users, why not let the users choose among and negotiate payments with competing research organizations? Why, for example, shouldn't OSHA, EPA, the Consumer Product Safety Commission, the Department of Energy, and a host of other agencies concerned with the health effects of chemicals be able to negotiate freely for the best service they can find, be it from the National Institutes, an EPA or NIOSH laboratory, or even a New York State laboratory?

  Even without opening up such a quasi-market, the government could very usefully modify its budget process to review common programs together, regardless of their organizational home. Every year, senior staff from OMB, the Science Advisor, and all the agencies sharing a common science function (be it weather research, forestry, or even inter-service aerospace investigations) would define the most effective program for pursuing their shared public goal by rank-ordering the components of each agency's work. They are the best critics of one another's efforts; together, they can find and spread efficiencies—the only non-zero sum escape from the painful rigors of the budget process open to them; and they will remember promises made but not respected when the group meets a year later for the next cross-department priority setting.

- The current discipline-focused, consensus peer review process for administering governmental research grants is unlikely to encourage fundamental jumps from a field's consensus or dominant technology; works against cross-disciplinary innovation; and is prone to subtle conflicts of interest and log-rolling within a field.

Why not see if sharply different, multiple, alternative "venture capital" channels might stimulate more adventuresome responses? Such an experiment might start with, say, ten to 20% of the budget in certain fields of applied research. These funds would be given to competing individuals, firms, and/or small panels to invest in the most promising portfolios of science these "investors" can find. They should, as much as possible, come from widely ranging backgrounds in order both to give those with ideas a broad range of potential sponsors they can approach and also to encourage experimentation across traditional boundaries. The "investors would be held accountable by rewarding them according to the success of their portfolios after several years by increasing or decreasing the size of the new funds made available to them (and, therefore, their remuneration, power and status).

This step toward speeding scientific innovation, even if initially modest in size, would probably be personally enticing to many of science's most innovative people. It would consequently reinforce Presidential efforts to make them take bolder, more strategic charge very usefully.

LEADING

Getting people's attention and changing their incentives are very important. Getting them in area after area, field after field to feel challenged and empowered to seize the initiative boldly, strongly, imaginatively is a great leader or manager's ultimate contribution.

The President could do a great deal to encourage such initiative. The public forum is always his to use. He can challenge, and he can recognize. He could, for example, sponsor an annual, heavily publicized prize competition for *highly* promising, practical, strategic new thrusts in science. It's hard to imagine *Science, Scientific American,* and others not willingly helping to get the word out if asked. It would also be easy to organize multiple review panels of senior policy people, the multiple panels emphasizing the President's stress on being open to new ideas and the quality and action orientation of the panelists being a chief inducement encouraging those with ideas to propose. Such encouragement to think should extend to scientists, scientific managers, and consumers, and their counterparts in other societies.

As the Chief Executive Officer of the federal government, the President can also engage his many line science managers directly. If he were to approach these tens of generally neglected officials, and ask them to find ways of stimulating bolder, more strategic science, he could energize several dozen reformist tigers, most of whom, in turn, influence much of private science. To succeed he would have to lead them as his managers, not try to regulate them through adversarial OMB or other staff minions. A Science Council of these line research leaders that met with the President periodically, was linked to him through his own Science Advisor, and was able to elect its own officers and hire its own modest coordinating staff would significantly help this functional cross-cut of the President's line managers respond to his leadership.

Again, these ideas are not specific proposals. They certainly are not a full program. Rather, they are simple, concrete examples of how a President, supported by a skilled Science Advisor, could create an environment that would so stimulate the creativity of many working in science that the field would learn routinely to step forward more boldly.

Need for a Science Advising Mechanism

Sidney D. Drell

Former British Prime Minister Harold Macmillan very persuasively stated the case for an effective scientific advisory apparatus to leaders of state in his book *Pointing the Way* (London: Macmillan, 1972). Lamenting the fact that our leaders have a woefully inadequate understanding of the high-technology weaponry they command, he observed:

> "In all these affairs Prime Ministers, Ministers of Defence and Cabinets are under a great handicap. The technicalities and uncertainties of the sophisticated weapons which they have to authorize are out of the range of normal experience. There is today a far greater gap between their knowledge and the expert advice which they receive than there has ever been in the history of war."

This is a dangerous problem that must be solved. Success in solving it will require efforts from both sides: from the scientists as well as from society's political leaders. The responsibility of the scientist is to speak accurately and responsibly on the technical challenges to society if and when he becomes involved in an advisory or public advocacy role addressing such problems. The government also must recognize its need here: It cannot dispense with scientists. Its obligation is to arrange for the best possible scientific analysis and advice before risking major decisions or raising unrealistic public expectations. Furthermore, the scientific advice must be neutral and free of political and doctrinal biases. This is not easy to achieve. To help protect itself against such biases, as well as mistakes—for scientists are no more than human—a government should create an advisory mech-

Sidney D. Drell, Professor and Deputy Director of the Stanford Linear Accelerator Center and Co-Director of the Stanford Center for International Security and Arms Control, has served in numerous government and academic advisory roles, including with the Arms Control and Disarmament Agency, the Office of Science and Technology Policy, and the Congressional Office of Technology Assessment. He is a MacArthur Fellow, has been a member of Jason since 1960, was a member of PSAC (1966–70), and is a member of the National Academy of Sciences.

anism that reaches out broadly, rather than rely on input from only one or two scientists.

President Eisenhower understood these issues well when he created, in 1957, the position of a full-time Science Advisor in the White House and also established the President's Science Advisory Committee (PSAC). These served the President and the nation well for more than a decade before they were disestablished in 1973. He also showed his wisdom when he dismissed the issue of the political affiliations of PSAC members by saying, according to his first Science Advisor, James Killian, that he liked scientists for their science and not for their politics.

Since the mid-1970s, after PSAC was abolished, numerous scientific groups and individual scientists have urged the federal government to reestablish an entity in the White House analogous to PSAC and headed by one strong Presidential Science Advisor. Perhaps two or three full-time senior advisors are needed in view of the very broad range of technical issues—including health, the environment, energy, and national security—that must now be formally addressed in formulating national policy.

I do not know of an effective substitute for a PSAC mechanism with rotating membership and a strong staff. It should support actively working panels that look ahead to future technological possibilities and that can anticipate their potential impacts on our security, our environment, or our economic and technological strengths. As Presidential panels with the full backing of the White House, they should have full access to whatever they require in order to anticipate and recommend ways of handling problems and opportunities before they blossom as crises or fade as lost opportunities.

A Presidential advisory structure can, in principle, present its analyses and advice directly and free of institutional loyalties or bias—that is precisely the function of staff in contrast to operational line managers and administrators. It is inevitable that recommendations of cabinet secretaries or agency directors are affected by the operational and institutional responsibilities they bear. A President needs what Science Advisors and PSAC can provide: independent and informed analyses of the technical issues that underlie and limit the political decisions that a President must make.

LACK OF COHERENT PLANNING

We have had no such effective mechanism since PSAC was abolished in 1973. The importance of recreating, sustaining and utilizing such a mechanism has become more and more clear in recent years. Our national science policy lacks coherent planning as to how to set priorities between short and long term goals. We see the once pre-eminent American space program fall into disarray, much of the high-tech leadership of American industry drift to foreign shores, serious environmental problems languish unaddressed, and more stories of defective weapons than of successes in arms control emerging from our national security efforts.

The need for an effective technical advisory mechanism for the President is also painfully clear in the aftermath of President's Reagan's famous Star Wars speech of March 23, 1983. In that speech, Reagan called on the scientists *"who gave us nuclear weapons to turn their great talents now to the cause of mankind and world peace, to give us the means of rendering these nuclear weapons impotent and obsolete."* He held out hope of a world freed from the nuclear threat of retaliation by advanced defensive technologies that ". . . *could intercept and destroy strategic ballistic missiles before they reached our soil."*

The issue raised by the President is one of profound importance. What the President has called for is nothing less than a fundamental change in the basic strategic relationship between the United States and the Soviet Union. Nor is he the first President to raise this issue in search of a safer world to be achieved by applying new technologies to strategic defense.

Every President since Eisenhower, upon entering the White House, has asked quite properly—can't we defend ourselves? Can't science and technology provide a shield against the threat of nucler annihilation? Can't we do better than living as mutual hostages under the condition of mutual deterrence? Upon further analysis and after receiving the best advice on the technical realities, other Presidents, before President Reagan, concluded that the answer was "No." This conclusion led, in 1972, to the negotiation and ratification of the SALT I Treaty strictly limiting the deployment of antiballistic missile (ABM) systems. This ABM Treaty is of unlimited duration, and is in force today.

It was, of course, proper and vital for President Reagan to ask the questions again in 1983, in view of the prodigious technical advances in the more than ten years since SALT I was negotiated. Do these advances now offer us new and better prospects for dealing with the nuclear threat as we look ahead into the future? This is a challenging question requiring thorough and dispassionate independent analysis and judgment. Unfortunately, that did not happen. President Reagan did not receive such advice when he gave his speech.

What is so regrettable is that, in contrast to previous occasions, this issue burst upon the political agenda in 1983 with no prior technical analysis. The President's speech was immediately followed by allegations from high Administration officials who made extravagant (and incorrect) claims about what could be done, leading to counter-allegations from many private groups and individuals. The ABM Treaty of 1972 became a pawn in the ensuing corrosive and divisive debate between large segments of the scientific community and our government. A number of independent analyses were subsequently published, but none could claim completeness of technical analysis based on full access to the classified technical data as well as unchallengeable scientific objectivity. Only now, four years after the President's speech, does the public have available a complete, thorough, fully informed and balanced analysis of many of the advanced technologies on which a nationwide strategic defense would rely. Thanks to the American Physical Society's study on the "Science and Technology of Directed Energy Weapons," which was based on access to the requisite classified information, the debate can be pursued at an informed level that should have been available—to the government as well as the public—before a change in policy was advocated.

This is just one major example of the fact that effective use is not being made of scientific input on technical issues at the highest level. An effective Presidential scientific advisory mechanism—and an interested President—are the two necessary ingredients of the remedy for this deficiency.

The Need for a New Start in Presidential Science Advice

A. Hunter Dupree

The President of the United States, like other responsible executives, requires a vast amount of information as he makes the decisions required by his office. It must come from sources at many levels both inside and outside the departments of the government and the Executive Office over which he presides. Since World War II, the departments and agencies have almost all taken into account the changing choices open to policymakers as a result of scientific research, and they have not been backward in urging on both President and Congress their changing requirements in money and trained personnel brought about by technological innovation, sometimes but not always based on scientific research.

The discovery of the chain reaction resulting from the fission of the uranium atom set up in the minds of scientists and ultimately of politicians and, beyond them, the wider public the belief in a one-way line of influence. Basic research led to applied research and then to development, out of which came a nuclear warhead. The culmination of the one-way influence was the uncontrolled explosion of a bomb out in the environment—as, of course, actually happened at Hiroshima and Nagasaki. To get from discovery, an action by members of the scientific community which took place in the controlled conditions of a laboratory, to the military application of force on chosen Japanese cities brought into play the fundamental institutions of the United States Government. The scientists in the laboratory, the political leaders who sanctioned the building of the bomb, and the members of the military forces which delivered it, were all human beings morally responsible for their actions. They felt that the success or failure of their actions would be

A. Hunter Dupree is the author of Science in the Federal Government: A History of Policies and Activities *and other publications. He was a fighter director and combat information center watch officer on the battleship* Tennessee *in the Iwo Jima and Okinawa operations. Dr. Dupree was Professor of American History at Brown University from 1968 to 1981, and has served on several panels in the Executive and Legislative branches of the federal government.*

measured by their position in the institutions of which they were a part—the scientific community, the Constitutional government of the United States, the military forces of the United States.

Obviously, the President of the United States is the only official on a level to comprehend all three of these groups. As the Constitutional head of the Executive branch of the government, he has responsibility for the functioning of all the departments and agencies, and he has the ability to call on them for technical information helping to make decisions. With the development of the tremendous technical capabilities of the mission agencies, the President can turn to the Department of Defense and to the individual services for information not only on how weapons systems work, but also on how their individual components work and how powerfully. They can tell him how a cruise missile compares to an MX missile or a B1 bomber or a sixteen-inch gun of the battleship *New Jersey*.

The agencies that are created to carry out missions are expert in interpreting the meaning of research—especially in mathematics, physics and engineering—as it bears on their ability to carry out their tasks, and they are often convinced that, if they were able to spend more on research, they would be better able to accomplish the missions that are their very reason for existence. They would ask for more in their budget presentations, secure in the knowledge that an elaborate set of deliberations preceded a decision to commit the nation to a major research program. It was even conventional wisdom among Presidential advisors that the hardest thing they had to do was to kill a program once started, even if it turned out to be as impractical and dangerous as the nuclear-powered airplane. Up to 1983, at least, the form of the assumption was honored that Presidential sanction was preceded by lengthy examination of the options and that he was guided by the best technical information obtainable.

THE SDI

The situation that has obtained since President Reagan's announcement of the Strategic Defense Initiative is unprecedented. Perhaps it is often called by a nickname—"Star Wars"—because of the lack of prior consultation with the scientific community. The President may have had private advice, and may have said to himself: The people who made the H-bomb should know what they are talking about. On the other hand, the mission agencies and the technical community in industry and the universities dependent on them for funding respond automatically with their part of the dialogue: Give us a trillion dollars and we will give you complete defense against nuclear missiles. The technical community is free to move straight to the business of spending the trillion dollars without asking whether the enterprise should be undertaken or not.

It is certainly a question of importance whether the technical advice the

President is getting is the best to be had. Does the research contemplated have a chance of producing the effects when applied to the mission of the government that its advocates say that it will? Much of the special apparatus for scientific advice to the President that was laboriously constructed between 1950 and 1972 addressed such middle-range questions as came out of the rivalries and differences of perception among the mission agencies. The scientific community, unlike the branches of government, does not have a constitutionally defined position, and it represents a different and broader mix of disciplines than just those mainly of interest to the mission agencies. The scientists must depend on the President wanting their advice, as Eisenhower did in 1957, and they have had to improvise ephemeral institutions such as the President's Science Advisory Committee and the Office of Science and Technology Policy to gain access to the President's inner circle of advisors. They have had to maintain a certain informality in order to comprehend the scientific community as it exists outside the government—in the universities and in industry. To get the independent views of scientists, who are well informed on the problems facing the President, but who are not beholden to the mission agencies, is the essence of the problem of making science policy in a democracy.

If the traditional structure to provide science policy advice to the President had survived and were serving President Reagan as it served some of his predecessors, some present problems would be at least addressed. The fundamental questions facing the President to which science policy is relevant lie, however, in an entirely different realm. It is not the one-way progression from laboratory to application that in itself requires the attention of the President and the policymakers at the highest level of government. Rather, after the applications have been made and the components developed into systems by development engineers, the resulting bundles of energy go forth into the social and biological environment that encompasses the earth. Some of this energy remains under control of the systems' designers, accomplishing their missions as they envisaged them. Some of this energy remains partially under human control but has effects at odds with the designers' intentions, to the point that the whole enterprise may become ironically counterproductive.

Some of the energy generated by modern technological systems goes out of control in a hyperbolic explosion, poisoning the neighborhood of the point of impact completely. The demonstration of the atomic bombs at Hiroshima and Nagasaki put the world on notice as to what could happen and raised the spectre of an extension of the neighborhood of the point of impact indefinitely. The explosion at Chernobyl demonstrated that even the most carefully controlled reactions have a potential for destruction comparable to the deliberately uncontrolled explosions.

The explosive release of nuclear energy is only a part of the historical situation that the President must come to sense at least intuitively. In increasing their ability to generate flows of energy, scientists have also demonstrated an unprecedented aptitude for creating electronic sensors and for manipulating the information they gain from them into networks far transcending the digital computers that have become so conspicuous at many levels of society. Our conceptions of the outermost galaxies and of the interior of single neurons in the human brain are now influenced by our enhanced means of comparing and processing information.

On the military side, the position of the President is potentially changed in undetermined ways by the envelopes of command and control in which the flow of energy is minimized and the flow of information maximized. As a story with unity, peopled with understandable human actors, the history of communication, command, and control has until recently impinged on the consciousness of people outside the military and technical establishments only fragmentarily. If it is ever put together in broad historical terms, it will rival the story of the nucleus itself as the symbolic plot of our era. The technicians trained in mathematics, physics, and engineering can produce the hardware—the radar, the computers, the spacecraft—that enclose and process the information. But as soon as that hardware goes out into the environment and performs in real time, it is impinging on the social and biological environment of the universe. Real time is history. The systems take in information, process it, and send out action signals that induce changes and necessitate another round. Research that gives the President information on the social and biological environment is what he needs to assess the changes wrought by technology. However much information he can command from the mission agencies leaves him still without means to evaluate the issues before him.

A HIGHLY FOCUSED CAPABILITY

The proposal of this paper is that a highly focused capability in evaluating technological systems in their social and biological settings be made available to the President in approximately the position once occupied by the Science Advisor, the President's Science Advisory Committee, and the Office of Science and Technology. In suggesting the introduction of social and biological research, there is no thought of banishing the capability in mathematics, physics and engineering that shaped the perspective of the old system. Rather, every major technological system must be examined both from the inside—technical feasibility—and from the outside—social and biological interaction.

A great many critics of the influence of the scientific community on Presidential policy will probably be jubilant to attack this proposal. Their conviction of the impracticality and irrelevance of all scientists and especially social scientists may make them read no further. Furthermore, they may be joined by veteran science advisors of the old school who feel that social science has made them vulnerable in the past and that chasing butterflies has nothing to do with national security. Such was the mindset that made social science go unmentioned in the act to create the National Science Foundation and, when support was smuggled in in the mid-1950s, it was deliberately limited to those quantitative studies that converged on the natural sciences. Many social scientists went along with this strategy, hoping to avoid criticism. The vast scope of federal support for the social sciences was hidden in many parts of the mission agencies of the government, and any effort to extract them—for example, to make a National Social Science Foundation—has been determinedly squelched by the social scientists themselves.

THE SOCIAL SCIENCES

We now know that a distinguished social scientist delegated by the Social Science Research Council seriously proposed an alternative scenario for the place of the social sciences in the post-World War II world. Talcott Parsons prepared a report that envisaged a foundation with the social sciences on a par with the natural sciences and one that did not hesitate to underwrite research applied to the great problems of society, confident that government support would not essentially threaten the autonomy of scholarly enterprise. He did not hesitate to include history among the social sciences. The report was never published, and might have remained forever buried if two editors, Samuel Z. Klausner and Victor Lidz, had not recently made it the centerpiece of a book-length analysis, *The Nationalization of the Social Sciences*.[1] They agree with the contemporary critics that the report never had a chance, but their reviving the discussion now means that the federal government's social science policy can be questioned even though fundamental discussion has been dormant since the 1950s.

Talcott Parsons, although he was not prominent in discussions of government policy for science after his abortive effort in the late 1940s, continued to think about the theoretical questions raised and, in 1970, when he retired from active teaching, he came back to the subject, extending his views on the social sciences to include biology as well.[2] Thus, even as the old machinery for science advice to the President largely disappeared, an alternative scenario was slowly being shaped in scattered places in the scholarly literature.

TECHNOLOGY ASSESSMENT

One does not have to look far to find a model for a science policy that shifts priority from weapons research and development to biological and social issues from the perspective of the global environment. Harvey Brooks, in arguing that the Strategic Defense Initiative is unparalleled as compared to earlier big science projects, says it "is best described as a large scale exploratory technology assessment, with very vague and open-ended technical goals, and considerable debate and disagreement as to its true strategic purpose."[3] The use of the term "technology assessment" points in the direction of research in the surrounding environment of whole interacting systems rather than limiting oneself to a single component, even if it is as powerful as an H-bomb. Brooks, in addition to being one of the most important conventional science advisors of the 1960s and 1970s, has played an important role in shaping the concept of technology assessment and getting it introduced into the government structure on the Congressional rather than the Executive side.

As chairman of the National Academy of Science's Committee on Science and Public Policy, Brooks appointed a Panel on Technology Assessment whose report, *Technology: Processes of Assessment and Choice* (1969), set the pattern for addressing the concern that "has mounted over society's seeming inability to channel technological developments in directions that sufficiently respect the broad range of human needs."[4] The panel contained a number of scientists and engineers, but social scientists, including historians, were well represented. One member had served in the Office of Science and Technology in the White House. For the first time in living memory, lawyers were much in evidence on a panel of the National Academy of Sciences. Milton Katz of Harvard Law School served on the panel, and the Executive Director was Laurence Tribe, just beginning his career in constitutional law.

Much of the discussion on the panel revolved around where in the government to place a technology assessment operation. One school wanted it close to the President as was the Science Advisor. Another group, of which I tended to be one, thought it important to give the office research capability in social and environmental systems in addition to the technological systems themselves. Therefore, the office should be in a position in the Executive branch far enough from immediate policy pressures to have some autonomy but close enough to have a channel of communication to the President. The final group, which included the lawyers, pushed for a position under the Congress in a position roughly analogous to the General Accounting Office. Since the whole study had been undertaken at the request of Representative Emilio Daddario, the tilt in the direction of Congressional advice was understandable. Indeed, this emphasis probably made possible the creation of the Office of Technology Assessment in the Congress in 1972, just the time of the collapse of the science policy structure in the Nixon White House.

Although the accomplishments of the Office of Technology Assessment may be considered by some to have been modest, from the point of view of this proposal for the future the experience gained is hard to overestimate. How can one study the policy issues that properly concern the President and Congress? What mix of disciplines should be represented on the staff? How should issues for study be chosen from all the potentially threatening situations that daily confront the government? How should they be insulated from political influence while coming to grips with politics both as a subject to be studied by social scientists and a necessary ingredient in even the most abstract of technological policy issues? Once some results are in, how are they to be displayed to policy-makers and made available to the general public? The OTA has given us a decade and a half of experience down on the firing line that is now available for scaling up in the Congressional setting, and most importantly for adaptation and transfer to the Executive branch.

NATIONAL SECURITY

The present hearings on the Iran-contra operations clearly reveal that advice to the President on national security must be overhauled. A virtually science-advisorless Administration has had a Ph.D. in nuclear physics as National Security Advisor and then has assigned him responsibilities for covert actions for which his CalTech education is at best irrelevant. Clearly, the national security mechanism must be overhauled, preferably by the most highly qualified leaders that the nation can muster.

Almost everything that the Science Advisor did under Eisenhower would now fall under the rubric of national security. When the inevitable Commission on the National Security Council is set up, deep thought should be given also to setting up an equally prestigious Commission on Science Advice to the President. It should seize the opportunity to wrest science policy from the dominance of the national security machinery and to set it up as it has functioned in earlier eras—advice drawn from all of science and scholarship and addressed to those problems that transcend the missions of the various departments. The United States is a major actor on the world stage, and what it does affects every society and every natural environment. The President, even while deluged by information and reports and petitions of every sort, must see above it to chart an overall course. He must have a sense of history as to where technology is going and what it means for humanity. The scholars of the nation must try to help him.

NOTES

1. Samuel Z. Klausner and Victor Lidz, eds., *The Nationalization of the Social Sciences* (Philadelphia: University of Pennsylvania Press, 1986).
2. A. Hunter Dupree and Talcott Parsons, "The Relations between Biological and Socio-Cultural Theory," *Bulletin of the American Academy of Arts and Sciences*, Vol. XXIX, no. 8 (May, 1976). Reprinted in Talcott Parsons, *Social Systems and the Evolution of Action Theory* (New York: Free Press, 1977), pp. 118–121.
3. Harvey Brooks, "The Strategic Defense Initiative as Science Policy," *International Security*, Vol. 11, no. 2 (Fall 1986), pp. 177–184.
4. National Academy of Sciences, *Technology: Processes of Assessment and Choice* (Committee on Science and Astronautics, US House of Representatives, July 1969), p. 1.

Government and International Relations: The Science of Living Together

Roger Fisher

The first time I heard the phrase "the science of living together" was in Moscow in June 1987. A Soviet colleague told me that at last he understood what I was about: I was insisting that we could think as clearly and rigorously about international negotiation and a good working relationship as we do about military technology. "You are telling us," he said, "that there is a *science* of living together."

As a lawyer, I have been reluctant to call what I do "science." Yet there is no doubt that the United States and other governments handle their international relations in a sloppy and dangerous way that cries out for the kind of organized clear thinking that is the essence of a scientific approach. For much of my life, I have been thinking and writing about how to conduct international differences. In a few pages, what basic advice would I give to a new President, Presidential Science Advisor, Secretary of State, or other official concerned with international affairs? It is a challenging assignment. Recognizing that a scientific quest never ends, and that all ideas are subject to challenge and revision at any time, here is a first draft.

LOOK FOR A METHOD, NOT FOR AN ANSWER

At the most fundamental level, the advice is not to look for "policies"— all-purpose patent medicines that the United States can apply from one situation to the next—but rather to improve the way we analyze and decide

Roger Fisher, Williston Professor of Law at Harvard and Director of the Harvard Negotiation Project, is author or co-author of a half-dozen books, including International Conflict for Beginners *and* Getting to YES: Negotiating Agreement Without Giving In. *He served with the US Army Air Force in World War II, in Paris with the Marshall Plan, and in the Office of the Solicitor General. Professor Fisher practiced international law in Washington before joining the Harvard Law School faculty in 1958, where he now teaches negotiation.*

what to do about international differences. We are less in need of policies
than of a way to organize common sense. Structure helps our own thinking
and makes it easier to work effectively with others. Here is one way to put
in clear and explicit form what many people approximate intuitively.

A BASIC FOUR-STEP APPROACH

I. What is the problem?
   (What are disliked symptoms that contrast with a preferred situation?)
II. Diagnosis: Possible causes and explanations?
   (What factors that we might be able to change are causing the symp-
   toms?)
III. Prescriptions: Possible approaches?
   (What general approaches might deal with the causes of the problem?)
IV. Specific action ideas?
   (Who could do what tomorrow to implement one or more of those ap-
   proaches? This fourth stage comes, for example, when ideas such as
   those advanced in this paper are being applied to a particular situation.)

In international affairs, our attention is often focused on a particular negotiation or crisis. What is happening in the arms control talks in Geneva?
Or what is happening today in the Persian Gulf? How the United States
handles particular negotiations and particular crises is important. We could
often do far better than we do. But the world does not start off fresh every
morning. More important than the way in which we deal with a unique
factual situation is the ongoing way in which we deal with other countries.
The pattern of interaction that we establish and maintain with each country
provides the all-important context within which the events of a given day
occur. Yet we often take that pattern for granted.

If our international relationships fare badly, it may be lack of hard thinking. Can we do better?

I. What Is the Problem?

Despite the almost constant insistence of the United States that it wants
"better relations" with the Soviet Union (and other countries), our relationships with most countries are best described as "poor." Even with big trading partners like Japan, our relationship is difficult. The patterns of interaction between the United States and other governments—the way we deal
with each other—seems often to damage rather than serve the interests of
both countries.

II. Diagnoses?

What are some possible causes and explanations? Governments deal with an unending series of discrete transactions and problems. On these, they try to influence each other through political, economic and military measures or through negotiation. Governments also have an ongoing pattern of inter-action with each other, a relationship that exists independent of a particular problem or issue. If the United States has poor relations with another gov-ernment, why? A relationship is not within the sole control of one party, but what factors that the United States might effect would help explain why our relationship with some countries is so poor?

We Have No Clear Idea of What a "Good Relationship" Is

We use the word "relations" in so many ways that there is no clear un-derstanding of the kind of relationship we seek. We confuse the goal of a good relationship with agreement, approval, friendship, and shared values. Our lack of understanding of what we mean by a "good relationship" be-tween two governments is demonstrated by the difficulty that even an in-ternational relations expert would have in suggesting how to measure whether, for example, France had a better relationship with Brazil than Canada did with China.

We Have No Clear Theory of How to Build a Good Relationship

We know that we are unlikely to turn a bad relationship into a good one by a strategy of appeasement, yet we do not hesitate to ask others to try to buy a good relationship by appeasing us. We suggest to the Soviet Union, for example, that a good relationship with the United States is contingent upon some substantive concession, such as getting out of Afghanistan, changing its policies on emigration, or accepting our Strategic Defense Initiative.

Sensing that a good relationship is reciprocal, we often behave as badly toward other governments as they appear to be behaving toward us. Yet there is no likelihood that reciprocating another government's bad behavior will improve the relationship.

Verbally Attacking Foreigners Is Often Good Domestic Politics

Leaders often see a short-term domestic political advantage in treating a foreign government as an enemy. The Soviet Union has long served as a useful whipping boy for American politicians. Yet, whatever policies the Soviet Union were to adopt tomorrow, the world would still face such enor-mous problems as those of the Middle East, South Africa, Central America, debt, poverty, hunger, population, the environment, education, trade, and development. Excessive criticism of the Soviet Union damages the relationship we are trying to improve and diverts attention from shared interests that we could better pursue side by side.

Prescriptions?

What are some general approaches for building a good working relationship? Improving the way in which the United States tries to exert *ad hoc* influence on other governments and the way it negotiates with them should in themselves tend to improve ongoing relationships. But the United States needs to devote explicit attention not only to how it deals with problems, but also how it deals with people—how it deals with governments and the human beings who constitute them. Briefly, this involves both clarifying the goal of a "good relationship" and adopting a general strategy toward building one.

The Goal: A Relationship That Deals Well with Differences

The more serious our differences with another government, the more important it is that we have a good way to deal with them. The quality of an international relationship we seek is not measured by the extent of shared values, or interests, nor by "friendship" and approval. What the United States needs and should seek to establish is a "working relationship"—one that will make it possible for us jointly to reach good outcomes efficiently for any difference, large or small, that we may face. With the Soviet Union, with our trading partners, and with our allies, differences are bound to arise. In every case we will be well served if we can jointly handle those differences in ways that are better for both of us than any available alternative, satisfy our interests as well as may be, avoid waste, strike both sides as fair, and produce practical commitments that are durable and easy to comply with. What are the dimensions by which we can measure that ability?

It appears that the quality of a working relationship can be measured by the extent to which the interaction between the governments partakes of the following elements:

(a) Rationality. When working on problems, reason should not be overwhelmed by anger, fear, hatred, frustration, or other emotions.

(b) Understanding. It is difficult to solve problems unless each government understands, empathetically, the other's perception of what the problem is, what caused it, what are possible options, and so forth.

(c) Communication. Such understanding and the ability jointly to deal with a difference are enhanced to the extent that there is effective and efficient communication between the two governments at several levels.

(d) Honesty. Communication that is dishonest or deceptive is worse than useless. The ability of two governments to deal well with their differences will be enhanced by the degree of honesty in their dealings. There need not be full disclosure, but there should be honest statements about the areas, such as intelligence and military codes, in which secrecy is being preserved and deception practiced.

(e) Non-coercive modes of influence. The acceptability of solutions will be greater to the extent that each government has been influenced by non-coercive means, such as persuasion, inspiration and example, rather than by threats of military or other action.

(f) Acceptance, respect. If we want to have a good relationship with another government, we need to accept them as someone with whom it is worth dealing. We may not agree with their views or conclude that their interests need be given great weight, but we should care about them and be open to learning from them.

It is no doubt possible—and certainly desirable—to improve upon this definition of a good working relationship. What is essential is that we have in mind some clear goal of the kind of international relationships we seek.

Pursue a Coherent Strategy for Building a Good Working Relationship

Often the best substantive solution to a problem lies in a bargain, a reciprocal exchange of *quid pro quo*. And it is also true that a good problem-solving relationship will be better for being reciprocal. There will be rationality on both sides, mutual understanding, good two-way communication, and so forth. But it appears that any relationship-building strategy based on reciprocity is doomed to failure. The Golden Rule of doing unto others as we would have them do unto us can be carried too far. Just because we would like another government to trust us is an insufficient reson for trusting them. Just because we might like them to yield to us does not mean that we should yield to them.

On the other hand, as suggested above, an eye-for-an-eye strategy in which we treat them as badly as we think they are treating us is no way to improve the relationship.

It appears that the best relationship-building strategy is one that is unconditionally constructive: with respect to each of the critical dimensions of a working relationship as defined above, we behave in a way that is good for the relationship *and is good for us whether or not they reciprocate*. Such a strategy can be summarized as follows.

An Unconditionally Constructive Strategy for Building a Working Relationship

(a) rationality. Even if they are acting from emotion,
   —be rational.
(b) understanding. Even if they misunderstand us,
   —try to understand them.

(c) communication. Even if they are not listening,
    —speak clearly, consult them before deciding on matters that affect them,
    and listen carefully.
(d) honesty. Even if they are trying to deceive us,
    —be reliable.
(e) non-coercive modes of influence. Even if they are trying to coerce us,
    —do not yield, but be open to persuasion, and try to persuade them.
(f) acceptance. Even if they reject our concerns as unworthy of considera-
    tion,
    —take their concerns into account and be open to learning from them.

Some will find it easier to understand this approach to a problem-solving
relationship by comparing it to that between an adult and a child. Even if
the child is having a temper-tantrum, does not understand the parent's concerns, and is not listening, the best advice to the parent is to be rational,
try to understand, and listen. When the goal is problem-solving, two heads
are better than one, but one wise problem-solver is better than none.

Such a strategy may take time and effort, but is essentially risk-free. The
only possible advantage given up is the chance to make a short term gain
by deceiving the other government—and that is certainly no way to build
a relationship. The strategy involves no substantive concessions.

Stop Verbally Attacking Foreigners

Leaders who want to help make the world a better place become trapped
in the hostility they help generate. No good was accomplished and much
time wasted during the years in which "Red China" was painted as an enemy. We do not help ourselves or anyone else by dividing the world into
good countries and bad ones. American leaders do the United States and
themselves damage by insisting that Nicaragua, Cuba, and the Soviet Union
are implacable adversaries. We should, of course, be realistic. Actions with
respect to all foreign governments should be based on an analysis of the
risks, not on optimistic "trust." If a government is well organized, however,
we can probably rely upon it to act in its own self-interest.

Since 1776, the United States has had a number of adversaries, Britain,
Canada, Mexico, Spain, Germany, Italy, Japan, and China during the Korean War. With each of these governments, we now carry on our differences
without serious threat of war. We should not use language that suggests that
adversaries are permanent. Treating them as fellow problem-solvers on a
fragile globe can become a self-fulfilling assumption.

To date, scientists have demonstrated more skill in blowing atoms apart
than in bringing people together. But the same kind of organized dedication
that produced the Manhattan Project during World War II can now be applied to improving the way we interact with other governments. Here is one

brief sketch of a nascent "science of living together" on this troubled globe. These ideas are greatly in need of improvement. But we already know a lot. My advice to new leaders concerned with international affairs is not to shoot from the hip, but apply a scientific approach to the way we conduct each international relationship. It may mean little more than applying organized common sense, but even that has been in short supply.

Science Advice to the President

Gerald R. Ford

In a publication dealing with the future of science advice to the White House, the Congress, and other leading elements of government, I hesitate to make predictions about the new discoveries of science and how they can be applied. I am confident, however, that science will continue to produce important and occasionally astounding ideas, and that engineers, industrialists, medical doctors, military weaponeers, and others will quickly convert these scientific discoveries into applications. What I can offer from my experience in both the White House and Congress are comments on the kinds of advice that is helpful and how it may get to the President.

From my observations, the leaders of our government are very conscious of the power of science and technology; many have a good understanding of scientific research processes, engineering developments, industrial production, as well as the other applications of science; some make it a principal activity to understand the details of government and non-government S&T programs and problems in order to handle their administrative responsibilities, their committee assignments, and/or their constituency interests. All of them, by their administrative assignments or their votes, can influence government funding, regulations, laws, and the establishment of a climate favorable to technical activities. More importantly, in doing so, they can shape the priorities and directions of research and be selective on many of its applications.

All of the above could give the reader the impression that these activities occupy much governmental leadership time and attention. In a sense they do, and in another sense, they don't. Most of the governmental scientific and technological issues are associated with large and complex affairs. There is much science and technology in matters of health, but government health programs go far beyond science and technology; in arms control, science and technology plays an important part, but foreign policy, defense policy, military alliances, and other considerations are overriding; in international competitiveness, there are such dominating factors as trade agreements, currency value, jobs, availability of capital, among many other items which

Gerald R. Ford was President of the United States (1974–1977).

are in fact more important than the science and technology, even though our science and technology capabilities are vital to our competitive strength. Thus, leaders of government need science and technology input in many forms. The major portfolios of defense, health, foreign affairs, space, commerce, etc., all contain items of science and technology. As issues in these major portfolios come through government processes, including those in the Administration and those in the Congress, the pertinent scientific research and development are judged on the basis of their importance to those larger governmental missions.

BASIC RESEARCH

Basic scientific research gets a somewhat different treatment in government. It has long been established that the federal government has a fundamental mission of funding basic scientific research, a necessary forerunner to so many vital needs of the country. There doesn't seem to be any serious political party division on the need for basic scientific research, nor for its funding by government. Of course, there are serious arguments as to which universities, research laboratories, or individual investigators get support, but we have developed pretty good schemes for awarding funds on the basis of merit, even though occasionally a political pork-barrel activity gets in the way. By and large, the whole treatment of basic scientific research funding in government is a rather smooth political process.

The biggest problem facing government, in both the Administration and the Congress, is to set the level of R&D funding. It is very difficult for government funding to match the cornucopia outpourings of scientific research. It has been my experience that all of the sciences present pretty good cases for going the next step in supporting their new ideas, but we have not yet been able to match fully the legitimate funding requests of science. So there is a problem of setting the budget levels for scientific research, with the result that there is competition among and between the various fields of science for funding of scientists, equipment and facilities. There is great need for the President and Congress to be in close contact with the scientific communities outside the government to help in arranging scientific research priorities.

Most of the scientists and engineers whom I've met take a very positive attitude toward the benefits to society that their work will give, and I do, too. Their enthusiasm for their work—what it does for society—presses them onward to secure funding or to get a favorable climate for their work. On the other hand, if you think of all the constituencies faced by politicians, you find many individuals and groups who are very disturbed by the changes which science and its derivatives offer to society. Many are deeply concerned about the side effects—sometimes even the primary effect—of an advance in science. And they are particularly worried if the pressure to advance a science or its application comes from a big institution. Government, industry, major private research laboratories all are recipients of criticism from many sources. It's pretty easy to see why: A new pesticide from an agricultural research laboratory may increase crop production, but it may also constitute a serious threat to groundwater supplies, birds and other animals, including the human; the production of fissile materials may contribute to the production of electricity in home, office, and factory, but it also suggests great problems of nuclear waste disposal. Even the biologists are often criticized for their use of animals in research and testing, and gene engineering.

SURPRISES

Beyond the special problem of the positive versus the negative, there is a great worry about the big surprises. Presidents don't like surprises. Each one wants both to be first to hear bad news so they can prepare to handle it, and to know about good news so they can take advantage of it. On the negative side, events like the Chernobyl or the Challenger accident clearly show that the system has failed, and that we ought to do better.

It is clear from polls that, on balance, scientific work is appreciated and the applications are wanted by society, but there are many signals from society that we should go slowly and carefully. So the Administration and Congress know that there truly is a balance that they must make. One of the assignments of the Office of Technology Assessment, Congress's science advising institution, is to make sure that new technologies are assessed with respect to their negative aspects as well as the positive. And scientific advice is asked of many units of this country, including the National Academies, the Office of Science and Technology Policy, professional societies, think tanks, etc., on adverse effects of technologies and scientific research.

So how can the President help in handling scientific and technological matters? How can the President find his proper positive leadership role in these areas? What bridges can be build directly or indirectly to the scientific community to assist him? For almost all of the past thirty years, there has been a White House Science Advisor to the President, who also directed a scientific office with a modest staff in the Executive office of the President. Though its initial establishment was actually an upgrading of a previously used advisory mechanism, it was a sharply pointed action to handle the surprise which our country received when the Soviet Union sent Sputnik into orbit. Once established, Eisenhower's new scientific advisory mechanism in the White House was used also to provide second opinions on the many new military weapons proposals which were flooding the White House and which would have broken the national budget if they were all supported. The White House science mechanism then gradually shifted over to consider civil scientific and technological issues. In fact, as the National Security Council grew in strength to handle the job of providing second opinions on military technology, the science office assumed a helpmate role, as it also did on science budgeting by the Office of Management and Budget.

A WORTHWHILE CONTRIBUTION

The scientific advisory structure has had its ups and downs, but generally has made a worthwhile contribution. Each President has handled it differently, depending on personal taste, White House staff structure and personnel, and especially the kinds of technological issues which emerged during a given Presidential tenure. In my Administration, the OPEC control of the Middle East oil triggered the oil crisis which reverberated through the economies of the world. There were many resulting implications for government science and technology, such that there resulted a great deal of reprogramming and budget reprioritization and even reorganization of departments and agencies which deal with energy. Today the big subject which needs lots of attention at the top of government is international competitiveness. What will tomorrow's big subject be? Perhaps the emerging biological science revolution will have the world in a spin, a situation in which governmental reprioritizing and reorganization thrives.

To help the President with the many S&T opinions coming from so many advocates and critics, he needs a science and technology helper to help examine the options. The President has the continuing task of being aware of the unfolding science scene and the evaluation of differing elements of that scene, including the long-term and short-term, positive and negative implications of science activity. For this, an Advisor who knows, and is part of, a broad science community in academe, industry, and government is needed as analyst, liaison officer, and gatekeeper. The President needs advisory help for his budgeting, programmatic and organizational decisions involving science. He needs a science and technology voice in the White House as he oversees the efforts of many agencies to play the government's role on such large-scale matters as international competitiveness. In my view, there is still a need for a strong White House Science and Technology Office. Without such competent technical assistance a President could, and probably would, make serious errors of judgment affecting our nation's future security, health, and prosperity.

Toward a Nation Healthy, Wealthy and Wise

Richard L. Garwin

The future of the United States is clouded by natural enemies, such as the AIDS virus, earthquakes, and volcanoes; by real or prospective military adversaries, such as the Soviet Union and Iran; and by domestic problems, such as functional illiteracy, drugs, self-serving bureaucracy, and a lack of attention to maintaining and building our physical and constitutional infrastructure.

Most would agree that the United States Government has a role in helping the nation realize a vigorous future in which these clouds are avoided, and that every tool of analysis and creativity should be bent to the support of these goals.

Never perfect, the employment of science and technology to foresee and determine the future has been substantially hampered, since the demise of the President's Science Advisory Committee in 1973, by the lack of a high-level group of outstanding independent scientists, charged with identifying problems and opportunities on behalf of the President of the United States, to whom the President can turn with his problems and who, in turn, are obligated to give their best efforts in an advisory capacity and in the extension of the Constitutional role of the President into the scientific domain.

Hardly needing examples is the endemic lack of warning of problems which could be attacked with profit when they are small, rather than waiting until they are large or overwhelming. Among these are the AIDS virus, military problems which could be solved by the application of technology outside the present bureaucratic structure, and the NASA Space Shuttle disaster with its impact on both civilian and military space programs. Identi-

Richard L. Garwin is IBM Fellow and Science Advisor to the Director of Research at the IBM Thomas J. Watson Research Center. He is a physicist, has some 34 US patents, is a member of the National Academies of Sciences and of Engineering, has been a consultant to the US Government and its contractors since 1950, and was a member of the President's Science Advisory Committee during the Kennedy, Johnson and Nixon Administrations.

fication of opportunities is another role for a scientific group, and the advancing of specific proposals to solve problems.

A SOUNDING BOARD

The President and the government, as a whole, lack a sounding board that would help to improve proposals or help reject them, and that would give some indication of reactions from the scientific community. The role of scientific analysis and invention in program evaluation is little understood by political leaders; one should neither accept nor reject a program as proposed without asking whether it can be improved through the application of existing technology and whether (if successful) it would be worthwhile. Program proposals and contractor reports are often artfully phrased to deny higher authority the ready insight into these questions required for proper evaluation.

Such a scientific group would be a corporate memory to identify resources, reports and people. Recent history is replete with a lack of awareness of problems (and reports proposing solutions) which had been studied before.

Such a technical panel could serve as a technical review panel to help the Office of Management and Budget (OMB) or the NSC judge the merits of programs, proposals or threats.

In the energy field, before deciding whether to pursue a program, it would be desirable to define and to determine the scope of alternatives, like drilling up and capping domestic oil fields in order to guard against interruptions in foreign supply.

On the intelligence or security front, it seems clear that information about espionage threats to the new Moscow embassy (in the forms of bugs and other sensors) was widely available in Washington, but was not thoroughly explored at the level of the Presidency.

The military ostrich revealed itself once again in the attack on the USS Stark when a US warship in the Persian Gulf was disabled the first time an attack was mounted.

BUREAUCRACY OUT OF CONTROL

Bureaucracy out of control is nowhere better exemplified than in the NASA Shuttle disaster, preceded in late 1979 by NASA's persuading President Carter that the health of the NASA Space Shuttle Program depended upon his forcing all future military launches onto the shuttle. Security aspects of this were addressed by the National Security Council, but without the vast resource of knowledge and experience which had been accumulated by the President's Science Advisory Committee and its panels up until the early 1970s.

The actual design error that led to the accident and the inadequacies of the shuttle program would very likely have been revealed by on-going interaction between NASA and a relevant PSAC panel.

PSAC would play the role essential to program choice, and one which should be noncontroversial—that of foresight. Such a group could attempt to look into the limited future as a surrogate for nature, identifying the likely course of events and allowing program proponents or authorities to determine whether they like that particular future or not.

On the military scene, there is an urgent need to consider options and problems of a full service—Navy, Army, Marines, Air Force—so that, for every proposed program, alternatives would be sought at that level, at a level above a Service, and at a joint level, including evaluation of the option, "No, not yet."

If a PSAC would be so beneficial, why do we not have one? It is not a matter of security *leaks,* or the leak of politically sensitive information. There was never even a charge of a leak of classified information from PSAC or its panels during the days in which such an organization existed. Nor was there any suggestion that members of PSAC or its panels used their knowledge of Presidential concerns or initiatives for individual profit or to do anything but advance these initiatives at a time before they were revealed to the public. That is not to say that world-class experts in a field, brought in to provide advice and judgment to the President, have not—on occasion—later used that same background to advise individuals or groups with goals opposite to those of the President—to attempt to terminate a program the President sought to continue, or to initiate a program the President thought was not in the net national interest. Fundamentally, however, the United States denies itself one of its principal strengths if the Administration does not make use of the best technical talent available to initiate and evaluate its options.

To attempt to suppress the flow of information to the technical community—or the writings or Congressional testimony of interested and competent people—would be to deny ourselves a strength and a fundamental Constitutional right which benefits not only the individual but society.

It would be desirable for a PSAC and its panels to work at as high a level of information as possible. To this end, it would help if the entire government provided analyses and not propaganda to the Congress in support of the chosen government program, in contrast to the more usual bureaucratic denial of alternatives. Furthermore, since the resources of the PSAC will always be limited, they should be saved, in large part, for those problems requiring confidentiality and privilege. This means that the Executive Office of the President ought to make as much use as possible of studies commissioned by the Department of Defense with the National Academy of Sciences, the American Physical Society, or other competent, independent organizations (with their own review mechanisms), in order to better aid decision-making in the armed services, and to provide better information to the Executive Office of the President.

CONCLUSION

It is in the very nature of things that one does not know whether the verdict on a program is "yes" or "no" until one does the study. But the purpose of thinking is to arrive at correct and useful answers—not to find arguments to endorse what has been decided on blind faith.

A President who understands that there are life-threatening hazards in the world—as well as astonishing opportunities—will seek the help of the best scientific and technical people in a President's Science Advisory Committee in order to have the best chance of identifying and reaching desirable goals for the nation and of avoiding disaster.

A View from the Sidelines

Eli Ginzberg

For just short of fifty years, I have been actively involved with the federal government—as full-time employee during World War II, as consultant to successive Presidents and various federal departments, and as periodic witness before numerous Congressional committees. These experiences have precipitated a number of conclusions about how our national government operates.

- Except for periods of major crisis, the decision-making scope for the President is relatively narrow. President Eisenhower noted with frustration that, were it not for Lyndon Johnson, he could get nothing done in the Senate.
- Even in periods of crisis and near crisis, the degrees of freedom available to the President are constrained because his decision arena is defined by the advice he receives from the key agencies—in foreign affairs, the National Security Council, the Departments of State and Defense (sometimes Treasury), and the CIA.
- While Presidents and the Congress are sensitive to the long-term consequences of the policies and programs that they accept or reject, as politicians they live in the short to middle-term, and their first and overriding objective is to find answers to agenda items that must be dealt with.
- Ours is a pluralistic society. Hence, however important the role of the federal government, particularly in foreign affairs, defense, and funding for research, what Presidents and Congress are willing and able to do depends heavily on the power and influence of non-governmental groups. One need only recall Eisenhower's trenchant address on the pervasive influence of the military-industrial complex.
- In the arena of science policy, there is a lesson in the fact that Vannevar Bush lost his fight with President Truman to establish the National Science

Eli Ginzberg is A. Barton Hepburn Professor Emeritus of Economics and Director of the Conservation of Human Resources at Columbia University. Author of about one hundred books, mostly in the field of human resources and health economics, Dr. Ginzberg is a long-term consultant to the federal government, foundations, and large corporations.

Foundation as a quasi-independent organization. It should also be noted that most federal support for R&D, with the exception of the biomedical arena, is linked directly or indirectly to defense—through appropriations for DoD, NASA, and DoE.

- The Mansfield Amendment placed severe restrictions on the capacity of the Armed Services to provide longer-term support for research in the basic sciences, and thereby tied governmental funding even more closely to weapons systems, moon shots, and engineering projects aimed at opening up new sources of energy.
- Inasmuch as OMB lacks a mandate or staff to do more than recommend minor adjustments in the budgets for R&D of the principal departments and agencies, and Congressional staffs are handicapped by limited access to information, the momentum of earlier decisions, and the local interests of key members of the Congress, the agencies' priorities—once approved—assume lives of their own. It takes a major failure to bring about premature termination of a program and a reallocation of funds.

A logical deduction from the foregoing is that the *structure* of the federal government makes it very difficult for the departments, the White House, or the Congress to obtain useful inputs from members of the scientific community, even if they see advantage to eliciting it. Herbert York and Harold Brown were able scientists who held senior positions in the Department of Defense; however, they had little more than marginal influence on the shape of the department's R&D budgets. The weight of departmental structures and processes suggests that the greatest leverage for improving the expenditure of R&D dollars would be gained by strengthening their scientific advisory mechanisms. Yet, the premature resignation of Emmanuel Piore from the chairmanship of the advisory group to the Office of Naval Research (which he had earlier helped to create), once he saw its function as simply helping the admirals "sell" their programs, and my own experience as a member of the Scientific Advisory Committee to the Air Force which I found served largely as window dressing, are bold indicators of the difficulty of changing the current system—at this basic level, where policies and programs are first fashioned.

When it comes to providing advice to Presidents, I have learned from my occasional interactions with eight of our chief executives, and close relations to a ninth, Eisenhower, that it all depends on the agenda of the President. If he desires advice from leaders of the scientific community, he has little difficulty obtaining it. But most presidents, with the notable exception of Eisenhower, have not seen the need to seek advice on scientific issues outside the Executive.

The interest of the President in seeking advice from the leadership of the scientific community is, however, only one facet of a much more complex issue.

Consider—In 1987 the following priority items would surely warrant a place on the President's agenda:

- How best to reconcile the conflicting opinions of his advisors (and NATO nations) about the discussions with the USSR re: arms reduction.
- Modifications in the SDI program in light of potentially restricted funding by the Congress.
- The level of appropriation requests for the Super Collider.
- Accelerating the level of federal response to AIDS.

But the 1987 Presidential agenda should also be concerned with other more difficult, if not intransigent, issues:

- Strengthening the research universities' infrastructure, including the upgrading of their laboratories and equipment.
- Determining the appropriate actions that the federal government might undertake—independently or in cooperation with the other sectors—to maintain and, if possible, increase the nation's talent pool in the face of adverse demographic trends.
- Exploring other approaches which might point directions to higher returns on current expenditures of R&D funds, and also pinpoint where new investments hold promise of high yield.

These items could be extended, but even a much longer list would not exhaust the barriers that lie in the path of improving the quality of advice from the scientific community to the federal Executive and the legislature. Some of the more important barriers should be noted:

- The difficulties of identifying the spokesmen of the scientific community.
- The frequently profound differences of values and opinions among members of the same discipline.
- The absence of any simple—or even complex—way of assessing relative claims for expanded support, as for instance between the advocates of Super Colliders and those who urge a crash effort to map the entire human genome.
- The overriding fact that breadth and depth of scientific knowledge and judgment are not necessarily sufficient to enable an advisor to the President to assess the options that the President confronts.

When it comes to advising members of Congressional committees, a review of the record suggests that more frequently than not, outside experts are scientists with a particular interest in—or commitment to—a program for whose funding they are lobbying. There is nothing improper or wrong about such "special pleading," but by the same token, it is no surprise that Congressmen tend to discount the testimony that experts offer.

The thrust of this analysis does not lead straightforwardly to a set of specific recommendations of actions that will assure that the federal Executive and legislature become the beneficiaries of informed advice about scientific matters from leaders of the scientific community. We have seen that most funding questions that shape federal science policy are directly linked to technological considerations, such as the purchase of a new weapons system—questions that inevitably fall within the preserve of the concerned department or agency. Every President must select the subjects that are high on his agenda and his sources of advice. And most Presidents have not recognized any urgency to open new channels of advice that the scientific community could provide. In fact, the recent record has been that Presidents have distanced themselves ever further from the science community.

I hold no brief for any particular reform: reestablishing the President's Scientific Advisory Committee; prescribing that every department have an assistant secretary for R&D; expanding the mission of OMB to include oversight of all federal R&D programs; strengthening the Congressional Office of Technology Assessment; working out new arrangements between the National Academy of Sciences (as well as the National Research Council) and the Congress and the Executive. There is little prospect that any or all of these would necessarily improve the quality of scientific advice available to the federal government.

My modest proposals focus on the following:

- The more effective use of educational and communication mechanisms to increase the public's scientific literacy and interest.
- Efforts to enhance the quality of science reporting in the daily, weekly, and monthly press. In the absence of a better-informed and -involved public in matters affecting science policy, neither the President nor the Congress is likely to reach out for informed consultative help.
- A stronger leadership role by the National Academy of Science in assessing the strengths and weaknesses of the R&D infrastructure and speaking with one voice to the Executive departments, the President, and the Congress about urgent (and continuing) ways in which they must seek to strengthen the nation's R&D efforts.

It is relatively easy to suggest mechanisms whereby the President and Congress might be able to obtain more and better advice from the scientific community. But the more urgent and continuing challenges appear to me to lie less in the domain of reforming the structures of the federal government and more in raising the literacy of the American people and the press about matters scientific. To these ends the scientific community has its work cut out: to improve its own house before taking on the unsolicited assignment of improving the structure of the federal government.

The Role of the President's Science Advisor

William R. Graham

From time to time, when I encounter a news or opinion article that outlines what the Science Advisor to the President does, and what he should do, I find it difficult to correlate these formal descriptions of the Science Advisor's role with the realities of a rapidly changing science and technology environment.

Both the office and the role of the Director of the Office of Science and Technology Policy are formally established by statute. According to Public Law 94-282: "The primary function of the Director is to provide, within the Executive Office of the President, advice on the scientific, engineering, and technological aspects of issues that require attention at the highest levels of government." This is the principal purpose and charge of the Science Advisor.

By statute, the Director of OSTP works for the President. Discussion of the Science Advisor's effectiveness often focuses on his relationship with the President, which today spans a wide range of activities, from personally briefing and counseling the President, to identifying issues, proposing and arranging Presidential activities, analyzing policy alternatives, preparing options for Presidential consideration, overseeing Presidential-level agreements in science and technology with foreign countries, and representing the Administration in ministerial-level science and technology activities overseas.

To function effectively, the Science Advisor must have access to a wide range of information and consultation with industrial, academic, and gov-

William R. Graham has been Science Advisor to President Reagan and Director of the Office of Science and Technology Policy since October 1, 1986. Previously, he was Deputy Administrator and then Acting Administrator of the National Aeronautics and Space Administration. Dr. Graham was a member of President Reagan's 1980 transition team. He has been a staff member of The RAND Corporation and an associate of an independent consulting firm. His doctorate, from Stanford University, is in electrical engineering.

ernmental sources, both domestic and foreign. Obviously, a wide range of sources and viewpoints provides the President useful alternatives in matters of policy formulation.

Advisory groups have been established to give periodic consultation to the Office of Science and Technology Policy and to act as a collection network for a broader spectrum of viewpoints. One advisory group that reports to the Science Advisor is the Federal Coordinating Council on Science, Engineering, and Technology (FCCSET), established by statute to be composed of the Director of the Office of Science and Technology Policy and one representative of each of thirteen federal agencies: Department of Agriculture, Department of Commerce, Department of Defense, Department of Health and Human Services, Department of Housing and Urban Development, Department of the Interior, Department of State, Department of Transportation, Veterans Administration, National Aeronautics and Space Administration, National Science Foundation, Environmental Protection Agency, and the Department of Energy. FCCSET and various committees that can be established under it (twenty-nine at present, with varying levels of activity) provide a direct link between government agencies and the science and technology communities.

Another advisory group is the White House Science Council (WHSC). The WHSC is a bipartisan group of nongovernmental scientists and engineers currently comprising three members from industry, two from the academic sector, and including the former heads of two national laboratories. The White House Science Council, established in 1981 under the authority of the Federal Advisory Committees Act, reports to and meets frequently with the Director of the Office of Science and Technology Policy. As required, the WHSC meets with the President and other senior members of the Administration to review issues identified either by the Director of OSTP or by the Science Council itself. Prior to the establishment of the White House Science Council in 1982, no comparable group had existed for about nine years. Prior to 1973, an earlier variant had been the President's Science Advisory Committee which, contrary to much of the currently fashionable rhetoric, filled the same advisory role.

Some of the reorganization proposals have advocated making the Science Advisor (1) head of a department of science and technology; (2) a member of the Cabinet; (3) a member of the National Security Council; and (4) a *de facto* fourth separate branch of the government with a corresponding *de facto* separation of powers.

Such recommendations reflect fundamental misperceptions concerning the involvement and function of the Science Advisor—at least in the current Administration. In fact, as well as in principle, the participation of OSTP in matters related to science and technology policy is both substantial and comprehensive. Giving Cabinet status to the White House locus of science advice, policy formulation, and coordination would bring with it substantial day-to-day operational, institutional, and (quite probably) regulatory responsibilities which could detract from providing sound and timely counsel to the President. In contrast, the Science Advisor is currently able to act as an objective arbiter of agency issues and to provide the President a source of advice unbiased by agency affiliation. This current role should be preserved.

To be useful to the President, the Science Advisor must participate in relevant meetings of policymaking bodies that report to the President. He must help the President form a consensus on important issues and must play a useful role in bringing issues into focus and formulating policy options and recommendations, in concert with his colleagues from the National Security Council, Cabinet-level policy councils, the Office of Management and Budget, and other agencies of the government. Development of the President's 1987 competitiveness initiative and superconductivity initiatives, review and policy guidance of the Space Station program, the superconducting Super Collider decision, and guiding the nation's science and technology relationships with foreign countries are illustrative examples.

Key to the Reagan Administration's accomplishments in those areas and many others is the President's strong commitment to science and technology in the affairs of the nation both at home and abroad. Nevertheless, like any Presidential advisor, the Science Advisor can be effective only when he or she has the President's confidence. While history will judge the current relationship, the present Science Advisor feels most privileged to serve President Reagan.

Science and Technology Advice to the President

Norman Hackerman

The desirability of establishing a federal Cabinet-level office to accommodate the importance science and technology have attained in national and international affairs has been debated continuously for some years. My negative position on this matter has already been stated.[1]

Without going into detail, the main reason for this position is the value of multiple approaches to the multi-faceted problems of 1) increasing our understanding of nature, 2) translating this understanding into technology, and 3) implementing this technology into a variety of products and services of use to ourselves and others.

All of this translates into material well-being by virtue of the positive effects on national health, national economic betterment, and national security.

The value of true understanding of the science and engineering enterprise at the highest levels of federal government could be simply the need to know how best to maintain that enterprise in a viable and healthy state. It is now a matter of equal importance to have a high order of technological sophistication in other matters of material consequence, however. In other words, the voice of technology—and therefore of science—is required in most matters politic.

The question then is how is this input best done? Perhaps the most appealing thing about a Cabinet-level office is the visibility and potential participation such a position offers. The disadvantages are sufficient to opt against this solution, however.

Norman Hackerman has been Chairman of the National Science Board, Chairman of Argonne Universities Association, and a member of the Defense Science Board. He is a member of the National Academy of Sciences and of the American Philosophical Society. Dr. Hackerman is Chairman of the Scientific Advisory Board of the Robert A. Welch Foundation, and is President Emeritus and Distinguished Professor Emeritus of Chemistry at Rice University and Professor Emeritus and past President of the University of Texas at Austin.

There are not many other possibilities. One, for example, is to use an independent agency—such as the National Science Foundation—as the apparatus and the National Science Board as the policy-deriving body. Indeed, this is the way the initial charter of the NSF can be read. The system as devised, however, did not work, mainly because it is an agency among agencies and the credibility of an unbiased approach to many issues would be hard to establish.

In fact, the best solution to this problem continues to be the invention of a Science Advisor as part of the President's staff. This individual can not only advise the President, but can also coordinate federal activities in science and technology, the assignment of the present Federal Council on Science and Technology, and, in addition, can chair a group like a President's Science Advisory Committee. The latter is a suitable and potentially effective means of tapping the best science and engineering capability in the country. The particular change here from the past is the chairmanship which hitherto was reserved for an outstanding individual outside of government. The present suggestion is aimed at adding power to the Advisor and making that position more attractive.

THE MAIN KEY

The main key to a successful system as described just above is the Science Advisor. That person must be knowledgeable, credible in the technology community, decisive, tough-minded, evenhanded, and *not* easily bruised. In addition, politics must not only not be anathema to the Advisor but must be recognized as the balancing factor that keeps us in the straits of democracy. The enterprise may work adequately without such a paragon, but it will work better to the degree the Advisor has these characteristics.

Apparatus has already been arranged to provide for cooperation within the government sector. The Federal Council on Science and Technology did function to accommodate cross-agency ties. Even if this provided information only, it is useful, and wherever it induces actual cooperation, it can be assumed to have provided even more benefits.

A PSAC-like group would be effective provided 1) it reorganizes its advisory character, and 2) the White House accords the advice given seriously, recognizing that it is in general not politically driven, i.e., is not idiotic because it may seem politically unfeasible.

The group should be of a size that does not impede action, thus some ten to fifteen members. It should be broadly representative of the basic sciences and engineering as well as of systems (atmosphere, oceans, etc.), aftermaths (environment, risk, economy, etc.), and social/political consequences generally. This is a vast spectrum so the word "broadly" is important.

Where more detailed expert knowledge is needed, it can be obtained via consultants and panels. The members of the group must be senatorial in outlook and not representative of their own fields of interest. They should deal only with the broad issues, albeit with consideration of details needed to reach policy conclusions.

The Science Advisor should chair both the advisory council and the co-ordinating council. In this way the Advisor is a full-fledged participating equal, rather than a staff officer. This provides a more authoritative base from which to provide guidance to the President and a better position from which to maintain status in the White House staff.

NOTE

1. *Technology In Society*, Vol. VIII (1986), pp. 111–113.

Science, Technology, and a World Transformed: Time to Upgrade the Government's Efforts

David A. Hamburg

Much of the technology that structures American lives today in ways we largely take for granted is of extremely recent origin. In 1900, there were few automobiles or household telephones; motion pictures were just getting underway; there were no household radios, no airplanes, no televisions, no computers. Today it is almost impossible to imagine a world without these technologies—and, in this country, without their presence everywhere. The world has been transformed by science and technology in this century—and the transformation is continuing, even accelerating, as the century comes to a close.

Through most of our history as a people, our economic success was in substantial part predicated on an open-minded, pragmatic orientation to technological utilization of natural resources for the general well-being. Much of this was based on a common sense approach to imaginative craftsmanship, as exemplified by many of our great inventors. Increasingly in the history of the country, the new technologies central to economic progress and national defense—national security in the broad sense—came to depend upon advances in fundamental science. Science and science-based technol-

David A. Hamburg, M.D., has been President of the Carnegie Corporation of New York since 1983. He served as President (1984–85) and Chairman of the Board (1985–86) of the American Association for the Advancement of Science. He was Professor and Chairman of the Department of Psychiatry at Stanford University from 1961–72; President of the Institute of Medicine, National Academy of Science, 1975–80; and Director of the Division of Health Policy Research and Education and John D. MacArthur Professor of Health Policy at Harvard University, 1980–82. Dr. Hamburg is a Trustee of The Rockefeller University and of the Mount Sinai Medical Center, New York. He has served on many policy advisory boards, including the Chief of Naval Operations Executive Panel and the Advisory Committee on Medical Research of the World Health Organization.

ogies have become a pervasive part of human experience in the 20th century and the key to future well-being. Science is not a separate activity, remote from the lives of people—however arcane it may be. Science provides the basis for most of the requirements for modern living and much of its promise for the future.

In recent decades, largely in the second half of the 20th century, science has been institutionalized on a vast scale for the first time, and the pace of advance in deep knowledge has accelerated dramatically—knowledge of the structure of matter and of life, of the nature of the universe, and of the human environment, even knowledge of ourselves. These scientific advances provide an unprecedented basis for technological innovation, especially in the context of political and economic freedom; and the pace of such innovation is now the most rapid in all of history.

These developments are intrinsically worldwide in scope. Many of our domestic problems are now more appropriately viewed as domestic aspects of international problems. This change in perspective calls for institutional innovations that have a chance of transcending traditional barriers—disciplinary, sectoral and national.

Moreover, the rapid and pervasive transformation resulting from science and technology calls for the strengthening of institutional capability for objective, scholarly analysis of critical issues based on a broad foundation of knowledge and experience. The government of the United States is in an extraordinarily strong position to stimulate and support such inquiries at a level far beyond what it is doing now.

Thoughtful policy-makers have increasingly felt the need for intelligible and credible syntheses of research related to important policy questions. What is the factual basis drawn from many sources that can provide the underpinning for constructive options in the future? Pertinent information is almost always widely scattered. Moreover, it is very difficult for the nonexpert and sometimes even for the expert to assess the credibility of assertions on emotionally charged issues. In the current process of world transformation, such studies are needed to tackle vital and complex issues in an analytical rather than a polemical way. This means a wide range of high quality information, analyses and options. Jumping to conclusions—or using a heavy ideological filter—can easily lead to major mistakes, missed opportunities, or even disasters.

SCIENCE POLICY

Science policy involves certain fundamental, recurring themes: 1) maintaining excellence, technical competence, and efficiency in the conduct of research; 2) broadening participation in the conduct of scientific activity and in the benefits of the applications of sciences; 3) shaping the uses of sciences towards widely shared ends—for example, the relief of human suffering, economic well-being, equitable distribution of resources, and peaceful resolution of disputes; and 4) the desirability of scientists participating analytically in the uses of science—at the interfaces of fact and value—neither avoiding nor dominating the processes by which the social uses of science are decided.

The nation needs several mechanisms, *both* governmental and non-governmental, for analyzing, thoroughly and objectively, the various options bearing on long-range science policy: what science can do for society, and how society can keep science healthy. The nation must capitalize on the extraordinary capability of our diverse nongovernmental institutions to get the best possible analysis and advice on long-term questions of great national importance. We are fortunate to have remarkable institutions that pull together the sciences very broadly and effectively. Such studies should include early warning signals on emerging problems; the identification of neglected opportunities; the formulation of new ways in which science and technology could contribute to the general well-being, here and abroad.

Medicine strives to honor its maxim: First of all, do no harm. So, too, in the era of world transformation by science and technology, policy-makers should strive for this maxim: First of all, get the facts straight. To do so requires casting a wide net inside and outside the government. Mechanisms to utilize a variety of inputs are of increasing value—drawing on technical competence broadly conceived from different sources, and striving to integrate information across methods, disciplines and perspectives.

For the Executive branch, a greatly strengthened Office of Science and Technology Policy in the White House can play a crucial role in performing such functions. Indeed, if properly constructed, the Office can provide a unique window on all of the opportunities related to science and technology as they impinge on every function of government. It might be assumed that this mainly means the Department of Defense and the science-supporting agencies such as NSF and NIH. In fact, it now means much more; increasingly, there are scientific and technological aspects to all the responsibilities of government.

Morever, the rapidly changing international economy is increasingly driven by developments in science and technology: witness telecommunications, biotechnology, computers—and the technical upgrading of established industries. No reminder is needed of the immense role of weapons in this picture. But the problem is not only one of hardware. It involves the uses of hardware, and the social impacts of technological changes. The behavioral and social sciences are more urgently needed than ever before to help sort out the vast economic and social changes taking place. In sort, the scope of opportunity and risk is much greater than it was such a short time ago as in the Administrations of Presidents Eisenhower and Kennedy when the science advisory apparatus worked so well.

THE SCIENCE ADVISOR

The President's Science Advisor is *not:* 1) a lobbyist for the scientific community; 2) an uncritical salesman for the President's policies; or 3) a wizard who personally covers all of science and technology in depth.

To do the job well, the Science Advisor must develop: 1) a relationship of trust, mutual respect, and open communication with the President; 2) a wide-ranging set of study groups to focus on important questions at the highest level of quality; 3) an ability to tap into the scientific community and its institutions in an ongoing, broad-based way—both in government and outside it; and 4) an earned reputation for integrity with no possibility of pre-cooked answers to technical or policy questions.

The Science Advisor needs a substantial staff—much larger than the present one; and a President's Science Advisory Committee. The latter can help to decide what needs to be studied in depth and how. It must be broadly composed, including physical, biological and behavioral sciences, as well as science-based professions such as engineering and medicine. It should be capable of dealing with military problems through appropriate study groups, but these should not commandeer its main energies. Still, it should relate systematically to the Defense Science Board and similar bodies. It should work closely with the Office of Management and Budget on a basis of clear communication and mutual respect. To be effective, OSTP cannot be distant from, subservient to, or arrogant towards OMB. The OSTP should also work closely with the Congressional Office of Technology Assessment which has become increasingly valuable over the short course of its existence.

More than ever, science and technology bear upon war and peace, health and disease, the economy and society, resources and the environment—indeed, the human future. Therefore, policy-relevant analysis must deal with the ongoing and potential applications of research and development in each sphere of life. Moreover, we will need to become increasingly analytical about the major facets of the scientific enterprise itself, including: 1) Science policy. What are the conditions under which science flourishes? 2) Technology policy. What are the conditions under which the science base can fruitfully be drawn upon for useful technological innovations? 3) Technology assessment policy. What institutional mechanisms and analytical methods are needed for ongoing assessment of major technologies with respect to the humane, constructive uses of technology?

With all our technical capabilities, tangible benefits, wealth, and optimism, we, nevertheless:

1) are in danger for the first time ever of totally devastating civilization and perhaps even extinguishing the human species in a nuclear war—and quite possibly before long in a bacteriological war as well;

2) are in a world in which about half the earth's people live in abject poverty under crushing burdens of illness, ignorance and disability;

3) are immersed in an ancient sea of prejudice, ethnocentrism and violence—now amplified greatly by modern weapons and telecommunications technology;

4) are generating a growing underclass of people gravely damaged for life—in the midst of unprecedented technical capability and affluence.

In addressing such crucial problems, there is a precious resource in the great scientific and scholarly community of the United States—and its links to the worldwide scientific and scholarly community.

One potential source of future strength lies in a dynamic interplay between the scientific community and the policy community—not only in military and health matters, where the concept is fairly well accepted, but over a wide range of economic and social questions. Among these, none is more important than finding ways to come to terms at last with the profound and pervasive human tendencies to generate deadly conflict.

Recommendations for Changes in Government Science Policy

Cyril M. Harris

Government's role in science and technology—from the office of the Science Advisor to the President to the Congress, agencies, and quasi-public organizations that determine agendas and provide funding—should be far more prominent than it is now. This role must be accepted as a crucial function of the federal establishment with high priority given to the responsibilities of oversight, policy-making, and thoughtfully designated support.

Scientific leadership at the federal level has so deteriorated in recent years that such action as does emanate from the federal government is almost entirely reactive—response to crisis that is rarely well-conceived, thought through to consequences, or sustained past the memory of the event that triggered it. The President's Science Advisor must be a first-class scientist and/or engineer chosen for broad-ranging scientific, administrative, and leadership skills and not primarily for political stance. He or she must have senior rank and regularly scheduled, frequent access to the President. The office itself must be given permanent status which is not subject to partisan pressures that can diminish its authority as the will of a new Administration dictates.

Among the areas in which policy changes are required are education, research, funding, and information exchange, and suggestions for some of these changes follow:

- Science teaching should be part of elementary school curriculums, beginning with the earliest grades, taking advantage of children's curiosity about the world around them.
- To improve the quality of science education at the high school level, a much larger pool of *qualified* science teachers is needed. A significant step

Cyril M. Harris, Charles Batchelor Professor of Electrical Engineering and Professor of Architecture at Columbia University, has served on numerous federal government and National Research Council committees. He is a member of the National Academies of Science and Engineering and of the American Philosophical Society.

forward would be to drop required "teacher education" courses for prospective science and mathematics teachers and to replace them with a master's level degree in the relevant discipline.

- Basic science and mathematics courses that enable students to function competently in an increasingly technological society should be required for high school diplomas.
- Basic college-level science and mathematics courses should be required for all college students, regardless of their choice of major.
- Science teaching laboratories in high schools and most colleges are woefully out of date. Massive funds are required to modernize them—funds that have not been—and probably will not be—available from state or local sources. A mechanism is required that will provide such funding from federal sources.
- Federal funds for scientific and technological projects should be granted only on the basis of peer review, and not because of lobbying by the applicant's institution or organization.
- There should be a greater funding support of venturesome individual research. Evaluation of such proposals is obviously difficult; but current practice tends to discourage the quirky and imaginative researcher, and as private or institutional funds grow increasingly tight, opportunities for such investigation shrink—almost certainly to the detriment of science.
- The designation of National Laboratories should be restricted only to those special fields of science or engineering where massive support at a single location is required. In recent years, some National Laboratories have been designated in specialties that require relatively few research scientists and relatively small-scale financial support. These have sometimes been the result of "pork barreling" by members of Congress, and are detrimental to the responsible allocation of resources and to appropriate scientific research.
- Government regulations regarding the interchange of new scientific and technical information between countries need evaluation. Very careful, dispassionate scrutiny of current policy is needed to ensure that any benefits of current restrictions are not outweighed by the harm done American scientific enterprise when it does not have access to the free flow of information. If such an objective review results in modification and simplification of these restrictions, the revised policy should be given widespread publicity.

Presidential Science Advising: A Memoir and a Prescription

Theodore M. Hesburgh

One of my earliest recollections of science advice to the President was a phone call from the White House in 1954. Sherman Adams was calling on behalf of President Eisenhower to ask if I would accept membership on the National Science Board. I countered by saying that my special fields were philosophy and theology, not science. He responded that the President wanted a philosophical and theological dimension among his advisors on the Board which was then only four years old. I then said that if the scientists on the Board were willing to listen to me, I was sure that I had a lot to learn about science and public policy from them, and indeed I did over the next twelve years.

One of the proofs of this is that, twenty-four years later, President Carter appointed me Ambassador and Chairman of the US Delegation to the United Nations Conference on Science and Technology for Development, to be held in Vienna two years later. Thanks to previous experience on the Board and other governmental bodies, I was able to assemble a magnificent delegation of scientists and to make some good recommendations to President Carter and Secretary Vance of the State Department.

Over all of these years and with several intervening Presidents, we were able to assure that the National Science Foundation kept its interest, concern, and support for basic research, the need for which after World War II gave it birth. We were able to insist that we enter the space age with a civilian agency, NASA, in charge, not the military. We initiated with Presidential and Congressional support many new national laboratories, such as optical astronomy at Kitt Peak, Arizona, and Cerro Tololo in Chile; radio astronomy at Green Bank, West Virginia; atmospheric sciences at Boulder, Colorado;

Rev. Theodore M. Hesburgh, C.S.C., became President Emeritus of Notre Dame University in 1987, after thirty-five years as President. He continues a distinguished career of public service, which includes 14 Presidential appointments and membership on the Carnegie Commission on Higher Education. He was awarded the US Medal for Freedom in 1964 and holds numerous honorary degrees.

and a score or more of others that have continued to serve well the national interest in science. I doubt that this would have happened without the enlightened advice that the President and the Congress were receiving from the National Science Board under the leadership of Detlev Bronk, who also presided over the National Academy of Sciences and was an active member of other advisory groups, such as PSAC. What began with Eisenhower grew, was further strengthened under succeeding Presidents, and was generally mirrored by other scientific groups advising the correlative committees and sub-committees of the Congress.

During recent years, all of this seems to have disintegrated, with the result that enormous scientific research programs, such as the Strategic Defense Initiative, have been launched to the dismay of the most competent scientists in the nation. Public relations seems to have taken the place of serious and solid scientific advice. Shadow has replaced substance to the consternation of truly competent people who were not even asked for advice. Not only were the mechanisms lacking, but also the will to do so.

Having personally witnessed the success of the former system of providing the best scientific advice to the President, I hope that a new administration will reinstate and reinvigorate the proven mechanisms of the past: a President's science advisor of high stature and a President's Science Advisory Committee. The nation deserves the best, and it is available for the asking.

"To Promote the Progress of Science . . .": Some Bicentennial Considerations

R. Gordon Hoxie

In observing the Bicentennial of the Constitution, we may well recall the mandate of the Constitutional Framers, "To promote the Progress of Science and useful Arts. . . ." The First Congress requested one of the Framers, Alexander Hamilton as Secretary of the Treasury, to advise them on the promotion of manufactures. His masterful response, his 1791 *Report on Manufactures,* provided a blueprint for a great industrial power. In it he wrote, recalling the 1775–1781 War for Independence:

> The extreme embarrassments of the United States during the late War, from an incapacity of supplying themselves, are still matters of keen recollection: A future war might be expected again to exemplify the mischiefs and dangers of a situation, to which that incapacity is still in too great a degree applicable, unless changed by timely and vigorous exertion. To effect this change as fast as shall be prudent, merits all the attention and all the zeal of our Public Councils; 'tis the next great work to be accomplished.[1]

National security was the primary engine which drove Hamilton to advance science and technology and to encourage invention, engineering, transportation, and trade policies. Lincoln, in the midst of a great Civil War in 1863, signed the charter of the National Academy of Sciences, an agency to advise the government on scientific and technical matters. Wilson, at the onset of World War I, had authorized the creation of the National Research Council as an operating arm of the National Academy of Sciences. Wilson, the former President of Princeton University, was rallying the scientists and engineers in the universities to help design the instruments of modern warfare and to serve as advisors to the War and Navy Departments.

R. Gordon Hoxie has served as President and CEO, Center for the Study of the Presidency, since 1969, and is the Editor of Presidential Studies Quarterly. *Earlier, he was President, C. W. Post College, and Chancellor, Long Island University. During World War II, he served in the Army Air Forces, and is a Brigadier General USAF (Ret.). He has served as a consultant to the Department of State and the Department of Defense.*

From Washington and Hamilton through Eisenhower and Kennedy, this linkage between science and technology and national security was fundamental. Then came the Vietnam War and the politicization of the scientific community, resulting in the 1973 termination of the President's Science Advisory Committee and the removal of the Science Advisor from the White House staff. The 1976 restoration of the President's Science Advisor in the Executive Office of the President had given him two masters, the Congress and the President. The Congress gets science and technology advice from the General Accounting Office and also from its own Office of Technology Assessment. It does not need the President's science advisory system.

The Science Advisor, in reality the Science and Technology Advisor, should not have to serve two masters. Ideally the Science Advisor should be an Assistant to the President, and the President should have his own science advisory committee. This was the effective system constructed by Eisenhower in 1957, and eliminated by Kennedy in 1962 on the advice of Richard Neustadt, who envisioned plural sources of power. The Science Advisor's primary responsibility should be to advise the President. It should *not* be to serve the science community, nor, indeed the Congress. His primary area of advice should relate to national security affairs. He should be a statutory advisor to the National Security Council, just as is the Chairman of the Joint Chiefs of Staff and the Director of the Central Intelligence Agency.

In the Eisenhower years, with the cordial support of General Andrew Goodpaster (the staff secretary) and the special assistant for national security affairs, a close relationship had developed between the Science Advisor and the NSC. This all changed with Kissinger as the Assistant for National Security Affairs under Nixon. With Kissinger there was great growth of the NSC staff, including its own science and technology capabilities, and the Science Advisor's relationship with the NSC was virtually cut off. This relationship needs rebuilding and statutory recognition. Further, the relationship with the Office of Management and Budget also needs strengthening. In accordance with Public Law 94-282, the Science Advisor is directed by the President to participate in budget recommendations to OMB. Indeed, the Office of Science and Technology Policy could be mandated to review all R&D budgets before they go to OMB. This authority should be limited to *total* budgets; the parts should be negotiable. The prestige and the value of the Science Advisor could further be enhanced by an annual report. This could be a major policy document like the President's annual Economic Report to the Congress, prepared by the Council of Economic Advisers. It would set the tone for science and technology policies.

FOCUS ON NATIONAL SECURITY

While the Science Advisor's advice to the President should be multi-faceted, including agriculture, arms control, energy, environment, medicine, space, transportation, and societal matters, and, in part, international in character, in keeping with international agreement, the primary focus should be *national security*. Again, this focus became confused in the mid-1960s as it came to relate to the Johnson's Great Society programs. Under Carter, the Science Advisor was virtually cut off from national security affairs. This was, in part, due to the hostility of much of the science community to the Carter Administration. This had been a hostility begun in the Johnson and Nixon years, abated briefly in the Ford Presidency; revived in the Carter years, it continues in the Reagan period, making, for example, the American Physical Society an unwitting ally of Common Cause in opposition to the Strategic Defense Initiative (SDI).

There has been some restoration of the primary security focus under Reagan. In keeping with this mandate, the Science Advisor needs ready access to the President, the Cabinet and Cabinet Councils, the National Security Council, the Office of Management and Budget, the Departments of State and Defense, and the President's Foreign Intelligence Advisory Board. Without losing this primary focus, he needs effective liaison to other departments including Commerce, Education, Health and Human Services, and Interior and with the National Science Foundation, National Academy of Sciences, National Academy of Engineering, and National Research Council.

Clearly there is needed as Science Advisor a person of stature and breadth of vision, respected in the scientific community, but not that community's servant. Clearly science advice and politics, like oil and water, do not mix. Edward E. David, Jr., member of the present White House Science Council, who had been Nixon's Science Advisor, warns that the 1973 abolition of the old Kennedy-created Office of Science and Technology had resulted from its strident advocacy. "From a purely operational viewpoint, offices with an advocacy rule and an outside constituency to serve can exist within the White House structure only so long as the cause is popular as perceived by the political arm of the White House." Dr. David concludes, "the Science Advisor's post must be filled by a statesman rather than an advocate, if it is to remain viable."[2] Franklin A. Long, who had served on the ideal President's Science Advisory Committee of the Eisenhower-Kennedy years, emphasizes the critical need for a science and technology "advisor that is close to the President and on whom he can have a special sort of reliance. Eisenhower," he concludes, "was the first President to face up to this."[3]

One of the great challenges of the remaining period of the Reagan Administration and that of Reagan's successor will be a rebuilding of trust between the Presidency and the science community. This is pointed out in the Op-Ed essay by Secretary of Defense, Caspar W. Weinberger, in *The New York Times*, August 21, 1987; therein, Weinberger counters the American Physical Society's "pessimistic study of SDI . . . containing important technical errors," and asserts, "By making perfection the enemy of the good, critics consign themselves to a fantasy-land."[4] Clearly a common ground for the common good must be rediscovered between the Presidency and large segments of the scientific community.

By contrast with the scientific community's cordial support of the President in the Franklin Roosevelt, Truman, Eisenhower and Kennedy Administrations, in the Johnson, Nixon, Carter and Reagan Administrations, that community's cordiality was replaced by sharp criticisms. While seeking to better relations with the university scientific community, other constituencies must also be considered. In terms of research and development, industry plays a major role. Indeed where the US government was in the past the largest R&D participant, today it is industry which expends 54% of all R&D funds. Keyworth and Graham, as Reagan's Science Advisors, have sought to emphasize the industry, university and government joint roles in an effective triad.

A DEPARTMENT OF S&T

Periodically, over the past century, beginning with the Allison Commission in 1884, Congress has given consideration to establishing a department of science and technology. But as William Carey, former Executive Officer of the American Association for the Advancement of Science, has observed, such a department would more likely end up a "Noah's Ark" than an effective national policy instrument. Fortunately many agencies like NASA and NSF cherish their independence to such an extreme that they would effectively block creating this conglomerate.

What is needed, then, is *not* a new department of science and technology but a better defining of the Office of Science and Technology Policy on the one hand and the President's Science Advisor on the other. The 1976 legislation had recognized that what had been created was not the final solution. It had encouraged additional study. But it had provided a long list of needs as Congress perceived them beyond the President's requirements for science and technology advice. It had the President's Advisor wearing several hats, advising the President, advising the Congress, and coordinating the execution of policy.

The President's Science Advisor should not be the creation of Congress. Congress now has its own sources of science advice. The Science Advisor needs access to the President. His primary responsibility should be that of the President's Science Advisor. To do this effectively, he should be in the White House as the Assistant to the President for Science and Technology. Essentially this had been one of the two principal 1950 recommendations of William T. Golden, the other being the President's Science Advisory Committee. The two proposals had not set well with the White House staff in 1950, and they would probably arouse similar opposition today. As George Reedy, veteran of the Johnson Presidency, expressed it in 1970, "to bring more assistants into the White House . . . increases the amount of jostling; the amount of elbowing; it places the 'rite of the long knives' on continuous run. . . . Believe me, any White House assistant with any sensitivity could

. . . write about the court of Paleologus in Byzantium; all he would have to do would be to . . . look up a few Greek names."[5]

Although White House staff resist all boarders as interlopers, there is something special in their resistance to Science Advisors. As Professor James Everett Katz has observed, "The chronic resistance of White House staff to Science Advisors and staffs is motivated by more than considerations involving power politics. The scientists are seen as being overspecialized and their advice as too esoteric and narrow for the Presidential level."[6] In 1957, seven years after Golden's recommendations, it had taken Sputnik and Eisenhower to get a Science Advisor on the White House staff and to constitute the President's Science Advisory Committee. Eisenhower was deeply grateful for the help of the Science Advisor and the PSAC in the last three, the most productive years, of his Presidency. Reflecting on it he concluded, "Without such distinguished help, any President in our time would be, to a certain extent, disabled."[7]

President Kennedy, on the advice of Professor Richard E. Neustadt in 1962, had supported the legislation which moved both the Advisor and the PSAC out of the White House and into the Executive Office of the President. There the Advisor, no longer a member of the White House staff, was subject to Senate confirmation. There the Congress could call the Advisor to appear before its committees. Senator Hubert H. Humphrey, chairing a subcommittee of the Government Operations Committee in 1958, had been miffed when Eisenhower's Special Assistant, James Killian, refused on grounds of Executive privilege to testify.[8] Since then, Humphrey was determined to get the Science Advisor out of the protective position of the White House staff. In part, Neustadt and Kennedy had succumbed to these pressures. This had deeply troubled both Kennedy's Science Advisor, Jerome Wiesner, and the committee. They recognized that the 1962 statute had both removed them from proximity to the President and had given them a second master, the Congress. The Science Advisor was no longer a member of the White House staff, being instead in the Executive Office of the President.

"THE RITES OF THE LONG KNIVES"

The real deterioration of the relationship of the Science Advisor and the PSAC with the President had set in under Johnson and climaxed under Nixon, with the discontinuance of the PSAC and the relegation of the Science Advisor to the National Science Foundation as an additional duty of the director. Reedy's 1970 warning about the "rites of the long knives" had been fulfilled. However, the politicization of the PSAC after 1965, with open criticism of President Johnson's and then President Nixon's Vietnam policies, had been a contributing factor. So also had been the leak to the press of PSAC criticism of the Administration's plans for a supersonic commercial aircraft. The criticism had contributed to Congressional rejection of the proposal. Moreover, Office of Management and Budget Director Roy Ash had made a convincing case for OMB's own science advisory role and that of the Department of Defense.

Realizing the mistake that had been made, Gerald Ford, only five days after he became President, instituted measures to restore a science advisory system in the Executive Office of the President. It was not, however, until May 11, 1976, that he could sign into law Public Law 94-282 establishing the present mechanism, the Office of Science and Technology Policy with a Director who would also serve as Science Advisor to the President. The fact that the Advisor is not on the White House staff posed no problem in the Ford Administration. In accordance with the President's desires, the Chief of Staff, Richard B. Cheney, gave him access to the President. Accessibility became a problem in the Carter and Reagan Administrations, however. Although being on the White House staff is no guarantor of accessibility, it helps. Moreover, it would remove the Advisor from the dilemma of serving two masters, the President and the Congress.

In essence, the position of Assistant to the President for Science and Technology would be parallel to that of Assistant to the President for National Security Affairs. Further, his relationship to the Office of Science and Technology Policy would be analogous to that of the Assistant for National Security Policy to the National Security Council. Just as the Assistant for National Security Affairs is the staff director of the President's National Security Council, the Assistant for Science and Technology would be the staff director of the Office of Science and Technology Policy. Reinforcing this relationship, the Assistant for Science and Technology should be made a statutory advisor to the NSC, like the Chairman of the Joint Chiefs of Staff and the Director of the Central Intelligence Agency. All of this would restore the primary focus of the Science Advisor to national security affairs. Other aspects of OSTP activities could be more effectively shared with the National Science Foundation. The President's Science Advisor should be relieved of peripheral time-consuming tasks such as chairing the Federal Coordinating Council for Science, Engineering and Technology and the Intergovernmental Science, Engineering and Technology Advisory Panel. With the support of the Office of Science and Technology Policy, the President's Assistant for Science and Technology should have a defined role in approving overall R&D budgets before they go to OMB. In point of fact it is OMB through the budget process which currently controls science policy. (To the credit of Keyworth, Reagan's Science Advisor (1981–85), he did secure substantial R&D increases for science and technology).

Essential to a better science advisory system is restoration of the President's Science Advisory Committee which the Assistant to the President for Science and Technology could chair. In its re-emergence it might more appropriately be re-designated as the President's Science and Technology Council. By its nature, like the NSC, it is only advisory. The term "council" is more prestigious than "committee." Neither the Council nor the Assistant to the President for Science and Technology would require Congressional approval. The National Science and Technology Policy, Organization, and Priorities Act of 1976 should be amended, however, with decreased extraneous responsibilities for the OSTP Director and increased for the National Science Foundation.

THE CHAIR

As to the Chairmanship of the Science and Technology Council, there are two schools of thought. When Eisenhower constituted it as the PSAC, his old friend, Isidor Rabi, had proposed an independent chairman, rather than the President's assistant. Nonetheless, Rabi had graciously stepped down as Chairman of the predecessor ODM Science Advisory Committee to make way for the Killian appointment. There is much to be said, however, for the independent chairman appointed by the President. Coincidental with the increasing problems of the PSAC in the Johnson Administration was the 1966 enactment of the Freedom of Information Act. In order to ensure the confidentiality of the deliberations of the proposed Council, a new Executive Order may be required.[9]

The proposed Council should be smaller than the original PSAC, perhaps no more than a dozen of the nation's most distinguished scientists. The present White House Science Council has done laudatory work, but it is the Science Advisor's council, not the President's. Among all of the former Science Advisors to the President, there is agreement that, whatever the exact name, the President's Science Advisory Committee should be restored. William T. Golden, the person who originally proposed such a body thirty-seven years ago[10] recently put the case for the restoration most eloquently when he wrote:

> . . . the President (and the Executive branch) needs the enrichment of novel, creative ideas and diversity of viewpoint on science and technology as aids to comprehensive consideration, policy formulation, and decision-making on a wide range of subjects relating to peaceful, to military, and to arms limitation and conflict-resolution issues. He does not now get much advice. What he gets is opinion from a Science Advisor who is limited by White House staff. The Science Advisor is served by his own small staff and by his self-selected White House Council, which does not have the stature of Presidential appointments nor the inspiration and effectiveness that would come from direct access to the President.

Mr. Golden concludes, "President Reagan, his successors, and the Congress should consider this salutary and relatively simple alternative to the illusory benefit and assured turbulence of a Department of Science and Technology."[11]

In the event President Reagan needs further counsel as to the wisdom of this recommendation, he might ask his good friend, Prime Minister Margaret Thatcher. She followed the Eisenhower (Golden) model with an advisory body of scientists and engineers appointed by and reporting directly to the "iron lady" herself. In addition, she has her Science Advisor, Dr. Robin Nicholson, who, together with the advisory body, is credited with much of the resurgence of British science, technology and industrial growth in the 1980s.

Here in the United States, both the needs and the opportunities are un-surpassed, requiring the "bully pulpit" of Presidential leadership. The President needs his own assistant unfettered by the myriads of little detail currently encompassing his advisor in OSTP. The President needs his own council, which can offer new vistas of leadership, restoring American competitiveness and American advance on new frontiers of science and technology. This is something to ponder when we consider the words of the Constitutional Framers 200 years ago: "To promote the Progress of Science." As we begin this third century under the Constitution, we shall either move ahead or move behind. Science and technology do not stand still. As Hamilton expressed it, three years after the ratification of the Constitution, this "merits all the attention and all the zeal of our Public Councils; 'tis the next great work to be accomplished."[12]

NOTES

1. Harold C. Syrett, ed., and Jacob E. Cooke, assoc. ed., *The Papers of Alexander Hamilton*. 26 vols. (New York: Columbia University Press, 1961–1979), X, p. 291.
2. Edward E. David, Jr., "Current State of White House Science Advising," in William T. Golden, ed., *Science Advice to the President* (New York: Pergamon Press, 1980), p. 55. See also Edward E. David, Jr., "Science Advising and the Nixon Presidency," in Kenneth W. Thompson, *The Presidency and Science Advising*, 3 vols. (Lanham, MD, 1986–87), III, p. 230.
3. Franklin A. Long, "New Perspectives in Science Advising," in Thompson, *op. cit.*, III, pp. 60–61.
4. Caspar W. Weinberger, "It's Time to Get S.D.I. Off the Ground," *The New York Times*, August 21, 1987, p. A27.
5. R. Gordon Hoxie, *The White House: Organization and Operations* (New York: Center for the Study of the Presidency, 1971), pp. 173, 182.
6. James E. Katz, "Organizational Structure and Advisory Effectiveness: The Office of Science and Technology Policy," in Golden, *op. cit.*, p. 241.
7. Dwight D. Eisenhower, *The White House Years*, Vol. II, *Waging Peace, 1956–1961* (Garden City, New York: Doubleday & Company, 1965), p. 224.
8. A Hunter Dupree, "A Historian's View of Advice to the President on Science: Retrospect and Prescription," in Golden, *op. cit.*, p. 179.
9. Harold C. Relyea, *The Presidency and Information Policy* (New York: Center for the Study of the Presidency, 1981).
10. Detlev W. Bronk, "Science Advice in the White House: The Genesis of the President's Science Advisers and the National Science Foundation," *Science,*

Vol. 186 (October 11, 1974), pp. 116–121; reprinted in Golden, *op. cit.*, pp. 245–256.

11. William T. Golden, "A Department of Science: An Illusion—PSAC: A Prescription," in Thompson, *op. cit.*, III: 117–119.

12. Hamilton, *Papers*, X, p. 291.

The Sublimation of the Science Advisor

Thomas H. Johnson

Scientists tend to be optimistic about the power of their own rationality. This is a direct—and very natural—consequence of their choice of profession, since science is founded on the conviction of the power of reason to understand the world. But the rationality of science and the rationality of scientists are different matters, and one does not necessarily imply the other. If scientists occasionally confuse the distinction in a flattering way, it has also become fashionable in recent years to use the negative sense of that confusion as a weapon to criticize science itself.

This confusion also colors the question of science advice to the President. Scientists believe, sometimes passionately, that the President should listen to what they have to say. But this is not the same thing as saying that the President should understand the opportunities and limitations posed for national policy by modern science and technology. Science policy cannot be separated from the politics of science, which, by common presumption, it is meant to regulate, but the higher aim of science advisory is to include scientific considerations in other kinds of policy decisions. Discussion by scientists of the roles of science advisory tends to be either Utopian, according to which everything that has happened has been insufficient to the desideratum of a rapt Presidential audience; or Arcadian, according to which things have been terrible recently, but the recreation of the President's Science Advisory Committee (PSAC) would restore the proper harmony between science and government.

Clearly the Utopian view is unrealistic. What is wrong with the Arcadian view is not that it is unlikely to occur, or that a new PSAC would be a bad

Thomas H. Johnson, Lieutenant Colonel, US Army, is Professor of Applied Physics and Director, Science Research Laboratory, at the US Military Academy, West Point, New York. His doctorate is in applied physics from the University of California at Davis/Livermore. Colonel Johnson was Special Assistant to the President's Science Advisor (1981– 82), and has served in the US Air Force Weapons Lab, the Lawrence Livermore National Lab, and US Defense Nuclear Agency.

thing, but that the traditional combination of Science Advisor plus PSAC deals rather poorly with two serious dilemmas inherent in our process of science advisory. It is important to understand the distinctions on which these dilemmas are based if we are to find a truly effective process.

DIFFERENT FUNCTIONS

The first dilemma arises from the fact that we wish the White House's apparatus for science advisory to perform two functions simultaneously, and that those two functions logically place contradictory requirements on that apparatus. In general, the functions can be summarized as the normal business of the Office of Science and Technology Policy (OSTP) and the occasional business of providing direct advice to the President.

OSTP itself performs quite a diverse collection of roles within the Executive Office of the President (EOP), in the Administration at large, and outside the government. The Director of OSTP makes frequent public appearances and statements to represent the Administration's policies, and performs both ceremonial and negotiating functions with other nations. The staff does many such things at lower levels, and its "answering the mail" functions take up about half its time. Within the government, OSTP coordinates technological issues among agencies, solving interagency technical problems before they must be raised to the President. In addition to brokering difficult issues, the Office attempts global planning of policy on matters as diverse as technology transfer, science education, and industrial competitiveness. Probably the most important staff role of OSTP is to assist other EOP staffs—the Office of Management and Budget and the National Security Council—to deal with issues involving technological judgments.

All of those OSTP roles require that the Office have an expert staff with diverse backgrounds. Even more important, they require a strong Director of the Office. The staff members, if they are competent, will be operating on their own all over the government, and occasionally in the public eye. Unless the Director has a firm hand on their agendas and their goals, the result will be chaos. Someone has to be responsible, and with so many activities of such potentially great import, that responsibility must be vested in the Director for both coordination and control.

But the Director of OSTP is also the Science Advisor to the President. In the latter capacity he is called on to assist on decisions in matters of even greater moment. In these matters the responsibility of judgment is not his, but the President's. It follows that the *sine qua non* of this role is the provision of advice based only upon evidence, and the clear demarcation of the limits of evidence and knowledge. Most difficult, he must frequently make judgments on the scientific components of larger questions without allowing those judgments to be colored by his views on the larger questions. Here, we cannot escape the problem of the rationality of the scientist himself. Like everyone else, he has prejudices, he has ambitions, and he makes mistakes. For this reason, C. P. Snow has argued powerfully (in *Science and Government*) that no head of state can afford to get his science advice from a single man. He must draw on some larger body of scientists in the hope that, when there is a diversity of judgment, he will be able to perceive the irrelevant influences. That is, the President does not simply find the average view or the best compromise among his advisors; rather, he uses their diversity of views and his knowledge of them to peel away the personal from the objective, and to assess the differing qualities of expertise and judgment. That is the sort of wisdom leaders must have.

The mere existence of some committee for science advisory does not solve this problem. The White House Science Council (WHSC) reports to the President only through the Science Advisor himself. The PSAC, although in theory directly responsible to the President, in practice saw him seldom and then largely ceremonially; they, too, depended on the Science Advisor. The corporate opinions represented in both WHSC and PSAC reports did not provide the President with any measure of the real diversity of opinion, far less of its sources, and the Science Advisor himself could act as a further filter.

Thus neither the WHSC nor the PSAC has been actually independent of the Science Advisor, or has been able to provide the President with a direct and diverse source of expertise. The case of President Reagan's strategic defense speech is frequently raised to argue a difference between the bodies; instead, it illustrates their similarity. The Science Advisor but not the Council was consulted, but the latter had in fact studied the relevant technologies and rendered a report. Simply replacing the WHSC with the PSAC would not have changed this situation in the least.

The dilemma here is the necessity simultaneously to provide strong leadership for OSTP and diverse resources of judgment for directly advising the President. The details of organization of the Office and of whatever advisory body exists matter a great deal, because those details determine who actually makes decisions and who is actually consulted, especially when much is at stake.

DIFFERENT STANDARDS

The dual foundations of scientific methodology are freedom and skepticism. Ideally, both information and individuals are free: Anything that is known will be shared, and anyone has the right to work on any problem. Further, it is not merely the right but the duty of scientists to be skeptical of evidence, of the interpretation of evidence, and particularly of conclusions. Anything may be legitimately questioned, and the natural presumptions are ones of doubt and independence, rather than of belief and adherence. Certainly there are many deviations from those values in practice: Because of competition, scientists refuse to share evidence readily; because of limitations on resources, scientists cannot choose their problems with real freedom; and because of social rigidity, one scientist's criticisms may matter much more or less than another's. Yet, in the end, evidence and predictive power do provide objective criteria, and scientists are educated to a culture whose belief in these values is extraordinarily strong and pervasive.

In government science advisory, however, the inherent values run almost precisely counter to these methodological values of science. First, advisors are, in general, asked to deal only with parts of problems. Scientific advice is sought on that aspect of a decision perceived by the official to require special expertise; the rest of the matter he reserves to himself, and the definition of the two regimes belongs to him. Second, advisors have in general neither authority nor responsibility. Even when their views are publicly identified with themselves (as in Presidential Commissions), they are free neither to choose the problem, make the final decision, nor act on the results.

Third and most important, advisors cannot insist on their public right to demur. On commissions and other public studies, one can ensure that one's views are expressed, either within the report or in a separate section of minority views. But in providing assistance directly to the President, particularly on important or pressing matters, advisors must be content to depose, and then remain silent as a decision is made and action taken. No responsible official can afford to have advisors who insist on always being right, or who feel that their responsibility to the public includes pronouncements of their dissent from some decision they would prefer to have seen made otherwise.

The dilemma here is thus the proper role of scientists whose best attributes result from their devotion to candor and skepticism, yet who must be asked to remain publicly silent concerning matters in which they consider themselves to have inside and expert knowledge.

DIFFERENT LOYALTIES

There are no straightforward solutions to these dilemmas. Once cannot satisfy the requirements of different functions by creating separate agencies and expect those agencies to work independently and well when their success depends on influence, and when all that influence stems from the same source of authority. An unhealthy competition would be inevitable. But if a single organization is required, how does one keep the OSTP role from becoming dominant?

Neither can one hope to indemnify the entire process against the failings of particular personalities; the design of any organization can only limit the extent of the impact. Thus, for instance, a good advisory apparatus will not assist a President who will not listen; nor can it cope completely with an ambitious or sychophantic Science Advisor; nor can it protect the President from self-righteous or disingenuous committee members. And it cannot satisfy committee members who honestly reckon that their advice has been misjudged.

SUGGESTIONS

I haven't a clean solution to all these problems; I doubt seriously that there is one. I shall merely make a few suggestions for patching up the existing process, in hopes that the advisory mechanism can evolve toward more satisfactory forms:

• Retain the Director of OSTP and make him simultaneously Chairman of the White House Science Council. Do away with the single title of Science Advisor to the President.

• Recharter the WHSC so that all its members become, in effect, Science Advisors. First, reduce its membership to roughly a half-dozen, so the President can get to know the members well. Second, have them all meet with the President on a monthly basis. Third, have the WHSC continue to conduct on-going and special studies with subpanels directed by one or two WHSC members and comprising distinguished scientists of varied backgrounds. Subpanel chairmen report to the President or to appropriate Cabinet officers. Fourth, allow the WHSC agenda to be set both by the President and by the members.

• Make it clear to members that the increased role of the WHSC carries real responsibilities similar to those of all government officials. That is, opposition to any policy position is permitted until the President has committed to a decision; after that, one is not free to criticize policies publicly. If this responsibility seems less than one's perceived duty to present opposing views publicly, one should first resign from the government.

• Recruit senior academics or industrial scientists as Associate/Assistant Directors of OSTP to avoid the creation of a staff eager to dominate the agencies or to carve out great careers. The honest broker function of OSTP is lost completely, particularly within the EOP, if the staff is easily perceived to have such goals. Similarly, neither the Director nor the other WHSC members can act as lobbyists for the interests of the scientific community. OSTP may assist the agencies in preparing cases for research support, but the personal access of the WHSC to the President is predicated on the absence of special interest, even when the members themselves believe that interest to be completely benevolent.

This program isn't likely to satisfy anyone in prospect. Scientists will feel that their lobbying access is reduced in terms of great budgetary stringency, particularly if the science advisory is explicitly decoupled from lobbying; but Cabinet officers and the multitudinous officials of the EOP will feel that, with the WHSC actually meeting with the President, scientists are being given too much access. The only people who might like it in the end are the Presidents, who, as far as I can tell, have always had difficulty finding any advisors who only talked about what they knew, and who then really knew what they were talking about.

Science Advice During the Reagan Years

G. A. Keyworth II

The election of 1980 reflected a shift in the national mood about government. In part, the voters were responding to a sense of national drift, and they chose someone who reembraced the idea of an assertive America and who wouldn't hesitate to use his Presidential podium as a "bully pulpit." To a lesser degree, the voters were responding to Ronald Reagan's campaign to reduce the role of a government that, to many Americans, had simply become intrusive. The combination of expectations—renewed economic and military strength, along with diminished government—set the stage for a new set of issues to dominate the political agenda.

If there is any single point that most distinguishes hypothetical from meaningful Presidential science advice, it is that national issues shape the agenda for everyone in the White House. Anyone who ignores that reality consigns himself and, more important, the expertise he can draw on, to the back benches. The two driving priorities that confronted me when I arrived in the White House in the spring of 1981 were rebuilding national defense, and strengthening the basis for US industry. There was a constant pressure to reexamine all federal programs in light of those priorities—something that turned out to be particularly pertinent for research and development.

Many in the science community were vocally dismayed that it took nearly five months into the new Administration until a Science Advisor was named. Many of them were additionally perturbed to learn that someone had been chosen from outside the traditional ranks of the science policy debate. I suspect many misread the implicit message. The Administration was com-

George A. Keyworth II was Science Advisor to President Reagan and Director of the Office of Science and Technology Policy (1981–85). Previously, he served at Los Alamos National Laboratory (1968–81), and became Director of its Physics Division. His doctorate from Duke University is in nuclear physics. Dr. Keyworth now heads his own consulting firm, the Keyworth Company, and is a Director of Hewlett-Packard Company.

mitted to a path of fundamental change, and it sought a new perspective of the role of government in science and technology. Many members of the Administration even saw the views of the scientific community as deriving from a political perspective that ran counter to the national sentiments that elected Ronald Reagan President. But, in the end, their choice reflected no more than the reality that science advice was seen as one of many inputs to decision-making and that whoever provided it would function as a member of the President's staff—not as a representative of the science community.

In terms of its relative priority on the national agenda, I think science wound up as one of the major winners during the Reagan years, with federal support for university basic research having nearly doubled by the early part of the second term. But the path was rocky, and one might not have predicted such an outcome in 1981. An interesting footnote is that, even after five years of conspicuous growth in federal support for basic research, many in the science community—perhaps even a majority—still held on to the preconception that the Administration's science policy was simply to "cut research" and that the President himself was anti-science. That perception was fueled early in the Administration when, indeed, science was caught up in a poorly thought-out effort by David Stockman, then Director of the Office of Management and Budget, to cut all "non-essential" federal programs by 10%. But that impetus, which was little more than a brief tactical foray by the zealous Stockman, was quickly reversed, primarily because the President himself believed in the importance of science and technology as essential drivers for both economic and national security. The program that emerged was one of selective growth for basic research at the same time that development programs, especially in energy, were scaled back. The persistent, almost reflex insistence within the science community that the Reagan Administration was anti-science—even anti-progress—which continued to be a constant drumbeat throughout the President's first term in office, served only to tarnish the credibility of a community for whom objectivity was expected as a professional requisite. Even the earnest efforts of my predecessor, Frank Press, who sought, as President of the National Academies of Science, to bring reason and facts to the debate could not restore full credibility to a community that was in such disarray.

EROSION OF EXCELLENCE

There were serious issues, other than funding, that I felt needed the objective participation of the science and engineering communities. In particular, I feared a diminishing standard of excellence in research and among researchers. There was creeping into US science a tolerance of mediocrity that threatened to undermine the very advantage we had enjoyed in science since World War II.

That situation was alarming for several reasons. One, our success in frontier research was a significant contributor to our national self-image as the Free World's leader. Two, we depend on science and technology more than any other country to maintain our well-being. Three, and perhaps the most serious consequence of all, such a trend would lose us the ability to draw our best young talent into science and engineering. And, four, it was going to be extremely difficult to build support for strong federal science programs unless those programs were of unblemished excellence.

I would pinpoint the sources of that mediocrity as: (1) the increasing isolation of scientific research from its application, and (2) the tacit belief that science, as a public priority, was above scrutiny. That latter perception led to and continues to promote arguments for funding science as a percentage of the federal budget. That attitude was displayed when the debate about priorities for funding biomedical research was reduced to counting the number of new grants the National Institutes of Health would make. All in all, the attitude reflected a complacency that could hardly withstand the kind of budgetary scrutiny that I saw developing.

My own early contribution to the unease in the community came in my first speech after being named Science Advisor. With much more forethought than some critics believed, I suggested that the federal government had an obligation to make choices about what it would support. I wanted particularly to make the point that mediocrity would flourish from the sentiment that support, once begun, would merely continue as an entitlement. We had allowed a situation to evolve where unproductive research was nonetheless allowed to limp along. Why not, I asked, be as forthright about reducing support for the less promising, more dormant areas of science as we were eager to increase support for others? After all, that's precisely what graduate students do in choosing their area of specialty.

Admittedly, at the time—mid-1981—we were girding for what looked like a future of severely constrained growth for federal programs, and a pruning of the withered branches would be a sensible means of assuring that the most important programs could continue to grow. The most visible application of pruning (some might extend the metaphor to call it "clear-cutting") was a consequence of the Administration's intentions to abolish the Department of Energy, redistributing its essential programs and eliminating many of the programs that had grown so fast during the 1970s and had so little *raison d'etre* in the 1980s. While that goal was never achieved, nonetheless we were successful in reducing the federal money being spent on energy R&D programs that had evolved without much attention to their ultimate economic feasibility, such as synthetic fuels. In particular, it was the savings in those energy development programs that enabled us to redirect substantial funding into basic research. The vigorous growth of the National Science Foundation, for example, was in part a result of pruning on a grand scale.

THE PUSH FOR BASIC RESEARCH

It is worth remembering that in 1981 the economy—peoples' visceral concerns about jobs and future, not economists' intellectual concerns about deficits—was a major election issue, and the Administration was looking for ways to rejuvenate American industry. Another major election issue was defense—and Ronald Reagan was swept into office as one of the most pro-defense Presidents of the century. In both cases technology and its antecedent, science, were seen as critical, incompletely utilized ingredients in raising our competitive profile. Those were among the most pressing policy issues confronting the Administration, and, consequently, they became dominant issues in OSTP. For that reason, we focused particular attention on the physical sciences and engineering.

In the case of industrial competition, we knew our industries had to continue to move up the "value-added" ladder in production as a way to differentiate ourselves from others, and especially as a means of countering the advantages of lower-priced labor and lower-cost financing that many foreign competitors had. That meant using what we had that they did not (our science), and that meant moving the results of research quickly from the lab to the marketplace. In defense, we were (and are) facing the consequences of continuous and aggressive Soviet growth in both strategic and conventional systems. By 1980, we were outmanned in both areas, and it was clear that future prospects would require us to find ways to get higher leverage from our spending on defense if we expected to counter the overwhelming Soviet numerical advantage. Again, that meant taking advantage of technology and, particularly, of our superior industrial capability to produce weapons and defenses that could exploit technology.

But it was becoming increasingly obvious that our national capabilities in engineering in particular, as well as in many areas of the physical sciences in some areas, had not kept pace with the demands we were placing on them. In 1981, we were facing serious shortages of engineers to meet existing industrial and defense needs, never mind to support growth. The exciting industrial climate was pulling engineers away from universities at all levels—both the B.S. engineers who might have, in the past, stayed in school to get advanced training, and their professors as well, who were being offered not only competitive salaries but, far more important for many, better opportunities to do research in industry. The engineering schools were facing an unprecedented increase in undergraduate enrollments at the same time they were contending with faculty shortages that looked like they might stretch on for a long time.

Among the agencies that supported basic research, we focused particular attention on the National Science Foundation because it, alone among the agencies, directs virtually all its funding to support basic research in universities. That put NSF, even though it is a relatively small agency, in a position of great responsibility, because it was on the line for maintaining the quality of what is one of the country's most important assets—our research universities. We saw NSF in three ways. First, and most important, funds spent through NSF not only supported some of the best science, but they also enriched the learning environment for graduate students, the best of whom often were supported for work on NSF-funded projects in the course of doing their dissertation research. Second, the rapid growth in NSF's budget was a symbol of Administration priorities for physical sciences and engineering and for highlighting the importance of universities. Third, NSF turned out to be an ideal breeding ground for new programs. (I give particular credit for making NSF into such a place to Director Erich Bloch, who came to NSF from an industrial career and managed to coerce a great deal of creativity and energy out of an initially suspicious, but eventually enthusiastic staff.)

The PYI Program

Three programs in particular illustrate the role of NSF. The earliest of them was the Presidential Young Investigators (PYI) Program. This was developed essentially as an incentive to attract more of the best new engineering Ph.D.s to teaching jobs, as well as to retain young engineering faculty who were tempted to move to industry. We also had two other objectives. One was to use the new program as a way to encourage better university-industry ties—a campaign that we waged throughout my time in OSTP (and one whose success has been so broad and pervasive that it must be attributed to changing times more than to changing federal science policy). To that end NSF offered a base grant to the PYI, then added matching funds to it based on the PYI's success in attracting non-government support. The other objective was, frankly, to let the PYI program symbolize our priority for university research.

The reception and implementation of the program was a telling illustration of the difficulty of coming into government and trying to change things. In spite of the widespread agreement on the problems that the PYI program was designed to address, we had a running battle with the bureaucrats at NSF whose instinct was to try to fit the new program into the mold of older ones. That resulted in an attempt to spread the awards out broadly over all engineering and science disciplines as if it were simply an add-on to the general funding pot for NSF. That, of course, was counter to its purpose of addressing the problem of shortages of engineering faculty. The other problem stemmed from the same misconception. In spite of explicit guidelines to the contrary, we were seeing the early PYI award recommendations heavily biased toward the oldest possible "young" faculty allowed. In one of my early encounters with the monumental resistance that tends to characterize a government bureaucrat's response to change, the NSF program managers were simply relabeling grants to younger researchers as PYIs, rather than using that program to attract fresh new Ph.D.s into academe. Both of those problems were eventually worked out, and NSF, when it began to get feedback from the outside world and to see the positive influence the program was having on young faculty, adopted its purposes with enthusiasm. (The PYI program became a source of increasing satisfaction when I could not visit a university campus without having a least one PYI seek me out to make sure we in Washington knew how effective the grant was in getting a new researcher's work off to a fast start.)

The second program at NSF is one that has begun to have profound effects on the way basic research is done in the United States. Interestingly, its origins were in engineering. In the early 1980s, both the industrial and academic engineering communities were closing in on a common conclusion—that there was an unacceptable gap between what was being taught in the nation's engineering schools and what was needed to accommodate to the rapid pace of change in technology. A strengthening of curricula in basics—physics, chemistry, biology, mathematics—had proven inadequate to prepare today's engineer to confront the information age. Having early decided to make this a high priority, we concluded that a multidisciplinary environment was essential to educating today's engineer. And, equally important, participation in that environment by industry researchers would cause it to adapt to change more rapidly.

Engineering Research Centers

The Engineering Research Centers were a response to that conclusion. Their immediate impetus was a briefing on the subject of "Computers in Design and Manufacturing" that was made to my office by the National Academies' Committee on Science, Engineering, and Public Policy in the fall of 1983. The presentation crystallized an idea—in effect, that the times were intellectually ripe to take on engineering research of a new level of complexity, and that this was an effort that would be best served by pooling the resources of both universities and industry. We were particularly struck by the dual advantages of bringing to bear superior combinations of research capabilities and of creating a wholly different educational environment for engineering students. That educational environment would be characterized by something common in industry, but, curiously, often missing from universities—problem solving.

Interestingly, it was some of the "second-tier" engineering schools, those with traditionally strong ties to industry, that were actually leading the way in trying to make this transition. The late George Low, then President of Rensselaer Polytechnic Institute, and the guiding force behind the COSEPUP briefings, was a forceful proponent of this problem-solving approach, and his efforts at RPI and with COSEPUP may turn out to have been among the most important stimuli for academic change in the 1980s. Participants from industry also brought important contributions to these deliberations. I well recall Jim Lardner, fresh from immersion in the John Deere Corporation's effort to improve their manufacturing processes, describing the future manufacturing engineer as "a decision node in a stream of information—from product conception to delivery."

Within a matter of months after that fall briefing, the National Science Foundation, working closely with the National Academy of Engineering, had put together a radically different kind of research support program at NSF. It would ask universities to propose the establishment of new, discrete Engineering Research Centers (ERC) that would be oriented around multidisciplinary approaches to solving complex engineering problems, that would reflect a mutual (i.e., university and NSF) commitment to long-term pursuit of the research, that would seek not only industrial financial support, but also industrial participation in the research and even in setting the goals for the center, and would establish an environment for training students.

As might be expected, there was apprehension on the campuses about this new mechanism. Some concerns stemmed from no more than resistance to change. (After all, university campuses are traditional, and traditionally resistant to change.) Some came from perceived disruption of trusted funding channels. Still more arose from fears that an increased presence of industry would distract attention from academic pursuits. (And industry had done little in recent years to merit more respect for their long-term vision of investment in R&D.)

But a more legitimate worry among some derived from realization that a disciplinary structure facilitated regulation of academic standards. That is, whereas a Physics Department knew what criteria its graduates should satisfy, how could similar assurances be met in a Composite Materials Center? Graduate education in the United States remains the world's premier; would the introduction of multidisciplinary centers threaten erosion of that excellence? Our intention was to build on that excellence, but we proceeded with caution, not knowing with certainty the full implications.

In any case, it was quickly evident that such concerns were not serious. The ERC program, under which a handful of new centers would be started each year beginning in 1984, struck a deafeningly responsive chord in the engineering research community. We decided to begin the program with about a half dozen centers—enough to assure variety in approaches, but few enough to assure extremely high quality among what we expected to be the models for many more to follow. To say the competition was vigorous would be an understatement. There were 148 proposals, from 106 different universities, requesting more than $2 billion—all competing to be among the first six centers. That was followed in the second round, the next year, with again more than 100 proposals.

In retrospect, I believe these centers, in similar form, would have emerged within a few years even without the presence of the federal program. That conclusion is based on two intertwined developments.

One was the obvious need and opportunity for universities to take a more active role in a national problem that they could hardly ignore—the direct challenge to American leadership in industrial technology by foreign companies and the threat to our economic health that resulted. The "land of opportunity" was no longer able to ensure that the next generation would have a better life—or as good employment—as the previous generation had enjoyed.

What had been glibly-mouthed pronouncements about improving the speed with which industry was able to capture the fruits of basic research became grim imperatives, and there was a mutual attraction between industry and universities as they saw a remarkably large area of overlap in their interests and competences. It should also be noted that the sometimes fiercely defended arms-length between large segments of academia and industry was a phenomenon peculiar to the 1960s and 1970s. It reflected the rapidly growing role of the federal government in providing research support to the universities, which made academia much more independent of industrial support than before (and eventually very dependent on government). But probably as strong a force for change was that the universities could no longer ignore something that had been obvious to industry, and more recently to academia's paying customers—the students. The divergence of interests, coupled with the deterioration of universities' facilities—to which both the federal government, by slowly funding in the 1970s, and universities, by consistently giving lower priority to facilities and equipment than personnel (always in the self-deluding hope that "next year" would see a windfall to correct the situation), contributed—brought matters to the point where universities were poorly preparing students for the worlds in which they would be working.

The second reason reflects changes in research itself. These were vividly brought home to us during the early 1980s in the course of those COSEPUP studies prepared by the National Academies. The shift, simply, was that many of the most important scientific questions were becoming "systems" problems. That is, knowledge and tools had matured to the point where it was possible to ask—and to have answered—very broad questions about nature. But such questions could neither be framed nor answered within the confines of traditional disciplines. It almost didn't matter what area of science or engineering was being assessed, because the conclusion was the same: The time was ripe, the tools were ready, and the community was poised to mount multidisciplinary efforts.

That conclusion, in one form or another, was the recommendation of about half the COSEPUP overview groups during the first three years. They ranged over agricultural plant science, neuroscience, materials science, cognitive science and artificial intelligence, engineering design, biochemistry, biotechnology process engineering, polymer composite materials, atherosclerosis, and parasitism. What we were seeing was evidence that the traditional disciplinary, or departmental, structure for organizing research in universities was increasingly imposing constraints on the kinds of problems that could be taken on effectively, and the response, whether stimulated by the federal government or not, would be the development of new multidisciplinary mechanisms for doing research.

By 1987, the idea of these centers for research has diffused well beyond NSF. Not only are most other federal research-supporting agencies developing their own versions as a means of addressing the... own missions, but similar plans are being made by state governments (which see these centers as major means for stimulating industrial progress in their neighborhoods) and by industry (which recognizes the value of centers as places for faster translation of knowledge into applications and for multiplying their own R&D efforts).

One of my colleagues in OSTP coined an apt descriptor of his considerable experience with government's all-too-typical contribution to programs conducted in the private sector. He often referred to "the dead hand of government," meaning that Washington had compiled a remarkable record of draining the innovation and creativity out of promising ideas, largely through the arrogance of remote managers who assumed they knew best about how the world ought to run. We bore that image in mind in the course of developing and launching many new programs, and that is why we so often tried to allow maximum flexibility on the part of the people doing the work, responding to changing climates in both science and industry, to set goals and take responsibility for getting there. That is why, from the start, the federal government restrained its usual enthusiasm for fine-tuning the structure and requirements for the centers it was encouraging and supporting. One of the particular consequences has been the stimulation of strong industry-university partnerships through shared interests and tasks.

BIG SCIENCE/BIG TECHNOLOGY: SSC AND THE NASP

In my earliest conversations with the President, he made it clear that he saw science and technology as a means for man to shape his own destiny. An eternal optimist, he expected his Administration to pursue policies that would reflect the importance of science to the nation. He was referring to two kinds of importance. One was the clear-cut relation between science, technology, and economic progress. His goal was to find ways to encourage and to allow American industry to be stronger competitors in the international market—not by manipulating trading conditions, but by making American industry better. And one of the cornerstones would be building on American science and speeding its translation into technology. He was far too experienced, however, to place much credence on such well-intended, but ineffectual, mechanisms as the Stevenson-Wydler mandate. Instead, he believed in a more passive role for government, encouraging the bringing together of provider and user. I have already discussed some of the policies that were built on that premise. But he also was referring to something grander as well. His vision of America was one of growth and of unlimited potential (his "morning in America" theme captured far more hearts and minds than did ideas like "limits of growth"). America's leadership in science and technology was among the most enduring post-war symbols of confidence in the future and opportunity for individual advancement through ability and effort. He saw science as future-oriented and as a powerful beacon for a democratic people—and he was naturally drawn to scientific and technological projects that captured and communicated that spirit, much as the Apollo project did twenty years ago.

But big projects do not, simply by virtue of their size, play that role, and often they convey the wrong symbols to the nation. My personal view was that Apollo was a superb example of a technology project that symbolized optimism and expectations for the future. On the other hand, I felt that the Space Station that was proposed in the early 1980s suffered from lack of purpose (and, concomitently, lack of definition) from the nation's point of view, and I argued strongly against it. After delaying a decision for three years, the President eventually endorsed the concept in the foremath of the 1984 Presidential election, although without requesting the requisite additional funding.

My opposition to that project, coupled with my opposition to hurried new construction of fusion research facilities and continuation of the Isabelle accelerator at Brookhaven National Laboratory, might have led some to think I had a bias against big science. Instead, I believe strongly in the symbolic value of choosing a large goal, then mustering a large effort to stretch for it. Perhaps the most notable example is the Strategic Defense Initiative, which is certainly ambitious, but was something we decided to proceed with, once we were satisfied that it was both feasible from a technological point of view, and immensely important from a defense point of view.

But two other projects very clearly illustrate the kinds of pursuits that the Administration believed embodied this idea of taking bold steps to build on what we do best, and in doing so to illuminate the possibilities that the future holds.

High Energy Physics

High energy physics has been a symbol of our commitment to fundamental research. And the promise it offers today, in pointing the way to a Grand Unified Theory for treating all natural forces in a single theoretical framework, is indicative of an intellectually dynamic field. A large measure of our broad scientific prowess has been stimulated by our pursuit of such fundamental science, whose mysteries have consistently attracted some of the brightest young people. But in 1981 we perceived a problem that threatened the continued vitality of that effort.

There is a price—a heavy price—that the nation is asked to pay to support leadership in physics. In the early 1980s, it appeared that we were not getting our money's worth. The construction of the Isabelle accelerator at Brookhaven National Laboratory was seriously off-schedule because of poor management, manifested as unsolved problems with the technical design. By 1981, it appeared that Isabelle would, in any event, be delayed beyond the point when it would be able to make a significant contribution to America's leadership in elementary particle physics. Yet there was immense reluctance on the part of much of the physics community to bite the bullet and stop the project. Much of the argument for continuation of Isabelle stemmed from a sense of "equitable distribution" of national resources. With major experimental facilities already in operation at Stanford in California, and at Fermilab in Illinois, Isabelle, in New York, was to be the East Coast's physics facility. And proposed additions and upgrades to both SLAC and Fermilab would provide important new experimental facilities—and quickly— yet Isabelle continued to drain off the funds available for high energy physics.

Isabelle was not a science issue anymore, but a political issue. So I decided to approach it that way. In 1982, we invited members of the High Energy Physics Advisory Panel (HEPAP) to the Department of Energy to a special Sunday morning meeting in Washington. I asked them to address a single issue: What step would ensure US leadership in high energy physics at the end of this century? Their recommendation was to build the Superconducting Super Collider, the largest purely scientific project ever proposed.

To their credit, the physicists, when confronted with that issue, were willing to take a stand—to shut down Isabelle in order that the SSC might be pursued. I felt comfortable in urging that action for two reasons. One, Isabelle was a loser. It was wasting taxpayers' money, and it was beginning to cast a shadow of failure over other parts of science. Two, I felt confident, even in 1982, that a campaign for the SSC would eventually succeed, because it was riding a tide of increasing public priority—and profile—for science and technology.

Once the physics community had agreed on the priority for the SSC, the Department of Energy began the study and design work that led, in 1987, to the President's decision to recommend construction of the SSC. The price tag—on the order of $5 billion—is steep, whether or not the cost is shared by other countries, and even amortized over the long construction period it represents a substantial increment to the amount of money currently spent on high energy physics. But it is important to remember that this is not simply an allocation of money to a sub-discipline of science. The SSC, somewhat like the space program, is a national effort, one that restates our determination to be the center for scientific thought and creativity. The pay-off will come not so much from quarks as from inspiration that spreads widely and from a continuing flow of the brightest young people in America into pursuit of science and technology—because the nation will have made it such a high priority. For my fellow scientists, that justification may seem vague, yet I believe it is the exactly the kind of thinking that won the SSC political support.

The National Aerospace Plane and SDI

The second example is of a project just as grand, though its goal is new technology. In 1984, I became aware of a program of classified research that had been going on for some years to develop a new kind of liquid hydrogen-fueled hypersonic airplane and which was reaching the stage where major decisions would have to be made about its future. This airplane, now known as the National Aerospace Plane, represented an astounding break-through in technology, because it combined both a Mach 20-25 airplane (five times faster than the "advanced" designs being touted by SST advo-cates of the day) and a direct flight into orbit of an air-breathing vehicle. The implications were stupefying—an airplane that could fly halfway round the world in two hours, and an airplane that could propel itself into orbit and deliver payload at a tiny fraction of the cost of today's rocket-propelled spacecraft.

In the spring of 1985, we faced a situation where we could have continued the development secretly (a policy that we would have no difficulty in get-ting strong military support for) or announce the project's goals publicly. It was an easy choice for most of us. I first described the plane in Congres-sional hearings in the spring of 1985 (hearings that had been called to drum up support for a much less ambitious, Mach 5 supersonic transport), and by the fall of that year it had been elevated to a fast-track program aiming at a prototype airplane in the air by the mid-1990s.

The reasons for going public with this program—and, by early 1986, the newspapers were filled with pictures of the President holding a model of the plane—were these: First, it was practical to expose much of the program without compromising those key aspects of technology that should remain classified. Second, at a time when American industry was battling foreign competition on most sides, this gave us a chance to demonstrate that one of our supreme industries, aerospace, was in a strong position to continue its leadership in the design and manufacture of aircraft. We served notice to the rest of the world that we intended to stay number one. Third, again we wanted to take advantage of an opportunity to display our ability to remain competitive by building on science and advanced technology.

There were those who said that the goal was too ambitious, that we would be better off biting off a smaller portion and, say, aim for a more readily attainable, liquid methane-fueled, Mach 5 supersonic transport. There are also those who say we ought to wait and see if someone else offers to build the SSC, or see if new superconductor technology might allow us to build it differently a decade from now. And there are those who recoil at the technical challenge of the Strategic Defense Initiative and plead instead for us to give it up. The position of the Reagan Administration has been consistent in each case—choose a worthy, achievable goal, and make the commitment to doing it. These decisions involved more than science advice. I could—and did vehemently—attest to the feasibility of each of these endeavors. But the President's decision took into account much more.

I believe these three large efforts—the SSC accelerator, the NASP, and the SDI—were supported by the President, in spite of his desire to diminish federal spending, because they captured three essential—and intertwined—national commitments. The SSC would focus a national commitment to fundamental research, while the NASP and the SDI would capture similar commitments to using technology for both economic and national security. While each project had its critics, many of whom feared the diversion of funds away from their own specialties, the President envisioned these projects as tools for leadership—components of his vision of a rejuvenated America. The fact that much of the scientific community failed to perceive this larger picture stands, I believe, as testimony to their diminished role and credibility in formulation of national policy.

R&D IN DEFENSE

When all the rhetoric and bombast from pro-defense and anti-defense forces are set aside, the primary reason for the rise in defense spending in the first Reagan Administration was that our relative strength *vis-a-vis* the Soviets had deteriorated, in some cases alarmingly and, without a change in priority, that trend would continue. The Administration believed that the weakening was already at a point of danger, and that it was being exploited by the Soviets in their efforts for global expansion during the 1970s.

This concern was not unique to the Reagan Administration. There was a new dimension to the East-West balance of power, however. Although Soviet military strategy was based in part on superior numbers of troops and weapons, they had persisted in diminishing the West's "force multiplier." This force multiplier, achieved by applying the West's stronger industrial, economic and technical bases to weaponry, had been, along with nuclear deterrence, a foundation of US and NATO strategy. The Soviet Union was simply developing better, more sophisticated weapons, and building them at a higher and more sustained rate than the West was. During the years of Detente, the West reduced its output. So the numbers game simply had gotten much worse. (As President Carter's Secretary of Defense, Harold Brown, noted: "When we build, the Soviets build; but, when we don't build, the Soviets still build.")

It was clear, by the late 1970s, that the Soviets were narrowing the technology gap that underlay the West's confidence in its force multiplier and even its nuclear deterrent. Their progress in aircraft, armor, air defense, intelligence, and communications, and in highly accurate "counter-force" missiles was rapidly bringing them qualitative parity and, in some cases, superiority. The crowning blow was in submarines: In 1981, we were assured that US superiority in submarine survivability represented a ten-to-fifteen year lead; by 1984, after the unexpected introduction of several new classes of highly sophisticated, and much quieter, Soviet submarines, that lead was reduced to five years. And many experts doubted that we retained any lead at all.

Erosion of our military technical edge, combined with the Soviet's numerical superiority, became a disturbing and difficult-to-dispute picture. Among the early responses in 1981 were programs to speed the introduction of new generations of weapons that would restore some measure of technological edge. But we found ourselves drawing on far-from-new designs and technologies in our haste to repair a bad situation. The MX missile was an essentially modern missile, but its basing modes became so varied as we wrestled with the growing Soviet counter-force arsenal that it suffered diminished political support and credibility. The B-1 was a resurrection of a 1960s program that had endured many delays, and the Air Force was divided in its appreciation of "Stealth" technology.

Although there were some notable exceptions, overall our defense systems suffered from many of the same ailments that we would come to identify in our industries within a short time: complacency, failure to speed new technologies into new systems, poor regard for building quality and reliability into the basic design, and slow learning of the lessons that our competition could teach us. In each case we badly underestimated how well our competitors could do when they focused their efforts on catching up with us.

OSTP was necessarily and, I believe, productively involved in many of the early policy decisions about modernization of strategic forces, and later about strategic defense. From assessing the enduring value of Stealth technology (of which I was, and remain, a firm supporter), to submarine survivability, to serving as a key spokesman for both "Densepack"—an Administration-backed basing mode for the MX missile—and the SDI, evaluating and advising on defense technology was an important activity in OSTP. Although that role has long been an underlying responsibility of the Science Advisor, it served to separate me further from my own scientific community that had become essentially pacifist in its attitude toward defense.

The anti-defense sentiments in the academic and scientific community had contributed to the host of major impediments to taking advantage of what should have been our greatest asset—US science and technology—for defense. There is obvious irony here, in light of the decisive edge that technology demonstrated during World War II and the leadership that defense played in supporting the post-war growth of our finest research universities. The Office of Naval Research, for example, predated the National Science Foundation, and until the debacle of the Mansfield Amendment, it and other defense agencies were among the most important and valued sources of support for university science. But as a result of various events—notably the Vietnam War—defense and universities withdrew from each other's company.

The consequences were twofold. First, defense lost the participation and thinking of many of the country's best scientific and technical minds. Second, defense found that it was running into problems finding enough good scientists and engineers to meet its needs, both in the uniformed services, and in civilian government laboratories as well.

The latter problem was primarily one of supply and demand. With the nation producing too few technically trained people, government found itself unable to compete with private industry for the people it needed. A special subcommittee of the White House Science Council, under the chairmanship of David Packard, set in motion several means of addressing that immediate problem by trying to establish greater flexibility in determining pay levels for technical personnel, in effect creating a fast track for advancement for those people who are willing to remain in government service. (David Packard later chaired the President's Commission on Defense Reform, an effort whose far-reaching consequences are likely to drive the defense debate well beyond the Reagan years.) The complaints we heard from the government bureaucracy about those approaches were similar to the complaints that universities heard from professors of poetry when they tried to set up differential salary scales as a means of attracting and retaining engineering professors: In effect, give the same special treatment to everybody! Universities and government will both find the battle to be worth fighting, but the longer-term solution for both will be to increase the supply of technical personnel in response to sheer demand.

The Defense Department had, in the 1950s and 1960s, been a dominant player in supporting the production of scientists and engineers, just as it had been dominant in supporting university basic research. In the 1970s, with DoD and academia finding each others' company less congenial, there was a progressive underinvestment by DoD in the production of both knowledge and personnel. And the civilian agencies did not pick up that slack. The results of that underinvestment have already been discussed (*e.g.*, deterioration of facilities, inadequate graduate student and post-doctoral support).

I call it underinvestment because DoD continued to expect to draw on the output of universities to meet its needs. Very early in the Administration, my office began to call attention to the disparity and, in light of the very large growth beginning to take place in DoD R&D, to encourage DoD to focus more attention and funding on university basic research. I think we made some progress, but not as much as we would have liked. Notwithstanding budgetary intentions, much of the funding for basic research is discretionary within DoD, and it often suffered in the face of urgent needs in applied research or development projects that cropped up. Still, the net direction was positive, and such new programs as those for university-industry cooperative projects, modeled on NSF's Engineering Research Centers program, began to reinstitutionalize support for academic institutions. We can expect the recent excitement about high-temperature superconductors to be another spur to better DoD-university linkages, because any successful applications program will require a strong basic research base to support it.

So to some extent the solution to this problem will be stimulated by perceived needs and opportunities. But I believe the real solution can only be achieved through changes in attitude. No amount of lobbying by the Science Advisor or some advisory body can force a new pattern on DoD. Nor do I point to DoD as the only party that has to change. The problem is not one-sided, and the academic community will have to show its own willingness to become involved in the debate and to suggest ways in which cooperation can be improved. Chasms between academia and defense come and go. Just as we are seeing a growing enthusiasm on campus for getting reinvolved in helping the country deal with problems of industrial competitiveness, we can hope to see similar reawakening of a sense of responsibility about defense—from the points of view both of responding to external threats and of having more voice in determining policy.

One point regarding defense R&D needs some additional exploration—the degree to which defense and civilian R&D are or are not mutually exclusive. It has become fashionable to discount the size of our federal investment in defense R&D when discussing the problem of industrial competitiveness. In a turn of a phrase the world's largest R&D enterprise becomes just one of the pack, and our competitors are extolled for their greater wisdom in concentrating R&D dollars where it will have commercial payoff. I disagree with that conclusion. Much of the R&D supported by DoD has application in both sectors, and in many of the most exciting areas of technology it is DoD that is supporting the most advanced work. It is true that we fail to take good advantage of some of it, just as it is true that we fail to take good advantage of the world-leading basic research done in our universities and federal laboratories. The solution is similar in both cases: Improve the transfer of knowledge, technology, and experience. The approach in the case of universities has been such mechanisms as engineering research centers, science and technology centers, industry-university cooperative programs, etc. The approach in defense R&D should be to bring more of the predominantly commercial businesses into defense work where they can not only breathe a greater degree of marketplace productivity into defense manufacturing, but can also participate in developing the newest technologies and speed their adaptation to commercial applications.

One of the more frustrating issues I carried away with me upon leaving OSTP remains technology transfer. The important content of this phrase lies, I believe, in the competitive advantage that can be captured by better teamwork between those conducting research and those developing products, or weapons. The distracting content, however, lies in that strong vestige of isolationism that surfaces as sheer paranoia about utilization of our technology by the Soviets or by our commercial competitors. And it has been the Department of Defense that has led this unconstructive chorus. Proof of Soviet exploitation of US technology is beyond dispute. And that is nothing new. The problem lies instead in our failure to exploit that technology for our own defense and competitiveness. That key to survival has been hampered by the DoD's effort to restrict technology utilization in the civilian sector, by its emphasis upon secrecy, and by its limitations upon research. And I believe the lack of familiarity with things technical, within both the Executive and Legislative branches of our government, has compounded the problem and impeded development of teamwork. This will doubtless be an important arena for future Science Advisors.

FORCING ADVICE ON THE PRESIDENT

The dilemma of the modern American Presidency has been discussed many times by other people, and I need not do more than acknowledge the impossibility by any single person filling all the roles that the public expects of him. President Reagan has often been criticized for lack of attention to detail. Yet his predecessor was equally criticized for obsession with detail. Let me merely state that my role was dramatically simplified by the President's remarkable ability to synthesize information—to develop a clear picture out of apparently overwhelming complexity. I mention this because it offers some contextual basis for the comments to follow.

I strongly believe that Presidents do and will continue to need direct, personal advice on scientific and technical matters that come before them. And I doubt that such advice can come solely from those whose primary responsibility lies outside the White House. Yet there remain so many misconceptions about how "the White House works" that it is difficult to maintain an objective discussion on how Presidential science advice can best be provided. First, people often focus, mistakenly in my opinion, on "access" to the President as the central measure. Assuredly this is important, but how that access is achieved is a far more central issue. And it is not mandated, whether by law or by physical proximity. It is achieved only by a common agenda and by genuine contribution. A President must accept input from the public, in all the ways that input manifests itself, because we are a democracy. But the White House is not a democracy, and the President selects from whom he will receive advice. Many scientists see the Science Advisor as their ombudsman. Yet nothing could be farther from the truth. The Science Advisor is merely a member of the President's staff—not a representative of the scientific community.

The government has more than 3,000 advisory bodies, most of them composed entirely of people from outside government. And there are many such mechanisms to insert scientific and technical opinion. But today's Presidents must struggle to maintain their own agenda, and so they will strive to seek counsel and input on issues that are high, and current, on that agenda. And that simple reality has often been overlooked when Presidential advisory mechanisms, such as the PSAC or the present White House Science Council, are examined. At any time there are unlikely to be more than a handful of pursuits that can engage the President's attention (and even they are regularly preempted by crises of all kinds). That means science issues have to have broad impacts to become Presidential issues. Many times an issue will have to wait, to gather momentum, before it has a broad enough impact to find its way onto the Presidential agenda. Environmental issues were premature in the 1960s; in the 1970s, they became important. The word "premature" is not a subjective measure nor is it an indication of value. I use it merely as a statement of political priority. We scientists often find this mismatch frustrating, but our predictive accuracy has not generated much confidence in the body politic, either.

The President's job, of course, is to set forth policy on a broad scale; others attend to the details and to the implementation. This does not mean that the President is not party to a regular stream of decisions about the implementation of science policy, but for the most part he chooses from options that are put forth by those to whom he has delegated responsibility. The allocations in his annual budget, for example, are largely decided in meetings with the Director of the Office of Management and Budget, agency heads, and White House staff. One of the Science Advisor's jobs is to focus on the major elements of the budget to make sure it reflects both the President's guiding policy (i.e., our emphasis on physical science and engineering in the form of new and expanded programs in the National Science Foundation or Department of Energy) and that it responds to research opportunities that have been identified in working with the science community. It is critical, therefore, that the Science Advisor have means of getting broad and frequent input from elements of the science community on the most important issues he is likely to have to deal with. It was not unusual, when I occupied that office, to have a dozen meetings a week with groups of scientists who had important issues to discuss.

My point is simply that the science advisory mechanism is most active— and most important—at the White House senior staff level, not at the Pres-

idential level. I point this out in partial response to those who would dictate
their own preferred mechanisms for making sure the President gets advice.
A favorite one is the reestablishment of the old President's Science Advisory
Committee, which would set up a dozen or so distinguished scientists who
would conduct studies on important science issues and report to the President
on their findings and recommendations.

PSAC has an interesting, even productive, history, but it ultimately self-
destructed when it failed to see its role in the same light as the President
did. That is, it began to be seen by the President as a group that was using
its position as a platform to advocate political actions—and to advocate them
not to the White House, but to the Congress and to the public. People complained when PSAC was abolished that it was performing a valuable role,
but that missed the point. Once it began to act as a "national" science advisory panel, it no longer played a valuable role for the President. There
are ample opportunities, such as in the National Academy of Sciences or
through powerful scientific organizations, for the science leaders to propose
policy. But common sense tells us that Presidents do not take kindly to
having their policy choices preempted by the very people who are supposed
to be helping them. And Presidents know, as does the public, that scientists'
opinions can be useful when focused on science issues, but that they abuse
a public trust when they stray from their areas of expertise and try to disguise
their actions by wrapping the cloak of science around them.

I have heard the arguments of those who would restore the golden age by
restoring PSAC. But I sense that much of the real motivation for such proposals is the barely concealed desire of the science community to tell the
President what it thinks is important—and, if he won't heed their advice,
to tell the Congress or the media or anyone else who will listen.

There is a very high level of frustration in science advising, and that holds
equally true at any level of government. Scientists are particularly ill-equipped
for negotiating, or even accepting, the compromises inherent in making public policy. They are often little more objective than the political ideologues
who are determined to see right and wrong answers to problems; effective
politicians—indeed, effective national leaders—are more likely to think in
terms of workable and unworkable approaches. One of the most consistently
offered bits of advice I gave to scientists, in particular when they were ad-
vocating some heartfelt new project, was to stay away from legislators and
politicians. All too frequently, the carefully orchestrated and negotiated plans
that we had made with key members of Congressional committees were
derailed by a delegation of scientists (especially my fellow physicists) who
could not resist going in person to explain why their pet project should take
precedence over defense, or Social Security, or Medicare, or whatever seemed
to be lower on their personal ranking of societal needs. Most frequent on
the list was the number of projects "that would require just the funds for a
single B-1 bomber."

Notwithstanding these potential traps in offering special status to scientists as advisors, I concluded early in my tenure as Science Advisor that we needed some kind of formal body of scientists to assist us in evaluating major issues of enduring importance. The White House Science Council worked very well—for three reasons. First, we made it clear from the start that this was to be advisory to me and that our deliberations were not to be discussed outside. Second, we appointed people who could work well together, people whose ideas could provoke strong argument but who could leave their personal agendas at the door. I made no attempt—or excuses about it—to assure that the WHSC was politically or even disciplinary balanced. (That did not make it any less intellectually independent or argumentative.) Third, I set the overall agenda based on my needs in advising the President.

Interestingly, few members of the WHSC objected to the lack of public visibility, and most were scrupulous in preserving the forum as one where we could say anything in the course of discussions without fear of it being repeated elsewhere. The WHSC dealt with some highly sensitive defense issues, as well as with more general issues such as funding for basic research and linkages to American competitiveness. I brought proposals to them, usually early in their formation, and I asked them to criticize or to propose alternatives. Or sometimes I simply shared the problems as they were developing and asked them to ponder them along with me. In turn, they told me when they did not have sufficient information to respond, and we would arrange for experts to come and talk to them before proceeding with discussion. The WHSC's importance was often unappreciated outside of government, but it had an enormous impact on the formation of science policy. The members were willing to forego visibility in return for a chance to be deeply involved in that process. They quietly made critical contributions to the shaping of the Administration's emphasis on basic research (including the Engineering Research Centers), and of the Strategic Defense Initiative and of strategic modernization, as well as dozens of other issues. Although the WHSC also conducted several major studies that eventually resulted in formal reports—such as the study of the federal laboratories and the study of the health of universities, both under David Packard's leadership—I always felt their private deliberations were by far the more important contribution they made to policy formulation.

Perhaps the most important measure of the WHSC's value came, however, not from me, but from the President. They became an accepted asset to the White House. They resolved major internal controversies (*e.g.*, an OMB-DoT debate over how to begin development of a new air traffic control system), had entire Cabinet meetings dedicated to their views (*e.g.*, an assessment of the role of federal laboratories in American science and technology), and even assisted in preparing major Presidential pronouncements (*e.g.*, SDI). But the trust they earned was by no means independent of the low profile they maintained. I only regret that their own satisfaction had to be largely vicarious, because implementation of their counsel often occurred months later and without attribution.

If one wants a model for what kind of science body can be effective in helping the White House develop policy that involves science, the WHSC is one that has tried and proven in today's climate. But I predict that, should a new President be persuaded that he needs a PSAC again, and if it is configured to emulate its predecessor, it will eventually meet a fate similar to its predecessor. Those who are willing to take that risk should bear in mind the cost of failure as well—the damage to the ability of the science community to influence policy as it should. That would be tragic.

TIME FOR A SCIENCE DEPARTMENT?

One fact underlies the debate about the role of the Science Advisor to the President—and of the auxiliary advisory mechanisms that the science community mounts: The Science Advisor has no line authority within the government. That is, I believe, an asset in performing the duty of advising the President. And, for that important function, the roster of key White House staff should continue to include a Science Advisor. But it is a strong deficit in implementing science and technology policy. Because such policies pervade so many of the nation's higher priorities, such as defense and economic competitiveness, I believe the time is ripe to develop a Department of Science and Technology. For a nation in which fully half of total R&D is provided by government, and much more of the basic research, maintaining the present priority below that of transportation, labor, etc., is surely anachronistic.

As a nation, we are perhaps more dependent on our strength in science and technology for economic growth and for national security than anyone else. Our problem is not that we do not adequately support research and development. I see, instead, that much of our difficulty in maintaining priorities and in speeding the use of science and technology for our own benefit stems from the subordinate role of science and technology in many of the government bodies responsible for its health.

The science community reacts strongly to suggestions that many of the science and technology supporting functions in government be collected into a single agency. They know that, particularly in science, there is no monopoly on foresight, and we need to offer multiple sources of support for research. That's a way to guarantee creativity and to prevent all proposals for support to have to pass through a "mainstream" strainer. I would join them in insisting that we maintain diversity in whatever funding system we have. But I wish, too, that they could see how tenuous is our present ability to maintain a coherent R&D program. I have myself been appalled at how little opportunity there is to defend priorities in the end. The science and technology elements of a major agency budget are often small in comparison to other operations, and they may barely surface for discussion in the ultimate budget decisions in the White House.

Priorities for science and technology should be thoughtfully established—and maintained. That would be greatly enhanced if the major science programs were brought under one managerial roof and, particularly, if the budget for large portions of science and technology were self-contained. Then, at least, tradeoffs would be made within a coherent policy.

But more important, when science and technology become the major concerns of a department, it not only makes it possible to plan more intelligently for long-term opportunities, but it makes it possible to create means for more coherent policies to speed the application of science. No one any longer would argue that we can continue to allow nature to take its course in allowing new knowledge to diffuse into applications, especially into industrial applications. Yet much of government science has traditionally operated with little regard for how it relates to the underlying industrial strength of the country. For example, I believe we would not have found ourselves, in spite of the billions we have spent in support of higher education in this country, with a situation where we have neither the laboratory facilities nor the faculty to provide superior technical educations to many of our students. Yet we have. Nor do I believe, under a better managed system, we would have allowed to develop a situation where American industry views cooperation with government laboratories as a descent into a bureaucratic quagmire where they face very real risks of losing more than they might gain.

I do not think there is likely to be a better time than the next few years to discuss this issue seriously, because the nation is becoming sensitized to the importance of science and technology in world competition. And, frankly, I believe the changes that have occurred in government science policy in the 1980s have created a markedly improved climate for looking seriously at what next steps to take to institutionalize those changes. With all respect to my fellow contributors to this volume, I would find such a debate—one which brings in the real-world perspectives of industrial and academic leaders— to be of far more interest and importance than extended discussions of traditional science advisory mechanisms among a small band of policy afficionados.

Science Advice for the President: Reflections from a Long Look Backward

Robert N. Kreidler

Nikita Khrushchev got me my first real job. Although I had been earning a paycheck since the age of 14—in high school, college, graduate school, and the Marine Corps—it was not until the fall of 1957 that I entered the world of the seventy-hour week. That fall, I was catapulted out of the Marine Corps and into the White House as abruptly as Sputnik was rocketed into orbit.

The assignment: Staff Assistant to the country's first Special Assistant to the President for Science and Technology and to the President's Science Advisory Committee as a whole.

The President was Dwight D. Eisenhower. The Special Assistant was James R. Killian, Jr., on leave from the Presidency of the Massachusetts Institute of Technology. The Staff Assistant—myself—was a fellow whose principal qualifications for his first job apparently were his pending employment with the Bureau of the Budget, some up-to-date security clearances, and great eagerness to start a career somewhere in government. More to the point, perhaps, was James Killian's willingness to place a bet on me. In any case, my nearly five-year stint on the White House staff included work for two Presidents—the first a Republican, the second a Democrat—and three Presidential Science Advisors. It was a heady experience, as first jobs go.

I describe these circumstances at the outset, so that readers may appropriately discount my still-firm conviction that there should be a Science Advisor at the right hand of the President (and a President's Science Advisory Committee chaired by that Science Advisor) to help him grapple with the scientific and technical complexities of matters of paramount importance to

Robert N. Kreidler, President of The Charles A. Dana Foundation since 1982 and former Executive Vice President of the Alfred P. Sloan Foundation, served as a Staff Assistant to the President's Science Advisors and the President's Science Advisory Committee in the Eisenhower and Kennedy Administrations from 1957–1962. For part of that period, he also served as the first Executive Secretary of the Federal Council for Science and Technology. He is a Trustee of Barnard College.

the nation. In the pages that follow, I describe the experiences that shaped that conviction and try to suggest how the important roles of the Science Advisor and the Committee may be strengthened and shortcomings and pitfalls of the past be avoided.

I cannot begin, though, without mentioning that a special issue of *Technology In Society* published in 1980 and also in book form, entitled "Science Advice to the President,"[1] is a treasure trove of insights into the value of a Science Advisor to the President and a President's Science Advisory Committee. Represented in that issue are all but two former Science Advisors, several former members of the Committee, high-level staff officers from both the Executive and Legislative branches of the federal government, scholars, historians, business executives with government experience, and President Gerald R. Ford.

In his introduction, the guest editor, William T. Golden (who, not so incidentally, first recommended the appointment of a Presidential Science Advisor in 1950), sets forth his own conclusions, noting that they are "consistent with the preponderant views of the other authors":

1. Science and technology advice are essential to the President as indispensable ingredients in a broad panoply of policy-making on domestic and foreign issues . . .
2. Congress also needs advice on scientific and technological matters . . .
3. The value of a Science Advisor to the President has been amply demonstrated in practice . . .
4. . . . The President's Advisory Committee should be reestablished . . . [and] the members of PSAC should be Presidential appointees . . .

In light of these conclusions, so forcefully reasoned and expressed, and buttressed by an extraordinary array of perceptive and candid essays, I am left free, here, to take largely for granted the need for the Special Advisor and Committee and concentrate, instead, on some personal reflections as to strengths that should be reinforced and weaknesses that should be avoided in re-establishing a strong science advisory apparatus to serve the President.

I say "re-establishing" because, despite the creation by law in 1976 of an Office of Science and Technology Policy within the Executive Office of the President, with a Director appointed by the President and confirmed by the Senate, science advice for the President has not been restored to the level of effectiveness that existed in the Eisenhower and Kennedy Administrations. For several reasons, symbolized by the fact that the Director of the Office of Science and Technology Policy reports to Congress as well as to the President, this system lacks the defining characteristic of the Special Advisor/Committee arrangement: *i.e.,* that special, direct, and essentially "personal" channel to the country's scientific community at large that gives the President an independent base of scientific and technical advice.

1957: THE CLAMOR FOR THE QUICK FIX

With the launching of Sputnik in the fall of 1957, and the ensuing public alarm that the nation was losing scientific and technological ground to the Soviets, came Congressional clamor for a Department of Science and Technology. Its proponents argued that only a full-fledged department, headed by a secretary with a seat in the Cabinet, could commandeer the resources for support of science and technology that were scattered throughout government. Only a full-fledged department, they said, would have the visibility and political clout to increase those resources sufficiently to enhance the nation's security, strengthen the economy, and restore "American leadership in science."

Counsel to the contrary, although quieter, was ultimately more persuasive. It argued that, because science and technology permeate our national life— and, in consequence, the missions of almost all agencies of government— they could not be squeezed into a single department without seriously compromising their role in an extremely wide array of government agencies and activities. In any event, President Eisenhower did not accept the prescription of a Department of Science and Technology for the sudden ills of the time. He moved swiftly to appoint James Killian as his personal Science Advisor and transferred the Science Advisory Committee from the Office of Defense Mobilization to the White House. The General had decided to take personal charge of the situation.

The winds of more dramatic change then subsided, at least, somewhat, but they periodically blew with renewed political force through the rest of Eisenhower's term in office. Both Killian and his immediate successor, George Kistiakowsky, were impelled to demonstrate that means other than a Cabinet-level department could strengthen science and technology in service to the government and the nation.

A CROWDED AGENDA

When Killian entered the White House, there were many problems more pressing—if not more distracting—than opposing creation of a Department of Science and Technology. These included, of course, helping the President respond to the urgent political necessity to get a US satellite into orbit— and quickly. The political pressure mounted when the first Vanguard attempt failed. More fundamental was the need to advise the President on the longer term organization of the nation's outer space program: For example, should it be under military or civilian direction?

Another paramount need was to advise the President about ways to bring greater coherence, order, efficiency, and economy into a host of national security and defense programs: the ICBM, the ABM, national security intelligence (especially communications intelligence and some exotic new high-technology intelligence capabilities), and the endless stream of advanced research programs advocated by the military services—the nuclear-propelled aircraft being a flamboyant example. These and a host of other national security issues converged on the Executive Office of the President, calling for major Presidential decisions and, in turn, on the advice Killian and Kistiakowsky provided for Eisenhower and on that Jerome Wiesner provided for Kennedy. While some of these issues are now dealt with elsewhere in government, many still require wise and experienced advice to the President himself.

On the domestic front, both the Science Advisor and the Committee confronted issues perhaps less dramatic, but no less compelling. Many went to the taproot of the strength in American science: support for basic research, the professional training of scientists and engineers, reform and modernization of science curricula in our secondary schools or at even lower levels, and financial assistance for higher education more generally. Other issues concerned the vitality of the scientific and technological infrastructure: identification and nurturing of neglected fields such as oceanography, developing the atmospheric and environmental sciences, dissemination of scientific information, modernization of scientific facilities and instrumentation, and revitalization of government laboratories from the National Bureau of Standards to the US Coast and Geodetic Survey—in some cases involving a redefinition of their missions.

This panoply of national security issues and domestic concerns confronted the Science Advisor and, to a lesser degree, the Science Advisory Committee, with their most persistent challenge, one most troubling to the President: how to set priorities among these concerns in a highly charged political atmosphere.

It was crucial that the Science Advisor and his small staff forge good working relationships, both with key individuals in the operating departments and agencies of the government and with senior staff officers in the Executive Office of the President—principally the National Security Council and the Bureau of the Budget (now the Office of Management and Budget or OMB). In any organization, there is an inherent tension between staff functions (in this case, represented by senior staff in the White House and the Executive Office) and line functions (represented by the departments and agencies). In the federal government, if only because of its vast size, these tensions are pervasive and powerful and an advisor to the President—whose value and loyalty to the man and the office require that he provide independent, disinterested advice—finds himself at their epicenter. All three Science Advisors whom I served handled this difficult situation adroitly. For Killian and Kistiakowsky, it was perhaps most difficult because the Eisenhower White House was a thoroughly staff-oriented operation. At least by contrast, the John F. Kennedy White House was free-wheeling, with distinctions between staff and line responsibilities not infrequently blurred or ignored.

Walking the tightrope between staff and line responsibilities was most difficult for the Science Advisor when it came to providing advice on priorities. Some members of the scientific community tended to view the Science Advisor as a friend in court, who should press the case for greater support, less government regulation, and more enlightened policies for strengthening American science. The poorer scientific agencies of government looked to the Science Advisor for help in increasing support for their programs or, which was sometimes true, restoring their faded luster. The larger purchasers of research and development, such as the Department of Defense, the military departments, and the Atomic Energy Commission, saw him at times as a useful ally, at times as a potent nuisance, and at times as irrelevant. The National Institutes of Health tended to ignore the White House and the Executive Office, preferring to do business with old friends of biomedical research in Congress, most notably Representative John Fogarty and Senator Lister Hill.

PRIORITY SETTING AND THE BUDGET

The Bureau of the Budget was a different player altogether. Traditionally staffed with career officers of high quality (although not always politically appointed Directors of equal caliber), it looked upon itself as a principal and professional staff arm of the Presidency. Elected Presidents and their appointed White House staffs, department secretaries, and agency heads came and went, but the careerists in the Bureau of the Budget remained at the pinnacle of federal government to serve the Presidency itself with loyalty and competence of a high order. Most germane to this discussion, the Bureau of the Budget (like OMB today) had unique influence and authority by virtue of its share of the power of the purse. Departments and agencies submitted their budgets, of course; but, subject to budget guidelines approved by the President (which the Bureau helped to frame) and to rarely successful appeals of its decisions to the President, the Bureau was the final arbiter of how much a department or agency had to spend. As such, it was the President's chief agent in setting and enforcing actual priorities in the Executive branch.

In carrying out this function, however, the professionals in the Bureau could not act capriciously or independently. They were recognized, even by their critics, as competent individuals essentially motivated by loyalty to the policies of the President. This required sensitivity to the needs of the departments and agencies carrying out those policies. In short, the professionals of the Bureau were negotiators, not confrontationists, and sought consensus. Senior staff of the Bureau welcomed appointment of a Science Advisor to the President and a President's Science Advisory Committee. In general, they had not been impressed with the idea of a Department of Science and Technology as a panacea.

The Science Advisors, for their part, wanted and actively sought a close working relationship with the staff of the Bureau. They knew that this was essential if they were to assist the President in the critical matter of setting priorities. The effective day-to-day liaison of the Science Advisor and his staff with the Bureau thus became another channel of advice to the President on matters involving science and technology.

If there were disappointments on the Bureau's part with this arrangement, they stemmed from the Bureau's desire for more active participation by the Science Advisor and his staff in coordinating science and technology throughout the government. The Bureau, at times, seemed obsessed with the notion that the Science Advisor should spend more of his time in that role. If there were disappointments on the part of the Science Advisor, who at the request of the President was immersed in national security affairs, they stemmed from demands by the Bureau for advice on managing the claims and counterclaims of a plethora of agencies involved with science and technology in their provincial domains.

ADVISING THE PRESIDENT

The first priority of the Science Advisor was to put in place an apparatus for providing orderly advice to the President on matters that were (or should be) of priority concern to him. The first step, mentioned earlier, was to move the Science Advisory Committee from the Office of Defense Mobilization to the White House and (in conformity to Golden's original advice to President Truman) to reconstitute its membership to the President's liking. The second was to recruit a very small staff, a White House constraint of considerable political importance. The third was to enlist some of the best scientists and engineers in the country, chiefly on an *ad hoc* basis, and to organize them into panels with specific assignments.

As Killian has noted, this panel format gave the Committee access to a range of experience far beyond what it could have mustered in its own ranks and made possible "intensive, highly specialized, and impressively thorough studies by talented scientists recruited from the national scientific community without being uprooted from their regular assignments."

I firmly subscribe to this flexible, innovative staffing approach and have adopted it time and again since leaving government as a preferred operational mode for several private foundations I have served. For this manner of organization provides many institutions with an array of talent and a quality of advice that no full-time staff can be expected to provide.

With this supportive advisory apparatus in place, the Science Advisor and Committee directed their attention to matters of major concern to the President. The President gave first priority to advice on the space and missile programs, the military budget, and other national security issues. He also gave priority, largely on the initiative of the Science Advisor and Committee, to advice on strengthening American science, improving science and engineering education, and promoting better organization and coordination of science and engineering activities within government.

Even a partial catalogue of responses to these concerns by the President's Science Advisors is impressive. The broad dimensions as well as the detailed specifics of these advisories are well spelled out by James Killian in his memoir, *Sputnik, Scientists, and Eisenhower,*[2] in George Kistiakowsky's diary, *A Scientist at the White House,*[3] and in the volume of essays mentioned earlier, edited by William T. Golden, *Science Advice to the President.* Some salient examples are repeated here for two reasons. First, they exemplify the kinds of issues on which a President needs *independent,* personal advice amidst the swirl of conflicting counsel—not infrequently controversial or parochial, sometimes self-serving—from many quarters in and out of government. Second, these examples confirm the relevance to the President of the advice offered because the public record now clearly demonstrates how often that advice was heeded:

National Security Issues

- A series of reports on the uses of outer space, the design of a civilian organization to develop and manage a national space program, and suggestions of individuals who might lead it. (The Committee's primer on space science and organization, entitled "Introduction to Outer Space," was enthusiastically received by President Eisenhower. He promptly authorized its public release, urging the widest possible readership, as a means to quell public concern over the perceived threat to our national security and leadership in science and technology precipitated by Sputnik.)
- Advising the President on missile programs: Thor, Jupiter, Titan I and II, Polaris, MIRV vehicles, and on antiballistic missile defenses.
- Recommendations, many highly classified, for extensive use of the most advanced scientific and technological knowledge for intelligence purposes—including reconnaissance satellites—as well as new, highly sophisticated means for communications intelligence.
- Advisory reports, insistently periodic, on the doubtful value and technical infeasibility of nuclear-powered aircraft, reports that helped to bring about cancellation of the project in the teeth of powerful pressures. Pressures of the intensity engendered by the controversy surrounding the nuclear-propelled aircraft and similar military fantasies so disturbed Eisenhower that he felt obliged to warn against them and their threat to the American way of life in his last major address to the nation, when he spoke of the danger of a growing "military-industrial complex."
- Long and intensive involvement by the Science Advisor, the Committee, and its panels—beginning in 1958—in the effort to achieve a nuclear test-ban agreement with the Soviets. These efforts resulted, in July 1963, in

a treaty banning tests in the atmosphere. The importance attached to nuclear testing by the military throughout this period (and since) make clear the President's need for technical views independent of those coming to him from the Department of Defense and the Atomic Energy Commission, both strong opponents of any test-ban agreement.

Strengthening American Science

Sputnik stirred not only wide public fears about the vulnerability of our national defenses, but also doubts about our world leadership in science and technology and about the quality of American education—education in science and engineering, in particular. Advice to the President and, in some cases, advisory reports to the nation made public by the President that originated in the President's Science Advisory Committee included:

- Larger appropriations to NSF for support of basic research and science education. In 1957, these were a meager $38 million, thus crippling the Foundation in pursuing its mission to build strong basic research capabilities in our universities and to improve science education.
- Strong support for the National Defense Education Act, signed by the President in 1958, which included the first federal loan program of student assistance for higher education.
- A report on "Education for the Age of Science," which recommended a doubling of national expenditures for education. Eisenhower released the report to the public with a statement that the strengthening of science education required the strengthening of all education.
- A report entitled "Scientific Progress: the Universities and the Federal Government,"[5] which pointed out the important relationship between basic research and graduate education and emphasized that scientific results are obtained and new scientists are trained as part and parcel of a simultaneous process within our universities. For this reason, the report argued, the government had a duty to promote the nation's security and welfare by supporting science in the universities.
- A report to the President recommending construction of the two-mile long linear electron accelerator at Stanford University. Approval of this recommendation was announced publicly by the President on May 14, 1959, with the statement that "I am recommending to the Congress that the federal government finance the construction as a national facility of a large new electron linear accelerator . . . which because of the cost [$100 million] must become a federal responsibility."
- A report on "Improving the Availability of Scientific and Technical Information in the United States." The recommendations in this report also were approved by Eisenhower, who directed that NSF assume leadership in improving the availability of scientific information. The recommendations, it should be added, were in stark contrast to a proposal backed by

Senator Hubert H. Humphrey, urging the federal government establishment of a vast, "national scientific and technical literature center."

Science Organization in Government

Although the Science Advisor and Committee, as staff to the President, had no responsibility or authority for managing research and development, they advised the President on ways in which the federal government could better manage R&D activities scattered throughout the Executive branch. They also advised the President on achieving better policy formulation and program coordination among government departments and agencies.

These two objectives had in any case become increasingly compelling to the Science Advisor:

- The volume of problems arising from program initiatives in the military and other agencies—initiatives too often lacking in sophisticated technical analysis or reflecting parochial biases—were threatening to destroy the critically important capacity of the Science Advisor and Committee to be selective and independent in focusing their energies on what they and the President perceived to be major national concerns. This pointed to the need for better management of R&D by the various departments of the Executive branch themselves.
- As part-time advisors, the members of the Committee were in no position to coordinate government programs. Although a series of Science Advisors tried to be helpful in this regard to the Bureau of the Budget, especially in coordinating programs that crossed departmental or agency lines, they operated under the severe constraints of lack of time, staff and authority. This pointed to the need for achieving better policy formulation and program coordination among government departments and agencies.

The record shows considerable responsiveness of the Science Advisor and Committee to the need for advice to the President on these organizational matters:

- The Defense Reorganization Act of 1958 included, as a result of a strong input from Killian in the drafting of the legislation, the establishment of a new position of Director of Defense Research and Engineering (now upgraded to Under Secretary) in the Department of Defense, reporting directly to the Secretary. Within the military departments, Assistant Secretary positions also were created, and scientists and engineers were appointed to fill them. The advice of the Science Advisor in making such appointees was frequently sought and heeded.
- Beginning in 1959, the Science Advisor and Committee urged establishment, within the Executive Office of the President, of a new organization

for arms limitation and control. The ensuing debate over whether such an organization should be a statutory part of the Executive Office of the President or of the Department of State continued for almost two years. It culminated in a bill, signed into law by President Kennedy in 1961, establishing an Arms Control and Disarmament Agency under the aegis of the Department of State. Among its other provisions, the legislation established the position of Assistant Secretary for Science and Technology in the new Agency.

- Within the Department of Commerce, a National Oceanographic and Atmospheric Administration (NOAA) was established to bring together diverse technical functions, once separately administered by such subordinate agencies as the U.S. Coast and Geodetic Survey and the Weather Bureau, to pursue new missions and programs in oceanography and the atmospheric sciences. While the early Science Advisors did not spawn this new organization, they helped lay the groundwork for it by recommending the establishment of a departmental post of Assistant Secretary for Science and Technology, with policy responsibilities for the agencies merged into NOAA and for the National Bureau of Standards and the Office of Technical Services.

- Among the proposals in the Committee's report entitled "Strengthening American Science"[6] was a specific recommendation to establish a Federal Council for Science and Technology, chaired by the President's Science Advisor. Membership in the Council was to be accorded to those government departments with substantial responsibilities in science and technology. Secretaries of the Cabinet departments were to designate as representatives to the Council policy-level officials able to represent their department as a whole. Independent agencies were to be represented by their agency heads. In approving this recommendation, Eisenhower said: "It is my hope that this new Council will improve the planning and management of government research programs and will facilitate the resolution of common problems and promote greater interagency cooperation."

The Executive Order establishing the Council, signed by the President in March 1959, reaffirmed the responsibility of NSF to develop national policies for the promotion of basic research and education in the sciences. The Executive Order abolished the long-established Interdepartmental Committee on Scientific Research and Development (ICSRD), composed of Civil Service employees with technical backgrounds from the same departments and agencies as the members of the new Council. By this action, it was hoped that the Council could exercise real policy authority in achieving better coordination among government programs. Dissenting howls from Civil Service scientists in government agencies, the former members of ICSRD— who claimed they were being cut off from influencing government-wide policies for the management of research by part-time scientists (PSAC members) and political appointees (FCST members)—led Killian hastily to reassemble them as a standing committee of the new Council, where they continued to function, as ineffectually as before, as a discussion group.

Both Killian and Kistiakowsky worked hard to make the Council a success, but, for both, its actual performance proved disappointing. Largely due to Kistiakowsky's tenacity and vigorous persuasion, there were some limited yet important advances. For example, a strong, well-coordinated national program in oceanography was developed and supported, and limited interdepartmental programs in the atmospheric and materials sciences were initiated.

In the large, however, the Science Advisors, and the interdepartmental councils and committees they tried to use—including subsequent ones under the aegis of the Director of the Office of Science and Technology and today under the Director of the Office of Science and Technology Policy—have failed to achieve, in my view, a fully effective system of policy formulation and program coordination for federal research and development.

SOME THOUGHTS ON THE PAST FOR A LOOK AHEAD

The principal conclusion that I draw from this long look backward, relying upon recollections of a singular personal experience concluded twenty-five years ago, was baldly stated at the outset. The President of the United States needs a full-time Science Advisor, supported by a part-time President's science advisory committee drawn from the scientific communities in our universities, various scientific organizations and associations, and industry. That is, he badly needs independent scientific and technological advice, which requires a means by which he can tap the scientific resources of the whole country.

The need and value of such an advisory apparatus at the immediate disposal of the President have not, in my view, been obviated by the strengthened scientific resources within the departments and agencies—with the inherent competition among them—or within the Executive Office—where the energies of the Office of Science and Technology Policy and the Office of Management and Budget are absorbed by matters of resource allocation, research and development management, and program coordination.

There are other lessons from the past which, if heeded, could enhance scientific advice for the President in the years to come. Many are rooted in the need for constraints on how the President's Science Advisors operate. In any organization, such policy and operating constraints serve to focus attention and energies on what the organization can do best and help it to avoid what it cannot do well or perhaps cannot do at all.

One of these constraints should be upon involvement of the President's Science Advisors in management and coordination of the expansive and diverse scientific and technical programs of government agencies. Such matters should be the principal preoccupation of the OSTP and the OMB, which can utilize the technical manpower in their own offices as well as the resources of the entire federal establishment.

Another constraint is the obvious need to avoid any semblance of representing the special interests of science or lobbying for support of those interests in the councils of government. This is not to say that science advice should not be offered, particularly at the request of the President, on such broad issues as improving the nation's scientific and technological capabilities in the interest of national security and welfare. But implementation of this advice, through advocacy of special investments in science and engineering, should be left to NSF inside government and to the National Academy of Sciences and other representatives of the scientific community outside of government. In its fledgling, budget-starved days, NSF was badly positioned to take on this task. Today, however, it is an influential agency with a large budget and its own board of outside advisors. It is quite capable of speaking out and being heard on specific programs and appropriations to strengthen basic research, science and engineering education, and our national scientific and technological leadership.

Another constraint on the President's science advisory apparatus should be to avoid becoming a job shop for the study of a wide array of problems involving science and technology. Such issues as cranberries and pesticides, acid rain, drug abuse, occupational health—the list is endless—probably should be assigned elsewhere for study and recommendations. For example, where advice from outside the government is deemed important, the National Academy of Sciences, with its large structure comprising the National Academy of Engineering, the Institute of Medicine, and the National Research Council could be used. The National Academy of Sciences, after all, was chartered by Congress to advise the government, at the request of the government, on just these matters, as well as to initiate advice on issues the Academy deems should be brought to the attention of the government.

The counterpart to this constraint, of course, is that the President's Science Advisor and the Committee should restrict themselves to basic problems of concern to the President and the country. They should be highly selective about the advice they offer. If they are, they will not be just another voice in government. Their advice will be more trenchant, more powerful, more sagacious, and more respected.

What, then, are the principal contemporary examples of problems of overarching concern to the President? What are the paramount issues where the President needs more and better independent scientific advice than he has now, concerns which his Science Advisors should help him address?

The most obvious and persistent concern is to provide for the nation's security. This is the overriding issue of our time, perhaps of any time, and today involves complex, multinational and multidimensional issues: avoidance of a devastating nuclear exchange between the super powers, containment of regional conflicts from escalating into broader ones, precipitation of accidental conflict by an idiosyncratic or alarmed misreading of events. In shouldering its premier responsibility to provide for the national defense, the military, quite naturally, turns to offensive and defensive military systems and strategies. Only recently has government initiative and organization become more strongly reflective of the opportunities to provide for the common defense through more comprehensive arms control and disarmament measures. On balance, national security policy still favors military doctrine: enhanced capabilities in strategic weaponry based on achieving superior numbers of weapons, their superior destructiveness, a superior diversity in the means of delivery, on the offensive side; and superior grand alliances, superior communications, superior military intelligence systems, and superior antiballistic, tactical and other weapons-specific systems, on the defensive side. Of more recent notoriety is the promotion of what might be described as an "offense/defense," the Strategic Defense Initiative (SDI) of "arming" outer space. On all sides—in strategic and tactical offense and defense and, consequently, in means for their control, containment, and perhaps to some degree abolition—there is a clearly perceived need for very superior science and technology.

Certainly in these gravest of matters, the President needs informed and independent advice. This is not to say that high-minded individuals in the defense establishment, the foreign policy establishment, and the military-industrial establishment do not have the best interests of the country at heart. They clearly do. But their individual perspectives are inevitably particular ones. They frequently are unable to place their interests in perspective, to adopt a more comprehensive view. And the President cannot provide the counterbalance alone. He needs advisors of scientific competence and prominence to stand up to those expressing more parochial opinions and speak with a strong, independent voice.

The world challenge to US competitiveness is another example of an area where the President urgently needs more and better scientific advice. Prior to Sputnik, American science and technology, when viewed at home and abroad, occupied a position of world leadership. It was a perceived threat to that leadership, represented by Sputnik, that alarmed the American public. Today, informed opinion of the international scientific community concedes United States leadership in pure science. But there is worry at home that even this leadership is eroding. Other nations, particularly Germany and France and, more recently, Japan, are increasing their support of basic research. More worrisome—and more immediate—our technological advantage, as measured by our industrial productivity relative to our major competitors, is declining rapidly. As reported by the President of the National Academy of Engineering, Robert M. White, at the Academy's 1986 annual meeting:

A phenomenon, the long-term consequences of which are poorly understood, is that product design, engineering, and software development increasingly are likely to be done overseas. The implications for maintaining the essential U.S. engineering capability are worrisome because of the implied erosion of the U.S. base in knowledge and know-how. Whether automobiles or refrigerators, computers or microchips, nuclear power or energy transmission systems, the likelihood is increasing that the systems are assembled from components designed, engineered, manufactured, and shipped from all parts of the world.

To help maintain our strong position in the international competition for technological leadership, and thus our domestic standard of living will require well-conceived, forward-looking national policies to guide our scientific and technological developments. Perhaps a new kind of Technological Capabilities Panel, established by a new President's Science Advisory Committee, is needed. Whatever the means of analysis, the development of such policies clearly can profit from advice to the President from a group of Science Advisors with deep and diverse roots in the scientific community.

Both national security and domestic welfare have reaped the benefit from American leadership in science and technology. In no small measure, furthermore, the international prestige of the United States is rooted in its extraordinary scientific achievements during and since World War II. As Killian said in his *Memoir:*

> The question of this country's position in world science is going to continue to come up, president after president, science adviser after science adviser; the new science advisory mechanism in the White House will thus find the question of how we maintain the quality and vitality of American science to be a matter of fundamental policy making at the Presidential level—fundamental for science and fundamental for our technology and our industrial strength.

NOTES

1. William T. Golden, ed., *Science Advice to the President* (New York: Pergamon Press, 1980).
2. James R. Killian, Jr., *Sputnik, Scientists, and Eisenhower: A Memoir of the First Special Assistant to the President for Science and Technology* (Cambridge, MA: MIT Press, 1977).
3. George B. Kistiakowsky, *A Scientist at the White House: The Private Diary of President Eisenhower's Special Assistant for Science and Technology* (Cambridge, MA: Harvard University Press, 1976).
4. President's Science Advisory Committee, *Introduction to Outer Space* (Washington, DC: US Government Printing Office, 1958).
5. President's Science Advisory Committee, *Scientific Progress, the Universities, and the Federal Government* (Washington: US Government Printing Office, 1960).
6. President's Science Advisory Committee, *Strengthening American Science* (Washington, DC: US Government Printing Office, 1958).
7. *Taking Technological Stock*, Report of the President at the National Academy of Engineering 22nd Annual Meeting (Washington: National Academy of Engineering, 1986).

The Science Advisor:
Who Needs One?

Donald N. Langenberg

To watchers, the signs are as clear as the autumn's first southbound vee of geese or the spring's first robin. Gaggles of politicians and reporters can be seen feeding and calling in small Iowa towns. The tentative first crowings and preenings of candidates for next season's leader of the flock can be observed daily. We already have the first reviews of the retrospectators, interpreting for us the historical implications of the Administration now nearing its end. There are even interpretations of the interpreters, analyses of the analysts. Yes, our republic will soon undergo another of its blessedly Constitutional transitions from one Administration to the next. Among those watching (and worrying) as the process begins again is a small but earnest group with a particular interest, namely the attitude of our next government toward the incorporation of scientific and technological expertise in its senior policy councils and, specifically, toward the office and person of the President's Science Advisor.

Why is this concern of any moment? And, if it is taken seriously, what is one to think about it? The answers to these questions are, of course, a matter of individual opinion. The opinions which follow, together with sundry assertions and admonitions, are those of a member of the academic science community with some brief but reasonably direct experience with science in Washington and with a couple of President's Science Advisors.

Let me begin by answering the question posed in my title. The President of the United States needs a Science Advisor—or someone equivalent—because the nation must have well-informed leadership as it confronts the growing variety of policy questions having scientific and technological elements. The notion that the President should have regular access to an in-

Donald N. Langenberg is Chancellor of the University of Illinois at Chicago. Previously, he was Professor of Physics at the University of Pennsylvania. He was Deputy Director of the National Science Foundation (1980–82) and Acting Director in 1980. He is a member of the Board of Directors of the American Association for the Advancement of Science and of the Alfred P. Sloan Foundation.

stitutional source of advice on scientific and technological matters first emerged in the Truman Administration, and was elevated to greater strength and effectiveness by President Eisenhower, though a generic source of such advice was provided earlier when President Lincoln chartered the National Academy of Sciences. The presence within the Executive Office of the President of a Science Advisor, with accompanying organizational apparatus, has been viewed with varying degrees of enthusiasm by Mr. Eisenhower's successors. Mr. Nixon's evident lack of enthusiasm led Congress to legislate the existence of a Science Advisor and of an Office of Science and Technology Policy within the White House. Unfortunately, it does not appear to be generally agreed that such an office and the purposes it serves are necessary and important tools of the nation's Chief Executive. This is surprising; the importance of access to technical advice in matters of state has been recognized for millennia. Kings from Babylon to Cuzco routinely retained scientists (astronomers) as a matter of course to advise on the timing of planting, harvesting, and other important events. That such expertise is viewed by some as irrelevant to national policy development in our intensely technological environment seems bizarre. Nevertheless, it is so. The implantation of a stable science and technology advisory mechanism in the upper reaches of the United States Government, one which is accepted as a valuable—even traditional—tool of government, will require continuing attention and patience from those who care and believe.

THE ADVISOR'S FUNCTIONS

What is a Science Advisor supposed to do? This is another question lacking a generally agreed upon answer. Many in the scientific community believe that the Advisor's principal function is to represent them in their never-ending quest for more federal funds. This is not a reasonable expectation. While the Science Advisor might properly be expected to take part in the shaping of the government's investment strategy for science and technology, he/she cannot compromise his/her credibility by acting as chief lobbyist for any special interest group, no matter how well intentioned. If the S&T community wants a lobbyist, they ought to go out and hire one. (Indeed, some do.) The Science Advisor must be the President's person, not someone else's.

So what does that leave for the Science Advisor to do? Merely to ensure that the making and implementation of federal policy in matters involving science and technology are illuminated by the best available scientific and technological understanding. That is a tall order, because it covers most things the federal government is concerned with, whether we realize it or not. To mention just a few recent examples, it would include everything to do with DoD's wares, hard or soft; the education of our people; the economics of social welfare programs in an inexorably aging society; AIDS, SDI, SSC, and a host of other acronyms representing expensive problems, most of which even a room-temperature superconductor won't solve. Given the paucity of miracles lately, perhaps we should be content with solid progress toward such a goal.

WHAT SORT OF PERSON?

And what sort of person should our next President seek? Obviously, no single person can possibly be expected to provide expert advice on all the necessary topics. Therefore, the Science Advisor must be able to tap the resources of an S&T community which has generally proved to be eager to provide advice. This probably requires that the Advisor be a scientist or engineer able to command the professional respect of that community. (The community is inclined to imagine that a Nobel Laureate or equivalent is required for such an important job, but experience shows that Stockholm's blessing is not an essential characteristic of an effective Science Advisor.)

The Science Advisor must be able to make complex and uncertain matters understandable to whatever diverse audience our citizens choose to install in the White House and on the Hill. One wonders whether a really good high school science department might not be a good place to look for such a person.

Most important of all, the Science Advisor must be seen as credible and trustworthy by his/her boss and the boss's closest associates. This criterion is, perhaps, the most difficult of all to satisfy. Why? Because any President's inner circle will naturally consist largely of people the President has found to be helpful, supportive and trustworthy over the course of his/her career in, guess what, politics. The path to certification as "distinguished, respected scientist/engineer" may run through thickets of politics, but it's not usually the kind of politics in which a President has been engaged. It is unlikely, therefore, that any of a President's old cronies will be distinguished, respected scientists/engineers, or that one of a distinguished, respected scientist/engineer's old cronies will be President of the United States. Hence, a newly appointed Science Advisor is likely to be a stranger to his new boss, and to most of his new associates. Under such circumstances, it is crucial that the Advisor quickly establish him/herself in a position which will allow him/her to be effective. To the extent that the Advisor has political views, no one should be surprised or affronted if they are similar to those of the President.

This intrinsic positioning difficulty cannot be surmounted by redrawing the White House organization chart or by fine-tuning legislative language. One might imagine a larger change which would increase the institutional stability of the S&T advisory function, while decreasing the importance of the Advisor's personality and probably also the directness of the connection with the Oval Office. That is, one might contemplate the consequences of imbedding the S&T advisory function in a Cabinet-level Department of Science and Technology. But that is a question for another occasion.

It seems self-evident to this writer that the White House cannot responsibly deal with many—perhaps most—of the issues which our President must face now and in the future without direct access to expert—perhaps even wise—advice from the nation's scientific and technological community. I hope that our next President will address this issue, concur, and use the mechanisms and resources readily available to assure him/herself of that access.

Confidential Advice in the Public Interest: PSAC's Dilemma

Joshua Lederberg

There has been substantial debate about the restoration of "PSAC," a President's Science Advisory Committee that was dismantled by President Nixon in 1972. I agree that his step seriously diminished the quality, breadth and impact of scientific advice to the Presidency in an era when this is most needed. It is important, however, that we explore some political realities that must be recognized and honored if a PSAC is to be effective. Recall that PSAC was a part-time body, one whose loyalty to the Executive was inevitably more tenuous than that of his appointed Science Advisor.

Paramount is the authentic need for a President to have advisors whose discretion and confidence can be trusted, however deeply they may disagree with him on specific issues. He deserves advisors who can bring a range of well-informed critical views to Executive policy-making, especially when new policies are being formulated—and this is eternally in the face of competing national needs and claims from special constituencies. To ensure that all of the relevant options and contingencies are thought about, nothing is more valuable than a candid devil's advocacy, which may be born out of principled dissent with his policies, but should be open-minded and restrained to be able to understand his logic as well.

I do not suggest that the most hostile opponents necessarily be sought on every issue; there will be ample dissent if any broadly constituted, experienced group of independent thinkers is recruited. Such "loyal critics" are unlikely to be recruited as full-time officials—in light of their motives as well as his. He is unlikely to confide in them, however, if they criticize his judgments in public as well as in private counsels. Obviously, they must

Joshua Lederberg, Nobel Laureate in physiology or medicine, is President of the Rockefeller University, and has had a long career in molecular biology research. He has been a frequent flyer on the shuttles to Washington for many years. He has sat on both horns of the dilemma he enunciates: at other—disjoint!—intervals, he was quite public in expressing his views, for example, as a weekly columnist for The Washington Post *(1966–1971).*

meticulously respect national security classification of data; but that is not the limit of their responsibility to the Executive. Their prestige as members of PSAC will give them advantages in public debate that a President would be loath to enhance for his openly avowed critics. As part-time, confidential advisors, they do not expect to resign if the President decides contrary to their convictions; but if they speak out inappropriately, they imperil the privilege of the Executive's confidence. The other side of the bargain is that PSAC not be exploited to win public support for the President's final policy positions.

The role of a PSAC then goes beyond that of the fulltime Science Advisor, whose position is obviously untenable in the face of a principled policy conflict. The Advisor does play an essential role as manager of the process, which, if done conscientiously, will be an affirmative search for the best informed, necessarily often controversial and disparate views on intricate technical questions.

The President plainly cannot effectively discharge his responsibilities without mobilizing good technical advice on a broad range of policies, in economic, domestic, foreign policy, national security, and a host of other domains. Discreet counsellors can be found as readily among scientists as among domestic and foreign policy advisers. Academic scientists must understand that they may be exposed to special pressures on campus and from the press and the Congress that could undermine their confidential relationship to the President. For many, especially those who are critical of a given Administration's policies, the prospect of being muzzled in public expression of their critical views may place them in a grave dilemma. The terms of the contract need to be spelled out carefully to nurture a new President's confidence and encourage him to call upon academic expertise to help serve the national interest. Regardless of how they may have voted, the expert's role is a depolarizing civility in the process of government between elections.

Despite episodic troubles, these issues were successfully faced up to during many years, during which PSAC thrived. Today, advisory groups analogous to PSAC continue to play a certain role within many government departments, even those pertaining to national security. Nor is the Nixon Presidency acclaimed as a prototype for how the White House should be managed in future. But it is important that scholars also understand and respect their peculiar responsibilities, if they are to lend their special skills to sensitive domains of government.

There is no way that advice of any kind can be forced on a reluctant President. One of our tasks is to revive a modus operandi that will show that the national interest is not in irreconcilable conflict with his political imperatives—and that better and more commendable, even more voteworthy, government will be the result.

Science Advising

Leon M. Lederman

William Golden's earlier compendium[1] contains all possible comments on the art and practice of science advising. Wisdom is truncated by the chemistry of the advisor and advisee. The President has available an awesome armada of potential sources of science advice if he feels the need for advice. Let's see: there is *the* Science Advisor and his apparatus in OSTP. There is PSAC or the White House Science Council equivalent (roughly). There is the NSF Director and the entire NSF with their manifold infinity of panels and boards. Occasionally, other Departments contain science, *e.g.*, Energy Research in DoE, Director Division of Research and Engineering of DoD, and the Defense Science Board. There is, for a small fee, the National Academy of Sciences and, through them, practically any scientist in the nation who has published two and a half refereed articles. The President can call on the patriots in our universities; he can, with a wink, assemble industrial scientists, scientists who can meet a payroll, and academic scientists who would dump anything and everything to even visit the White House Office Building.

Any thesis that the President's advisory system is weak cannot be supported, unless someone would propose something really bold, *e.g.*, that a group be empowered to teach the President quantum mechanics while he is under the influence of sodium pentathol or something.

Although the Congress is clearly a much more difficult entity to advise, a plethora of entities is also in place. We start with OTA, proceed to the GAO, the Library of Congress and then note that the National Academy of Sciences is available here, too, as are an infinite number of witness-experts testifying before a like number of committees. An excellent example is the monumental study of science policy issues by the House Committee on Science and Technology, chaired by Don Fuqua, in the 1985–87 period. A more dramatic example was the late and much-lamented Joint Committee

Leon M. Lederman, high-energy physicist, has been Director of Fermi National Accelerator Laboratory since 1978. He is a member of the National Academy of Sciences, and has received numerous awards, including the National Medal of Science in 1965.

on Atomic Energy—the green-covered, fine-printed reports of this committee constitute a library of science, science history, sociology, and politics. A wise person in search of science education can read here the elegant testimony of Nobel Laureate after Nobel Laureate, straining to be clear to the lawyers of this powerful committee. What more noble motivation than next year's budget allocation?

Here again, the only dramatic innovation would be a Constitutional amendment which would require each member of Congress to pass a science literacy test.

Passing over the Supreme Court, where can we go for advice on how to improve the advice to government? I have only one positive and not too impractical suggestion. It came from my mentor, Professor I. I. Rabi, and was given to his younger colleagues some time after the Oppenheimer affair and after only twenty years of his own experience. (He now has another twenty-five or so years, but I doubt if he has changed his mind). Rabi's admonition went something like this: Advisors come and go. Power in this country belongs not to advisors, but to elected officials. If you scientists want your advice to be heeded, *get elected! Run for office!*

Suppose the 400,000 or so scientists in this country established a fund of $10 million, to be available for any Ph.D. with a good publication list who wanted to try for Congress? Most of these candidates would have no political liabilities, and would know a lot about education and the importance of science and education in modern society. Even more, they'd know the limitations of science and their arguments in corridor and committee would be persuasive. Rabi's utopian idea was to have a government, not excluding the Supreme Court, sprinkled with people well trained in science. That's my proposal too!

NOTE

1. William T. Golden, ed., *Science Advice to the President* (New York: Pergamon Press, 1980).

Quality of Technical Decisions in the Federal Government

Gordon J. F. MacDonald and Charles A. Zraket

The paradigm of a Science Advisor to the President, supported by a President's Science Advisory Committee, evolved from a seminal report written by William T. Golden in 1950.[1] During the decade that followed, growing public and political recognition of the influence of science and technology on society led to increased interest in Golden's proposal. The concept's gradual evolution was punctuated by the launching of Sputnik thirty years ago. This event reinforced the perceived need for a stronger voice of science in the White House than the part time position their existence could provide. The conditions that aroused this recognition of need in the 1950s are similar to those present in the late 1980s. The careful planning that went into the appointment of a Presidential Special Assistant for Science and Technology and the definition of that role remain relevant today. The underlying character of the concerns that led to President Eisenhower's action has a persistence and timelessness that suggest the nation will face similar concerns in the coming decades.

Gordon J. F. MacDonald, geophysicist, is Vice President and Chief Scientist of The MITRE Corporation. He was a member of the President's Science Advisory Committee under President Johnson (1964–68) and of President Nixon's Council on Environmental Quality (1970–72). He has been a member of the Defense Science Board, and has served on numerous advisory committees for NASA, the Department of State, the National Science Foundation, and the National Research Council. He is a member of the National Academy of Sciences and of the American Philosophical Society.

Charles A. Zraket is President and Chief Executive Officer of the not-for-profit MITRE Corporation, engaged in systems engineering, planning, and research work in national defense and civilian areas. He is an Overseer of the Center for Naval Analyses, a Trustee of the Hudson Institute, and a member of the Council on Foreign Relations.

THE LATE 1950s AND THE 1980s:
CONTRAST IN PROCESS

The long-term danger of inflation, the growing balance-of-payments problems, declining US industrial competitiveness, and increasing deficits were as great a concern during the last years of the Eisenhower Administration as they are for the Reagan Administration. The antagonistic pulls between greater defense spending and lower taxes dominated discussions of economic policies in the 1950s, as they have in the 1980s. During his last years in office, Eisenhower hoped to devote a major effort to arms control, only to be hindered by the downing of the U-2. After a massive defense buildup during the first six years of his Administration, Reagan wished to proceed with arms control negotiations in his last two years, only to be slowed by the Iran-Contra controversies.

The similarities in the major themes of the 1950s and 1980s continue down to details. Arms control proposals of the 1950s centered on agreements regarding limitations of nuclear tests; radioactive fallout had preoccupied scientific and public opinion since the irradiation of Japanese fishermen on the *Lucky Dragon,* one hundred miles downwind of an extremely dirty American bomb test. The early proposals concentrated on a comprehensive test ban covering tests in space, atmosphere, oceans and underground. The reactions of national laboratories having responsibilities for maintaining the nuclear stockpile was swift. The laboratories and defense contractors argued and lobbied against any ban on testing. Their principal arguments were based on the proposition that the Soviets would cheat. The schemes proposed for anticipated Soviet cheating included the suggestion that a nuclear weapon set off in an underground cavern would produce a seismic wave corresponding to only a fraction of its true power because of the air separating the explosion from the rock walls of the chamber. This and similar proposals for Soviet cheating, such as tests beyond the sun or the far side of the moon, challenged the scientific capacity of the Administration. Eisenhower was well equipped to deal with these technical complexities, as first James Killian, and later George Kistiakowsky oversaw the analyses of outside experts, including Hans Bethe, Robert Bacher, and Lloyd Berkner.

The thorough analyses and clear-cut debates between proponents and opponents of arms control placed the well-prepared United States delegation in an advantageous position in negotiating with the Soviets. The negotiations eventually led to an aboveground test ban during the Kennedy Administration, demonstrating over the following years that arms control agreements could not only be negotiated, but also implemented. The Special Assistant for Science and Technology, drawing on the resources of the President's Science Advisory Committee (PSAC), was the President's main source of technical information on the proposed test ban during all of these discussions, preparations and negotiations. Follow-on efforts to achieve further progress in arms control during the early 1970s were weakened, in part, by inadequate White House science counseling. Treaties of 1974 and 1976 that sought to deal with underground testing exempted explosions below 150 kilotons, not the five to ten kilotons that were the focus of discussions in 1960.

During the 1980s, the issue of a comprehensive test ban arose again with Gorbachev's prolonged moratorium on any nuclear test. While the State Department favored negotiations aimed at lowering the 150-kiloton threshold, the Department of Energy with its weapon laboratories, the Defense Department, and defense contractors vigorously opposed any move away from the 150-kiloton threshold. In addition to the possibility of Soviet evasion, the validation of the nuclear stockpile and the requirements of a new generation of nuclear weapons for the Strategic Defense Initiative (SDI) were advanced as reasons for maintaining a high threshold. The validity of these arguments rested on the complex questions of seismic detectability, weapon reliability, and the practicality and effectiveness of esoteric weapons such as x-ray lasers.

The Reagan Administration, unlike the Eisenhower Administration, lacked an effective mechanism to judge the technical merits of the various claims. Further, there was no ready means by which the Administration could secure disinterested but expert advice, if it had so desired. Without an effective science advisory mechanism, questions were not raised concerning the judgments of the interested parties, the Departments of Energy and Defense. Into this vacuum moved Congress, which, in 1987, attempted to legislate a unilateral United States threshold of one kiloton. Rather than entering into any negotiations from a position of strength based on analysis and debate, it was obvious—not only to the Soviets, but to the world—that the United States did not have a unified position, and in fact, was in disarray on this issue.

The contrast in the way the Eisenhower and Reagan Administrations dealt with analogous test ban issues well illustrates the values inherent in the position of a Special Assistant for Science and Technology. While not as grand as the question of the feasibility and desirability of SDI, the issues of a comprehensive test ban clearly underline the differences between the Eisenhower and Reagan Presidencies in dealing with closely similar technical problems. (Even the Strategic Defense Initiative has links to the Eisenhower Administration. Kistiakowsky records in his diary that on August 25, 1960, Si Ramo talked about a proposal from the Space Technology Laboratories of the Ramo-Wooldridge Corporation for an AICBM system. The system would consist of a swarm of tens of thousands of small satellites that would pounce on any missile as it is being launched. Kistiakowsky remarks that the proposal would probably be "fantastically expensive," but the idea might be important. The proposal resurfaced in the 1960s as the Air Force's BAMBI, and was later abandoned, but not forgotten.[2])

SCIENCE ADVICE AS QUALITY CONTROL

Eisenhower's letter defining the terms of reference of the appointment indicates the care and thought that went into defining the role of the Special Assistant for Science and Technology.[3] The letter, sent first to Killian, then to Kistiakowsky, and also used by Kennedy in appointing Jerome Wiesner, spells out the responsibilities for oversight of all science and technology programs in the government, with emphasis on activities related to national security. Indeed, Eisenhower's letter to Kistiakowsky singles out three agencies for special attention—Department of Defense, Central Intelligence Agency, and the Atomic Energy Commission, whose weapons functions were assigned to the Department of Energy in the 1970s.[4]

The special attention given to matters of national security in Eisenhower's terms of reference follows from a number of considerations. The importance of defense to the nation is evident. Expenditures for the security agencies' technical programs far exceed those of any other federal agency. National security is dependent on weapon systems whose lifetime is measured in decades. The development and acquisition of systems that can reliably operate and counter foreseeable threats for tens of years require the highest level of technical insight and judgment. Importantly, the details of such systems are often highly classified. In some program areas, such as stealth technology, the underlying concepts are classified, as well as the technologies themselves. Detailed knowledge of such systems is restricted to the funding agencies, government laboratories, and defense contractors, all of whom have special interests to protect. The classified nature of many national security programs precludes the open inquiry and critique that are essential to quality control for an open scientific enterprise.

In the absence of strong scientific and technical oversight from the federal government, the surveillance of technical decision-making falls on Congress. That institution, though strengthened since the 1960s through the establishment of the Office of Technology Assessment and through greater recognition of the need for technical staff competency, falls far short of what is required in disinterested assessment of decisions on which the future of the nation rests. Daily parochial demands of constituents, the need to focus on broad political issues, and the requirement for reelection diffuse well-intended efforts of members of Congress and largely prevent them from playing substantive roles in technical oversight.

Implicit in Eisenhower's assignment of broad oversight of science and technology to the Special Assistant was the requirement to maintain quality control of the entire federal scientific enterprise. Indeed, the quality control function is a Science Advisor's most important responsibility and must be carried out in a variety of ways. The essential first step in maintaining and enhancing the quality of technical decisions is to ensure that the highest caliber of people are involved in technical decision-making. Achieving the highest quality membership of the President's Science Advisory Committee involves numerous considerations. PSAC, with a panel structure, provides an interface of the White House with the technical community. When compromises in selecting PSAC members are made (such as requiring geographical diversity, as was the case in the Johnson Presidency), the stature and, thus, the effectiveness of PSAC is diminished.

The Science Advisor, working with the Cabinet officers and agency heads, can play an essential role in identifying and recruiting highly competent scientists and engineers as candidates for the position of Assistant Secretary, the level where many technical decisions are made. This function was clearly anticipated in Eisenhower's terms of reference when he directed Cabinet officers to consult with the Special Assistant for Science and Technology on staff appointments. In carrying out this function, the Science Advisor, working with PSAC, must not only identify appropriate candidates, but convince them to serve in government. This is an ongoing process, since there is always personnel turnover, even during a four-year Administration. The task of recruiting becomes more difficult as an administration draws to a close, but even so, in the last two years of the Eisenhower Presidency, Killian and Kistiakowsky were able to bring highly able scientists into government, particularly the Defense Department.

At times, improving the capacity for making quality technical decisions involves the creation of a new organizational framework. Killian, in responding to a suggestion from John Wheeler, Eugene Wigner, and Oskar Morgenstern, set in motion a sequence of events that led to the formation of JASON (a group of scientists who now work in-depth on national security matters while maintaining a primary affiliation at a non-governmental institution, often a university). Killian noted that better mechanisms were needed to allow more first-rate scientists to contribute to national security, and do so in an atmosphere in which the work might proceed creatively, with a minimum of restrictions. Since Killian's 1958 initiative, JASON to this day has provided a steady stream of reports and studies on some of the most complex technical issues faced by the Defense Department.

Quality control can be exercised through reviews of selected programs by the Science Advisor's staff and/or panels of PSAC. Given the magnitude of federal technical programs, the degree of selectivity must be very great. Criteria for selectivity include existence of unexpected technical obstacles or lengthy delays due to technical problems, as well as program importance. Reviews by a group within the Executive Office of the President can have a number of therapeutic effects. To prepare for a PSAC review, a program is critically examined from inside the responsible agency. Often this internal review can provide means for program improvement. Because of the command nature of a White House oversight, the principals within the department housing the program are far more likely to focus on potential problems. Further, the attention drawn to the program by high-level review can enhance the morale and the productivity of participants. As a result of both internal and external reviews, program managers are much more likely to become aware of defective concepts, faulty designs, inadequate performance, or even unnecessary programs. During the Eisenhower and Kennedy Presidencies, the staff of the Science Advisor provided an exceedingly useful service in facilitating communication between parts of the bureaucracy, while arranging for and participating in the program reviews. Indeed, Robert McNamara is reputed to have asked how Jerome Wiesner, with a minute staff, could know as much or more than the Secretary of Defense about his defense program, when he had far greater resources available.[5]

The importance of the quality control function of the Science Advisor is well illustrated by the management of technical affairs in the Eisenhower Administration. Eisenhower strengthened technical management within the Office of the Secretary of Defense by creating the position of Director, Defense Research and Engineering, a position initially occupied with great distinction by Herbert York. During a period of intense research on ballistic missiles and a buildup of defense forces, the new office oversaw the development of a new technology, the ICBM force, with great success. Responsibility for ICBM became the subject of bitter debates among the services, all of whom wished primary responsibility. Despite the divisive nature of these conflicts, York's efforts led to the deployment in the 1960s of the basic strategic weapons of the 1980s—land and submarine-based ICBMs and the B-52s.

The organizational form developed from the Eisenhower conception of a science advisor aided by an outside committee has been adopted and maintained by numerous industrial organizations to help achieve technical quality control. IBM has a Chief Scientist aided by a small staff who, together with an outside group of scientists, assist management in evaluating IBM's research program, as well as new product lines and the means of manufacturing them. General Motors has a similar structure, and other companies, large and small, have followed suit by creating organizations that are similar in function, though differing in detail.

Despite the success of the organizational mode in various settings, no serious attempt has been made in recent years to reestablish it within the White House. The history of the abandonment of the science advisory concept is well known. President Nixon did not like nor did he trust the advice he received on the antiballistic missile system and the supersonic transport. He also resisted the muted warnings concerning the war in Vietnam. Nixon strongly believed that he was not being well served by his own Science Advisor and science committee; his convictions were reinforced by admonitions from his budget officers that his advisory scientists were no more than advocates for more money for science and, indirectly, for their own research. The mistrust of the advocacy role of the Science Advisor and PSAC persisted through succeeding Administrations; it was this mistrust that demolished the advisory mechanism so carefully crafted during the Eisenhower years.

The successful implementation of the quality control function requires that the advisory apparatus be recognized as interest-free by the more-or-less permanent civil servants staffing the Office of Management and Budget (OMB), by the President's political advisors, and by the managing agency heads. If a President is to control the federal scientific enterprise, he must have an advisory apparatus that has the confidence of other members of his Presidential staff. Most importantly, there must be harmony between his Science Advisor and those having responsibility for managing the fiscal affairs of the Administration, as well as with those whose primary responsibility is managing the federal enterprise. Above all, advice that is confidential must remain so, regardless of final policy decisions. Public airings of private counsel destroy the confidence of the President in his advisors, even that which is built over years of service.

Science and technology will continue to grow in significance. A President can only manage the federal technological enterprise if he has the staff resources that permit him to ensure decisions that are technically sound. While political factors may determine the final outcome of any decision, the technical information should be available in a form that is as free of conflict of interest as possible. The organizational arrangements that were designed to make this possible worked well during the closing years of the 1950s; there is no reason to doubt that the same framework will work for the nation in the late 1980s and beyond.

NOTES

1. Golden, William T. "*Government Military-Scientific Research: Review for the President of the United States, 1950–51,*" 432 pages, unpublished. Available at the Harry S. Truman Library, Independence, Missouri 64050; the Herbert Hoover Presidential Library, West Branch, Iowa 52358; the Dwight D. Eisenhower Library, Abilene, Kansas 67410; and the American Institute of Physics, New York, New York 10017.
2. George B. Kistiakowsky, *A Scientist in the White House* (Cambridge, MA: MIT Press, 1977), p. 388.
3. James R. Killian, Jr., *Sputnik, Scientists, and Eisenhower: A Memoir of the First Special Assistant to the President for Science and Technology* (Cambridge, MA: MIT Press, 1977), especially Appendix I.
4. George B. Kistiakowsky, *op. cit.*, pp. 1–3.
5. Jerome B. Wiesner, "Why We Need a Tough National Science Advisor," *The Washington Post*, May 24, 1987.

Science Advice to the President

Paul A. Marks

I would like to address the need for an adequate mechanism for providing advice to the President in the formulation of federal policy over the broad range of areas related to biomedical and behavioral research, health care and disease prevention—"health-related science and technology." While there is a clear need for this function, there has been in fact, a lack of an effective advisory structure for the President which provides a comprehensive capability to cover these critically important areas so basic to the nation's welfare.

Understandably, scientific and technical advice to the President has been dominated by advisors expert on issues particularly related to national defense and space technology. This is appropriate, but should not and does not preclude the President's need for scientific and technological advice in the health sciences and related areas. The objective of the advisory structure should be to facilitate the President in his policy decision-making by apprising him of the state of biomedical and behavioral research, identifying neglected as well as promising areas for initiatives, and advising on short-term and long-term priorities across the broad spectrum of health sciences and technology. At the same time, the advisory structure should be available to assist other branches of the Executive, such as the OMB, during the formulation of health policy and health budget. The advisory system must be sensitive to and cognizant of the President's wishes, policies and goals, and aware of public concerns and aspirations.

Paul A. Marks, M.D., has been President of the Memorial Sloan-Kettering Cancer Center since 1980. Previously, he was Vice President for Health Science and Professor of Medicine at Columbia University. He has served on the President's Cancer Panel and the President's Biomedical Research Panel and numerous other federal and New York State Advisory groups. Dr. Marks is a member of the National Academy of Sciences and of the Institute of Medicine.

WHY HEALTH SCIENCES ADVICE FOR THE PRESIDENT?

If there is to be excellence in the nation's biomedical research and health-related programs, there is a need for continuity of direction and stability of support. The nature of biomedical research is inherently a long-term enterprise. Meeting the challenges of the health of our people—AIDS, cancer, drug abuse, aging, health care costs, access to necessary health care—all require both short- and long-term commitments. There are many other issues that underscore the need for effective advice to the President in the formulation of federal policies in these areas—such as the increasing regulatory processes of the federal government in health-related areas ranging from recombinant DNA techniques to federal reimbursement for health services. Biomedical research and health-related issues are important aspects of our international relations and foreign policy. Other nations, particularly developing countries, often view our scientific and technological expertise as the direct basis of our economic and social well-being and wish to share in the benefits of that expertise. This represents important opportunities for us. Multinational cooperation may be a vitally important resource in our own efforts to make progress in one or another health-related area, for example, vaccines and AIDS.

All of these, and the many other health-related issues with which today's President must deal, are greatly affected and complicated by rapid advances in science and technological knowledge and achievement. To deal wisely with these issues, it is helpful for a President to have broad technological literacy, but it is essential that he have a strong advisory staff support.

We increasingly must look to scientific and technological advances to help solve such complex problems as improving our health, feeding the world's growing population, contributing to the growth of our economy by generating jobs and productivity, and meeting opportunities for international cooperation. These issues impinge on and are interwoven with the fabric of domestic and foreign policy formulation.

The advisory structure for the President should not be primarily concerned with the welfare of biomedical science and health-related technology, as important as these are, for such science and technology will flourish as our country flourishes. Many have expressed concern that United States science and technology are sliding from a position of world leadership. The federal government is the dominant source of funding for both biomedical research and health care in this country. If the President's policies over the broad range of health-related issues are to be successful, it is essential that he be informed as to the current state of science and technology and be advised as to the best judgments with respect to future opportunities and likely developments. While this is not unique to the health-related sciences, it is unique for the lack of an apparatus for comprehensive, balanced science advice to the President.

PSAC

During the period of the President's Scientific Advisory Committee, which existed from 1951 to 1973, there was a presence of experts in health sciences and mechanisms for providing PSAC with access to qualified experts on specific health-related sciences issues. President Nixon abolished the Science Advisory Committee and this markedly narrowed access to an effective science advisory system to the President. Ironically, it was at this time that the President's Cancer Panel was established under the National Cancer Act of 1971, and, owing in part to the effective relationship with Presidents Nixon and Ford, provided a valuable asset in helping the President set priorities for the National Cancer Program and for biomedical research broadly. Admittedly, it was administratively unorthodox. Yet, the impressive advances in biomedical research facilitated under this program are now beginning to give us the knowledge needed to make fundamental attacks on many diseases that make up today's health agenda in cancer, as well as AIDS and other viral infectious diseases, atherosclerosis, diabetes, genetically determined disorders, and a host of others. Unfortunately, there is a widespread perception that during the late 1970s and 1980s, advice to the President in the area of the health sciences has had neither the coherence nor the effectiveness commensurate with the breadth of the problems.

It is generally recognized that the most comprehensive policy tool for the President is through the budgetary process. Furthermore, the President and other policy-makers must make priority decisions on the basis of imperfect indicators and information from disparate sources, laced with uncertainties. It would be desirable for the President to have balanced, comprehensive and soundly based health science advice, drawing upon expertise from the federal government, state and local governments, industry, universities and even foreign sources in making his choices and establishing his priorities in the political context of his office.

PRESIDENT'S HEALTH SCIENCES ADVISORY PANEL

In developing a health sciences advisory panel for the President, as in other areas, it is preferable to avoid unnecessary proliferation of organizational units operating in the same arena. The advisory panel should be mandated to meet periodically with mission agencies and the relevant government structures to provide an opportunity for coordinating the elements of its advice.

The very nature of biomedical research and health-related issues requires continuity. Long-range planning for science and technology in the health areas is both necessary and difficult. Policy-making in this area must have Presidential perspective. The degree to which any White House office can engage in long-term planning is limited. Further, there is always the danger in over-planning in a rapidly changing scientific environment. The President receives advice from many sources and is influenced by many factors and is the final integrator.

A Presidentially appointed panel, specifically constituted and staffed to provide advice to the President across the broad range of issues related to health, could be an effective mechanism to support Presidential policy decisions in these areas. The politics of such decisions must be the province of the President. The panel should regularly report to the Science Advisor to the President and be available for direct consultation with the President. The panel's advice exclusively through an intermediary such as the President's Science Advisor may function, but may not be an entirely satisfactory substitute for the option of a direct relationship if the President so desires it.

The OMB, as the predominant agency in establishing the President's budget, should have access to the President's Health Science Advisory Panel. The panel should include—but not necessarily be restricted to—biomedical scientists, clinicians, other health professionals, social scientists, and public members of stature, wisdom, discretion, independence and patriotic dedication. The panel must have the capabilities necessary to conduct timely, high-quality policy analyses needed to support their participation in the process of advising the President. The panel should have access to mission agencies, national academies, professional groups, academic and research institutions, industry, and other individual consultants as necessary and desirable. It is important that they tap broadly the resources of the United States in these areas. In addition, consultation abroad should not be neglected because other nations are growing strongly in biomedical research and biotechnology.

Pluralism and diversity of ideas should be obtainable in such a forum. Issues should be addressed with suitable depth of analysis to provide the President with realistic policy options. This could require the use of supplementary *ad hoc* committees, not necessarily Presidentially appointed, on specific issues. Such committees would consist of qualified individuals and one or more members of the parent panel. Such subcommittees could evolve into standing subcommittees.

The problem of advising the President on biomedical and health care matters is not basically different from advising him on any other scientific and technological issues. Presidents do not usually have as strong foundations in the health sciences as they may in matters related to national defense. Nevertheless, health-related issues are becoming an increasingly important part of our national agenda, as well as our international agenda. We need only cite the part health issues play in exchange programs with the USSR, China, Third World Countries, and our competitive position in biotechnology—one of the fastest growing sectors of our economy—with Japan and Western Europe—to mention two areas.

Health care expenditures are second only to our defense budget and rising rapidly. Access to health care and its rising costs are not usually viewed by some as components of science advice to the President, in fact, resolution of these issues is critically dependent on having the best and most reliable information on the relevant health sciences and technologies.

Advice to the President must be broadly conceived. It must assist the President in translating into political terms the implications of scientific and technological developments. The Health Science Advisory Panel and, in particular, its chairman, must know and understand the problems of the President.

APPOINTMENT OF THE HEALTH SCIENCES ADVISORY PANEL

Members of the panel should be Presidentially appointed. On the one hand, the nature of the issues related to health are such that continuity in analyses and policy recommendations is essential. On the other hand, the President must have confidence in the members of the panel. However, if all members of the panel change with each Administration, it may both become political and lose continuity. A reasonable compromise might be that the chairman and vice-chairman of the panel serve at the pleasure of the incumbent President, but other members of the panel, while appointed by the President, should have sufficient tenure to overlap Administrations. Such members of the panel should not be considered by the scientific community or the world at large, as creatures of a particular President or to have a particular political orientation. It is important that they be viewed as scientists, clinicians, health professionals who are objective, independent, and not of a visible political complexion, expressing their advice in a way that is understandable to the President and the public. Scientific advisory groups to the President always generate certain anxieties among other groups in government, as well as non-government institutions and individuals. Nevertheless, if the President desires it, such an advisory panel can serve him and his office well. For the advisory panel to function effectively, the President must want its advice.

Another issue is the relationship of such an advisory panel to the President to the Legislative branch. This is a matter of opinion. I believe that the President is best served by having his own advisors working directly for him without division of loyalties. Relationships with the Congress should be with the knowledge and perhaps the permission of the President or by request of Congress through the Office of the President to have the chairman of the advisory panel or committee members testify before them.

In summary, fulfilling the President's and the nation's ambitious expectations for science and technology as they relate to the health of our people involves a national commitment to research development and innovation among several sectors, including the government, industry, academia, and the public, playing complementary roles. Scientific advancement and technological achievement pervades all areas of government responsibility and the health of our people is certainly no exception. It follows that the President, as our chief policy maker and implementor, should be well served by an adequate and effective mechanism for advice on issues related to health care and disease prevention.

Federal Policies Affecting the Research Strengths of Universities and Colleges Need Better Coordination

Walter E. Massey

Since the establishment of the National Science Foundation in 1950 and the Science Advisory Committee in 1951, a number of mechanisms and processes have evolved with the goal of providing coordinated planning and oversight for science and technology activities throughout the federal government. The relative effectiveness of these various structures is usually a function of the influence of the President's Science Advisor, the Office of Science and Technology Policy (OSTP) and, in some instances, the Director of the National Science Foundation and the National Science Board.

The need for a system that allows for coordinated planning across all major research-oriented federal agencies is clear and well recognized. Although a number of interagency and multi-agency committees now exist, the problem has not been solved. Invariably and understandably, each federal agency sees its highest priority as generating the resources to support its own programs; and each agency has a loyal, vocal and underfunded constituency to which it must pay particular attention. The problem is exacerbated by the numerous Congressional authorization and oversight committees whose jurisdictional assignments cause them to focus on and be concerned with only one or two agencies. In the absence of effective, collaborative interagency planning, important areas of science and technology may not receive sufficient attention, and major initiatives that require more resources than are available from any one agency may not be undertaken.

Walter E. Massey, a physicist, has been Vice President for Research and for Argonne National Laboratory at the University of Chicago since 1982. Previously, he was Director of Argonne National Laboratory (1979–84). He was a member of the National Science Board from 1978 to 1984, and is President-elect of the American Association for the Advancement of Science.

239

The difference an activist influential Science Advisor can make in these matters is quite substantial and important. This is demonstrated by at least two recent examples: the development of a long-range plan for major research facilities in materials sciences, and the initiation of the Engineering Research Centers (ERCs) and the subsequent Science and Technology Centers. Both of these initiatives were very much the result of the leadership provided by George Keyworth.[1] Although these initiatives have their major homes in one particular agency (the ERCs in NSF and the materials sciences research facilities in the Department of Energy), they clearly require the support of and resources from other agencies.

One important area that rarely receives a coordinated government-wide perspective is the role of universities and colleges in our research enterprise, and their importance to the health and vigor of science and technology in the United States. About one-half of all the federally funded basic research in the US is carried out in universities, and universities and colleges are the unique source of our human resource base for science and technology.

Yet there does not exist an established system or mechanism within our federal structure that views universities from an institutional perspective and assesses the effects of various federal policies on the ability of these institutions to contribute to the nation's research and development activities. The different agencies and offices within the federal government have particular views, interests and perspectives that color their interactions with universities. The research funding agencies, such as the National Institutes of Health and the National Science Foundation, see universities primarily as research-performing organizations that also train graduate students and provide a place for postdoctoral researchers to mature and develop.

The Department of Education apparently sees universities and colleges as educators of undergraduates and recipients of federal funds for financial aid. Indirect costs and financial accountability are issues that dominate interactions between OMB and universities and colleges. To agencies concerned with generating tax revenues, these institutions are classified together with other not-for-profit organizations, such as museums, zoos, symphony orchestras, and foundations, and are held to be subject to the same federal tax or fiscal policies that apply to all not-for-profit institutions.

A SERIOUS LACK

The absence of an established mechanism among these agencies to review federal policies that affect the research and development strengths of universities is a serious lack. A strong case can be made that such coordinating activities should exist in OSTP and be a responsibility of the President's Science Advisor. Fortunately, George Keyworth did assume this responsibility and attempt to exercise this kind of oversight and coordination through the appointment of the "Panel on the Health of U.S. Colleges and Universities,"[2] convened under the auspices of the White House Science Council. This, however, was a one-time effort, and the long-term effects of this report are yet to be seen.

The importance of universities and colleges in our science and technology effort was underscored and emphasized in this report. The opening paragraph of the Executive Summary reads, "The health of U.S. society is uniquely coupled to that of its universities. To a greater degree than any other country, this nation looks to its universities both for new knowledge and for young, trained minds prepared to use it effectively. But just at a time when much is expected of our universities, after more than a decade of retrenchment and belt-tightening, they find themselves with obsolete equipment, aging facilities, and growing shortages of both faculty members and students in many important fields."

The panel reached a number of conclusions and made several recommendations to agencies in the Executive branch, as well as to Congress. Among its findings are, "A healthy university system is the basis of our future. In any ranking of priorities for allocating research and development support—both federal and private—universities must rank first." The report made recommendations that called for significant increases in funding for research and development at universities and for funds in support of facilities, equipment, and the "university infrastructure." It also called for changes in the federal tax code, as well as for simplification and improvement in the reporting and management of indirect costs. It recommended decreased paperwork on federal grants and contracts, stability in research funding, and significant increases in scholarships and fellowships. Although the report appeared to be well received by the federal agencies that support research and development, as well as the most important Congressional committees, its recommendations have apparently had very little effect. Since the report was issued in February 1986:

- The OMB attempted to institute guidelines for recovery of indirect costs that would have significantly decreased the federal government's share of support of research at universities.
- The Department of Education proposed sharp reductions in financial aid at the undergraduate level, without apparent recognition that universities and colleges would have to assume the burden of supporting students who were not supported by federal scholarships, thus decreasing the amount of institutional funds available for research-related activities.
- A tax code was implemented that severely restricts the ability of universities to use tax-exempt financing for renovation and construction of research facilities, at the same time that federal agencies are requiring increased cost sharing by universities.
- The NSF communicated its intentions to decrease the amount of academic year salary support for researchers, as well as summer salary support.

In each of these instances, the particular agency and/or Congressional committee acted from a perspective that, given its own interests, appears to be quite appropriate; and from that perspective, the action is probably seen as having a modest (if any) negative effect. Taken together, however, the accumulation of these various actions, if undertaken, would be profoundly negative for the health of universities. The problem, to reiterate, is the absence of an agency, group, or committee within the federal government charged, on an ongoing basis, with monitoring such policies and actions, and assessing their effects on the research strengths of our universities. I recommend that such a committee or board be established on a formal basis, either through legislation or by Executive order. Let me suggest two possible mechanisms by which this might be accomplished:

- There could be established within the OSTP a permanent "Committee on the Health of Universities and Colleges in the Research Enterprise." This committee would monitor the programs and policies of all federal agencies that significantly affect universities and would make reports and recommendations to the President's Science Advisor on an annual basis, at appropriate times to be included in the formulation of the federal budget.
- The Federal Coordinating Council on Science, Engineering and Technology (FCCSET) might be asked to undertake this role. This council already exists and is designated as the central coordinating body for federal science and engineering activities. It consists of the director of OSTP and representatives of each of the major research agencies. If a representative from the Department of Education were added to this group, and if the chairman of the committee were given the explicit responsibility to have the committee function as a body concerned with the health of colleges and universities in their research roles, this mechanism might prove more effective than having a committee in the office of OSTP.

I am sure there are a number of other ways by which this problem could be addressed, but I am convinced that unless we do improve the present situation, our ability to sustain the nation's strengths in science and technology will be severely impaired.

NOTES

1. Dr. George Keyworth was the President's Science Advisor and Director of the Office of Science and Technology Policy from 1981 to 1985.
2. Report of the White House Science Council "Panel on the Health of U.S. Colleges and Universities," February 1986, Office of Science and Technology Policy, Executive Office of the President, Washington, DC.

Science Advice to Government

Alan H. McGowan

It is a truism—but nonetheless compelling—that, in the twentieth century, almost the twenty-first, science advice to the government is crucial. What is not so obvious is the form the advice should take, and how the advisors should be organized.

It is also true that, for advice to be effective, it has to be wanted. Unwanted advice has sometimes had interesting consequences, particularly in the science field. Thus, for example, when President Nixon didn't like the advice he was given by the President's Science Advisory Committee—and, particularly, when some of the members went public with their positions, he abolished the Committee. Although Congress, seeing the need for science advice in the White House comparable to that being given them by their own Office of Technology Assessment, created the Office of Science and Technology Policy, its powers were so limited by both Congress and the President (being afraid of past experience) that top-notch scientists refused to fill the post, and those who did take it have not been able to provide the kind of independent advice that is so important.

Given the many scientific controversies which have swirled around the White House, and the seemingly unresolved questions still at issue, one has to ask if the exercise has made any difference. Jerome Wiesner, President Emeritus of MIT and Science Advisor to Presidents Kennedy and Johnson, makes a compelling case that it has. It did so, however, because the Presidents wanted it; President Eisenhower, dismayed over Sputnik, rescued the office from a minor post in the Office of Defense Mobilization and made it report directly to him (thereby realizing the original proposal made by William T. Golden); Presidents Kennedy and Johnson wanted the advice, thought they needed it, and, therefore, listened. Presidents after them have not wanted it, have not listened, and have either ignored or abolished the office.

Congress, for example, seems to want the advice given to it by its Office

Alan McGowan is President of the Scientists' Institute for Public Information (SIPI); is a member of the Science and Law Committee of the Association of the Bar of the City of New York; was Chairman of the Youth Council of the AAAS; and is an active member of committees of the New York Academy of Sciences and of the AAAS.

of Technology Assessment. This, of course, is, in no small part, due to the extraordinary skill exhibited by its leaders, particularly the current incumbent, John H. Gibbons; nonetheless, the Office thrives because of its perceived need by a Congress faced with technological and scientific issues every day of its existence.

Nor should we forget that PSAC was not the first attempt to bring the scientific community into contact with the workings of government. The National Resources Planning Board (and/or organizations with similar names) existed from 1933 to 1943, a decade filled with first peacetime and then wartime emergencies which increasingly took on scientific hues. It was killed, ironically, by Congress (simply by appropriating no money for it); again, one of the compelling reasons for that action was that Congress did not like or agree with its reports (unlike PSAC, it made its recommendations in public documents). In classic form, it killed the messenger, although many of the reports had seminal value, and have shown their worth even today. Had the country paid attention to some of the warnings then, it would have been saved a lot of grief in later years.

Congress and the President, in the long run, are reflections of the public that elect them. If the President does not want science advice, at least part of the reason is that the public doesn't see its importance. In the decade and a half after Sputnik, the American public looked to the scientific community for leadership, and the scientists responded with an active PSAC, with the most prestigious scientists serving on it and devoting a good deal of effort to its work; the same was true of the National Resources Planning Board in the decade following 1932. When the public becomes ambivalent about science—as it did in the late 1940s and as it is now—the political leadership can turn away from scientific advice.

This thesis obviously deserves a great deal more exploration and debate than is possible here. The implications, however, are interesting; what matters is not the form of science advice or the particular structure of the group giving the advice, but the level of acceptance or desire for it among the public and, therefore, among the politicians.

Scientific literacy—or at least some level of understanding by the public of the role science and technology play in our complex economy—is the key. The form of science advice may vary, and perhaps should, as old forms wither and indicate the need for new ones to take their place; the need for it has to be indicated by the public, so that politicians cannot turn away from it to pursue politically expedient, even though scientifically unwise or impossible, ends.

Science and the Federal Government

David Packard

As we approach the last decade of the twentieth century, science has become pervasive in much of the work of the federal government, and extensive science and technology advice is being provided for a wide range of activities throughout the government. Some departments have established standing committees to obtain scientific advice, such as the Defense Science Board of the Department of Defense; special committees are appointed to provide advice on specific subjects. Many of the federal laboratories have committees of scientists to provide advice and council and to evaluate the quality of their work. In recent years the Congress has taken a much more active role in considering budget proposals that involve science and technology, and the Congress has become involved in designating specific research projects at some of the federal laboratories. Extensive scientific advice is provided the Congress in hearings held to consider these matters.

The economy of the country has also become much more dependent on science and technology, and the ability of many industries to compete in the international marketplace is now largely determined by their leadership or lack of it in high technology. Since the federal government has a vested interest in the welfare of the US economy it has properly been seeking advice about what can be done to maintain our worldwide competitive position. The Administration has appointed committees to consider this area, and the Congress has also held hearings, seeking scientific advice. There is

David Packard is chairman of the Board of Hewlett-Packard Company, which he and William R. Hewlett founded in 1939. He was Deputy Secretary of Defense for three years until December 1971. He was Chairman of President Reagan's Blue Ribbon Commission on Defense Management, which submitted its final report in June 1986. Mr. Packard is Past President of the Board of Trustees of Stanford University; a member of the White House Science Council and of the National Academy of Engineering; a Trustee of the Herbert Hoover Foundation and of the American Enterprise Foundation; and is Vice Chairman of the The Nature Conservancy. He has been Chairman of The Business Council, and a Director of several major corporations and of the Stanford Research Institute and the Committee for Economic Development.

no lack of scientific advice for the federal government on many important issues at this time.

With this large and important involvement of the federal government with science and technology it is certainly appropriate to ask whether the government is receiving the best possible advice from the scientific community of the country, and also to ask the corollary question, "Is it accepting and acting on the best advice available?"

In exploring the issue, it will be helpful to review briefly how and why the federal government became so heavily involved in science and technology. It is especially important to make note of the serious deterioration of the environment in which science and government must work that has occurred during the past two decades.

THE HISTORY

At the beginning of World War II, the scientific community of the country was mobilized to assist in the war effort. Vannevar Bush was appointed by President Roosevelt to head the program. By the end of the war, 30,000 scientists, doctors and engineers were working on new weapons and new medicine. It is noteworthy, in light of the tight bureaucratic control over such activities today, that the Congress gave them money in lump sums, and trusted them to decide how to spend the money. Their success in the development of radar, electronic counter-measurers, the proximity fuse, and other scientific military equipment, and, of course, the atom bomb was the critical determinant of the favorable outcome for the United States and its Allies. Much of this work was done with the cooperation of our Allies, particularly Great Britain, but scientists in Germany and Japan were not able to keep up with the military technology developed by the Allies during the war.

At the end of the war, Vannevar Bush, who had provided the leadership for this wartime effort was convinced that a similar program should be established for the peacetime period of the country following the war. That was done, implemented first by the Office of Naval Research, and then by the National Science Foundation, which was established in 1950. The initial activity was to support a number of research programs at universities across the country in fields that might be useful in the peacetime economy. Scientists also continued to support the government in the development of military technology as the confrontation with the Soviet Union began to unfold, and they assisted in the development of our strategic nuclear forces throughout this period. In the early years after the war, the US relied on manned aircraft for the delivery of nuclear weapons. US leadership in aeronautical science was largely the result of the outstanding work of the National Advisory Committee for Aeronautics, which was established during World War I and which was one of the few scientific endeavors that worked on national problems during the two decades between the wars. After the Soviet Union launched Sputnik in 1957, a crash program was undertaken to develop and deploy the Minuteman System of land-based missiles and the Polaris System of submarine-launched missiles. In the early 1960s, the Apollo Program was undertaken with the stunning success of landing a man on the moon in 1969. There were also major successes in medicine, resulting from the close and effective cooperation between the scientific community and the federal government during the war, and the National Institute of Health is still receiving major funding from the federal government.

Vannevar Bush, in recommending this program of research and development after the war, made the following statement in his book, *Science, The Endless Frontier*, "On the wisdom with which we bring science to bear in the war against disease, in the creation of new industries and in the strengthening of our armed forces depends in large measure our future as a nation."[1] By the late 1960s, it was quite evident that the effective working relationship between the scientific community and the federal government had achieved what Vannevar Bush had predicted.

A FAVORABLE ENVIRONMENT

This great achievement was possible because of a very favorable environment during this period. National Security and International Affairs were dealt with on a bi-partisan basis in the Congress, and there was discipline among the Congressional subcommittees. The news media was protective of the Office of the President, and reasonably responsible in dealing with matters of national security. There was also a generally good rapport between the President and the scientific community of the country. This favorable environment began to deteriorate toward the end of the Johnson Administration, and has become much worse since. The trauma of Vietnam and the Watergate affair took its toll, and national attitudes deteriorated badly in the 1970s. Today, we have a highly emotional adversary atmosphere in Washington, a partisan division in the Congress on national security, international affairs, and, for that matter, almost everything else. We have a news media that seems intent on damaging the federal government whenever possible, and altogether too many people involved in our national affairs seem to be putting their self interest ahead of the welfare of their country. In this environment, it is not surprising that the scientific community is also often divided in the advice it gives the government.

It is difficult to see how this adversary environment will improve in the foreseeable future, unless there is a crisis of some kind. Recommendations to improve the quality of scientific advice for the federal government should be made with the understanding that the environment is not likely to improve and may, in fact, become worse.

There is another reason why scientific advice to the government is likely to continue to be fractionated. We are becoming much more concerned about the uncertainties of the future. For example, contaminants in the air we breathe or in the water we drink can now be measured in parts per billion, and at these low levels we do not know how much is dangerous for human consumption over long periods of time. We know that some pollutants from civilization affect the upper atmosphere of the earth and, at some level, are likely to cause dangerous changes in the weather. Even the scientists who study these problems can not agree on their predictions. Scientific research during the past two decades or so seems to have increased the uncertainties of the future rather than reducing them as one might expect.

What then can be said about the future of scientific advice to the federal government in light of the current environment? Although scientists will continue to disagree on many important issues, there are some important issues on which they can or should agree, and a concerted effort in areas of agreement would be an important contribution to the national welfare. There are three areas of particular importance to a successful relationship between science and the federal government that have deteriorated since the mid-1960s and that must be restored for the United States to sustain world leadership in technology in both the commercial and the military field.

First and perhaps most important there should be no disagreement on the fact that we must educate enough scientists and engineers to meet the future needs of our country. We are not doing so today as is clearly indicated by several recent reports. The Report on the Health of US Colleges and Universities by a panel of scientists, engineers and educators, under the sponsorship of the White House Science Council[2] provides a good analysis of this problem and has some constructive recommendations.

Second, we need a better working relationship among the the scientific community, the federal government, and the private sector, business and industry. This relationship has greatly improved during the past few years. Industry is sharing the burden with the government in providing more funding for research and education at colleges and universities, and private foundations are also beginning to provide more funding. There is still, however, much to be done in this area. For example there is a great deal of important new technology being generated in the federal laboratories that is not being effectively used by business and industry.

Third, we need to do a better job in converting new technology into useful products. This, too, requires a better working relationship among the parties involved. This problem has received considerable attention from the private sector and there has been good cooperation from the universities and the government. Unfortunately, in the important area of National Security, the time required to convert new technology into useful weapons has increased substantially. It is generally agreed that the US is ahead of the Soviet Union in most areas of scientific technology in the laboratory, but it now takes so long to field weapons using new technology that we are not able to take advantage of whatever lead we have. This problem is caused by an over obsession in the DoD about technology transfer and the imposition of unwieldy contracting procedures on DoD by the Congress. For example the Polaris System of submarine-launched missiles required slightly over five years from the beginning of development to deployment. That was done in the late 1950s, and a major military system program has never been done as well since that time. Today a comparable new weapon program would require ten years or more.

These three subjects should be first priority items for the scientific community, the President of the United States, and the Congress. While there will continue to be disagreement on what should be done, particularly in the area of national security, there should be no disagreement that, whatever we decide to do, it should be done much more efficiently.

There are other areas in which there is likely to be general agreement within the scientific community and between it and the other parties involved. In these areas, science and technology advice to the President could be much more effective than it has been. If the scientific advice were more unified and more forceful, it would clearly have a larger impact.

A RECEPTIVE PRESIDENT

What can be done to make the President more receptive is a more difficult matter. President Reagan is prone to accept recommendations that have a dramatic or a political impact, and that is likely to be the case, at least, with most Presidents. Here, a more concerted effort with his advisors could be useful, but on major issues, particularly those involving national security, the President is most likely to decide himself on what scientific advice to accept, and it will not always be that of the majority of the scientific community of the US. This is not anything new or unique to the United States. In his Godkin Lecture at Harvard in 1960,[3] C. P. Snow describes Winston Churchill's allegiance to the scientific advice of F.A. Lindeman, who, in the early days of the war, thought there was no future for radar. Fortunately, the advice of Sir Henry Tizard prevailed, because he was supported by the bureaucracy and the military on the importance of radar. Lindeman was a strong advocate of strategic bombing, while Dr. Tizard and his associate scientists thought it would not be cost-effective and, in this case, Lindeman's advice prevailed. Cost-effective or not, it would have been politically impossible for Winston Churchill to have refused to proceed with strategic bombing at that time.

This case highlights another problem with the advice of scientists on major issues that receive the attention of the President. Many if not most of these issues involve consideration of factors that are not scientific in addition to those that are. There is no evidence that the judgment of scientists on factors that are not scientific is any better than well informed persons who are not

scientists. It is, therefore, possible for the President to make the right decision, even if it is not supported by a majority of the scientific community.
In a democracy, the will of the people will ultimately prevail on critical
issues of national importance, but it may take some time for the people to
become well enough informed to make good judgments. The right decision,
whether it be the one recommended by the Scientific Community or not, is
not likely to be achieved quickly on some of the complex issues we have
to deal with at the present time.

Scientific advice to the federal government has made an invaluable contribution to the welfare of the United States over the entire span of years
since the end of World War II. It has been more effective at some times
than at others. There will be continuing changes in the environment that
may make this advice more difficult to implement. It is important that the
people across the country, as well as those in the government, are continually reminded that the US scientific community is a great national asset
and ways must be found to continue to encourage advice from its distinguished members both to the federal government and to the organizations
and people in the private sector. Scientists should recognize that their advice
is indispensable on scientific issues, but their advice on other matters deserves no special credibility over other well-informed people.

The United States is being challenged as never before in peacetime in
high technology, which is the practical application of science, both in the
commercial and the military arena. Our country sorely needs a renewed sense
of dedication and teamwork among the scientific community, the Office of
the President, and the Congress. The payoff would be tremendous, and it
really won't cost very much.

NOTES

1. Vannevar Bush, *Science: The Endless Frontier* (Washington, DC: US Government Printing Office, 1945).
2. C. P. Snow, *Science and Government* (Cambridge, MA: Harvard University Press,
   1961).
3. *Report of the White House Science Council Panel on the Health of U.S. Colleges
   and Universities* (Washington, DC: Office of Science and Technology Policy,
   1986).

Science: Advice and Vision

Heinz R. Pagels

In 1917, a newspaperman interviewed Julius Rosenwald, a successful merchant who had already built a vast business empire, and asked him about his need for counsel. Rosenwald, to the newsman's surprise, replied, "The commonest and shabbiest thing in the world is advice. A normal man does not require it. His conscience or intellect is sufficient." Rosenwald was referring to business advice, but his remarks, in the view of many contemporary decision-makers, could just as well apply to science advice. Who needs science advice?

The argument that scientific advice and expertise must be channeled to our political leaders to serve the national interest is based on the recognition that we live in a complex technological society. The future of our nation, its international competitiveness, its military security, and the health and welfare of its citizens are critically dependent on our management of science and technology. The argument goes on to assert that political decisions should be informed by the findings of science, or else the decision-makers proceed at risk to the nation; no one should decide in ignorance of the facts. Yet, reality, in this instance, differs from its favored interpretation.

Political decisions, such as the decision to advance a nuclear energy program, or a health care program, while they are informed by science and technology, are primarily political decisions. In other words, the key factors are economic and social pressure groups, lobbies, the need for jobs in a specific industry and, most significantly, the perceived popularity of the decision with the electorate. Scientific knowledge and advice can and will be

Heinz R. Pagels is Executive Director and Chief Executive Officer of The New York Academy of Sciences. He came to the Academy after 18 years at The Rockefeller University where he continues to hold an Adjunct Professorship in Physics. A Fellow of the American Physical Society and the AAAS, Dr. Pagels is Vice President of the International League for Human Rights, a member of the Council on Foreign Relations and trustee of the New York Hall of Science, and member of the New York City Partnership and the New York Bar Association. He is the author of The Cosmic Code: Quantum Physics as the Language of Nature *(1982) and* Perfect Symmetry: The Search for the Beginning of Time *(1985).*

used by whatever interest group thinks it will serve its purposes and will be discredited by its opponents.

The decision-making process in our society is extraordinarily complex; it is essentially political, and science plays but a small role in it. Presumably, scientific criteria can help define the boundaries of a political issue that has a technical component. Establishing such boundaries would be helpful if politics were a strictly rational process. But political leaders, on more than one occasion, have promoted programs that require, in effect, a repeal of the laws of nature—they step right over the boundaries. In that instance, the decisive veto is cast by nature, and order is restored by natural rather than social law.

Scientists are intellectually committed to the idea that the facts should speak for themselves, that truth has priority over opinion and power—a commitment that is essential to the conduct of scientific inquiry. "Yet scientists," as one politically astute friend accused me, "are a bunch of political virgins." They do not play the political game and are often poor players when they do—they have little idea of what goes on in the mind of a political decision-maker. Politics, like science, is a professional activity that requires special knowledge, experience and expertise. Were scientists to accept the perception that they are but just another interest group, they might become more effective (if that is what they want) in influencing decisions. This agenda, however, speaks to scientists of the priority of power over truth, in direct conflict with how they want to see themselves.

The advice of scientists and engineers is hardly equivocal, as any politician can testify. It is possible to assemble experts that stand on both sides of an issue. Furthermore, the procedural pressure in the science-based political decision-making process moves the debate to areas of maximum scientific ambiguity. No rational person will fly in the face of hard facts; but interpretations are another matter. The scientific facts may help define the boundaries of a contested area but they do not define that area itself.

Political leaders can take or leave scientific advice. Some years ago, the science advisors to President Nixon were asked to study the supersonic transport (SST), and then informed him that, for economic and environmental reasons, the SST should not be built. Their advice was confidential. Mr. Nixon, with his usual candor, spoke with complete accuracy when, in effect, he informed the public, "I have consulted with my scientific advisors and I have decided to proceed with the SST." The Congress, however, took another view and voted against the SST, the science advisors were abolished, and France and England went on to demonstrate how much money could be spent on a SST as a national symbol of aeronautical prowess.

In other instances, political leaders accept the advice of some scientists to their subsequent chagrin. President Ford was clearly ill advised when he mobilized the national health facilities to combat a swine flu epidemic that never materialized. Yet, politically, he had little option, once confronted with the choice, for the cost would have been very high if the epidemic did, in fact, occur. President Reagan might have avoided much criticism and gained more support had he consulted broadly about the technical possibility of a defensive space shield. Even if he knew about the vast difficulties of implementing his missile defense program, he might still have gone on to propose it for strictly political reasons, not the least of which was to bring the Soviets to the bargaining table.

Scientists and politicians live in different decision-making worlds, and it is as difficult to educate a politician about science as a scientist about politics. Scientists in the government complain that after spending years "educating" members of Congress about the nature of science, its prospects and limitations, to the point of true communication, the Congressmen lose their jobs at the ballot box, or through retirement. Scientists can afford to take a long term point of view; politicians usually can not.

Scientists and politicians in our society are influenced by very different components of our culture: they often look at the world differently, but each is effective in its own way. In spite of their differences, it is clear that neither group can avoid the consequences of accommodating the other if our republic is to prevail in the future. Over the last decades, especially since World War II, a bureaucratic infrastructure has arisen in the government that mediates the flow of information from the practicing scientists and engineers to the political leadership. The future of this system of science advice ought to be reexamined, especially in view of the fact that the nature of scientific inquiry, the relation of science to society, and the very architechtonic of the sciences is, itself, changing. Science has become both more complex and more influential in the lives of ordinary citizens.

The US government has a vast, institutionalized structure to provide science advice. It is broadbased, pluralistic, diverse and, on the whole, excellent. The government and military can, in principle, if not in practice, draw on the consultative scientific resources of the entire nation—all the experts in industry, government and universities. In this regard, the OTA and the National Academy perform their services well. Usually, the government relies on a small number of experts, some of whom put themselves forth for such purpose out of a sense of patriotism, vanity, or both. When avoidable, science advice should not be gratuitous, but needs to be solicited by educated users. We should bear in mind the thoughts of Mr. Rosenwald, that advice is "the commonest and shabbiest thing in the world." Science advice should fill a real—not a perceived—need. One way to guarantee that is to establish a "market mechanism" for science advice to the government.

If we look at science advice to the Executive branch, then I think that a solitary "science czar," a Cabinet officer, would not serve the President well. A science advisor should, however, sit on the National Security Council. Science is complex, reflecting the complexity of nature itself, and the scientific advisory structure to the President and Congress should reflect that complexity if it is to serve the truth, a truth which is seldom simple. Or, to put it in the language of computer architecture, I am opposed to the "sequential processing" of science advice to the President or Congress—a hierarchical system. I prefer a "parallel processing" model for science advice, both because it is less likely to propagate serious errors and is superior at pattern recognition. Many parallel channels of information—a pluralistic rather than hierarchical system—would serve the President best. It is the way a brain, rather than a machine, works.

The courts of this nation have a real need for accurate and balanced science advice, and no adequate institution exists to serve this pressing need. Our society dumps its most urgent problems into the courts, especially complex and controversial issues that the law makers won't touch. While the parties in dispute are free to bring in their experts, the judge could use a little help, too. It is not beyond the resources of this nation to set up a science advisory institution, similar to OTA, that might help the courts. I do not have in mind "a science court," but rather, a scientific advisory system to serve as "a friend of the court," to be solicited in time of need. I have no idea what the legal and other obstacles to such a suggestion might be, but it seems worth exploring.

The kind of science and technical advice that I have been describing, while important, is generally in the form of how to build a better toaster, what to do if the old one breaks, or the environmental impact of the same. I think that scientists can serve a higher purpose in the government—a purpose that draws on the inspiration that led them into science in the first place.

A society needs a vision of the future that promotes the self confidence that enables it to move onward. Science, as the dominant intellectual framework of our time, can provide that vision. In this century, humanity made the first preliminary contact with the invisible forces of existence—the quantum atom and the molecular order of the living cell, forces that reveal a complexity hitherto unimaginable. Scientists are now exploring this complex domain of existence and their discoveries will alter the course of our civilization. This age of scientific exploration is in its infancy. New, emergent sciences of complexity will alter the architectonic of the sciences and the very conduct of inquiry itself. A new natural reality is being revealed. The societies that master the new sciences of complexity and the reality they reveal, will become the cutural, economic and military superpowers of the next century.

It behooves our political leaders to be aware of the magnitude of this development and to guide its creation. Scientists could serve no greater national purpose than to transmit this vision of the human future—a new synthesis of knowledge touching all components of human life, an enterprise transcending parochial national boundaries, carrying us deep into the order of the human body and eventually lifting us to the stars.

The Dilemmas of Decision-Making from AIDS to SDI

David Perlman

Today's spectacular advances in science and technology demand critical policy decisions at levels of complexity more and more difficult for government leaders and the public to understand. The need for disinterested, expert advice on issues of research and development priority, of technical feasibility, of fiscal and environmental impact, and of quantifiable risks and benefits grows ever stronger.

Government policy itself, of course, must continue to be made and implemented with the consent of the governed, but the decisions should be truly informed, and providing the information to government leaders without political bias requires input from independent scientific and technical specialists. They may quite properly be recruited from the ranks of those whose philosophies are compatible with the leaders who select them, but pre-eminent professional competence should be the first criterion for recruitment. Mere yea-sayers can lead unwary Presidents, Cabinet officers, and the Congress to disastrous decisions.

In more innocent days a generation ago, fewer difficult questions seemed to require technical answers, and government—perhaps less plagued by intractable social and political problems—showed a greater willingness to accord high priority to scientific ventures whose utility could be only dimly perceived, if at all.

Consider this description of the state of physics presented by a panel of scientists to a Congressional hearing nearly 30 years ago:

"Physicists now comprehend not only the structure of stars, the motion of our own and other galaxies, the curvature of space, the possible ways in

David Perlman, Associate Editor of the San Francisco Chronicle, *reports on science and science policy, is a past president of the National Association of Science Writers, and a member of the Committee on Public Understanding of Science & Technology of the AAAS. In 1974, he was a Regents Professor at the University of California, and, in 1986–87, was a Carnegie Corporation Fellow at the Stanford Center for International Security & Arms Control.*

which our universe has evolved, but also matter on a finer and finer scale: from familiar objects to molecules; then to the atoms of which the molecules are composed; the internal structure of the atom with its electrons orbiting around nuclei; the nucleus itself, made of protons and neutrons and the mesons which bind them together; and lately even something of a picture of the inside of the proton itself, complex and containing yet other particles. We are peeling an onion layer by layer, each layer uncovering in a sense another universe; unexpected, complicated, and—as we understand more— strangely beautiful."[1]

That description of the state of physics in 1959—a bit on the optimistic side, perhaps, but focused solely on the elegant and intellectual aspects of scientific inquiry—came from a panel appointed jointly by President Eisenhower's Science Advisory Committee and the General Advisory Committee of the Atomic Energy Commission. It was chaired by Dr. Emanuel R. Piore of IBM, and its poetic evocation of the pure mysteries that high-energy physics might probe to enrich our culture was influential in persuading Congress to appropriate the $114 million that funded construction of one of the world's great fundamental physics facilities: the Stanford Linear Accelerator Center.

It is worth noting, too, that the cost estimates prepared by subsequent advisors proved so precise that the builders of SLAC brought their immense project into full-scale operation on time and within budget. As plans for a superconducting Super Collider move forward, the advisory processes that led to SLAC could well serve as a model.

Early in President Kennedy's Administration, when the young leader sought to give the world convincing evidence of America's capacity to forge far ahead of Sputnik, solid scientific advice informed him—well before his public proclamation of the goal—that a manned landing on the moon within a decade was both technically and fiscally feasible. The advice proved dramatically correct.

Contrast that history of Presidential scientific advice against the current situation when such critical policy issues as the regulation of biotechnology, expanded AIDS testing, priorities for space exploration, and—above all— the pace of strategic defense research are being addressed after only limited and often highly politicized scientific and technical advice.

A GROWING CRISIS

A growing crisis in the balance of nuclear terror exists today as arms control efforts between the United States and the Soviet Union move on a frustratingly erratic path—one moment toward apparent agreement, the next toward mistrust and recrimination, and then again toward precarious agreement.

Late in the 1970s, for example, laser researchers exploring high-intensity

X-ray beams for biomedical research began to suggest potential military applications, if laser energy could be pumped with nuclear explosives.[2] At the same time a group of retired military men supported by the Heritage Foundation developed the "High Frontier" concept of strategic defense against nuclear attack relying heavily on kinetic energy weapons deployed aboard fleets of satellites.[3]

By 1980, "High Frontier" became a national political movement, while X-ray laser research accelerated secretly at the Lawrence Livermore National Laboratory, with no public proclamation of national necessity. On November 14 that year, an underground nuclear test in Nevada code-named Dauphin demonstrated that lasing generated by the energy of a nuclear explosion was indeed possible. A year later Livermore launched its high-priority "Project Excalibur" to develop the nuclear-pumped X-ray laser weapon, and Edward Teller, a close but unofficial adviser to President Reagan, proposed that such weapons might be "popped up" from submarines to destroy enemy strategic missiles during their initial boost phase.[4]

Quietly, and without wide public knowledge or open political debate, research by the national laboratories and aerospace contractors into an array of exotic defense systems accelerated throughout 1981 and 1982. Then on March 23, 1983—convinced by the arguments of Teller and the "High Frontier" advocates, President Reagan called on America's scientists to devise new defensive systems that would make all nuclear weapons "impotent and obsolete." SDI, the Strategic Defense Initiative, was born, and the media—enthralled by the apparently daring expansion of defensive weapons into space—dubbed its concepts "Star Wars."

The President's speech announced a policy decision of overwhelming significance. In his own White House Science Council, an expert panel prepared a strong report, warning that there were no ballistic missile defense technologies on the horizon that might change the existing strategic balance, but Mr. Reagan was never given that report. So the President enunciated his vision of a strategic defense with no purely disinterested technical advice—and only later did he name the Fletcher and Hoffman expert panels to examine the technical and political approaches that might conceivably bring SDI to reality. Still later, after analyses by technical experts at the Congressional Office of Technology Assessment, by the Stanford University Center for International Security and Arms Control, by other scientific and cost-benefit specialists and, finally, by a distinguished American Physical Society panel and a team at Livermore, both armed with relevant classified data from the Star Wars organization itself, did truly informed public debate over SDI become possible, and informed discussion of the project's role in arms control become part of the 1988 Presidential campaign.

Many experts now argue that, had President Reagan been given the benefit of prior study and recommendations from a thoughtfully constituted scientific advisory committee, the bruising political battles and the pace of the

Star Wars enterprise itself might have been far more rational. SDI research plans might also have become far less entangled with other arms control issues, less embroiled in conflict with the Anti-Ballistic Missile Treaty, and less provocative to the Soviets who accord high priority to their own destabilizing research into strategic defense systems.[6]

Instead, our current Administration has seen a different and diminished role for its science advisory institutions. Dr. George A. Keyworth, the President's Science Advisor from 1981 to 1985, became an apologist—advocate is perhaps a more genteel word—for Presidential policies often based on wishful thinking and ideology, and the White House Science Council either remained silent or did little more than back him up.

Here, for example, are Dr. Keyworth's comments on a controversial proposal to create a Cabinet-level Department of Science and Technology:

> There's only one man who matters—the President. We have a President who's very pro-science, is very cognizant of what the word competitive means, and has a clearer view of the future than most people do. I believe from his position he has a better ability than I do to see the pros and cons of this particular proposal.[7]

In that same discussion Keyworth offered other revealing thoughts about the current Administration's view of the proper role for science advisors in the White House:

"This is the President's home," Keyworth said, "and we are guests here. The WHSC (White House Science Council) members behave like very dedicated and responsible guests."

As advocate and, indeed, polemicist, rather than disinterested advisor, Keyworth could also leap into the political lists during his White House tenure, and one of his favorite targets was the press. "We're trying to build up America," he declared, "and the press is trying to tear down America. . . . for some reasons that I just do not understand, much of the press seems to be drawn from a relatively narrow fringe element on the far left of our society . . . there's an arrogance that has to do with the power of the press. . . .

"The President has, among his greatest attributes, a deep sense of the American public. In many ways the President is the embodiment of the American public—that's the way he thinks. The President is aware of what most Americans want but the arms controllers lose sight of: Arms control has as its objectives: 1) stability and 2) reductions . . . In that context Salt I does not meet the public demand; Salt II does not meet the public demand. We need something bigger, bolder and more responsive to public concerns. . . . What the president has proposed (in SDI) is to develop the means to intercept ballistic missiles—this is a technical point but it's very important—in the *boost phase* before they multiply. We didn't have the means to do this ten years ago, or even five years ago, but today we believe we possess the technology."

Such oratorical advocacy of an issue like SDI, rather than expert, disinterested, and quiet counsel, is by no means a unique example of the wrong role for official science advisors.

AIDS

Consider the lethal and so far insoluble problem of the AIDS epidemic. It is impossible today to determine what, if any, advice emanated from the President's science advisors when the epidemic was first detected in 1981 and in the years following as its death toll grew. Fortunately, scientists at the National Institutes of Health, and major university research centers, as well as epidemiologists at the Centers for Disease Control quickly recognized the nature of the threat. Ultimately the AIDS virus was isolated and a test for antibodies to the organism was developed. But what scientific advice did the President get that might have impelled him to break his long silence over AIDS and proclaim a national policy for combatting the disease? There was no word from the White House on such critical issues as the need for major new funding to expedite AIDS research, education on prevention for young people, proposals for mandatory antibody testing, the costs (both social and financial) of quarantining AIDS victims. What we saw, as the AIDS epidemic spread and something like panic arose in many American communities, was Presidential inattention, and finally confusion among his high-level advisors: His Surgeon-General, Dr. C. Everett Koop, for example, pressed for candid education in the public schools about AIDS and sexual activity, and prescribed widespread use of condoms for those of whatever age who are sexually active.[8] At the same time, the President's Secretary of Education, William Bennett argued that school programs on AIDS must focus on abstinence, and insisted that condoms should not be offered to sexually active teen-aged youngsters.[9]

In the field of biotechnology, without the presence of a strong Science Advisor it is difficult for any President to make considered judgments on the degree to which genetic engineering—born in the laboratory barely fifteen years ago[10]—can, in fact, be harnessed to meet human medical and agricultural needs; or what regulations to propose for the burgeoning biotechnology industry, or what patent policies to advocate for animal life endowed by the genetic engineers with valuable new hereditary traits.

There are other decisions in biomedical technology that call for Presidential leadership—particularly where they involve delicate issues of ethics and privacy and access: Federal support for such life-prolonging medical technologies as organ transplants, and for future technologies such as artificial hearts, requires policy decisions that will ultimately involve many billions of federal dollars. Regulation of fetal research, of new techniques for in vitro fertilization and surrogate motherhood requires government decision-making that is both technically sound and humanly sensitive.

Ever since disaster struck the Shuttle Challenger on January 27, 1986, both the President and Congress have needed the most expert and dispassionate scientific analysis of the many options available for America's future in space:

Should we fund a new Heavy Lift Vehicle for SDI? Deploy the Space Station whose cost estimates have already soared from $8 billion to $32 billion? Pursue or abandon our long-deferred unmanned missions like the Galileo probe to Jupiter, Magellan to Venus, Ulysses to the sun, and the Hubble Space Telescope to scan the entire known universe? Should we join the Soviets to roam the surface of Mars and bring back samples of the Martian soil?

Wolfgang K. H. Panofsky, director emeritus of SLAC, served on President Kennedy's Science Advisory Committee in 1963 and 1964, and provided critical technical advice that made the Limited Test Ban Treaty of 1963 possible. Today he argues that the once-high standing of science advisors in the White House and the major Cabinet-level agencies has been badly undercut.

"Scientific competence among the advisors has receded to much lower levels," Panofsky says, "so policy often gets made without paying attention to technical and scientific realities. Even the President's Science Advisor doesn't have a high degree of stature, and unfortunately part of the job description today is that he must be an enthusiast for SDI."[11]

A Presidential Science Advisor can be independent, yet entirely compatible with his boss, Panofsky says. "It's perfectly reasonable for the President to select an Advisor who is compatible with his philosophy, and he should be ideologically in tune with the President, but selecting him because he already has a strong position on specific issues is a different matter. A President must choose between having a confidential Advisor and having a public spokesman for the President's science policy. Now we have an Advisor who is actually a vocal spokesman on specific issues, and you can't do that—he should only be giving confidential advice to the President. The President may not accept the advice, but being an Advisor is in many ways incompatible with being a spokesman. It's obvious to the public, the press and the Congress today that the Science Advisor is only a policy spokesman for the President, and that most of the independent experts in the Cabinet are either not sufficiently independent or not sufficiently expert."

To an outside observer, science-based policy decisions at the White House and in Cabinet departments often appear to suffer from inadequate background information, and at times from conflicting advice by "experts" pushing their own political agendas. The Departments of Interior, Energy, Health and Human Services, Agriculture, Transportation and Defense, in particular, badly need strong science advisors at the undersecretary level, with regular direct access to their chiefs. In the White House, a new Presidential Science Advisory Committee, well-staffed and headed by a scientist with the highest credentials and holding the President's confidence, can be critically important to any future Administration that seeks to enhance America's scientific and technological preeminence, to restore its industrial competitiveness, and to strengthen its national security.

Notes

1. 86th US Congress, Joint Committee on Atomic Energy, subcommittee hearings, July 14–15, 1959, p. 527.
2. David M. Ritson, "The Nuclear-Pumped X-Ray Laser, a Weapon for the 21st Century," *Nature,* August 7, 1987.
3. Lt. Gen. Daniel O. Graham, USA (Ret.), "High Frontier: A New National Strategy," High Frontier, Inc., Washington, D.C., 1982.
4. Ritson, *op. cit.*
5. See, for example: Ashton B. Carter, "Directed Energy Missile Defense in Space," US Congress Office of Technology Assessment, OTA-BP-ISC-26, April 1984; "Ballistic Missile Defense Technologies," OTA-ISC-254, September 1985; "Anti-Satellite Weapons, Countermeasures and Arms Control," OTA-ISC-281, September 1985; "Ballistic Missile Defense," a report from the Stanford Center for International Security and Arms Control, April 1985; "Directed Energy Weapons," a report by the American Physical Society, April 1987, published in *Reviews of Modern Physics* (1987); Lowell Wood and Gregory Canavan, "Joint Statement," in response to the APS Report, House Republican Research Committee, May 19, 1987; and "Responses to Critiques by Wood & Canavan," APS Directed Energy Study Group, June 18, 1987.
6. "Soviet Military Power," US Department of Defense, 1987.
7. Interview in *SIPIscope,* January–February 1985, Scientists' Institute for Public Information, New York.
8. *Los Angeles Times,* October 22, 1986.
9. *San Francisco Chronicle,* March 17, 1987.
10. Stanley Cohen, Annie Chang, Herbert Boyer and Robert Helling, "Construction of Biologically Functional Bacterial Plasmids in Vitro," *Proceedings of the National Academy of Sciences,* November 1973.
11. W. K. H. Panofsky, personal interview, June 1987.

To Foster Science
Restore University Autonomy

Gerard Piel

This memorandum is about science, but its subject is the state of the country's universities. It is addressed to all who will listen but especially to the President's Science Advisor and to the members of the President's Science Advisory Committee (if one is re-created, as it should be) and to concerned members of Congress.

The state of the universities is parlous. Like the hole in the ozone layer, it cannot be fixed overnight. As with the ozone layer, we are doing things to our universities that we may not be able to fix a generation from now. If the country's scientific enterprise is to thrive, some significant part of the public funding of science must go to restore the integrity of the universities which that funding has been subverting.

The university is where the work of science gets done. Thus, 116 out of the 122 Nobel prizes bestowed on American scientists since the end of World War II went to scientists in our universities. That is, moreover, 51% of all the prizes awarded. The record tells us that American universities have been performing well two functions that uniquely define the university as an institution. The first, is to elect from each generation of students those who are best qualified to carry forward the dissemination and advancement of human understanding. The second is to set those chosen few free, each to find the question that interests her or him, and to pursue it wherever it may lead for as long as they live.

These four decades have also seen the federal government take over from private philanthropy the funding of the rising costs of doing science. The

Gerard Piel is Chairman of the Board of Scientific American *and was one of its founders in 1946. He was President of the American Association for the Advancement of Science (1985–1986) and Chairman of the Board (1986–87). He is a Trustee of the American Museum of Natural History and of the New York Botanical Garden. He was twice elected an Overseer of Harvard University and is a member of the American Philosophical Society and of the Institute of Medicine. He is the author of numerous articles and books on education, science, and public policy.*

cumulative flow of federal funds into our universities now exceeds $50 billion. From the legislation that appropriated all that money, however, it is clear that no more than 5% of it was intended to support scientists in pursuit of their chosen interests and almost none of it for support of the universities. The money was appropriated to buy the results—the uses—of the work.

This is in accordance with the implicit bargain between university scientists and the federal government that started the flow of funds and has kept it growing almost ever since. That was not, however, the arrangement first sought. In 1945, in *Science: The Endless Frontier,* spokesmen for the scientific community showed that the universities could no longer support the increasingly costly work of their scientists—no longer make good, that is, on the promise to set them free to work on questions of their own choosing. Those spokesmen called upon the federal government to make this disinterested undertaking to the country's scientists through a National Science Foundation. In return, they promised practical results.

Federal funding was immediately forthcoming. The established agencies of the government were eager to buy those results. With funding suddenly so generously available, few scientists regretted the five-year delay in the establishment of the National Science Foundation. Fewer still agitated for increase of the modest appropriations with which it started.

SCIENCE IN JEOPARDY

The big money for science in our universities has come from the "mission" agencies with the biggest appropriations. The military and paramilitary and the health agencies have supplied more than 85% of the cumulative flow. To the universities these huge funds, from year to year as much as 30% of the total expenditures of the 100 "research" universities, have been flowing on terms that have now put the institution of the university and the scientific enterprise of our country in jeopardy.

The money goes not to the universities, but through the universities to the scientists. It goes not to the support of the scientist, but to the "project"; not for the long term of uncertain inquiry, but for the short term of fiscal management; not for the work, but for the utility of its prospective results. At issue somewhere in every grant or contract has been the delicate question whether the work is on behalf of the mission of the granting agency or work the scientist would be doing anyway—or on a grant from another agency. That ambiguity now compromises even the funding from the National Science Foundation; it has had its big increases in appropriation—it crossed the billion dollar line in 1985—for "Research Applied to National Needs" and presently for "knowledge transfer for national competitiveness."

Over time the ambiguity has been resolving in favor of the granting agency. As the presidents of the leading research universities not long ago complained, "'mission-oriented' grants are now 'task oriented.'" For the Strategic Defense Initiative, Pentagon granting officers are pressing funds on university scientists against the settled consensus of the community that the Initiative is infeasible.

The saving virtue argued for this style of funding is that the funds are awarded by peer review. That honorable procedure has detached the scientist's loyalty from the community of scholars in the university, however, and tied it more closely to the invisible college of peers in the same line of work. Most scientists recoil from any suggestion that their universities might have any say about the funding of their work from external sources. A few are beginning to share my misgivings, however, about the deteriorating terms on which they solicit and accept federal funding.

During the first two decades of their "federal period," the universities grew with the growth of federal funding "largely outside of organized faculty influence and control," in the words of Clark Kerr. In the past two decades, it is the dearth of federal funding that has been subverting their autonomy and has set university scientists and administrators hunting for support from industry on terms that put the motivation of the work and the publication of its yield under cloud. During the last two years, the National Science Foundation, flying the competitiveness banner, has been funding the creation in the universities of "institutes" for engineering and goal-directed research in which governance is to be shared with parties from outside.

With the universities unable to secure the freedom of scientists to choose their own questions, choices are being made for scientists by a half dozen federal granting agencies. No matter how considerately those agencies administer their grants and contracts, their missions and research interests taken together must leave large gaps in what would be the 360-degree horizon of the country's scientists free to look where they choose. Before the end of the century, we shall have occasion to declare the most painful of all regret: at what did not get done.

Consideration of measures to reduce the crushing federal pressure, to restore autonomy to the universities, and to secure again for university scientists the freedom to do their own work should begin with recognition that the federal presence in the universities is decisive. It can be exerted as well for conservation of these vital national, natural resources as for exploitation of them.

A PROPOSAL

My modest proposal is that some significant part of the public funding of science should go to the universities in the form of institutional grants. This is not a new idea. You should know that it excites strong resistance in the scientific community and little enthusiasm from university administrators. R. A. Millikan tried to keep any suggestion of it out of the National Science

Foundation legislation. Its advocacy, in turn, by each of the few Congressmen ever interested in science policy (*e.g.,* by Carl Elliott, Henry Reuss and E. Q. Daddario) was stifled in the hearings. When Jerome Wiesner floated the idea in the Kennedy White House, he had to add: "I suspect neither the funding agencies, the universities, nor the individual researchers will welcome this suggestion . . ."

Welcome or not, I recommend that we convene a Constitutional convention of the parties concerned to design the instrument and the policies for the administration of university grants. It should be possible to get these parties to buy at least the venture capital needed to put the young scientist, on first tenure-ladder appointment, in action. At present, the assistant professor has little more than a license to go hunting in the granting agencies—there to adapt or to disguise his or her new question to fit funding for already certified old questions. If the university can no longer support a life-long career in science, it should have the funds to launch the career of a scientist it has trained and chosen. That is a first step back to autonomy.

A Prescription for Science and Technology Advising for the President: An Interview by William T. Golden

Frank Press

Mr. Golden: Frank, you are outstandingly well qualified to advise on why every President of the US needs independent advice on science and technology issues and on how best to assure him of advice that he will seek and consider. You were Science Advisor to President Carter, you were a member of PSAC under President Kennedy, and you have been a member of the National Science Board. You have been a member of the National Academy of Sciences for many years and are serving a second six-year term as its President. You know academia from professorships at Columbia, CalTech, and MIT. You have been closely involved with industry. And you have served on many official missions to the Soviet Union, to the People's Republic of China, to Japan, and to the NATO countries.

The purpose of collecting this volume of essays by well qualified individuals of diverse experience and viewpoints, regardless of their political orientations, is to attract attention to the great and growing need for dependable science and technology advice to the highest levels of government. The approaching 1988 elections create opportunity to draw attention to the science and technology advisory functions and to review them. In this way, one hopes to influence the candidates for high office, Presidential office and Congress, to reflect about this function as an essential

Frank Press is President of the National Academy of Sciences, serving his second six-year term. He was Science Advisor to President Carter (1977–80) and has been a member of the President's Science Advisory Committee (1961–64) and of the National Science Board. He has been on the faculties of Columbia, Caltech, and MIT in geology and geophysics. He has served on numerous government and scientific boards and has received numerous awards.

ingredient in government policy-making and decision-making. So, let us have your thoughts.

Dr. Press: Let me give you at least my own point of view from the vantage point of somebody who served as a consultant to Kistiakowsky and to Killian, and was on the President's Science Advisory Committee (PSAC) during the Kennedy Administration with Jerome Wiesner as the Science Advisor, and who later had the job himself.

There is no question that in this day and age, when science and technology are such an important part of almost everything in front of the President, that there should be a science person at a high-level position in the White House. In that respect, you were very prescient forty years ago when you pointed this out. To close the circle, Jerry Wiesner's recent op-ed article in the *Washington Post* made the same case, referring to your earlier contribution. It was very timely.

But I think that from what we've learned in terms of past Presidents and past Science Advisors and their influence, the office and the concept have to be changed somewhat. That's the main thrust of what I would like to say to you.

I believe that the Science Advisor should be an office that is not legislated, like the OSTP office, which by statute is part of the Executive Office of the President, not part of the White House. That's a distinction that not too many people know about. The Executive Office of the President is a different entity from the White House itself and the White House Office. And any office that is forced upon the President by legislation rather than initiated from within is looked upon with suspicion and as an intrusion.

Congress in its wisdom wanted to have science advice at the highest level and, as you know, during the Ford Administration, the National Science and Technology Policy Organization and Priorities Act was passed. I don't believe that was the way to do it. You can't force it on the President. You create the office, but it's isolated as an office that is more responsive to Congress than to the President. I believe that future Presidents, because of the way society is going, will want a science advisor. This will be especially true for the younger breed of Presidential candidates. Every one of them—and I speak to most of them on both sides of the aisle—understands the importance of a White House Science Advisor.

All of this comes down to the following proposal: The President's Science Advisor should either be named as an assistant to the President, which is a very high-level position, or should be given a Cabinet position without portfolio. Either of those would be acceptable, and either would work very well.

It would be unprecedented. The other Science Advisors were special assistants. I believe that the time has come to name the Science Advisor an assistant to the President in the White House rather than in the Executive Office.

The President's Science Advisor in that position will need a professional staff without question, because the agenda is so broad. There is no individual in this vast country of ours that knows everything, from health to environment to technology to defense to space to the frontiers of science. So that person will need a strong professional staff, perhaps twenty to twenty-five people.

Even with a professional staff, that person will need strong contacts with the best scientists in the country, the best engineers, and the best physicians through a network that will become very important. The issues will require expert advice that will mostly be found outside the government.

Now, there are a number of ways to handle this. There are those who believe in a strong PSAC concept, a Presidentially appointed panel of advisors, perhaps in the mold of the PSAC under Wiesner, which was the best PSAC. It's a very good concept. It has a record of success. But I think some changes would be required.

You cannot be a PSAC member two or three days a month and then be a dean, a working scientist, a provost, or a vice president or CEO of a corporation. If you want to be fully briefed on what is going on currently within the government—the issues and the problems—then it takes a stronger time commitment. Without these briefings and without this knowledge, there's only so much that you can contribute. To be involved and to be a problem-solver, or the source of new ideas, requires a commitment of several kinds—a time commitment, which I think should at least be half-time, and a disciplinary commitment that as long as you're involved in the President's family, you take all of your concerns directly to the President and not outside. Now, the scientists I know of the caliber of PSAC members want to be involved with strategy and tactics. They're smart. They're competent. They know the issues. But they have to agree to these conditions. You can't look at PSAC problems two days a month and then go home and do your other job. You come in, you shoot from the hip, you can't give it your best shot because of time and discipline. So I believe that a PSAC, a Presidentially appointed PSAC with a chairman as the Science Advisor to the President, is perhaps the best solution, if you can do it the way I've described.

Mr. Golden: Let me just repeat that. You think the best solution would be to have a President's Science Advisor who would be Chairman also of a Presidentially appointed President's Science Advisory Committee.

Dr. Press: Yes, with the understanding that the PSAC members give the time that's required—I think it's about half time—and sign onto the White House Staff discipline that I've described.

There are alternate versions of this. You might have a small council, analogous to the Council of Economic Advisers, who are full time. You'd have a chairman, the President's Science Advisor, and very distinguished people as deputies, all of whom would be full-time Presidential appointees.

Now, there are alternate schemes, one of which I used when I was in the White House. It again recognizes that the President's Science Advisor needs to bring experts in to help him with these problems. The way I organized it, because President Carter did not want a PSAC, was to bring in special panels on an issue-by-issue basis. I had a special panel on the MX. I had a special panel on the Test Ban. I had a special panel on space policy issues. I had a special panel dealing with ozone and the ozone standards for the country. I brought these experts in from across the country. They were fully briefed and didn't have to spend full time because they were already experts and didn't have to learn new material.

Mr. Golden: I might comment that CO_2, radioactive waste disposal, certain genetic engineering issues would be comparable topics today.

Dr. Press: Yes. To continue, I had 20 or so panels, as was required. And it worked. It was an alternative for a President who didn't want to build up large staffs in the White House. Many Presidents feel the efficiency of smaller staffs is very important to them. Then they can track everything. They know everybody, and they know what's going on. With large staffs, there are too many people floating around with White House passes, and you lose control. Too many people speak in the name of the President. That was President Carter's attitude, and that's why we used this other approach. So, these are the different models for doing things.

The main point is that the President's Science Advisor has to be on the White House staff, I think, as a Cabinet officer without portfolio or an assistant to the President. That's more important than the title of Director of the Office of Science and Technology Policy (OSTP).

Those are the changes I would make. Whether the Presidential candidates in the years ahead would accept my proposition, I don't know. As I mentioned before, in my discussions with some of the younger governors and senators, I have the feeling that they would accept this notion because they appreciate the role of technology and its importance to this nation. The older generation may prefer a conventional, traditional White House staff. It remains to be seen.

Mr. Golden: As is now being done, with the Science Advisor and the OSTP being several notches down from the President . . .

Dr. Press: Exactly. . . .

Mr. Golden: Well, that's a very clear prescription, and one which I find congenial. What would you think about the practicalities in relation to the Congress? After all, there is now an Act: OSTP exists by Congressional Act. Do you foresee a problem with that?

Dr. Press: This could be handled in a number of ways. The President could accept the OSTP Act, and simply give the Director of OSTP the title of Assistant to the President on top of all that. Now, I'm sure that his White House counsel will say to him, "Mr. President, do you want an Assistant to the President who is required to testify before Congress?" I don't know what the answer will be.

Mr. Golden: Well, if you were President, you'd rather not.

Dr. Press: In which case, I would advise the President to use his reorganization authority. I believe that if the President went to Congress and said, "If the purpose of your legislation is to make sure that I have requisite advice from the best scientists in the country, then I propose to do that by going even further than your statute, by putting the Science Advisor into the White House with the title, Assistant to the President, or with the title, Cabinet officer." I believe that Congress would be very supportive, because it's really what they wanted, only a more powerful position than they themselves enacted.

Mr. Golden: Congress would be concerned, I should think, about losing access on occasion to the Science Advisor, and that becomes a problem. But it was dealt with satisfactorily in the past, and also now there's the Office of Technology Assessment where the Congress has some staff of its own. Does that seem to you to have a bearing? My impression is that the OTA has been a useful entity.

Dr. Press: I agree with that, but that's another matter. You see, if they want to be able to call my assistant to the President down for testimony, . . . I just don't know how the President would react to that. What is he going to say? It's Presidential privilege and I can't answer that question. So it's an issue that they would have to face. I don't lobby Congress, but I would try to impress upon Congress that, if we have a President who wants to make his advisor an Assistant or give him Cabinet status, Congress should accept it because that's exactly what Congress wanted to accomplish in the legislation.

So that's the way I would like to see it. I think there's a readiness in the years ahead.

Mr. Golden: Well, that's the point, that's the trend among the younger public servants and aspirants.

Dr. Press: I see that in the younger governors, the younger senators who are potential Presidential candidates. I think they understand this.

Mr. Golden: Well, that would be my impression also. Frank, do I understand, in summary, that your ideal resolution of this, the ideal revision of the status of science advising to the President, would be to have a President's Science Advisor and a President's Science Advisory Committee. They might have different titles, but in any event, the President's Science Advisor would be the chairman of the PSAC, whatever it may be called, and the President's Science Advisor would be an active, full-time member of the President's staff, an Assistant to the President or a Cabinet officer without portfolio. He would have such staff as he might need, which might be twenty-five professionals, more or less. He would have the President's Science Advisory Committee, which would report to the President as well as to him, as the old model was; and I'm proceeding a little further, you didn't say that.

And those members of PSAC would be expected to spend half time, more or less, this would not be just a couple-of-days-a-month kind of thing or a one-day-a-week kind of thing, either, but would require a very substantial commitment of their time and would be a very important part of their lives; and they would, indeed, be better in that role by reason of spending the other half of their time out in the actual world of academia or of industry or finance and would therefore be in touch with national and world affairs. And you have what might be called a fall-back position that could be somewhat less desirable. It seemed to be your second choice: a mechanism in which there would be a President's Science Advisor of the same kind plus a body comparable to the Council of Economic Advisors, perhaps five other members, all of them full-time people and all of them Presidential appointments and all of them members of the White House Staff and not of the Executive Office of the President.

Dr. Press: That's pretty close.

Let me just summarize it succinctly. This is in the order of priority:

1. There should be a President's Science Advisor with the title of Assistant to the President or Cabinet member without portfolio.

2. The Advisor should be backed up by a committee or a board of people, mostly from the outside. If it's in the form of a President's Science Advisory Committee, then it will require the disciplines I've mentioned: a major commitment of time, at least half time, and the discipline of . . .

Mr. Golden: Loyalty to the President . . . privacy.

Dr. Press: Not loyalty so much as not opposing the President publicly while in office. Failing this structure, the President's Science Advisor might establish *ad hoc* committees in different areas as the need arises. That's my lower priority.

Mr. Golden: Failing a PSAC.

Dr. Press: Failing a PSAC, if the President didn't want a PSAC. Failing that.

Mr. Golden: A Carter mode that you employed, faute de mieux.

Dr. Press: Exactly. That's right.

So those are the possibilities there.

The Science Advisor needs a staff because he's going to have to comment on agency programs where the agencies have hundreds and hundreds of scientists and engineers. The Advisor needs a small staff of perhaps twenty-five. On top of that, he needs a budget with a couple of million dollars a year—which I had, but which may not have survived in recent years. This is required to cover studies and analyses and do the necessary research rather than having to sponge off of agencies. It's very important to be able to commission the Academy or the Institute of Medicine or some university to look into an issue.

Mr. Golden: Without having to scrounge.

Dr. Press: Without having to scrounge for money. Yes.

And that's it. I believe that what I've described is a very powerful mechanism, more powerful than ever before. Maybe the times are ready for something like this.

Mr. Golden: Now, in your summary, you didn't refer to the Council on Economic Advisers as a model.

Dr. Press: I just left it out accidentally.

Mr. Golden: I see. But that would be a subordinate role and a fall-back position.

Dr. Press: That's after the PSAC, a smaller group, full time.

Mr. Golden: Thank you, Frank. That's a very clear description, analysis, and prescription.

May we talk more generally. A point I want to make is that every President's Science Advisor, and there have been twelve of them so far (Oliver Buckley, Lee A. DuBridge, I. I. Rabi, James R. Killian, Jr., George B. Kistiakowsky, Jerome B. Wiesner, Donald F. Hornig, Edward E. David, Jr., H. Guyford Stever, Frank Press, George A. H. Keyworth, II, and William R. Graham), has had a different job. Each one would describe the elephant differently, because each one had a different President. The elephant was different, and the world was different, and the job was different. And, of course, organizational changes occurred also. Do you agree that that will continue to be true in the future because of the interplay between the Science Advisor and the President and because "the only permanent thing is change?"

Dr. Press: Yes.

Mr. Golden: Frank, I wonder whether you would comment about the personal relationship of a President's Science Advisor to the President—a relationship which can be generalized to many advisors at high levels. For example, how does one go about telling the President things that he may not want to hear but that the Advisor thinks he should hear and consider. Closely involved is the relationship of privacy that has to exist between any individual and the person he is advising. I would guess that there were occasions in which you told President Carter things that he might have preferred otherwise, and in some instances he might have taken your advice, and on others he might not have; and on still others he might have been stimulated to seek other opinions.

Since I have played roles as assistant to two very able people, though in very different organizational settings, I am mindful of how useful it can be to an intelligent, open-minded, high-ranking person to have someone near him, in whom he has confidence for judgment and loyalty, who will tell him that he's wrong, or tell him that he's blind to matters.

Dr. Press: I was very pleased to see an analysis (Walter Williams, "The Carter Domestic Policy Staff," *Research in Public Policy Analysis and Management,* Vol. 3, pp. 23–67) of the Carter Administration and of the staff of the Carter Administration by a professor at the University of Washington. This is what he said. It's the best compliment that anybody ever paid me. He interviewed all of the Presidential assistants, and he said that everybody agreed that Frank Press was balanced, called it as he saw it, never went beyond his own expertise, and therefore had enormous respect from all of the other staff members.

I did tell the President that he was wrong on a number of issues. For example, I told him he was wrong on the MX. I told him that the position he was about to take on air quality standards for the country was based on very poor data, and I told him that his goal of 20% solar energy by the year 2000 could never be achieved. He espoused the goal anyway, but he had at least heard a cautionary point of view.

There were a number of other situations like that. In the Carter White House, what I did was not unusual. People said what they thought, some on political grounds, some on other grounds, and I did it on issues I knew about, feeling confident that I had a proper base and credibility to make that kind of judgment. He listened but did not necessarily follow the views, although often he did.

Mr. Golden: That's what you would picture as an intimate, mutually trusting relationship that ought to exist between a President's Science Advisor and the President.

Dr. Press: I didn't go outside and argue against the MX publicly. But everybody in the Cabinet knew my views on it.

Mr. Golden: Would you comment on the relations of the National Academy-National Research Council with the government and how these touch on the Presidential science-advisory mechanisms.

Dr. Press: Let me put it in perspective. The Academy's relationship with the government is a very close and intense one, but it is not with a single place in the government, it is with hundreds, literally hundreds of different parts of the government, many places within the NSF, within HHS, within Interior, within NASA, within the Department of Energy. Included within that list is the OSTP; they've asked us for help and we've obliged. Our contacts with Congress are really accelerating very rapidly with requests to undertake important substantive analyses and studies for them.

So I would say that our contact with the White House is not one that exceeds the many contacts that we have with the rest of the government and Congress.

Mr. Golden: Thank you, Frank, for your interesting, practical, and helpful observations.

Scientific Mediation and Technology Policy Convergence

Joel R. Primack and Nancy E. Abrams

In matters of technology, there is, in the United States, constant dispute. Our political system and legal procedures provide a large and shifting selection of moments when arguments can be made, and combatants value their rights to use these opportunities. What our system lacks are equally powerful methods for achieving technical and political concensus—for resolving disputes over technology policy in ways that are generally accepted to be technically sound and politically legitimate. In this article, we discuss two practical methods which, if used seriously, could not only advance the resolution of the problems to which they were applied, but also substantially raise the general level of debate and understanding about technology in this country.

"Scientific Mediation"[1] is a relatively simple and inexpensive procedure which can be extremely useful to policy-makers. It is designed for the very common situation where a decision regarding a technology must be made while significant scientific uncertainties concerning the consequences of utilizing the technology still exist. (It is only appropriate in situations where experts can legitimately differ, not in fake disputes like that, for example, between the Tobacco Institute and the American Cancer Society, where only large transfusions of money keep one side alive.) In legitimate technical

Joel Primack is Professor of Physics, University of California, Santa Cruz. His research is on cosmology and particle physics, and he is an originator of a current leading theory of galaxy formation. He wrote Advice and Dissent: Scientists in the Political Arena *with Frank von Hippel, and helped to create the American Physical Society's program of technical studies on public issues and the AAAS Congressional Science Fellowship Program.*

Nancy Abrams is a lawyer and mediator who has developed alternative methods of dispute resolution for the Ford Foundation, the Congressional Office of Technology Assessment, the Government of Sweden, and private clients. She is the author of many articles on the application of innovative dispute resolution to scientific controversies and peace.

disputes, there are generally scientists with impeccable credentials to be found on both sides of the question, and the decision-maker has no way of choosing whom, if anyone, to believe, except on the highly unreliable basis of preference for the personality of a particular scientist or, in a misguided use of democracy, the sheer weight of numbers of scientists on one side rather than the other. As Einstein said when told that Hitler was having a hundred eminent professors compile a book disproving relativity, "If it were true, one professor would be enough." Scientific Mediation allows the decision-maker, as well as eventually the press and public, to understand the technical dimension of the policy dispute, and to make an intelligent decision on that basis.

HOW IT WORKS

This is how scientific mediation works.

1. The decision-maker, whether it be a judge, a government agency, or for that matter a corporation, determines what the question is. It must be a primarily technical, not political or economic, question. The most extensive use of Scientific Mediation so far has been in Sweden, where it was first applied to the question: "Is the electric utilities' plan for nuclear waste disposal safe and adequate?"[2] This is a largely technical question, even though it involves other elements.

2. The decision-maker then brings together three people: A) a mediator, who need not be a scientist, but must understand the technology policy-making process and be regarded as a person of stature by everyone involved; and B) two reputable scientists from relevant fields who hold opposite views on the policy recommendation, presumably because of their differing underlying scientific opinions. Each must be acceptable to the constituency for that position. (If there are three legitimate positions, then three scientists will be chosen. For the sake of brevity, however, we will outline the procedure on the assumption of two sides.)

3. The two scientists first list, in writing, the main areas on which they agree. This step, analogous to the making of stipulations in law, greatly narrows the dispute, since between any two scientists in the same or related fields, there is usually far more agreement than disagreement, and seeing this is important not only for the decision-maker, but for the scientists themselves.

4. The scientists then list the fundamental points relevant to the issue on which they do not agree.

5. With the help of the mediator, they now embark on the main task of Scientific Mediation: to explain in writing for each of the listed points precisely why they take the positions they do. Each must explain his/her reasoning to the satisfaction of the other one, and since both are experts, they cannot talk past each other. This step in practice resembles

cross-examination, except that the scientists do it with each other. There is no grand-standing and no audience. It is done in private with, at most, the mediator present.

6. They list and explain the areas, if any, in which further research is required before a responsible decision on the current question can be made.

Scientists generally collaborate only with other scientists with whom they agree, and so this is not a familiar task for them. The mediator throughout has three crucial responsibilities:

A) To help smooth and maintain the working relationship.

B) To keep the discussion relevant to the policy decision.

C) To be sure the final product is in clear English with a minimum of technical jargon.

During the fifth step, the personal biases and assumptions of the scientists will surface and be separated to a great extent from their scientific opinions, because what has generally happened is that they have used these, as we all do, to fill in the gaps in their knowledge. They will probably not agree on a policy recommendation in the end (although on several occasions in Sweden, this unexpectedly occurred), but agreement is not the goal of the procedure. The goal is a readable report, signed by both scientists, which lays out the range of possibilities, explains what still needs to be known by a responsible decision-maker, and clarifies the nonscientific beliefs or even biases that may cause a person to come down in one place on that range rather than another.

The procedure is inherently unbiased and fair, and cannot be stacked like a committee. Each side has its say, in a finite amount of time, and the end result is that the reader of the report is in a far better position to make an intelligent decision than by simply relying on the prepackaged word of a scientist or committee.

TPC

But what about the big technological issues that involve political, economic, ecological, and even moral dimensions? For example, how should the United States handle its nuclear waste problem? Or the AIDS epidemic? Or the arms race? Scientific Mediation can only be used on small aspects of such issues. We propose another procedure for such major questions, which we will call "TPC," standing for "Technology Policy Convergence" or, alternatively, "The Public Counts."[3]

TPC requires the government to accept the premise that the public matters, and should be listened to. The problem from the point of view of many decision-makers and experts, however, is that the public is narrow-minded and ignorant. People with strong opinions object to new technologies (or support them, for that matter) without understanding either the needs and trade-offs of the larger political entity or the underlying technical issues. The preferred solution is frequently to exclude the public as much as possible. But it is then hardly surprising that disputes persist, and views become even more polarized.

It is true that much of the public is ignorant, but what goes unrecognized is that, on forefront technological issues, everyone, including the experts, is ignorant of the big picture. We will use nuclear waste disposal as an example to illustrate the method of TPC, although it could probably be applied to anything from health care priorities to national defense strategies.

TPC works like this. The people ultimately responsible for nuclear waste disposal should put forth a plan as to how they propose to do it. The federal government has volunteered to shoulder this burden, although we believe it should belong to the nuclear utilities. But either way, the plan should be constructed as a BEST FIRST EFFORT. It must not be a laundry-list of options but a complete plan, covering each step from extraction of spent fuel rods from the reactor to the form and location of the waste thousands of years in the future. It should also contain an explanation of the reasons behind the main technological choices, as well as unvarnished worst case analyses. It is to be understood, however, that the plan is a first draft only, and that criticism of the plan will be incorporated into the next iteration and not be taken as adversarial.

The plan should then be published and opened for scrutiny by a wide range of institutions with relevant expertise, such as universities, state governments, industry groups, energy agencies of foreign governments, and most especially public interest groups. These citizen groups must be adequately funded by the government to hire sympathetic scientists and engineers to perform a thorough analysis of the plan. At least one review, possibly by the White House or a special commission set up for the purpose, should be performed using Scientific Mediation, since this is the only procedure specifically designed to bring out the real trade-offs, both qualitative and quantitative, in such a technical plan.

The plan and reviews should then be discussed at a conference or series of conferences in major political centers such as Washington, DC. This would assure both attentive and sophisticated press coverage and attendance by the largest number of relevant decision-makers. The general understanding that would emerge from an effort of this kind is an absolute prerequisite not only to the development of a safe long-range plan but also to any kind of meaningful public participation, because it would only be at this point that the issues would be defined clearly enough so that the public could competently decide what was worth supporting.

The next version of the plan would likely be of incomparably higher quality, as well as being far more acceptable for implementation in a democratic society. This procedure would result not in perpetual confrontation, but in eventual convergence. And it would bring us, as a society, closer to the goal of civilized cooperation that is becoming ever more crucial to human survival.

NOTES

1. Nancy E. Abrams and R. Stephen Berry, "Mediation: A Better alternative to Science Courts," *Bulletin of the Atomic Scientists*, April 1977.
2. Nancy E. Abrams, "Nuclear Politics in Sweden," *Environment,* May 1979.
3. Nancy E. Abrams and Joel R. Primack, "Helping the Public Decide: The Case of Radioactive Waste Management," *Environment,* April 1980. Reprinted in Robert W. Lake, ed., *Resolving Locational Conflict,* (Center for Urban Policy Research,Rutgers University, 1987). A shorter version is Nancy E. Abrams and Joel R. Primack, "The Public and Technological Decisions," *Bulletin of the Atomic Scientists,* June 1980. Sweden has followed an interactive process such as we propose in developing its nuclear waste ("KBS") plan, which is now in its third iteration.

Presidential Science Advising and the National Academy of Sciences: An Interview by William T. Golden

I. I. Rabi

Mr. Golden: Rab, your paper in the first volume of this series, Science Advice to the President, *published in 1980, was replete with vivacity, charm, and wisdom. Now, seven or eight years later, I hope you'll express your up-to-date thoughts about science and technology inputs to the highest levels of our government.*

Dr. Rabi: Well, I'm discouraged about the trend and the situation. The culture of our government officials is apparently not up to science. There's been a great departure from the roots: arithmetic, common sense, and the like. The President's Science Advisor and the President's Science Advisory Committee have not played effective roles since Nixon abolished them. Like many good intentions, the idea has gone sour, because the subsequent Presidents have not appointed PSACs and President Reagan has downgraded the Science Advisor's office and wants only advice and ideas that please him. The Advisor's job has been to back up the President—not to help him decide, but to back him up whatever his decision was. That is as far from science as you can get.

Mr. Golden: You told me that you want to comment about the National Academy of Sciences, which plays a very important role in this whole process of the evaluation of science and technology and of providing sci-

I. I. Rabi (b. 1898), Nobel Laureate in physics (1944), was a member of the original President's Science Advisory Committee (Office of Defense Mobilization), was its Chairman (1956–57), and continued as a PSAC member until 1960. He was a member of the General Advisory Committee of the US Atomic Energy Commission (1946–56) and its Chairman (1952–56). Dr. Rabi has served on many US Government and UN boards, and has received numerous honors and awards. He is University Professor Emeritus at Columbia University, and is a member of the American Philosophical Society and of the National Academy of Sciences.

ence and technology advice to the President and to the Congress and, in a sense, indirectly to the Judiciary and to the American public.

Dr. Rabi: The Academy should play a role, a central role; it is organized to do that. It was organized in such a brilliant way that it is in government and yet out of government. What has happened with the Academy is that we've added new divisions in recent years, like sociology and economics, that really have no place there. I think there should be no place in the Academy for activities that aren't connected with hard science, for a very simple reason: The hard sciences are an essential element of our culture and the novel element in our culture for the last few hundred years. Sociology and economics are valuable in themselves, but they're not science in the sense of physical and biological sciences. When the Academy speaks on such subjects, however, it speaks to politicians who feel they are just as capable of talking about such subjects as are the scientists, maybe more capable.

Mr. Golden: You mean when they talk about economics or the other social sciences as distinguished from the physical and biological sciences?

Dr. Rabi: Yes. And I think it's disastrous. We did that with the President's Science Advisory Committee—I recall Moynihan and some others. And, of course, those social scientists are very knowledgeable; they know all the gossip and so on—very impressive that way. And pretty soon the hard scientists are cowed and don't speak with their own voices. But we really need their input, however naive it may appear at certain times. It's an absolutely essential element.

Another thing: the Academy has grown, and there are too many people in it for intimate, collegial discussions. When any group goes above a certain size, it's run by an in-group. People like to be elected. And, of course, greater size makes the President of the Academy and the other officers very busy just running the show, in an administrative and fund-raising sense. And it becomes so diverse that they look for all sorts of work which, although important, can be done as well by other groups.

So I think the Academy is over-expanded. Too many members, too much staff. It's too big an organization and requires a lot of money just to keep alive. I have quit going to meetings. It's not interesting. I can't find the essential people I want to talk to. They're lost in the crowd. Maybe I'm showing that I'm an old man.

Mr. Golden: Well, you show that you haven't lost your alert, independent-spirited, mature judgment. You've certainly retained your sense of humor. When did you stop going to the Academy meetings? How far back?

Dr. Rabi: Oh, it must be some ten years ago. The Academy has greatly increased in membership and budget in recent decades.

Mr. Golden: Was it different under Det Bronk? You used to go regularly when he was President—and you were younger. That's quite a while ago.

Dr. Rabi: That's quite a while ago. Then he was followed by Fred Seitz and then by Phil Handler, and now by Frank Press. Fred Seitz changed the scene. He brought in the engineers, put them on an equal level with the scientists; and that, I think, was devastating because, whatever you can say about the engineers (and they're wonderful and essential people), they're not scientists. They don't have that kind of thinking. And they have a lot of money. They feel, therefore, that they're very powerful and right. It is said that Britain and the US are two people separated by a common language, and I think that's the scientists and engineers. They're really very different. I was interviewed by some Japanese a few years ago on just that question. And it occurred to me to say that the difference between them can be best illustrated by the difference between poetry and advertising. Advertising lives on poetry, part of the language and so on, images—that sort of thing. But, of course, advertising is not poetry. Basically they're very different. So you can sense the underlying cause of my discontent.

Mr. Golden: So you would not have created a National Academy of Engineering; or, if it had been created, you would not have placed it in this close affiliation and parity with the National Academy of Sciences.

Dr. Rabi: That's right. They could be by themselves. Any connection of engineering with science can only degrade science. Science is other-worldly; engineers are practical people. And the people who get elected are not necessarily great engineers; many of them are heads of corporations and very valuable to our culture, but not to our science. And I have similar views about the Institute of Medicine. They're different; they have very different outlooks.

Mr. Golden: Well, if the National Academy of Sciences were disaffiliated from the other two, what would you visualize it doing that it isn't doing now?

Dr. Rabi: It would have to continue to supply studies and advice to the government, as it was founded to do. So much depends on the President of the Academy and the staff of the National Research Council. They have somehow or other to imbue the government with the spirit of science, which is a cultural thing. When you have that, you have a different slant on everything; at least, everything which concerns the government. So I can't be specific. And, of course, it should be recognized that by stepping into all sorts of issues, taking on all sorts of questions, they lose their mystique. It's only the very fundamental questions that should be addressed.

I'll comment on a specific major topic for its value as an example. Recently, a question came up about the report of the American Physical Society that studied Star Wars; and then it was pointed out there was another opinion. So there are these two sides that differed. You realize that on the one side you had some of the most eminent scientists and engineers in the world, and on the other side had people who had a vested interest—government employees and so on. Which side should you select? Common sense tells you right off; you don't have to be the common man, which I define in Nixon's terms—don't have to be an expert. Did I ever tell you about Nixon's definition of "common man"?

Mr. Golden: No.

Dr. Rabi: On one occasion, Nixon, I, and our host—a man who had headed the Arms Control and Disarmament Agency and who had been high in the Department of Defense—were talking, and Nixon referred to the common man, and then began to define what he meant: Who is the common man? He said, "Well, it could be the president of a bank or the publisher of a newspaper, the head of a labor union, the superintendent of schools," and went on that way—this was the man in the street. I thought it was a wonderful definition.

Mr. Golden: Well, do you think that the Academy's effectiveness is impaired by reason of getting the bulk of its funds from the Congress, by appropriation? Do you think it can be independent?

Dr. Rabi: I don't know. When it gets to be this big and has to live (I don't know how many employees it has, it's a large number), then you can't be independent. You must keep yourself going; there are mouths to feed.

Mr. Golden: You've indicated that you'd prefer the National Research Council to be a smaller undertaking, with fewer jobs.

Dr. Rabi: We have all these think tanks around—God knows, the place is full of them. Very bright, very well-paid people. No need for the Academy to duplicate this stuff.

Mr. Golden: What could the Academy do to be uniquely helpful to the Congress; and I take it you are also thinking of the Executive branch?

Dr. Rabi: Oh, helpful to the whole country. It is an independent body, with carefully selected people, American citizens. When problems come up in any important field, the Academy can be asked for advice. The Academy, through its structure, can bring in very good people. That's what the President's Science Advisory Committee was able to do because of its composition: marshall the whole, enormous scientific effort from the large number of qualified people in our country.

Mr. Golden: You served as a member of PSAC for many years, from its early years; and you were its chairman for a time. It has been abolished. Do you think it has outlived its usefulness? Or would you like to see a PSAC restored to existence?

Dr. Rabi: I don't see how the President can do without one. You see, he's tried to do without a PSAC. He's gotten into one mess after another. Of course, the President has to have the capacity to use it. It should consist of people who are themselves sufficiently important that he could dare to make a decision stand up before the country, if he had their backing. And also sufficiently important that they can't ignore them. I'm not saying he should always take their advice but he should understand it, consider it, and not ignore it.

A PSAC could be of great use to the President. You asked what use it could be. It could give him confidence, if it's sufficiently well established—confidence when he takes their advice and protection if he does, on either side. And the President had that.

Mr. Golden: You're thinking especially of President Eisenhower.

Dr. Rabi: Yes, I'm thinking especially of Eisenhower. Kennedy was not quite so good, because Jerry Wiesner, for all his great gifts, was no match for McGeorge Bundy; so he got shut out of foreign policy. Bundy was head of the National Security Council: a very important position.

Mr. Golden: So you would restore a PSAC. We're talking here in the hope that your thoughts and those of others in the book I'm assembling, will stimulate thinking among candidates for the Presidency in 1988, and thereafter, in the hope of influencing them to make more effective use of scientific and technological advice in the determination of federal government policies over a broad range of issues that will affect the lives of all of us.

Well, Rab, let me shift a little here. What roles do you see for the National Academies of Science and Engineering and the Institute of Medicine, as distinguished from the role of a President's Science Advisor and a President's Science Advisory Committee?

Dr. Rabi: Well, a President's Science Advisory Committee should be concerned with the problems that come before the President. They're there for the President, for no other purpose. The Academy is there as a group that meets periodically and discusses scientific matters. They can discuss matters of public affairs, but there should be a scientific base. So it's an entirely different thing. In their capacity as members of the Academy, they are apolitical. As advisors to the President, the other group are—must be—politically sensitive. The President is and must be political.

Mr. Golden: What would you see, then, as the Academy's role? Do you agree that the Academy should do particular study jobs, as they do now, directly and via the National Research Council?

Dr. Rabi: I think they could do study jobs, but very selectively.

Mr. Golden: And the wide variety of studies that are undertaken by the National Research Council?

Dr. Rabi: I don't see why our great governmental laboratories and other organizations, public and private, can't do many more of those study jobs.

Mr. Golden: You mean the private, not-for-profit think tanks?

Dr. Rabi: Yes.

Mr. Golden: The bulk of the think-tank money does come from the government.

Dr. Rabi: Yes, we're using them anyway. I don't see why the National Research Council, the NRC, should be so heavily involved. And putting the work under the Academy tends to lower the Academy's stature. With the think tanks you know who they are: this one is a conservative group, that one is less conservative, and so on. Their characters are recognizable. When the National Research Council engages in such work, some of it anyway, it reduces the Academy and its organizations to the think-tank level.

Mr. Golden: Rab, you were talking about the National Research Council doing work that you believe could just as well be done by some of the private, not-for-profit think tanks. You were saying that the National Academy, by running an NRC, was reducing its stature and level. Would you want to continue your comments about that?

Dr. Rabi: Well, I like that way you said it. I believe that the Academy should avoid doing anything in competition with what can be done as well by private groups. Private groups are responsible to whoever hires them. The Academy is national, they work for the United States, for the government, whether it's for the President or the Congress or other branches of government. It represents, we hope, the best the United States can offer.

Let's not get in a position that you go into a court where they have their experts on both sides. The Academy should never get into that position. Some of the things that the Academy has addressed itself to are also being worked on by other groups outside. This is all right under certain circumstances, but should be carefully scrutinized.

Mr. Golden: If I understand you correctly, Rab, you would have the Acad-

emy do a limited number of studies when asked by the government (which could be the Congress or it could be the President) on major topics, and confine itself to them. And it should limit the relatively large number of jobs undertaken through the National Research Council. Is that what you've been saying?

Dr. Rabi: Yes, but perhaps I don't know enough about the present situation. It's easy to say more than one knows.

On a related subject, some members of the Academy have felt very strongly that the Academy made damn fools of themselves in recently rejecting for membership a noted sociologist. And it made a big splash in the newspapers. You saw that?

Mr. Golden: Yes, I did see that.

Dr. Rabi: That was very unfortunate.

Mr. Golden: Well, the Academy members are always either going to elect people or not elect them, aren't they? There has to be an election process. Differences of views are not a fault of the Academy; indeed, in a way, they are a great strength.

Dr. Rabi: No, no, it's not the fault of the Academy. I wasn't at the meeting, but this particular instance, in the way it occurred, was unfortunate. It demonstrated that the sociologists shouldn't have been in the Academy at all.

Mr. Golden: You mean any sociologists?

Dr. Rabi: Yes, *any* sociologists.

Mr. Golden: And the point you're making is that the Academy should confine itself to the physical and biological sciences and mathematics?

Dr. Rabi: That's right. Sociologists have no unique thing to bring to the Academy. The fact that you can have controversy within a discipline, controversy over issues that very often can't be decided, is significant. It is not true of the hard sciences, at least very rarely.

Mr. Golden: Well, I'm sure it happens. After all, consider the Jim Conant incident many years ago. There was a revolt against electing him President of the Academy, and Det Bronk became President. You were probably there. What about that?

Dr. Rabi: Well, that's minding its own business. People say it's political. Most of the members just didn't like him personally.

Mr. Golden: Didn't like Dr. Conant?

Dr. Rabi: Yes. That's right. His fellow chemists. And I can understand that, though I had great respect for Conant.

Mr. Golden: But his fellow chemists, or some of them, anyway, didn't care for him?

Dr. Rabi: That's right; enough to defeat him.

Mr. Golden: I think Ken Pitzer was one of the leaders of that revolt. Do you recall? He was at the Atomic Energy Commission at the time. Must have been around 1948.

Dr. Rabi: I don't remember whether Ken was involved. I know some of those who were. I felt resentful of Conant at the time. Anyway, I think Bronk was a better President than Conant would have been.

Mr. Golden: That's past, however. That's interesting chit-chat about history. We're concerned with the history of the future, Rab, aren't we?

Dr. Rabi: I think we've sort of run our course. There's been a decline since about the end of 1960. A general decline in the country.

Mr. Golden: In the country as a whole?

Dr. Rabi: In the country as a whole, and these other things are symptoms of it. Intellectual and perhaps moral decline. I was alarmed, troubled, at the power of the President: This young man said, "We'll go to the moon."

Mr. Golden: Kennedy.

Dr. Rabi: Yes. And, by God, we went to the moon. It wasn't a thought-out thing, this enormous project. And the same sort of thing is Reagan saying, "We'll do the SDI—Star Wars." Both of those decisions were for political reasons. They certainly didn't have the backing of the Department of Defense. It's the power of Presidency. And unchecked. Kennedy was and Reagan is popular. Now Reagan seems to want the power of an absolute monarch.

Mr. Golden: Well, not quite.

Dr. Rabi: I mean, he had the Congress cowed and until recently he could do anything, almost anything.

Mr. Golden: You're talking about the SDI?

Dr. Rabi: The SDI is one, but there were all sorts of other things. For example, war against the Central Americans. This sort of thing. The point is, you begin to worry about democracy—that we could vote for him. The facts are all against him. His record in California was dreadful. So as I said, I'm discouraged. When I look at this new set of candidates, I wonder whether we've extended democracy too far. That's the general idea. Who would ever have made what's-his-name President? The football player.

Mr. Golden: Football player? Well, I don't know—what's the allusion? You mean somebody who was the President?

Dr. Rabi: The Vice President who then became President.

Mr. Golden: Well, gosh, you can't be referring to Harry Truman, because he wasn't a football player, he was a haberdasher.

Dr. Rabi: I mean Ford.

Mr. Golden: Oh, was Gerald Ford a football player? I didn't remember that. Well, that's a cultural matter.

Let's turn to the fundamentals. Rab, recently you were talking about the importance of science and its being a separate, very special element in our society, world society and culture. Rab, put it in your words.

Dr. Rabi: Science is the basic element, the novel element in our culture over the last four or five hundred years. It's overwhelmingly powerful; but unless understood, unless we learn to live with it congenially, it can destroy our country and the world.

Mr. Golden: And you were saying that the National Academy could be increasingly influential with the President, any President who has the will and the capacity to understand such matters—as you felt President Eisenhower did. And with other facets of the government. Those were about your words.

Dr. Rabi: Yes, in conclusion, I think every President should have a Science and Technology Advisor and a PSAC. And I think that the National Academy of Sciences has been and can and should be a strongly supportive and influential part of the advisory mechanism to the President and to the Congress—and to the American people.

Science Policy—Theory and Reality

Simon Ramo

The American society is now highly technological, and is becoming more so every day. We sow, reap, cook, communicate, manufacture, travel, clothe, entertain, educate, research, manage, cure and kill by highly technological means. Yet our government at the very top finds it difficult to include important science and technology dimensions when making its decisions. The demanding issues of our time, like avoiding war, building the economy, curbing terrorism, or fighting poverty, are viewed there as purely social-economic-political, as distinct from technological. But all these "non-technological" issues intersect, and science and technology facets are in the middle of every intersection, sometimes originating or adding to the problems, more often offering possibilities for solving them, and very frequently providing opportunities which if grasped would enable the nation to rise to new higher levels of productivity, satisfaction of needs, and happiness.

Inadequate appreciation of science and technology creates distortions of the White House's priorities and imbalances its agenda. Meanwhile, whether understood by government leadership or not, science and technology-based matters are having increasing impact. Thus, computer systems made possible by information technology advance alter productivity and employment patterns more than can minimum wage laws. Broadened global communi-

Simon Ramo, recipient of the Presidential Medal of Freedom, the nation's highest civilian award, and of the National Medal of Science, is Director Emeritus and co-founder of TRW, Inc., one of the world's largest technological corporations, and was Chief Scientist in the development of the US Intercontinental Ballistic Missile. Dr. Ramo was Chairman of the President's Committee on Science and Technology under President Ford, and has also been a member of the Advisory Council to Secretary of State Kissinger on Science and Foreign Affairs, The White House Council on Energy Research and Development, the National Science Board, and the Council of Scholars of the Library of Congress. A Visiting Professor at Caltech, Dr. Ramo has been a Regents' Lecturer at the University of California, a Fellow of the Faculty of the Kennedy School of Government at Harvard, and Chairman of the UCLA School of Medicine Planning Committee. He is the author of several textbooks in science, engineering, and management that are in worldwide use.

cations and transportation resulting from technology breakthroughs speed up and link the world's operations more than can trade negotiations. Military technology superiority is more basic to national security than draft legislation. And, at a time of intolerable budget deficits, over one hundred billion dollars a year of government funds are being expended on science and technology-based programs, not all wisely.

Technology advance is now globally pervasive. All nations today perceive their technological strength to be critical to their economic growth, standard of living, and national security. This is creating a world technology Olympics where to win many events is to be safe and sound, while to score too rarely can be disastrous. Technology is accordingly involved now in virtually every international issue with which the government must deal.

The United States can hardly expect to maintain, let alone enhance, its standard of living by furnishing low-price labor to the rest of the world. We must be instead a leading producer of scientific discoveries and technological products and services. Since we possess limited resources and our nation is a hybrid of free enterprise and government control, both the private and governmental sectors must optimize their efforts in science and technology. Government-private cooperation to some extent is now essential for setting goals, priorities and strategies.

THE NEED FOR SCIENCE ADVICE

With the world as it so plainly is today, it would be natural to expect a strong presence of science and engineering competence in the White House, where government leadership, integration, and focus must originate. As the President ponders the nation's present and future, leading scientists and engineers, it would seem, always would be on hand. They would mix with the staff members we have come to expect in the White House, people skilled in practical politics, public relations, law, government bureaucracy, diplomacy, economics, intragovernmental in-fighting, and communications with the media. The President and the two or three principal deputies who work out his program, we would further assume, would understand the need for identifying and considering the science and technology aspects as they work out problems of national security, taxes, global economic competitiveness, domestic economic growth, energy, the environment, national communications, and transportation, education, budgets, appointments to key government positions, government reorganizations, and all the rest.

This has not been happening, however. Some dozen Science Advisors have occupied offices in the Executive Office Building adjacent to the White House for most of the past thirty years. But after Kennedy, the individuals who held the office never actually met enough with the President to come to understand each other's thinking. Not all participated in important White House staff meetings. All communicated adequately with the third echelon of OMB (Office of Management and Budget) on the budget allocations for pure research, but seldom, if ever, conferred alone with the OMB head or the President's chief of staff. All Science Advisors employed committees of distinguished engineers and scientists, but, after the early years, such committees did not affect White House positions significantly. Science Advisors sometimes took strong stands on large NASA or Defense Department or Department of Energy or other government projects, but, in recent decades, those stands rarely carried noticeable weight in determining whether to initiate, defer, or halt such projects.

The science office was established by President Eisenhower in response to the traumatic shock from the Russian Sputnik launch in October, 1957, not because the White House of that period had seen the need and created the office independently. (More precisely, it was re-established in full accord with the proposal for a full-time Science Advisor to the President and a President's Science Advisory Committee approved by President Truman in December 1950 and appointed by him, in dilute strength, a few months later.) After Kennedy's assassination, the Office of Science and Technology (or, as it came to be called in a later rebirth, the Office of Science and Technology Policy) ceased to be a strong component of White House decision-making. The really influential White House staff leaders proved not capable of sensing when science and technology were important ingredients, as they often were, in the problems they were busy with. They did not think it necessary for the Science Advisor to be kept informed of White House matters so he could elect to inject a contribution. They expected the Science Advisor, as is customary for narrow specialists, to wait to be called on before participating.

Knowing this condition to be unsatisfactory for the United States in today's world, many have regularly suggested formulas to improve the situation. Some think the answer is to reestablish the President's Science Advisory Committee (PSAC), abolished by Nixon when he simultaneously rid the White House of the Science Advisor and his staff. Others propose creating a new Department of Science with a Secretary of Science in charge. Still others would like a re-designation of the President's Science Advisor as Counselor to the President with full Cabinet rank, or the creation of a Council of Science Advisors (*a la* the Council of Economic Advisers). But all these proposals seem to me to ignore two very important real-life circumstances.

First, a Science Advisor and a supporting committee or other unit cannot introduce science and technology competence into the long-range planning of the White House, its choosing of goals for the nation, or its setting of a strategy to meet those goals, if in reality such functions are not being performed in the White House. It is close to accurate, too close for comfort, to say that recent Presidents and their key aides have been totally occupied with crises and short-term issues. They take for granted such long-term goals as that the United States must remain strong militarily, strong economically, and strong technologically. But what they really spend most of their time thinking about and acting on are matters needing immediate handling. The pattern of America's selfish-interest-constituency democracy (probably the best democracy in the world, and certainly the best and only one we have) causes our government to act on a political expediency basis rather than through steady, consistent, well-thought-out policies. A science "policy" office doesn't fit well into a White House that operates this way.

Policy deliberation surely should include selecting goals, examining alternatives, setting priorities, and evolving strategies for implementations. But in America goal articulation has become little more than the emitting of motto-like phrases by political leaders at election time: decrease the size of government, lower taxes, strengthen the military forces, cut spending, eliminate poverty, broaden opportunity, protect the environment. Doing little policy formulation of significance has become the way of life because originating policy implies making long-term plans that will be adhered to (a political unreality) and because conjuring up policies satisfactory to diverse political constituents is so difficult.

The other circumstance that has prevented recent Science Advisors from contributing significantly to the President's performance of his duties arises from a fundamental of the American culture. Those well suited to running for and being elected President are not likely to possess, as a result of any direct experiences, a solid feel for the way science and technology impact the society. The same is true of the one or two people the President will select as his chief deputies. Together they do not have the background, and once in office neither the time nor the interest, to broaden themselves so as to be able to include science and technology considerations in their problem-solving work days.

NO RADICAL CHANGES

The probability of radical changes taking place in the American pattern for managing our democracy is essentially nil for many decades ahead. We are likely to see greatly improved White House handling of issues having important science and technology ingredients only when favorable accidents occur. For instance, the President or one of his truly influential deputies may just happen to possess an unusual appreciation for science and technology. (Nelson Rockefeller as vice president was such an accident.) Or maybe someone will come along whose first career was in science and technology and who shifted later into political pursuits that finally lead to a powerful White House post, conceivably even the Presidency. Another lucky accident might be the appointment as Science Advisor of an individual whose talents outside of his or her science or engineering training, or whose geographically common roots, causes that person to enjoy close friendship with the President or his principal advisors. (Jerome Wiesner was perhaps such an accident, and Frank Press might have been, despite his Columbia-Cal-tech-MIT background, had he been born in Plains, Georgia.) Some competitive country's activities, or natural causes, or the weaknesses of our own system may cause the occurrence of a severe disaster, a horrible threat, or a critical dilemma, with a very clear science and technology base, one that scares and fascinates the citizenry so much that the White House suddenly is forced temporarily to elevate the stature of the science and technology office, as happened with Sputnik.

I cannot suggest how to increase the chances of such accidents occurring. Without them, we shall simply have to wait patiently for a greatly broadened appreciation by average Americans of the importance of science and technology in the attaining of their goals in life. In the United States, when we have a severe shortcoming, the way we overcome it is always by a two-step process. Step Number One, absolutely mandatory: the problem gets worse, so bad, in fact, that hardly anyone can miss realizing it exists. Then, and only then, Step Number Two takes place: the voters demand action to solve the problem. I may have appeared pessimistic in the foregoing, but I am optimistic when I think of this two-step process. Are we not now progressing so well with Step One that Step Two is sure to follow one of these days?

Step Number One will result from the increasing evidence of our world technology leadership decline, our poor quality of science and math education in the primary and secondary schools, our decreasing production of Ph.D.s in physical science and engineering, our low rate of investment in productivity increases, our highly political and often misguided selecting of multibillion dollar space and defense projects which are vastly over-promised to get funding and then are vastly overrun in price and time and underdone in performance, and finally the regularly delayed, low-priority appointment of the President's Science Advisor when the post becomes open and the persistent low rating by the White House of that office's function. Step Number Two's arrival may become apparent in some future Presidential campaign when building American science and technology resources will have become a priority political issue, maintaining American world leadership in science and technology a long-term goal, and active science and technology wisdom in White House deliberations an accepted must.

Memorandum to the President-Elect Re: the White House Science Advisor

Donald B. Rice

During most of the post-World War II years, the staff of the President has included a Science Advisor, currently the Director of the Office of Science and Technology Policy. Since this is only one among many Executive Office components, and since one of your predecessors (Richard M. Nixon) chose to do without, since many federal agencies and offices relate to science, you may well wonder if it is a necessary element of your White House operation.

The argument of this interregnum memo is "Yes, but. . . ." *Yes*: This function can help you formulate sounder policies and generally promote a higher quality administration. *But*: Getting the right kind of help from this part of your White House is not automatic, even given an enormously qualified appointee. You, yourself, will have to give the function personal attention, and set guidelines for its operation.

There are two overarching reasons for maintaining the post of Science Advisor and bolstering it with back-up staff.

- You will want your decision-making to be as informed as possible. Because many of the issues crossing your desk—domestic, defense and international alike—will be at least quasi-scientific in character and content, a properly structured means of tapping into this knowledge base and directing scientists' talents to pressing problems can significantly improve your decision-making process. In this role, the Advisor's mission is to provide you with objective, scientifically sound, analytically based inputs.

Donald B. Rice, President of the RAND Corporation since 1972, supervised federal budgets for numerous areas serving science and technology while serving as Assistant OMB Director from 1970–1972. He has served on the National Science Board, the Defense Science Board, and various scientific advisory committees, including the Killian Committee. Dr. Rice holds degrees in engineering, industrial management, and economics.

He or she will be one among several sources of relevant information on any given decision, and will be required to work collaboratively with the Executive Office staffs responsible for domestic policy, national security policy, and the federal budget.

- The health of the nation's scientific enterprise and the pace of technological development are matters of Presidential concern. The second mission of the Advisor, then, is to help you formulate policy for science and technology and to bring better coherence to the federal programs in these areas. This role also requires collaboration with others, especially the Office of Management and Budget and federal agency officials.

Defining these two purposes also exposes the tensions between them, however. There is at least an appearance—if not the reality—of conflict between advising the President on policy and program issues and "representing" a scientific community that is heavily supported by federal funds. The Advisor will feel strong pressures from that "constituency" to devote the bulk of his efforts to policy for science and technology and to funding for federal programs. Yet the more he does so, the more the other senior members of your staff will try to wall him off as a representative of a "special interest" planted in their midst.

Your appointee and his agility in avoiding the horns of that dilemma will be the keys to success. He or she should be skilled in analysis as well as in science or engineering, possess a passion for getting at the facts, and be willing to sublimate ego and subordinate personal views in order to play honest information broker on your behalf. The challenge will be to find all this in someone who has sufficient standing in the science and technology community to be credible in the role.

Having recruited such a figure, you should lay down some marching orders:

Tell the Science Advisor-designate to concentrate on providing sound information in support of your decision-making and to expect to work in tandem with your other key advisors. This will make it more likely that the generalists on your staff will work with him rather than around him. You can count on natural bureaucratic and political forces to divert enough of his energies to issues of policy for science and funding for federal R&D programs.

Let him know that you will hold his advice on policy and decisions to the same standards of logic and inquiry as is expected of scientific research. Urge him to reach out, not only to the country's best scientists and technologists, but also to the best in policy research and analysis. Explain that you look forward to direct contacts, and will always have time for him when necessary, but that one of his primary responsibilities is to contribute to the staff work you get from OMB, your domestic advisor, and the National Security Council.

Aside from procedures, what general guideposts should you and your Advisor keep in mind? A short list might include these points:

- For some long-term problems—toxic waste, acid rain, and AIDS are examples—effective policy is heavily dependent on understanding the current state of knowledge. Knowing what we don't know about these issues is crucial to projecting the effects of alternative policy interventions and for guiding the research process to better informed future decisions. Here, the information-gathering must not be confined to asking the best chemists, atmospheric scientists, and biologists to marshal established data, although that's an essential first step. Top-flight policy analysis will also be needed. And it must be performed by those—be they physical, biological or social scientists—who have learned to apply the methods of scientific inquiry across and beyond academic disciplines.
- Both of you should be cognizant of the nonscientific elements in science-related issues. Some major decisions, such as whether to build a space station or a superconducting supercollider, are suffused with science and technology content. But they also have their non-scientific aspects, as can be seen by the somewhat unseemly competition among the states for hosting the supercollider. Other broad issues facing our society, such as productivity, competitiveness, and the quality of education, also have science and engineering ingredients. But the connection, while widely believed to exist, remains unmeasured. Solutions here will involve many other realms of policy, and the role of science and technology will probably be taken more on faith than on calculations.
- Occasionally, segments of the scientific community produce results that are more political than scientific. One classic case was the contention, in the early 1970s, that a supersonic transport would destroy the ozone layer. A more recent example involved certain work on the topic of nuclear winter, subsequently exposed as both biased and sloppy. Bad though it is, such "science" can achieve wide currency in the media and the public mind. In those instances, the President's Science Advisor can provide a useful service by fashioning and disseminating an objective, valid treatment of the issue.
- You will have to decide whether you want independent, scientific reviews of major defense programs. I vote "yes," provided it is done selectively and in cooperation with the Secretary of Defense. But you should remember that most Secretaries have opposed it.

What must you do to secure the right kind of support on questions such as these?

The first requisite is to construct a decision-making process that regularly organizes all relevant information and options for your review. Create the demand for well-informed decision-making and your Science and other senior advisors can manage the staff activities to satisfy it for you. Beyond that, your displays of interest and curiosity concerning scientific matters will make it much easier for the Science Advisor to summon the best and the brightest to your aid. You could further bolster his effectiveness by seeing to it that some of your other Cabinet and senior staff appointees also have technical credentials. Conceivably, this might even improve performance in those positions.

Almost forty years ago, the late Justice Felix Franfurter pointed out that "there is a good deal of loose talk about science in politics. If by 'science in politics' is meant the availability of an irrefragable fund of knowledge in the possession of a few wise people who could, out of hand, solve the connundrums of government, it is merely another romatic delusion. But if by science we mean an intellectual procedure and a temper of mind, there must be science in government, because science dominates society. It then becomes a question of how much science government employs and how good it is."

And, I might add, at what level and how well it is employed.

Science and Technology Advice to Government

David Z. Robinson

Comparing the present period to the past two decades, the role of scientists in affecting decisions of the federal government seems to be waning in the Executive branch, increasing in the Congress, and essentially non-existent in the judiciary. On the other hand, basic science continues to get substantial funds from both the Executive and the Legislative branches.

THE EXECUTIVE BRANCH

The Executive branch took the lead, using science advice with the establishment of the President's Science Advisor and the upgrading of the President's Science Advisory Committee in 1958. Since then, the scope and influence of science advice has varied in rough proportion to the Advisor's access to the President. The zenith seems to have been reached in the late 1950s and early 1960s. The nadir was doubtless the period from 1973 to 1974 when the Advisory Committee and the position of Advisor were abolished. At present, there is a Science Advisor, but he has little real outreach to the scientific community. There are advisory committees, but they do not publish the results of their studies. The Executive, however, continues to support basic research and, despite budget cuts in many agencies, the National Science Foundation gets strong support.

THE CONGRESS

Meanwhile, the Office of Technology Assessment, a relatively recent addition to Congressional Agencies, has conducted technical analyses (including two on the SDI program) that have had wide acceptance. After a shaky

David Z. Robinson was a member of the staff of the Office of the President's Science Advisor from 1961–67. He was a physicist at Baird, Inc., from 1949–1959 and 1960–1961; a staff scientist at the Office of Naval Research in London (1959–1960); and Vice President for Academic Affairs at New York University (1967–70). Since 1970, he has been at Carnegie Corporation of New York as Vice President and, since 1986, as Executive Vice President.

start in the late 1960s, OTA has become a respected part of the Congressional scene. Furthermore, there are now in Congress a number of interns and staff with scientific training.

THE COURTS

Explicitly disinterested technical advice has seldom been requested by the courts, although expert testimony arranged by plaintiffs or defense is a frequent feature of the adversarial process in a wide range of civil actions with technical or scientific dimensions. The Supreme Court has had no science advisor in preparing what might be considered scientific pronouncements on such matters as the age at which a fetus can live outside the womb, and on the validity of statistical analysis relative to racial bias in the imposition of the death penalty. The recent series of cases regarding the requirement to give equal time to teaching creation science, if evolution was taught, provides a mixed picture. While most judges believe that mandating "creation science" involves religious intrusion into science teaching, some judges (including two Supreme Court justices) have disagreed. None has called on scientists in any cases that have gone beyond the lowest level, since the judicial appeals process does not allow for such intervention.

THE FUTURE

The future role of science and scientists in improving the work of top-level government officials will depend on two factors. The first is the belief on the part of the politicians that such advice is essential to their effective performance. Even if the desire exists, there may be need for institutional change to allow for appropriate input.

The Congress

The greatest chance for institutional change may lie in the Congress. OTA has been effective, and interacts with the staffs of committees who request information. There are three other Congressional agencies, however, that have separate staffs—the General Accounting Office, the Congressional Research Service, and the Congressional Budget Office. Although there is information exchanged between these agencies on the projects they are working on, there are no joint products. A mechanism for producing such products could be worthwhile.

OTA is supervised by a bipartisan Technology Advisory Board of twelve members—six from each House. At the present time, the Board not only approves projects, but must vote to release reports after they have been prepared and cleared by advisory committees. Although the Board has always voted to release reports, the vote to release the report on the Strategic Defense Initiative in the last Congress was only seven to five in favor. If the quality of the reports is compromised by the need to pass a political litmus test, then the value of OTA will be seriously diminished. Perhaps the Board should be limited to approving projects, rather than approving results.

A third problem is that OTA can work only on requests from a committee of the Congress. Of course, friendly committees could be relied on to ask important questions, but it might still be useful to have some independent authority for the OTA staff.

Finally, the strength of the President's Science Advisor in the Kennedy and Johnson Administrations was enhanced by a close relationship with the Office of Management and Budget, including participation in appropriate budget preparation sessions. An equivalent relationship with the Appropriations Committees of the House and Senate would be quite worthwhile. The Appropriations Committees now rarely ask for information. The review of the Strategic Defense Initiative to be released in 1987 is a relatively rare exception.

All the above improvements call for better management of the Congress, and some of them are quite fundamental, involving jursidiction, influence and independence. Congressional staffs, however, have grown enormously, and there is great need to rethink the management. Of course, this is a larger and much more important job than appropriately using technical advice. Focusing on improving the organization of Congressional staff, however, in order to get and use technical advice might lead to important institutional change, and might be easier to do.

The Executive

A future in which a President had interest in and respect for scientific ideas would be ideal. Such a President might try to re-establish a President's Science Advisory Committee. It is not clear that a part-time committee could be as useful today as it was in the past. Increased staffing of the Science Advisor's Office of Science and Technology Policy would be advantageous, as would agreement to look into the problems in the Department of Defense.

The OSTP worked best when the agencies of the federal government were competent scientifically, particularly when there was a good scientist at a high level, either as an Assistant Secretary or in some close relationship to an agency or department head. Top-level advice in the Executive branch must go well beyond the President, if the needs of the country are to be met.

The Courts

The judicial system of the country operates in a very special way. Evidence is given at the lowest level, but there are layers of appeal where no new evidence is taken, but where matters of law are discussed. This cumbersome system insures the rights of individuals, and accommodates to judges of varying competence. Furthermore, the system deals with individual cases, and this, in itself, makes scientific generalization difficult. It seems hard to see where and at what level scientific advice would be most useful. District Court Judge Charles E. Wyzanski appointed Professor Carl Kaysen, a Harvard economist, as a special master when he heard the anti-trust case against the United Shoe Machinery Company in the early 1950s, and special masters can be appointed when the judge requires it. Given the self-confidence of judges at the appellate level, it is hard to believe that they would be willing to ask for outside scientific advice, although they could remand cases to the district courts for additional evidence. Until the time comes that judges are sufficiently educated in science to know what they don't know, it is unlikely that there can be much change.

Some Thoughts on the Management of Technologies in Medicine

David E. Rogers

I am a physician. During my career I have been successively a bench researcher, the professor and chairman of a Department of Medicine, the dean of a major medical school, and for the past fifteen years, the president of The Robert Wood Johnson Foundation—a large philanthropic organization devoting its resources to improving the health and medical care of Americans. These qualifications permit me to address problems in science and technology as they pertain to personal health and medical care, but not in a broader context. Thus I will recommend a look at three areas where changes in our way of doing things might make medical care more effective and less costly.

Background

All Americans are vividly aware of the fact that American medicine, the way it is organized, how it is delivered, and how we pay for it, is undergoing rapid and profound change. At present the American public worries the most about the escalating costs of medical care. But, as the many steps to restrain growth in medical care expenditures are moved into high gear, other problems facing medicine, concerns about access to care, its quality, and its equitable distribution, are once again receiving more interest. These concerns stem from increasing evidence suggesting that some of these cost containment measures are eroding access to care and may be reducing its quality, particularly for those who are black, hispanic, poor, and uninsured.

The advancing sophistication of medical technologies has played an im-

David E. Rogers is currently Walsh McDermott University Professor of Medicine at Cornell Medical College. He formerly held positions as President of the Robert Wood Johnson Foundation, Princeton, New Jersey; Dean of The Johns Hopkins School of Medicine, Baltimore; and Professor of Medicine at Vanderbilt University. He is the author of numerous articles in the fields of infection, medical education, and American health care policy.

portant role in the changing face of medicine. Technologies have permitted us to greatly improve our ability to diagnose and treat many diseases. At the same time most (but not all) technologies have contributed to the rapidly increasing costs of care. Lastly, technologies by their very nature have placed an unfortunate but increasingly wide emotional moat between the physician and his or her patient. Thus doctors are viewed as colder or less caring then in times past.

What might be done to more effectively harness and deploy our powerful new medical technologies while improving health outcomes? Let me suggest work in three areas.

1. Significantly increase federal funding of health services research.

   Despite the 400 billion spent yearly on health and medical care, solid knowledge about the ways to deliver medical care more effectively and efficiently are sadly lacking. We need much more careful studies on how medical care is organized, how it is deployed, its quality, its effectiveness, its distribution to different groups (the very young, the very old, minorities), if we are to improve our performance. In recent years, however, we have sharply curtailed the research studies which might yield answers to such questions. Between 1977 and 1987, the dollars directed at these questions by the National Center for Health Services Research fell from $28 million to $18.2 million. In my judgment, this is extremely short sighted. During a period of change, where better information on how to make the most of our medical know-how at the least cost is critical, we have sharply curtailed precisely the kinds of studies which might tell us how to do so. This is analogous to discharging the Army intelligence corps, while combat troops remain in the field preparing for a tough battle, the outcome of which is in doubt.

2. Move swiftly to develop both the methods and the mechanisms for better determining the effectiveness and potential cost benefits of new medical technologies before their introduction into the mainstream of medical practice.

   Overuse of technologies is an increasing worry for American medicine. Because of swift progress in biomedical research, new and often very expensive technologies are being introduced at a bewildering rate. Many are swept into the mainstream of medical practice without adequate evaluation of their potential usefulness, hazards, and costs.

   Many have proved to be life saving, and some have reduced costs. Recent examples of technologies which were widely adopted in the absence of adequate data regarding their usefulness, however, would include internal mammary ligation and other operative procedures for coronary artery disease, lumbodorsal sympathectomy for hypertension, gastric lavage for peptic ulcers, and carotid endarterectomies to prevent strokes. Careful objective evaluation of these technologies was not done until they

were in widespread use. Studies performed after the fact have clearly
shown their effectiveness falls far short of what was originally suggested.

There is also evidence to suggest that it is the widespread use of more
and more "little ticket" laboratory technologies per patient which have
contributed to most of the escalating costs. For example the number of
laboratory tests performed on a patient with a perforated appendix moved
from 5.3 in 1951, to 14.5 in 1964, to 31.0 in 1981! Similarly, laboratory
procedures performed on a patient who had suffered a myocardial in-
farction jumped from 12.8 in 1964 to 37.5 in 1981. There have been no
significant differences in morbidity and mortality in either case. Nevertheless, it is also clear that introduction of expensive "big ticket" technologies fuel the flame. For example coronary artery bypass grafting was
done 138,000 times in the United States in 1982. The net cost per procedure was then about $16,000. Thus performance of this surgery rep-
resented a $2.5 million expenditure. As yet another example, it costs
between $250,000 and $300,000 a year to operate a computerized tom-
ography scanner. The United States has about 2,000 of them, thus CT
scanning costs the United States about $500 million per year.

Many of the new technologies represent major advances in the management of human disease, but some do not. Clearly what is much needed
is a strong, well-financed Office of Technology Assessment, public or
private, with the mandate to make proper and adequate evaluations of
new technologies before their entry into the general medical market place.
The nation started down this road 10–15 years ago, but we have recently
faltered badly in the funding and support of such an office. Establishing
such an authority would swiftly pay for itself and probably avoid a significant amount of the human suffering and misery which can accompany
the use of a procedure of doubtful value.

3. Make the financing of medical care "neutral" toward the use of medical
technology.

Our present reimbursement practices have helped create such problems. They vastly over-reward physicians for the use of technologies,
many of which are invasive and uncomfortable. Not surprisingly this has
lead to significant overuse of bronchoscopes, gastroscopes, colono-
scopes, and the like. While such procedures are often defended as "insurance" against malpractice suits, it seems clear that fiscal rewards for
such practices are generally the motivating force for using them. It has
been shown, for example, that a general internist can triple his or her
income by simply using many approved but unnecessary technologies in
his or her practice.

Obviously, the use of such technologies is often important for the proper
practice of high quality medicine. Doctors should not be penalized for
employing them. On the other hand, he or she should not be rewarded
for their overuse. A reimbursement system which sharply lowered the

reimbursements for technologies and placed more value on the use of the physician's cognitive skills is much needed today. Physicians should be paid for the use of their heads and hearts and hands, not just their technological equipment.

Attention to these three problems—all of which have the potential for sensible resolution—could do much to improve American medical care while keeping the rates of escalation of its cost those that the American public could afford.

Advising the President on Science and Technology: Why Can't We Get It Right?

Robert M. Rosenzweig

Why do we continue to find it so difficult to build into our governmental processes a reliable capability for supplying the President timely, relevant, and politically useful counsel on the scientific and technological aspects of issues that come before him? I believe that the answer to the first question is reasonably clear, while the answer to the latter is anything but. For the sake of brevity, I will sketch the reasons for both in outline form.

1. While many scientists appear to believe that science advising is uniquely difficult to implant in the structure of government, the fact is that technical advice, generally, does not fare well when it is separated from operating responsibility—a powerful factor in agenda-setting—and from political accountability. One model, commonly cited with envy by scientists, is the Council of Economic Advisors, established in 1946. The experience of the CEA is actually quite mixed. Clearly, it has never been the sole source of economic advice reaching the President and, more to the point, it has rarely been the leading source. Indeed, in some Administrations and at some times in all Administrations, the CEA, often the bearer of unwelcome counsel, has found itself very much on the outside looking in.

The CEA does provide an advantage for which there is no counterpart in the science and technology area, namely, a professional staff capable of supplying sound, regular analysis of economic issues which the Council can use to advise the President, should he wish to hear or heed their advice. The Office of Science and Technology Policy should provide that capability, but in the Reagan Administration it has, with a few notable exceptions, failed

Robert M. Rosenzweig has been President of the Association of American Universities since 1983. He was associated with Stanford University for many years, and was Vice President 1974–83. Previously, he served in the US Office of Education (1958–62), and was a Congressional Fellow of the American Political Science Association.

to bring together a staff group that could hold its own with other aggregations of talent in the agencies and in the Congress.

2. The CEA experience is also as good an example as any of the fact that governing is grounded in politics, which in a democracy means, above all, electoral politics. Advisory institutions that are not attuned to that cycle and advisors who are not sensitive to it are going to fail, no matter how technically sound their advice may be. The great trick, in this aspect of democracy as in all others, is to have the skill to put sound technical knowledge to the service of the needs of political leaders. People with that skill are in short supply.

3. It is also clear, from the CEA experience and from the history of science advising, that Presidents who do not want to be advised will be unmoved by any institutional arrangements for advising them. Richard Nixon did not want science advising and took steps to be sure he would not get it. Ronald Reagan does not want to hear the predominantly pessimistic views of scientists on the feasibility of SDI, and it has been arranged so that he does not. In such circumstances, no amount of skill will inform policy with sound technical content because other actors—senior White House staff, agency heads, or OMB, to mention but three—will dominate the process.

4. In any large organization—and government certainly is that—what is important will often be pushed aside by what is urgent. In the context of science advising, science may be important, but technology is more often urgent. To put the same point differently, as they are seen by policy-makers, science demands money, technology solves problems. For most of the post World War II period, science dominated the national agenda and technology came along behind. That relationship has been changing in recent years, but the change has not yet been incorporated into the thinking of scientists about science advising. Until it is, there is likely to be continuing resistance among policy-makers to advice that seems to them to be of dubious immediate relevance to the problems they face.

5. Finally, everyone who has written about any aspect of advising Presidents or other policy-makers has noted the central importance of the personal relationship between the Advisor and his client. For Presidential science advising, it is the single most important element because of the structure of science within the government. Science and technology are now everywhere. At least six agencies of government are major players in science and technology, and almost all others are developing stakes in the game. When necessary, the heads of those agencies are, themselves, science advisors to the President. They have their own avenues of access to him and, if they see the Advisor in the White House as their adversary, they will not cede their places to him.

From the foregoing, it is easy to see why science advising is so difficult and why it has had such an uneven record of success over the years. It will always be difficult, but it may not be hopeless. The key is whether or not the next President will want advice that is tailored to his needs, rather than the political/bureaucratic needs of the Executive departments. He will get plenty of the latter in any case; will he want the former?

Perhaps. Just as Sputnik helped President Eisenhower value in-house science advice and the space program helped President Kennedy to the same understanding, the next President may see the connection between science and technology policies and the massive economic problems the nation will face during his term, and will want loyal, unself-interested help in sorting through the problems and opportunities he will face. That seems to me the new and hopeful element in the picture. If, however, political energies are spent on an effort to establish a Department of Technology, then the opportunity will be lost. If such an effort fails, it will still have succeeded in diverting attention from what is most needed. And if it were to succeed, then a new bureaucratic/political competitor for attention will have been created, and the job of putting knowledge to the service of policy will be no closer to completion.

Federal Policies for Academic Research

Roland W. Schmitt

We have become so accustomed to having the federal government, an institution driven by political motives, support research and, specifically, academic research, that the marvel of it is gone. Yet many politicians who consistently vote to appropriate the funds for this activity undoubtedly feel sympathy for the view of Queen Juliana of Holland, who was heard to exclaim, "I don't understand computers. I don't even understand the people who understand computers." The same is surely true for science and scientists, technology and technologists.

Technical people and politicians hold different attitudes toward key elements of the scientific and technical enterprise. For example, quite a few politicians regard peer review, a tenet of the scientific community, as an "old boy's network," preserving the privileges of those receiving the bulk of federal support. To them, the largesse of the federal government for research should be spread around "equitably." To the technical community, it should be targeted at excellence—as judged by them.

The advice one gives to politicians, then, cannot be couched in terms that appeal only to the cognoscenti of science and technology, especially when it pertains to academic research. Yet it must rest on foundations of good policy for academia and the federal government, both. So, before addressing the question of advising the federal government about academic research, let's look at the substance of some issues.

A shift is occurring in the balance of forces that govern federal support of research. It is driven by disappointment. Past policies have not adequately protected the US advantage in high-tech industries and international competitiveness. "Why," it is asked, "do we win so many Nobel Prizes and yet lose so many industrial battles?" From the perspective of the academic research community, the fault may seem to rest elsewhere. But I do not be-

Roland W. Schmitt is serving his second term as Chairman of the National Science Board. He is Senior Vice President for Science and Technology of General Electric Company, and is a member of the National Academy of Engineering.

lieve this view alone is tenable; instead, we have to re-examine the underlying motives for federal support of academic research and see whether today's
realities call for new policies. And we must do this while preserving our
ability to win Nobel Prizes.

PUBLIC SUPPORT OF RESEARCH

Four main rationales drive the public support of research. Briefly they
are: 1) the desire to answer enduring, fundamental questions about the universe, nature and man; 2) the appeal of a frontier to be conquered—a uniquely
American rationale, rooted in our history; 3) the usefulness of science; and
4) the political appeal of many scientific projects and programs.

The first rationale dates back to at least the sixth century BC. It remains
the most prevalent motivation of individual researchers. Scientific research,
at this level, is akin to other areas of human creativity, with the constraint
that, in science, man's creativity must answer to nature's reality. But, with
this rationale alone, support for research would be not much greater than
for the arts and humanities.

The second rationale is the appeal to Americans of the frontier and the
pioneer. In 1890, Frederick Jackson Turner, a historian, noted that the geographical frontier in the US ran deep in our psyche and, as it vanished, was
being replaced by other symbolic frontiers. Vannevar Bush, the engineer,
educator and administrator, who was asked by Franklin D. Roosevelt in
1945 to recommend how science could be applied as effectively to civilian
pursuits as it was being applied to win World War II, used the frontier
metaphor in his famous report, *Science, The Endless Frontier*.

In the United States, we take it for granted that pushing back frontiers is
a strong rationale for public activity. We should remember that our view is
not universal. Listen, for example, to the director of Japan's Sony Research
Center, Makato Kikuchi. "In Japan," he writes, "no matter which way you
go, at the end of the road there is an ocean. What a feeling of security. It
is like being rocked in a giant cradle."

Bush's frontier rationale was accepted, but the details of his own views
on organizing US science were not. In place of a system in which the federal
government would take explicit responsibility for the health of the entire
science and technology base of the nation, we got a different concept: federal
support provided through mission-oriented agencies and a National Science
Foundation that, with only modest perturbations, has been a supporter of
pure science, as defined and identified by academics.

The third rationale is the usefulness of science. This usefulness had been
recognized even before Francis Bacon made clear that it could often be inextricably tied up with science's intellectual value. Bacon's link between ideas
and works has since been better appreciated in the United States than in
most other nations, including his own.

Finally, the fourth rationale, science as an object of legitimate political attention, dates far back into our nation's history. Though it may not matter much to scientists exactly where the superconducting Super Collider is lo-located, it matters a great deal to the people whose local economy will benefit by many millions of dollars a year. And many politicians have noted the value of research intensive universities in regional economic development.

The order of these four motives for government support of research is the order of increasing appeal to federal politicians and administrators who are responsible for supporting research. Yet it also represents the order of decreasing appeal to the academic researchers who receive federal support. For the two decades since Bush's report, this dichotomy was reconciled by the belief that satisfying the first two rationales—answering basic questions and pushing at frontiers—would act more or less automatically to produce the right outcome for the second two rationales—utility and political value. That has proven to be only partly true. Its limitations have now become too important to ignore.

SCIENCE, TECHNOLOGY AND INTERNATIONAL COMPETITION

We have moved into an era of intense worldwide competition in technology-based industries. One revolution follows another: polymers, microelectronics, computers, biotechnology. These changes force us to reexamine our assumptions regarding the operation of these four rationales.

In the post-World War II era, when modern science policy was shaped, we didn't need to think clearly about the relationships among science, technology, and international competition. So we didn't. We assumed that basic research, though driving technological progress, was distinct from and superior to that progress. Listen for example, to J. Robert Oppenheimer, who could say: "Why do we seek new knowledge? To this question there is not one answer, there are two. They are disturbingly unrelated. One answer is that new knowledge is useful. The other answer is that the getting of it is ennobling."

This attempted separation of pure and applied research even pervaded industrial laboratories. In 1957, when I became head of a research group at General Electric's corporate laboratory, the theory was in full sway. My group and another were assigned to do basic research. We were to pass on our ideas to other groups that would turn those research results into inventions. They in turn would pass the inventions on to others that would turn the inventions into commercial products or processes.

But this "assembly line" did not work. Each group did its own job well. My group's output included scientific discoveries that won a Nobel Prize and put four of our 25 people into the National Academy of Sciences. It also, later, through other routes led to several small entrepreneurial businesses. Yet the invention groups were filing patent applications based not on our ideas, but on their own. And the development groups were paying only marginal attention to either of the other activities.

Since then, the Japanese have provided an even more impressive refutation of that assembly line view of innovation. Their approach has been to develop skills in emerging technologies and use them to innovate bit by bit in the context of strong, continuing interactions of technology, design, manufacture, and markets. True, they have not so far contributed greatly to pioneering advances in science and technology. But they have often transformed those advances into commercially important items more quickly and effectively than we have. In Japan the academic research system has neither possessed the same vigor nor been as closely related to industry as in the US.

These arguments might lead one to conclude that all is well with our academic research system and that our problems of competitiveness must be addressed by industry. There is much truth in this. US industry does need to improve the way it manages and utilizes science and technology. Many books have been written on the topic. But, in addition, I believe that federal support for academic research will not grow in a healthy fashion, and will not maintain the strong academic system needed by the US without changes. Academic institutions themselves will have to respond more directly to the interest of the federal government in economic impact and regional development. Can these interests be served without undermining the traditional strength and productivity of academic research? I believe the answer is "Yes," but it will involve changes and risks.

RESPONSIVE POLICIES

Governments want to see science and technology contribute to the general welfare. Leaving aside the specific governmental functions such as defense, this means economic development and jobs. On two main points, these federal interests seem to conflict with the tenets of academia: the organization of campus research and the distribution of funds for research. In both cases, though, I believe there are solutions that are responsive to federal interests but that also preserve the essential integrity of the research enterprise as viewed by academic scientists and engineers.

The organization of academic research has been driven principally by opportunities arising from the advance of science itself, and by using them to conquer frontiers. The individual academic investigator, the pioneer, has been at the heart of the system, and much federal support has been in the form of grants to individual investigators, each devoted to a particular discipline. Yet industrial technology usually depends on multidisciplinary effort and such effort tends to be appealing to government officials and politicians. Some of the better supported initiatives of federal agencies have been responsive to this interest—for example, DoD's University Research Initiative and NSF's Engineering Research Centers. Many academic researchers are apprehensive about these developments, fearing they will distort traditional interests and values. Yet, there is nothing in either initiative that will necessarily weaken the production of creative, forefront research results, provided such centers are well conceived and operated. Indeed, similar modes of organization have already arisen in academic institutions themselves. The disciplines around which universities are organized are superb categories for teaching—for transmitting knowledge. But nature doesn't necessarily partition itself into disciplinary segments, nor can its secrets always be plumbed by the mind and instruments of a single investigator. Thus, many centers of research, combining the efforts of a number of investigators and cutting across conventional academic lines, have originated on campuses. The experience of academic institutions in operating these self-generated centers should help them respond to federal interests and to do so in a manner compatible with the tenets of productive basic research and with maintaining the linkage between research and education so vital to training the next generation of scientists and engineers.

The second issue—distribution of funds for academic research—is in some ways more difficult. Politicians know that strong academic research contributes to economic development. They further note that the geographical distribution of funds for academic research is concentrated in the leading research universities. For example, of the top twenty-five university recipients of federal research funds, only one is in the south and south-central region. Many politicians wish to have these funds distributed more "equitably." Indeed, the organic act for the National Science Foundation explicitly requires attention to geographical distribution. But, most scientists and technologist believe that research funds should be allotted solely on the basis of excellence; there is good evidence that top people and top institutions contribute inordinately to progress in science and technology.

Can we respond to the political interests without undermining the processes that make science work? I believe that the key is to devise programs—as NSF has already done to some extent—which support efforts to nucleate and grow new centers of excellence wherever the talent and determination arise. It will be far better to create new foci of excellence that can compete with the older ones on the basis of merit than to be forced to distribute research funds on purely political grounds.

In summary, to get growing support for academic research means to serve the objectives of those who supply the funds. And those objectives tend to center on the last two rationales for federal support—utility and politics. Failure to respond with suitable programs risks not only stagnant support but, even more ominously, direct political intervention. This has already occurred for academic facilities where "pork barrel" appropriations have been growing. It would be even worse to have it occur with research programs and thus threaten the standards of quality and integrity of the research process itself. Fortunately, ways are being devised to meet the political objectives and yet preserve the integrity and productivity of academic research. They do require some changes on campuses. These changes are not only within the bounds of good research policies, but in some instances might even reinvigorate some of the people and institutions who pioneer them.

EFFECTIVE ADVICE

Academic research is a vital and important component of the US research system. Both government and industry are dependent on it—even beyond its role in education—to a greater degree than in most other nations. Yet, today, federal impact on its health and well-being is spread across numerous agencies. In view of the trends presented above, the question is whether the federal system today is adequate to insure the future health of academic research and to foster the changes needed.

At present each agency goes its own way with only modest and sporadic coordination. The Office of Science and Technology Policy is in position to provide strong coordinated leadership, but whether it does or not depends solely on the issues that the incumbent puts at the top of the agenda. The National Science Board, the only statutory governing board of a federal agency, has a commission to render broad policy advice on science and technology. In reality, though, it has no jurisdiction over and little influence on the policies of other federal agencies such as DoD, DoE, and NIH. Other advisory boards such as the Defense Science Board and the Energy Research Advisory Board have their own mission-specific agendas. DoD's University Advisory Board, the National Academies' Government-University-Industry Roundtable, and others also play specialized roles in aspects of academic research policies.

The system has worked reasonably well so far. There have been exceptions. The issue of research facilities at universities still festers with the result that the political pork barrel is encroaching more and more into this important domain. The issue of overhead on government research contracts—quiescent for the moment—is sure to erupt again. But the real question is whether the system will be adequate for addressing the deeper changes in academic research discussed above. The answer is that there are no institutional structures to assure coordinated federal leadership. Thus, individuals in key positions will have to put these issues at the top of their personal agendas and work with each other. It is an answer that may leave many uncomfortable, but it is a better answer than an intricate new bureaucratic structure.

Technological Advice to the President: A Two-Way Street

Robert C. Seamans, Jr.

There are conflicting opinions on the contemporary role of science and technology advisors to the President and other high-level government officials. Some feel that such advisors are held in low esteem, and their views are not sought except to justify decisions already reached. Others note that the scientific and technical people differ on key issues, and wonder whom to believe. Still others are mystified by the seemingly avoidable failures that occur on complex technological endeavors. When such failures occur, it may be difficult to disentangle the roles of the initial advisors, the designers, the contractors, and the operators, but there will often be public criticism of those involved in the technical decisions.

The decision-making process is a two-way street that requires understanding on the part of advisors as well as recipients. In this paper, I've elected to approach several of the issues involved in the process by drawing on my experience as Associate Administrator of NASA when John F. Kennedy was President. During the early days of his Presidency, decisions were reached that dramatically changed the objectives of manned space flight.

UNPREPARED FOR DECISION

James E. Webb was appointed Administrator of NASA in February 1961, four weeks after President Kennedy's inauguration. Soon thereafter, David Bell, Director of the Bureau of the Budget, asked Webb to submit recom-

Robert C. Seamans, Jr., Dean of the School of Engineering (1978–81) of the Massachusetts Institute of Technology, has been Secretary of the Air Force, Associate and then Deputy Administrator of NASA, Administrator of ERDA, President of the National Academy of Engineering, and an Overseer of Harvard University. He is a Trustee of the Carnegie Institution of Washington, the National Geographic Society, the Woods Hole Oceanographic Institution, and the Museum of Science (Boston) and a Senior Lecturer at MIT.

mendations for any changes in President Eisenhower's programs that were felt to be necessary. Webb agreed with his NASA associates that funds should be requested for manned space flight beyond the yet-to-be-flown Mercury missions in low earth orbit. An advanced manned program, ultimately called "Apollo," had been opposed by the previous Administration. Bell advised NASA that President Kennedy did not have time to review such proposals in depth and, consequently, decisions on the future of manned space flight should await the following year's budget cycle. At a meeting on March 22, 1961, Bell's statements were confirmed by the President.

A CHANGED ENVIRONMENT

Yuri Gagarin's successful earth orbital flight for the Soviet Union on April 12, 1961, had a dramatic worldwide impact. It also inspired criticism of the US space program in general, and of NASA in particular. NASA's new Administrator and his deputy, Hugh L. Dryden, were summoned before a special session of the House Space Committee the very next day. The Caucus Room of the House was "standing room only," and the general tenor of the session was a deep anguish over the US's poor and declining posture *vis-a-vis* Soviet success in space exploration. Congressman James Fulton, the Republican Minority leader on the committee, wanted to know why NASA wasn't working three shifts a day, seven days a week on the Mercury mission. Such questions were skillfully addressed by Webb and Dryden.

The hearings before the House Space Committee returned to normal attendance the next day with a presentation by George Low on manned Apollo studies. Low, the Director of Manned Space Flight at NASA Headquarters, was discussing his first viewgraph when Congressman King from Utah interrupted with a question related to a Biblical story. "Weren't we like the ancient leader who lost his army because he underestimated his adversary?" he asked. Congressman King followed his rhetorical question by asking whether or not the Soviets planned to land men on the moon in 1967, the fiftieth anniversary of the Russian Revolution. I stepped into the breach, and explained that we were not privy to Soviet planning. Then I was asked whether the US could land men on the moon in 1967. I responded that success would depend on the support of the President, the Congress, and the public at large, but if there were a national mandate, I believed such a mission would be possible. I based my answer on the results of the extensive research that NASA had already completed.

In response to White House concerns about NASA's Congressional testimony, Webb sent a memorandum defending the NASA Congressional witnesses to President Kennedy's aide, Kenneth O'Donnell. Webb noted that members of the committee, almost without exception, were in a mood to find someone "responsible" for losing the space race to the Russians, and also to let it be known publicly that *they* were not responsible.

A PRESIDENTIAL REQUEST

I never learned how President Kennedy reacted to the combative mood of Congress and NASA's response, but I do know from his memorandum to Vice President Lyndon Johnson that he did not like the US being thought of as "second-best in space." His memorandum of April 20, 1961, asked whether there was any chance of "beating the Soviets," and if so, how. He asked for a report at the earliest possible moment. The Vice President held a number of meetings in his inimitable "let's-reason-together" fashion, and then turned to Secretary of Defense Robert S. McNamara and Webb for their views, to be submitted by May 8, the day before the Vice President was leaving for an inspection tour of Southeast Asia.

FORMULATING RECOMMENDATIONS

Astronaut Alan Shepard successfully carried out the first manned Mercury flight, a suborbital mission, on May 5. Many in the US and abroad saw the lift-off on television. The effect of a previously announced, openly viewed, successful flight was a big "plus" for the US, and it gave NASA credibility at a crucial juncture in its history.

Webb met with Secretary of Defense McNamara at the Pentagon on May 6. I found that McNamara was not one for extensive pleasantries. Even as we sat down at his conference table, he suggested that each agency outline its recommendations, and then an attempt could be made to integrate them into a single government program. There was little overlap between the specific projects recommended by NASA and the Department of Defense, hence the discussion revolved primarily around President Kennedy's concern for a mission that might outdistance—or, at least, neutralize—the Soviet's advances in space. McNamara asked whether a manned planetary goal would give the US a greater opportunity to be first. I answered that landing men on the moon and returning them safely appeared possible, but that a one- to two-year mission to Mars would involve technological and physiological consequences well beyond our present capabilities and understanding. McNamara advised us that the Department of Defense had already prepared a classified report outlining the Soviet capabilities and containing the DoD recommendations to counter the implied Soviet "threat." He suggested that NASA's recommendations for manned lunar landing should be added to this document. Webb agreed. On May 8, 1961, prior to the White House ceremony to celebrate Shepard's successful Mercury mission, McNamara and Webb signed the report containing their recommendations. Later, at a formal luncheon, Vice President Johnson eulogized Shepard and NASA, and then left for a meeting with President Kennedy. As he walked from the room, the Vice President was carrying the manila envelope containing the NASA-DoD report.

THE GOAL IS DEFINED

On May 25, 1961, President Kennedy delivered a special message to Congress that included the exhortation, "Now it is time to take longer strides . . . before this decade is out, of landing a man on the moon and returning him safely to earth." The first draft of the section of the message that related to space exploration had been sent to NASA for comments. In the draft, the date for the lunar landing was 1967. NASA argued that the reputation of the US should not hinge on such a tight time constraint, and hence the reference to "decade" was used to provide more flexibility.

TECHNICAL ALTERNATIVES

The selection of the mission mode was the most difficult, most important, and most controversial of the technical decisions that had to be made following the President's recommendation to Congress. A number of possibilities were suggested, but the two most widely accepted were "Direct Ascent" and "Earth Orbit Rendevous." The first would use a single launch vehicle large enough to land men on the moon with sufficient equipment to make the return passage. In the second mode, smaller launch vehicles would take a variety of modules into earth orbit which, when brought together, assembled, and checked out, would permit the lunar mission to be conducted the same as with "Direct Ascent."

Soon after these design studies were initiated, I received the first of several letters from Dr. John Houbolt, a NASA research engineer. He wondered if I remembered the discussion about "Lunar Orbit Rendevous," the scheme for landing men on the moon that he had discussed with me during my first visit to Langley Research Center in September 1969. He then asked whether Brainerd Holmes, the Associate Administrator for Manned Space Flight, was evaluating this scheme in comparison with the other possibilities. I forwarded Houbolt's letter to Holmes with a transmittal note saying that the concept appeared attractive, and asking for his evaluation. Several months later, Holmes told me that he and his management council favored Houbolt's approach.

DEBATE AND RESOLUTION

Technical matters of great importance were reviewed by Jerome Wiesner, the President's Science Advisor, Wiesner's staff, and the President's Science Advisory Committee. They were uniformly unhappy with the recommendation for "Lunar Orbit Rendezvous." Many reasons were advanced for this displeasure. Foremost was the danger of rendezvous and docking in orbit around the moon. If this maneuver failed, the two astronauts who had been to the moon could not return. NASA agreed that the risk existed, but pointed out that other and greater risks would be minimized by this approach.

Webb responded to Wiesner's concerns in a letter dated August 20, 1962. He ended his letter by noting that study of this special configuration was continuing, and stated that the "constructive criticism by eminently qualified men is of tremendous value, and we look forward to further discussion."

The further discussion took place under unusual circumstances. President Kennedy had not yet visited any of the NASA installations. A blue-ribbon group, including the President, the Vice President, McNamara, Wiesner, the British Minister of Defense, and others set out on a space safari, with Huntsville as the first stop. While at Huntsville, the group was escorted through the large cavernous assembly area, with press and Huntsville employees cordoned off at a safe distance. Half-way across the floor, President Kennedy turned to Webb, and asked him if he agreed with the criticisms about the "Lunar Orbit Rendezvous." A verbal free-for-all ensued, and the winner wasn't immediately selected.

"Lunar Orbit Rendezvous," however, did become the mode chosen for the Apollo mission, with President Kennedy ultimately supporting Webb and his technical team.

THE ACHIEVEMENT

Apollo 11 blasted off from Cape Canaveral the morning of July 16, 1969, after many equipment and operational tests on the ground and in space. Eagle, Apollo's lunar lander, touched down on the lunar surface four and a half days later. Astronaut Neil Armstrong was seen on television by more than a billion people as he descended from the lunar lander, and took his "one single step for man, one giant step for mankind." The next day, Armstrong and Edwin E. Aldrin, Jr., rode the ascent stage from the lunar surface to a successful rendezvous with Michael Collins, who had remained aboard the return capsule in orbit around the moon. The three astronauts were successfully recovered in the Pacific Ocean after their four-day return passage, and were welcomed aboard the USS Hornet by President Richard M. Nixon.

When the Apollo 17 mission was completed in December 1972, ten more astronauts had walked on the lunar surface. The achievements of the Apollo missions, coupled with results from the unmanned scientific satellites of the same era, were widely acclaimed. During the decade following the President's bold decision, the United States had clearly become pre-eminent in space.

CONCLUSIONS

Those advising the President or other high-level government officials on scientific and/or technical issues must understand that there are usually many factors other than science and technology that influence the final decision on any question. The President must be concerned with the economy, national security, societal needs, and political forces. Hence, on complex issues, the President must be given time to weigh information and to understand the benefits and risks. In recognition of the severe time constraints on the President, advisors must prepare and present recommendations as succinctly as possible. When differences exist, alternatives must be presented with the pros and cons outlined, and with judgmental differences, if such exist, carefully explained.

Conflicting views make a President's decision more difficult, but he is well advised to listen to the diverse opinions, lest he be co-opted by a single small group. In furtherance of this need, a President should have close advisors who can act as devil's advocates to flush out differences and force protagonists to assess and to present their arguments carefully and thoroughly.

The process of determining a plan of action isn't always neat and tidy, and may appear protracted and frustrating, especially to those deeply involved. It is better, however, to take the time to consider alternatives than to suffer the consequences of unrealistic decisions.

At a time when our future hinges on the proper use of technology, even our robust nation cannot withstand too many failures. Scientists and engineers have a responsibility to provide advice in appropriate forums. Presidents and other high-level officials have the responsibility to provide such opportunities so that they can receive thoughtful information on which to base their decisions. Only in this way can our democracy endure.

Matching Reality to Need

Frederick Seitz

There are several levels at which individuals or groups may advise the President or the Executive agencies concerning matters related to science or engineering, but two are most important. The first is open advice such as may appear in books or journal articles, in the familiar Congressional testimony, or even in so-called open letters.

The second is much more highly privileged, such as by advice that is given privately on request, for example, as a member of staff, as a consultant, or as a member of an advisory committee.

The two kinds of advice need not be substantially different but they carry quite different levels of responsibility. This difference is not always appreciated by scientists and engineers who may have their own agendas or loyalty to a constituency somewhere "out there." On the other hand, the difference is clearly understood and appreciated by seasoned politicians. Generally speaking, I will focus here on the second form of advice with emphasis on advice given to the President.

In this connection it should be borne in mind that Congressional committees, and indeed the government as a whole, learned soon after World War II that, whenever issues related to science and technology having strong political content, and in which personal perceptions as well as well-founded technical facts play a prominent role, came to the fore, it was always relatively easy to find individuals with good professional qualifications to argue, even vehemently, in support of either side. This has in fact been something in the nature of an Achilles heel in the process of providing technical advice to the government.

The environment within which the President acts and his needs differ not only from one Administration to another, but can change radically within a given Administration as we have seen clearly within recent decades. More-

Frederick Seitz is President Emeritus of The Rockefeller University and Past President of the National Academy of Sciences (1962–69). A physicist and generalist, he has been involved with national science policy since World War II, and has served on many advisory committees, including PSAC.

over, the task of heading the Executive branch has changed substantially in the past twenty-five or so years because both the Legislative and Judicial branches of the government have, with some success, sought to expand their own powers at the expense of the Executive. This has made it necessary for the President to be much more cautious in forming his circle of most intimate advisors.

VARIOUS AGENDAS

President Kennedy, partly, but not entirely as a matter of personality, felt free to give his advisors great latitude within the Executive offices. His successors have been much more guarded in dealing with their advisory structure. This situation could change again, but only if there is much more concurrence in our society regarding national goals than we have had in the past two decades or so. Even then, however, much will depend upon the President's own perceptions as well as that of his Cabinet concerning the extent to which he needs advice beyond that which he can obtain directly through his own offices and agencies.

President Truman, for example, depended very much on advice which came to him through the Executive agencies, although even he decided to override the recommendation of the highly prestigious General Advisory Committee of the Atomic Energy Commission with respect to work on the development of fusion weapons after balancing in his own mind the recommendations of the committee against opposing views concerning the national interest.

Initially, President Eisenhower relied mainly on advice he derived through the agencies until he was caught by surprise by the launching of Sputnik in 1957. He then took special steps to fill a major gap in his own advisory structure by the creation of a Scientific Advisory Committee. It is difficult to know to what extent he believed that there would be a permanent need for such an apparatus, but it was, in effect, abolished early in 1973 by President Nixon. It is also worth noting that, when Senator Melvin Laird was asked to serve as Secretary of Defense by President Nixon in 1969, he insisted, as a condition of his acceptance, that the President's Science Advisory Committee cease devoting attention to the activities of the Department of Defense. This indicated that, by that time, a relatively free-running committee was not regarded as an unmixed blessing everywhere in the Executive branch. In this connection, I might add that I believe, as a result of firsthand knowledge, that President Johnson would probably have reorganized the science advisory structure in the White House had he ultimately decided to run and been reelected in 1968.

It is also very important to note that the advisory apparatus created by President Eisenhower, and then expanded by President Kennedy with the addition of an Office of Science and Technology which could include a relatively large working staff, came into being under Executive orders so that its responsibilities were directed primarily to the President.

OSTP

As Congress gained power following Watergate and desired more access to White House affairs, it agreed in 1976, with the concurrence of the Ford Administration, to create the Office of Science and Technology Policy in the Executive offices. This was to be headed by a Science Advisor to whom the Congress would have access when it so desired. While this action might, in a sense, be regarded as a triumph for the recognition of the importance of science and technology in the Executive offices, it also meant that the President's Science Advisor would no longer be, so to speak, an exclusive advisor to the President. The value of the Advisor would depend to a considerable degree upon the relationships between the President and the Congress which as we have seen can be quite variable.

For a period of perhaps two years after President Carter took office, relations between Congress and the Executive were relatively tranquil. As a result the President's Science Advisor (Frank Press) was able to develop good working relationships with the President on a number of major issues. Eventually, however, rising monetary inflation, the troubles in Iran, and the Soviet invasion of Afghanistan came to dominate national attention. Matters related to science and technology slipped into the background.

A SCIENCE COURT

Are there new alternatives that might be put into operation at a sufficiently high level that would command significant attention, in spite of the differences that might arise between the Executive and Legislative branches? Nearly twenty years ago, a highly imaginative engineer, Arthur Kantrowitz, proposed that it might prove possible to achieve widespread concurrence on issues involving science and technology by creating what he termed a Science Court. This body, which would be relatively independent of government and managed by well-recognized professionals, would review topics having technical content and render judgment in somewhat the manner in which the Supreme Court adjudicates matters in its own domain. It was suggested that such a body, presumably being apolitical, would receive widespread and respected attention when the government is formulating policy.

Regardless of the merits of such a plan, and quite apart from the details of the form it might have taken, this suggestion came under attack from individuals who rightly or wrongly feared that such a "court" could become packed or slanted in some consistent way which would make its advice suspect so that it would contribute to rather than alleviate controversy.

In actual fact, our government already has such a semi-private organization available to it, namely the National Academy of Sciences, which was created in 1863 in response to the Civil War and which has evolved its structure over the decades so that it now includes a large, full-time staff working within the framework of the National Research Council, and has intimate working relationships with the National Academy of Engineering and the Institute of Medicine, all of which were created under the terms of its original charter of 1963. It is obligated to advise all branches of the government on request.

The leaders of the National Academy of Sciences have learned over the years that their effectiveness is greatest when the organization is able to deal with topics of two types, namely matters of an almost exclusively technical nature having great public interest and on which professional advice is widely welcomed, or with issues of primarily professional interest such as those related to promising frontiers of basic research. In such cases, the professional knowledge of the scientists and engineers is put to work at its best.

The effectiveness of the Academy is less apparent when it attempts to grapple with policy issues that have a very high level of political content and in which the objectivity of those involved in the studies can be called into serious question. Taken as a whole, the Academy has, with occasional lapses, used sufficiently good judgment in handling its activities over the decades that its opinions are usually taken seriously. Even then it has been attacked from time to time by so-called public interest groups because its committee meetings are usually held in private. It would probably be exceedingly difficult to create another such "independent" organization from start in the present environment.

CONCLUSION

In trying to pull these thoughts together I come, more or less reluctantly, to the conclusion that far more important than innovation in the science advisory structure is the need for our country to achieve some form of concurrence regarding a variety of national and international affairs. Only then can we expect to achieve a state in which the means by which advice on matters related to science and technology enters governmental affairs can become a truly significant issue. Achieving concurrence will require strong leadership, particularly in the White House, but also in the Congress—with a good measure of bipartisan agreement. Moreover we seem to reach out for strong leadership only at a time when a state of national crisis is widely recognized. Perhaps the time is ripe for such recognition but I am inclined to think it lies farther ahead, at some time in the 1990s. Perhaps, when that occurs, the Congress and the President would agree harmoniously to rewrite the legislation governing OSTP so that the Science Advisor is once again a privileged advisor to the President.

A Case for Evaluating the Nature of Scientific and Technological Advice to the Federal Government

John Brooks Slaughter

> No nation can maintain a position of leadership in the world of today unless it develops to the full its scientific and technological resources. No government adequately meets its responsibilities unless it generously and intelligently supports and encourages the work of science in university, industry, and its own laboratories.—Harry S. Truman, September 6, 1950

Supporting science is a necessity for all great nations and certainly for the United States. Science extends and refines our understanding of the physical universe from the smallest to the largest scale in both space and time. This investment in knowledge opens the door to an expanding human dominion over resources and processes of the physical world. The investment also contributes to society a range of abilities and opportunities which surely would not be available otherwise. It is important to recognize that opening the door is necessary but not sufficient for the ultimate realization of these benefits of society. For that to happen, the great wealth of knowledge we are accumulating must be communicated and applied in a deliberate way.

The conduct of science and technology in America has evolved over the past forty years into a well-organized collaboration between government, industry and academe. Although the structure changes little over time, the relative involvement of each of these participants may vary significantly on even an annual basis. The seminal role of the federal government in funding

John Brooks Slaughter is Chancellor of the University of Maryland College Park (since 1982); was Director of the National Science Foundation (1980–82); has his Doctorate in Engineering Science from the University of California/San Diego; was a staff member of the Naval Electronics Laboratory at San Diego (1960–75); received the Distinguished Service Award of the National Science Foundation (1979); was a Board member of the AAAS; is a Director of the Monsanto Company, Martin Marietta Corporation, and other corporations; and is a member of the National Academy of Engineering.

and encouraging research and development (R&D) is the most critical factor in the equation. Congressional decisions about financing Presidential funding requests for agencies, such as the National Institutes of Health, the National Science Foundation and the Department of Energy, for example, are the throttle that controls the levels of scientific effort throughout much of the science and technology establishment. Changes in taxation policies and incentives for corporations to invest in R&D influence the role that industry plays in the arena. Cyclical oscillations in these policies and in Congressional appropriations produce perturbations that affect the generation of scientific knowledge, the extension of the knowledge into processes and products, and the development of the human resources required to maintain our national presence.

For the most part, the President of the United States through the Executive branch of the government sets the priorities that emerge ultimately in the form of Congressional budget decisions. The Office of Management and Budget (OMB), the Executive agency for establishing and promulgating the federal budget, is responsible for providing the Administration's budget levels for each agency of the federal establishment. For this process to work well, considerable interaction must take place between OMB and each agency to ensure that those activities supported by the President exist in the budget at funding levels appropriate for the accomplishments expected in a given fiscal year.

If the President and the Congress are to be in a position in which choices can be made that are wise and consistent with the nation's needs and aspirations for science and technology, mechanisms must exist for the provision of advice and counsel from the scientific and technological communities to the White House and the US Congress. The primary arrangement for this to occur is through the Office of Science and Technology Policy (OSTP), headed by the President's Science Advisor. The Science Advisor draws upon many sources, inside and outside government, to access the national knowledge base of science and technology.

One principal source of knowledge and studies for this purpose is the National Research Council, the operating arm of the National Academy of Sciences, the National Academy of Engineering and the Institute of Medicine. Although technically a private, non-governmental entity, the National Research Council, an outgrowth of the nineteenth-century Congressional action which established the National Academy of Sciences, occupies and deserves an exalted place in the hierarchy of organizations participating in the process of recommending priorities for federal investments in science and technology. Its reach spans a range which includes defense, space, energy, transportation, health and other fields and disciplines vital to our national capacity for leadership in research and development. Of all the advisory mechanisms in place, the National Research Council is the least politicized and the most effective in providing scientific and technological advice to the government. It should not, however, be the sole source of advice, but rather serve as a model for other policy-making bodies.

THE CASE

This essay argues that it is necessary to have the most sophisticated and objective mechanisms for providing scientific advice to the government in a research and development environment that has become increasingly more complex, competitive and contentious. Some examination of the nature of the advice sought, how it is provided, and how it is used by the President, the Congress and governmental agencies may reveal the kind of advice that is required if we are to retain our positions at or near the top of those nations with a developed capability in science and technology.

An example which reflects that complexity, competitiveness and contentiousness in the globe-circling activity designed to produce superconducting materials that can carry electrical energy with effectively zero resistance at temperatures considerably higher than previously thought possible. Superconductors are important not only because of their inherent phenomenological considerations, but also because of the public policy issues that are being challenged as scientists in government, academic and industrial laboratories work feverishly to make technological breakthroughs, as corporate executives ponder the readiness of their companies to develop products emanating from those breakthroughs, and as economists and politicians question our national capacity and resolve to compete in the international marketplace that certainly will exist.

The rate at which all this is occurring strains credulity. It was in April 1986 that two scientists at the IBM Research Laboratories in Zurich discovered that a compound of barium, lanthanum, copper and oxygen was superconducting at 30 Kelvin. Ten months later, Paul Chu, a University of Houston researcher, developed a ceramic compound that operated with superconductivity at 98 Kelvin. At that point the race to be first in superconductors became more exciting and more competitive than the Triple Crown of horseracing. In May 1987, IBM announced that it has the capability to produce a superconducting material that has 100 times the capacity to carry electrical current than was previously possible. The idea of superconducting supercomputers or magnetically levitated bullet trains has now become much more than a science fiction story-line.

The list of potential uses is mind-boggling if superconducting materials can be made to exist at or near room temperature, the goal of the frenetic, worldwide scientific activity. But science and technology may end up taking a back seat in this race very soon. Marketing strategies, trade policies, long-term financing, and return on investment are likely to be more important in determining who will be able to benefit most from the new developments.

There are those who believe that, while the scientific contributions will be made by American scientists, it will be the Japanese who introduce the first products. This view lends credence to the witticism that the development of a new product is a three-step process: First, an American firm announces a new invention; second, the Russians claim they made the same discovery twenty years ago; and third, the Japanese start exporting it.

After years of seeing foreign competitors capitalize on the fruits of the American research enterprise, many people in this country view the current efforts to develop high-temperature superconductors as the final chance for the US to reclaim international technological supremacy. For years now, we have been watching with interest that has developed into fear as the Japanese have cornered the consumer electronics market, and now also lead in capital items such as power generators, machine tools, and construction equipment. The fear of seeing superconductors become, like semiconductors, lasers, color TVs, and VCRs, the province of the Japanese has introduced a unique degree of anxiety and paranoia into the research and development picture. It is this state of our national mental health which must be taken into consideration when formulating the scientific and technological advice provided to the government.

A similar case can be made for the scientific and technological activity underway in the field of biotechnology which has emerged from the discovery of deoxyribonucleic acid (DNA), the genetic blueprint of life, by Watson and Crick in 1953. This finding has led to new ways to grow disease- and pest-resistant plants, to develop higher protein grains and livestock, to produce hybridomas that manufacture specific types of antibodies, and to discover medicines that can be selectively targeted. But these potentialities bring questions that require more than scientific knowledge to comprehend and answer. There are issues of ethics, of economics, of politics that must be confronted as we proceed with the research and the application of gene splicing and switching. Science advice to the government must take into account these dimensions.

CONCLUSION

The process followed by the National Research Council, which was referred to earlier, musters the kind of broad-based resources to advise the government on matters ranging from ethics to engineering. The strength of this process—its access to knowledge in a range of fields, its nonpartisanship, and its in-depth research—should be replicated by other agencies in order to develop a range of organized sources of objective scientific and technological advice. Too often the Executive branch, in particular, becomes the captive of advisors who are more ideological than objective and who are too limited in their perspectives and the depth of their knowledge. Under such circumstances, the value of the advice given is rendered suspect.

New knowledge gained from grappling with scientific questions is the intellectual raw material for economic progress. As an industrial nation with a high standard of living, there is only one way we can compete in an international marketplace in the long run. We must be smarter than others. The year's discoveries from our sometimes abstruse research in physics, biology, chemistry, oceanography or engineering will, years from now, be the basis of new industries and innovations in old ones. Investing in research and in those institutions responsible for conducting research is the best way to create and preserve, rather than deplete and dismantle, a natural and national resource.

Science Advice to the Seats of Power in Government

H. Guyford Stever

This subject, science advice to government, is not a new one; in fact, it is very old. It is a shock to some of us in the larger science community (science and its applications) when we realize that we have been advising government for half a century. Some in our community have occupied positions of science and technology decision-making, as well, and have been, in fact, the recipients of the advice to government from our own kind in the private sector. To experience both sides of this advice exchange is a rewarding experience which more of our kind should try.

Though our generation did not invent science advising, we certainly have helped it to flourish at all governmental levels. In suggesting the future of science advice to government, it will be difficult to propose ideas or organizations which do not exist, or have not been tried before. In fact, we really should ask the question, "Don't we want more of the same, only better?"

From my early days in science, half a century ago, I noted that scientists like complete control of the direction and use of their work. As a young professor at MIT, I recall James R. Killian, Jr., Science Advisor to President Eisenhower, often making the statement in speeches and in conversations that "scientists should be on top, not on tap." In fact, many of the Science Advisors I know preferred the decision-making role to the Advisor's role.

Looking to the future, we must remember that some of the best scientific advice has come outside normal channels. In actuality, many scientists chafe at the prospect of going through channels with their scientific advice, and seek ways around them. An example of this occurred in the early 1940s

H. Guyford Stever was Science Advisor to President Ford and Director of the National Science Foundation. He has been President of Carnegie-Mellon University, Professor of Aeronautics and Astronautics at MIT, and Chief Scientist of the US Air Force. He is a Director of several major corporations, including TRW, Inc.; Goodyear Tire Company, and Schering-Plough Corporation. Dr. Stever is a member of the National Academy of Sciences, and is a member and Foreign Secretary of the National Academy of Engineering.

when a group of leading European scientists, who had taken refuge in the United States from the horrors of Nazism and Fascism, found a way to get directly to the President to advise him that an atom bomb project should be started. They got what they wished in part only, for President Franklin D. Roosevelt then turned to the science structure which he had set up in the US Government, under Dr. Vannevar Bush, to lead the program until it was turned over to a truly centralized and authoritarian organization, the United States Army, for the development of the atom bomb. This example also illustrates a common characteristic of this kind of process in that the scientists who gave the original advice were restive, dissatisfied with, or even rebellious toward the kind of leadership that the program actually got.

I believe that informal channels of science advising will continue to exist, and will grow in the future, especially due to the greater openness of our government to the opinions of the population expressed to the Congress and elected officials who are becoming ever more sensitive to the power of science. With the increasing popularity of the Congressional committee hearings and the growth in use of local, regional and national hearings by the departments and agencies of government, there are many opportunities for self-appointed advisors. And the direct influence of constituents on their own Congressmen is a potent factor.

THE FORMAL MECHANISMS

What of the future of the formal science advising mechanisms in our government? Before we look at them, we should ask several questions: Who needs science advice, who wants science advice, who accepts science advice, and who uses science advice? The real test of science advice is to get over the hurdles suggested by such questions.

When looking at the foci of science power in the federal government, and the number of chains of science advising they possess, one suddenly realizes that the science advice business is a very large one. The collective budget must be a good fraction of a billion dollars. The budget of the National Academies complex alone, making hundreds of studies per year, approaches $100 million a year, and that complex is only one of many scientific advice suppliers to government. This leads me to a principal theme, that we have plenty—perhaps a plethora—of scientific advice. What we need to look at is the quality of advice, the screening and selection process, and how to get the best advice used.

At the top, the President has a formal scientific advisory unit. Both Houses of Congress, with their many committees through which they deal with major issues involving science, have large numbers of staff members, many with science backgrounds. Advice is also received from their constituents, from their formal hearings on scientific issues, and from specially appointed scientific groups. But scientific advising in government goes far beyond that.

All departments and agencies with Presidentially appointed officials have both formal and informal channels of scientific advice, sometimes peopled from their own internal organizations, but quite often additionally from the private sector.

The number of agencies in which science and technology play important primary roles has grown substantially in recent times, and one wonders whether this growth of science-oriented agencies is going to continue, or whether we have finished our entrepreneurial days in the invention of scientific agencies. Perhaps now we will simply readjust existing agencies as new pressures develop. But in the past fifty years there have emerged the National Science Foundation; the Atomic Energy Commission, which went through two or three transformations in to the Department of Energy; the Department of Transportation; the National Aeronautics and Space Administration, which resulted from a major reorganization of the National Advisory Committee for Aeronautics; the Environmental Protection Agency, practically a new unit; within the Department of Commerce, the National Oceanographic and Atmospheric Administration; within the Department of Defense, the Defense Advance Research Project Agency; and many more. Of course, the Presidential Office of Science and Technology Policy and the Congressional Office of Technology Assessment should be included.

Institutional innovation has, indeed, been the mark of the past. The thrust has slowed down to a considerable extent, however. Just as in the industrial world, perhaps we are now going through a consolidation period with mergers and takeovers and turf battles, which will end with our current agencies assuming any new kinds of problems that emerge from the scientific community. For example, there doesn't seem to be a new agency emerging from the rapidly growing biological science revolution. It seems to have been absorbed in existing agencies, the Department of Health, the National Institutes of Health, the National Science Foundation, the Environmental Protection Agency, etc. And we have progressed a long way into the new information revolution, including its telecommunications and computer sciences, and we have not invented an agency for it, although some existing agencies have greatly increased their work in the field. Perhaps we can conclude that, in the future, we shall work our scientific advice into the existing very powerful scientific agencies.

There is a great temptation to try mergers and reassignments of various departments or parts thereof to form a new Science Department in order to get greater effectiveness, to eliminate overlapping responsibilities, and to save money. These are worthwhile goals, but most of these combinations seem to suffer in being conglomerates without sharp foci. Of course, when a scientific activity is weak in an agency, or its mission has become obsolete, action should be taken. I, however, prefer to see science and technology efforts connected with many mission agencies in order to strengthen each of them. Additionally, this ensures that the different views and approaches on science and technology matters must be compared and handled at the highest levels of government, instead of in a single, lower-level agency. It requires, of course, strong attention at the top of the total science and technology field in order to achieve those worthwhile goals above.

IN THE CONGRESS

On the Congressional side of things, the committee activities have grown in the handling of scientific issues. The principal major institutional invention for Congress in recent times, the Office of Technology Assessment, has already assumed the important role of option comparisons, and probably could absorb other important responsibilities for Congress.

We can go deeper into the governmental structure to find additional centers of scientific power. In addition to those major units that are directed by Presidential appointees, there are many units of government which are run entirely by employees of the government and even major contract laboratories and think-tanks. Each one of them has a degree of scientific power and also gets a lot of scientific advising.

All of this seems to be a long-winded way of saying that we have a great variety of scientific advisory structures. Also many scientists and engineers who have taken positions of leadership in these agencies have become part of the power structure where they are the advisees and decision-makers instead of the advisors. They are the ones who can decide whether a piece of advise is, in fact, reasonable and useable.

This complex interplay of science decision-making and science advising is a very healthy one. I believe that it is one of the strengths of our country, in that we permit so many of our experts in science and engineering to participate in the complex process which ends in decision to use certain scientific ideas. We can complain all we like about various elements of the system, but many of us are involved. Quite often elements of the advisory structure are misused. Scientific advisory committees are often composed of people who already see eye-to-eye with the government leaders whom they advise. There are times when environmentalists feel that their input has been neglected; and the large-scale technically oriented companies often point out that the research and development climate that government sets is very poor because of a lack of understanding in government agencies.

Scientists and engineers, like most people in society, like to use their special power—in this case, scientific expertise—to further their own set of values on issues larger than science. Advisors of government, although they are asked primarily because of their special expertise and experience, often include value judgments together with their scientific advice. Sometimes their expertise is taken and their value judgments are rejected; sometimes both are taken; sometimes both are rejected; occasionally, the expertise is rejected, and the value judgment is accepted. Sometimes government officials select specific scientific advisors primarily because their value judgments agree with the official opinion. But all of this shows that we have a democratic process, and that no one is completely suppressed. No one loses completely his freedom of expression, if he is in the scientific advising channels. The mass of advice from the greater science community to top levels of government, however, reflects widely different value judgments on many applications of science, sometimes on basic research itself, for example, as in the case of the use of animals in experiments. I would not, in closing this discussion of value judgments versus expertise and experience (they are not in opposition to each other, but they are different matters), that, in the long run, those who accept full-time decision-making positions in government have the privilege of making the final value judgments, as well as selecting which expert advice to follow. If they are elected or appointed officials, there are processes by which the country can get rid of them if it is dissatisfied with the value judgments they are making, so there are limits to their power.

THE FUTURE

So what is our future? There will be a continuation of an outpouring of scientific advances. I once thought that molecular and atomic phenomena were becoming rather fully developed, only to be greeted by masers and lasers and solid-state and the modern development of molecular structures in biology, DNA, RNA, the genetic revolution, the understanding of the large molecule groupings in cells, etc. Think of the applied revolutions based on molecular phenomena! Many have been generated in recent years, and there doesn't seem to be any reason why they should stop. Nuclear physics does not seem to be moving as rapidly, but there has been some progress there, too. The earth sciences, oceanography and atmospheric science, geology and geography have much to offer. Everywhere we turn, scientific fields are outpouring, and the institutional structure we have to apply the discoveries of scientific research in practical applications are thriving. There will be great need for science advice as these fields of science continue to progress.

What about the advisory structure at the top where large-scale policy decisions are effected? I am very suspicious of highly centralized institutional arrangements for science and technology. I think that our institutions, both the public and the private ones, work best in a pluralistic, decentralized way. I do not see that there are important ideas in science and engineering that do not get the attention of the top decision-makers in our country. Clearly, more scientists themselves should be willing to take decision-making posts in government. It is particularly disappointing that a number of highly qualified people have turned down such posts as the Science Advisor to the President of the United States in recent times; it is a weakness of the scientific community that many of its members have been unwilling to throw themselves into some of the political turmoil that goes with such an important post. To be sure, one cannot be a scientific dictator in any of these positions, but one can still make a very great contribution in them.

The Science Advisor—or, more correctly, the Science and Technology Advisor—to the President of the United States has an important post. The President is at the top of the decision-making on all scientific issues, and it is important for him to have someone to keep him up to date with scientific and technological progress, someone to make sure that he is in touch with first-rate people in the science and engineering fields, someone who can help him understand the options suggested by so many different sources. I would hope that future Presidents make it a practice of getting an advisor who works well with the rest of their White House organizations, for that is a requirement of the job, and, at the same time, is well accepted by the science community for his competence and experience.

At the top level, there is one institutional unit which is lacking, in my opinion. That is a Presidential Science and Technology Advisory Council (PSTAC). We need a top-level, Presidentially appointed group, small in number, but high in professional experience and competence, to complement and supplement the Science and Technology Advisor to the President. Its job would be to help select the important scientific and technological action options for the President from all the many advisory inputs from all governmental levels.

We don't necessarily need many new institutions or new positions. What we need is a strengthening of the quality of the advisory mechanisms we now have and, concurrently, a strengthening of the positions of science and technology decision-makers in government. Scientists and engineers—at least, a good number of them—must throw themselves into this complex political activity in order to get the best for our country in science and technology.

Science Advice in the Government: Formulation and Utilization

Gerald F. Tape

The formulation and utilization of science and technology advice by the federal government has been under continuing study and change since World War II, when it was recognized that science and technology would play an ever-increasing role in the nation's security and economic growth. Recommendations came from within the government, both the Executive and the Legislative branches, and from independent individuals and organizations.

The most successful and extensive use of such advice occurred during the decades of the 1950s and 1960s. This was a period of strong Presidential leadership and receptivity for science, and it culminated in the development in the White House of a strong advisory mechanism, namely, the Science Advisor and staff and the President's Science Advisory Committee. The essays presented in the book, *Science Advice to the President*, edited by William T. Golden (New York: Pergamon Press, 1980) summarized well the evolution, successes and failures of that post-World War II period. There is no need to repeat that history here. Rather, let us examine the next decade in the light of past and present experience, and suggest where and how the nation can best be served when issues involve a science and technology component.

In addressing science and technology advice for the highest levels of government, one needs to consider how science and technology impact decision-making in the three branches of government.

Gerald F. Tape has been President of Associated Universities, Inc. (1962–1963 and 1969–1980); Commissioner, US Atomic Energy Commission (1963–69); US Representative (Ambassador) to the International Atomic Energy Agency (1973–77); a member of the President's Science Advisory Committee (1969–73); Chairman, Defense Science Board (1970–73); and is a member of the National Academy of Engineering.

JUDICIARY

Courts must base their decisions on the law and the information presented to them. Judges are not free to inject their own knowledge; an understanding of the subject matter is important, however. It is important that lawyers presenting a case understand the role of the science or technology involved, and utilize expert witnesses to provide, for the record, the facts and their relevance to the issues. It is difficult to visualize how a formal advisory mechanism could serve the judiciary as it is now structured. The Department of Justice, however, has access to all of the resources of the Executive branch, including reports of advisory bodies, in preparing for the prosecution or defense of cases involving national issues that impact on—or are impacted by—science and technology.

LEGISLATIVE

The principal responsibility of the Congress is the enactment of legislation. Laws arise from issues that develop from the public and from the Legislative and Executive branches of the government. Legislation covers a wide spectrum from policy and its implementation, programs and budget, procedures and practices, to detailed orders. The available mechanisms for advice are many. For science and technology, the most important are the Congressional hearings and, in response to members' requests, reports and studies by the Office of Technology Assessment, the Congressional Research Service, and the General Accounting Office. From time to time, the Congress has mandated studies by the National Academies of Sciences and Engineering. In my opinion, the Congress now has available a sufficient number of qualified sources and mechanisms for advice. The difficulties, when they arise, are more apt to be in the manner in which expert advice is used or not used in order to achieve particular objectives of individual members. That is beyond the control of the advisory structure itself.

In general, witnesses from the Executive branch are invited to testify at hearings. To the extent that the Executive branch has done its job well, there should be less need for replication of a science and technology advisory structure in the Congress. To the extent that the Executive branch ignores, without good reason, science and technology advice in proposing legislation, the more the Congress will need to look for independent advice.

The Congress would be well advised to give greater attention to the rate of funding for major new research facilities. Each project requires an Authorization Bill that specifies the scope and an Appropriations Bill that specifies funding. The tendency has been to fund major research facility projects at a less than the optimum annual rate, the assumption being that a year or two of delay doesn't matter. As a result, the total cost of each project is increased, and research results to be obtained following commissioning are delayed. In an age of competition, we need to hold down investment costs and to obtain the return (research results) at the earliest date. The argument often used for stretching out projects through funding delays is that more projects can be underway at the same time. In my view, it is always more cost-effective, on a national basis, to start and finish each research facility on the optimum design and construction schedule. If some projects have to wait, they should be given a firm planning start date, so that design of the facility on the basis of the then-expected state-of-the-art technology can proceed. The Science Advisor, Office of Management and Budget, and the Congressional Budget Office could be helpful in providing guidance.

EXECUTIVE

The operations of the federal government are carried out principally by the departments and agencies. As in any major business, however, there must be a centralized focus for policy and programs. Also, the establishment of common practices and procedures, to the extent feasible, is desirable. For the United States, these responsibilities are shared by the President and the Congress with the initiation of actions generally coming from the Executive. As such, the President, with the advice and support of the various White House offices, is responsible. Matters affecting and affected by science and technology are become ever more important in Presidential decision-making.

A President, in discharging his responsibilities, is faced with many choices. Advocates both internal and external to the government abound. Each department and agency should take an advocacy position in the discharge of its responsibilities. Centralized evaluation and priority setting are required. Objectives must be established, priorities set, conflicts resolved, and quality performance achieved. Where science and technology issues are present, the President needs advice that can be best integrated by a strong and well-informed Science Advisor. While his office has a crucial role, other White House offices, especially the Office of Management and Budget, must also be involved.

An extensive science and technology advisory apparatus now exists in the Executive branch. Many departments and agencies utilize advisory bodies drawn from the public, especially where programmatic needs are better served by advancing the frontiers of science and in developing and applying new technologies—Department of Defense, Department of Energy, National Institutes of Health, National Science Foundation, and National Aeronautics and Space Administration, to name but a few. The same is true of some regulatory bodies—Environmental Protection Agency, Nuclear Regulatory Commission, Food and Drug Administration, for examples. Today's drive for competitiveness at home and abroad is putting more pressure on development and application of advanced technology for the marketplace. Industry, university and government interaction is vital. External advisory bodies are necessary to provide a broad perspective and interaction with the working community of scientists, engineers and managers.

A SCIENCE AND TECHNOLOGY PRESENCE IN THE WHITE HOUSE

The White House staff is an assemblage of experts having many specific and often diverse interests, for example, foreign policy, domestic policy, national security, etc., each with a political overlay. And yet the unifying factor is support of the President and his program. Decisions can rarely be based on factual knowledge alone; public perception and political factors must be considered. The issue is how, in such an environment, the White House science and technology presence can best serve the President and the nation. In the most general terms, the best arrangement consists of an influential Science Advisor, a competent staff, and a body of external advisors. The Science Advisor is the key to this arrangement.

Within the government, the Science Advisor must have the confidence of the President, the White House staff, and the departments and agencies with which the office interacts. Outside of the government, he or she must have the confidence of the community of scientists and engineers and of their institutions—universities, industry, and national centers. The confidence of the leaders of science and technology in other countries is also required in order to support U.S. foreign policy and to promote increasingly important international collaboration in science. The totality of the communities to be served presents an enormous task for the Science Advisor.

Assistance comes from two sectors, internally from experienced and competent staff and externally from a body of Science Advisors. The staff must provide support to the Advisor in all areas, but probably the most important is the maintenance of smooth working relationships within the White House family (National Security Council, Office of Management and Budget, staff), and with other government units. The external advisors, acting individually or collectively on committees, must recognize that their advice must be objective and sound, and that they have special obligations when working in the White House environment.

The principal responsibility of the Science Advisor is to bring the benefits of the country's science and technology endeavors to bear in achieving national objectives; in other words, to serve the nation. At the same time, the Advisor must oversee and assure the health of the national science and technology program. Only by initiating and maintaining forefront programs can we expect to compete in the broadest sense. The totality of science and engineering—education, basic research, engineering, and application as carried out in the universities, industry, and national centers—must be considered. The Advisor must be a voice *of* science in order to provide public understanding and to indicate directions and opportunities for the future, and a voice *for* science where there is concern for the health of the enterprise.

The Science Advisor must operate in a political environment. A successful Advisor finds ways for science and technology to support politically motivated objectives as well as political support for science and technology objectives.

EXECUTIVE BRANCH SCIENCE AND TECHNOLOGY ADVISORY STRUCTURE

All departments and agencies must be encouraged to utilize science and technology advisory bodies. The purpose is to support high-quality priority programs and to identify new opportunities. Such bodies do, of course, now exist, especially in the mission-oriented agencies. Effective advisory mechanisms at the department and agency level should reduce the need for White House and Congressional duplication. There are often, however, cross-agency technical conflicts which are best resolved at the White House level.

In the White House, there now exist the Science Advisor to the President, the Office of Science and Technology Policy, and the White House Science Council. I see no need for a major change in the organizational structure; the necessary elements are in place. Success or failure in the discharge of responsibilities is more a function of individuals and relationships and the support provided by the President and the Congress than of the organizational structure.

Some will argue for a reincarnation of the President's Science Advisory Committee, appointed by and reporting to the President. Such an advisory structure carries weight and has prestige. Its reports are addressed to the President; a Presidential response is expected. Implementation of recommendations carries the Presidential imprint. Yet there can be problems, as we know from past experience. Some recommendations are better handled by direct action between the Science Advisor and the affected agencies; only a few recommendations require Presidential action, and these could easily be identified by the Science Advisor. Certainly, the White House advisory structure is there to assist and not to create difficulties for the President.

In my view, the present form of a Science Advisor to the President and the White House Science Council is a reasonable compromise. Fundamentally, effectiveness is dependent on the principals involved and their interest in and receptivity to maximizing the use of science and technology in support of major national goals and solving national problems.

THE COMING DECADE

Times have changed. In the decade of the 1950s and much of the 1960s, the country was primarily concerned with national security and "keeping ahead" of the Russians, whose rapid progress in nuclear weapons development and the Sputnik space shock placed heavy emphasis on military and space competition. At the same time, the US enjoyed a generally recognized leadership role throughout the world in standards of living, professional achievements, and international relations. There was a favorable balance of trade, a reasonable federal deficit, and continuing economic growth. The Western world and many developing nations looked to the United States for leadership, cooperation and assistance.

Today, the situation is drastically different. There is continuing emphasis on national security, but there is also increasing recognition that simply increasing the nuclear arsenals of the superpowers is not a viable option. More attention is being given to arms control and the concomitant question of threat evaluation and verification of agreements. There is a marked increase in competition from abroad in the domestic marketplace, the US trade balance is unfavorable, and the American can-do approach is being taken over by other nations. Competitiveness is not a political buzz-word; it is a fact of life.

The decay of competitive strength, an unfavorable trade balance, the federal deficit, national defense, and space and domestic issues must continue to receive attention at the highest levels by the Executive and the Congress. Many of these problem areas are interrelated. All, in varying degrees, have science and technology components. But advanced technology, while necessary, will not alone solve the problems. In every instance, major reforms in the conventional way in which the government and industry have done business in the past will need to be instituted. "Overhead," whatever its source, has been allowed to increase dramatically. A glaring example is the time it takes to obtain authorization and to complete a major project or to bring a product to the marketplace as compared to performance by foreign competitors.

The White House science advisory mechanism can do more than identify priorities and opportunities for the support and application of science and technology or resolve technical conflicts. It can help bring realism to the decision-making process by pointing out the limitations of science and technology and indicating where other actions are required to effect solutions. For example, since many nations, in time, will be able to reach the same technological plateaus, the competitiveness edge will ultimately be determined, not by technology, but by the effectiveness of personnel involved, both labor and management.

The need to address major issues that have high science and technology components, such as arms control; nuclear proliferation; affordable, viable military forces for the twenty-first century; security of command, control and supply; industrial competitiveness, etc., is obvious. In addition, I urge that issues where decisions are influenced by factors such as personal risk, perception, and emotion be addressed. The balancing of personal risk versus societal risk has been most difficult to achieve. Hard decisions are needed, especially in the regulatory area. In many instances, a mandated reduction of risk to persons is associated with an increase in societal risk or cost or both.

To illustrate with an extreme example, elimination of pesticides and fertilizers in agriculture would result in major reductions in productivity and higher costs that would impact most strongly on lower-income persons. Personal risk is frequently judged on the basis of public perception, enhanced by the "might happen" mentality. Public education is needed. The President and his staff and the Congress and, above all, the public need to understand, and to be able to balance the risks to persons in taking a given action as well as the risks to society, *i.e.*, the nation, that would be involved in not taking that action. These are important matters; they affect national and economic security in areas such as defense, energy, food supply, health, industrial activities, and transportation. The degree of acceptance of risk is also a major factor in international competitiveness. There is no such thing as a risk-free society.

CONCLUSIONS

The United States, in the coming decade, is facing a number of serious problems. From a past position of having exploitable technology, financial resources, and production know-how in achieving—with little competition—a position of international leadership, we are now faced with playing catch-up. While concentrating on superpower military confrontation, we are in danger of losing the economic war to some of our friendly nations. The civilian economy needs enlightened governmental cooperation and assistance. Leadership, focus, and commitment to a long-term strategy are needed. Most of all, the country must pull up its socks and face the reality of the times.

Science and technology have played an important role in the past. We relied on advancing technology to provide solutions to problems that would have otherwise had less desirable results. Technology supported industrial activity, which, in turn, supported higher wages. There are still plenty of opportunities, and we need strong research and development programs that will generate new opportunities. But, most of all, we need to emphasize the effective application of developed technology and the roles to be played by labor and management.

The current problems are not all with the government, although the problems that the government faces are probably central; industry also has its problems. The private sector's concern for the next quarter's financial statement is a fundamental deterrent to pursuing major, long-term developments. The short attention spans of most Administrations and of individual members and committees of the Congress also fail us where long-term program interest and support are necessary.

Many issues, not all of a science and technology nature, will need to be addressed. Anti-trust considerations dictate the need for competition, *i.e.*, multiple suppliers. When there was little foreign competition, multiple US suppliers were required. Now, for some products, there are no US suppliers, a situation often of major concern to the Department of Defense. Government initiative and leadership can stimulate desirable changes in all sectors, technical and administrative, public and private.

This is the time for the President to call upon the Science Advisor to take the lead in recommending initiatives that will

- make the combined R&D output of the universities, industry and national centers more focused and effective in restoring the civilian industrial sector to a worldwide competitive status:
- lead to formulation of a technically sound, viable, affordable year 2000 military force;
- identify changes in legislation and practice that will allow science and technology programs to be carried forward on a more timely and cost-effective basis in both the public and the private sectors;
- identify changes in legislation and practice that will accelerate and promote the industrial development and marketing of advanced technology products; and
- identify and monitor new directions in science and discoveries that have the potential of enhancing or protecting the country's future industrial competitive and national defense positions.

In summary, the nation is in a precarious position; it must not be allowed to drift. Changes in motivation and practices are needed; personal and institutional objectives must be reconciled with national goals. The special interests of many individuals, groups, organizations, companies, etc., may have to be set aside in the interest of national recovery. Let us start where the issues have a more factual and objective base and thus may be more tractable—science and technology.

With the leadership and strong support of the President, the start can be made with a White House science and technology organization that must include an influential Advisor having the confidence of the President; a knowledgeable, effective staff; and a body of recognized, objective advisors having outstanding credentials, especially in science, engineering and management.

The Future Role of the Science Advisor

Edward Teller

Science and technology have thoroughly changed our lives. A change in our way of thinking is much less in evidence. The split of our society into two cultures—the new culture of science and the old culture of the humanities—comes close to a case of public schizophrenia. Our political leaders are in real need of reliable scientific information. Unfortunately, the proper lines of communication are underdeveloped. Neither good intentions nor legislation will change that condition rapidly.

That good communication is possible can be seen by examining a peculiar example: the island of Taiwan. In the past thirty-five years, the population has grown from eleven million people to almost twenty million. At the same time, the living conditions there have progressed from extreme economic misery (an average income of $144 per person per year) to the borderline of prosperity—an average income of $3,750. The change is a result of the application of technology in both agriculture and industry. It is not a coincidence that almost half of the high ranking government leaders of Taiwan have advanced degrees, mostly earned in the United States, in mathematics, physics, chemistry, agriculture or engineering.

No one should expect that a similar miracle could or should occur in the United States. But we must continue to work on the difficulties of understanding that exist between the two cultures. The President's Science Advisor will continue to have an exceptionally difficult task. The following suggestions are made with the hope that they will lead to some improvement in the cooperation between government and science.

Edward Teller, nuclear physicist, is a Senior Research Fellow at the Hoover Institution, Stanford, and Associate Director Emeritus of the Lawrence Livermore National Laboratory. He was active at Los Alamos, and was a major figure in the development of the hydrogen bomb. He has been a member of the General Advisory Committee of the Atomic Energy Commission, of the President's Foreign Intelligence Advisory Board, and the White House Science Council. He has been awarded the National Medal of Science and the Enrico Fermi Medal. His latest book is Better a Shield Than a Sword *(1987).*

A SCIENCE COURT

The role of the President's Science Advisor includes answering specific questions, drawing attention to new possibilities or new dangers, and clarifying scientific issues. In connection with the last responsibility, a proposal made by Arthur Kantrowitz could go a long way toward correcting some of the confusion and fear connected with current scientific topics. His suggestion is to establish a Science Court, which the Science Advisor could use as an effective tool for public education.

The findings of a Science Court would be binding on nobody. The Court would have one purpose: to provide reliable scientific opinion on questions of national interest. Nuclear reactors and nuclear waste disposal is one. The risks of various curative drugs, which the Food and Drug Administration handles in a rather restrictive manner, is another. The comparative risks of pesticides and pests is a third.

The Court would be made up of three to five scientists selected to serve as judges. Each case would be heard by a different group of competent scientists, who have a reputation for decent judgment but who are not specialists in the particular field in question. The National Academies of Science, Engineering, and Medicine could provide a great number of suitable people—scientists who don't have a strong position on either side of a question, but who can distinguish science from pseudo-science.

The procedure might be as follows. When a disagreement or an apparent disagreement between scientists arises on a topic with political ramifications, the Science Advisor could call for an advocate to be selected from each side. Those selections should be left to the two opposing parties. The selected advocates would be ratified by the Presidential Science Advisor.

After the two advocates are designated, each would select a member of the Court from the list of potential members, and one or more other Court members would be selected by the Presidential Science Advisor with advice from the National Academy. The case, pro and con, would then be presented to the assembled Court. Each of the proponents could adduce evidence and introduce witnesses. The witnesses could be cross-examined by the other side. The advocates would offer summary statements, but the Science Court would draw up one or more concluding opinions.

Scientists are said to be objective. That is true in regard to their own narrow fields, where they can be disproved. If they imagine that they are objective beyond that field, outside their specialty, they will be less self-critical and less objective than others. It is up to the scientists serving as judges to be as objective as ever possible.

The advocates, on the other hand, should not even try to be objective. They should marshall all effective arguments supporting their position. Thus what the Science Court could provide is an adversarial procedure that would allow factual information to be brought to public attention and would provide assistance to the public in drawing reasonable conclusions.

Contrast that procedure with what happens today. In those few cases where the subject attracts enough attention and a major panel is convened, the pressure on the panel members for unanimity is great. Yet, unanimity is apt to lead to error. The other possibility is hardly better. The findings of the panel are so watered down by compromise as to be meaningless.

An adversarial procedure would provide a full hearing of the arguments for and against the question. That type of procedure has proved one of the pillars of democratic society in all kinds of disputes. The only difference would be that when the judges have spoken, unanimously or otherwise, their decision binds no one—not the President, not the Congress, not any court of justice. A Science Court would clarify the extent to which scientists disagree and whether the disagreement is substantive or based on value judgments. Disagreement among scientists has led to confusion among the public. Identifying the basis for scientists' disagreement would produce elightenment.

If the court managed to clarify some of the difficult cases that affect public policy, it would more than have proved its merit. If its findings stood the test of time, it would acquire prestige. Then indeed the Science Court would provide guidance for the people, for their representatives, and for the Administration itself.

If the public were better informed on scientific topics, the Science Advisor would be much better able to perform his other roles of providing advice on specific issues and alerting the President to needs and possibilities. The Science Advisor should not have a big permanent staff. The advisory function should certainly not become a big department.

A Science Advisor should have as little power as possible. Scientists are not used to power, and they may not be properly limited in the ways in which power is used. Scientific problems are well-defined, and have only one correct answer. Political problems are ill-defined, have many possible answers, and often require compromise. Scientists are poorly trained for making the types of decisions required in politics.

AD HOC PANELS

Use has been and should be made of *ad hoc* panels, composed in each case of the best experts available on specific, concrete scientific questions of particular urgency. As a rule, these panels should function for half a year or so and then go out of business. Many more scientists would be involved, and they would be involved where they can do the most good. Any real scientist knows his limitations. He knows he can give advice on few topics. But on those topics he can give good advice.

I think that *ad hoc* panels, having less prestige and more insight, are particularly appropriate for the function of a scientist. A scientist is at his worst when he pontificates. He is at his best when he makes a remark about his own special area of study. In that sense, a Science Advisor should not be an all-wise man. He should be a conduit that makes available the best advice that is possible in each case. Decisions, however, cannot and should not be made by any expert or panel of experts. They must be made by the elected leaders themselves. The power must remain where the populace has placed it.

A Science Advisor should not be someone who speaks only when spoken to. A Science Advisor must have access to government leaders when he recognizes that an important issue is not receiving adequate attention. A recent example concerns strategic defense. Advances in science or technology changed the character of ABM defense. From both open sources and intelligence reports, it was clear that the Soviet Union was hard at work on new defense technologies and that the United States was ignoring them. President Reagan, after consulting with his military and scientific advisors proposed to the scientists of our country that the possibility of defense against weapons of mass destruction be thoroughly explored. One result was bitter public controversy; another, less widely noticed outcome is that the President's original proposal for research on the subject has been universally accepted.

There is a final simple requirement for doing a good job as a Science Advisor—the Science Advisor should give advice that is advantageous to the nation, not advice advantageous to science. On some occasions, both interests may be served by the same action, but an advisor should never influence policy to produce advantages for science alone.

I am a scientist. I like to see advantages for science. But, if the Science Advisor believes that his main job is to promote science, then he becomes nothing more than a lobbyist. He may be successful in one case or another, but in the long run the effort will be resented and will not be successful. The Science Advisor may advise actions that are advantageous to science only in so far as they are clearly necessary for the country as a whole. That requires a great deal of self-criticism on the part of a Science Advisor. His heart is, for good and natural reasons, on the side of science. He must subject himself to careful self-questioning about whether he is moved by his preference for science or by the broad interests of the country as a whole.

The practically impossible job of the Science Advisor has always been frustrating. Even if the Science Advisor enlightens the public with the help of a Science Court, and even if he provides good advice aided by appropriate *ad hoc* committees, his job will remain frustrating. But I hope that, by implementing such programs, he may establish some oases of success in the desert of frustration.

Presidential Studies
and Science Advising

Kenneth W. Thompson

For the scientist, three problems present themselves in evaluating science advising. Each relates to a function of the Science Advisor. The first is the advocacy function which persons in government and political scientists take for granted but scientists may not fully comprehend. A former Cabinet member warned that science advising in the White House could readily become one more example of special pleading for a powerful constituency to which the Advisor is beholden. Civil rights and economic interest groups turn to Advisors who plead their cause. The Cabinet member was sufficiently concerned about an Advisor playing such a role that he recommended that Science Advisors should be assigned to Cabinet-level departments instead. According to this view, the Advisor inescapably is cast in the role of advocate for the scientific community, a group that is large and influential with research needs that dwarf any other research group. To the extent the Advisor is a middleman between the government and scientists, he must maintain their confidence and trust if he is to call on them to serve the nation. It is inconceivable that the government can ever retain a sufficient body of scientists within the government to provide authoritative research and information on the many science problems that arise. Thus the task of the Advisor is likely to remain very heavily one of identifier, catalyst, coordinator, and organizer of science resources outside government.

Some would go one step further in describing the Advisor's functions. They see the Advisor as essentially a cheerleader. Much of science is beyond the understanding not only of the man in the street, but of the trusted public servant. In the 1960s, a little group of thoroughly competent scientists saw themselves as science interpreters. Men like Lloyd Berkner sought to explain

Kenneth W. Thompson has been Director of the White Burkett Miller Center of Public Affairs, University of Virginia, since 1978, and also J. Wilson Newman Professor of Government and Foreign Affairs there. He was Vice President of The Rockefeller Foundation (1961–74), responsible for international education, the humanities and arts and the social sciences.

complex realities in science to the uninformed and the uninitiated. Such a need clearly exists within government as well. Someone must identify, explain, justify and defend science. The mere availability of scientists is not enough. Intense competition for scarce resources demands a strong effort to publicize and praise science. It demands, in effect, a cheerleader who leads the march toward acceptance of a controversial policy. A recent example is the action taken by Reagan Science Advisor Jay Keyworth, who spearheaded the campaign for the Strategic Defense Initiative.

A third need is for what analysts have called a grand conceptualizer. Someone must help the President in determining priorities. The urgent problems and research needs of scientists are virtually unlimited. Moreover, not every urgent problem can be clarified and ameliorated through study and research. Either the data or means of study may be lacking. Someone close to the President must guide an Administration's thinking concerning problems that deserve the highest attention and those that are amenable to study and improvement. Presumably, the Science Advisor should have such a mandate.

"A FOURTH-TIER PLAYER"

Yet this role for the Science Advisor would appear utopian and exaggerated to those who have occupied that post. In practice, Philip Smith sees the Advisor as "a fourth-tier player in the hierarchy of the presidency."[1] I am reminded of the statement of Dr. Daniel Ruge that the position of the Presidential phyician which he occupied in the first term of the Reagan Administration was that of a "blue collar worker." If formal designations of Advisors have validity, it must be validity with political content. The Science Advisor, like the Presidential physician, the latter especially where the 25th amendment is concerned, must make their way in a highly competitive political environment. The White House staff is increasingly a battlefield for a host of special interest groups each claiming a slice of the political and budgetary pie. The Science Advisor and especially his or her staff must live in such a world for as Sidney Drell has written: "What you need on the staff are highly qualified people who've got 'street smarts.' Through their contracts they know where to go in the various agencies, where to get the answers, how to ask in a way that is not confrontational so that they get shut out, and how to use the fact that they are asking in the n ie of the President."[2]

In Miller Center Forums with former Science Advisors, science w. .ers, and political observers, I am impressed with how often certain references recur. Is is said that "Science Advisor A" came to Washington believing that his scientific standing and the sheer political weight of his sci ntific judgments would produce policy results. Advisor A was deposed tc think that the mere act of sending a memorandum up the line was equiva nt to making policy, given the mandate and prestige of the Advisor. S h an attitude calls to mind Paul H. Nitze's comment about intellectuals outside government who imagine that filing a report or submitting a paper was a contribution to foreign policy. In Nitze's words, the only way to influence foreign policy is to be present to fight for points in the report or paper when it is discussed.

John Walsh has written that the disappointments of the partisans of science advising as a strong influence in the White House are the result of "somewhat exaggerated expectations."[3] Because scientists, in particular, may sometimes have expected too much, their mindset has led them to overlook political factors and limitations. He notes that Lee DuBridge had been enormously influential throughout the 1950s. He contributed far more to the growth of federal science affairs than he is credited with doing. The scientific community, however, was at odds with government in the late 1960s, and DuBridge resigned about eighteen months after he took the job, less than the half-life of most Science Advisors. Walsh explains: "He [DuBridge] was regarded by Nixon loyalists as a kind of ambassador or envoy from the scientific community, not as a loyal staff man or team player."[4] For the mature scientist, life as a team player in an alien setting among persons whose main achievement is successful electioneering often proves difficult. A Nobel Laureate and a campaign advance man are not drawn easily and naturally to one another.

THE EXTERNAL ENVIRONMENT

The Miller Center discussions also found discussants putting emphasis on the external environment as it affects science advising. Several made the point that it is tempting to look back to a golden age of science advising and attribute it wholly to the quality of scientists and the impact made possible through organizing the efforts of a critical mass of extraordinary scientists. No one questioned that the era of Killian, Kistiakowsky, Wiesner, Hornig and DuBridge, "before the fall" with Richard M. Nixon, was a notable period in the mobilization of first-class science talent. It was also the time, especially during the years of Killian and Kistiakowsky, of Sputnik. At every level, from elementary school science education to the most advanced scientific research, political incentives bound up with the national objective of "catching up" with the Russians pushed science ahead. Of the Kennedy era, Walsh writes: "Wiesner had had a pre-existing personal relation with Kennedy, but it seems to me that the key point is when Wiesner was there, resources were available for expansion."[5] The earlier postwar years were a time of science expansion and almost every university had a good chance of obtaining financing for a new basic science building. Vietnam created a wholly different social and political atmosphere and some of the constraints introduced then have continued down the present. Shifts in national priorities have also impacted on science. One such change has been the broadening consensus that something should be done to enhance the nation's economic competitiveness in the world. Here, although science has a role to play, the forms of cooperation between government and business are more difficult to discover. The elements required for cooperation in the use of the Science Advisor in matters affecting space and defense fall more readily into place than they have with advice on industrial development.

In these and countless other sectors of science and government, both science scholars and Presidential scholars quite clearly have contributions to make. In one important sector, however, the responsibility of students of the Presidency is unique. Their task in studies of the institutional Presidency is to describe, analyze and evaluate the organizational patterns, political forces at work and options of key offices and agencies within and outside the White House. Thus Professor Erwin Hargrove of Vanderbilt University recently completed a series of studies of the various Councils of Economic Advisers in postwar Presidencies undertaking to offer general principles and conclusions on their functions. Considerable monographic work is underway on the work of the National Security Advisor and the National Security Council. A few studies are available on the Domestic Council and other inquiries are being made of environmental policies and programs.

To pose the problem of science for Presidential scholars in simplest terms, how is the President to organize the work of a specialist group in any functional area where there is no overall policy? It is possible to argue that the Council of Economic Advisers functions which relate to national economic policy, grounded in historic American views of the economy and the particular economic philosophy of a President coming into office, can be focused within the framework of a broad but coherent policy. Similarly, the government has a national security policy and certain controlling views of the national interest to guide the National Security Advisor. By contrast, the Science Advisor operates without significant guideposts of this type. He is an expert on science who must guide generalists on public policy within a White House structure that seemingly is weighted so that science, compared with economics or national security, has a relatively low priority and even lower visibility.

Left unanswered is the question how science advising is to be located and institutionalized. Should the Science Advisor be inside or outside the White House? Who should select the Science Advisor and his or her staff? What should be the profile of a Science Advisor? What should be his relation with and responsibility to his constituency, the science community? What should be the mandate of the Science Advisor and who should determine the mandate? What are the implications of the fact that the OSTP is established by statute and its Director must be confirmed by Congress? Does the statute make it easier or more difficult for the Science Advisor to serve the President? How large a staff does the Advisor need, and what proportion should be career personnel with ongoing assignments, and how many should be appointed anew by each President and each Science Advisor? What are the necessary and essential relations the Advisor should seek with the Congress, and to what extent should the Science Advisor see himself or herself as primarily the President's person?

As the central questions are posed about Science Advisors, they clearly fall broadly within the sphere of competence of political scientists, historians, and legal scholars who study the Presidency. It would seem important that whoever undertakes to answer such questions be able to move back and forth between research findings on such bodies as the Council of Economic Advisors and other advisory groups? How does their function bear on the form institutionalization has taken and should take, and what is the historical record of experience in each of the several "arenas of power," to draw on Theodore Lowi's concept. It behooves those who would prescribe change or improvement in science advising to examine the broader record and institutional memory existing in the other arenas of politics.

To suggest that institutional comparisons may be useful is not to claim that the experience in other arenas can point the way to improvements in science advising. The reason Presidential scholars may have contributions to make is precisely because no clearcut answers suggest themselves. The experience that is being recorded and organized for study, say, on economic advising and the analysis that Hargrove and others have devoted to the problem may at least offer certain lessons.

THE PRESIDENT'S VIEWS

Another way to view the question is to ask how does the President or any particular President conceive the role of science advising. This approach requires getting into the mind of the President. It is an approach with which Presidential scholars are familiar. In foreign policy studies, the task of the observer is to look over the shoulder of the decisionmaker examining the options he is considering and seeking to understand the constraints under which he is acting. It would mislead to suggest that scientists have no role in responding to such questions. Plainly, their knowledge of substance places them at the highest level among those with a right to speak. Moreover, many have had greater experience in government than theorists of administration. Yet the central point is that the unique contribution of Presidential scholars is likely to be in the institutional and administrative areas. Foundations or academies with scientists as presidents should take note and be more responsive to the need for such studies.

NOTES

1. Kenneth W. Thompson, ed., *The Presidency and Science Advising*, Vol. I (Lanham, MD: University Press of America), p. 4.
2. *Ibid.*, Vol. IV (forthcoming), pp. 31–32.
3. *Ibid.*, Vol. IV, p. 48.
4. *Ibid.*, Vol. IV, p. 51.
5. *Ibid.*, Vol. IV, p. 54.

Science and Technology Advice: Some Observations

Alvin W. Trivelpiece

Even after six years as the Director of the Office of Energy Research at the Department of Energy and as the "science advisor" to three Secretaries of Energy, I am still not certain that I know what science advice is as distinct from any other kind of advice. Does science advice mean that only scientists are qualified to give it? Does it mean it is derived by scientific methods and that it's the same advice that would be given by any scientist, since the conclusions upon which it is based were objectively determined? Does it mean that the advice is devoid of political content or spin and, therefore, can be trusted?

To whom is this "advice" to be given and how is it to be acted upon? What happened to technology or engineering advice? What about the political or economic consequences of science advising? Are economists or politicians to be brought in, since scientists know nothing of these matters?

The point is that science or technology advice is not a simply defined pure entity. Rather, it is merely one more element in a cacophony of advice that the Executive and Legislative and, to a lesser but growing extent, the Judicial branches of government receive all the time.

In fact, in my opinion, the government is awash in advice on matters pertaining to science and technology. This, then, raises several interesting questions. If they are getting all this good advice, why aren't science and technology getting better financial support from the government? Or maybe science and technology are being supported at a level appropriate to the advice given. Why does the government continue to support projects and

Alvin W. Trivelpiece has been the Executive Officer of the American Academy for the Advancement of Science since April 1987. Previously, he was Director of the Office of Energy Research, US Department of Energy (1981–87). Earlier, he served as a corporation officer and was Professor of Engineering at the University of California/Berkeley and Professor of Physics at the University of Maryland. He has been a Fulbright Scholar and a Guggenheim Fellow, and is co-author of Principles of Plasma Physics.

programs that are outmoded, obsolete or stupid instead of excellent and exciting ones that we recommend? Don't they understand? Obviously "we" must give them more advice until "they" see it our way. Well, I believe that "they" don't know what to do with all the "advice" that "they" are getting now. It is not because the advice is unsound or that "they" are not smart enough. Rather, I believe that it is, in part, that we are usually telling them what we want them to do for us, instead of attempting to learn what it is that they need answers to in order to solve their problems.

In the Executive branch, there is the Office of Science and Technology Policy (OSTP), whose Director serves as Science Advisor to the President and also is responsible for the White House Science Council. Some of the Cabinet agencies have senior science and technology advisory committees (for example, Department of Defense has the Defense Science Board; Department of Energy has the Energy Research Advisory Board) as well as many technical advisory committees that report at the assistant secretary-level and at various program levels. The National Science Foundation has the National Science Board and a plethora of other program advisory committees—similarly, with the Environmental Protection Agency, the National Aeronautics and Space Administration, the National Bureau of Standards, and others. In addition, the National Academy of Sciences and the National Academy of Engineering prepare numerous reports on many matters pertaining to science and technology for both the Congress and the Administration.

CONGRESSIONAL FELLOWS

In the past fifteen years, there has been a rapid build-up of the number of Congressional fellows (and staffers) with advanced degrees in various fields of science and engineering who provide direct input to the members and to key committees concerned with these subjects. In addition, many scientists and engineers make individual visits to many Congressmen and their staffs to "advise" them. One has only to examine the hearing record of some of the authorization and appropriation committees concerned with science matters to see that advice is not in short supply. Trade associations as well as scientific and engineering societies inundate the Congress with reports, position papers, and testimony. There is also the Office of Technology Assessment, the Congressional Research Service, and even the Government Accounting Office providing advice or information on scientific and technical subjects. How, you ask, can the Congress then continue to do such outrageous things as fund facilities for which they have not sought out "peer" review to determine the proper priorities?

What all this boils down to is that it is easy to give advice. Having it taken seriously is another matter. This requires that the advisee trust the advisor. Trust requires time to establish, and is not easily given. This is particularly true in the shifting sands of politics where the motives of the advisor are sometimes questioned in terms of whether the advice is being given for the benefit of the advisee or the advisor. In this regard, science advice (whatever it is) is no different. In my experience, however, I have found that many scientists and engineers believe that it is or, at least, that it should be treated objectively and taken more seriously because it is "more objective."

Such a belief probably stems from scientific value systems combined with a lack of understanding of certain aspects of the political process. For the most part, scientists are aloof from the political system, and are not involved in the grassroots efforts that result in the selection and election of candidates for national political offices. There are never any effective "scientists and engineers for" efforts for Governors, Representatives, Senators or the Presidency. As a result, there usually are no members of the new teams coming to Washington or going to the statehouses who are or have recently been working scientists or engineers.

In the case of the Presidency, the new team fills all the various "special assistant for . . .", etc., positions mostly with those individuals who have had a long association with the party and the new President—individuals whose trust and loyalty are not questioned. Somewhere in this process, it is realized that the position of the Director of the Office of Science and Technology Policy also needs to be filled. Since this position cannot be filled by a nonscientist member of the new team, an outside search for a suitable candidate is initiated. This process usually involves asking several prominent scientific leaders if they are interested in the position and, if not, do they have any recommendations for someone who might be. When a candidate with suitable scientific credentials and the minimum acceptable political credentials has been identified, cleared, nominated, confirmed, and sworn in, the new Administration has usually already been in office for several months.

TWO HANDICAPS

This means that the new "Science Advisor" starts with two handicaps. The first is that he was not likely to have been involved with the team that developed the campaign position papers well before the election and, thus, is not likely to be deeply involved in the transition process immediately thereafter. The second is that, by the time he arrives on the scene, many of the decisions affecting science and technology have already been made, and these have been made on some basis other than an in-depth understanding of the science-intensive elements of the issues. These handicaps, coupled with the expectation of the science community that their special interests will be communicated directly to the President by the Director of OSTP, make this a very tough job. The early days of an Administration are mainly driven by economic, international and political imperatives that do not generally require any detailed understanding of science or engineering—although I believe that they should. Thus, even after he arrives, there are not a lot of opportunities for a new Science Advisor to get involved in the day-to-day management problems at a level that establishes a sound basis for trust. Once a basis of trust is established, then advice is more likely to be routinely sought and sometimes taken. This is true for the Cabinet agencies, as well.

Most scientists, engineers, and many others believe—and correctly so—that science and technology are central elements that drive a significant fraction of our economy. Thus, they have trouble understanding that political leaders don't appreciate this, and that these leaders don't give science and technology a more central role in government planning and management. This creates animosity between the science community and the Administration. This animosity is usually not well disguised and makes it even more difficult to establish effective communication where matters of importance require it.

Another problem relates to the tensions that sometimes result from the plans and actions of Cabinet officers, who have effective line management control of most of the Executive branch functions of government, and the activities that the various staff members at the White House would like to see carried out. In the final analysis, most Cabinet members have a better chance of prevailing in matters where they have taken strong stands. Everyone knows of exceptions to this and so do I, but, from my experience, I would place my bet on the Cabinet member in almost all circumstances.

The point is that advice, science or otherwise, to the President or elsewhere in the Executive branch, does not necessarily lead to direct action, but usually must be implemented by Cabinet officers or other subCabinet line managers. If they don't agree with what is proposed or recommended, they can usually stop the action, even though they may not be able to implement their own plans of action. This doesn't mean that the various science and technology advisors in the Executive branch are without influence. Quite the contrary. They can and do have considerable influence, but, starting as unknowns to the political team and promoting programs and activities that seem to nonscientists as peripheral to the mainline government functions, they have their work cut out for them.

NO EASY SOLUTIONS

Are there any solutions to this problem? Not any easy ones. But, as a first step, I believe that scientists and engineers need to try to see the problems from the perspective of those in government on whom we would inflict our advice.

In that regard, I have come to the opinion that science and technology advice is going to have to begin to be organized and introduced at the grassroots political level. As distasteful as scientists and engineers find the political process, they are going to have to get much better at working within the system. We have been lucky in that, in many cases, our advice is eagerly sought out. The benefits and, in some cases, the problems caused by science and technology are matters of growing interest. But the competition for money and other resources is getting much tougher, and we cannot take for granted that our advice will continue to be sought or even listened to to the degree it is today. In addition to being taken seriously as scientists and engineers, we need to be taken seriously in the political arena as well.

The chances of getting the Secretary of Energy to visit some laboratory or facility was always enhanced if the trip included a political element. Several efforts to get the President to visit scientific facilities failed because, in competition for his time, many factors such as politics have to be considered. In most cases, the collateral political benefits were too small. This is our failing, not that of the politicians.

Senators and Representatives are more likely to visit laboratories, universities, and military bases in their districts because there is a closer constituency relationship. In the future, we are going to have to take better advantage of this to the benefit of science and technology. By this, I don't mean the grubby business of hard-ball politics—to get a new facility for the state or district or prevent something from being killed off. Rather, I mean taking advantage of the political process to gain access to those political leaders whom we wish to have trust us. This means learning what they want help with in the way of sound technical advice, and then giving it without partisan or other political spin.

If the thrust of my remarks seem pessimistic, I don't mean it to be. I believe that the system works much better than most of those outside of government know. Just because a particular decision didn't go the way some believe it should have on purely scientific merits, doesn't mean that those involved in the decision process were ignorant of the facts or didn't understand what was at stake. In most of today's decisions, there are many elements that come into play. Science and technology are but two of them.

Science Advice to the President

John G. Truxal

Events of the past fifteen years clearly indicate the valuable role which would be filled by an effective mechanism for science/technology advice to the Executive branch of the federal government. Analogous mechanisms are important in the Legislative and Judicial branches as well; this essay will focus on the most pressing deficiency, currently in the Executive branch.

The desirable role for science advice ranges over a wide variety of issues—from those with major media and public attention (SDI and AIDS as recent examples) to those with much less public awareness (*e.g.*, the serious deficiencies of the Communications Privacy Act of 1986 or the regulation of ocean disposal of waste). The large majority of the current issues in the political arena currently involve significant technological content; intelligent decisions depend on proper assimilation and weighing of the limitations and capabilities of modern technology.

To be effective, the science advisory system must establish continuing communication between the political decision-makers and the strengths of the science/engineering community. Our experiences of the past thirty years seem to indicate that achievement of this goal depends on at least three major characteristics of the science advisory mechanism.

CONTINUOUS, BROAD EVALUATIONS

The US political process responds to perceived crises and opportunities, and often responds rapidly. As an election approaches, the system is unusually receptive to technological initiatives with clear appeal to the electorate (*e.g.*, the federal coverage of dialysis treatment enacted as the last

John G. Truxal, Distinguished Teaching Professor at the State University of New York at Stony Brook, has served as a consultant to several government agencies and industrial organizations. He is active in the minorities-in-engineering effort and the New Liberal Arts Program of the Alfred P. Sloan Foundation. Dr. Truxal is a member of the National Academy of Engineering and a Fellow of AAAS, IEEE and ISA. From 1970–1972, he served as a member of the President's Science Advisory Committee.

legislation before the 1972 election). The system responds to publicly recognized crises (the National Maximum Speed Limit of 1974, or the current movement toward a national policy for controlling AIDS).

Such technological responses are frequently put in place on very short notice. When the time for political action arises, the leaders have to move rapidly—a time constraint totally incompatible with the careful study of the science and technology. If the science advisory mechanism requires a year for evaluation of a new initiative, the political leaders will have long ago turned their attention to more urgent problems.

The only feasible way for a science advisory system to work requires initiation of policy/science studies well in advance of the political need. Thus, the system must have a continuing set of studies underway, and the set must anticipate political opportunities. During the 1960s, the President's Science Advisor and the President's Science Advisory Committee attempted to respond to this challenge.

Since prediction of crises and opportunities is likely to be wrong frequently, the science advisory system must continually pursue a wide range of studies—many of these will never prove useful, others will suggest specific opportunities to the political leaders, a few will respond to crises. If this conclusion is accepted, it follows that the science advisory mechanism must be of reasonable size—in terms of both full-time professional staff and part-time consultants involved over long time periods.

Furthermore, both the staff and the consultants should be drawn primarily from the group of individuals who are at the forefront of their fields and have an understanding of the broad implications of technological change. This constraint means that both staff and consultants will normally be middle-aged, with impressive achievements within their own careers. The entire group should encompass people from the range of disciplines, including social scientists and humanists.

TIES TO EXECUTIVE BRANCH

The science advisory office obviously can only be effective if the director (presumably the Science Advisor to the President) is able to bring science and technology information into the political decision process at an early stage. If the Science Advisor has a firm relationship with the President and key White House staff members, there is no problem.

Undoubtedly this relationship will vary markedly as the particular individual serving as Science Advisor changes, and it certainly will depend on the particular President. Consequently, it would seem that the effectiveness of the science advisory system will depend on the establishment of strong relations with Departments within the Executive branch.

One approach to realizing such relations would be to have each specific member of the Science Advisory Committee (or the group of continuing consultants) primarily responsible for science advice in the area of one department. That consultant would then be selected initially with the approval of the Cabinet member guiding that department. While one does not want to complicate the already difficult task of selecting consultants (and full-time staff members), the process is an opportunity to establish strong communication links to the decision-makers.

RELATIONS TO INDUSTRY

The science/technology advisory system should have strong representation from technological industry for several reasons. First, a large fraction of the significant research is done in industrial laboratories (obvious for the applied research, but also true to a less, but appreciable extent for the basic research). Historically, science advising has been drawn disproportionately from academia. In some important areas of technology, critical knowledge resides primarily in industry.

Second, a primary concern of the science advisory system in the next decade will undoubtedly be US international competitiveness. This topic covers a range of policy issues in which highly significant knowledge resides in industry leaders, individuals in leading business schools, and social scientists—all groups poorly represented in past science advisory systems.

Third, many of the recommendations of the Science Advisor will require public and political understanding, challenges where industry can be a major help.

CONCLUSION

The above paragraphs emphasize the view that the system generating science/technology advice for the Executive branch should be an on-going activity, continually studying major issues and areas of science/technology to be poised to give advice at the moment politically opportune. The advice needs to flow to all receptive segments of the Executive branch.

Furthermore, the focus of the work should be on the technology and applied science—on issues which impact public policy and the citizenry. These are issues in which there is normally no single, correct answer; the science advisory system should exist to communicate the characteristics, limitations, benefits and risks of the technology.

A SPECIFIC EXAMPLE

One specific example illustrates these points. The effects of non-ionizing, electromagnetic radiation on human beings are scientifically uncertain. Recent research indicates there may be significant biological (if not health) effects at levels below the existing federal standards. Indeed, there is some possibility that the fields associated with electric blankets and common kitchen appliances may warrant concern.

Clarification of these questions requires extensive research under difficult constraints—*e.g.*, scientific and ethical feasibility of such research on human beings, or impossibility of adequate longitudinal studies. Clearly, if this problem is judged significant, the realization of a research program should be the responsibility of the science advisory system. The results of the existing research efforts need to be communicated to the appropriate government agencies (OSHA, Commerce, EPA, etc.) Without an effective science advisory system, the communication between the science/technology constituency and the governmental agencies occurs only in fits and starts, often in response to particular media concern.

Science Advice Thirty Years Later

Alvin M. Weinberg

In 1957, when the President's Science Advisory Committee was established, science advice to the government was unorganized and sporadic. Today, thirty years after Sputnik, scientific advice pervades our governmental agencies and departments: Such advice is, above all, institutionalized and bureaucratic. Moreover, this pattern has spread to the Legislative branch, especially with the establishment of the Office of Technology Assessment, as well as the more traditional entities, such as the Congressional Research Service of the Library of Congress and the General Accounting Office.

Does the President need a powerful entity, such as the old PSAC, in the present environment, an environment very different from the one that existed in 1957? I suppose the most persuasive argument favoring re-establishment of such an entity is the imbalance that now exists between the scientific apparatus of the Executive departments and of Congress, on the one hand, and of the Presidency, on the other. Even though the President is supposed to be in control of the Executive departments, in fact, very often he must balance national interests against the parochial interests of his departments. Simply as a matter of self-defense, one might argue, the President needs his own scientific entity.

Yet the President's power in the extremely important allocation of resources to various scientific enterprises remains secure. The Office of Management and Budget, as well as the Domestic and Economic Policy Councils, are his creatures; and the course of science within government is probably still influenced more by decisions of the OMB and the Executive Councils

Alvin M. Weinberg was Director of the Oak Ridge National Laboratory (1948–1973); Director of the Office of Energy Research and Development in the White House (1974); and Director of the Institute for Energy Analysis (1975–1985). He served on the President's Science Advisory Committee from 1958 to 1961. For his contributions to the development of nuclear energy, he received the Enrico Fermi Award, the Harvey Prize, the Heinrich Hertz Award, and the Atoms for Peace Award. Dr. Weinberg is a member of the National Academies of Science and of Engineering, the American Academy of Arts and Sciences, and the American Philosophical Society.

than by any other actors. The relation between OMB and the Science Advisor or PSAC has always seemed to me to be ill-defined. In the cases with which I am familiar, OMB called the shots much more than did the Science Advisor. This certainly was the case when I served in the White House in 1974 as a token scientific presence there in my capacity as Director of the Office of Energy Research and Development, and I have no reason to believe that this has changed or is likely to change. Where funds are to be allocated, OMB must be superior to any scientific advisor whose responsibility hardly includes the fiscal state of the country as a whole. This intrinsic and fundamental weakness of any scientific advisory apparatus of the President must be recognized.

Management of science and allocation of resources to science is, perhaps, the less important function of a scientific presence in the White House. More important is advice on broad questions of public policy that are not themselves scientific, but that surely involve scientific issues. During the first PSAC, the formulation of policy on arms control and, perhaps, the decision to send a man to the moon were the most important such issues. On the decision to send a man to the moon, PSAC was ignored. (I recall how Jerry Wiesner casually told the Committee, just before we broke up to catch afternoon flights, that President Kennedy had decided to send a man to the moon. PSAC had never been asked whether to do so, largely, I believe, because most of its members were against the mission.) On arms control, PSAC's views were extremely important and greatly influenced our country's policy. Nevertheless, even here, PSAC's views were, in part, ignored: One hundred ABM launchers were deployed around Grand Forks despite the all but unanimous vote by PSAC against ABM.

Today's Science Advisor is less visible and presumably has less power than did yesterday's. Have the two functions of the Science Advisor—management of science and formulation of public policy involving scientific components—been handled notably worse in the Reagan Administration than in previous Administrations where the roles of the Science Advisor and of PSAC have been more obvious and important than they now seem to be?

In respect to the management of science, I believe most would agree that this Administration has been enlightened and constructive. Perhaps the best indicator of this is the fate of the National Science Foundation: Its budget has continued to rise and, indeed, the budget for all of science has risen. Insofar as one can equate generous support of science with enlightened management of science—a position I suppose more popular with scientists than with the Secretary of the Treasury—I would say that, yes, the Executive branch has displayed an intelligent sensitivity toward the scientific enterprise as a whole, at least as intelligent as other Administrations in which the scientific advisory apparatus was better structured.

What about the other aspect of scientific advice—formulation of broad policy having scientific components? By far the most important such policy has been the Strategic Defense Initiative. This is regarded almost universally by the academic scientific community as a disastrous failure: Had the President had impartial and independent scientific advice, he would never have embarked on so hare-brained a scheme.

Two points must be remembered before one draws this conclusion. First, this is not the first time that a decision was taken by a President that was contrary to the general view of the scientific community, if not to his science advisors. As just noted, Apollo and the limited deployment of the ABM were precedents. The second point is, however, much more telling. Despite the wisdom that has become conventional in most academic scientific circles, the case against SDI is not as powerful as some would have us believe. Had President Reagan *had* an independent PSAC, it would almost surely have recommended against SDI, and its advice, reflecting the arms control dogma of the past thirty years, would probably have been wrong.

The usual arguments against SDI are both technical and political: Technically, it cannot work, and politically, it upsets the structure of deterrence upon which the peace of the world depends.

These arguments are valid, but only if the world is viewed in its present configuration, with 10,000 strategic warheads on each side. Of course Star Wars can't work against 10,000 warheads and 90,000 decoys, but this is the wrong question. The right question is: At what level of disarmament and arms control does Star Wars work? And how does one work out a crisis-stable path to this configuration in which perhaps a few hundred strategic warheads are confronted with magnificent defense. This is the question that should be asked by the analytical strategists. President Reagan—on grounds that went ever so far beyond simply game-theoretic analysis and were largely instinctive, not scientific—concluded that a defense-dominated world with few offensive weapons and many defensive weapons is one well worth striving for. His appeal to the scientists to figure out how to achieve this world was not frivolous—but only if one interpreted the task to include visualizing a future in which strategic warheads have been drastically reduced. That Reykjavik and Secretary Gorbachev have placed such possibilities on the negotiating table shows the method in the President's madness, as well as the impossibility of seeing all contingencies.

Much of the scientific community chose not to see—or to take seriously—the full implication of President Reagan's vision. This reflects not only upon its collective judgment, but, worse, it possibly illustrates the weakness in an advisory structure that becomes too heavily institutionalized. Its thinking becomes channeled and conventional, just as does the thinking of any bureaucracy.

My purpose here is not to explain why I believe the President was more correct than his detractors. It is, rather, to argue that the decisions on scientific matters and on broader policy having scientific components of this Administration has not been notably worse than in previous Administrations where the Science Advisor had more bureaucratic status and, in some ways, *eg.*, the SDI decision, I would say it has been better.

This is not to say that science and technology policy are without fault. In particular, I despair of our country establishing an energy policy, in particular, a policy toward non-fossil energy systems. But this is a side issue. I believe the SDI decision and the generally constructive pursuit of science policy within the Reagan Administration demonstrates that, in 1987, unlike 1957, advice to the President on science policy—without benefit of PSAC, but with a Science Advisor and the Office of Science and Technology Policy working closely with OMB and with the Executive Councils—is not ineffective. As for the SDI decision, only time will tell who is right and who is wrong. The decision was, in any case, much more political than scientific and, as in all such instances, must reflect the President's—not his Science Advisor's—views.

Repairing Radar for the Ship of State

Edward Wenk, Jr.

For twenty-six years, I served in Washington, D.C., as a public servant, the latter half in four science advisory roles in the US Congress and to three Presidents. It was like living in the eye of the political hurricane. In being directly exposed to such turbulence, it was hard to know from what direction the wind was blowing. In the seventeen years since, separated from that venue and protected by the serenity of academe, I have been studying political meteorology. That is, I have been trying to understand what was going on so as to discern patterns that could be employed in the future steering of technology by public policy, to extract benefits with a minimum of adverse side effects.

At the heart of the matter is a premise that the future is a matter of choice and not chance. Although I first encountered that aphorism in Planned Parenthood many years ago, I can think of no more trenchant statement of our situation. In a dangerous and complex technological world, being both alive and free must be our fundamental goal for which technology is increasingly our most powerful and influential means. Meeting our responsibilities to humankind and not just to our tribe, today, will depend on our decisions to create the futures we want and head off those we do not. How, then, can we make such fateful choices?

THE CONTEXT FOR PRESIDENTIAL CHOICE

Despite a nostalgia if not myth about key decisions being made in the marketplace, I have observed that such choices are made primarily as public policy. The individual assigned the greatest influence on that future is the

Edward Wenk, Jr., became a technical advisor to Congress in 1959, subsequently serving on science policy staffs of Presidents Kennedy and Johnson. Subsequently, he was founding director of Congress' Science Policy Research Division, then appointed Executive Secretary of the Council on Marine Resources and Engineering Development under Presidents Johnson and Nixon. In 1970, he joined the faculty at the University of Washington, heading the Program in Social Management of Technology. He is a member of the National Academies of Engineering and Public Administration.

President of the United States. In following the Constitution, both goals and means are ultimately set by the CEO of the nation. In a technological world, our President is systems manager.

That the President needs help is self-evident. What may not be widely recognized in a technological milieu are the extra stresses attending matters of choice: Facts are more complex, often couched in mists of probabilities. The range of choices is greater. The consequences of error are more potentially lethal to society and hazardous to the prestige of the decider. Amidst a high noise level, new fashions shift the social agenda, while narrow self-interests squeeze out any dedication to the commonweal. Technological delivery systems become more interdependent so that individual initiatives are constrained by actions and reactions of others over whom there is no control.

These are the external sources of difficulty. Internal to the decision process are other problems: Stamina may be inadequate to the challenge of problem solving, or political will inadequate to prevail over obstacles. There may be too little information to steer by, or communications may be distorted or blocked. The steering mechanism may be disabled by incompetence, error, exhaustion, self-delusion, bias, venality or hubris. Most seriously, the machinery may have lost a capacity to learn so as to withstand shock with spontaneous versatility for rearrangement and resilience.

In this discussion, incidentally, there is an unstated premise that government is not just a power broker. It is also a steering system. That concept implies both clarity of goals and a powerful guidance system for safe navigation—thus, the role of navigation aids, especially of advisors. It is this notion that sparked President Eisenhower's 1958 appointment of James Killian as Special Assistant for Science and Technology.

TECHNOLOGY, NOT SCIENCE

Before examining ingredients of such advice and counsel, we should recognize that, for the early years of such a post, it was science and not technology that was accorded primary attention. That members of the auxiliary President's Science Advisory Committee were primarily physicists and chemists, with few from life sciences and virtually none from behavioral sciences, would tend to confirm that orientation.

Today, the situation has changed. Far more issues on the President's agenda depend on the structure and processes of technology than on science. We may thus need to understand better the fundamental connections between technology, people and politics. For example, we need to recognize technology as more than science and engineering, more than hardware. Technology is a social process. Each technological delivery system involves a constellation of people and institutions in an intricate web of communications, using a wide range of knowledge beyond the purely scientific.

We must also face the reality that all technologies have side effects, that they act as a two-edged sword. In addition, all have inordinate capacities as organizing principles to concentrate wealth and power; an examination of public and private organizations created in the last two decades would substantiate that phenomenon.

To inquire further, we discover that, as well as amplifying human muscle and the human mind, technology functions as a social amplifier. It stretches the economy. It magnifies risk. It increases demands on our institutions, especially on government. It tends to promote human greed. With these interactions, it amplifies distinctions of who wins and who loses, and how much, so it stimulates conflict.

Historical analysis of performance of the science advisory function, including two generations of the Office of Science and Technology, reveal a flutter and flounce when issues became heavily loaded with civilian technology. Understanding of the social, political, economic, legal and ecological connections was too elementary. In contrast, the National Council on Marine Resources and Engineering Development, created in 1966 by Public Law 89-454, led to what is now referred to as the "Golden Age" of marine policy. One reason for its extraordinary success lies in its perspective of technology-intensive public policy rather than science.

THE ROLE OF INFORMATION

Given these stark features of the technological milieu, political decisions become critically dependent on information—technical information *in* the system; and management information *about* the system. Expert knowledge is necessary but not sufficient. Also involved is appreciation of the social and economic context and constraints; the past behavior of key participants; a map of delivery organizations, their linkages and aspirations; a memory of past performance; and a view of the way ahead, both opportunities and obstacles.

LOOKING AHEAD

To be sure, the future is always uncertain. But if decisions fail to recognize the prevalence of technological side effects so as to practice the equivalent of preventive medicine, we will be constantly buffeted by surprises, using an increasing fraction of our wealth and political energy in fixing up things that should never have been permitted to occur.

It is this doctrine of anticipation that is the newest tool in the palette of science and technology advice. It is also the one least used, partly because our entire society fastens pathologically on the short term.

This author had much to do with the 1964 origin in the Legislative Reference Service of the concept of "technology assessment," what is later termed "TA." The concept was influential in three statutory products. The first is the well-known section 102(2)c in the 1969 National Environmental Policy Act (NEPA) Public Law 91-190, requiring impact analysis of technological initiatives in advance. The second was creation in 1972 of the Office of Technology Assessment, Public Law 92-454. The third product was a future focus in the National Science and Technology Policy, Organization and Priorities Act of 1976 that recreated the Presidential advisory function, Public Law 94-282.

Quite apart from expanding the theater of parameters in technological choice by looking at broader social, economic, political and ecological effects, TA also can illuminate future consequences of today's options. This aid to choice then exposes a remarkable connection between technology and culture. In the time period when TA attracted the eye of the US Congress (and also that of Senator Patrick Moynihan in his 1969 advisory to President Nixon) came recognition of an emerging cultural shift. Previously, during and after World War II and through the early years of the Space Race, the key policy question being asked of technology was, "Can we do it?" Can we build nuclear weapons, land a man on the Moon, (and today, can we build a Strategic Defense)? Beginning in the early 1960s, however, a second question was being asked, "Ought we do it?"

That is what lies behind TA and NEPA and much contemporary legislation intended to protect the public interest from the harmful effects of technology.

Yet, today, even asking this second question is not enough. In the face of so many weapon systems that malperform, the tragedies of *Challenger* and Chernobyl, we suddenly stumble over the shock that a concentration on the purely technical ingredients of technology and its uncritical advocacy by those hypnotized by technology's promises or expecting to profit therefrom ignores essential issues, and even Constitutional principles: those affected by technology have a right to know in advance of their exposure to risk. Democracy does not accept unchallenged the role of innocent bystanders. Yet we find that the apparatus for technological delivery, not the technical precocity, seems repeatedly to fail. Thus, the third question we must ask is "Can we manage it?"

THE ROLE OF VALUES

There needs to be a clearer recognition that much of what passes for innovative benefit to society has its roots in purely commercial motivation. The exposure of shabby ethics in some sections of Wall Street is in part a consequence of the new power of computers.

So we must recognize that at the root of most technological decisions is an exercise of values, values held in common by the society, but also values held by the individuals in power, both giving and receiving science advice.

The validity of decisions made with the assistance of science advisors cannot be judged only from the technical virtuosity demonstrated. It must be judged on the basis of long-term consequences through effects on the fundamental creed of the society being served. Have the future generations been taken into account as legal as well as hypothetical constituents?

The social management of technology becomes a matter of moral vision as well as technical. Those considering impacts of our most powerful technologies must understand people as well as machines, be sensitive to the reality that all technologies have human service as an end, and be willing to accept the personal risk of being sharply separated from an exhilarating political environment by acting on the basis of what they consider right, rather than simply to be loved by uncritically (and even illegally) following preferences of the leader.

FORESIGHT

The roots of science and technology advice thus lies in ethics. But the wings lie in foresight, in the notion of radar for the ship of state to detect opportunities as well as hazards. The Science and Technology Policy Act of 1976 made this concept abundantly clear.

In Section 101(a), the Congress finds that the general welfare requires "vigorous, perceptive support and employment of science and technology in achieving national objectives" with "long-range, inclusive planning"; that capabilities should be directed toward "anticipating and resolving" critical problems; that funding "represents an investment in the future"; that capabilities must be strengthened for "technology assessment.and for technological planning."

Section 102(b) on implementation calls on the federal government to "anticipate future concerns to which science and technology can contribute." Section 102(c) on procedures expects particular attention to problems that are exceptionally "long-range, geographically widespread or economically diffused." Thus "while maximizing the beneficial consequences of technology, the Government should act to minimize foreseeable injurious consequences."

Section 205(a) on duties of the recreated Office of Science and Technology Policy, expects it to collect information concerning trends, and to "initiate studies and analyses, including systems analyses and technology assessments of alternatives," and to "identify and assess emerging and future areas in which science and technology can be used effectively" in the national interest.

If those provisions were not sufficiently explicit, in Section 206(a), the OSTP Director is to "describe situations and conditions which warrant special attention within the next five years," with the five-year outlook updated annually. In effect, this required five-year outlook was a metaphor for a doctrine of anticipation.

I can report first-hand, incidentally, from my role as advisor to three entities who drafted this policy—staff of the Senate, staff of the House of Representatives, and staff of the Office of Management and Budget—that his introduction of these notions created little fuss at a time when all three were behaving as adversaries because they were believed to be philosophical ornaments of little political significance. That may explain why virtually none of these provisions has been implemented, and why this neglect has not been the subject of Congressional investigation.

Systematic, sensitive foresight is not an ornament. As the Bible states, "without vision, the people perish." Yet, science and technology policy, its roots of ethics and its wings of foresight, languish at a time in history when a more acute vision of the future is critical to survival. To be sure, it is difficult to mobilize a constituency for such abstractions, unlikely that there is sufficient political mileage in such a stance that national leaders will risk some of their political capital on such advocacy.

LESSONS

In a future with more technology, not less; with dangers ever more potentially lethal; and with choices ever more perplexing, future Presidents, and indeed candidates for President, may wish to ponder their own consciousness of "the situation." Then, whatever it may contribute to popularity, in the public interest, they might act to deal with the processes of choice as well as with the substantive issues. For without a healthy mechanism for choice, there is a higher probability that all short-term solutions ultimately go awry.

Candidates should call for vigorous implementation of the 1976 science and technology policy that, over a decade ago, provided the tools for the social management of technology, to create those futures we want and head off those that a human society cannot tolerate. That would be one way we could make the US Constitution ever more viable in the third century of American democracy.

REFERENCES

Porter et al., Alan R., *A Guidebook for Technology Assessment and Impact Analysis* (New York: Elsevier, 1980).

Wenk, Jr., Edward, *Tradeoffs–Imperatives of Choice in a High-Tech World* (Baltimore, MD: Johns Hopkins University Press, 1986).

The Rise and Fall of the President's Science Advisory Committee

Jerome B. Wiesner

Few institutions of the federal government have had as rapid a rise to prominence and lapse into oblivion as the President's Science Advisory Committee (PSAC). Few institutions have been punished as thoroughly for doing a good job. And few institutions are needed more right now. The position of the President's Special Assistant for Science and Technology still exists, but it has been reduced to a meaningless role. Recent administrations have rejected the use of a formal science advisory committee altogether, and have made other arrangements to assist the President on technical matters. The current Administration, for example, depends more upon the agencies that sponsor individual programs to evaluate them, and on an inchoate collection of informal advisors.

In this article, I am going to examine the costs to the nation of the rise and demise of the President's Science Advisory Committee and the diminished role of the President's Science Advisor with regard to Presidential decision-making, and show why some form of thorough institutionalized review process is necessary to assist the President in the management of the nation's scientific enterprise. In the US form of government, the President is the only official who represents the nation as a whole. He must play a central role in balancing the priorities of the nation, and especially those aspects that are dominated by the federal government, as is the case with science and technology. The kind of assistance he has in making these decisions determines the thrust and the quality of the scientific and technical programs. It is vital that it be sound and, as far as possible, objective.

A flood of recent events and problems are directly traceable to the absence of a Presidential advisory group: The Challenger disaster, the unproven and exaggerated claims about military inferiority and need for excessive amounts

Jerome B. Wiesner was Science Advisor to Presidents Kennedy and Johnson (1961–64). He has been Dean, Provost and President of the Massachusetts Institute of Technology, and is the author of Where Science and Politics Meet *(New York: McGraw-Hill, 1965).*

of new military technology and hardware, the exaggerated claims of Soviet cheating on arms agreements, the disregard by the responsible agencies of serious environmental and public health problems, and the loss of competitiveness of much of American industry. Vital decisions that will not only shape the long-range future of the US but of the world are being deferred or undertaken without adequate debate or regard for their impact on other programs. Environmental destruction is an example of decisions deferred, vast expenditures for SDI, decisions inadequately considered. Many technical programs are operating without careful, knowledgeable supervision and thus fail, or at least waste large sums of money. The Packard Commission, appointed by President Reagan to examine Pentagon operations, made these points emphatically.

It may be sheer coincidence but the disintegration of the US space program, sliding from a position of world leadership to one of embarrassment, has paralleled the decline of Presidential science advising. Last year, American space scientists had to send their instruments for investigating Halley's Comet on Soviet space probes, and American companies wanting to launch communication satellites are looking to European companies for launchings. Even more serious in the long run than the deterioration of the space program, much of US industry, both low and high tech, has gradually slipped out of competitive range of industries in other nations, most notably in price, but often in quality as well. And this is despite the fact that US research activities remain among the world's best. While many factors helped bring the world's strongest industrial complex to its present dilemma, Presidential actions and inactions played a major role.

OVEREMPHASIS ON FINANCING

The problem clearly lies in a national inability to allocate and manage our resources rather than in technological incompetence. I believe that an overemphasis on government financing for space and military technology, without supervision or adequate consideration of the costs or need, is at the root of the problem. The federal government has inadequate processes for setting priorities among the vast demands made on it for technological innovations, development and production. It has not set priorities for balancing resources between government requirements and the needs of civilian industries. For example, the expensive space shuttle went on—and went under!—in spite of ample evidence that it was not needed for any contemplated space activity. In the area of national defense, too, many unnecessary defense programs have been pursued. The result has been a systematic, decades-long diversion of manpower from productive civilian industry and education. Lest someone else point it out first, I should also note that much of the basic research that has given the United States its leadership position was undertaken for defense purposes. But we are not getting that lift from our defense research today. Quite the reverse, in fact. We now have a crisis which we must face squarely if the United States is to recover the momentum of its scientific enterprise.

I want to focus on PSAC, and the office of the Science Advisor, and examine why our recent Presidents and their advisors have been so opposed to the mechanism developed by Presidents Truman and Eisenhower to provide assistance in their efforts to understand and be in control of the federal role in funding and encouraging science and technology, and then I want to suggest how to recover from the present difficulty.

The demise of the President's Science Advisory Committee parallels a growing US tendency to disregard inconvenient facts in arriving at decisions. This tendency is particularly strong on matters of defense. The fear of the Soviet Union has long provided an excuse for exaggerating the threat in order to justify many unnecessary technical developments and military purchases and to hide the damage being done to the US science and technological enterprise by the Pentagon control of employment for many technically trained persons and funding for much advance research. But forty years of priorities tilted heavily towards the military, even taking into account the positive achievements, have overall brought US civilian technology to its present position and, ironically, have had the net effect of continuously increasing our real national danger.

Because of the dominance of federal funding, the ability of the United States to manage effectively the wide-ranging and complex issues raised by the rapid advance of technology rests on the government, and thus ultimately with the President. This has been true since the end of World War II. Before the war, science and technology were primarily private activities. Technological decisions were made by play of market forces and research decisions were dictated by intellectual curiosity. Since the war, bureaucratic objectives and military profits have invaded a once-benign scene. In addition, increased technical complexity and the imposition of military secrecy have shut out public understanding and participation from decision-making. Thus many technological choices—particularly the major ones—became the sole responsibility of a well-informed President.

It is my observation, based on personal experience with the scientific advisory apparatus used by four Presidents, that scientific advisory groups always generate major anxieties among other groups in the government, as well as industrial firms looking for work. It is often said that PSAC had undue influence in the Eisenhower and Kennedy years. But the fact is that this fear of undue influence of science advisors on the President did not start with the creation of the office; it has existed ever since science and technology became a vital aspect of national life. Witness the concerns about the role of Vannevar Bush, Karl Compton, Robert Oppenheimer, and many other scientists during World War II.

Basically the question of who provides the advice boils down to a competition for control of Presidential decisions. For a President, the task is to adjudicate the rivalries among many contenders who join together only to confront him. The challenge is to retain control of his information sources and thus his freedom of decision. I watched at close range the game played by the Pentagon against four Presidents; for example, practically the only times the members of the Joint Chiefs agreed was when they were attempting to persuade the Secretary of Defense or the President to accept their proposals. Otherwise, in their advisory capacities, one could always predict their positions on any subject by identifying the vested interests of their individual services. Because, as I said earlier, so many of the dominant issues of our times involved military technology, the perceived need for secrecy has been added to the obvious barrier of technical complexity, and the combination has led most citizens to shy away from sticking to strong views that contradict those of a President, even when the facts appear to support their position. Edward Teller has long argued that secrecy in technical fields does much more harm than good, and should be eliminated. I agree with him completely.

THE TRUMAN DECISION

President Truman faced the question of technical decision-making as soon as World War II ended. Troubled by inter-service battling over which of them should have the responsibility for the many new technologies that were evolving, and especially by the continuing controversies about nuclear weapons, Truman commissioned a study of how to get himself better information and advice. He persuaded William T. Golden, a prominent financier, who had had considerable experience with wartime Navy Department's research and development efforts, and who afterward had been assistant to Lewis Strauss in the first three years of the Atomic Energy Commission, to study the problem, and make recommendations about what to do. In the Fall of 1950, Golden filed a report that proposed a full-time Scientific Advisor to the President, to be assisted by a Scientific Advisory Committee of highly qualified scientists. Golden's recommendation was opposed in varying degree by the heads of most governmental agencies, and by many individuals working directly for the President. Lewis Strauss, among others, opposed the Golden proposal vehemently. In fact, during most of the Eisenhower presidency, Lewis Strauss struggled to control the technical information channels to the President. I know from personal experience that, on occasion, he privately contradicted the advice of other officials and even gave erroneous information to President Eisenhower.

After months of debate, despite the opposition, Truman and his White House assistants decided to acccept Golden's recommendations—in Principle, to appoint a Presidential Science Advisor and to establish a Scientific Advisory Committee. But the opponents of Golden's plan succeeded in weakening it. The new Committee, established in 1951 by President Truman, was placed under the Director of the Office of Defense Mobilization, instead of reporting directly to the President. To make matters worse, the Director of Defense Mobilization, General Lucius Clay, was not particularly interested in the problems the Committee was created to address, and he did not give it much attention. His successor, Arthur Flemming, however, did appreciate the important role of science and technology, and did involve the Committee in his efforts to help the President understand the national security problems of the period.

But these compromise decisions badly undercut Golden's plan for a technical advisory system; however, the most serious problem that resulted was the separation of the functions of the Advisor and the Advisory Committee. The quality of the advisors was high. Oliver Buckley, a distinguished scientist, just recently retired as President of the Bell Telephone Laboratories, was appointed Science Advisor, and a distinguished group of scientists, among them I. I. Rabi, Lee DuBridge, Jerrold Zacharias, Robert Bacher, James Fisk, George Kistiakowsky, Edwin Land, and others of similar international fame became members of the initial Committee. Members of this early group shared an important characteristic in addition to their outstanding scientific reputations—they had all been deeply involved in the wartime research and development effort. Many of them had worked together on the atomic bomb project and on radar. So they brought a vast fund of knowledge about nuclear and other military matters to the Committee. They were undoubtedly the most knowledgeable group in the government regarding the new military technologies.

Buckley and the Science Advisory Committee functioned more or less independently. The Committee had its own chairman, I. I. Rabi of Columbia University. The compromise arrangement of responsibility and agency oversight was further handicapped by the fact that Buckley was not very active. He was in failing health and, in addition, believing that the role of Science Advisor should be primarily a responsive one, he did not undertake any personal initiatives. Later Science Advisors made a practice of alerting their employer to potential problems. The Rabi Science Advisory Committee was somewhat more active than Buckley's, but because it had not been given any specific assignments and because it did not meet often and had little staff help, it did not provide much assistance to President Truman either.

Dwight Eisenhower made somewhat greater use of this original Committee, perhaps because of the close personal relationship between the President and Dr. Rabi that went back to Eisenhower's term as President of Columbia University. For example, the Committee sponsored the 1954 Technological Capabilities Panel that gave direction to the US missile and reconnaissance program, and the famous 1957 Gaither Committee study on civil defense. Both of these studies were undertaken in response to the President's growing concern about the Soviet missile program and the increasing danger to the American people.

SPUTNIK

It took the shock of the Soviet Sputnik in 1957 to realize the Golden proposals. President Eisenhower was upset by how little he had been told about the difficulties of the American satellite, Vanguard. He had earlier been persuaded to announce that the United States was going to launch the world's first artificial moon, and so the Soviet accomplishment and the world's response was a source of major embarrassment to him. The Russian feat led to a widespread belief that the Soviet Union had surpassed the United States in technological strength. The entire scientific and educational system came under fire, and Eisenhower faced a rising clamor for decisive actions to correct the situation. Although he doubted that the allegations were true, he did not believe that the same individuals who had allowed the situation to develop should be asked how to correct it. He also realized how isolated he was, and began to search for a way to obtain his own information about technical problems. His solution, used soon after the launching of Sputnik in the fall of 1957, was to appoint Dr. James Killian as his Special Assistant for Science and Technology, and move the Advisory Committee into the Executive Office of the President, where it could provide him with independent evaluation of the government's many scientific programs. Its members quickly developed a close rapport with the President, who turned to it frequently for help. President Eisenhower provided Dr. Killian with a letter of appointment spelling out, in great detail, his responsibilities and giving him wide-ranging authority.

So encompassing was this letter that, when I became Science Advisor to President Kennedy in 1961, he used this same letter to define my responsibilities. This essentially gave me total oversight to all science and technology programs in the Government and in related education programs. Because of this enormous range of responsibilities, PSAC and I were very careful in our selection of programs, and I always checked with the President before starting any major new projects.

The new team of Science Advisors and the President's Science Advisory Committee responded with a frenzy of activities. I became a member of the Committee in the spring of 1958. PSAC's first tasks were to bring order to the space program and sort out the conflicting allegations about relative positions of the US and Soviet science and education programs. An operating procedure rapidly developed based on the *ad hoc* committee study process of earlier times, but changing it to a continuing process. As its main source of information, the committee used advisory panels. Typically a panel would be chaired by a member of the advisory committee, and would include scientists and engineers from universities, industry and the government, selected for their expertise in the field under review. Sometimes other PSAC members in addition to the chairman would be included in the membership.

In the Eisenhower-Kennedy period, a major role of PSAC and the President's Special Assistant for Science and Technology was to screen the avalanche of military and space projects confronting the President, and attempt to provide sufficiency within a manageable budget. Such a task can only be done by a technically competent group with a non-vested interest. Advisors from industry and the defense laboratories are usually competent, but hardly unbiased, so that PSAC depended heavily upon university-based experts plus those from industrial laboratories such as the Bell Telephone Laboratory, whose duties gave them a high degree of independence.

PSAC quickly showed the value of continuity in following individual programs. It also provided another important feature. Because PSAC often met as a group, it was able to provide perspective and balance on the many programs and fields contending for attention. Each panel reported its progress to the monthly meetings of the full Advisory Committee, bringing it up to date and generating questions that needed further clarification. The collective knowledge and experience of the whole Committee contributed significantly to the ultimate recommendations that were made to the President. Dr. Killian and the PSAC members who prepared the plan approved by the President then played a major role in its implementation. The President had a major influence on the focus of the PSAC studies. For example, he wanted to establish a civilian space program, and the Committee worked toward that end. They worked hard to develop the proposal for an agency that ultimately became NASA.

NUCLEAR WAR

As President Eisenhower became increasingly involved with military R&D and space programs, PSAC did too. A 1956 Chief of Staff study predicted massive carnage and destruction in the United States if a nuclear war occurred. The report stimulated the 1957 Gaither Panel study which confirmed the conclusion of the military study that even with extensive defenses, both passive and active, many tens of millions of Americans would be killed in a major nuclear war. The Gaither Panel also voiced serious alarm about the speed and scale of the Soviet missile deployment effort. These reports gave a sense of urgency to the US missile program, and also heightened Eisenhower's determination to moderate the arms race. He became particularly committed to an exchange of military information to lessen tensions, and to a test-ban treaty to halt the development of new weapons.

In 1958, as he became increasingly dedicated to halting the arms race, President Eisenhower asked the Science Advisory Committee to help him. I vividly recall the drama of the moment. Referring to the Gaither Panel's Report, he pounded his desk and said, "You can't have that war. There aren't enough bulldozers in the country to scrape the bodies off the streets. Why don't you help me prevent it? Neither the Defense Department or AEC will give me any help. They have other interests."

With this challenge, many of us on the PSAC Committee turned our attention to the technical questions of the test ban and other disarmament efforts. That moment changed the focus of the rest of my life, though I didn't realize it at the time. This switch had major repercussions for the Committee, too. It made PSAC the President's main source of technical information on arms-control and also, which was important to its ultimate fate, the target of weapons advocates' wrath, a situation that continued as long as PSAC survived. In 1960, after President Kennedy asked me to be his Special Assistant, and I agreed, he approved the Committee set-up as it was operating and, in fact, at my suggestion, he retained the members. In this way it was my hope to give the Committee a non-political character, so that it could be maintained intact—with the exception of the special Assistant—through subsequent Presidential transitions. And actually, President Nixon followed this practice, too, at the start of his Administration.

I said earlier that I am convinced that if there had been adequate Presidential-level overview of technical programs in recent times, similar to that provided by PSAC, the Challenger explosion would not have happened. The PSAC Space Panel would certainly have detected the problems with the booster rocket early on and alerted the Administrators of NASA and the President. PSAC also had developed a source of information, in addition to its own reviews, that might have alerted it to the shuttle troubles. The Science Advisor's staff had acquired an unanticipated and important role in the overall science management process. Without planning to do so, PSAC became the ombudsman for Federal science and technology programs. The staff became a group to whom workers on government programs, aware of faulty designs, poor manufacturing, inadequate performance, unnecessary programs, or other problems could appeal when their concerns were ignored within their own organization. Scientists and engineers realized that the PSAC staff provided a channel that they could use with the confidence that they were not risking the traditional fate of the whistle-blower. We made no effort to encourage this channel, but neither did we discourage it. Robert McNamara once asked me how it was that the few people in my office knew much more about Department of Defense R&D and procurement difficulties than he did with his large staff.

Although the immediate cause of the Challenger disaster was the explosion of a solid-fueled rocket, the real reason for the failure was that President Reagan did not have his own technical review team. All the groups involved were under extreme pressure to maintain a launch schedule at all costs. They ignored numerous warning signals. In technical jargon, the President had no feedback. He received no independent information or advice to help him judge Challenger or any other technical program for which he was responsible, or, for that matter, the soundness or need for any of the proposed new programs that flow into the White House continously, such as most notably, the SDI.

It may well be that President Reagan did not want such help. Attempts by individuals to give him access to other views on the existence of the now discredited "window of vulnerability," for example, were certainly repulsed. Nor has the President given opponents of the SDI a hearing. Perhaps Oliver Buckley was right after all, when he said, "You can only give advice to someone who wants it."

In all fairness, I should make it clear that President Reagan did not create this situation; he inherited it. But some of his closest advisors were among those who helped bring it about. It was President Nixon who abolished the Science Advisory Committee and the post of Special Assistant to the President for Science and Technology. He got rid of them because he did not like the advice that they were providing on issues ranging from the controversial anti-ballistic missile system and the proposed supersonic transport aircraft to the performance of military equipment in Vietnam. Their evaluations were negative, while he was getting more optimistic information from other sources. He finally abolished PSAC and the post of Science Advisor after a few frustrated members of PSAC—wrongly, I believe—publicly opposed the ABM and supersonic transport. In doing this, they violated the long-standing and proud tradition of confidentiality of the Science Advisory Committee. Previous Science Advisory Committees and Science Advisors had frequently given advice that was not followed because of nontechnical factors the President chose to emphasize, usually financial or political, but always in the past they had been given a thorough hearing, and they remained publicly silent.

President Nixon upset some of the PSAC members by refusing to hear their views. He did not want to hear the facts. In a sense, he chose to kill the messenger. In later years, Presidents Ford and Carter made arrangements to get their own assistance on technical questions. President Ford faced an anti-PSAC bias that lingered on after President Nixon, and so never was able to create an adequate advisory system. President Carter appointed a Special Assistant for Science, but didn't reestablish a Presidential Science Advisory Committee with anything like the extensive capabilities of the original committee. Dr. Frank Press, Carter's Science Advisor, made extensive use of advisory panels, but did not use a PSAC style group to achieve integration and continuity.

President Reagan's operating style dictates altogether different ways of making technical decisions. He uses the buddy system, which in the end, proved disastrous. Reagan has made no effort to get independent advice about technical questions such as the shuttle, or SDI, perhaps because he did not know that he needed it. He trusted the advocates who had surrounded him during his campaign for the Presidency, and heeded their advice.

It is true that Reagan was turned down on the position of Science Advisor by a number of very good scientists who might have had some influence. They drew back when they learned about the limited role they were going to have, and especially that their information and advice would flow to the President mainly through his Chief of Staff; that, in fact, they were being asked to be an advisor to a Presidential aide. George Keyworth accepted the position, despite the limitations, and thus served the President and the country poorly.

Much of the Reagan defense and disarmament policy stems from the views of Edward Teller and the nuclear bomb laboratory staffs. The intense lobbying efforts of Teller and his like-minded colleagues with members of Congress blocked Eisenhower completely in his quest for a total nuclear test ban, and forced President Kennedy to settle for a partial nuclear test ban, instead of the comprehensive ban that he wanted. Though their efforts did not stop President Nixon's achievement of a limitation on anti-ballistic missile systems, they did fight it, and their contemporary counterparts are doing their best to undercut it now, fifteen years later. They and their advocates representative of a particular, interested point of view now dominate whatever scientific decision-making occurs at the White House level.

In addition to wasting money and increasing the danger of nuclear war, the continuing weapons programs, both R&D and manufacturing, have diverted resources from productive efforts, especially technical manpower, which is badly needed in the civilian sector. The lure for industry of the easy profits available on military programs, plus the intense concentration of the leadership and the public on defense issues, has been an important factor in the decay of the nation's civilian industry. The problem today is not missile balances with the Soviet Union; it is reclaiming American independence from what we were warned about: the military-industrial complex.

Rapid changes in technology mean that there is never a stable moment. Some observers of the military scene hope for a time when the opportunity for new and more fantastic weapons will not exist and a non-threatening world will just happen. A political expert on the arms race calls himself a short-term hawk, a middle-range owl, and a long-term dove. He does not understand the flow of technology. Its course does not change direction by itself. In technical development, one idea engenders another. This vicious cycle can only be broken by human intervention—not by another invention—by people limiting weapon development and choosing more benign uses of technology. Otherwise, the scale of technical activity devoted to arms will continue to grow until it transforms all society into a military camp. The civilian economy, the true basis of our national security, will decline, thus increasing the fraction of our resources devoted to arms, with a continuing loss of civilian technical leadership.

THE FUNDING PROCESS

The tradition in the federal government is for the various Executive branch agencies to propose their most ambitious programs to the President with the expectation that they will be pruned back. Usually, the total requests far exceed the financial resources available, and it becomes the President's task to choose those that appear most important and in the best interest of the nation. Obviously, a President cannot be expected to understand all of these highly complex demands, or even have much time for them. So, for the initial choices, a President must depend upon the Cabinet officers and other agency heads and their staffs, as well as the Office of Budget and Management, which works with the departments to prepare their budgets. But, ultimately, it is properly the President, as the one official responsible for the welfare of the country as a whole, who must choose.

As the scientific problems that face the various agencies have expanded, so have their funding needs, and the problem of selecting among them grows more difficult. I have estimated that, left to normal growth, technical programs double in cost in approximately six years. The GNP, at its best, used to double in twelve years. So the President's difficulty in making choices increases each year. This is why budgets grow so continuously.

THE FUTURE COURSE

What can be done to reverse the decline in the US technological well being? We are faced with two separate challenges. First, the President must resume control of the federal scientific enterprise. He must take back control and oversight of these vast resources from the military/industrial complex. Second, we must simultaneously revitalize the civilian science and technology enterprise, all of it—education, basic research, and civilian application of technology. We should buy only the few military systems needed to insure national security, and direct the rest of our vast technical resources to rebuilding the nation's civilian industrial base. An essential part of this task is to build the Presidential science advisory mechanism back up in a way that would regain the confidence of the Congress and general public in the government's decision-making process. This will not be easy, given the recent history. But it must be done.

An independent investigation is needed to explore the overall problem posed by science and technology for the future well being of the nation. To make a start, we need to reestablish PSAC, and utilize the position of the Science Advisor as it was in the past.

Some scientists who have been involved with the Presidential advisory process believe that the President's Special Assistant for Science and Technology should be a member of the Cabinet, a member without portfolio. He or she would thus be subject to Congressional approval, so as to provide a check and a degree of public exposure. Others propose that the entire Science Advisory Committee also be subject to Congressional approval, and that PSAC should be answerable to Congress. Such steps would institutionalize the activity and probably give it obviously needed status. On the other hand, it is probable that exposing the science advisory function to political processes in such a manner would deprive the President of an opportunity for the intimate, confidential relationship that existed under Eisenhower and Kennedy. Such a relationship can be the best guarantee of objective, politically uncontaminated advice and information.

I believe that several additional steps could be taken quickly to improve the Presidential process and the quality of the US technical establishment. First among these would be to relax the secrecy imposed on military/technical matters. Secrecy is ostensibly imposed to keep information of military systems from potential opponents. Experience shows that its main role is to keep the American public in the dark. Too often secrecy is applied selectively, more to win debates than to protect information. Some of the best analysis of military technology has been provided by independent studies based upon fundamental physical facts, not secret knowledge.

A new PSAC should give equal attention to the problems of civilian, or private-sector science and technology. This would be a new task. During my term as Science Advisor, a PSAC panel began to examine the problems of civilian technology. In retrospect, I can see that our focus was too narrow. Our concern was for those industries that were not employing R&D effectively. But some of the panel's observations were on the mark. For example, it expressed concern about the lack of R&D in the steel industry. Not only was that industry not doing any significant R&D, it was ignoring what was being done overseas. It was fast becoming obsolete. That was long ago, in 1962. A member of my staff predicted that the American steel industry would be dead in twenty years. Actually, we did not know how to stimulate civilian industries' uses of R&D. The National Science Foundation has had some modest successes with its experiments in this area, but we really do not know what to do to restore the US position of leadership. Tax credits for R&D seem also to have helped. But the basic problem of maintaining a competitive industrial base obviously needs more than just better R&D, although this is essential. This is a problem that the PSAC process will not solve, except to the degree that it can stimulate science education and basic research. But regular PSAC review could clear the biggest obstacle from the path. It could prevent the colossal waste of technical manpower that the federal government now subsidizes, drawing too many of the best technical people into working on high tech weapons of war that are not needed, are not productive and with luck will never be used. We need to give a healthy peace that same priority.

If a study committee were to be set to work on the problem, public consideration and debate on its findings would in itself improve our position in scientific and technological research, development, and deployment; and the economic, social and security benefits to the nation as a whole and to the entire international community would be commensurate.. Perhaps such a study would suggest a more effective Presidential advisory system. If so, it could be adopted after appropriate consideration. But we should not allow the hope for an ideal solution to leave the President and the nation floundering and at the mercy of random and unidentified forces. We have an effective model: a President's Science Advisor in the White House and a President's Science Advisory Committee. Let's use it. Let's get our technological priorities straight.

NOTE

1. A detailed history of this activity can be found in the book, *Sputnik, Scientists and Eisenhower* by James R. Killian, Jr. (Cambridge, MA: MIT Press, 1982); and William T. Golden's book, *Science Advice to the President* (New York: Pergamon Press, 1980).

Over-Regulation: Required or Ridiculous?

Rosalyn S. Yalow

Executive, Legislative, and Judicial branches of our federal, state and local governments need to search for more effective science and technology advice, rather than responding to the loud voices of political activists.

The time has come for government at all levels to re-examine laws and regulations promulgated by a phobic fear that we are in the midst of a cancer epidemic which is a consequence of radiation and man-made carcinogens. The facts are that, according to the American Cancer Society statistics, other than the dramatic increase in smoking-associated cancer of the lung, which began in men about 1930 and in women about 1960, the age-adjusted cancer death rates have in fact fallen strikingly over the past half-century. The decrease by three-quarters in the cancer of the uterus death rate is undoubtedly due to the widespread use of Papanicolaou's stain test which has permitted early diagnosis and treatment. The stomach cancer death rate, however, has fallen to one-fifth and liver cancer death rate has fallen to one-third the 1930 levels. These decreases are not due to dramatic improvements in therapy, but are probably a consequence of decreases in the natural carcinogens in our diet. Is it the improved refrigeration or the use of pesticides and fungicides that slow the growth of insect infestation and mold contamination that has resulted in so dramatic a decrease in cancers related to food intake? Bruce Ames, who developed the Ames test for mutagenicity, has written that public health could be endangered by banning the use of ethylene di-

Rosalyn S. Yalow received her A.B. from Hunter College in 1941 and her Ph.D. in nuclear physics from the University of Illinois in 1945. When radionuclides became available from the Oak Ridge reactor at the end of World War II, she joined the Bronx Veterans Administration Hospital to set up a radioisotope service which would assure that biomedical investigation with and clinical application of these materials would proceed pari passu. Together with the late Dr. Solomon Berson she developed a technique known as radioimmunoassay which permits measurement of hundreds of substances of biologic interest in blood and other body fluids. For this discovery she received a Nobel Prize in Physiology or Medicine in 1977.

bromide (EDB) as a fumigant since its ban would result in an increase of natural carcinogens that would put us at much greater risk than that from EDB.

The "Delaney Clause" of 1959, which prohibits the use of any food additive that at any dose level produces cancer in any animal, should be replaced with laws and regulations that would permit the establishment of a *de minimis* for potentially toxic substances. An amount so low as not to be of regulatory concern could be that for which any possible effect would be hidden in the "noise of the system", *i.e.*, the random variation in natural disease processes or the variability of carcinogens found naturally in food. The amount of nature's mutagens and carcinogens we regularly ingest probably exceeds by a factor of 1,000 to 10,000 those associated with man-made chemicals. These natural carcinogens are found in foods, such as celery, figs and parsley; in spices, such as mustard, horseradish and pepper; and in the burnt and browned material in our toast, hamburgers, steak and, of course, coffee. When we regulate, let us not forget that people who have consumed a meal containing fried pork or bacon have easily detectable levels of mutagens in their urine. Unless we are prepared to avoid all foods containing natural carcinogens, it would appear to be too stringent to ban additives with a carcinogenic potential that is small compared to those we readily accept in our daily diet.

Let us consider the use and abuse of the Superfund for the clean-up of hazardous materials resulting from human activities. Historical records had shown that a radium processing plant had been in operation at a site in Northern New Jersey for about a decade. The plant was abandoned more than sixty years ago. With federal money potentially becoming available, the New Jersey Department of Environmental Protection (NJDEP) undertook an investigation as to the possible extent of radioactive contamination in the vicinity of the original plant. Studies in 1983 revealed that such contamination did exist. A decontamination program was begun at a cost of several million dollars. The contaminated soil has been stored in drums—with no place to go because of a variety of legal complications.

To put this issue into a proper perspective, it is necessary to appreciate that the total amount of radium involved is estimated to be 0.5 Curies (Ci). This is to be compared with the emissions from model coal-fired power plants which range from 0.02 to 0.7 Ci radium per year, so that, over sixty years, the lowest emitter spewed forth 1.2 Ci.

While the New Jersey authorities have been unable to resolve the problem of what to do with 0.5 Ci of radium because of public reactions and legal controversy, a new problem arose. In December 1984, a worker on his way into Pennsylvania's Limerick nuclear power plant triggered a radiation detector alarm. Soon thereafter it was recognized that radon contamination in homes in the Reading Prong area, stretching from Pennsylvania through northwest New Jersey into New York and in Clinton, New Jersey, and perhaps elsewhere in the country may exceed levels found in uranium mines.

Estimates from government agencies have suggested that up to one-quarter of the 130,000 per year lung cancer deaths could be due to indoor radon levels. Congress was quick to respond. Legislation has been introduced to mandate a nationwide survey of radon in schools, and to earmark $30 million in federal funds to help states develop programs to deal with the radon problem.

Are these actions really necessary? In 1930, the lung cancer death rate was only 5% of what it now is—although radon has always been with us. One might claim that there was underdiagnosis of lung cancer in the 1930s, but, by 1970, the age-adjusted lung cancer death rate among Mormon women had hardly risen since it was still uncommon for these women to smoke. Further evidence that the major fraction of lung cancer in non-smokers is probably not associated with radon exposure comes from histologic studies since the cell-type found in cancer of the lung in non-smokers differs from that found in uranium miners.

The use of irradiation of food to preserve and protect it from contaminants is regulated by the Food and Drug Administration (FDA), since irradiation is considered to result in "food additives." The international community has been enthusiastic about the potential use of irradiated food. A 1981 World Health Organization document states "all the toxicological studies carried out on a large number of irradiated foods, from almost every type of food commodity, have produced no evidence of adverse effects as a result of irradiation." Nonetheless the American people have not been well informed that food-irradiation does not present a health hazard and that it would permit us to have a greater variety of high-quality and safer food products were this process to come into more widespread use in the United States.

Still another unsolved problem is what to do with our garbage. Surely we will soon run out of landfill space. To what extent can we recycle? Is the picture of the barge Mobro from Long Island plying its way up and down the Atlantic trying to unload its tons of smelly garbage a harbinger of things to come?

It seems very exciting to pour billions into a Superconducting Super Collider or sequencing of the human genome. We are bombarded with the "War on Cancer" or the "War on AIDS." Perhaps we would be able to pay for these advances if we did not continue to waste money on problems that at the current state of science we should better be able to solve in a more rational way than is current practice. The above examples illustrate the need for informed, unbiased and responsible science advice to the highest levels (as well as to lower working levels) of our federal, state and municipal governments. All too often government calls on the National Academy of Sciences and other respected scientific organizations for advice—and then fails to listen.

Thinking About Science Advice

Adam Yarmolinsky

If you want to think about science and technology advice, it helps to compare that advice with other kinds of advice that affect decision-making in the Federal government; political, social, economic, even moral or ethical advice.

Scientific and technological advice is not so different from most other kinds of advice. The subject matter it deals with is not more complex than the subject matter of other kinds of advice—although it may appear so at first; on the average it is probably about as uncertain, and it is as likely to be wrong, or at least inappropriate.

But it does differ from other kinds of advice in at least two respects: It generally requires more patience to absorb, because it rests on factual and methodological assumptions that politicians don't know as well as they know the bases for other kinds of advice.

At the same time, it is subject to a kind of verification—up to a point—that is not generally available with other kinds of advice. At least the early steps in the process by which the advice is arrived at can be tested by replicating them in a way that is not often possible with other kinds of advice.

Lastly, the subject matter of science and technology advice is fundamentally more resistant to manipulation, more intransigent, than the subject matter of other kinds of advice. We can (sometimes) change the results, but we can't change the rules.

The present low estate of science and technology advice to the President is more evident than the relatively healthy state of science and technology advice to the Congress. It may be worthwhile to examine the reasons for

Adam Yarmolinsky, Provost of the University of Maryland, is a lawyer who has been a professor in the University of Maryland Policy Sciences graduate program, at Harvard Law School, and at the University of Massachusetts. He served in the Kennedy, Johnson and Carter Administrations: in the Pentagon (as Principal Deputy Secretary of Defense for Security Affairs, 1965–66), White House, and the Arms Control Agency. He received the Distinguished Public Service Medal of the Department of Defense in 1966, is a member of the Institute of Medicine, is Chairman of the Board of Trustees of Bennington College, and is a Fellow of the American Academy of Arts and Sciences.

the difference, with a side glance at advice to the Judiciary branch, in order to consider what changes in attitudes and practices might improve the quality and sharpen the impact of advice to future Presidents.

If you want advice, the first thing you need to do is to ask for it. Free advice is known to be worth about what you pay for it. Since advice to Presidents is usually paid for in the coin of recognition, advice unsought and unacknowledged is not likely to be of the highest caliber.

The contrast between the glory days of the President's Science Advisory Council (PSAC) under Presidents Eisenhower and Kennedy, and the thready pulse in the life-line between the Reagan White House and the scientific community underlines the point. PSAC worked so well because its members knew that their advice was sought after, and would be taken seriously. Thus it responded to the first distinguishing character of science advice, the need for lay recipients of that advice to pay attention and listen patiently.

It worked also because it replicated, on a small scale, the process by which scientific information is validated. The group process, both within the Council and in its task forces, gave scope to the peer review process on which the advance of scientific knowledge depends—the second distinguishing characteristic referred to above. In the same fashion, the group process within the Congressional Office of Technology Assessment, and in its task forces, functions for the Congress today.

THE ADVISORY PROCESS

The President's Science Advisor can facilitate and expedite communication of advice. He and his staff cannot substitute for a group of advisors who still devote themselves more or less full-time to the practice of science. And the relationship is not helped when the office itself is left vacant for long periods of time. The advisory process reaches (what one hopes is) its nadir when, as in the case of Edward Teller and the Strategic Defense Initiative, the President acts on the advice of a single member of the scientific community, quite isolated from his peers, whose ideas are rejected by a clear consensus of expert opinion.

The reliance on expert consensus does raise a problem which can be described as the "They laughed at the Wright Brothers" phenomenon. The simple answer to the argument that the scientific community tends to overlook or even to resent saltatory innovations is that it just isn't so. For every case of a Barbara McClintock, whose discoveries about plant genetics were ignored for almost a generation, there are scores—hundreds—of Watsons and Cricks, Einsteins, Fermis, Rabis and Bohrs. Further, scientific advance is essentially a cooperative endeavor, and the vision of the lonely researcher must be joined with the contributions of other lonely researchers to achieve more than partial truths.

Paradoxically perhaps, the collaborative effort seems more valuable in hard science than in social science and policy analysis. The "big science" social experiments of the 1960s and 1970s yielded a good deal less than their champions promised. This was partly because the experiments were not set in the same time-frame that constrained the decision-makers. They took too long. Decisions on housing or welfare or education or employment policy could not wait on the results of massive surveys. But it was also the case that the experiments tended to demonstrate the obvious. They simply did not produce that counter-intuitive insight that is the hallmark of creativity—and that helps the decision-maker at a critical point. Such insights are more likely, it seems to me, to come from independent, even isolated inquiry and reflection: a Moynihan report, or Tom Schelling's work on deterrence.

Hard science, on the other hand, accumulates policy-relevant insights by a process of accrual, depositing grains of insight, that slowly build into a critical mass or, to vary the figure, by chipping away at the intransigent granite of the physical world. And decision-makers need to understand the potentials—and the limitations—of the physical world as they are slowly revealed by the integration of the work of individual scientists. Just because of the intransigence of that world, understanding what cannot be changed is at least as important as figuring out how to change it.

EXCLUSIVE ADVICE

In one respect, at least, effective advice to the President must depart from the model for scientific inquiry: Advice offered to the President on any subject, must be the exclusive property of the person being advised, not to be shared with the general public or with interest groups, special or general. Otherwise the advisor becomes a mere lobbyist, and the President must discount the advice, in order to avoid the impact of public knowledge of the course being pressed on him by a presumably trusted advisor. The need for confidentiality is less when the advisors are dealing with the Congress, at least where the advice is sought by a Congressional committee, or committee staff, rather than by an individual member.

There is, of course a spectrum of advisors. The spectrum goes from the full-time member of the White House staff whose behavior should reflect the passion for anonymity, once embraced by Presidential advisors, but now more honored in the breach, to the member of an *ad hoc* advisory committee, whose widely known views on the subject matter of the committee's work may in fact have determined the invitation to join the group as a representative of one part of the opinion spectrum. Somewhere in the middle are members of a PSAC, which performs a continuing advisory function on a wide range of issues. Such individuals must continue to speak and write. But on specific questions put to them by the President or a White House staff member, they ought to preserve silence, at least in their corporate responses. These responses are often protected under the classification given the nature of the inquiry. But even where they are not so protected, the reports themselves need to be controlled by the authority that requested them, subject initially to the leakage generated by pressures within the system. At the same time, individual PSAC members will continue to express their views, but if the system is to work, they must remain mute on the advice they have conveyed as a corporate body, at least until the recipient sees fit to release it.

The issue of confidentiality only emphasizes the importance of trust and confidence in the relationships between politicians and scientists. Jerome Wiesner, who served as Science Advisor to Presidents Kennedy and Johnson, and later as President of the Massachusetts Institute of Technology, once observed that the questions that confronted him in the White House turned most often on scientific issues, while the questions that confronted him at MIT were more likely to turn on political issues. I suspect this was so because the academic community was more comfortable with and better able to reach agreement on scientific facts than on political ideas, while the political community had the reverse disposition.

Trust becomes especially important, therefore, to bridge the gap. But the trust that is needed to validate scientific advice is not trust in individual scientists; it is rather trust in the scientific enterprise, born of sympathy for and confidence in what is described in the ceremonies for academic degree recipients as "the fellowship of educated men and women" and "the ancient and honorable company of scholars."

Further light is thrown on this relationship by the way courts handle scientific advice. Our judicial system is an adversary one, in which we leave it up to the litigants to bring out the story by contesting each other's versions of the truth, each one bringing on his own gaggle of experts, with the judge acting only as an umpire, enforcing the Marquis of Queensbury rules. The system works tolerably well, and proposals to modify it by allowing the judge to find his own experts have been rejected by most students of the problem. It works, in part, because the courts' freedom of action is so narrowly circumscribed by legislation and Executive action.

But the Executive and Legislative branches do need to pursue their own experts, on whom they can rely in their much broader scope of decision-making. The representatives of all the interests affected by governmental decision-making will have their experts to bolster their arguments. The President and the Congress still need a body of impartial expertise to interpret what they are hearing from the contending multitudes. Until the relationship of trust and confidence is reestablished between the President and the scientific community at large, the advice will not be fully offered or, if offered, will not be properly heard.

PART 2

CONGRESS

Scientific Advice to the Congress

Philip H. Abelson

There are marked differences between the Executive branch and the Congress in the ways in which scientific advice enters the respective systems and is utilized. The President can have a Science Advisor as a channel for studies and information. In turn, the Advisor has a staff and an advisory body composed of distinguished scientists and engineers. In addition, within the Executive branch, there is a large body of competent scientists and engineers in such organizations as the National Institutes of Health, the National Science Foundation, the National Bureau of Standards, the Geological Survey, the National Aeronautics and Space Administration, and the Department of Agriculture. The scientific resources that Congress has must serve 435 representatives and 100 senators. A complicating factor is that each Congressman has a special constituency, and the interests and concerns of the constituents differ. For example, low oil prices are good news to the northeast states. They are bad news to Texas. The result is that Capitol Hill is intensely politically oriented.

A major development has been the fragmentation of power in the House of Representatives. In an earlier day, the Speaker and the chairmen of the major committees held the power. In the past decade, however, a great proliferation of committees and subcommittees has occurred. There are now more than 150 of them. Chairmen of these bodies maneuver to increase the scope of jurisdiction of their empires.

Congress as a whole and the individual members do not lack for information. If anything, there is an overload. Washington has become a great center for those who would influence the government. The number of lawyers licensed to appear before the District of Columbia bar has risen to 45,000. The number of trade and professional associations—many dealing with mat-

Philip H. Abelson, physicist, was editor of Science *from 1962 to 1984. He is presently Science Advisor to the American Association for the Advancement of Science. He was President of the Carnegie Institution of Washington (1971–78); has served on numerous federal advisory committees; and is a member of the National Academy of Sciences, the Institute of Medicine, and the National Academy of Public Administration.*

ters of science and technology—with offices or headquarters in Washington has risen to around 3,000. Much of the efforts of these associations is devoted to trying to influence the course of legislation. Congressmen are prime targets. Often the goals of the various supplicants are contradictory and the information supplied slanted.

Other sources of information include Congressional staff, hearings, visits and letters of constituents, the Congressional Research Service, the Office of Technology Assessment, the General Accounting Office, the Congressional Budget Office, and the National Research Council. In addition, what appears in the news media is closely followed. For example, advances in superconductivity which enjoyed press attention stirred interest in Congress and led to requests for a report by the Congressional Research Service and to possible legislation.

An important fact of life on Capitol Hill is the magnitude of the Congressional staff. Congressional employees now number about 40,000. Of these at least 20,000 are professional people. The staff has become so powerful that it is often referred to as a separate branch of government.

CONGRESSIONAL STAFF

Members of the Congressional staff serve at the pleasure of Congressmen who appoint them. Each Senator and Representative has an allowance to pay expenses, which include salaries of assistants. In addition, when they are chairmen of committees or subcommittees, they have additional staff. There is a very close relationship between Congressmen and their Congressional aides. If a member becomes chairman of a powerful committee, one of his staffers will often become the top legislative aide for that committee. The legislative aides and to a lesser extent other members of staff have important functions. They develop information concerning potential legislation; they write the legislation; they prepare talking points concerning it. If there are hearings, the staffers are present, and they coach the Congressmen, feeding questions or comments to them. The staff interacts with staffs of other Congressmen, gathering intelligence about prospects for passage and negotiating support for the legislation. When bills have been passed in both houses, the legislative aides have important roles in the conference that adjusts differences in the bills of each body and in preparing the final language.

The terms of office of Congressional staff are longer than those of many members. Staffers are highly professional; they have very broad knowledge of issues, personalities, and how the Congress functions. In effectiveness with respect to making things happen, they are often superior to freshman Congressmen. A major center of scientific and engineering expertise for the House of Representatives is the staff of the Committee on Science, Space and Technology. Out of a total of 80 staffers, about a third have advanced degrees in science or engineering. Sprinkled among the many offices on

Capitol Hill are about thirty Congressional Fellows that are selected by and supported financially by various scientific and engineering societies. A further discussion of the Fellows program will be provided later in the text.

The Congress has a magnificent resource in the Library of Congress, often called the best library in the world. The staff is called on to provide information ranging from quick answers to simple questions to detailed studies by the Science Policy Research Division of the Congressional Research Service. The Science Policy Research Division has a professional staff of thirty-seven who are expert in a wide range of scientific and engineering disciplines. They turn out 100–200 reports a year with a median of 20 pages. In addition they respond to some requests with one- to two-page memos totalling about 500 a year. Their products are well-regarded on the Hill, and are said to be objective and free of political ideology. The reports and especially the memos are prepared with a fast response time. Congressional staffers can initiate action by a simple phone call. To obtain information for longer, detailed studies, staff often consult experts by phone. They also send out drafts to experts for review.

OTA

The Office of Technology Assessment is valued for its comprehensive studies, often book-long in length. These publications contain analyses and recommendations that often lead to legislation. OTA has funds to contract out all or part of a study. Its products contain a blend of solid science and technology placed in the context of policy considerations. In forming study committees OTA is careful to include representation of the interested public.

The General Accounting Office was established to monitor the expenditures of the appropriations made by the Congress. As science and technology have impinged more and more on our lives, the competence required at the GAO has evolved to include scientists and engineers. This part of the staff has become increasingly active in preparing worthwhile reports. One entitled "Alternative Fuels. Status of Methanol Vehicle Development" is particularly impressive.

The National Academy of Sciences was chartered to advise the government when requested to do so. Presently the operating arm—the National Research Council—has a budget of more than $100 million a year. Most of this derives from many hundreds of contracts with Executive agencies. Since 1971, Congress in legislation has requested a total of eighty-five studies. Thus there has been comparatively little formal interaction between the NRC and Congress. Recently there has been increasing informal interaction. Personnel have been recruited to the NRC who previously had served on staff on the Hill. Established friendships and trust provide a mechanism for reliable transfer of information.

Hearings are an important source of scientific and technical information to the Congress. In some instances, the Congressmen and the staffs are already knowledgeable about the topics, and they know ahead of time the testimony that is likely to be presented. The purpose of such a hearing is to provide a "paper trail," that is, a written record. In some instances, however, hearings are the fastest way to inform the Congress when a new development occurs. By judicious use of the telephone, staff can identify the key experts and arrange to have them appear as witnesses to present written material and late-breaking data during a question period.

FELLOWSHIPS

One of the most constructive developments in the provision of scientific advice to the Congress was the establishment of Congressional Science and Engineering Fellowship Programs in the early 1970s. At that time, the American Association for the Advancement of Science, the American Society of Mechanical Engineers, the Institute of Electrical and Electronic Engineers, the American Physical Society, and the American Chemical Society began programs. These organizations subsidized the salaries of their fellows, who spent a year on Capitol Hill. Initially, Congressmen were cool to the programs. Among other concerns was their opinion that the two different cultures of science and politics might be incompatible. There is an old saying about the difference between scientists and politicians that goes, "When a scientist makes a statement, other scientists ask, 'Is it true?' When a politician says something, other politicians ponder, 'Why did he say it?'" The Congressmen were also suspicious that the scientists might have hidden agenda incompatible with theirs.

The Congressional Fellows programs have been quite successful. The number of sponsoring societies has increased. Requests by Congressmen for Fellows exceed supply by a factor of five. A total of 360 Fellows have served their year. Many have remained on the Hill or in Executive agencies. Others have gone back to academe or to industry, where their experience has proved valuable.

The Fellows are selected by the sponsoring societies and are chosen from a large crop of applicants. They usually come to Washington early in September each year and immediately undergo a two-week period of intense structured briefings arranged by the American Association for the Advancement of Science. This provides exposure to aspects of the legislative process and issues before the Congress. The Fellows also visit a number of Congressional offices, and finally choose one where personalities and issues seem most attractive. On joining the staffs of the Congressmen, the Fellows quickly become immersed in the activities. Being highly intelligent and motivated, they soon make themselves useful and valued. They furnish information in their area of expertise, write speeches for members, prepare press releases on many subjects, give briefings, assist in legislative debates, and help arrange for hearings on scientific and technical matters. In many instances new skills must be developed in order for the Fellows to be effective in their roles within Congress. Among the requirements for all Fellows is a high tolerance for ambiguity, flexibility, adaptability, and the ability to work under occasional severe pressure.

As the Fellows demonstrate loyalty, intelligence, good judgment, and expertise, they are often given increased responsibilities, and may be architects in drafting important legislation. Satisfaction with the Fellows program continues to mount, and it receives excellent marks with Congressmen and their staffs. A key ingredient is the matter of trust. The typical Congressmen has a limited background in matters scientific and technical. He is subjected to an overload of conflicting and slanted information by persons with axes to grind. He very much needs and values having around him people who can be counted on.

In summary, many mechanisms are available to provide scientific and engineering information and advice to the Congress. The mechanisms are being improved, and the Congress can match the Executive branch in drawing on expertise for any given issue involving science and technology.

Reflections on Science, Technology and Congress

Emilio Q. Daddario

The present concern about American productivity and the nation's ability to compete in a world that has become so rapidly globalized has initiated a period of self-examination. We are in another of those introspective times when Americans raise critical questions about their institutions and the direction their leaders are taking them. They do so with that combination of rationality and emotion that is so often the prelude to change, setting the stage for public policy determinations which will decide whether the United States will proceed with the knowledge, optimism and vision that have been characteristic of its world leadership. Whatever the direction, whatever our course of action, the United States will be the key world player, even though it is no longer the completely dominant force, a role to which it became so comfortably accustomed during the decades following World War II.

The stakes have never been higher, for what we do will affect our internal social and economic order, as well as determine whether the world will continue toward better economic integration or become fragmented by protectionism. It is a role that calls for the marshalling of our best talents, and of special significance will be a visible, understandable and substantive reaffirmation by the Executive and Legislative branches of our government that the progress of pure and applied science is essential to the national interest. This is a crucial time for an assessment that will underscore and build on our successes, weed out and recoup our failures, and determine a national strategy simultaneously to compete and to lead in a world where startling new technologies regularly ambush our own most promising developments.

Our need to call on the best advice to set out such a strategy does not necessarily preempt what is presently in place. The Executive and Legis-

Emilio Q. Daddario was a member of Congress (1958–71), author of legislation forming the Office of Technology Assessment, Director of the Office of Technology Assessment (1973–77), and Chairman of the American Association for the Advancement of Science (1978). He is Co-Chairman of the American Bar Association-AAAS Conference of Lawyers and Scientists, is a Trustee of Wesleyan University, and is a member of the Institute of Medicine.

lative branches of government that deal with the everyday planning, review and monitoring of responsibilities are well supported by established and experienced staffs. Despite their existence, however, and squarely in the face of our brilliant scientific and technological innovations, "competitiveness" has induced over two hundred members of Congress to form a caucus to meet a perceived international challenge. A consultant group hired to advise them states that

> what has happened is that the economic game has changed. Competition for markets, jobs and tax revenue is no longer local, state or national; today the competition is global and we are losing in that competition.[1]

Although that advice appears to focus Congressional attention on our industrial sector, the rapid trend toward internationalism also affects our academic enterprise, since the latter provides much of the scientific and technological foundation on which our industry is built.

As in most cases, this is not a problem without antecedents, and it almost axiomatic that, whenever there is concern about our economic well-being, our decision-makers see a need to examine the effectiveness of the nation's scientific and technical capability. In 1963, the Congress asked the National Academy of Sciences to determine

> what level of Federal support is needed to maintain a position of leadership through basic research in the advancement of science and technology and their economic, cultural and military applications.[2]

The reply to that specific question, one of several, indicated the question implied we were taking too much for granted in the assumption that such leadership could be assured continually. Dr. Verhoogen, one of the panelists, said

> The U.S. has mastered . . . the technology of many fields, but brilliant engineering achievements are not to be seen exclusively in the U.S. and our technology supremacy does not extend to all fields.[3]

In that same report, Drs. Teller, Kantrowitz and Bode spelled out a supporting concern about our ability to convert basic research into applications, and warned that, while the US still enjoyed a highly favorable balance of trade, both in payments for technical know-how and in the export of products based on sophisticated technology, it could soon fall behind, as it has already in the sale of some industrial products. Now that we have reached that point, questions are raised quite predictably as to our ability to convert knowledge into application across the board.

Since our technological developments are directly dependent on basic science, the education and research role of our universities needs to be better understood. Educators are rightfully proud of an educational system that has produced scientists and engineers whose ability to apply scientific discovery to practical problems deserves much credit for the maintenance of our nation's stability and security for a good portion of this century. They realize also that their successes, ever harder and more costly to come by, have led to increasing levels of government support, higher justification requirements, and uncomfortable scrambles for tax dollars.

THE CHALLENGE

At the 1987 Annual Meeting of the National Academy of Sciences, Erich Bloch, Director of the National Science Foundation, issues a challenge that has been before us for decades:

> The requirements of the Nation, the changes and opportunities in science, the institutional needs of science and engineering, and the relationships among the parts of the enterprise are such that the community needs to reconsider its central purpose.[4]

Even though Mr. Bloch carefully emphasized increased NSF support for education, human resources, and the disciplinary base of science and engineering, it was only his initiative affecting institutional innovation that drew public fire. "Why, since the great university centers have accomplished so much, did he want to fix something that ain't broke?" That was the question, both proper and predictable. It seems an ultimate axiom that talented people prefer to do pure science, and a lesser one that the emphasis on pure science undermines applied science. Yet the latter is gaining adherents as many of our technological initiatives are picked up outside the boundaries of our fifty states where, it is claimed, other nations allow us to go through the expensive process of research, development and design, and then place their bets on their own versions of those technological prospects that show optimum consumer promise.

Mr. Bloch has thought all this out. The research institutions may not be broken, but he sees some cracks, and seeks

> "these changes because we need ways to bring new knowledge more rapidly to the marketplace. We need more integration between researchers in industry and academia. Through this mechanism (the NSF Science and Technology Centers), we hope to improve knowledge transfer, an area where as a country we are being outpaced by our competitors.[5]

A SERIOUS WARNING

Even though Mr. Bloch was not pressed to spell out what those *cracks* consisted of, his warning is a serious one. The effective promotion of pure and applied science is handicapped by the complexity that links them. And our frustration over the ability to direct knowledge to specified ends becomes particularly vexatious when we see ourselves threatened by the encroachment of foreign manufacturers in areas which we previously dominated.

The fear of foreign competition is not new, however, and there are other warnings to build on. In 1967, the National Academy of Sciences prepared a report for the Congress dealing with the "special problems of effective applications of the resources of science to advances in technology,"[6] entitled, "Applied Science and Technology Progress." Its introductory section pointed to

> the tension between the mission-oriented institution and the research-oriented university that arises not so much because both want to perform research with a limited pool of resources, but rather because the mission-oriented institution depends for much of its intellectual stimulation and for its staff upon the university. Yet the university, with its dedication to basic research, tends to relegate applied research, and those who are dedicated to it, to a secondary position."

To overcome the tension, Dr. Teller recommended that

> the NSF and other government agencies . . . pay particular attention to the creation of an educational system that serves the applied science community as a whole, . . . not support . . . independent applied science projects except in direct support of an educational effort . . . and establish close links between outstanding applied science laboratories and appropriate academic institutions to direct their programs toward applied science under the leadership of the best men in the field.[7]

At a time when concern about our ability to convert knowledge into marketable products raises the spectre of a declining economy, Mr. Bloch has asked the American science community to "reconsider its central purpose." That consideration would have added weight if the Congress were to become involved by asking the same question. An analysis of that "central purpose" touches on institutional changes that could profoundly affect our entire educational and research personnel and goes beyond the Congressional requests that led to the reports on "Basic Research and National Goals" and "Applied Science and Technological Progress." The theme is a continuing one, however, and the National Academy of Sciences, now including the National Academy of Engineering and the Institute of Medicine, should be asked to complete the trilogy.

The previous reports, the first ever performed for the Congress by the Academy, purposefully avoided in-house Executive and Legislative advisory mechanisms in an effort to achieve a fresh sense of impartiality and independence. In a preface to the "Applied" report, George P. Miller said, ". . . this report . . . is another significant milestone in Congress's method of gathering talented, objective assistance to its use." It is a method particularly adaptable to an examination of institutions whose leaders recognize the concerns that have placed them under public scrutiny, understand their individual strengths and weaknesses, have varying ideas that need to be fought over and reconciled, relating to the roles they and government should play, and who, by the very nature of their daily tasks, are susceptible and receptive to change.

This is an occasion when the government should seek specialized advice. If there are to be reforms or shifts in emphasis in the ways the scientific and technical communities go about their business, the recommendations should come from them. The strategy by which it presently accomplishes its "central purpose" is a formidable challenge in itself, and considerable thought has been given to personal and institutional adjustments that might additionally hasten the adoption and application of research results. Improvements in that process, difficult to come by at best, are understandably complicated by the phenomenal growth of our total basic and applied effort.

The Director of the National Science Foundation, with the legislative mandate to improve the linkage between knowledge and development, has asked for help in that regard. That help can best come from the people who practice science and engineering. It is in the national interest for the Congress, which issued the mandate in the first place, to give them the chance to create and suggest expeditious ways to widen the horizons of research, learning and development.

NOTES

1. Charles McMillion of the Congressional Leadership Institute, "Technological Competitiveness: Meeting the Economic Challenge," presentation to the ABA-AAAS Conference of Lawyers and Scientists, June 24, 1987.
2. "Basic Research and National Goals," report by the National Academy of Sciences to the US House Committee on Science and Astronautics (1965).
3. *Ibid.*
4. Erich Bloch, Director of the National Science Foundation, "Scientific Leadership and Economic Competitiveness," remarks to the National Academy of Sciences, April 28, 1987.
5. *Ibid.*
6. Letter from Fred Seitz, then President of the National Academy of Sciences, to the Honorable George E. Miller, USHR, May 25, 1967.
7. Edward Teller in "Applied Science and Technological Progress," a report prepared by the National Academy of Sciences for the US House Committee on Science and Astronautics, 1967.

Science and the US Senate

Pete V. Domenici

The United States Senate is not a cross-section of America. The framers of the Constitution never anticipated it would be. So today, sixty-five of our 100 Senators were trained as lawyers.

A dozen Senators have a business background. There are four farmers, two bankers, plus a variety of other occupations, from a former social worker to a former pro basketball star.

With all this talent, one broad discipline is missing. Not a single member of today's United States Senate is a scientist. The closest we come is our civil engineer (Senator Evans of Washington) and our astronaut (Senator Glenn of Ohio).

We have a nonscientific Senate confronting a world of scientific challenges and opportunities that dwarf those available to previous generations. We seem likely to accomplish more scientific breakthroughs during the next three decades than we achieved in the past three centuries.

Yet only a couple of members of the United States Senate might be able to run a proper test-tube experiment.

Should we worry? Should we toss all those lawyers onto the street, replacing them with physicists and biologists for the Next Scientific Revolution?

Probably not. Lawyers make good legislators not because they have studied "The Law," but because they know how to ask questions, key questions.

Let me cite an example that involved me, a lawyer and non-scientist, several years ago. At that time, the Environmental Protection Agency, with great fanfare, had issued a report declaring that acid rain was, essentially, good for you, or at least good for crops.

At the same time, Congress was embroiled in a debate over whether to require pollution scrubbers at coal-fired power plants. Would this report stampede Congress into looser pollution standards?

Pete V. Domenici has been Senator from New Mexico since 1972. He is ranking Minority (Republican) Member of the Committee on the Budget and of the Committee on Energy and Natural Resources. He was Chairman of the Senate Budget Committee (1981–86).

The evening the report came out, my staff and I looked through it to prepare for a hearing the following day. We noted that the broad conclusions were based on single tests of several crops at a single plant. I didn't have to hold a Ph.D. to know that EPA couldn't reach valid scientific conclusions until it repeated that or any experiment again and again.

So the next morning, I questioned an EPA official about this. He had not looked carefully at the study. He returned to his office in such frustration over the study's inadequacy, I heard later, that he yanked his telephone out of the wall. The report sank from public sight.

My point is that Congress usually does pretty well in evaluating science. We have scientists on our staffs, and we regularly ask scientists in government, industry, and back in our home states to critique one another. We then sift out the logical conclusions. I am particularly fortunate because two of the most important scientific facilites in the world, the Los Alamos and the Sandia National Laboratories, are located in New Mexico, providing me with unusually sound advice.

ENCOURAGING SCIENCE

But in America, in 1987, we have reached a time when we need to do more than evaluate science. With the opportunities that exist in the next few years, we must focus our laws and efforts in a way that encourages science, particularly the transfer of our scientific accomplishments from the lab to the production line.

The problem is this: America seems awash in Nobel Prize winners. All the great scientific breakthroughs occur here; then all the production takes place abroad.

We hear so much about what we call "competitiveness," our ability to market products to the world. I am convinced America can strengthen our competitiveness far more effectively by unleashing our vast scientific knowledge than by passing a dozen new trade laws.

Earlier this year, the industrialist David Packard in testimony to the Senate Budget Committee, made an extremely astute observation. It was this:

> Raw materials and natural resources are no longer the foundation of our economy. Knowledge is now the most important element in our economy.

We are in the business of selling knowledge. We are producing it. But we must use it. We must apply it.

A key tactic in reaching our goal must be to use more efficiently those national laboratories, such as Los Alamos and Sandia. We have nine around the nation, all operated by the Department of Energy. One of every six scientists in the United States is employed in the national laboratory system. Each lab has a mission set by Congress, a mission involving the defense of America.

Yet these labs offer far more. They offer a pool of talent, a reservoir of opportunity, like none other in the world. The defense missions of the labs must never be compromised, but much other activity and science goes on there that can be utilized throughout the economy.

To use the labs to their capability, we must make some radical departures. Louis Pasteur wrote in 1871: "There are science and the applications of science, bound together as the fruit to the tree which bears it." Basic science and its applications to benefit mankind are linked tightly. If we forget that, we are missing Pasteur's point.

The Department of Energy is quite proud of the fact that twenty-seven new companies came into being last year as spin-offs of research that was undertaken somewhere in the national labs system. That is twenty-seven new companies created to convert the results of breakthroughs into practical products and ideas.

That sounds exciting. And, of course, it is. But compare that rate of spin-off with the rate at just one private institution, the Massachusetts Institute of Technology. MIT's overall budget is less than one-tenth of DoE's labs budget. Last year, MIT research produced spin-off companies equal to the entire DoE effort.

AN AGGRESSIVE APPROACH

While such comparisons may be misleading, those numbers tell us something. If we are to be competitive in the world, we simply must take a more aggressive approach in extracting our scientific achievements from the laboratory and putting them onto the production line.

Two huge, exciting issues confront mankind, issues that offer vast opportunities and great challenges to science and industry. Each is an issue that all the trade laws in the world will not affect one bit.

The first is superconductivity.

The second is the human genome.

No one can argue with the value of developing room-temperature superconductors, or mapping the human genome down to the last chromosome and base.

Exploring the opportunities of superconductivity could produce a leap forward in our standard of living far beyond the dreams that came from landmarks like the lightbulb, the telegraph, or nuclear energy. Whoever turns theory into practice will dominate much of industrial development in the 21st century.

Unlocking the human genome would mean advances in human health to a degree that would make antibiotics pale in comparison. Unlocking the sequence of the human genome will give us access to the genes that control the form and function of the body. That, in turn, will give us the knowledge to control and repair and prevent diseases and conditions affecting the body.

Whoever finds the key will dominate pharmaceutical and medical developments in the 21st century.

And we can not just "let it happen." My concept, put forward in legislation as S. 1480, will encourage the national labs to work with industry and with universities to tackle these great scientific challenges in a more coordinated way.

For example, we could put together a Human Genome Consortium to integrate the best talents of the labs, industry, and the universities, giving the Consortium a mission and a timetable.

We must get on the move. The Japanese and others are determined to get there if we fail.

These achievements will happen. They will happen in our lifetime.

The question we must face is "Will they happen in America?"

Federal Investment in Science and Technology: Priorities for Tomorrow

Don Fuqua

Over the decades since World War II, there has been a steady increase in the degree to which science and technology pervade our everyday existence. Scientific and technological advances influence almost every aspect of our lives, from national security to the food we eat, from the national economy to the clothes we wear, from physical health to mental development and, most particularly, our national industrial status in the international arena, one of the prime determinants as to the quality of our future way of life.

There is every indication that this trend will continue. It is axiomatic, therefore, that a strong national program of scientific research and technological development is an absolute essential to a nation's socio-economic well-being, if not its very survival. Such a program necessarily involves a significant amount of federal government support—in fact it is often said—accurately, in my estimation—that science today lives or dies depending on the amount of federal dollars budgeted for research. This heavy dependence on federal support runs head on into the urgent need to reverse the trend of huge annual deficits in the federal budget.

This does not mean we can no longer afford a robust federally funded science and technology effort. It does mean that the Administration and the Congress must take a careful look at the priority accorded research among other pressing national needs; must determine anew whether the mechanisms and funding levels that have evolved over the years constitute the current

Don Fuqua has been President and General Manager of the Aerospace Industries Association of America, Inc., since January 1987. As such he is a leading spokesman for the US aerospace industry. Before joining AIA, Mr. Fuqua served twelve terms as a US Congressman from Florida. He became Chairman of the House Science and Technology Committee in 1979, after having served on the Committee since 1963. He was Chairman of the Subcommittee on Space Science and Applications from 1971 to 1981, and also served as ranking majority member of the House Committee on Government Operations.

optimum approach to the government investment in science and technology; and must review and perhaps reshape the policies that govern federal support for research, in order to provide contemporaneous direction for the challenges that lie ahead.

I feel qualified, on the basis of extensive experience in science-related areas, to offer some views pertinent to those ends. I was privileged to serve for twenty-four years on the House Committee on Science and Technology, eight years as its chairman. More recently, as President of Aerospace Industries Association, I have been associated with an industry whose capacity for scientific/technological advancement is second to none. This longtime exposure to science matters has bred some hopefully constructive judgments as to where we, as a nation, should be headed in science and technólogy and what the best routes are for getting there. The subject is, of course, extremely broad and the interests of clarity are better served by focusing on some selected areas of particular importance.

BASIC RESEARCH

Even in times of special attention to deficit reduction, the need to invest in the nation's future dictates strong federal support for basic research, fundamental investigation intended to expand human knowledge without regard to the possibilities of practical application. In my view, current funding, although not insubstantial, is sufficient, to at least 1% of the overall federal budget from its current level of 0.8%

UNIVERSITIES

American research universities generate most of the nation's new scientific knowledge in addition to providing basic training for the nation's scientists and engineers. The federal government is providing effective support for basic research at both public and private universities, but such support has declined in recent years. Federal support for basic research at universities should be brought back to its former level of 0.2% of the Gross National Product.

An acute need is revitalization of the infrastructure, the physical plant universities use to conduct research. Universities have not been able to modernize their plants to match the needs of rapidly advancing technology with the result that facilities, equipment and instrumentation are generally obsolete. There have been many instances in which college researchers, moving to new jobs in industrial laboratories, do not know how to operate the laboratory's advance equipment.

Some immediate direct action must be initiated, and government intervention is essential because the problem has grown to the point where the universities are incapable of solving it on their own. I have proposed a remedy whereby a portion of the annual research money distributed by the main federal agencies would be set aside to finance consruction and renovation of university research facilities. That seems to be an effective way to solve the immediate problem, but there would still remain a need for a mechanism to assure continual updating of the infrastructure over the long term. That next step, however, cannot be taken until infrastructure adequacy is restored.

Over two centuries of our nation's history, a national university system has evolved. Although its growth has been somewhat haphazard, it is a vitally important asset that must be recognized by the federal government and fostered as a system. I do not suggest that we create a new bureaucracy for system oversight; I believe that adequate mechanisms are already in place within the Department of Education. A special office or branch of that department should be charged with conducting a systematic program to deal with problems of higher education, to monitor and supervise government-funded support of university research, and to provide guidance as to how the system can remain viable and vigorous.

BIG SCIENCE/LITTLE SCIENCE

The obvious difference between "big science" and "little science" is scope and funding. Little science is typically a grant-funded project carried out by an individual at a university laboratory. Higher on the scale are science/technology programs whose costs run to the tens of millions, hundreds of millions, even billions. Big science and little science are often in conflict with regard to funding allocations, particularly when the overriding consideration in government budgeting is deficit reduction, and we cannot finance all the research that needs or merits doing. We must prioritize.

The federal government has an equal responsibility to both big science and little science. Realistically, however, there will be proposals for large-scale research programs that must be accorded a measure of priority because of their extraordinary promise of future benefit to the nation. Such programs must be federally supported because only the federal government has the capacity and resources for the undertaking, and with limited money available for science in general, approval of a superscale program could have serious adverse impact on small science funding. The Administration and the Congress must exercise care in authorizing such "megascience" programs to insure that the indicated benefits justify the effort, that the program is a sound investment for the nation, and that its approval does not entail severe impairment of the small effort.

INTERNATIONAL COOPERATION

Science and technology activities have long been conducted on an international basis, particularly in the aerospace world where company-to-company or nation-to-nation cooperative agreements are commonplace. There is an evident trend toward greater internationalization. The reason is simple: money. Research to extend the frontiers of human knowledge is very expensive and it becomes more so with each increment of advance. We are reaching the point where certain research programs of immense scale are beyond the funding capability of any single nation; we may, therefore, be approaching a time when science endeavors will routinely become international efforts.

If such efforts are to be successful, a first requisite is establishment of some sort of international decision-making mechanism. The participants will have to look at the "big picture," in each major discipline that lends itself to large-scale cooperative programs, projecting twenty-to-thirty years into the future. From that perspective, they will have to negotiate the parceling out and balancing of national responsibilities and the geographical locations of cooperative program elements. These superscale research projects will, of necessity, be spearheaded by the major industrial nations. Every effort should be made however to include developing nations, their participation structured according to their capacity to contribute.

HEALTH RESEARCH

Among specific categories of research, medicine is perhaps the one of broadest interest. For some time, the federal government has been providing strong support for research over a broad spectrum of health-related classifications: degenerative diseases such as cancer or cardiovascular failure, contagious diseases, organ transplants and general improvement in surgical techniques, congenital deformities, advanced investigations such as gene manipulation, and fundamental problems of hygienic and sanitation, to mention just a few.

In these and other areas, progress has been impressive and US life expectancy has increased dramatically. The degree of progress would seem to indicate that we are devoting a reasonable portion of our tax dollars to this field of research. There remain problem areas, of course. I do not feel, however,that quantum increases in medical research funding would lead to commensurate achievements, because research ideas take time to mature and because the number of "breakthrough researchers" is limited—and they are, in all probability, adequately funded. I advocate maintaining the pace and scope at which medical research has advanced in recent years.

EDUCATION

I believe, as do many, that the future US competitive posture in defense and world trade is dependent, to a significant degree, on the quality of scientific and mathematical education provided Americans. There is special concern about these areas of education today. The greatest weakness is the dearth of competent math and science instructors at the pre-college level.

The system has thus far provided no solution, so we must consider unconventional approaches. I recommend such measures as special inducements for prospective science and mathematics teachers, special classes conducted by local industry representatives, and routine competency examinations for science/mathematics capability. I also advocate an increase in federal funding for pre-college science education.

DEFENSE RESEARCH

Evaluation of funding adequacy and overall direction of defense research is beyond the scope of this discussion, but there is one fact that bears mention: Although military R&D in general has grown dramatically over the last several years, the basic research portion of the defense budget has not kept pace and has, in fact, declined. This point is emphasized by the fact that basic research conducted by all federal agencies in Fiscal Year 1986 ran about 14% as a percentage of all federal R&D, basic research by the Department of Defense, in comparison, was below three percent—despite the fact that overall military R&D represents well above two-thirds of all federal R&D.

This neglect of basic research by the Department of Defense is a matter of concern, because basic scientific research—no matter what agency conducts it—is the underpinning of our future national technological capability. I believe, therefore, that the basic research effort within the defense program should be provided additional resources. Also, it seems likely that interaction between non-defense agencies and DoD would be beneficial to our national research advancement. The National Science Foundation, which has the prime responsibility for the nation's basic research effort, could work with DoD to assure that proper investments are being made in fundamental research areas important not only to defense, but to the future national technology base.

One other aspect of defense research merits mention: the Mansfield Amendment that required the Department of Defense to support only research directly related to DoD's mission. That amendment was in effect for only one year—1970—but its impact has lingered. For seventeen years, it has exerted an inhibiting effect on R&D by limiting innovation and creativity, and it has been responsible, in part, for the decline in military basic research as a percentage of the defense R&D budget. I feel strongly that the Congress should specifically disavow this amendment, even though it is no longer in force.

SPACE RESEARCH

Since much of my experience has been directly related to space research, this discussion would not be complete without comment on the goals of our civilian space program.

Space offers a number of direct benefits in commercial development and scientific gain, but perhaps its greatest long-term value is that it is a technology "driver"; meeting space goals forces a stream of advancements across a broad spectrum of scientific and technological disciplines. The broader technology base, in turn, benefits national security, industrial competitiveness and a generally elevated standard of living for nation's people.

All this is true only when there is sufficient force to drive technology, in other words, when the space goals are sufficiently advanced to *demand* significant technology advancements. Ideally, we need a space program that thrusts at the limits of human capability and thus exerts the maximum driving force.

Do we have such a program? The NASA/international Space Station, currently the centerpiece of our space effort, is a technologically demanding step in the right direction. But in the larger sense, the Space Station is not in itself so much a goal as an enabling system, a means to even greater ends. There is need—and NASA and the Administration are now considering options—for a bold and challenging long-range plan.

The National Commission on Space presented an absorbing scenario for the next fifty years: manned space stations in low and high Earth orbit, manned way stations operating between the Earth and its moon, a lunar outpost by 2005, a full-fledged colony on the moon by the year 2020, and a permanently manned settlement on Mars by 2028.

I applaud the Commission's imaginative vision and I feel that the program it offers is technically feasible. But I have reservations about the timetable, considering the current and predictable climate of fiscal austerity. I suggest an interim goal—development of the lunar outpost for occupancy within the first decade of the 21st century. Accomplishment of such a challenging objective would drive and engender enormous technology advancements and would, in addition, firmly establish US leadership in space.

Science, Technology and Law in the Third Century of the Constitution

John H. Gibbons

Our preference for muddling through has had its day, and it will not be good enough for the third century of the Constitution.—William D. Carey

Science, technology, and law are rooted in mankind's unending search for knowledge, comfort and harmony. Despite these concurrent origins, practioners of science and technology on the one hand, and law on the other, remain largely ignorant of the others' mysteries—the scientist's reaction to the intricacies of policy-making parallels the politician's aversion to the laboratory, to the uncertainty inherent in research and, sometimes, to the constraints on decision-making that are the outcome of analysis.

These respective illiteracies create serious handicaps. Few would deny that science and technology more deeply affect governance than ever before. Traditional boundaries—physical, political, cultural, and ethical—are breached by developments in science and technology. Resolution of the ensuing controversies requires that political leaders make their decisions and compromises based on clear, objective, accurate and unbiased information.

Yet technical information is often diffuse, judgmental, uncertain—and subject to rapid change. It is rare that "the facts" ultimately are at issue in policy debates, but rather unknowns and reasonably disputed claims. Science tells us what we *can* do, law whether we *should*. And scientists, like other experts and laymen, are replete with personal goals and viewpoints. When they enter the policy arena the effect on policy-makers can be disquieting. The impact, in fact, is not unlike that created by competing shamans whispering in the chieftain's ear: tribal warfare.

Over the past fifteen years, the Legislative branch has found it increasingly important to have access to non-partisan analysis of technology, especially its implications. Congressional committees have added staff trained in science and engineering, and they have been around long enough to de-

John H. Gibbons has been Director of the Congressional Office of Technology Assessment since 1979. Earlier, he served for many years as a research physicist and administrator at Oak Ridge National Laboratory.

velop expertise in policy analysis. Committee staff, generally more issue–oriented than the personal staff of members, has grown at a swifter pace than personal staff. And fellowship programs designed to lend scientific support to committees have been initiated. At the same time, Congressional support agencies, broadly shared resources, have garnered increasing support, enabling a more sophisticated analytical approach to socio-technical issues in the Congress.

Creating the Office of Technology Assessment, in 1972, was a step Congress took to match changes in governance to the changes wrought by technology, and to bridge the gap between science and law. Congress saw a threat to the balance of power in the federal government. Faced with a deluge of complex technological proposals sent to it by an Executive branch resplendent in scientific resources, Congress felt increasingly ill-equipped to evaluate those proposals. They designed OTA to be a balancing resource, to draw together national wisdom on technical issues, critically review and analyze information, develop findings, describe options, and accurately translate and communicate the results to Congress. An explanation of how and why OTA works and some general observations on the importance of scientific understanding in governance and the transferability of OTA's experiences follow.

SENSE AND SENSIBILITY

Intellect distinguishes between the possible and the impossible; reason distinguishes between the sensible and the senseless. Even the possible can be senseless.—Max Born

OTA is a *technology* assessment agency because while pure science may be socially and politically neutral, its application is not. OTA analyses generally produce reports identifying where consensus on a technological issue exists, explaining the reasons for disagreements among the experts, and suggesting plausible options for federal action. These options represent choices reasonable people of various philosophical persuasions might make given scientific and political realities, and the implications of such choices. An OTA analysis attempts to distinguish not only between the possible and the impossible, but also between the realms of the sensible and senseless. Upon reaching that point, the political sensibilities of Congress must then be brought to bear.

OTA's founders embedded in its authorizing legislation several features that helped the agency develop into an essential, trusted party to the decisionmaking process. Chief among them are:
• An active, bi-partisan, bi-cameral Congressional Technology Assessment Board (TAB), which meets every few months to establish overall agency

policy, review activities, and consider proposals for initiation of assessments (generally requested by committees of jurisdiction);

- An assignment to examine emerging technologies not only in terms of direct, technical impacts, but also to consider indirect implications, including physical, biological, economic, social and political effects;
- Specific designation of OTA as a shared Congressional resource, to be responsive to requests for analysis from committees in both the House and Senate, and from both sides of the political aisle; and
- Hiring and contracting flexibility, vested in the Director, which helps assure that the proper balance between institutional memory (dependent upon long-term staff) and changing needs for specialists can be struck and helps avoid political bias in the staff.

The fact that OTA extensively involves the principal stakeholders and interested public in its work by use of advisory panels and reviewers, while retaining full responsibility for the finished product, has contributed to its level of credence and political acceptance and also its high standing in the technical community.

FULL AND INFORMED DEBATE

A sense of the future is behind all good politics. Unless we have it, we can give nothing—either wise or decent—to the world.—C. P. Snow
A people who mean to be their own governors must arm themselves with the power which knowledge gives.—James Madison

Full and informed public debate, a cornerstone of our democracy, is a major reason for including technical information in the policy process. Besides the direct utility of the studies to the requesting committees, OTA's results serve to help strengthen public awareness not only of the issues, but also of the existence and diversity of various mechanisms to redress them. OTA's work helps focus the political debate and narrow and resolve differences. Authoritative, policy-relevant, but *non-partisan* studies help members with different political perspectives understand the issues and choose positions that comport with their political agendas or represent reasonable compromise. OTA's unique approach allows it to be not only politically neutral but also "technology-neutral," *i.e.,* OTA is viewed as neither for nor against technology, per se. It is *not* by advocacy of a particular position, but rather by comprehensive analysis, exploration of impacts, and development of authoritative, trustworthy, and understandable options and choices that OTA best serves the Congress and the nation.

OTA is Congress's principal response to their challenge, as policy-makers, to communicate with scientists/technologists. It assures that science and technology have a voice in policy, but that it also remains only one of many. What about elsewhere in the government?

In the Executive branch, the mission-oriented Cabinet-level departments constitute an in-house source of advice, but also of powerful advocacy, to the President. Other mechanisms have been used (off and on) by the White House since Harry Truman and Dwight Eisenhower, such as the Presidential Science Advisory Committee, the Office of Science and Technology, and now the Office of Science and Technology Policy. These offices have not only drawn upon the Executive agencies, but also have theoretically provided ready access outside government to national scientific and technical information. Unfortunately, they also easily slip into an advocacy role for the causes of the mission agencies and S&T in general.

Special, painstakingly chosen commissions and advisory boards are also sometimes appointed to temper the mission-orientation of the President's permanent sources of scientific advice. But, in addition to being selected for political compatability, they lack continuity, institutional memory, and sometimes even the ability to effectively communicate results to the Administration and Congress.

There are other offices of the President that can play important roles in technology assessment. The Council on Environmental Quality, the Council of Economic Advisers, the Domestic Council, the National Security Council, and *especially* the Office of Management and Budget have played vital, albeit changing, roles from one Administration to another. Generally, they have served as flywheels, adjudicating for the President the positions of different agencies and advocates.

Nonpartisan information is, of course, available to the Executive branch from outside sources. The National Academy of Sciences/National Academy of Engineering is an excellent source of independent advice, providing one-stop access to the US science and engineering community, but is also an advocate for science and technology. OTA's reports, though directed to a Congressional audience, are equally available to the Executive branch. Were our government a parliamentary system, OTA would be serving double-duty as advisor to the legislator and the executive, but—for the very reason that Congress created OTA in response to Executive power—it might be unwise for the Executive branch to rely too heavily on Congress to set the agenda of analysis or on OTA to carry out the analyses, develop findings, and provide policy options.

Perhaps a framework, similar to OTA, could be created within the Executive branch to provide for continuity, quality control, and delivery of analyses to the Executive and the interested public. A feature of such an organization could be that it would not make specific policy recommendations. It would, rather, present findings, help focus the debate on the most essential differences to be resolved, and provide a spectrum of policy choices or options for the President's *political advisors* (a different group of people, *e.g.*, Cabinet officers) to consider. Such an organization, to be effective, would have to consider impacts that transcend strictly technical issues, and include social, economic, environmental, and other ramifications. It could be the focus for a number of present activities, including the Council on Environmental Quality and a variety of Commissions.

The information provided by such an organization would ultimately be used to justify decisions that also involve other considerations inherent in governance, but it is important that the analytical information itself constitute an unbiased point of departure. Most difficult issues are not just "scientific" or "technical" but inherently multifaceted. It is all the more important, then, to assure that technical issues are not misrepresented or misunderstood.

LIMITS TO THE SCIENTIFIC METHOD

Between the idea and reality
Between the motion and the act
Falls the shadow—T.S. Eliot

My objective in raising the question of how to provide science and technology advice to the President is not only to be certain that the Chief Executive and his political advisors have the best non-partisan information available, but also to raise public understanding about socio-technical issues and the proper role of technical experts in decision-making. A troublesome and historic misperception about the power of science—attributing to it awesome and unrealizable capabilities to achieve societal goals and resolve societal ills—has worked in recent years to the disadvantage of both scientists and policymakers. We critically need scientists in the policy arena, but must recognize the limits of both their information and their objectivity, and reassert the important roles that ethics, morals and religious values also play in policy-making.

OTA succeeds in the Legislative branch because it fills a critical communication gap between scientists and policymakers by reducing the shadow cast by technical uncertainty and disagreement among experts. OTA distills technical information for laymen and then steps back to witness the mysteriously exquisite process of negotiation and resolution within Congress. I believe the Executive branch could benefit greatly from similar assistance.

Acknowledgment. The assistance of Holly L. Gwin of the OTA staff in the preparation of this essay is gratefully acknowledged by the author.

Science and Technology Advice and Education: A Long-Term View

Bill Green

The Challenger tragedy and the economic threats involved in the United States trade deficit suggest that, while necessity is the mother of invention, failure can be the father of innovation.

Both the space program and international trade are examples of arenas in which the federal government needs solid, honest and long-range scientific knowledge.

When dealing with trade, the word "competitiveness" fairly leaps off the lips of every corporate manager, economist, and social scientist in our country. It also has made its way into the consciousness of elected officials and bureaucrats in Washington. But in question is whether we are getting the kind of scientific and technical advice that will assure our competitiveness in this ever more "high-tech" world. The jury is still out on that question, but there are some positive signs.

As a member of Congress who serves as the Ranking Republican on the House Appropriations Subcommittee funding four science-oriented agencies—the National Science Foundation (NSF), the National Aeronautics and Space Administration (NASA), the Office of Science and Technology Policy (OSTP), and the Environmental Protection Agency (EPA), I have direct experience with the manner in which the Congress and the President get science advice. I also carry a personal interest in scientific advancement and its potential for improving our lives. Finally, even placing aside the "hype" surrounding competitiveness, I believe we must continue to grow scientif-

Congressman Bill Green is the only New York City member of the House Appropriations Committee and is Ranking Republican on its HUD-Independent Agency Subcommittee which appropriates funds for NASA, the EPA, the Council on Environmental Quality, the National Science Foundation, the Department of Housing and Urban Development, the Veterans Administration, and several other agencies. He is also Co-Chairman of the Environment and Energy Study Group in Congress, and has been active on a wide range of energy and environmental issues, including acid rain and ozone depletion.

ically if we are to remain a strong economic and political force in the world. To do this, the federal government needs good technological advice.

THE PRIMARY SOURCES

Let's consider the primary sources of scientific advice for the Congress and the President:

- The President has, within the White House, the Office of Science and Technology Policy. This small outfit (fifteen people and a 1987 Fiscal Year budget of $1.949 million) serves as a source of "science and technology advice for the President and other organizations within the Executive Office of the President; provides for coordination and policy analysis of research and development programs of the federal government; and conducts research and analyses, with the Office of Management and Budget, of research and development programs of the federal government."[1]
- The National Science Foundation, a research-oriented independent federal agency providing funds to universities and researchers to develop scientific and engineering base. (Its FY 1987 budget is $1.624 billion.)
- The Office of Technology Assessment, an agency within the Legislative branch, whose duty is to provide detailed analyses of major public policy issues related to scientific and technological change to both Houses of Congress. Its budget is $16.5 million.
- The National Research Council, an arm of the National Academy of Sciences, is unique among these as its independent status permits it to be less affected by political pressures and allows it to function as a reasonably objective voice in science and technology policy. Its role in identifying the problems with NASA's solid rocket motors caused both the Administration and the Congress some embarrassment.
- In addition, most major federal agencies have advisory groups within their structures. Because these internal organizations are rarely free of the pressures that affect their own agencies, however, their success or failure in providing advice usually depends on their ability to make agency heads take notice.

Cases such as the Challenger accident and our trade deficit forced us to recognize the relative paucity of resources we devote to science and technology. Only about seven out of every thousand Americans receive degrees in engineering. In Japan, the figure is forty. Furthermore, over 50% of the Ph.D.s awarded by our universities since 1980 go to non-US students. This should not be viewed as cause for xenophobic alarm, but rather as an indication of the poor status of our scientific and technological "labor force." This does not augur well for either the quality or availability of scientific advice for our nation.

The one positive result of the Challenger tragedy, however, is that it has drawn attention to the shocking way in which *available* scientific advice, both within and outside of NASA, was ignored; engineering advice was taking a "back seat" to launch pressures and the need to enhance the international status and profitability of the space shuttle.

Are we learning from these mistakes? In the months since the Challenger disaster, NASA has been subject to intense public scrutiny and criticism. We have now recognized that much of the engineering opinion ignored or overlooked suggested that reliance on the shuttle as the nation's single means of space transport was wrong, and that some design elements of the system were inherently flawed. Yet, even as I write this, NASA is moving forward on another controversial great new leap into space—the Space Station.

THE SPACE STATION

Since 1984, the first year of funding for this program, I have been openly skeptical of NASA's insistence on a permanently manned configuration for this project. In my discussions with space scientists and in an informal poll I took in 1984, I was shocked by the ambivalence and often outright animosity members of the science community felt toward this program. The Station reminded them of another big-ticket NASA item of years past, the Shuttle. During its development, the Shuttle attracted almost all available monies from science programs within NASA and, since the Shuttle's first launch, the science community felt that NASA's focus was commercial launches, defense launches, and then—if time and space permitted—science launches.

In the early planning of the Station, many scientists saw NASA's science money going into what promised (and what is proving to be) a very expensive item, around $12 billion in 1984 dollars, for a station that will be significantly smaller than envisioned in 1984. They were skeptical and even downright hostile as the Station plan seemed to downplay scientific experimentation in favor of a dramatic manned "hotel." Today, the Station is delayed in getting started (although not entirely through the fault of NASA), and has doubled in price. But, finally, through the Congress's insistence, which was based to a large degree on scientific advice, NASA is stressing the scientific and technological uses of the station, and reluctantly has agreed to a man-tended configuration before assembling the full Station. This I view as a victory for good sense, as well as one for sound scientific advice: Most scientists I spoke with agree that the technological advancements engendered by the necessary automation and robotics on a man-tended Station will be significant and will assure us some early scientific return from the Space Station.

And, since the Challenger accident, advice within NASA, through its own Mixed Fleet Task Force, and advice from outside NASA, from sources as disparate as the Congressional Budget Office and Dr. Thomas Donahue,

Chairman of the Space Science Board (in an opinion expressed independently of his duties), have urged NASA once again to use Expendable Launch Vehicles (ELVs) to launch payloads and to build and supply the Station. The reasoning is that the use of these reliable vehicles will free up the Shuttle for more science-based missions, particularly with its uniquely outfitted laboratory, the Spacelab, on board.

NASA reluctantly came around to that view, and is now contemplating what would have been heresy only a few scant months ago: the idea of building a new unmanned launch vehicle structurally based on the Shuttle to assist in building and resupplying the Station. Would NASA have continued to reject such advice absent the Challenger tragedy? Certainly the advice was there, yet the continued (and, in hindsight, amazing) successes of prior Shuttle flights allowed NASA to ignore much of the advice. The agency certainly will be less likely to do so in the future.

SCIENTIFIC ILLITERACY

Let me return to the matter of education for another area in which scientific pressures produced a positive development in public policy. For years, reports from a variety of independent and government sources have warned that our country's children were relatively illiterate in math and science. The statistics I quoted earlier on percentages of students in those technical areas point out the fact that not nearly enough young men and women are getting involved in science and math *at an early enough age to cause them to become career choices*. To many high school and college students, math and science are frightening, mysterious, and to be avoided, if possible.

Several years ago, I hosted a Congressional forum in Manhattan with business executives and educators who were worried that industry, in need of scientific minds, was hiring so many science/math educators that fewer minds would be trained for the future.

The consequences of this are apparent to anyone who sees Japan's technological edge increasing to the point where the research and development of Japanese automobiles is done in Japan by Japanese and the building is done by American workers in Ohio.

A report by a Commission headed by William Coleman, a former Cabinet official under President Nixon, entitled "Educating Americans for the 21st Century," and numerous other studies have concluded that undergraduate and secondary education is in dire need of government assistance. For several years, those of us with active interests in this issue have pressed the National Science Foundation and the Department of Education to increase the amounts they budget for pre-college science education to reflect that priority.

This year, $30 million was added to the National Science Foundation's Science Education budget specifically for this purpose. I take some pride in pointing to that fact, since it reflects one instance in which Congress took some action specifically based on sound scientific advice. In addition, I believe the coming years will see a continuing emphasis on funds for math and science studies, especially in pre-college and college studies. I cite that as one example of where the Congress received good advice and acted on it.

IMPROVING THE QUALITY OF ADVICE

A question now arises as to what we can do to improve the quality of advice available to the President and Congress. And certainly the quality of advice available does not matter if we are not willing to listen to it. Given the Challenger accident, I suspect that NASA and the Congress will be much more attentive to scientific advice in that area in the future and, I would hope, in general.

One specific recommendation I would make is for a strengthening of the Office of Science and Technology Policy within the White House. It is now too political in the sense that it reflects the biases of the Administration (for example, in regard to the Strategic Defense Initiative) to the detriment of contrary thoughts and other programs. It would be difficult to completely depoliticize this office, but we do need someone close to the President with a sound scientific and technical background who can give clear, cool advice and assist in plotting science policy for our nation. That would demand a larger budget than the paltry one currently requested by the White House, yet to spend that money on an OSTP with a narrow agenda would be a mistake.

The overall problem seems to be two-fold. First, the resources devoted to developing long-range (educational) and immediate (advisory) scientific knowledge need to be augmented. That, I believe, is slowly happening. Second, the resources we expend are worth nothing if we ignore sound scientific and technical advice in favor of mere wishes and political goals. The Challenger accident and our economic problems have shocked us into a degree of attentiveness, and I hope it will continue.

NOTES

1. Executive Office of the President, Office of Science and Technology Policy, Budget Submission, FY88, p. 1.

Congress Needs Informal Science Advisors: A Proposal for a New Advisory Mechanism

James Everett Katz[1]

These are times that try the souls of those concerned about the quality of science and technology advice in the federal government. The editor of this volume has pointed out that science advice to the President is in low estate, perhaps close to nadir. Other commentators have observed that many forms of scientific and technical advice are increasingly politicized, by-passed, or ignored. To address this situation, many leaders of science continue to call for greater involvement of scientists in advising public officials. For example, in her capacity as president of the American Association for the Advancement of Science (AAAS), Anna Harrison urged the input of scientists in public policy in order to improve the state of the nation and the world.

I support her and others' calls. My concern in this article is with science advice[2] to the US Congress, an area which has often not met with success.[3] Our contemporary situation reflects the poor fit between what is needed by legislators in the way of science advice and what is provided to them. Devising a mechanism for getting good scientific advice to the Congress would mean better policy for two reasons: Congress would have the tools to counterbalance the sometimes incomplete or biased information which the Executive branch provides to it,[4] and would be better equipped to tailor decisions according to the varying needs and situations across the diverse face of America.

I propose that this goal be pursued by getting scientists more involved in Congressional decision-making through voluntary, informal advisory panels

James Everett Katz, a sociologist working for Bell Communications Research (Bellcore), is currently investigating the social impact of technology. During the early 1980s, Dr. Katz served as a staff member of a US Senate committee. He is the author of Presidential Politics and Science Policy, Congress and National Energy Policy, *and several articles on science, technology, and public policy. He received his Ph.D. from Rutgers University and has held fellowships at Harvard and MIT.*

on the local level. But in order for such an idea to work, scientists must be willing to interrupt their studies long enough to bring their talents to bear on the chaotic, rough-and-tumble world of politics. They must come forward, on their own initiative, to offer their service to lawmakers in Congress. It is greatly needed for the following reasons.

The separation of powers is alive and well, meaning that the Executive branch does not necessarily share information with the Legislative branch. It, at times, uses or releases reports for its own or the Administration's purposes. To illustrate, during the debates over the Supersonic Transport Plane and the deployment of the anti-ballistic missile, respectively, certain documents were withheld or selectively released in order to bolster the Administration's position. Another example may be seen in the economic impact statement prepared by the Reagan Administration for the Clinch River Breeder Reactor. Independent scientific groups, such as the Union of Concerned Scientists, evaluated this report and found it highly biased and incomplete.[5] Moreover, in contrast to the Executive branch's multitude of formal science-oriented agencies, commissions, panels and grant and contracting programs, Congress has only three agencies with science and technology components: the Congressional Research Service (CRS), the General Accounting Office (GAO), and the Office of Technology Assessment (OTA).[6] The committee and personal staffs also possess some scientific expertise in some cases.

While each of the Congressional agencies mentioned above is doing an important job with very limited resources, and often provides important scientific analyses and interpretations in a timely manner, their operations are limited by countless rules and regulations. This is especially true for the OTA, which is also the only Congressional staff agency devoted solely to technology policy questions. It is not allowed to respond to requests from individual members, only from its board. Studies done by the OTA can take two to three years, whereas a member of Congress often needs to become informed about and vote upon an issue in a matter of days, sometimes less. Moreover, it is virtually impossible for OTA to provide information about the consequences of decisions for the member's own state or district. (Rarely would an agency researcher be familiar with the local situation of a member's district.)

The GAO and CRS, two other avenues open to Congress members for scientific advice, are thinly staffed for what is required of them. The CRS alone handles about half a million Congressional requests for information each year; it is difficult for CRS staff to focus on long-term questions and national needs since they are constantly "putting out fires." The problem has become exacerbated due to constraints on budgets, which have meant reduced services and lower staffing levels. Moreover, these agencies can become bogged down in day-to-day concerns like any other bureaucracy, reducing their effectiveness for individual members of Congress needing to get expert assistance quickly. Bound by countless rules and procedures, these agencies might be creatures of Congress, but certainly not creatures of individual Congress members. The staffs, like those of OTA, would also be unfamiliar with the specific problems and conditions of a member's district. Consequently they cannot provide the intimate and direct advice so often needed by lawmakers.

The rules governing staff agencies are necessary and proper and the limitations understandable. Yet members of Congress and their staffs do need scientific advice framed within the context of their particular state or district. They need to be alerted to science-based problems *before* they come for vote in Congress and to have technical issues presented in a way that makes sense to their unique position as elected representatives of particular districts or states. Because of their very nature, the support agencies cannot provide such intimate, direct, and "early warning" advice to lawmakers, nor can they readily report on a situation in a particular district or state.

Another important source of science advice are the specialists on many members' staffs. In fact it has been argued by some that each staff should have a bona fide scientist on its payroll, and there are those that do. The AAAS helps out by providing each year through its Congressional Fellows program a total of one or two staff members to work *gratis* for members of Congress. A few other scientific associations have done the same. But this is an expensive program (both in terms of the direct costs of supporting the Fellow and indirect costs of supporting the staff to solicit applicants, choose the incumbents, and administer the program) and no more than a few of the 535 Congressional offices can be provided for. Further, these Fellows may be unfamiliar with the legislators' districts. While clearly, to varying degrees, the suggestion of having scientific specialists on staff has been sporadically adopted, in my experience those who plan to stay in Congressional staff positions quickly "go native." The prospects are not good for professional scientists who become staff members in terms of retaining their standing with their fellow researchers. One study shows that the more involved in politics a scientist becomes the more he or she is looked down upon by colleagues who are still active in research.[7] But more important is that, shortly after arriving on Capitol Hill, these individuals usually become operators, just like any other staff member. They become socialized into the culture of Capitol Hill and in a sense are captured by the Capitol Hill process. Partly they are forced to do this. If they continued to talk and act like scientists, no one would listen to them. Thus they would be ineffective.[8]

Of course Congress is a Legislative branch, and not charged with carrying out directives or administering programs, so it has little to gain and much to lose by having a large bureaucracy of its own. My argument is that the dearth of guidance it receives on science and technology matters can be corrected through supplementation. A role should be created for scientists that would permit them, as it were, to put one foot into the political arena while keeping the other foot—and most of the weight—in the scientific arena. This new role would permit them to contribute to effective science advising while retaining their primary allegiance to and attention on scientific research. It could be done specifically in the following manner:

Scientists on an independent, local basis could form small volunteer advisory committees (of perhaps three to seven experts) for their members of Congress, operating closely with members and their staffs in a *confidential*, informal manner. These committees would be drawn from each member's district—from industry, academia, and the public sector. They would be familiar with the unique situation of their particular legislative district. In the very few cases where there are no scientific bodies present in the district, scientists could be drawn from neighboring areas. While each committee would have a permanent core, it could easily be enlarged or reorganized on an *ad hoc* basis for particular issues, *e.g.*, radioactive waste disposal, or for a particular policy area, *e.g.*, nutrition programs. Through their professional network, advisors could contact other specialists and organize into panels on an as-needed basis.

Confidentiality would provide not only a greater latitude of opinion, but also greater flexibility. As circumstances change, so too could the advice of the panel's experts. Since future facts cannot be known, advice from experts about the future is certainly not infallible. With confidentiality and informality, advisors need not be in a position of staking their reputations on a prediction about which, in any event, they cannot have 100% certainty.

There will be temptations on both sides to seek advantages beyond simply providing access to the best possible scientific advice. Legislators may seek endorsements from the scientists and scientists may push for preferential treatment in terms of funding or site selection for research programs. (The relationship between scientists and politicians is already fraught with temptations. To illustrate from my personal experience as a Congressional staff member, I will summarize what happened at a meeting between a prominent scientist from a large university and Congressional staff members who worked for a representative in whose district the university was located. A staff member asked the scientist, "Is there anything our office can do for you in terms of helping your institution get grants?" This is politics "as usual" and quite a different thing than what I am recommending.) My proposal calls for high moral conduct on both sides. Neither side must use this as an opportunity to grind its own ax or the program would fail, with the nation as the loser. I believe a statement of ethics—a code of conduct—should be agreed to between the parties involved. Perhaps the scientific societies would draw up a model set of guidelines, which could be readily adopted by each legislative office and scientist-participants. To show the kind of standards I mean, it is worth relating the response of the scientist to the above-mentioned staffer's overture. The scientist said he was not interested in having funds channeled by means of political leverage to his university, and that, furthermore, he hoped that no staffer could do so. He went on to state that funding for research should be based solely on merit; if this staffer could influence the process, then others could, too, to the disadvantage of those who deserved it based on the intrinsic quality of their work. This statement illustrates the moral posture that I believe the Congressional science advisor should take.

In addition to having the panels be confidential, local, and endowed with a code of ethics, another all-important aspect would be informality. Informality would provide the crucial element of timeliness to the proceedings. We scientists may find it difficult to fully appreciate the time pressures under which members operate; routinely, they are required to make crucial "yea or nay" decisions on issues having to do with science or technology with almost no notice. While we would prefer to "wait until all the facts are in," they must, perforce, come up with a decision, and it would behoove us all if they were able to avail themselves of expert advice beforehand.[9]

The Fellows program of AAAS and other societies is an important step in the right direction and more should be done to bolster this form of public service. Yet it is vital that scientists as individual citizens step forward on their own state or district's behalf, in order to provide direct and personal contact between members of Congress and their district's scientific community.

Doubtless, some members of Congress have little interest in scientific advice, either because they are going to stick to their position no matter what the facts seem to indicate, or because they are afraid of scientists turning against them and embarrassing them in public. But based on my experience as a Congressional staff member, I believe that many members of Congress do wish that they had advisors who could help them sort out the facts, who could tell them—from a relatively objective scientific and technical standpoint—what the situation is, and who did not have self-interested motives behind their reports. These Congressmen and women would welcome such panels. Success will breed growth.

I would mention, in addition, that with more and more programs being developed and implemented at the state level, state legislators might wish to consider a similar advisory mechanism to assist their deliberations as well.

NOTES

1. The views expressed in this article are those of the author and may not reflect those of Bell Communications Research or its owners. I would like to thank Robert E. Kraut and Tom K. Landauer for their helpful comments.

2. I will use the terms "science" and "scientist" to also mean "advanced technology" and "technologists."

3. As illustrations, see Richard Barke, *Science, Technology, and Public Policy,* (Washington, DC: CQ Press, 1986); Harvey Brooks, "The Resolution of Technically Intensive Public-Policy Disputes," *Science, Technology & Human Values* 9:1 (Winter 1984), pp. 39–50; *Science and the Congress,* Third Franklin Conference Proceedings (Philadelphia: Franklin Institute Press, 1978); S. D. Fries, "Expertise Against Politics: Technology as Ideology on Capitol Hill," *Science, Technology & Human Values* 8:3 (1983), pp. 6–15; B. M. Casper, "Rhetoric and Reality of Congressional Technology Assessment," *Bulletin of the Atomic Scientists* 34:2 (1978), pp. 20–31; and Eilene Galloway, "Scientific Advice for Congress," in S. Lakoff, ed., *Knowledge and Power* (New York: Macmillan, 1966), pp. 359–376.

4. For example, see Joel Primack and Frank von Hippel, *Advice and Dissent* (New York: Harper & Row, 1974); and H. L. Nieburg, *In the Name of Science* (New York: Quadrangle, 1966).

5. See James E. Katz, *Presidential Politics and Science Policy* (New York: Praeger, 1978), pp. 188–205; and James E. Katz, "The Uses of Scientific Evidence in Congressional Policy-Making: The Case of the Clinch River Breeder Reactor," *Science, Technology & Human Values,* Winter 1984, pp. 51–62.

6. The National Research Council (NRC) is sometimes requested by Congress to undertake studies; often two years pass between the time the Congressional mandate is issued and a report by the NRC is released. Since any study authorized by Congress is coordinated and administered by an Executive branch agency, and the NRC undertakes study on its own and the Executive branch's behalf, the NRC must be viewed as a governmental—not a Congressional—science advisory service agency. The length of time usually needed by the NRC to fulfill a Congressional request is significant in the light of the recommendation I make later in this article.

7. Daniel Melnick, V. L. Melnick, and H. H. Fudenberg, "Participation of Biologists in the Formulation of National Science Policy," *Federation Proceedings* 35:9 (1976), pp. 1957–1962.

8. For a discussion of the differing ways scientists and politicians look at the world, see James E. Katz, "The Uses of Scientific Evidence in Congressional Policy-Making," *ibid.*

9. My recommendation for informal science advisors is designed only to supplement—not replace—other important sources of Congressional science advice. The other sources are both varied and vital to producing sound policy decisions. Industrial, labor and public interest groups, scientific societies, and the National Research Council are among the many groups which, on their own initiative, bring science advice to Congress and respond to Congressional requests for advice. Occasionally, even individual employees of the Executive branch use back channels and private meetings to provide scientific advice to Congressional offices (advice that is sometimes divergent from the official positions these employees are required to maintain in public statements). Yet almost never do these important sources provide advice tailored to the particular needs of individual members of Congress nor can they do so in the informal manner I am recommending.

Science Advice, Government, Education and the Economy

John Kerry

America's leadership in science and technology is crucial to maintaining a strong competitive posture in the international economy of the future. The federal government, through the NSF and other agencies, plays a very important role in supporting basic research in science and science education, which makes our position of leadership in science and technology possible. The Congress also plays an important part in this process through its functions of oversight, authorization and appropriation.

There is no more critical issue for the future of this nation than the question of how we maintain our tradition of excellence in science and technology, and thus our ability to compete in world markets in the changing and highly competitive environment of the new international economy.

In this context, the role of science advice in government becomes increasingly important. Good science advice is essential to wise decision-making in both the Executive and the Legislative branches of the government. Unfortunately, the position of the President's Science Advisor has become increasingly politicized.

It is no secret to anyone in the scientific community that, in the past few years, the role of the President's Science Advisor has changed that of a distinguished, independent member of the scientific community to that of an advocate of the President's policies, such as the Strategic Defense Initiative, a highly controversial program. Nor is it a secret that loyalty to the SDI program has become a litmus test in choosing a Presidential Science Advisor.

These are not healthy developments for science policy in the United States. The President—and Congress—need to have access to top-quality, unbiased scientific advice from those who can best represent the entire scientific community. We need a Presidential Science Advisor who can best represent the

John Kerry, US Senator from Massachusetts, is a member of the Committee on Commerce, Science and Transportation, and of the Committee on Foreign Relations. Previously, he was Lieutenant Governor of Massachusetts.

431

entire scientific community. We need a Presidential Science Advisor who can follow in the footsteps of James Killian and Jerome Wiesner, not those of Oliver North. It is my hope that we will soon see a return to science advice in the White House which contributes objectively to the thoughtful formulation of national policies.

PARTICULAR CONCERNS

Several recent trends in US science and technology lend a sense of urgency to my concerns. I would single out four areas of particular concern.

First is the eroding base of our university research enterprise. Some of our brightest investigators are being forced to work with outdated equipment in antiquated facilities. Construction and renovation of academic research facilities could amount to from $5 billion to $20 billion over ten to twenty years, according to some estimates. Costs for closing the gap between present university instrumentation and that required to ensure maximum productivity from creative and innovative researchers may alone be as much as $1 billion. In the face of this need, however, we have seen federal obligations for academic research and development plants decrease by 90% (in constant dollars) between 1966 and 1983.

Second is the direction R&D spending has taken during the past two decades. Primary in the significant rise in R&D expenditures over the 1982–86 period has been the major increase in Department of Defense (DoD) support. One major factor has been the rapid increase in funding for the Strategic Defense Initiative (SDI). National Science Foundation Director Erich Bloch recently emphasized that only a little more than a quarter of all federal R&D effort goes into civilian research. Indeed, US civilian R&D, as a percentage of Gross National Product, is now below that of Japan and West Germany. Moreover, as Dr. Bloch also noted, DoD funds are largely directed to shorter term development efforts with roughly only 3% going to basic research.

Third is the growing recognition of the importance of science and technology to economic health, to developing new products, to creating new jobs, and to increasing productivity. This has been dramatically illustrated in my own state of Massachusetts, where our blends of mature industries and high technology enabled the state to weather the recession of the early 1980s and emerge into a period of economic growth.

And fourth is the fact that we stand at the threshold of many exciting developments in fields such as biotechnology, advanced materials, microelectronics, and, perhaps, superconductors. We need to take steps to maintain our position of leadership in these areas. Without support from government, America's high technology industry is in danger of falling behind those of Japan, Europe and the Soviet Union.

NATIONAL SECURITY AND COMPETITIVENESS

Today, our national security strongly depends upon our ability to compete in international markets. That ability, in turn, depends upon a sound research base, which is able to fuel the technology and innovation needed to sustain our economic leadership. In order to maintain our position of leadership, we need strong support for science in the Congress and from the President.

I am encouraged that federal support for the National Science Foundation is scheduled to increase this year and to double over the next five years. The share of research dollars that is devoted to basic civilian research is dropping, however. This is a disturbing trend in light of the concerns I have indicated.

Investment in basic science and engineering is essential to improving our international competitiveness, and to reducing the trade deficit. From our history of support for basic research at America's colleges and universities has come America's history of scientific excellence, technological preeminence, and our many Nobel prizes in science. We need to strengthen support of basic research in science and engineering, we need to attract more young people to science and engineering, and we need to make greater investment in the infrastructure of science and engineering—equipment, instrumentation and facilities.

THE NEED FOR NEW TECHNOLOGIES

In recent years, America has gone from being a creditor nation to being a debtor nation, and one with a growing trade deficit. Trade protectionism is not the answer to this problem. Developing new technology is the only real solution. My own state of Massachusetts has been a leader in the development of new high-technology industry. This is due, in large part, to the spin-off effect from over one hundred colleges and universities located in Massachusetts, including such world-renowned institutions as Harvard and MIT. Joint university-industry partnerships in research are very important to encouraging innovation in technology and continuing the trends which were started along Route 128 in Massachusetts.

One of the most fundamental issues in science and education today is the question of how we can give all our children, regardless of social background, a good opportunity to participate in the modern world of high technology. We must make greater efforts to link the science-rich and science-poor sectors of our society. Women and minorities are greatly underrepresented in science and engineering in the United States. We need to broaden the pool of scientific talent in this nation, both in the interest of equal opportunity and in the interest of science.

We have, in the United States, the largest and most respected scientific community in the world, yet our precollegiate science education is at a low point. We must connect the scientific talent of our universities, colleges, corporate laboratories, and national laboratories with the elementary and secondary schools, thereby strengthening the national capacity for broad education in the physical, biological and behavioral sciences.

Leadership in science and technology is critical to our future as a nation. Good science advice and support for science in government is essential if we as a nation are to remain competitive in the world economy in the future. The President's Science Advisor has a crucial role to play in ensuring that the United States retains its traditional position of leadership in science and technology. We can no longer take this position for granted.

While I am encouraged by the support for science indicated by increases in the NSF budget, I am also mindful that the trends outlined above give rise to serious cause for concern about the direction that US science and technology are taking. Our government must begin a process of addressing these concerns, so that America can remain the world's leader in science and technology. To this end, it is essential that we seek, attract and hold strong independent science and technology advisors at the highest-level organizations in the Executive and Legislative branches of our government—with a maximum of quality and a minimum of politics.

Science and Technology Advice for The President and Congress: The Need for a New Perspective

Robert A. Roe

Scientific and technological expertise and advice have existed at the highest levels of American government since the beginning of our nation's history. Our first President was a civil engineer, and our third, Jefferson, possessed such skill and wisdom in matters of science and technology that his eminence in these areas has become part of our national legend. Despite their own expertise, these two, along with most other American Presidents, sought counsel on science and technology issues.

Today's formal and institutional framework for scientific and technological advice at the government's highest strata is a direct outgrowth of the major role that science and technology played in winning World War II. Nevertheless, more than forty years down the road, it is easy to lose sight of how significant an influence the broad historical context of World War II had on our current conception of science and technology advice.

Franklin Roosevelt's war-time Office of Scientific Research and Development, and its prescient Director, Vannevar Bush, left a remarkable record of achievement. From that emerged, within all branches of the Department of Defense, an indelible stamp of respect for science. Near the close of the war, Bush was commissioned by President Roosevelt to conduct a study of the role and function of science as it relates to the national welfare. When the study's seminal report, *Science: The Endless Frontier,* appeared, the cornerstone was laid for the federal government's support of basic research.

Robert A. Roe has served in the US House of Representatives since 1969. A senior member of the Committee on Science, Space and Technology, he was elected to be its Chairman at the beginning of the 100th Congress. Congressman Roe, trained in engineering, is one of the few members of Congress with a technical background.

During the ensuing five years of debate and discussion, the general configuration of the National Science Foundation emerged and the Organic Act
establishing NSF became law in 1950.

In the same year, William Golden was serving as Special Consultant to
the Director of the Bureau of the Budget to carry out a review of the government's scientific activities at President Truman's request. In a memorandum to the President, he suggested the need for a post of a Science Advisor
to the President. Golden's outline for the primary functions of the Science
Advisor's responsibilities was developed through a series of consensus-building
discussions with scientists and engineers in and out of government, as well
as with non-scientific government officials. Two out of the three primary
functions envisioned for the Science Advisor's role were national security-
related. The Advisor would keep himself informed and current on all R&D
programs of military significance within the various government departments; he would have to be prepared to establish a civilian R&D organization comparable to Roosevelt's war-time office; and he would be responsible for offering advice to the President on scientific matters, especially
those of military significance.

After ideas for the proposed position were debated and discussed, and the
machinations of politics followed their due course, what emerged for that
time was a chairman of a Science Advisory Committee attached to the Office
of Defense Mobilization. This arrangement was effective in 1951 and, given
world events, was a practical and even predictable framework. The Korean
conflict had begun the year before and the struggle between the Communist
and non-Communist worlds was battled out in Asia until the 1953 cease-
fire. The war in Korea surely kept the military importance of science in the
forefront. This recounting is more than historical litany; it describes the root-
ing of Executive science advice, first and firmly, in the national security
arena.

There were only a few years between the end of the Korean War and the
Russian launch of Sputnik in 1957. The superiority of American science
was questioned and the consequent space race between the United States
and Russia found the very same "Cold War" competitors squared-off against
each other—not in military conflict—but involving the same symbolic importance of winning.

From 1951 until the shock of Sputnik, the Science Advisory Committee
remained institutionally associated with the Office of Defense Mobilization.
During this period, however, the Committee developed a growing relationship directly with President Eisenhower. Sputnik was a catalytic event that
compelled the show of prominent and public affirmation that American science was still preeminent. As a consequence, the President elevated the Science Advisory Committee to White House status, converting it into the President's Science Advisory Committee with a first-time, full-time Presidential
Science Advisor.

THE SPACE EFFORT

Space had become, for many people, the primary symbol of world leadership in science and technology. Although the National Aeronautics and Space Administration (NASA) was created as the country's civilian space agency, and the Space Act of 1958 was absolutely explicit that activities in space should be devoted to peaceful purposes for the benefit of all mankind, we were still racing the Russians to get up there.

The next catapulting event occurred in the spring of 1961, when Yuri Gargarin orbited the Earth and returned safely. By late May, President Kennedy made a public commitment for America to land a man on the moon within a decade. This announcement had the profound effect of mobilizing the nation's vast scientific, technical, and engineering resources toward the lunar landing goal; and America reached the moon in the summer of 1969.

In the Eisenhower Administration and the early part of the Kennedy Administration, when the President was able to receive first-hand, personalized science counsel on national problems, the national problems were, for the most part, heavily tilted toward national security issues.

In 1962, the position of the Science Advisor and his staff was moved from the inner circle intimacy of White House staff, where it had existed since 1958, to the larger and less personal arena of the Executive Office. This new arrangement created some formalized protection against potential abolition of the position with changing Administrations, made the position subject to Senate confirmation, made the Advisor available to testify before Congress, but most importantly, moved the Advisor and his staff—the newly created Office of Science and Technology—into an isolated compartment in the long corridor of Executive Office organizations. With this institutional shift came a vastly expanded array of responsibilities, broadly described and perhaps increasingly more difficult to carry out from the less strategic position in the Executive Office.

There was not much time between this change and the abrupt and tragic end of the Kennedy Presidency, the accession of Lyndon Johnson to the White House, and the national embroilment in Vietnam. The Vietnam War consumed much of the attention and energy of President Johnson and of President Nixon during his first term. The conflict in Southeast Asia was divisive for the whole nation and resulted in divided opinions among the scientific community as well. The Science Advisor and his enlarged but more remote organization worked on a variety of important science and technology issues, but matters of military significance were again in the forefront for the nation. There was a growing polarization of ideas and people in the Nixon Administration which increasingly complicated the environment, and in 1973 the President cavalierly abolished the position of Science Advisor, his staff—the Office of Science and Technology—and the Presidential Science Advisory Committee.

A quick scan of this historical context reveals a pattern for roughly the first twenty-two years (1951–1973) of formal science advice to the President that is still not easily recognized from the vantage point of 1987. Despite the fact that the Science Advisor and/or the Science Advisory Committee did not focus solely on issues of military scientific significance, the conception of this advice was crafted from war-time achievement, found its sealegs during the Korean conflict, and landed in the White House for the space race. For the major portion of those twenty-two years, one fundamental historical pattern prevailed. With few respites, America was either involved in armed military conflict in Asia, testing wills with the Soviets over Cuba, or focused on recapturing the science and technology stronghold of space from the Russians.

If a judgment of those first two decades of experience in formal science advice were the object here, the commentary would be highly laudatory of both the outstanding personnel and the unique and professional practice of their advice. The nation had good fortune in having diverse and unusual talent to call upon. Our objective here is different, however. We must be able to read the broader arc of the past as a road map that directs us to the future. From this retrospective observation, we can extract an important and new understanding for the prospective direction of science advice.

NEW CRISES

The tight historical time frame of a series of significant events coalesces with the passage of time. But the year 1973 brought more than the dismantling of the Science Advisor's position and office. In that same year, the nation saw, in rather quick succession, the Arab oil embargo, the resignation of the Vice President, the Watergate Crisis, the completion of US combat troop withdrawal from Vietnam, and a Congressional vote to end the bombing of Cambodia.

The oil embargo was a global event that fundamentally altered both the world balance and perspective. It made 1973 a watershed year. Although hindsight informs us that America made a major shift in 1973, this change did not filter swiftly into the national conscience. The back-to-back events of military disengagement in Southeast Asia and the overnight chaos wrought by the disappearance of our oil supply-lines from the Middle East moved us swiftly from the era of an almost continuous focus on some form of military competition (since World War II) directly into an era of global economic travail. Although the "Energy Crisis" had been waiting in the wings for some time, had been predicted by a fair number of astute observers, and had been the subject of some important studies by the previous Office of Science and Technology as early as the mid-1960s, 1973 marked its crushing debut in the world economy.

Thus, in broad generalization, the first era of "formal science advice" could be termed the "national security era of science advice." The Committee on Science and Technology was the primary force behind the reinstatement of the White House science apparatus. After intensive hearings, the Committee drafted legislation to which the White House, under President Ford, was amenable. When the post of Presidential Science Advisor was reestablished in 1976 with the new Office of Science and Technology Policy, it was set essentially into its previous institutional mold and mission, but it surfaced on a dramatically changed national and international scene.

Economic problems had begun to eclipse military security issues. By the end of 1973, inflation reached an annual rate of 8.8% and represented the largest increase in any year since 1947. The fuel shortages brought on by the embargo caused a sharp drop in demand for gas-guzzling automobiles. The prosperity supported by cheap energy was crumbling, and the ponderous burden of energy costs began to take their toll. The second oil shock in 1979, resulting from the crisis in Iran, saw the Japanese capture roughly 25% of the US auto market.

The re-established Science Advisor's post was filled in early 1977. In the ten years since then, and more accurately from the early 1970s, we have been in an era of increasing economic concerns. Although at the moment inflation and unemployment are down, the enormity of the federal deficit is straining our resources, our trade balance is unfavorable, and many of our strategic industries are struggling to survive.

SEEKING SOLUTIONS

During the decade since 1977, there have been many efforts to find solutions, *i.e.*, the late 1970s Carter Domestic Policy Review on Innovation, the landmark Stevenson-Wydler legislation, the Reagan-appointed Presidential Commission on Industrial Competitiveness, and a recently initiated Study of Technology Policy being conducted by the Committee on Science, Space, and Technology.

The Science Advisor and the OSTP still exist, however, on the periphery of the very issues to which they should be capable of making major contributions. More than ever, there is a need for science and technology advice at the highest levels of government, but the perspective of how that advice fits into the resolution of current national problems needs to be altered.

There is a growing understanding in all sectors that science and technology are components of almost every important issue facing the nation. Yet today, the conception of the role of science and technology advice, and the structure through which that advice must operate, keeps it bound to another era. It is advice that comes to us in isolation rather than in integration with the other factors of which it should be a functioning part.

Historically, and until the mid-1950s, economists used the traditional forces of land, labor and capital to portray and predict economic conditions. To that a fourth force must be added, technology. It is widely held that anywhere from one-third to one-half of all our growth has come from technological progress, and that technology is the main driving force behind long-term economic growth. The new understanding of the role of technology in economic expansion seems to make it both unreasonable and unrealistic to separate the government's most prominent position of scientific and technological advice from the economic planners and predictors.

Today, we are experiencing a rapid shift from a domestic economy/domestic marketplace to the new global economy/global marketplace. Technology has been a major force in bringing about this shift. Technology has brought dramatic change to transportation and communication, and drawn the world's industrial nations into closer proximity. This, in turn, has made three out of the four economic forces, that of labor, capital and technology, more fluid and mobile and thus less confined by national boundaries. What was once considered America's own domestic market is now considered, by the rest of the industrialized world, the choicest territory for selling its wares. The implications of this major economic transition are multifold and require a new perspective of what constitutes science and technology advice in contemporary society.

Almost eight years ago, Lewis Branscomb wrote: "The Science Advisor should be an active participating member of the President's team for addressing public policies for economic matters. . . . Most important, in my view, would be a bridge to the Council of Economic Advisers and the President's Special Trade Representative, as well as to the Treasury. The effectiveness with which the nation's technological capabilities are nurtured and applied, substantially determines domestic economic well-being and foreign trade competitiveness." This commentary was insightful and visionary almost a decade ago. Now it is practical guidance that can help us redefine our conception of what science and technology advice should encompass, as well as what it might be expected to help us accomplish.

At this juncture, however, I would be averse to recommending any specific institutional changes until this new perspective could be comprehensively explored through a series of hearings that the Committee on Science, Space, and Technology would conduct in order to gather expert opinions from diverse constituencies on the subject. It would be necessary to elicit opinions from representatives of the economic, financial, industrial, academic and governmental communities, as well as from the traditional science and engineering communities.

When approaching such a task, it is important to keep in sharp focus that whenever change is proposed, the objective and direction of that change should be carefully questioned and clearly understood. For the nation, excellence in science and technology is a goal, not for mere prize-winning incidents or experiences, but more importantly for what it represents in terms of sustaining economic health and maintaining national security; and our most secure national defense resides primarily in a stable economy capable of responding to any critical national need. Well-positioned and integrated science and technology advice can provide us with the long-range perspective that is frequently absent in national planning.

THE ADVISORY PROCESS

The process of providing this advice to the President, on one hand, and to the Congress, on the other, must be understood as two separate and distinct issues. In order to be effective, the advice must be carefully adapted to the unique nature of the branch concerned. The Executive branch is focused toward the central figure of the President. No matter how the information and advice is formulated, it is eventually directed to a singular focus. It is here that we must elevate as well as integrate the role that science and technology play. Only in this way can we reap their benefits for our long-term objectives. We cannot realize our expectations for economic growth if we isolate and ignore one of the most formidable forces of that growth.

Providing science and technology advice to the Congress is, in many ways, a more complex problem. Any advice to the Congress must evolve from the understanding that although the term "Congress" suggests a collective disposition, the national legislature was designed institutionally to represent population segments and geographical sections. In Congress, there is no center or focal point. No advice can be directed toward the Congress in totality. Nevertheless, the configuration of the Congress can lend itself to advice at several levels. Individual members of both the House and Senate can be informed and counseled by frequent contact with prominent scientists, engineers and economists in their own constituencies. It is important that the contact not emanate from crisis advice, but rather evolve from regular, informal visits or communication. The committees and subcommittees on which members serve provide a second level of opportunity for science and technology information, perspective, and impact. This can occur by assembling staff with broad expertise, and by tapping our great public informational and advisory reservoir through the Congressional hearing process. Hearings provide an environment where the diverse aspects of an issue can be explored and debated. Dissimilar disciplines and divergent views provide an important perspective for policy decisions.

The Office of Technology Assessment, which was established specifically to assess the impact of technology, provides yet another level and aspect of science and technology counsel to members of Congress. On the roster of government organizations, the OTA is still relatively new, but its reputation for highly competent analysis has created increasing requests for its work from an ever broader circle of members.

Since there are so few members of Congress who have either a scientific or technical background, members must develop sensitivity for the integral and substantial role of science and technology through repeated and often random exposure to this reality. This places a significant reponsibility on representatives of the scientific and technical community, utilizing especially their professional organizations.

Fundamentally, Congress is advised through its individual members, and then through the workings of the committee system. It may appear at first glance an uneven process of miscellaneous exposures. The problem of integrating scientific and technological information with other information, both general and specialized that members of Congress must assimilate, is a microcosm of the larger task of serving in the Congress. Each member will perceive the responsibility differently and perform the task accordingly. It is indicative of the great potpourri that we call democracy.

Our past experience with science advice is primarily concerned with counsel to the Executive branch where the advice can be centralized and focused. The dispersed and diffused composition of Congress does not lend itself to singular proposals or arrangements. Those concerned about science advice might be wise to accept and respect that eventuality.

The wisdom of the Founding Fathers in creating three distinctly unique branches of our government is manifest. They not only intended to create a separation of powers, but also a subtle mixture of composition and control. The bicentennial endurance of their creation becomes the strongest judgment of their work. In addressing this new perspective for science and technology advice, we, as planners and proposers of change, should begin from this fundamental understanding.

Fulfilling the Science and Technology Advisory Needs of Congress

Jeffrey K. Stine

Obtaining reliable and independent advice on scientific and technological issues has been of growing importance to the US federal government since World War II. Despite the distinct needs of all three branches of government, most observers and commentators have concentrated on the advisory apparatus available to the President. The experience of advising the Executive Office on matters of science and technology has, therefore, set the standard model for providing such advice to the Congress and to the Judiciary, but, although a central office of science and technology advice may be appropriate for the Executive branch, it is not necessarily appropriate for the other two branches of government. The differing functions, compositions and organizations of the three branches demand advisory systems sensitive to particular characteristics and needs. The mechanisms adopted by the Congress are illustrative of this point, for its multilayered and seemingly disconnected advisory system has, by and large, worked.

Through the 1950s, although it had a Legislative Reference Service (established in 1914 within the Library of Congress) through which members could obtain specialized information on political, economic, and cultural matters, Congress tended to use scientific and technical information provided by the Executive branch agencies. This channel supplemented committee hearings, where experts representing various interests were asked to testify. Following the launch of *Sputnik* and the establishment of the National Aeronautics and Space Administration in 1958, the need for specialization became more apparent. In response, Congress formed the House

Jeffrey K. Stine is an independent consultant, specializing in the history of science and technology. He served as an American Historical Association Congressional Fellow with the House Committee on Science and Technology (1984–85), where he wrote A History of Science Policy in the United States, 1940–1985 *(1986), the first background report for the Committee's Science Policy Task Force.*

Committee on Science and Astronautics and the Senate Committee on Aeronautical and Space Science to deal with space and science issues. This reorganization had important ramifications for the formation of federal science policy (previously the domain of the Executive branch); for, prior to this time, Congress had had no vehicle for reviewing the government's overall research program or for discussing unified, systematic approaches to solving the nation's scientific research problems or setting national science and technology policy.

The creation of the Presidential Office of Science and Technology in 1962 and the growing magnitude of federal support for science and technology simply intensified Congress's need for its own bipartisan advisory system. In 1963, a bill to create a Congressional Science Advisory Staff was introduced in the House of Representatives, and in the Senate a bill was introduced to establish a Congressional Office of Science and Technology. Although these initial attempts to institute a special staff of Congressional science advisors failed, they expressed deep-seated concern within the Congress, and a different approach was taken the following year. The Legislative Reference Service (later renamed the Congressional Research Service) established a Science Policy Research Division in 1964. The new division could provide both quick responses and in-depth studies in response to Congressional requests, and it immediately began hiring its own scientific and technical experts. Other divisions within the CRS also made occasional contributions to science and technology advice when appropriate. In addition, the House Committee on Science and Astronautics added to its professional staff and assembled a Research Management Advisory Panel made up of experts from across the country.

THE NAS ROLE

Congress also began to turn to the National Academy of Sciences for independent advice on matters dealing with science and technology. From its inception during the Civil War, the Academy had advised the federal government upon request, but such work had heretofore been oriented primarily toward the Executive branch. In 1961, the Academy established the Committee on Government Relations (renamed Committee on Science and Public Policy [COSEPUP] in 1963) as a means of expanding its participation in the formation of national science policy and to provide advice concerning the status and needs of particular scientific disciplines. Under the chairmanship of George B. Kistiakowsky, a former Science Advisor to Presidents Eisenhower and Johnson, COSEPUP cultivated close working relations with several federal agencies and departments, and began preparing a number of detailed studies at their request. The Academy leadership was also interested in improving its organization's relations with Congress, especially in light of a desire to enlarge the Academy's science policymaking role. A formal agreement was reached in December 1963 in which the National Academy of Sciences would advise the Congress on science policy issues. More specifically, it was decided that COSEPUP would undertake a series of studies for the House Subcommittee on Science, Research and Development which would be financed by and made available to Congress. As a result of this arrangement, three studies were ultimately prepared.

Despite the usefulness of these studies and the link to the scientific community which COSEPUP offered Congress, close and sustained working relations between COSEPUP and Congress were never developed, primarily because COSEPUP and the National Academy of Sciences had continued their Executive branch orientation. Key COSEPUP and Academy members maintained strong ties (official and unofficial) with numerous executive agencies and advisory groups, and conducted a multitude of studies for these organizations. As a consequence, it was difficult for COSEPUP to remain completely impartial and detached when working for Congress. In addition, the requirement that Congress reimburse the Academy for studies done by COSEPUP made it administratively difficult for individual committees to maintain a continuous relationship with COSEPUP because funds for such external advice were not a normal part of a committee's budgetary authority.

The Congressional need for science and technology advice expanded further during the late 1960s as society grew increasingly concerned about the unanticipated environmental, social and economic consequences of new technologies. Many members of the technical community were optimistic that such consequences could be systematically forecast. To avail itself of advice concerning the potential ramifications of new technologies, Congress established the Office of Technology Assessment (OTA) in October 1972. OTA was organized so that its permanent staff could be supplemented through the liberal use of outside consultants, contractors, and advisory panels. This structure allowed it to tap the nation's top scientific and technical experts for in-depth analyses. As Congress expanded its oversight function over the Executive branch agencies during the 1970s and 1980s, it relied increasingly on the independent science and technology expertise provided it by CRS and OTA, and, to a lesser extent, on the appropriate offices of the other Congressional support agencies—the General Accounting Office and the Congressional Budget Office. Occasional and more limited input was also provided by two other Congressional groups—the Environmental and Energy Study Conference and the Congressional Clearinghouse for the Future.

All these groups now provide Congress with reliable and relatively unbiased presentations of what is or is not known about a particular science or engineering topic. But the most effective means for Congressional Members to attempt to understand a scientific or technical problem or recommendation—and especially the debate over such problems and recommendations—remains the committee hearing, where members control who testifies and can ask their own questions according to their own level of understanding or their own interests. Although the hearing process offers important opportunities for gaining information and advice, its effectiveness is dependent upon sound preparation—largely the responsibility of Congressional staff members, who are engaged in selecting topics for hearings, selecting and sequencing the witnesses, briefing members and formulating questions to be asked the witnesses, and drafting follow-up questions. Staff members also help summarize hearings, and draft and revise legislation. It is thus the staff who, behind the scenes, helps frame the debate and helps put Congressional Members at ease with scientific and technical issues. Because the permanent staff forms the heart of the Congressional science and technology advisory apparatus, it is imperative that Congress continue to be able to attract scientifically and technically trained individuals to assist it. Yet the practical demands of research careers, academic tenure, or industrial competitiveness can frequently discourage scientists, social scientists, and engineers from taking such posts.

THE FELLOWSHIP PROGRAM

One method for providing Congress with a fresh, rotating supply of scientifically and technically trained staff members is the Congressional Fellowship program, which allows participants to spend a year on Capitol Hill. Several professional societies—including the American Chemical Society, the American Geophysical Union, the American Physical Society, the American Psychological Association, and the Society for Research in Child Development—participate in this program, which began in 1973 and is administered by the American Association for the Advancement of Science, a pioneer in the program. Fellows come from universities and private industry, and range from physicists fresh from a post doc to full professors in child psychology. Each participating society sponsors one or more persons to serve on a Congressional staff for one year. Although many former Fellows have stayed on or returned to Washington, most return to their universities or companies, thus helping to extend informal advisory networks to the Congress.

To fulfill its funding and oversight roles properly, Congress must have its own bipartisan science and technology advisory apparatus, free of agency or disciplinary bias. It should not, and cannot, be expected to rely on the expert advice of the Executive agencies on which it must keep both a critical and nurturing eye. This need for an independent advisory system seems best met through refinement and improvement in the existing multilayered approach.

Science Advice to the Congress: The Congressional Science and Engineering Fellows Program

Michael L. Telson and Albert H. Teich

This paper is intended to provide a brief introduction to the history and contributions of the Congressional Science and Engineering Fellows Program. Since 1973, this program has given scientists and engineers the opportunity to spend a year serving as professional staff members in the offices of Senators or Representatives or on Congressional committees. The fellowships are sponsored by a number of scientific and engineering societies. The American Association for the Advancement of Science (AAAS) serves as a coordinating body, sponsoring two Fellows and providing an "umbrella" for the programs of the other societies.

The paper first reviews the context in which the program was created in the early 1970s, and the personalities and events that led to appointment of the first group of Fellows in 1973. It then describes the nature of the program as it now exists and explains briefly how it works. It discusses ways in which the program has made a difference—particularly the network of former Fellows who have stayed on as Congressional staff, or are working in other areas of government. Finally, it touches on the future potential of the program.

BACKGROUND

The role of Congressional staff has changed enormously since the early 1970s. The most obvious change is the dramatic increase in numbers—from

Michael L. Telson is the energy and science analyst for the Committee on the Budget of the US House of Representatives. He was an AAAS Congressional Fellow with the Senate Energy Committee in 1973–74.

Albert H. Teich is the head of the Office of Public Sector Programs at the American Association for the Advancement of Science. This office is primarily responsible for running the Congressional Fellows Program.

The views expressed in this paper are those of the authors and do not necessarily represent those of their respective employers.

about 11,000 in 1970 to 19,600 in 1987. (These numbers reflect committee and members' staff only, and do not include such Congressional support agencies as The Library of Congress, the Government Printing Office, the Congressional Budget Office, and the Office of Technology Assessment.) There are many reasons for this change, but most observers believe that a central factor was the desire on the part of Congress to counteract what its members perceived as the growth of Presidential power and initiative and the consequent decline in the role of the Legislative branch. Congress, it was felt, lacked access to the kind of specialized expertise available to the Executive branch, and more staff was needed to give it a source of independent advice and judgment. (Ultimately, these concerns also led to the establishment of the Office of Technology Assessment and the Congressional Budget Office.)

This concern coincided, in the early 1970s, with a decline in the seniority system and a rebellion by younger members of the House of Representatives who sought to wrest some of the power from entrenched committee chairmen. As a consequence, many new subcommittees were created and the power of the full committee chairmen was reduced. The increased dispersion of power required new staff for the new centers of power. At the same time, the importance of science and technology in public affairs was growing at a rapid pace, and both political leaders and members of the science and engineering communities were becoming increasingly concerned about Congress's perceived weakness in this area.

ORIGINS OF THE PROGRAM

It was in this period of ferment that the AAAS became actively interested in creating a Congressional Fellows program—an idea that had surfaced occasionally at AAAS Board and staff meetings for some years. Scientists had a long tradition of offering science advice to the Executive branch of government—one that had become especially strong during World War II and was greatly strengthened in the aftermath of Sputnik. Scientists had relatively little experience in working with Congress, however. By the early 1970s, the Nixon Administration had become rather disenchanted with the formal science advisory process, allowing it to languish and eventually abolishing the White House science office entirely. The attitude of the Administration, combined with the ascendance of Congressional power, provided a favorable climate for the creation of a Congressional Fellows program— one that would help scientists better communicate with the Legislative branch of government.

The American Society of Mechanical Engineers (ASME), the Institute of Electrical and Electronics Engineers (IEEE) and the American Physical Society (APS) were entertaining similar thoughts at that time, and they joined with AAAS to create the program and appoint the first "class" of Fellows in 1973. Several people played important roles in this effort, including AAAS members Joel Primack of the University of California at Santa Cruz and Frank Von Hippel of Princeton, who had studied the role of scientists in the political arena and subsequently published a book on the subject; AAAS treasurer William T. Golden, who had long been involved in providing science advice at the White House; and AAAS staff member Richard A. Scribner, whose responsibilities included public affairs.

Primack and Von Hippel, together with William Drayton, began the process of locating potential Fellows. Golden anonymously contributed the initial funding which made it possible for the program to go forward. Scribner, with the guidance and encouragement of AAAS Executive Officer William Bevan, as well as President Leonard Rieser and Chairman Glenn Seaborg, energetically developed the program. Seven Fellows were placed in Congressional offices in the fall of 1973, three by AAAS (including one of the authors of this article, Telson), two by APS, and one each by IEEE and ASME.

From the beginning, the program was viewed as having multiple objectives:

- to create a cadre of Congressional staff who would understand science and engineering, and who would enhance the capabilities of Congress to deal with these issues;
- to create a group of scientists/engineers who would learn the ways of Congress, and return to the science/engineering community at large and help that community improve its abilities to affect public policy;
- to expose Congressional staff and members of Congress to ways of thinking in scientific/engineering fields; and
- to make it easier for the general scientific and engineering communities to deliver their messages to Congress more effectively, by achieving the prior objectives.

AAAS, which had long seen itself as a convening and coordinating body for its nearly 300 affiliates, agreed to assume responsibility for coordinating the fellowship programs of the other scientific and engineering societies, for organizing an orientation program for the Fellows, for identifying opportunities in members' offices and on committee staffs, and for helping to match the individual Fellows to the most appropriate opportunities. The orientation program was intended to last about two weeks and to provide an introduction to the Washington policy scene, its institutions, actors, issues and processes. The societies decided that the fellowships would last for a one-year period in a single office, rather than being split into two terms of six months—one in the House and one in the Senate—as was done in the pre-existing American Political Science Association Congressional Fellowship Program.

THE PRESENT PROGRAM

At present (1986–1987), the AAAS Fellows program consists of twenty-two Fellows working in Congressional offices (with an additional twelve "Science, Engineering and Diplomacy Fellows" in an analogous program sponsored by the State Department and the Agency for International Development). The twenty-two Fellows are sponsored by thirteen different scientific and engineering societies. AAAS continues to serve as the "umbrella" organization, while sponsoring two Fellows of its own.

AAAS receives about sixty applications each year, and interviews about eight finalists in the Spring. The AAAS Fellows receive a stipend of $26,500 per year from the Association, plus nominal moving and travel costs. Occasionally this is supplemented by sabbatical pay from the Fellow's home institution. The Congressional office in which the Fellow is placed does not pay the Fellow.

Fellows arrive in Washington for the two-week orientation program early in September, after which they interview with a number of Congressional offices and arrange their placements. The orientation period includes meetings with Congressional staff and members touching on most aspects of Congressional activities. One indication of the program's success is the fact that demand for Fellows from Congressional offices is strong and has grown year by year, far exceeding the number of fellowships. Most Fellows, in deciding where they will serve for the year, are able to choose from among offers from several offices.

HAS THE PROGRAM MADE A DIFFERENCE?

There is little doubt that the program has made a difference in relations between the scientific and engineering communities and the Congress. Between September 1973 and August 1987, some 402 Fellows have gone through the Congressional and Diplomacy Fellows programs. Among these alumni (excluding the most recent class), twenty-two are now working in Congressional staff positions; eighteen are at the Congressional Office of Technology Assessment (OTA); fifty-five are in the Executive branch of the federal government; seventy-two are in private industry; ninety-five are in academic posts; and 104 are in other positions.

The program's objectives, as listed previously, have been well served. Relations between Congress and the scientific and engineering community are on a much different plane today than they were in 1973. Communication is easier and much more frequent. There are a substantial number of Congressional staff (including former Fellows and others) who came from the scientific and engineering communities. There are also a large number of Fellows who have been through the program and who have returned to research and administrative careers in universities, industrial laboratories, and other institutions, enriched by the experience and able to assist their colleagues in making their voices heard in Washington. And, significantly, there are now a great many Congressional staff and members of Congress who have had the experience of working closely with technically trained individuals, and gained a better sense of how to integrate scientific and technical judgments with other considerations in dealing with public policy issues.

It is also worth noting that several former Fellows hold very responsible positions in the Congress and the Executive branch. For example, Leonard Weiss (IEEE, 1975/76) is now staff director of the Senate Committee on Governmental Affairs; Paul Gilman (AAAS, 1978/79) is administrative assistant to Senator Pete V. Domenici (R-NM); and Andrea King (American Philosophical Association, 1984/85) is administrative assistant to Representative Richard Gephardt (D-MO). Also, Thomas E. Cooper (ASME, 1975/76) has been Assistant Secretary of the Air Force for R&D; and Alton Keel (American Institute of Aeronautics and Astronautics, 1977/78) has been deputy director of the National Security Council and is at present US Ambassador to NATO; while Frederick Bernthal (APS, 1978/79) is a commissioner on the US Nuclear Regulatory Commission.

Former Fellows are now also at the Office of Management and Budget (OMB), where Norine Noonan (American Chemical Society, 1982/83) is acting chief of the Science and Space Branch, and Jack Fellows (American Geophysical Union, 1983/84) is the examiner for the National Science Foundation. Other alumni serve on the staffs of the House Budget; Education and Labor; Energy and Commerce; Rules; and Science, Space and Technology Committees; the Senate Energy Committee; the Joint Economic Committee; and in the offices of Senators D'Amato (R-NY), Glenn (D-OH), Harkin (D-IA), Inouye (D-HI) and Simon (D-IL), as well as Representatives Brown (R-CO), Dymally (D-CA), Gregg (R-NH) and Schneider (R-RI).

These individuals, along with the other Fellows who have gone through the program, represent an important resource to the scientific and engineering communities, as well as to the federal government and to the nation at large. While Fellows' interests include technical subjects, the most successful often go far beyond these limits into a wide range of subjects of concern to their members or committees. Fellows provide technical expertise and judgment to their members and committees, helping them deal more effectively with technically based issues. Their knowledge and contacts also help the Fellows bring to the surface issues of scientific and technical interest and get these issues on the Congressional agenda. Fellows have served as points of contact in members' offices for scientific institutions in the members' states or districts, and have participated in developing initiatives that serve scientific ends as well as constituent needs.

FUTURE POTENTIAL

The Fellows program has made a clear difference in all of the areas mentioned previously. Can it continue to make a contribution? The answer is clearly "yes." The problems are far from solved. The number of technically based issues facing the nation—from SDI to economic competitiveness to AIDS—is growing daily and the need for technically trained staff is growing in tandem. The number of new Fellows arriving each year and remaining on the Hill is barely sufficient to offset losses to attrition.

Many parts of the Congress are just beginning to recognize the need for science and engineering Fellows. The past year (1986/87) marked the first time a Fellow had served with the Speaker of the House. No Fellow has yet served on the Appropriations Committee in either house. Each year the program seeks to enlarge the scope of its placements while continuing to place Fellows in those offices that have made good use of them in the past.

The orientation program alone is of great utility. It affords an opportunity for those involved with the program to keep in touch with Congressional concerns on a yearly basis. This includes the Fellows and alumni, as well as the participating societies and their staffs. The orientation provides the new Fellows with an intimate view of the Washington policy environment, and reminds those in the environment of the quality of the Fellows and the value of the program as a whole.

There is much work yet to be done. The benefits of the program are regarded by many as an exponential function of the number of Fellows that have been through it, and as it grows, the program continues to evolve. New societies join the program, taking the place of those that have chosen to discontinue their fellowship activities. A significant step took place in 1986 with the publication, by AAAS, of a directory of former Fellows, and the subsequent formation by a number of former Fellows of an "alumni association." As the program approaches the middle of its second decade, AAAS and the other sponsoring societies can be proud of their achievements, but they can ill afford to slacken their efforts.

PART 3

JUDICIARY

Science and Technology Advice in the Judiciary

Danny J. Boggs

It is a commonplace that our society is becoming increasingly technological and scientific, and that it is becoming increasingly litigious. The increase in the supply of lawyers over the period 1970–85 was about as rapid as the increase in scientists. Thus, the interplay between these two burgeoning fields is likely to be very important in the waning years of the second millennium and into the third.

In addressing this interplay, and asking the question how judges are to obtain, analyze and use for decision scientific information and judgment, we must keep in mind the type of decisions judges are called on to make. Those decisions may have far reaching impact, but they arise in the context of a particular case. Judges are not usually asked to decide, for example, whether the one-hit model of cancer causation is correct or not. Instead, we are asked to decide whether exposure to a *particular* agent caused *this person's* cancer. The case-specific nature of our law is both its glory and the despair of systematizers. Anyone can bring a suit, if they feel aggrieved. No research model is required. At the same time, courts have no power to act in the absence of such a suit. Thus, judicial intervention and decision will always appear haphazard in contrast to the type of agenda the Executive and Legislative branches can pursue.

This leads to recasting our question as two. What kind of scientific and technological questions should we (and do we) ask courts to solve? And how can courts best acquire the type of knowledge that allows them to do their best at answering the questions?

Many of the most noted science-related cases have come out of review of federal regulations. Perhaps maddeningly to scientists, such cases are

Danny J. Boggs is a Judge of the US Court of Appeals for the Sixth Circuit. Previously, he had extensive experience in the federal government: as Deputy Secretary of the Department of Energy; as Special Assistant to the President; as Assistant to the Solicitor General, Department of Justice; and in other capacities. He also served in the Kentucky government, and engaged in the private practice of law.

455

generally not supposed to turn on the ultimate "truth" of the scientific judgment reached by the regulating agency. That is a judgment for the agency itself to make. The judicial function is primarily to assure that prescribed procedures have been followed, though such procedures generally include a requirement that the decision be a "reasoned" one. Thus, if the agency has strayed too far from what the reviewing court thinks the science supports, it may find such a decision not "reasoned."

For the most part, however, scientific questions arise from a court's familiar function of fact-finding, though now the facts have become much more complicated and elusive. It is no longer "Did Smith hit Jones?" or was a certain machine defective. These questions may have involved some technical knowledge, but were amendable to decisions by processes that seem familiar. The classic statement of this use of technical evidence was in *Frye v. United States,* a 1923 case where scientific evidence was ruled admissible when it was "deduced from a well-recognized scientific principle or discovery, . . . sufficiently established to have gained general acceptance in the particular field. . . ." With the profusion of new scientific knowledge and increasing controversy over what techniques are accepted in the field, we have moved to a new level of complexity in courts' addressing of scientific issues and in their need for scientific advice.

In theory, at least, a federal trial judge's ability to obtain information and judgment is almost unlimited (and most states follow the Federal Rules). He may appoint his own expert witnesses (Rule 706 of the Federal Rules of Evidence), allow reports and tests of many types to be admitted as evidence, and otherwise overcome any obstacles to placing before him (or a jury, should the rules and/or the choice of the parties result in a jury) any evidence needed.

USE OF INFORMATION

At the trial level, the more compelling question is what is he to do with this information. Let me contrast two recent trials before Federal judges: *Wells v. Ortho,* concerning a charge that spermicides caused birth defects, and *Johnston v. United States,* concerning a charge that low-level radiation from radium paint in aircraft dials caused cancer. (*Wells* is printed in volume 615, page 262, of the Federal Supplement, a set of books reporting decisions of federal trial courts. *Johnston* is printed at volume 597, page 374.)

Judge Shoob, in Georgia, found that the spermicide was the cause of the birth defects. Judge Kelly, in Kansas, found that low-level radiation was not the cause of the injury claimed there. Judge Shoob ruled against what a poll of scientists in the field would probably would have said. Judge Kelly ruled in the same direction as the majority of experts in the field. Yet each made full use of the panoply of powers indicated above. They both heard extensive evidence and made a decision based on their understanding of the science and the credibility of the witnesses. From a process point of view, they did the best that was available under our system. Undoubtedly, some commentators will think one or the other (though probably rarely both) was wrong. The fact that most observers will tend to lean in the direction of either generally greater sympathy to claims of injury in the face of disputed scientific evidence or greater skepticism in the face of the same evidence should alert us to the fact that it is not a simple "scientific" question that we face, though scientific evidence may well be relevant.

One commentator (Wendy Wagner, in Yale Law Journal, volume 96, page 428 [1986]) calls such questions "trans-science."[1] Commentators such as Bernard Cohen and Bruce Ames often rank certain controversial risks with homely comparisons to the risk from gaining one ounce of weight or eating one teaspoon of peanut butter. To some these comparisons are compelling. To others, even so apparently insignificant a risk is repugnant if imposed on the unwilling or unknowing, and thus those who are imposing should be liable if there is any colorable basis that the risk resulted in harm.

These latter judgments are peculiarly legislative, and legislatures could do much more to ease the lot of judges, and make decision more transparent and rational. To make an analogy, courts could take evidence and strain to ascertain a safe driving speed in good conditions in each individual auto accident case. But legislatures have given us a standard, by setting speed limits. At least in standard conditions, you can't argue that driving within the speed limits is dangerous (and driving above the limits is usually strong evidence of negligence). Many of the individual scientific issues addressed by courts could be addressed legislatively. Exposure to asbestos for over "x" years could trigger liability. Exposure to radiation below "y" could be conclusively not a basis for suit. Courts could then play their more traditional fact-finding and rule-applying role with greater precision and guidance to the conduct of others. This has been done in areas such as Black Lung Disease, where most decisions are made by reference to standards set by the legislature.

McCleskey v. Kemp, a recent landmark Supreme Court case (reported in volume 55 of the periodical *United States Law Week,* p. 4537), dealt with a mathematical study purporting to show that race (of the victim, not the criminal) affected imposition of the death penalty for murder. Although this seems like science also, such a study could rarely be affirmatively conclusive, because there may be factors that we haven't considered. And it can't really be negatively conclusive either, because you may explain away differences by adding factors, but maybe those explanations aren't the real ones. Which returns you to meta-issues such as whether *any* distortion or disparity is tolerable, is the death penalty intolerable *a priori,* or is it *a priori* tolerable as a democratic decision (the ultimate decision reached by the majority of the Supreme Court).

CONSTITUTIONAL ISSUES

Constitutional issues are different, precisely because they are not susceptible to resolution by the clean cut of the legislative sword. If the Supreme Court says a result is compelled or forbidden by the Constitution, only the extraordinarily difficult process of Constitutional amendment can change the decision. We must begin from a document largely constructed 200 years ago. Whether a judge is an "interpretivist" or an "expansionist," you have to start with the Constitution. A judge may limit his consideration to the words, history or structure of the Constitution (as in an article by Robert Bork, in the Fall 1971 Indiana Law Review, p. 1) or go to the spirit, values or penumbras of it, but the judge still must start with the document. And it says virtually nothing directly relevant. In the entire text, there is scarcely a word, other than the Patents Clause, that appears to recognize any special place, rules or problems arising from science. Yet the old concepts have to try to reach new issues.

Such questions include *what* is life and, now that it can be "made," is making it a "useful art" or "science" under the Patents Clause. In a case called *Diamond v. Chakrabarty,* (printed in volume 447 of the United States Reports, p. 303), the Supreme Court said yes. They include issues of conception and life in *Roe v. Wade,* the abortion case, and issues of when does death occur. Many of these are not strictly "scientific" issues. Instead, they are problems that may have been implicit or hidden in the past but have become visible or salient because we can now know and do things we could previously only guess at or imagine. We can create in fact the dilemmas that were once only law school hypotheses or bull-session chatter. Issues like neomorts, the use of fetal brain tissue, or frozen embryo conception arise from science, but are not scientific questions in the same sense as risk analyses. Science can tell us how a six-week fetus differs from a 36-week one by all kinds of scientific and physical measurements, but it can't tell us when life begins.

But, as courts are asked to make frontier-type decisions, science can play a role in telling us some of the likely consequences or possibilities of a decision either way. If you believe that man must not alter the gene pool of other creatures, the ice-minus experiments must be stopped, but not for any "scientific" reason. If you think a current experiment looks harmless, but are simply troubled about where it might lead, science may be able to add something.

A word on appellate courts. The Supreme Court and the Circuit Courts of Appeals (where I sit) are not just a larger group of judges answering the same questions. We're supposed to look at the *standards* of law, and less at the *application*. We have a firm principle that the trial court (or jury) finds the facts, and we just see if they applied the right law. But there's a catch (there always is, in law.)[2] If those findings are "clearly erroneous," we can overturn them. How then are we supposed to get the scientific information and wisdom to do that?

It can come from trial itself. We can see obvious errors in the arguments and analysis at trial. We can read the science ourselves, and try to judge. But should there be another trial or argument before us just on the science? Can you have non-lawyers argue the science? That has not usually been allowed, and if the real skill involved is argument, not science, that might not really help. There is a real reluctance in higher courts, unable to devote the time the trial court did, to overturn uncertain judgments. That was probably why the higher courts all let *Wells* stand, though it has been much criticized.

Bad scientific decisions by individual courts aren't fatal to scientific advance, or the social good; they just may slow things down a bit. The Legislative branch can always step in and make sweeping decisions to avoid difficulties raised by courts. I think, however, we could allow reviewing courts more latitude, if they chose, in scientific cases. This could be done by statute, allowing them to conduct their own mini-trial, taking evidence and opinion, with a more expansive review of lower court findings that rest on basic scientific issues.

THE QUALIFICATIONS

So the question returns to *who* judges, not just *how*. Are all judges equally qualified to decide scientific questions? Although cases are generally assigned by a random process among a number of trial judges, there is an informal adjustment process. Chief judges at times do seem to assign or transfer cases informally to those who can handle them best. This could be done more fully and systematically by establishing some basis in court rules. This does not mean that only or predominantly scientifically trained judges should be used for this task, merely that those who feel better qualified to assess scientific controversy, or who are so judged by their peers, should be given those tasks.

I conclude by noting that obtaining the proper relationship between courts and scientific issues is not primarily one of the technicalities of science advice. As I have tried to demonstrate, there are many ways for judges to get advice, but there is always the primary question of the attitude and philosophy of the decision maker. Just as there have always been plenty of sources of advice on morality, philosophy, economics and social thought, yet judges have frequently made decisions that seemed wrong to some, merely extensive exposure to even the best scientific thinking will not inevitably lead to an indisputably correct result. The most we can do is to try to improve the processes for the presentation of scientific material and the willingness and ability of judges to assess them as fairly and knowledgeably as possible from a lay prospective.

NOTES

1. Derived from Alvin Weinberg of Oak Ridge National Laboratory, "such questions . . . seemingly are part of science, yet in fact transcend science, . . ." *Science,* Vol. 174 (1971), pp. 546–47.
2. Harry Kalven, a great law teacher and constitutional scholar, said that the law is "analytically dense" in the same sense that there is a mathematical concept of the "density" of a set of numbers. That is, a set of numbers is "dense" if, no matter what two numbers in the set are given, another number in the set may be placed between them. Thus, the set of real numbers is "dense," but the set of integers is not. Law is "analytically dense" in the sense that, between any two cases which appear to be fully explained by a set of rules, another case can be postulated in which it is uncertain or arguable as to what rule or set of rules governs.

New Interfaces of Science and the Law

Bennett Boskey

The past two decades have seen notable growth in the connecting links between science—or science and technology—and the law.

This is not to suggest that they had hitherto been wholly separate. For example, the Constitution itself, in Article I, Section 8, contemplated the early establishment of a patent system by conferring on Congress the power "To promote the Progress of Science and useful Arts by securing for limited Times to Authors and Inventors the exclusive Right to their respective Writings and Discoveries." The prompt implementation of this provision by the First Congress meant that, from the beginning of the Republic, the federal courts have been to a significant degree at the cutting edge of technology—with responsibility for deciding, for instance, whether, in the light of the prior art, the claimed invention is sufficiently novel to sustain the validity of the patent, whether the accused device is an infringement, whether the patent has been misused commercially in a manner which should bar a recovery, and a host of other questions requiring some understanding of technology if the law is to be prudently and justly applied.

One of the best known patent cases in our history is the Supreme Court's decision in 1888, occupying an entire volume of the United States Reports (126 US), sustaining by a vote of 4-to-3 the validity of Alexander Graham Bell's two principal telephone patents; and over fifty years later, in 1943, the Supreme Court had occasion to decide, by a vote of 7-to-2, that one of Marconi's basic United States patents on the wireless was not valid because its claims were "anticipated by the prior art." Needless to say, such issues can be exceptionally complex, and may call for a combination of innate wisdom and acquired knowledge not readily in the armory of every federal judge.

In many other areas also, as American law has developed over the past

Bennett Boskey is a practicing lawyer in Washington, DC, who was, some years ago, Deputy General Counsel of the United States Atomic Energy Commission. He is also a member of the Council and Treasurer of The American Law Institute.

two centuries, the law has had its necessary interconnections with science and technology. In contractual disputes and other commercial matters, a genuine understanding of how a product is made or is used or affects third parties may be fundamental to knowing what the controversy is really all about and how it should be equitably resolved. In tort law, which since World War I has developed along so many new lines, it is the technology that often determines what constitutes a dangerous instrumentality for which a higher degree of liability may be imposed; likewise, science and technology may be critical to such decisions as what emissions are a nuisance that ought to be abated, what is a safe place for an employee to work, or even the fundamental question of what are the proper standards for measuring due care or negligence or gross negligence in a particular case.

MARKED TRANSFORMATIONS

If these and other interconnections between science and the law have been part of the landscape for so long a time, why, then, is it fair to say that the past two decades have witnessed some marked transformations in the relationship? A number of contributing factors can be discerned.

One is what has come to be known as the post-World War II "litigation explosion." In comparison with other countries, the United States is an incredibly litigious society. A kind of mystical force seems to propel Americans into the courts to seek resolution of controversies of all kinds. This results in clogging the dockets of the courts, in producing inordinate delays before cases can be finally determined, and in greatly escalating the costs of litigation. But it also means that large classes of people may have an interest in the outcome of one lawsuit or a related group of lawsuits. The many thousands of Vietnam veterans having an interest in the Agent Orange litigation would be an example. The many thousands of workers and their families having an interest in the asbestiosis litigation would be another. The millions of smokers, living and dead, and their families having an interest in the tobacco litigation would be still another.

The aggregate monetary stakes in such court actions mount to almost astronomical levels (and, incidentally, help to produce various liability-insurance crises, as well as novel efforts to obtain the protection of the bankruptcy courts). The issues involved center largely—but by no means exclusively—on scientific data often turning on debatable extrapolation from known facts. Expert testimony abounds—extensive, learned, and frequently contradictory. Judges and jurors must grapple with such evidence as best they can. It is small wonder that such intersections of science and the law— on the massive scale that the United States legal system has not only permitted, but encouraged—compel these disciplines to become far better acquainted. And even if various aspects of the movements for legal reform— among them, alternative dispute resolution mechanisms, or no-fault-liability scenarios, or caps on damages awardable—do prevail in whole or in part, it seems unlikely that this need for close acquaintance between science and the law will be diminished.

THE ENVIRONMENT

Another influential factor has been the emergence of serious and widespread environmental concerns not only in the United States, but throughout much of the rest of the world. In the United States this has produced extensive legislation directed toward cleaner air, cleaner water, cleaner ground, and reasonably safe industrial operations. The legislation normally is not expressed in terms of absolutes, but rather may aim at having some optimum balance struck. Typically, this calls for determinations by a federal regulatory agency—sometimes supplemented by or interacting with state regulatory agencies—and hence brings into being an encyclopedic array of regulations and adjudications. Much of this turns squarely on available scientific data, often characterized by incompleteness and inherent uncertainties. Because our laws tend to favor a high degree of judicial review (though with appropriate deference to what is called the "expertise" of the agency), the courts become the final arbiters of whether the agency's utilization of the scientific data comports with the applicable statutory provision. Thus a recent (July 1987) unanimous *en banc* opinion for the eleven active judges of the United States Court of Appeals for the District of Columbia Circuit starts with the observation that "Current scientific knowledge does not permit a finding that there is a completely safe level of human exposure to carcinogenic agents"; it goes on to rule (some forty pages later, after cutting through the thicket of obscure Congressional legislative history relating to technology) that, under the Clean Air Act, the Environmental Protection Agency, in regulating hazardous pollutants, including carcinogens, cannot consider cost and technological feasibility in determining what is "safe," but must base the determination solely upon the risk to health.

REGULATORY AGENCIES

Still another influential factor has been the rapid proliferation of regulatory agencies, both federal and state, to which have been delegated substantial responsibilities in fields where scientific and technical data will often be crucial. The environmental aspect has already been referred to. But there is much more. Federal Trade Commission proceedings have become a haven for statistical and scientific studies of the most varied kinds (and the most varied quality). The Federal Aviation Administration must rely on complex technical data in discharging its responsibilities for aviation safety. The Food and Drug Administration must assess complex biological and scientific data in ruling upon new drug applications. The Nuclear Regulatory Commission must apply a combination of intuition and scientific data—much of it hypothetical in nature and based on assumptions as to "worst cases"—in determining reactor safety. Among the current phenomena having a largely medical science orientation is the formulation of governmental responses to the newly perceived menace of AIDS. The list could go on and on. And the proceedings in which these matters are considered at the agency level— whether rulemaking or adjudicatory—are almost invariably subject to judicial review.

THE COMPUTER

The final influential factor I shall mention is of a more general nature. It is the settling in of the computer age. Like other segments of society, lawyers and law students and judges and court administrators are becoming immersed in computerization. Much can be gained, for example, from the virtually instantaneous data retrieval systems which facilitate examination of the legal precedents, or from a court's ability painlessly to extract a computer run which furnishes a current statistical measurement of its own performance.

Computerization is not without costs in terms of additional problems being spawned for the legal system—problems such as the new threats to some fundamental rights of privacy, or enhanced ways of stealing proprietary data, or the uncovering of new lacunae in the copyright laws. But whatever solutions may be forthcoming to minimize such costs, there is a rapidly spreading appreciation of the affirmative benefits, both substantive and administrative, which the legal system can obtain from the computer revolution. The potentialities for classifying and utilizing scientific data, and for conducting analytic studies genuinely pertinent to the case at hand, are increasing enormously. This presages greatly enlarged opportunities for developing and using scientific data in legal proceedings. Plainly, the computer is here to stay, and the legal system is seeking to digest its implications.

Does all this mean that lawyers and judges should train themselves by obtaining a degree in engineering or advanced physics or computer sciences or biophysics? Of course not—though there might well be occasions when such a degree would be helpful. Does it mean that the Harvard Law School should gently float down the Charles River to merge with MIT? Again, of course not—though some lawyers might feel this would bring a useful infusion of talent into MIT. But it does mean that increased scope and encouragement should be given to the interdisciplinary studies, which so many of the law schools have begun to undertake with other faculties at their universities. It likewise means that much is to be gained by increasing the substantive dialogue between lawyers and judges on the one hand and scientists and engineers on the other. For better or for worse, science and law are destined to move ahead in company with one another. It is essential that each profession gain a better understanding of the other than now prevails.

On Limiting the Scope for Scientific Evidence

Richard A. Epstein

Judges are not scientists, although there may be a few among them who have had scientific training. But even if they were, their scientific training would be of limited service to them in dealing with the expert evidence that scientists routinely proffer in an ever-widening range of administrative and legal disputes. No scientist today knows a tiny fraction of the scientific information that is accumulated daily. Judges, who are often drawn from the ranks of former English and history majors, can hardly be expected to do better.

The question then arises, how should judges respond to their fated ignorance of scientific matters? One possible stance is that the judges could assume a role of deference on scientific matters. This attitude could manifest itself both in the review of administrative action and in the use of scientific evidence in ordinary jury trials.

Starting with the administrative agencies, special tribunals, such as those dealing with medical or environmental issues, could be staffed with scientists who make technical decisions—decisions that judges, in turn, would review only to see that the procedural requisites, such as hearing and notice, are fully complied with. The advantage of this system is that judges are not required to speak on matters of which they are ignorant, while scientists for their part are not required to educate judges on technical information that is beyond their power to learn. There is, at least at first blush, a division of labor in which each side is assigned to the task it does best.

But there are weaknesses to this approach as well. When science comes into the legal arena, it comes on both sides of an issue. Any expert has loyalties to clients that can, and perhaps must, interfere with the lofty de-

Richard A. Epstein is Professor of Law at the University of Chicago, where he is Editor of the Journal of Legal Studies. *He has written and taught on a wide range of subjects, including contracts, property and torts. Mr. Epstein is a member of the American Academy of Arts and Sciences, and was a Fellow at the Center for Advanced Studies in the Behavioral Sciences (1977–78).*

tachment and neutrality that lie at the heart of the scientific enterprise. The judicial approach that allows scientists free reign on matters of fact does not settle the question of which scientists should prevail when the experts themselves disagree. There was a time when the faith in expertise was so great that government scientists and administrators were trusted to make the final determinations themselves, as parties above the fray. Yet today this view has rightly been subjected to unrelenting attack, on the ground that service to government, far from insulating scientists from political influences, exposes them to pressures far beyond those that judges face in their ordinary work.

There is, moreover, room for that pressure to exert itself. Much of the scientific evidence of relevance in ordinary administrative work is not descriptive, but predictive. And if the question is whether a given drug is likely to cause certain kinds of injury, the answer typically rests upon uncertain extrapolations from uncertain evidence. Thus if it is known that a given drug causes damage in high concentrations in some, but not all, laboratory animals, it is an open question whether the drug will cause, and if so, how often, damage in human beings when used in far lower concentrations. The question of whether to allow the drug on the market or to keep it off thus depends as much on the attitude that scientists take towards risk, as it does on the scientific evidence. But that having been said, the claim that scientific expertise must be respected becomes problematic. In making choices about the socially acceptable level of risk scientists do not have any special competence that is denied to judges. The polar solution in administrative cases, then, does not work. Yet it is far harder to find some intermediate position that demarcates the zone of expertise from the zone of judicial control. It should, therefore, come as no surprise that modern administrative law has not generated any uniform attitude to agency expertise, but instead runs the gamut from "hard look" to "hands off." What else could be expected?

JURY TRIALS

A similar problem exists in the context of ordinary jury trials. The recent upsurge in cases of product liability and medical malpractice, for example, has placed far greater scientific demands upon judge and jury alike. In the traditional intersection collision between two automobiles, the jury could be trusted to decide which driver had the right of way, and which had prudently observed the rules of the road. Even if the instruction of the judges left something to be desired, as they frequently did on issues of both negligence and causation, jurors could fill in the gaps from their own experience. Judges of course reserved some power to overturn jury verdicts when they were against the manifest weight of the evidence. This system seems to have worked pretty well on balance.

The modern cases where battles between experts arise are, however, those in which the jury is deprived of its experiential base. Its task is accordingly more difficult and its judgments more suspect. Yet, by the same token, the reviewing judge is hardly better able to deal with the information, and is more exposed to criticism if his stated, written reasons turn out to be erroneous. So there is a tendency to give the jury very broad sway, notwithstanding its limited competence.

In drug cases, for example, one inescapable question is whether a given drug was the cause of a given kind of condition. The Bendectin cases illustrate just how difficult these determinations can be. Large numbers of plaintiffs have sought to recover for birth defects which they allege were caused by Bendectin, taken by their mothers in the early months of pregnancy. In order to establish this causal linkage, the plaintiff introduced evidence about the chemical composition and activity of the drug, the likelihood of its constituents to cause injury, the results of various *in vivo* and *in vitro* studies, and extensive epidemiological evidence. The defendant drug company, Richardson-Merrell responded in kind with evidence on all these counts, and introduced the results of the systematic studies conducted by the F.D.A., which suggested that the case against Bendectin had not yet been made, so that the drug did not have to be withdrawn from the market.

With a record this complex, there is something to be said on each side of the question, so that it is only a matter of time before different juries reach inconsistent verdicts upon the causation question. Judges then have to decide whether to overturn the verdict, but they too can act inconsistently. And that is precisely what happened, as the plaintiffs lost in most cases but still prevailed in some, even after the judge reviewed the jury verdict.

As with the appeal to experts in administrative tribunals, there is no obvious way to proceed once the experts have disagreed with each other. My own belief is that once the F.D.A. has resolved the causation question for itself, then no individual jury should be allowed to reach an independent judgment of its own. Bad judgments may be a way of life, but inconsistent judgments are an avoidable cost of the legal system. The practice, of course, today is otherwise. Each jury and each court was allowed to go its separate way, so that in the end Bendectin was withdrawn from the market, if only because its manufacturer could not run the risk of enormous litigation expenses and the prospect of being held liable for substantial punitive damages.

THE DILEMMA

There is a universal proposition which says that it is far easier to pose a dilemma than it is to resolve it. That proposition surely holds with the use of scientific information in judicial determinations. By now the horns of the dilemma should be evident. Judicial deference permits bias to permeate scientific judgments. Judicial control requires judges to make decisions on matters that are outside their technical competence. There is no set of rules that will make this dilemma go away, especially if we take as given the substantive legal rules that are used to decide various legal disputes. To be sure, it is possible to limit the problem around the edges. Expert witnesses might not be allowed to testify if they spend most of their time in court and little at the scientific bench. Independent experts might be appointed by the court, at least, in some cases. And the priority between administrative determinations and jury verdicts could be worked out in a general way, and in advance, to eliminate the risk of inconsistent determinations.

Yet I suggest that the best place to seek relief is not by revising the law of expert evidence, but by looking at the substantive laws themselves. The modern crisis with scientific evidence has arisen, in large part, because the legal system, both through its legislatures and its courts, continues to expand the areas of control that it exerts over the life of its citizens. When the classical liberal philosophy of natural liberty and limited government prevailed, there was a strong presumption that the role of government was to insure that individuals did not use force and fraud against their neighbors, so that each person had a zone of freedom in which he could make out his own life choices. Today the modern view is that the protection against force and fraud is only the first function of government, so that it is also strictly necessary to protect people against their own incompetence by making decisions for them which they are deemed not able to make for themselves.

The shift in general social attitude has profound effects in the kinds of cases that work themselves into the legal system. In drug cases, for example, the role of government is not solely to insure that companies disclose the risk of their products before they are placed on the market. Instead, it is to determine whether it is proper for consumers to be allowed to use those products at all, even on a doctor's advice, which can be given with a detailed knowledge of both the available treatments and the patient's conditions. The narrower question of disclosure clearly requires the collection, evaluation and use of expert evidence, but the later question of marketability surely gives far greater scope for their expert evidence, and places far greater strains on judicial competence.

Similarly, in modern product liability cases, the older tests of liability asked whether product contained a latent defect which caused harm in its ordinary use. Expert testimony was therefore necessary to determine whether as metal pipe contained a latent crack which caused a boiler to explode. But today the modern rules allow judges and juries alike to make extensive cost-benefit studies to determine whether products whose dangers are obvious should be marketed at all. Again the scope for expert evidence becomes far greater than it was under the earlier, more limited, regime of liability, without there being any systematic evidence that the increased scrutiny improves the level of products that reach the marketplace.

The same kind of story can be told in subject area after subject area: labor relations, antidiscrimination laws, criminal responsibility, utility rate making, antitrust, corporations, and securities. In virtually all these areas, the best approach to the intrinsic difficulties of handling scientific evidence is by indirection. The substantive rules should be reexamined to see whether they could be simplified to reduce the dependence that the legal system must place on expert evidence. If there are fewer complex laws, then there will be fewer occasions for expert evidence to misfire.

Judicial Understanding of Science

Edward Gerjuoy

The notion that the legal profession, including the judiciary, would profit from a better understanding of science and technology is not novel. As long ago as 1836 a legal scholar declared:[1]

> Hence, legislators, courts and lawyers are often obliged to resort to the evidence of those who have made physics and mental philosophy their peculiar study: and it is very clear that this can be done with assurance of correctness, only when the *examiners*, as well as the *witnesses*, are in some degree enlightened on such subjects. (Emphasis in the original).

In more recent years, many law schools and bar associations have made serious efforts, described by Professor McKay elsewhere in this volume,[2] to familiarize would-be and practicing lawyers with science and practicing scientists. Such efforts also have been fostered by the National Conference of Lawyers and Scientists (NCLS), established in 1974 under an agreement between the American Bar Association (ABA) and the American Association for the Advancement of Science (AAAS). The ABA and the AAAS each appoint nine members of the NCLS, which meets several times a year to discuss the appropriate uses of science and technology within the legal system; when warranted, the NCLS organizes specialized conferences relating to its broad subject.[3]

Recent years also have witnessed the publication of numerous books[4] and articles[5] about the interactions between law and science, as well as treatises[6] aimed at educating lawyers with specialized practices in the details of pertinent particular technologies. Many of these articles, including a useful re-

Edward Gerjuoy has a Ph.D. in physics from the University of California/Berkeley, and was a university physics professor and researcher for many years before receiving a J.D. and passing the bar. He is a member of the American Bar Association (ABA) Section of Science and Technology Council, and of the ABA/American Association for the Advancement of Science National Conference of Lawyers and Scientists, and, until very recently, was Editor-in-Chief of the Jurimetrics Journal of Law, Science and Technology. *Dr. Gerjuoy is a former member of the Pennsylvania Environmental Hearing Board, and presently is of counsel to the Pittsburgh law firm of Rose, Schmidt, Hasley & DiSalle.*

search compendium,[7] have been published in the *Jurimetrics Journal of Law, Science and Technology,* the quarterly joint publication of the ABA Section of Science and Technology (which has over 3,000 members) and the Arizona State University College of Law Center for the Study of Law, Science and Technology. The *Jurimetrics Journal* "is a forum for the publication and exchange of ideas and information about the relationships between law, science and technology in all areas, including . . . the uses of science and technology in law practice, adjudication, and court and agency administration." *Jurimetrics* is by no means the only law journal concerned with the relationships between law and science, however. The many widely read but more narrowly focused (than *Jurimetrics*) journals on environmental law, intellectual property law or medical law also are concerned with those relationships as, surprisingly often, are articles in non-legal journals such as the AAAS weekly publication *Science*[8] and the Massachusetts Medical Society weekly, *New England Journal of Medicine.*[9]

THE LAW-SCIENCE OVERLAP

The preceding paragraphs provide an introduction to the institutional and library resources in the law-science overlap area that increasingly are becoming available. For law and science issues whose resolutions do not hinge upon detailed knowledge of a particular science or technology, for instance, the proper criteria for admissibility of scientific evidence at trial, these resources[10] should prove very helpful to sitting judges, both lower court and appellate. These resources will be at most indirectly helpful, however, to those judges who, as so often happen in modern litigation, find themselves grappling with recondite issues requiring more than a superficial understanding of a specialized scientific field. In the famous Agent Orange litigation, one of the Vietnam veteran plaintiffs died of cancer at age 45, after fathering two children, one born dead after a five-month pregnancy and the second apparently unusually sickly; Judge Jack Weinstein had to decide whether these medical disorders had been caused by the plaintiff's exposure to the Agent Orange herbicides.[11] There is no reason to think that, during the years preceding the Agent Orange trial, Judge Weinstein (who is not a scientist) would have, could have, or should have found the time to gain the enlightenment in oncology, epidemiology and pediatrics needed to render his decision—which in this case was against the aforementioned veteran—with the "assurance of correctness" that David Hoffman envisaged. Science and technology simply have "progressed" too far beyond their 1836 boundaries. Today, even a trained scientist often is barely more knowledgeable than a layman about the almost innumerably proliferated specialized scientific and technological areas outside the scientist's own specialty. I consider myself—and believe I am considered—a broadly trained, competent physicist, but the very large proportion of the immense amount of scientific expert testimony I heard during my tenure on the Pennsylvania Environmental Hearing Board was well outside my physics-professional ken. Being a physicist could not directly help me to decide, as I have had to decide, which of two opposing soil scientists had correctly characterized the soil types on farm land where residential septic tank pumpings were being disposed, or whether the silt discharged into a stream from a surface coal mine would imperil natural trout spawning in the stream.

We may conclude that almost all cases involving specialized scientific issues inevitably will be decided by judges who, whether or not they have been trained in science, will derive their understandings of those specialized issues from the parties' presentations at trial, not from any pretrial scientific education. Moreover, because of our adversarial system of justice, the basic thrust of this just-stated conclusion will remain valid, even in those rare cases wherein the judge's own scientific speciality is very pertinent to the scientific issues at bar. The so-called adjudicative facts, on which any particular judicial decision is based, must be arrived at solely from the record made in open court; even if the judge is a more competent scientific specialist than the testifying experts, it is improper to denigrate the expert testimony, which was subject to cross-examination, in favor of the judge's own opinions, which the parties had no opportunity to rebut.

On the other hand, it must not be forgotten that judges, though bound by the case record, can importantly influence that record. In the interests of justice, the trial judge, without usurping the cross-examiner's role our judicial system reserves to the parties' advocates, can and should question witnesses for the purpose of clarifying the record; in the same interests an appellate judge can and should order the parties to re-brief specialized issues which have not been usefully addressed, or to newly brief critical, previously unaddressed issues which have escaped waiver under the appellant court's procedural rules. For the exercise of these judicial functions, as for the earlier mentioned function of ruling on scientific evidence admissibility, it is highly desirable that a judge have more than a nodding acquaintance with science, even if the judge's own scientific knowledge lies outside the specialities directly germane to the issues which must be decided. Especially important is a comprehension of what may be termed the sociology of science, *e.g.*, of its reward mechanisms, of ways by which scientists and scientific journals achieve prestige, of the peer review process for publications and grants, etc. Without such comprehension judges (like juries) will be unable to evaluate the comparative professional reputations of competing scientific experts, or (if the finder of fact is a jury) to frame questions to those experts which will elucidate their reputations for the benefit of the jury. For instance, judges regularly should inquire whether the lists of publications offered in support of scientific expert witness qualifications were in refereed or non-refereed journals, and should establish on the record the distinctions between refereed and non-referred articles. The attorneys who appeared before the Pennsylvania Environmental Hearing Board soon learned to anticipate such inquiries from me; there was the happy concomitant result, welcome to any judge, that fewer obviously poorly qualified expert witnesses were called to testify.

COMBINED DISCIPLINES

The best way to gain a non-trivial understanding of science is to be a scientist. In general, US judges are attorneys, who come to their judgeships from the practicing bar or from law school professorships. I do not recommend that we appoint judges who are scientists, but have no legal training; even a specialized panel like the Environmental Hearing Board had to rule on many purely legal issues, *e.g.*, of standing to appeal, right to intervene, statutory construction, estoppel, etc. Therefore the best first step toward instilling a better understanding of science into our judiciary is to award more law degrees to persons who have been working scientists, or at least science graduate students. Law schools should actively recruit such persons, and our bar associations should actively attempt to acquaint the scientific community with the intellectual excitement, not merely the financial rewards, that a successful legal career can furnish. I add that, in so writing, I do not want to discourage law schools from admitting more bachelors of science; at this time, however, American colleges typically are not conveying to their undergraduate science majors the quality of scientific sophistication judges should have.

Law students receiving their J.D.s today will not substantially penetrate the judiciary for two decades or more; in the meantime, much can be done to improve our present courts' abilities to cope with complex issues of law and science. Courts which expect to have to decide such issues should seek law clerks with scientific training. Judges should be kept currently informed about the resources described at the beginning of this paper. Those resources should be supplemented with regularly offered short courses about the sociology of science and related relevant subjects, designed for sitting judges who are not scientifically trained. Such related subjects might include, for example, distinguishing between the two types of uncertainties that inevitably attach to scientific opinions: (a) those that arise from inherent deficiencies in present experimental and theoretical knowledge and (b) those that result from the fact that different scientists can arrive at different answers even when applying well-established knowledge to well-posed problems. When these uncertainties make legal decisions difficult, judges should be relying on the opinions of the best-qualified experts for uncertainties of type (b), but probably would do best to rely on their common sense for uncertainties of type (a). Similarly, judges should be educated in what is meant by the "scientific method" and in the distinctions between science and what may be termed pseudoscience, on which distinctions there now is a considerable literature.[12] Measures of the sort just described will not immediately resolve our present judiciary's difficulties with issues of law and science, but in time should significantly alleviate those difficulties, which is all that realistically could be hoped.

NOTES

1. David Hoffman, *A Course of Legal Study* (Baltimore: 1836), reprinted in the series, *American Law: The Formative Years* (New York: Arno Press, 1972), p. 698.
2. Robert B. McKay, "Science and Technology: Advice to the Judiciary," this volume.
3. *Inter alia,* Symposium on Science and Rules of Evidence (April 1983), 99 Federal Rules of Decision (F.R.D.) 188 (1983); Symposium on Science and the Rules of Legal Procedure (October 1983), 101 F.R.D. 599 (1984); and Workshop on Scientific Fraud and Misconduct (September 18–20, 1987).
4. Illustrative titles are: Michael J. Saks and Richard Van Duizand, *The Use of Scientific Evidence in Litigation* (National Center for State Courts, 1983); and J. D. Nyhart and Milton M. Carrow, *Law and Science in Collaboration* (National Center for Administrative Justice, 1983).
5. Under the heading, "Science and Law," in the American Association of Law Libraries Current Law Index (to legal periodicals), there are 92 distinct entries for the years 1980–86.
6. Cf., *e.g.,* Max Schwartz and Neil Forrest Schwartz, *Engineering Evidence* (Shepherd's/McGraw-Hill, 1986), with Cumulative Supplement.
7. Frank L. Huband and Stephen B. Gould, "Catalog of Research on the Use of Scientific Evidence in Legislative, Judicial and Executive Decision-Making," *Jurimetrics* 23 (Spring 1983), p. 279.
8. *E.g.,* Francis E. Sharples, "Regulation of Products from Biotechnology," *Science* 235 (March 13, 1987), p. 1329; Bernard D. Davis, "Bacterial Domestication: Underlying Assumptions," *ibid.;* and "The Ice-Minus Case and a Scientifically Informed Judiciary," Letters to the Editor, *Science* 237 (July 3, 1987), p. 10.
9. *E.g.,* D. A. Kessler, S. M. Pape and D. N. Sundwall, "The Federal Regulation of Medical Devices, *New England Journal of Medicine* 317 (August 6, 1987), p. 357; and William J. Curran, "Compulsory Drug Testing: The Legal Barriers," *New England Journal of Medicine* 316 (February 5, 1987), p. 318.
10. See the materials cited in Notes 3, 4 and 7, as well as, for example, Frederick B. Lacey, "Scientific Evidence," *Jurimetrics* 24 (Spring 1984), p. 254.
11. *In re Agent Orange Product Liability Litigation,* 611 F. Supp. 1267 (E.D. N.Y. 1985). See also, P. Schuck, *Agent Orange on Trial* (Cambridge, MA: Harvard University Press, 1986).
12. *Inter alia* Martin Gardner, *Fads and Fallacies* (Dover, 1957); Martin Gardner, *Science, Good, Bad and Bogus* (Prometheus, 1981); Carl Sagan and Thornton Page, *UFOs. A Scientific Debate* (New York: Norton, 1972); various articles in *The Skeptical Inquirer,* the quarterly journal of the Committee for the Scientific Investigation of Claims of the Paranormal, *e.g.,* Carl Sagan, *Night Walkers and Mystery Mongers: Sense and Nonsense at the Edge of Science,* Vol. 10 (Spring 1986), p. 219.

Science and Technology Advice to the Judiciary

Robert B. McKay

For 200 years, the Constitution of the United States has acknowledged the relationship between science and technology and law only in the provision that "The Congress shall have Power . . . to promote the Progress of Science and useful Arts, by securing for limited Times to Authors and Inventors the exclusive Right to their Respective Writings and Discoveries" (Article I, Section 8, Clause 8). Other provisions in that rather open-ended charter, however, have permitted subsequent interpretations that provide protection for privacy rights; enable government to regulate nuclear power and industrial safety; and encourage efforts' to advance inquiry into the emerging frontiers of science.

While the specific advances of science in the last two centuries could not have been imagined by the drafters of the Constitution, it is no accident that the way was left open for such developments. The emergent ideas of seventeenth- and eighteenth-century science allowed a break with the medieval notion of a divinely ordained social hierarchy. Heinz R. Pagels, Executive Director of the New York Academy of Sciences, states the matter succinctly:

> In the view of the deistic founders of our nation, God set the great Newtonian clockwork of the universe in motion and then left it to run its course, much as the Constitution was designed to set in motion the social dynamics of the nation. The English and French social thinkers, from whom Jefferson, Franklin, Adams, Madison, Hamilton, and others drew inspiration for their political ideas, were profoundly influenced by empiricism, a philosophy that developed from the eighteenth century triumphs of science.

Robert B. McKay has been Professor of Law at New York University School of Law since 1953, and was Dean from 1967–75. He was President of the Association of the Bar of the City of New York (1984–86), and is a Governor of the American Bar Association, and has been Chairman of the Section of Legal Education and Admissions to the Bar. Dr. McKay was Chairman of the Attica Commission (1971–72) and Director of the Institute of Judicial Administration (1980–83). He is a Trustee of the National Judicial College.

Indeed, as Pagels also reminds us, Jefferson was one of the first Americans to master calculus, and he invented the best metal plow of his time. Franklin, well known for his experiments in electricity, was also the first to dissolve carbon dioxide in water, in the process "inventing" soda pop.

Despite the openness of these individuals and others responsible for the Declaration of Independence and the Constitution and for the close relationship between science and government, during most of the intervening two centuries, science and government have been more separate than involved in joint endeavors. To be sure, there was, almost from the first, legislation defining the rights of authors and inventors. But the National Science Foundation was not established until 1950, and it was not till early 1951 that President Truman created the science advisory organization that was reinforced immediately after Sputnik by President Eisenhower with James Killian, Jr., as President's Science Advisor with a distinguished President's Science Advisory Committee.

Since the creation of that apparatus and that Foundation, there has been at least a nominal working relationship between science and the two political branches of the government. The third branch, however, has remained somewhat more distant, almost resistant, to the need for interconnection between science and the judiciary.

This reluctance of the judiciary to embrace the newest developments of science is not altogether surprising. Lawyers and judges are, by inclination and training, disposed to look to the language of the law in constitutions, statutes and prior decisions for guidance to resolution of current disputes. Commonly, the law is regarded as self-contained, requiring little or no external support beyond careful exposition of the facts and the law. Lawyers and judges have even been somewhat reluctant to use the information available from such social science disciplines as criminology, psychology and sociology, and the hard sciences are typically regarded as still less likely to aid in the resolution of disputes.

SCIENTIFIC ILLITERATES

Perhaps equally important in the failure to make effective connection between science and law is the regrettable but indisputable fact that most lawyers and judges are scientific illiterates. For those interested in a career in the law there is little encouragement to study mathematics, physics and chemistry or to comprehend the significance of biomedical research that aspires (or threatens) to change the very nature of the human body and/or personality.

In the simpler world of 200, or even 50 years ago, that separateness might have been understandable, even not particularly harmful. But in a world in which the government reaches into every crevice of public and private life, and in which science dominates so many of the decisions, it is no longer acceptable for the courts to stand apart from modern knowledge. Examples abound:

- The right of privacy, defined in constitutional terms, implicates medical knowledge about the viability of the fetus and the protection of individual personality from computer invasion.
- The communications "revolution" affects personal and business activities from telephonic communications to banking transactions in ways that are certain to involve judicial intervention.
- The operational safety of nuclear reactors is subject to judicial scrutiny for final determination.
- Recombinant DNA and experimentation on the human genome are likely to involve disputes that require judicial intercession.
- Industrial safety and product liability issues are typically resolved in the courts.

John Brademas, President of New York University, has said, quite properly, that "the agenda of science is much too important to be left to the scientists." If that is a plea for effective interaction among all knowledgeable decision-makers, the appeal is unquestionably sound. The counterpoint, to borrow the same format of expression, is that "the agenda of the judiciary is too important to be left to lawyers and judges."

It may be that scientists (and others) do not understand very well the sometimes mysterious ways of the law. The regrettable fact is that lawyers and judges know even less about the practical—let alone the theoretical— workings of science. A better communication between these inextricably related disciplines is vital to the increasingly important role of the judiciary in resolving disputed issues that affect not only the scientific community, but, as well, all persons who must live and function in this increasingly complex world.

GOOD NEWS

If the continuing lack of comprehension between science and law is the bad news, there is, fortunately, also good news. The Bar is beginning to wake to the knowledge deficiencies of its constituents.

While legal education can scarcely be said to have embraced science as part of what is generally perceived as an overloaded curriculum, courses and seminars are not uncommon in Patent Law, Copyright Law, Law and Economics, Environmental Law, Computers and the Law, and Forensic Medicine. All involve some knowledge of various aspects of science and its application to law.

Continuing legal education has gone further than the basic legal education program in offering specialized instruction in many of the cross-over situations in which science and law increasingly intersect.

The most encouraging developments are taking place in the hundreds of state and local bar asociations, usually through their committee activities and bar association publications. A few representative examples, taken from the organizations I know best, must be sufficient.

American Bar Association Sections include those devoted to Natural Resources Law, Public Utility Law, and Science and Technology, as well as many committees and subcommittees devoted to developing more information and better coordination with the science community. The most dramatic example is the relatively young Science and Technology Section (established in 1974), which includes the following divisions, each with several committees: Aerospace Law, Communications Law, Computer Law, Government Policy and Regulation, Life Sciences and Physical Sciences, and Technology in Legal Practice and Judicial Systems.

The enthusiasm for science and technology in the substantive sections of the ABA does not seem to have carried over to the Judicial Administration Division (which includes most members of the judiciary who are members of the ABA). Of the dozens of committees, there appears to be only one, on Modern Technology in Courts, as part of the National Conference of Special Court Judges, that seems likely to focus on even a limited aspect of science as it relates to law.

The New York State Bar Association has sections or committees on Health Law; Food, Drug and Cosmetic Law, Environmental Law; Mental and Physical Disabilities Law; Medical Malpractice; Public Utilities Law; and Biotechnology and the Law. Manifestly, lawyers in these units either have or must acquire scientific knowledge which they will then apply to judicial or legislative proceedings.

The Association of the Bar of the City of New York has about 120 working committees, of which, by my calculation, at least 18 have some more or less direct involvement with science issues. Without indulging in the tedious task of listing those committees, perhaps it is more useful to identify the actual work product printed in the Association's *Record* in the few months between November 1986 and May 1987: "Legalization of Nonprescription Sale of Hypodermic Needles: A Response To The Aids Crisis" (Committee on Medicine and Law); "An Analysis of Proposed Charges in Substantive and Procedural Law In Response To Perceived Difficulties In Establishing Whether Or Nor Causation Exists In Mass Toxic Tort Litigation" (Special Committee on Science and Law); "The International Protection of Technology: A Challenge For International Law Making" (Lecture by Nicholas deB. Katzenbach); "Standards For Obtaining Stays In The Courts Of Appeals From Final Nuclear Regulatory Commission Orders Granting Reactor Operating Licenses" (Committee on Nuclear Technology and Law); and "Acquired Deficiency Syndrome (AIDS): A Selective Bibliography of Legal, Social And Medical Aspects."

There is, you see, hope that the legal community will prove itself adaptable to the newly perceived need for better communication between science and law, just as the Constitution has always demonstrated its flexibility in adjusting to changing circumstances. In view of this demonstrated willingness to accommodate to scientific information, it is time for the scientific and legal communities to get together to devise the most effective means for accomplishing that result. The nation's judges deserve and urgently need the combined assistance of the scientific community and the legal profession.

Improving the Courts' Ability to Absorb Scientific Information

Maurice Rosenberg

In an ever more complex world, the courts increasingly are asked to re-solve disputes in which decision turns on scientific data. The case may de-pend on the results of

- epidemiological studies of the health histories of veterans exposed to Agent Orange; or
- demographic studies bearing on racial or gender bias on the job; or
- consumer surveys showing the defendant has marketed a product so similar to the plaintiff's the public is confused as to its source; or
- sociological studies on whether disqualifying persons with anti-capital punishment views produces juries that are too prone to vote "guilty"; or
- statistical data on the frequency of death, illness and injury from a growing list of products and contaminants; and so on.

The science advice the judiciary needs falls into two categories. In one, the court's scientific findings will affect the interests of the immediate par-ties and of almost no one else; in effect, their impact is limited to the single case. These findings are called "adjudicative facts." In the other category, the findings provide the factual basis for the way the court formulates a rule of law of general applicability. Those findings are called "legislative facts." They are the kind of facts an alert, responsible legislative body would seek to assemble before choosing a statutory solution to the problem addressed.

In both types of cases, the courts need evidence that experts can supply, but there the similarity ends. The two situations raise significantly different problems and require equally different solutions. A few examples will make

Maurice Rosenberg is Harold R. Medina Professor of Procedural Jur-isprudence, Columbia University School of Law. He was Assistant At-torney General of the United States (1979–81), heading the Office for Improvements in the Administration of Justice. Mr. Rosenberg was President of the Association of American Law Schools (1972–73), is the author and co-author of several books, and is a member of the American Academy of Arts and Sciences.

this clear. Suppose the dispute relates to whether a nuclear generating unit failed because of improper design by the defendant rather than poor maintenance by the plaintiff; or to whether the chemicals that defendant buried in landfills years before account for exaggerated levels of disease in the local population. The resolution of that kind of adjudicative fact dispute calls for sophisticated scientific evidence. For the parties, victory usually depends on which scientific explanation of the occurence can be advanced most persuasively. To make its strongest case each side retains a team of experts who tend to adopt severely partisan stances. Typically, they offer diametrically opposite opinions on the key technical issues, leaving the judge and jury more confused than helped.

Early in the 1960s, the judiciary in several jurisdictions tried to remedy the difficulties caused by partisan experts' testimony in personal injury lawsuits by creating "impartial medical panels." In Pittsburgh and New York, for example, the courts appointed well-known doctors from various medical specialties as neutral advisers to the judge and jury. Their function was to diagnose, evaluate and explain the medical evidence whenever the parties' doctors disagreed about what the evidence showed. After a flurry of interest lasting a few years, the impartial panel idea fell into disuse. Many members of the bar were against the panel plan, apparently because they believed the judge's and the panel's influence over the disputed issues frustrated the working of the adversary process.

In recent times, various proposals to provide high-level courts with scientific experts as staff aides have not been well-received, despite the fact that "technical advisors" are firmly established and well accepted in the Court of Appeals for the Federal Circuit. The advisors in that court are trained in law and also hold advanced degrees in a scientific or technical speciality such as physics, chemistry or engineering. They assist the judges in patent cases and other lawsuits that turn on scientific proof. A major reason the technical advisor model has not been accepted for other courts is that the legal profession is generally wary of allowing in-court experts to speak inaudibly and anonymously to the judges in ways that may determine the results of sharply contested cases.

A better solution to the problems of unbridled and unhelpful partisanship may be to adapt the practice employed in voluntary arbitrations to the process of resolving adjudicative fact disputes calling for expert scientific information. The National Academy of Sciences or a similarly respected professional group might create panels of outstanding scientists who have not taken partisan positions on important scientific issues before the courts. When an issue arises in a lawsuit, the court would have authority under the rules to require the parties to agree to the appointment of one or more experts from the designated list of experts in the relevant specialty. The selection procedure would resemble the practice followed in selecting arbitrators: each side would have the right to strike names off the list until one or more names remained. Neutral experts chosen in this manner would be the only experts who could give evidence. In the federal courts, authority for this procedure may already exist in the rule providing for pretrial conferences. At the conferences, the court has the explicit power under the rule to limit the number of expert witnesses the parties may call. While the rule does not expressly so state, it may implicitly permit the judge to limit the experts to the ones the parties have chosen from the panel.

Even more urgent than improving the way courts obtain scientific data on case-specific issues of adjudicative fact is the need in the sphere of legislative fact-finding. The judiciary's current method of absorbing scientific information on legislative facts is haphazard, unruly and unreliable. One study of appellate litigation reported that 40% of the cited references to the scientific literature came via the court's independent research, unaided by the lawyers or the record made in the lower court. (*See* T. Marvell, *Appellate Courts and Lawyers* 192 [1978].) The appellate judges (including justices of the United States Supreme Court) simply took "judicial notice" of the materials they cited. That is, they or their law clerks found the materials in the library, read them, and used them.

To a large extent, the appellate courts have no alternative but to employ that kind of judicial notice, for the litigants are less likely to fill the information gaps in legislative-fact disputes than to help the court in adjudicative-fact situations. The parties' first priority, understandably, is to win the case. Assuring that the courts make "good law" in the process is not a vital objective. Except where it would induce a favorable decision, they have little incentive to spend great amounts of energy or money to provide the courts with the kinds of scientific data a responsible legislature would insist upon before making a law.

A major defect in the courts' self-help in this area is the tendency to use scientific studies, reports and data that are *methodologically* unfit for judicial consumption. Since neither the judges nor their clerks have been trained in scientific research methods, their use of flawed materials is not surprising.

A possible remedy suggests itself: creating a public agency to act as an information resource for the courts with regard to the methodological acceptability of scientific and technological research findings. The agency, probably at the national level, might be a consortium of scholars and scientists drawn from the National Academy of Sciences, the Library of Congress, the National Institutes of Health, the National Science Foundation, the National Endowment for the Humanities, and other entities. Its mission would be to receive and catalogue scientific studies that qualify for judicial attention. The criteria for determining whether a study qualifies for approval would not be agreement or disagreement with its content or recommendations, but only a finding that its design and methods fall within the range of accepted standards of scientific inquiry. These standards would be akin to standard accounting principles in financial practice.

Procedures would be developed to regulate the manner in which courts utilize studies on file in the depository. For example, a study found acceptable in its methods would be available for judicial notice if and only if timely notification were given to the parties and an opportunity afforded them to submit briefs supporting, contesting, or commenting on the material the court proposes to use. The comments could go both to the methods and the substance of the study. If a party so desired, it could submit any other relevant materials. Use by the court of studies found acceptable as to research methodology would not in the least inhibit resort to other materials.

Procedures would also be devised to assure a full and fair opportunity for researchers whose proffered studies were not at first approved to obtain a second review. Of course, the review process should not be unreasonably elaborated since the litigants will be free to offer studies not on file.

Although this proposal is not free from difficulties, it offers a way to improve the judiciary's ability to absorb scientific materials in discharging the courts' important law-declaring function. It deserves a trial run.

Technology and the Courts

Patricia M. Wald

We live in a high-technology society in which law and science inevitably mix. Issues of science and technology come to federal courts in different ways. Old-fashioned common-law torts, where one person is accused of negligently injuring another, now are likely to turn on scientific evidence about causation or state of the art evidence on technology. The Agent Orange, DES, and Bhopal litigations come to mind. Federal appellate courts also review for reasonableness the decisions of a wide variety of administrative agencies which frequently involve science and technology. For example, the United States Court of Appeals for the District of Columbia has ruled on Food and Drug Administration decisions about the acceptable threshold level of carcinogenic additives in food and whether the Nuclear Regulatory Commission has adequately considered the risk factors in plant siting that might contribute to a nuclear disaster.

While there are persistent grumblings that judges get their scientific facts wrong or that they are unable to correctly assess the value of scientific evidence, being misled on occasion by the personality or persuasiveness of the expert witness, it seems unlikely that Congress will soon remove these cases from our jurisdiction. Indeed, in the Clean Air and Clean Water Acts, Congress has mandated judicial enforcement of a series of "technology-forcing" laws designed to push industry to the outer frontiers of technology in order to minimize the discharge of harmful pollutants into our air and water.

Nor do I believe it would be a good idea to curtail judicial review of cases involving scientific and technological material or even, as some suggest, to channel them into a special Science Court. Even if we were to require all challenges to governmental action implicating science or technology to be

Patricia M. Wald is Chief Judge of the United States Court of Appeals for the District of Columbia Circuit, of which she has been a member since 1979. She was formerly an Assistant Attorney General for Legislative Affairs at the United States Department of Justice (1977–79), Litigation Director for the Mental Health Law Project (1975–77), and an attorney at the Neighborhood Legal Services Program. She has written numerous articles on criminal justice, juvenile rights, administration of justice and mental health law.

initially tried before agencies, those agency decisions should not be immunized from generalist court review. Agencies, by combining all three government functions—legislative, executive and adjudicative—into a single institution, inevitably create some potential for arbitrary or even biased decisionmaking.

The independence of the federal judiciary, guaranteed by the Constitution's life tenure and salary protection clauses, offers a nonpoliticized check on such decision-making that is not available elsewhere. We read too often in the papers about instances of specialized agency personnel who are supposed to base their decisions solely on scientific evidence turning out to be motivated by political and bureaucratic pressures to give up the check of judicial review too casually. Furthermore, the need for specialized agency policy-makers to explain their complex and arcane decisions to generalist judges is probably a good thing. Given the profound implications for our citizens of these decisions, they need to be judged by the humanist as well as the scientist viewpoint.

It, therefore, makes eminently good sense to think about ways judges can become more scientifically sophisticated. Right now, few of us have any training in the methodologies of science. Nor, unlike either the Executive or the Congress, do we have scientifically trained persons to consult for advice. Indeed, our ethics constrain us from talking to any expert, however "neutral," on our own. All of the information we get must come from the lawyers through the adversarial process or be contained in the record of the administrative proceedings we are reviewing. Some judges hire law clerks with expertise in science, but this is an *ad hoc* process at best; most judges simply cannot predict from year-to-year what kind of cases they will be assigned so as to know what kind of specialist they will need, *i.e.*, an engineer, a biologist, a physicist.

Suggestions have been made that an advisory corps of scientists be established for the courts at large to use. Cost considerations aside, there are obvious problems as to how the areas of expertise would be chosen, given the increasing specialization of science and technology; how the time of the experts would be allocated between courts, since it is evident that each court could not afford its own advisory corps; and whether there really are such beings as "neutral" experts. Judges also must operate on quick time-frames; our court alone processes hundreds of cases with scientific or technological aspects every year. For it to be helpful, we would have to get our advice quickly.

It might be that on-call panels of scientific advisors could be assembled from which judges could select appropriate counselors with the knowledge of and opportunity to object by counsel on both sides. That expert's opinion, in turn, would be subject to comment by the parties. Some trial courts have already experimented with appointing "court experts" under Federal Rule of Evidence 706 to critique the scientific evidence and testify or file reports for the court's use. In appellate review, however, the situation is particularly tricky, for the expert's role can be one of clarification only as to what is already in the record; the judge must assess the reasonableness of the agency's position on the basis of what was before the agency, not what is before him now.

At this stage, with a minimum of experience to draw on, it is hard to say how much the creation of an auxiliary science and technology consultancy for the courts would improve their performance in complex cases or whether such a service could be successfully integrated into the court's way of doing things. Some judicious experimentation would help although it is well to remember that science is not the only unfamiliar terrain in which judges must tread. Competing versions of history, differing theories and evidence about behavioral sciences, and various schools of economic theories pose the same danger to a judge of losing her or his footing in an alien discipline.

LEGAL, FACTUAL AND POLICY JUDGMENTS

If we were, however, to experiment with scientific counseling for the courts, we should start by distinguishing between several different types of judgments that a court makes which implicate science and technology: legal judgments, factual judgments, and policy judgments. Legal judgments, such as "pure" issues of statutory interpretation, are least likely to involve complex scientific or technological matters, although, at times, they may. If Congress writes a complex statute, using detailed scientific terminology, and a question arises about Congressional intent, the court will have to educate itself in the scientific subject about which Congress legislated. Factual judgments on the other hand are quite likely to turn on an assessment of scientific or technological evidence. Thus, whether a certain drug causes cancer is a factual issue which must be decided on the basis of scientific data, often in statistical form. (A *caveat* is in order: Science almost never answers such a causation question definitely. Rather, the scientist will only state what the *probability* is that a drug will cause cancer under certain conditions.) Finally, the most difficult judgments courts are called upon to make are essentially public policy judgments. The question whether a certain drug presents an *unreasonable risk* to human health is a policy judgment that is qualitatively different from the factual judgment about whether the drug causes cancer. Even taking the factual judgment as a given, one can still dispute the policy judgment. Despite known risks, a drug may provide such valuable benefits that the risks are reasonable.

In tort law, judges are allowed to decide for themselves or with a jury what constitutes an "unreasonable risk" upon the basis of the scientific facts which have been presented in court. In order to evaluate the underlying scientific evidence about the dimension of the risks, judges need familiarity with the scientific method. But for the policy judgments surrounding the question of whether the risk taken was a reasonable one under all circumstances, judges need a different sort of skill: the ability to engage in risk-benefit analysis. It is, of course, true that when an appellate court passes on an agency's risk-benefit analysis, it is supposed to give great deference to the agency's policy judgment, not only because the agency has greater "skill" in making these value judgments, but because it is a more appropriate political institution for making these delicate and agonizing choices. When an appellate court questions an agency's policy judgments in the scientific or technological area, it is usually because the agency failed to adequately consider an important factor in the overall risk-benefit analysis, not because we are second-guessing its policy conclusions. In light of the major role that risk-benefit assessments play in administrative decisions in the area of science and technology, however, we must target the goal we expect to accomplish by giving our judges a scientific education. Training in the basic scientific methodology may enable the judges to understand the factual predicates for the agency's decision better, but it may not contribute much to their evaluation of the reasonableness of agency policy judgments about the risk/benefits of a particular decision.

No one suggests that the courts should be the prime risk manager in our society; that job belongs to the administrative agencies. But many argue that judicial review should be aggressive enough to assure that an agency's decision to accept or reject a risk is not way out of line: in legalese, "arbitrary" or "capricious." That kind of review entails comparing the risks of alternative courses to the one under review, an assessment, as it were, of the "risk portfolio."[1]

For example, it is frequently pointed out that underregulation, as well as overregulation, entails social and economic costs. The agencies themselves, however, are often not adept at this comparative risk approach, and provide little or no information to the courts about it in the record. Thus, the court itself may have to require the agency to show that its failure to regulate or to regulate more or less rigorously in a given case is reasonably consistent with a risk portfolio strategy. If courts became sufficiently familiarized with risk management techniques to conduct a meaningful and intelligent review of the agency's decision to regulate or not to regulate, they could contribute more meaningfully to the development of this critical technique in the agencies and in the law itself.

In sum, a top priority may be to educate judges in the techniques of risk-benefit analysis to give them a better perspective for coping with the complex technological and scientific policy judgments that come into their courts. Judges might also need more basic scientific training to make factual judgments about the underlying scientific and technological evidence that confronts them at trial or in the appellate record. Risk management education is, however, probably the highest priority to provide the overarching framework for more technical inquiries. "Crash courses" away from the courthouse, cassettes, and in-house seminars might begin to fill the short-term gap. But law-school education would be even better for the next generation of lawyers, law clerks, and judges.

To conclude: Science and technology have invaded our courts and are here to stay. If, as a society, we want better judicial resolutions of cases that involve complex scientific and technological matters, then we must figure out some way to make our judges more adept at handling scientific evidence and the policy implications of new technology but always within the confines of their own discipline and ethical restraints. The time may finally have arrived to turn society's as well as the judiciary's attention to this issue.

NOTE

1. See, *e.g.*, Stewart, "The Role of the Courts in Risk Management," *Environmental Law Reporter* 16:10208 (August, 1986); Huber, "Safety and the Second Best: The Hazards of Public Risk Management in the Courts." *Columbia Law Review* 85:277 (1985); and Yellin, "High Technology and the Courts," *Harvard Law Review* 94:489 (1981).

PART 4

APPENDICES AND INDEX

Observations on Presidential Science-Advising: An Interview by William T. Golden (Summer 1979)

George B. Kistiakowsky

The interviews here combined were conducted at Professor Kistiakow-sky's house on Cape Cod in the summer of 1979 while he was undergoing treatment for a major illness. Editing was completed too late for inclusion in *Science Advice to the President* (1980). The article remains timely, and is now presented for its wisdom, its piquancy, and its historical significance; and to fill the lacuna in that volume which included essays by every other Presidential Science Advisor (except the first, Oliver Buckley [appointed by President Truman], who died in 1959).

Mr. Golden: Dr. Kistiakowsky, it is well known that, since your tour as Science Advisor to President Eisenhower in 1959 and 1960, and your subsequent membership on PSAC, and since the publication in 1976 of your book, A Scientist at the White House, *you have retained a lively and independent interest in the subject. Will you please express informally at this time your practical insights concerning science advice for the President, based on your own experience and subsequent reflections?*

George B. Kistiakowsky (1900–1982) was Science Advisor to President Eisenhower (1959–60), and a member of the President's Science Advisory Committee (1957–63). He was Professor of Chemistry at Harvard (1937–71). Dr. Kistiakowsky was awarded the Medal for Merit (1946), the Presidential Medal of Freedom (1961), and the National Medal of Science (1967); and received numerous other honors. He was a member of the National Academy of Sciences (Vice President, 1965–73) and of the American Philosophical Society.

Dr. Kistiakowsky: Generally speaking, PSAC was not very influential until the stimulus of Sputnik. The heyday of Presidential science advising for ten years—from 1957 to 1967, roughly defined—was due to a very unusual confluence of circumstances of development. For one thing, the federal government essentially lagged in allowing for the growing importance of technology in the state and progress of American society. It isn't that there weren't good scientists in the government, but they were in the lower ranks, and they simply had very little access to policy-making. Recall, for instance, how that Secretary of Commerce—Mrs. Hobby, I think her name was—fired Dr. Astin as Director of the National Bureau of Standards over the battery additive, which was, of course, a total fraud. And that sort of thing took place time and again. I recall that, when I was in the White House, I invited all the members of the Federal Council on Science and Technology, which was just under Cabinet level (second- and third-level people in each Department) to a dinner, an informal dinner I gave them; and one of them, a no. 2 man in one of the old-line Departments, arrived already well oiled and had some more to drink and then launched into an appalling attack on all things having to do with research. He didn't attack me personally, but he attacked the Director of the National Science Foundation, the Administrator of the Space Agency, and the Director of Defense Research and Engineering, who were all there in person, and told them that they were all involved in a rip-off of the American taxpayer, that what they were doing was worthless and should be stopped forthwith. And in that line continued a long monologue, interrupted by some of the people who finally left in disgust. And he used four-letter words and that sort of thing. Now, he was a lawyer, and after I complained to the White House about the performance, I was received with amazement because they said that they hired the man because they felt that the Secretary of that Department was so political that he would not understand the importance of Research & Development.

That sort of thing was then very strong. And, therefore, with the coming of Sputnik and sudden enormous concern of Eisenhower (and attacks on him, too) that we were not staying on top, there arose a very strong objective reason for invigorating science-advising on the top level. The President could not get advice of that kind from his Cabinet or even from his National Security Council members. They were just not qualified to give it to him. And a more qualified person, like Alan Waterman, the Director of the National Science Foundation, was too shy and too modest and didn't venture beyond his narrow bailiwick. So that was the reason. Kennedy continued this concern.

Then, after that, we had a sequence of Presidents who were out-and-out politicians, who were therefore not interested in the substance of issues, but only in their impact upon society—politics, in other words. They preferred to let the substance be digested at lower levels of government. Of course, matters reached a real absurdity in the Nixon Administration, a farce, when Magruder, who was a salesman for the SST (supersonic transport), was hired by the White House to start a great program of new technologies, instead of relying on the existing Science Advisor, Edward E. David, Jr. And another was a farcical performance when somebody cooked up the idea of Project Independence for Nixon: how to make the country independent of imported energy in five years. Nixon handed it to the Chairman of the Atomic Energy Commission, again by-passing the Science Advisor. And she (she's now the Governor of Washington, Dixie Lee Ray (I always mix her with that stripper, Gypsy Rose Lee, although their figures aren't quite the same) came back with a program which, of course, Nixon touted, not understanding what was involved. Eventually, when you really analyze it, it amounted to this: Give the Atomic Energy Commission a lot of money and it will solve the problem. That was all there was to that Project Independence, and it died, not yet born—before the egg was fertilized. Well, the whole thing became almost farcical, I think, because the Presidents felt that—to define themselves politically— they must assert that they had had some scientific advice, so somebody was appointed, but not used. Ed David, being very intelligent, managed to do some useful things on lower levels. But, frankly, I think that, after that, Guy Stever was not given much opportunity and his performance was not effectual.

Of course, in the meantime, you see, the federal government grew enormously heavy with scientific bureaucracy, technical bureaucracy—staggeringly large increases—with the creation of a great many highly technical agencies, like the Department of Energy, the National Aviation [sic] and Space Agency, the Environmental Protection Agency, and the various regulatory organizations, like the Nuclear Regulatory Commission. You can go through one after the other and you'll find dozens of these agencies which are loaded with technically trained bureaucrats, and the Presidents clearly prefer this arrangement to any other one. It seemed to me that creating the Department of Energy was a catastrophe, because it allowed the appointment of Schlesinger and complete domination by the old Atomic Energy Commission bureaucracy, which I consider the most rotten bureaucracy in Washington. It's arrogant, it's self-sufficient, it's indifferent to the public good, and, in all respects, I say it's the most rotten bureaucracy in town. And that crowd is really controlling the whole Department of Energy, plus the elements which infiltrated into it from the oil industry. So this Department, which is supposed to represent the public, actually is run for the nuclear industry and for the oil industry.

To me, this shows the inherent incompetence, intellectual incompetence, of Carter and his staff, to have allowed this sort of thing to happen instead of strengthening the parts of the energy function already existing in separate government agencies and giving the Science Office in the White House the powerful integrating role. He should have told all those characters: "Frank Press is speaking with my voice. When he says something, you do it, as much as if I were ordering it directly." Well, it's a different way of doing things, and that's why I'm very much disappointed that things are going the way they are. And then there's this business of Carter saying during his campaign that he was a physicist. Then he quickly corrected himself, saying he was a nuclear energy engineer, which he has a claim to, but a feeble claim, and it amounts to about as much as his assurances that he will be against the Washington bureaucracy and that he will be fully truthful (not lie) to the American people and a few other things.

Thus, the role of the President's Science Advisor has been greatly downgraded. It is still a very useful one—in some respects, important. But it is certainly not one which aids and influences the President on major policy-making. The President's Science Advisor and the PSAC were designed to influence major policies. They did so to some extent in the beginning and substantially in the late 1950s and the early 1960s, certainly during the Eisenhower years. In the Eisenhower years, to a large extent, the role of Killian and myself was in the domain of national security. But, additionally, outside of that area there were some things done that were importantly influential.

For instance, there was the report of the President's Science Advisory Committee on graduate schools, research, and graduate training, the Seaborg Report on Graduate Education. The President approved that report, and it had a very major impact on government policy, because, until then, the federal government bought research as any other commodity. That's the way everything was formulated: to buy the package. But, thereafter, it was clearly understood that higher education, including the training of scientists, was part of the process for which the federal government was giving money in grants or contracts via the Department of Health, Education and Welfare, the National Institutes of Health, etc. Those grants were to be of a general support character in substantial measure, rather than restricted to specific objectives. So I think that was a very important contribution on the part of PSAC in my time. In Killian's time, of course, there was the creation of the Space Agency—that was very important. As Science Advisor, he played a major role in its creation.

After Kennedy came in, however, the Science Advisor found himself confronted with two very strong personalities in the national security area, namely, McNamara and McGeorge Bundy. In contrast, Killian—and, particularly, I—had a relatively easy time and were, in effect, able to dominate or strongly influence the White House staff people and also the Secretary of Defense. Tom Gates had so much difficulty trying to control the Services that he welcomed our help consistently, such as telephoning me and asking me personally to take on a job involving the Joint Chiefs of Staff which was too hot for his office to handle. It was concerned with adjudicating a squabble between the Air Force and the Army. But McNamara and Bundy felt that the Science Advisor, the third in the group, made a crowd and was not necessary. They gradually managed substantially to reduce the role of the Science Office of Jerry Wiesner, who was very able and dedicated, and, when Don Hornig came in, that process was essentially completed. This was under President Kennedy and then under President Johnson.

On the other hand, of course, the Science Advisor was given a very much bigger domain, management domain, in domestic affairs, that is, in civilian affairs. These were of growing importance in government activities as time passed. The attitude of the government changed. Eisenhower used to frequently talk about the private sector of the economy, into which he didn't want government to intrude. Kennedy and Johnson, however, were very much activists. So the Science Advisor's Office still remained extremely important in contributing to policy formulation.

The Science Office should continue, now and in the future, to influence major policies. But it is much more difficult now. The enormous growth of scientific bureaucracy, the technical bureaucracy within the government, makes it far more difficult for the Presidential Science Office to challenge the proposals, the policies, advanced by the various bureaucracies, the various agencies of the government. They function more cleverly (capably?) now.

Also, the issues are much more complicated now. And greater technical sophistication has been developed in the operating agencies. The Departments and agencies are frequently just as parochial as they were twenty years ago, if not more so, but they're better informed. They are more fully staffed and are better able to justify their points of view and to present them in more detail. Therefore, they are more difficult to challenge. And, of course, at present, the Office of Science and Technology Policy has only a small staff and low visibility.

Mr. Golden: Will you comment on the role of PSAC, the President's Science Advisory Committee?

Dr. Kistiakowsky: It was not always very helpful, still it was occasionally extremely helpful. Because of the broad experience of the membership, it sensed the fraudulence, intellectual fraudulence, of some of the proposals before government. And it could alert the Science Advisor that this or that Department or agency was trying to pull a fast one. I remember things like that happening, and I'm sure they happened before and after me. Well, PSAC doesn't exist anymore. Frank Press, the Director of the Office of Science and Technology Policy, seems to operate with a collection of rather junior assistants. He must get along somehow without the occasional—but important—help of a PSAC.

PSAC was helpful both with ideas and with a kind of supportive stature. The help was mostly with ideas and with criticism. Stature was helpful, too. Friendly but unrestrained criticism was able to strengthen the views that the Science Advisor eventually put forward. It is very important.

Mr. Golden: Dr. Kistiakowsky, may we turn to the future?

Dr. Kistiakowsky: Now where we are going from here on into the future, I really don't know. I think to a very large extent it depends on what kind of President we're going to have. If we have more of what we've been experiencing, I don't think the country will be in very good shape, because the President is obviously unable to get real control of the federal bureaucracy. I mean, for example, the Department of Energy, which— as is now coming out gradually—was not carrying out his orders, and was doing some things which were explicitly favorable to the oil industry, and that sort of thing. And he is unable to work with Congress. (Also, if he runs for re-election, Congress will—as likely as not—get into the control of the Republicans, because he will not provide any strength to the Democratic candidates, since he may just barely squeak in.) So I see very little hope coming on the federal government scene.

Mr. Golden: Perhaps you will express your views on the Presidential candidates and prospects.

Dr. Kistiakowsky: I don't think there is much point in my going one by one analyzing the consequences of the election of various people as President. But, *faute de mieux*, I'm for [Senator Edward] Kennedy. I have some doubts about him, relating to the past, but I think his record as a Senator is very impressive, though I do not *always* like what he proposes. I think he's going a little too far, particularly in enlarging the role of the federal government, that is, continuing in the spirit of the '60s—for example, the extensiveness of his National Health Insurance proposal. I think the most important element is that he gets able people to work for him. The mafia that Kennedy will bring into the White House—and, of course, he will bring a mafia—will be so superior to that sad gang from Georgia, which is really no better than the gang that Nixon brought from southern California. And the only thing they learned from Nixon's example is that they are being much more cautious.

And on the Republican side, I don't know; I can't get enthused about any of them.

Mr. Golden: Let's look at this in a more abstract and theoretical way, since we should plan for a long future and there will be a succession of Presidents. Would you agree that the interrelationship between the President and his Science Advisor, the personal rapport, is crucially important for success, as it is in all human relations, in bureaucracies or elsewhere? Your successful experience demonstrates that.

Dr. Kistiakowsky: You were referring to my experience with President Eisenhower, and Jim Killian's. Eisenhower was a receptive person and people could work with him.

Mr. Golden: Continuing with the future, in what areas do you think the President will need scientific and technological advice, and how should he go about getting it?

Dr. Kistiakowsky: Under present conditions, issues other than military are much more important in the public eye. Public welfare progress, as distinguished from national defense efforts, has become an area in which science and technology should play an increasing role. These are areas which the President of the United States, whoever he is, has to take strongly into consideration in his political policies, domestic as well as foreign. Not only in the future, but already in the present and for some years past, a rather substantial fraction of issues coming to the President (and I want to exclude purely political issues having to do with the election)—or that should come to him for resolution because of their national importance— have substantial technical input. That, of course, is true of a majority of issues in the national security area. It is very heavily true in the area of energy, it is true in the whole balance between environmental protection and economic progress. Here you've covered three huge areas already, and there are other areas that are involved, such as health, and perhaps agriculture. Certainly health.

It seems to me completely logical that a scientific advisor should be among the assistants having direct access to the President. Perhaps there should be a Chief of Staff. Eisenhower had several chiefs of staff, and one of them, Adams, was terrible because he was so domineering. But General Persons, who succeeded him, was very easygoing. There were several things that he insisted he be informed about, but that was the limit of his involvement. We got along fine and got to be very friendly, and he even took a little practical joking from me, and everything was just dandy.

I would think that—just as the President has to have a political advisor who can tell him how Congress and the public will react—he should have a legal advisor, and economic advisor and a national security advisor. Similarly, he has to have a science and technology advisor. I think the word "science" is overworked, because the issues coming to the President are not strictly scientific issues. Even in my time, I think I spent less than 10% of my time on science as distinguished from technology. And that technical advisor ought to be a senior person who can speak as a co-equal with such individuals as the Director of the Bureau of the Budget and the President's Counsel, the advisor for National Security Affairs (NSC), and so on. That was essentially my situation.

Of course, this situation doesn't exist now, and it did not exist in Nixon's time or in Ford's time nor, for that matter, did it exist in Johnson's time after his first two years in office, when he got wrapped up and pinioned in Vietnam. He essentially rejected Hornig as part of the Eastern Establishment, which he began to hate and suspect, and so on.

So I think a President's Science Advisory organization is something which the country needs and should have. But what the more detailed structure should be and how it should operate, I really can't say, because I think that would be up to the President. But the Science Advisor has to be on such a level that—although with some deference—he can speak to the Cabinet-level people. And he should feel clearly superior organizationally to the next lower levels, that is, the Under Secretaries and Deputy and Assistant Secretaries.

That is the level where he ought to be, and the President would have to deputize him eventually as the oversight over interagency types of issues when more than one agency is involved. Essentially the Science Advisor would be delegated authority to speak for the President in defined areas. Now what sort of an office that entails, I think depends upon the temperament of the President. First of all, I think that the office should not actually manage anything, in the sense of being an operating department. That would be catastrophic, because that would immediately reduce its effectiveness. But the size of the office—the structure of it—depends very much on the kind of assignments—specific assignments—the President gives. If the President wants to have the man (or woman) very largely as a policy advisor and not as a supervisor-coordinator of the way the Executive branch carries out the Presidential orders, why then, the office itself can actually be very small. Under those circumstances, it should, however, have very large tentacles, reaching into the entire national technical community. It should have the ability to draw on talent, at a moment's notice, to consult on an issue that confronts or is being presented to the President.

If, on the other hand, the President wishes his Science Advisor to do quite a lot of coordinating, of interdepartmental collaboration and guidance, then, of course, the office would have to have much more in the way of full-time personnel, and these tentacles that I have described to the national community would become less important. To do both policy guidance and interdepartmental coordination to a great extent is, I think, too much for an individual.

Mr. Golden: Please tell us more about the perils of interdepartmental coordination.

Dr. Kistiakowsky: Interdepartmental coordination is a very hazardous area, peppered with land mines. I had a lot of problems between the Space Agency and the military. They were repeatedly dumped in my lap, and were a continuing problem. A transitory interdepartmental issue was the cranberry episode. Then, of course, the underground atomic device test was an interdepartmental affair. It probably cost me more time than any other single issue. And I went on the job with specific instructions from the President—oral instructions to get the job done. I was involved very heavily in the underground test, but you wouldn't call me the actual coordinator. It was, however, an active role on a specific piece of business. It was not just a matter of policy guidance; it was a matter of negotiation and coordination of people with very different views.

Hans Bethe eventually pulled away. He changed his mind only about one particular technical issue. When the Big Hole Theory was developed, that was still before my time, and it embarrassed Killian. Bethe asserted that the theory of the Big Hole was nonsense, was wrong. And Killian accepted Bethe's view and told that to Eisenhower. And then, sometime later, Bethe had to admit that he was wrong and the theory was correct. And that caused Killian to change his mind. He switched his mind completely, and at the last meeting which he and I had with Eisenhower—he was saying goodbye immediately after my swearing in or maybe just before—he told Eisenhower (making my job infinitely more difficult) that, in his—Killian's—opinion, the Test Ban Treaty was inadvisable, because it couldn't be monitored on account of the Big Hole. This, of couse, was nonsense, because, when you analyze the Big Hole, you realize that it was a totally unrealistic concept. Theoretically, it was right, but nobody in his senses would ever try to cheat the Test Ban Treaty by digging big holes. It's just that simple: both for the difficulty of doing it and because the great mass of rock and earth that you took out of the hole would show up on the surface and result in your being caught.

Now Killian really switched his mind. Later, he went back into partial support of the Test Ban Treaty, but without the enthusiasm that he had showed prior to the spring of 1959. Hans Bethe simply felt so embarrassed by that blooper that he withdrew from active involvement more and more. That is too bad because he was very good.

Mr. Golden: Dr. Kistiakowsky, will you please expand your comments about a President's Science Advisory Committee (PSAC), which was eliminated by President Nixon and which many people think should be re-established in some form.

Dr. Kistiakowsky: Frankly, I don't know whether a President's Science Advisory Committee should be reconstituted; I have no judgment on the subject. It would be impossible to recreate the old PSAC, because it was oriented very heavily on national security issues. It consisted almost exclusively of individuals who had very rich experience of full-time government-related jobs during World War II. And they felt at home with government matters, because they had these years of practical experience in World War II, and had fulfilled highly responsible civilian positions. And then they went back to academic and other civilian jobs, refreshing their contacts with science. That was a unique combination which we cannot have anymore, because many of the people who go into government and some ranking military officers in retirement tend to accept administrative jobs thereafter. Very frequently, these are in the aerospace and related industries, in the military-industrial complex, if you wish to call it that. And, therefore, they are in danger of being biased. Thus I don't think they should be used for PSAC-style committees. I have grave doubts about including people from the major aerospace and related industries, however able and basically honorable, because they are really part of the military-industrial complex.

I think it would be very difficult to find appropriate individuals now who have had enough government experience to understand what is being talked about in dealing with government issues and who then went and got jobs which left them without conflict of interest. Those jobs are really few and far between. They would be academic jobs, mostly, small industry maybe, foundations possibly. So I don't know if you can put together any very helpful group of advisors. Relevant issues have become so enormously diversified that one cannot, in a committee of workable size, have experts in every field. Incidentally, the old PSAC was pitifully weak in the life sciences, though Caryl Haskins was outstandingly wise and able.

Maybe one should have completely separate groups, one in the physical area, ranging all the way from engineering to pure science; another in the life sciences, again ranging from medical and pharmaceutical and environment—biomedical matters—to pure science. And maybe the two separate committees might function quite well, the Science Advisor being the bridge between them. Because I certainly know that, in the PSAC, at least in the 1960s when I was still a member, I heard the life scientists and medically oriented people complain that 90% of the time the whole conversation, the presentations and so on, were incomprehensible and uninteresting.

Mr. Golden: You've said nothing about social scientists on a PSAC. There have been a very few included over the years.

Dr. Kistiakowsky: I think that was a mistake. I wouldn't have any. I think the social sciences should be dealt with by other parts of the Presidential organization, such as the Council of Economic Advisers. Which social scientists should be included in PSAC? Sociologists? Economists? Why? James Coleman was on for a while, and Herbert Simon and Patrick Moynihan. Simon won a Nobel Prize, but PSAC is not his business.

The PSAC and the Science Advisor should not be expected to present a final integrated judgment. They should provide an input to the President covering science and technology involvement. And, in the end, the President is the one who integrates. Therefore, making the PSAC charter too broad would be a terrible mistake. For the same reason, I would not include in PSAC people who are dedicated to the military, because the military have a very strong input to the President. PSAC should be critical of the military insofar as it deals with these problems, as it was when I was a member—a kind of counterforce.

Mr. Golden: Finally, let me ask your views about science and technology advice for the Congress. Do they need it? I presume the answer is yes. How should they get it?

Dr. Kistiakowsky: Many Congressmen and Senators now have technically trained people on their staffs. Sometimes they're good people. They also have available to them all of the science service in the Library of Congress, which does specific jobs and does them very well. They search for the available information, prepare review articles, and the like. That's very useful. Then the Office of Technology Assessment could be extremely helpful and powerful, if Congress would let it. But, again, Congress won't let it be more than it is by political interference, by keeping the budget down, and by limiting the staff size. The example of the old Joint Congressional Committee on Atomic Energy is a shocker. They presumed themselves to know the technical aspects, and they got terrible results like spending well over a billion of really good dollars on aircraft nuclear propulsion, because they thought it was a good idea.

Yes, Congress needs science and technology advice, but, fundamentally, we have to remember that Congress is a law-writing organization and that is something entirely different from the Executive branch of the government. And so the need for scientific information in Congress is very much less than it is in the Executive branch. And, by the current statute, they can call on the Director of the Office of Science and Technology Policy, who, with his other hat, is also the President's Science Advisor. Frank Press appears to have handled this delicate dual-role usefully and well.

Mr. Golden: Thank you, Dr. Kistiakowsky, for your independent, candid and spirited and vivid observations. They will enliven future discussions.

Back to Science Advisers

Hans A. Bethe and John Bardeen

Science increasingly transforms the military, political and economic landscape in which governments must operate. Nevertheless, since 1972, scientific advice to the United States Government has been remarkably haphazard. For that and other reasons, the nation is embarked on vast programs based on the misconceptions that we have an unlimited supply of scientific talent and that there need be no relationship between cost and benefit.

The prodigality has a hidden price: It is destroying our ability to compete in international markets, which we created. We must recapture our traditional pragmatism, or the foundations on which our security rests will crumble away.

We once had a sound scientific advisory apparatus. Established by President Dwight D. Eisenhower, it was headed by a full-time science advisor who was chairman of the President's Science Advisory Committee, composed of prominent scientists and engineers whose appointments were not correlated to Presidential elections. This system provided advice relatively uncontaminated by personal ambition and political bias.

The committee played a crucial role in many national security initiatives, including establishment of the post of director (now under secretary) of defense for research and engineering, and also the Defense Advanced Research Program Agency. It supported the development of missile-carrying submarines, the most survivable part of our strategic forces. It fostered innovations that led to surveillance of the Soviet Union by planes and satellites, and it started the research that led to today's excellent capability to detect underground nuclear weapons tests.

In 1972, President Richard M. Nixon liquidated the entire Science Advisory Committee organization because it had opposed two of his pet projects: deployment of antiballistic missile defenses and construction of a

Hans A. Bethe and John Bardeen are Nobel laureates in physics and emeritus professors of physics at, respectively, Cornell University and the University of Illinois.

Copyright © 1986 by The New York Times Company. Reprinted by permission.

supersonic transport. Mr. Nixon's subsequent about-face on the antiballistic missile, and the bitter English-French experience with the Concorde, soon confirmed the committee's judgments. Though the post of science adviser was eventually re-established, it never regained the status it had when it was backed by a body with the standing of the committee.

The Strategic Defense Initiative provides a telling example of what can happen when a technology program is launched without proper technical advice. President Reagan's "Star Wars" speech was prepared without consultation with experts in the Pentagon or his own science adviser, George Keyworth, until only a few days before the speech was given. And while the White House Science Council had a panel examining related technologies, and had met five days before the speech, it was not consulted.

At the time, there were few scientists who thought there was any prospect of fulfilling the President's dream of making nuclear weapons "obsolete." Three years and billions of dollars have not changed that consensus. A recently declassified report refutes claims by members of the Administration that the Initiative has scored "monumental breakthroughs." From interviews with many scientists at the weapons laboratories, the report concludes that their Initiative research "has resulted in a greater understanding of program difficulties, which are much more severe than previously considered." The scientists themselves resented the fact that "the progress their research has achieved has been inflated."

Perhaps the country can afford this $30 billion gamble. But top-flight scientific manpower is a rare commodity, and we cannot squander so much of it on nonproductive endeavors. Our manned space program illustrates this point. While Apollo was a great technical achievement, its cost was far greater than the dollars spent. Superior technical talent tended to gravitate to Apollo and the military programs, at the expense of civilian industries, allowing Japan to establish its dominance in consumer electronics and other markets.

Unfortunately, it has taken the Challenger disaster to bring the scientific community's concerns with our space program to the attention of the public and the Government. In particular, the great majority of space missions, whether military, scientific or commercial, would be cheaper and infinitely safer without man in space. And the tragedy itself shows what can be in store when technical judgments become subservient to schedules and politics.

If we are not to commit further follies, we shall have to recreate a scientific advisory system that has sufficient independence and prestige to give advice that is politically unpalatable. An Eisenhower advisory committee, even if composed largely of scientists from the weapons labs, would have made it perfectly clear to Mr. Reagan that his vision of defending cities against nuclear attack had no basis in scientific knowledge.

The Carnegie Commission on Science, Technology, and Government

William T. Golden

The Carnegie Commission on Science, Technology, and Government was established by the Carnegie Corporation of New York in 1988, under sponsorship of its president, David A. Hamburg, to assess and recommend improvements in the mechanisms by which the federal government and the states incorporate scientific and technological (S&T) knowledge into policy and decision making on the wide range of topics in which such elements should be considered. The Commission's special focus has been on the organization of government as it affects decision-making processes, rather than on specific policy options. Its goal has been a nation better prepared to respond to the opportunities and hazards of scientific and technological advances.

The Commission was established as an independent, bipartisan body with a 5-year charter. In addition to eminent scientists and engineers, the Commission and its Advisory Council included former officials who have served at high levels in all branches of government, as well as leaders from the private sectors of American society. The Commission's studies on Congress have been guided by a separate advisory council of more than 40 senators and representatives.

The Commission's work has been carried out largely through task forces addressing organizational entities and issues that cut across several governmental sectors and departments. The Commission has also sponsored a variety of consultant studies, seminars, and workshops.

The Members of the Commission and of its Advisory Council are listed on pages 513–515; staff, senior consultants, and assistants to task force chairmen are listed on page 515.

Though formally dissolved, as planned, on June 30, 1993, the Commission will continue to exist for several years in a less structured form to distribute its publications, promote its recommendations, and be available for consultation. It is encouraging several science-based, not-for-profit organizations to carry on related activities.

Organizations examined by the Commission include the following:

- Executive Office of the President
- Congress
- Judiciary
- Federal Regulatory Agencies
- State Governments
- Nongovernmental Scientific Organizations
- International Development Organizations

Task forces have also considered topics that cut across organizational boundaries, which include the following:

- National Security and International Relations
- Economic Performance
- Environment and Energy
- K–12 Math and Science Education
- Long-Term Science and Technology Goals
- The Quality of Federal Scientists and Engineers
- Federal Environmental R&D Programs

The Commission's publications are listed beginning on page 516. Among the most notable are:

- *Science & Technology and the President* (October 1988)
- *E³: Organizing for Environment, Energy and the Economy in the Executive Branch of the U.S.Government* (April 1990)
- *New Thinking and American Defense Technology* (August 1990; Second Edition May 1993)
- *Science and Technology in U.S. International Affairs* (January 1992)
- *A Science and Technology Agenda for the Nation: Recommendations for the President and Congress* (December 1992)
- *Science and Technology in Judicial Decision Making: Creating Opportunities and Meeting Challenges* (March 1993)
- *Science, Technology, and Government for a Changing World* (April 1993)

Much of the Commission's work on governmental organization and decision-making processes has been pioneering. While Hamburg and the Carnegie Corporation expected the influence of the Commission to be primarily long term, some fruits of its efforts (e.g. improvements in the Presidential science and technology advisory organization) are already evident. Consideration of many issues are still *in utero*, but lively. Most of the benefits should continue to emerge and evolve in the months and years ahead.

The Commission aimed to stimulate interest and discussion, that would lead to action by influential individuals and agencies within and outside of the government. It has not sought credit, nor to establish paternity (which is difficult to prove and often impolitic to claim). But it is clear that its activities have helped to activate latent substrates and to stimulate salutary ferment involving both lively and dormant issues. An arresting example of the latter is the Commission's major recommendation to greatly strengthen the capability of the State Department in science and technology matters by improving career opportunities and, creatively, by establishing a science and technology advisory apparatus in State comparable to that which supports the President.

It is worth mentioning the following points:

1. The Commission Task Forces have had gratifying cooperation from all levels of government, both during the development of their reports and after the reports have been completed. Individuals from institutions outside the government have been generous in giving their time to review reports and discuss issues.

2. Generally, intended recipients have carefully considered Commission reports. When appropriate, Commission members and staff have met with agency and organizational representatives to review findings, and to make certain that they understood, whether or not they agreed with, the rationale behind the recommendations.

3. Some of the Commission's recommendations have been implemented or approved for future implementation. In certain cases, modifications have been made. New institutions such as the "Carnegie Group" of international science advisers, the newly labeled Advanced Research Projects Agency, the Critical Technologies Institute, and the Science and Technology work of the Federal Judicial Council could have a permanent effect on the way that government institutions use knowledge of science and technology matters.

4. The Commission has received substantial press coverage, and over 200,000 reports have been distributed. Many of these were distributed in response to specific requests.

5. Two Commission members (William J. Perry, Deputy Secretary of Defense, and Sheila Widnall, nominated to be Secretary of the Air Force), four Advisory Committee members, and seven members of task forces

have been appointed to high government positions in the new administration. A senior staff member, Mark Schaefer, has been appointed Assistant Director of the Office for Science and Technology Policy (OSTP) for Environment.

More specific comments follow on the work of the Commission as it relates to each of the three branches of our federal government and to the States.

EXECUTIVE BRANCH

At the White House level, key recommendations of the Commission's first report, *Science & Technology and the President*, were implemented by President Bush. Others had made similar recommendations. President Bush upgraded the post of science adviser to Cabinet rank and re-established the President's Science Advisory Committee (PSAC), renamed the President's Council of Advisers on Science and Technology (PCAST). Another recommendation, the early appointment of the science adviser, was implemented promptly by President Clinton.

Action has been taken on the following Commission recommendations aimed at encouraging the federal departments and agencies to work in concert on program development and policy integration:

- Economic performance: The Defense Advanced Research Projects Agency has been renamed the Advanced Research Projects Agency and its mission has been broadened to strengthen its linkages to high-technology, commercial industry. A new Economic Security Council has been established at a high level in the White House.

- K–12 math and science education: The Department of Education and the National Science Foundation have signed an historic memorandum of cooperation, and an Executive Order has been issued requiring all S&T agencies to become involved in K–12 math and science education.

- Environmental policies: The Commission's views on the need to link the economy, energy, and the environment in the development of national policy (symbolized by E^3) have been widely accepted. The White House Council on Environmental Policy has been replaced by an Office of Environmental Policy to develop environmental policies in the context of other national policies.

At the international level, a new worldwide consultative mechanism of donor organizations is being established to assess research needs and help mobilize resources for environmental R&D, especially in developing countries. An informal "Carnegie Group" of S&T advisers to the heads of government of the Summit countries (United States of America, Canada, United Kingdom, France, Germany, Italy, and Japan), Russia, and the European Community was established under the auspices of the

Commission. It has met five times and has decided to continue meeting on a regular semi-annual basis in different member countries. Pursuing modified patterns, and influenced by the Commission, groups of high-level science and technology advisers have been convened in Mexico for the Western Hemisphere (and Spain and Portugal), and in Kenya for African Countries. Action has not yet been taken on the recommendation to strengthen the coupling of science and foreign affairs by appointing a Science Counselor to the Secretary of State and a science advisory committee to parallel the White House S&T advisory structure. Efforts to strengthen the State Department's sensitivity and capability in science and technology matters will continue. The need is recognized. The implementation will not be easy — as post-World War II history demonstrates. Career opportunities must be created and traditions recognized. But, as Spinoza said long ago, "Omnia praeclara tam dificilia tam rara sunt."

Strong interest has been shown by the National Academy of Sciences in following up the Commission's recommendation that a non-governmental National Forum on S&T Goals be created to define goals for S&T in the context of national and social policy goals. The American Association for the Advancement of Science, the National Academy of Public Administration, and the New York Academy of Sciences are among other well-established organizations that may carry forward, each in its own way, some of the activities of the Commission.

LEGISLATIVE BRANCH

The Carnegie Commission's Committee on Science, Technology, and Congress, chaired by former Congressman John Brademas, completed a series of three studies on how Congress uses information and advice, as well as the procedures by which it develops and oversees the implementation of science and technology policy. These studies were guided by a bipartisan advisory council of more than 40 current senators and representatives and their staff's, who met regularly with members of the Committee and its staff. The Committee also sought the advice of a broad range of individuals in academia and nongovernmental organizations, including current and former Congressional Science and Engineering Fellows, who have expertise and first-hand experience in congressional operations.

The Committee's first two studies examined how members request, receive, and use information and advice from individuals and organizations outside Congress as well as from the four congressional support agencies: the Office of Technology Assessment, the Congressional Research Service within the Library of Congress, the General Accounting Office, and the Congressional Budget Office. The reports present a number of recommendations, which include the establishment of a bipartisan

Science and Technology Study Conference within Congress to facilitate
the discussion of issues among senators and representatives and also the
organization of a private, nonprofit institute to function as an information link between Congress and the scientific and engineering communities. The reports also recommend expanding the Congressional Science
and Engineering Fellows program, and strengthening the capacity of the
National Academy of Sciences and the congressional support agencies to
provide Congress with information and advice. To this end, members of
Congress are working to establish a Study Conference, and the Commission is facilitating the organization of a nonprofit institute. The National
Academy of Sciences has developed a new report summary series directed to Congress, and the Commission has sponsored an outside study
of ways to improve and expand the Congressional Fellows program. The
Commission also sponsored the preparation and publication of a very
useful book entitled *Working with Congress: A Practical Guide for Scientists and Engineers*, written by William G. Wells, Jr. (Washington, DC:
AAAS Press, 1992).

The third and final Committee report evaluates the inner workings of
Congress and the challenges that members and their staff face in addressing scientific and technical issues. The report takes a fresh look at committee structure, the role of the leadership, and the budget, authorization,
appropriations, and oversight responsibilities of the legislative branch as
they relate to science and technology. Fortuitously, the development of
this report parallels Congress's own internal examination of these issues
from a broader perspective. The Commission's Committee on Congress
has provided the Joint Committee on the Organization of Congress with
a wide variety of information and advice on issues pertaining to science and
technology.

JUDICIARY

Recent developments in both law and science have coincided to bring
increasingly complex issues before the courts for resolution. New kinds
of cases involving scientific and technological information are entering
the courts in large numbers, before science has adequately explored the
issues. In particular, the dramatic growth in toxic torts and environmental litigation has put new pressure on the legal system, which is simultaneously being asked to adjudicate issues on the frontiers of science and
to develop theories of substantive law. This pressure is intense because
of the large numbers of people involved and the profound social, economic, and public policy concerns raised by these new legal claims.

In 1989, Congress established the Federal Courts Study Committee,
with members appointed by the Chief Justice to survey the state of the
federal judiciary. A working group of the Carnegie Commission on Science, Technology, and Government aided the study committee's review

of the use of scientific and technological information in the judicial decision-making process. The Federal Courts Study Committee's final report in 1990 reflected several important issues raised by the Carnegie Commission. Acting on that report, the Judicial Conference of the United States, the policy-making body of the federal judiciary that is chaired by the Chief Justice, acknowledged the increasing importance of economic, statistical, and natural and social scientific data in both routine and complex litigation. As a result, the Conference called for the Federal Judicial Center (FJC), which is the research and education arm of the federal judiciary, to undertake a comprehensive examination of how courts handle scientific and technological issues.

In the summer of 1992, the Federal Judicial Center's Board of Directors approved a proposal by Judge William W. Schwarzer, director of the FJC, to launch a 3-year pilot project on judicial management of scientific and technological evidence. The proposal was developed with the active encouragement of the Carnegie Commission. The project is designed as an institutional base for a resource center that will complete, disseminate, and maintain a S&T manual for federal judges; develop S&T components for judicial education programs; identify needed research and planning to improve the judiciary's ability to handle S&T information; and engage the S&T communities in these activities.

The FJC is also developing protocols in the areas most frequently encountered by judges, such as toxicology, epidemiology, and biostatistics. These protocols, created jointly with members of the scientific community, will provide suggested questions for judges that will permit quicker and more effective rulings on challenges to expert testimony, whether those challenges are based on the qualifications of experts, the validity of the theory on which the expert is relying, the reliability of the data underlying the theory, or the sufficiency of an expert's opinion to sustain a verdict. The Carnegie Corporation of New York has funded the pilot project through the Federal Judicial Center Foundation. The creation of this pilot program represents a recognition, by the leadership of the judiciary, of the need to place a high priority on improving the process by which cases involving S&T information are adjudicated.

The substantive interface of science and law was considered by the Supreme Court of the United States in the case of *Daubert V. Merrell Dow Pharmaceuticals, Inc.* The case presented the issue of the appropriate standards of admissibility of scientific and technological expert testimony — a subject of central concern to the Commission's Task Force on Science, Technology and the Judiciary. The Commission therefore decided to file an *amicus curiae* brief, on behalf of neither party, which proposed new criteria for admissibility, focusing on the methodology used by the "expert" in reaching his/her conclusions and whether the conclusions were strong enough to meet the plaintiff's requirement for burden of proof. The National Academy of Sciences, the American Association for the Advancement of Science, the *New England Journal of Medicine*, and some 20 other organizations also submitted *amicus* briefs.

In June 1993, the Supreme Court ruled that judges have a duty to act as "gatekeepers" on the use of expert witnesses. The stated criteria were fully consistent with the Commission's brief. The decision will enhance the important role of the Federal Judicial Center's project on judicial management of science and technology evidence since the judges now have a clear duty to understand the scientific methodology to be used by potential expert witnesses.

The development of substantive law by the Supreme Court and the establishment of innovative procedural techniques by the Federal Judicial Center should begin to have an effect on individual federal courts by late 1993.

THE STATES

Many of our 50 state governments have established science and technology advisory and promotional organizations. Largely for competitive economic reasons, but partly in response to cultural and educational concerns, increasing attention is being paid to science and technology issues. The Commission established a Task Force on Science, Technology, and the States under the active and effective leadership of its Advisory Council member, Richard F. Celeste, former Governor of Ohio. It has been functioning promisingly.

The Carnegie Commission on Science, Technology, and Government has been unusual among commissions in the emphasis it has placed, from its inception, on aiming for remedial action, rather than just publishing reports and relying on nature to take its course. In its quest for effective remedies, it has probed for areas susceptible to organizational improvement. It has tried to devise ideal prescriptions or practical palliatives. It has welcomed, and indeed actively sought, the ideas and solutions of incumbents and others. And it has been relentless, this side of fuse blowing, in promoting its ultimate recommendations.

Though the Commission can be credited with some immediate achievements, its effectiveness can be fairly assayed only over a span of years, or perhaps a decade. It has been an initiator, a participant, and a catalyst, stimulating the involvement of other organizations and individuals. To the extent it should prove effective, it will be the consequence of the work of many hands.

The central role of David Hamburg, president of the Carnegie Corporation of New York, must be emphasized. His vision led to the creation of the Carnegie Commission on Science, Technology, and Government. His ability to attract men and women of outstanding ability, patriotism, relevant experience, and dedication was vital in assembling an effective team of distinguished Commissioners, Advisory Council members, and staff. He opened many doors and was always welcome. And he footed the bill: some $11 million for the five years, all from the Carnegie Corporation of New York. If the efforts of the Commission prove to be salutary, as now seems likely, this will have been a sound investment. Andrew Carnegie would have approved.

Members of the Carnegie Commission on Science, Technology, and Government

William T. Golden (Co-Chair)
Chairman of the Board
American Museum of Natural History

Joshua Lederberg (Co-Chair)
University Professor
Rockefeller University

David Z. Robinson (Executive Director)
Carnegie Commission on Science,
    Technology, and Government

Richard C. Atkinson
Chancellor
University of California, San Diego

Norman R. Augustine
Chair & Chief Executive Officer
Martin Marietta Corporation

John Brademas
President Emeritus
New York University

Lewis M. Branscomb
Albert Pratt Public Service Professor,
    Science, Technology, and Public Policy
    Program
John F. Kennedy School of Government
Harvard University

Jimmy Carter
Former President of the United States

William T. Coleman, Jr.
Senior Attorney
O'Melveny & Myers

Sidney D. Drell
Professor and Deputy Director
Stanford Linear Accelerator Center

Daniel J. Evans
Chairman
Daniel J. Evans Associates

General Andrew J. Goodpaster (Ret.)
Chairman
Atlantic Council of The United States

Shirley M. Hufstedler
Attorney
Hufstedler, Kaus & Ettinger

Admiral B. R. Inman (Ret.)

Helene L. Kaplan
Attorney
Skadden, Arps, Slate, Meagher & Flom

Donald Kennedy
Bing Professor of Environmental Science,
    Institute for International Studies and
    President Emeritus
Stanford University

Charles McC. Mathias, Jr.
Attorney
Jones, Day, Reavis & Pogue

William J. Perry*
Chairman and Chief Executive Officer
Technology Strategies & Alliances

Robert M. Solow
Institute Professor
Department of Economics
Massachusetts Institute of Technology

H. Guyford Stever
Former Director
National Science Foundation

Sheila E. Widnall
Associate Provost and Abby Mauze
    Rockefeller Professor of Aeronautics
    and Astronautics
Massachusetts Institute of Technology

Jerome B. Wiesner
President Emeritus
Massachusetts Institute of Technology

----

* Through February 1993

Members of the Advisory Council, Carnegie Commission on Science, Technology, and Government

Graham T. Allison, Jr.
Douglas Dillon Professor of
    Government and Director,
    Strengthening Democratic
    Institutions
John F. Kennedy School of Government
Harvard University

William O. Baker
Former Chairman of the Board
AT&T Bell Telephone Laboratories

Harvey Brooks
Professor Emeritus of Technology
    and Public Policy
Harvard University

Harold Brown
Counselor
Center for Strategic and
    International Studies

James M. Cannon
Consultant
The Eisenhower Centennial Foundation

Ashton B. Carter
Director
Center for Science and International
    Affairs
Harvard University

Richard F. Celeste
Former Governor
State of Ohio

Lawton Chiles
Governor
State of Florida

Theodore Cooper*
Chairman & Chief Executive Officer
The Upjohn Company

Douglas M. Costle
Former Administrator
U.S. Environmental Protection Agency

Eugene H. Cota-Robles
Special Assistant for Human
    Resources &Affirmative Action
National Science Foundation

William Drayton
President
Ashoka: Innovators for the Public

Thomas Ehrlich
President
Indiana University

Stuart E. Eizenstat
Attorney
Powell, Goldstein, Frazer & Murphy

Gerald R. Ford
Former President of the United States

Ralph E. Gomory
President
Alfred P. Sloan Foundation

The Reverend Theodore M. Hesburgh
President Emeritus
University of Notre Dame

Walter E. Massey
Director
National Science Foundation

Rodney W. Nichols
Chief Executive Officer
New York Academy of Sciences

David Packard
Chairman of the Board
Hewlett-Packard Company

Lewis F. Powell, Jr.†
Associate Justice (Ret.)
Supreme Court of the United States

Charles W. Powers
Managing Senior Partner
Resources for Responsible Management

James B. Reston
Senior Columnist
New York Times

Alice M. Rivlin‡
Senior Fellow
Economics Department
The Brookings Institution

Oscar M. Ruebhausen
Retired Presiding Partner
Debevoise & Plimpton

Jonas Salk
Founding Director
Salk Institute for Biological Studies

Maxine F. Singer
President
Carnegie Institution of Washington

Dick Thornburgh
Former Undersecretary General
Department of Administration
    and Management
United Nations

Admiral James D. Watkins (Ret.)§
Former Chief of Naval Operations

Herbert F. York
Director Emeritus
Institute on Global Conflict
    and Cooperation
University of California, San Diego

Charles A. Zraket
Trustee
The MITRE Corporation

----
*   Died April 1993
†   Through April 1990
‡   Through January 1993
§   Through January 1989

Carnegie Commission on Science, Technology, and Government Staff

Headquarters Office, New York

David Z. Robinson
Executive Director

Maxine L. Rockoff
Senior Administrator

Jesse H. Ausubel
Director of Studies

Jeannette L. Aspden
Managing Editor

David A. Kirsch
Program Associate

Lori Skopp
Program Associate

Dolores Locascio
Administrative Assistant

Paul Harris

Washington Office

David Z. Beckler
Associate Director

Mark Schaefer
Senior Staff Associate and
Director, Washington Office

Steven G. Gallagher
Senior Staff Associate

Jonathan Bender
Program Associate

Alexandra M. Field
Program Associate

Christina E. Halvorson
Program Assistant

Bonnie P. Bisol
Office Manager

A. Bryce Hoflund
Secretary/Staff Assistant

Senior Consultants

William D. Carey
Senior Adviser to the President
Carnegie Corporation of New York

Thomas F. Malone
Sigma Xi

Walter A. Rosenblith
Massachusetts Institute of Technology

Assistants to Task Force Chairmen

Christopher Coburn
Task Force on Science,
Technology, and the States

Kathryn L. Edmundson
Committee on Congress

Rollin Johnson
Task Force on K-12 Mathematics
and Science Education

Maryann Roper
Task Force on Development
Organizations

Formal Reports of the Commission

Science & Technology and the President (October 1988)

E³:Organizing for Environment, Energy, and the Economy in the Executive Branch of the U.S. Government (April 1990)

New Thinking and American Defense Technology (August 1990; second edition May 1993)

Science, Technology, and Congress:Expert Advice and the Decision-Making Process (February 1991)

Technology and Economic Performance:Organizing the Executive Branch for a Stronger National Technology Base (September 1991)

In the National Interest:The Federal Government in the Reform of K–12 Math and Science Education (September 1991)

Science, Technology, and Congress:Analysis and Advice from the Congressional Support Agencies (October 1991)

Science and Technology in U.S. International Affairs (January 1992)

International Environmental Research and Assessment:Proposals for Better Organization and Decision Making (July 1992)

Science, Technology, and the States in America's Third Century (September 1992)

Enabling the Future:Linking Science and Technology to Societal Goals (September 1992)

Partnerships for Global Development:The Clearing Horizon (December 1992)

Environmental Research and Development:Strengthening the Federal Infrastructure (December 1992)

A Science and Technology Agenda for the Nation:Recommendations for the President and Congress (December 1992)

Facing toward Governments:Nongovernmental Organizations and Scientific and Technical Advice (January 1993)

Science and Technology in Judicial Decision Making (March 1993)

Science, Technology, and Government for a Changing World:The Concluding Report of the Carnegie Commission on Science, Technology, and Government (April 1993)

Risk and the Environment:Improving Regulatory Decision Making (June 1993)

Science, Technology, and Congress:Organizational and Procedural Reforms (Expected release: Fall 1993)

Consultant Reports

Strengthening the Policy Analysis and Research Role and Capability of the Office of Science and Technology Policy, Executive Office of the President, Background Paper, William G. Wells, Jr., and Mary Ellen Mogee (May 1990)

The Work of the Federal Courts in Resolving Science-Based Disputes:Suggested Agenda for Improvement, Report of a Working Group, Carnegie Commission on Science, Technology, and Government (1989); Reprinted in:*Federal Courts Study Committee Working Papers and Subcommittee Reports*, Vol. 1 (July 1, 1990)

The Role of NGOs in Improving the Employment of Science and Technology in Environmental Management, Background Paper, Charles W. Powers (May 1991)

The United States as a Partner in Scientific and Technological Cooperation:Some Perspectives from Across the Atlantic, Consultant Report, Alexander Keynan, Carnegie Commission on Science, Technology, and Government (June 1991)

Procedural and Evidentiary Mechanisms for Dealing with Toxic Tort Litigation:A Critique and Proposal, Consultant Report, Margaret A. Berger, Carnegie Commission on Science, Technology, and Government (October 1991)

The Budget Process and R&D, Consultant Report, Willis H. Shapley, Carnegie Commission on Science, Technology, and Government (April 1992)

The United States and Development Assistance, Background Papers for the Task Force on Development Organizations, Carnegie Commission on Science, Technology, and Government (June 1992).

Reports Sponsored by the Commission

Copies of these reports are available from the publishers:

Recruitment, Retention, and Utilization of Federal Scientists and Engineers:A Report to the Carnegie Commission on Science, Technology, and Government, National Research Council, Committee on Scientists and Engineers in the Federal Government, Alan K. Campbell and Linda S. Dix, editors, National Academy Press, Washington, DC, 1990.

Science and Technology Leadership in American Government:Ensuring the Best Presidential Appointments (the Dam Committee Report), National Academy of Sciences, National Academy of Engineering, National Institute of Medicine, Committee on Science, Engineering, and Public Policy, National Academy Press, Washington, DC, 1992.

The Prune Book:The 60 Toughest Science and Technology Jobs in Washington, John H. Trattner, Madison Books, Lanham, MD, 1992.

Working with Congress:A Practical Guide for Scientists and Engineers, William G. Wells, Jr., sponsored by the Carnegie Commission on Science, Technology, and Government and the American Association for the Advancement of Science, AAAS, Washington, DC (December 1992)

Improving the Recruitment, Retention, and Utilization of Federal Scientists and Engineers, Report to the Carnegie Commission on Science, Technology, and Government by the National Research Council, National Academy Press, Washington, DC (January 1993)

Index of Names

SALVE REGINA UNIVERSITY

3 3759 00125 9755